"In this erudite and thought-provoking book Lee Barrett provides a penetrating study of Augustine and Kierkegaard, adroitly demonstrating the interactions between the theological concerns of these two seminal thinkers. By organizing his study around the themes of *eros* and *kenosis,* journey and desire, Barrett skillfully articulates an Augustinian-Kierkegaardian vision of the Christian life that speaks powerfully today. Essential reading for anyone interested in the theological Kierkegaard."

— **DAVID R. LAW**
University of Manchester

"Kierkegaard scholarship has long needed a definitive study of the Augustine-Kierkegaard relationship; and this is it. . . . This book will be valuable not just for students of Augustine, at the dawn of state-sponsored Christendom, or of Kierkegaard, at its twilight, but also for anyone who wants to understand the whole of Western Christianity at its heart."

— **ANDREW J. BURGESS**
University of New Mexico

KIERKEGAARD AS A CHRISTIAN THINKER

C. Stephen Evans and Paul Martens
General Editors

The KIERKEGAARD AS A CHRISTIAN THINKER series seeks to promote and enrich an understanding of Søren Kierkegaard as a Christian thinker who, despite his many critiques of Christendom, self-consciously worked within the Christian tradition and in the service of Christianity. Volumes in the series may approach Kierkegaard's relationship to Christianity historically or topically, philosophically or theologically. Some will attempt to illuminate Kierkegaard's thought by examining his works through the lens of Christian faith; others will use Kierkegaard's Christian insights to address contemporary problems and competing non-Christian perspectives.

That Søren Kierkegaard profoundly influenced nineteenth- and twentieth-century theology and philosophy is not in doubt. The direction, extent, and value of his influence, however, have always been hotly contested. For example, in the early decades of the twentieth century, German theologians Karl Barth, Dietrich Bonhoeffer, and Emil Brunner all acknowledged deep debts to Kierkegaard, debts that would echo through the theological debates of the entire century. In spite of this, by the middle of the twentieth century, Kierkegaard was also hailed (or cursed) as a father of existentialism and nihilism because of his appropriation by Heidegger, Sartre, and others. At the same time, however, he was beginning to become the reveille for a return to true Christianity in North America through the translating efforts of Walter Lowrie and David Swenson. At the beginning of the twenty-first century, Kierkegaard's legacy is once again being seriously and rigorously debated.

While acknowledging and affirming the postmodern appreciation of elements of Kierkegaard's thought (such as irony, indirect communication, and pseudonymity), this series aims to engage Kierkegaard as a Christian thinker who self-consciously worked as a Christian in the service of Christianity. And, as the current discussion crosses the traditional boundaries of philosophy and theology, this series will necessarily do the same. What these volumes all share, however, is the task of articulating Kierkegaard's continuities with, challenges to, and resources for Christianity today. It is our hope that, in this way, this series will deepen and enrich the manifold contemporary debates concerning Kierkegaard and his legacy.

EROS AND SELF-EMPTYING

The Intersections of Augustine and Kierkegaard

Lee C. Barrett

WILLIAM B. EERDMANS PUBLISHING COMPANY

GRAND RAPIDS, MICHIGAN / CAMBRIDGE, U.K.

Published 2013 by

Wm. B. Eerdmans Publishing Co.

2140 Oak Industrial Drive N.E., Grand Rapids, Michigan 49505 /

P.O. Box 163, Cambridge CB3 9PU U.K.

Printed in the United States of America

19 18 17 16 15 14 13   7 6 5 4 3 2 1

Library of Congress Cataloging-in-Publication Data

Barrett, Lee C.

Eros and self-emptying: the intersections of Augustine and Kierkegaard /
Lee C. Barrett III.

pages   cm.   — (Kierkegaard as a Christian thinker)

Includes bibliographical references and index.

ISBN 978-0-8028-6805-3 (pbk.: alk. paper)

1. Augustine, Saint, Bishop of Hippo. 2. Kierkegaard, Søren, 1813-1855.
I. Title.

B655.Z7B37 2013

230.092'2 — dc23

2013031424

www.eerdmans.com

To my wife Betty,
who has been my beloved companion and support on this road;

to my brothers William and John,
who have shared much of the journey with me;

and to my nephew Spencer,
an aspiring pilgrim.

Contents

Foreword

It is impossible to escape the long shadow that Augustine has cast over the Christian theological tradition. Theologians will invariably find themselves wrestling with Augustine's direct or indirect influence whether it is exerted in terms of the framing of particular questions, the definition of categories, or the determinations of particular conclusions. Søren Kierkegaard, a nineteenth-century Danish Lutheran, was no exception. But how exactly did Kierkegaard engage, and find himself engaged by, Augustine's legacy?

Boldly leaping into this discussion with both feet, Lee Barrett launches the KIERKEGAARD AS A CHRISTIAN THINKER series by offering a wide-ranging and compelling account of what he calls the "intersections" of Augustine and Kierkegaard. His investigation carefully and thoroughly examines various intersections that emerge within textual matters (e.g., Kierkegaard's reading of Augustine's texts), historical concerns (e.g., the manner in which Augustine's texts and ideas were mediated through Kierkegaard's teachers), stylistic or rhetorical choices (e.g., the connections between the modes of writing employed by both), and a wide range of theological perspectives and conclusions (e.g., considerable agreement concerning the *telos* of human existence). As a result, Barrett opens a trail through the manifold complexities of Augustine and Kierkegaard that forces us beyond any simple declamations; Barrett clears a path that leads us to the places where we can clearly see and feel the deep connections and occasional disagreements between these two giants in the Christian tradition.

Two further comments are helpful for orienting Barrett's account. First, Barrett is first and foremost a Kierkegaard scholar and not an expert on Augustine, a conclusion that is amply supported by his manifold contributions to the International Kierkegaard Commentary, the Søren Kierkegaard Society, and the Kierkegaard Research: Sources, Reception, and Recourses project. Therefore, Barrett's account begins and ends with a focus that is guided by Kierkegaard's life and writings. This volume does appear in a series devoted to Kierkegaard's thought after all. Recognizing this reality, however, is not to say that Barrett is unfair to Augustine—far from it. Rather, it is merely to suggest that a volume written by an Augustinian scholar may look very different from what you will find in the following pages . . . although that, too, is a needed volume.

Second, to suggest that Kierkegaard is Barrett's first love would be to miss the larger picture. For Barrett, as this volume frequently illustrates, Kierkegaard and Augustine are worthy of attention because they assist us in the ongoing task of theology. Barrett is unashamedly a theologian, and for him theology is a work that necessarily serves the Christian life. For this reason, he begins and ends with the theme of an individual's journey home to God, a theme that permeates the thought of both Augustine and Kierkegaard.

To draw these introductory comments to a close, please allow a personal anecdote from one of us. Nearly a decade ago at an academic conference, Paul heard Barrett offer a few remarks devoted to Kierkegaard's relation to Augustine. What struck Paul, in ascending order of relevance, was (a) he had never heard a paper solely dedicated to relating these two figures before; (b) Barrett clearly grasped the depth of the material he was talking about; and (c) Barrett's suggestions concerning the theological connections between Augustine and Kierkegaard seemed surprising and yet oddly sensible. Since that conference, Paul has been hoping that Barrett would find the time and energy to return to the intersections of Augustine and Kierkegaard in a sustained way. That time has come. We are extremely grateful and excited that this volume is now appearing in the KIERKEGAARD AS A CHRISTIAN THINKER series.

C. STEPHEN EVANS
PAUL MARTENS

Explanation of the References

The references to Augustine's works are to the series *The Works of Saint Augustine: A Translation for the 21st Century* (Hyde Park, NY: New City Press, 1997–). Rather than referring to page numbers, the notes refer to that series' system of dividing the text into books, chapters, and sometimes paragraphs. For many of Augustine's volumes, book divisions appeared in the early manuscripts, chapter divisions were added in the fifteenth-century printed editions, and paragraphs were often numbered in the seventeenth century. The editors of the most recent English translation of Augustine's complete works have chosen to use all three sets of divisions in those instances where all three have been in use. As a result, when there are both chapter numbers and paragraph numbers, the paragraph number will be in parentheses. For example, with regard to the *Confessions,* "IV, 3 (9)" means: book IV, chapter 3, paragraph 9. If the paragraph numbers are consecutive, not starting over with a new book, often a period will separate the chapter and paragraph numbers. This practice has usually been followed by other editions and translations of Augustine, which are legion. Thus the reader can, by using this citation system, find the reference in other editions and translations.

The references to Kierkegaard's major books are to the series *Kierkegaard's Writings* (Princeton, NJ: Princeton University Press, 1978-1998), under the general editorship of Howard V. Hong and Edna H. Hong. The references to Kierkegaard's journals are to *Søren Kierkegaard's Journals and Papers* (Bloomington: Indiana University Press, 1967-78), also edited by Howard and Edna Hong. For this series, I have given the volume number and the entry number. For papers and notebook entries not found in the

Hong series, I have cited *Kierkegaard's Journals and Notebooks* (Princeton, NJ: Princeton University Press, 2007–). For this series, I have provided the volume number and page number because the system of enumerating the entries is too cumbersome. Because the citations of Kierkegaard's texts are frequent and recurring, and because the sigla are simple, I have embedded them (in parentheses) within the text.

Sigla

AN	See *OMWA, PV, AN*
BA	*The Book on Adler,* trans. Howard V. Hong and Edna H. Hong (Princeton, NJ: Princeton University Press, 1995).
CA	*The Concept of Anxiety,* trans. Riedar Thomte in collaboration with Albert B. Andersen (Princeton, NJ: Princeton University Press, 1980).
CD	*Christian Discourses* and *The Crisis and a Crisis in the Life of an Actress,* trans. Howard V. Hong and Edna H. Hong (Princeton, NJ: Princeton University Press, 1997).
CI	*The Concept of Irony, together with "Notes on Schelling's Berlin Lectures,"* trans. Howard V. Hong and Edna H. Hong (Princeton, NJ: Princeton University Press, 1989).
CUP	*Concluding Unscientific Postscript to "Philosophical Fragments,"* 2 vols., trans. Howard V. Hong and Edna H. Hong (Princeton, NJ: Princeton University Press, 1992).
EO 1; *EO* 2	*Either/Or,* 2 vols., trans. Howard V. Hong and Edna H. Hong (Princeton, NJ: Princeton University Press, 1987).
EUD	*Eighteen Upbuilding Discourses,* trans. Howard V. Hong and Edna H. Hong (Princeton, NJ: Princeton University Press, 1990).
FSE, JFY	*For Self-Examination* and *Judge for Yourself!* trans. Howard V. Hong and Edna H. Hong (Princeton, NJ: Princeton University Press, 1990).
FT, R	*Fear and Trembling* and *Repetition,* trans. Howard V. Hong and Edna H. Hong (Princeton, NJ: Princeton University Press, 1983).
JC	See *Pf, JC*

JFY	See *FSE, JFY*
JP	*Søren Kierkegaard's Journals and Papers,* 7 vols., ed. and trans. Howard V. Hong and Edna H. Hong, assisted by Gregor Malantschuk (Bloomington and London: Indiana University Press, 1967-78).
KJN	*Kierkegaard's Journals and Notebooks,* ed. Niels Jørgen Cappelørn et al. (Princeton, NJ: Princeton University Press, 2000–).
OMWA, PV, AN	*On My Work as an Author,* "The Point of View for my Work as an Author," and "Armed Neutrality," trans. Howard V. Hong and Edna H. Hong (Princeton, NJ: Princeton University Press, 1998).
PC	*Practice in Christianity,* trans. Howard V. Hong and Edna H. Hong (Princeton, NJ: Princeton University Press, 1991).
PF, JC	*Philosophical Fragments* and *Johannes Climacus,* trans. Howard V. Hong and Edna H. Hong (Princeton, NJ: Princeton University Press, 1985).
PV	See *OMWA, PV, AN*
SLW	*Stages on Life's Way,* trans. Howard V. Hong and Edna H. Hong (Princeton, NJ: Princeton University Press, 1988).
SUD	*The Sickness unto Death,* trans. Howard V. Hong and Edna H. Hong (Princeton, NJ: Princeton University Press, 1980).
TA	*Two Ages: The Age of Revolution and the Present Age. A Literary Review,* trans. Howard V. Hong and Edna H. Hong (Princeton, NJ: Princeton University Press, 1980).
TDIO	*Three Discourses on Imagined Occasions* trans. Howard V. Hong and Edna H. Hong (Princeton, NJ: Princeton University Press, 1993).
TM	*"The Moment" and Late Writings,* trans. Howard V. Hong and Edna H. Hong (Princeton, NJ: Princeton University Press, 1998).
UDVS	*Upbuilding Discourses in Various Spirits,* trans. Howard V. Hong and Edna H. Hong (Princeton, NJ: Princeton University Press, 1990).
WA	*Without Authority,* trans. Howard V. Hong and Edna H. Hong (Princeton, NJ: Princeton University Press, 1997).
WL	*Works of Love,* trans. Howard V. Hong and Edna H. Hong (Princeton, NJ: Princeton University Press, 1995).
WSA	*Works of Saint Augustine: A Translation for the 21st Century* (Hyde Park, NY: New City Press, 1997–).

Augustine and Kierkegaard: Rivals or Allies?

Intellectual historians of very different stripes have linked the names of Aurelius Augustinus and Søren Kierkegaard with surprising frequency, even though the careers of the two Christian thinkers were separated by almost a millennium and a half. It is indicative of this trend that the magisterial encyclopedia of Augustine studies, *Augustine through the Ages,* boasts a lengthy article comparing Kierkegaard and Augustine, while it contains no such essay comparing Augustine with Schleiermacher, Barth, Tillich, or even Rahner.[1] Sometimes the purpose of this widespread association of the two authors has been to contrast them as if they defined the opposite poles of the theological spectrum. According to some historians of Christian thought and Western philosophy, Augustine was the archetypal apologist of a totalitarian church, while Kierkegaard was the quintessential proponent of individualistic piety.[2] From this perspective Augustine was the promulgator of authoritarian and allegedly objective doctrines, while Kierkegaard was the advocate of passionate religious subjectivity.

But other interpreters have portrayed Augustine and Kierkegaard as close theological kindred, insisting that both of them practiced a similar and distinctive "existential" way of thinking about God and human life.[3] Typically, these interpreters have hailed this unique way of doing theology

---

1. See John Doody, "Kierkegaard," in Allan D. Fitzgerald, *Augustine through the Ages: An Encyclopedia* (Grand Rapids: Eerdmans, 1999), pp. 484-86.

2. See, e.g., Walter Kaufmann, *Critique of Religion and Philosophy* (New York: Harper, 1958), pp. 19-24, 153-55.

3. See, e.g., Paul Tillich, *A History of Christian Thought,* ed. Carl E. Braaten (New York: Simon and Schuster, 1967), pp. 67-78, 103-33, 458-76.

as one of the most significant trajectories in Western religious and philosophical thought. In this view, Augustine and Kierkegaard shared the conviction that the desire to know and experience God was inextricably bound together with the individual's quest for self-transparency and self-integration in a fractured and opaque world. With this connection established, Augustine's and Kierkegaard's self-involving approach to religious reflection has then been juxtaposed to the more "systematic" academic styles that dominated theology in the late Middle Ages and the post-Reformation periods.[4] After surveying this abundance of rival assessments of Augustine and Kierkegaard, it could easily be concluded that two entirely different theologians have lived named Aurelius Augustinus, as well as two different Danish authors named Søren Kierkegaard.

The texts written by Augustine and Kierkegaard are sufficiently elusive and polyvalent to sustain both sets of interpretations. Viewed in one way, Augustine and Kierkegaard appear to be diametrical opposites; change the angle of vision slightly, and they appear to be remarkably similar. This ambiguity is to be expected, for both thinkers wrote in ways that resist facile appropriation and demand personal investment from their readers. Authors who hope to catalyze a profound transformation in their readers, as both Augustine and Kierkegaard attempted to do, usually produce books that are amenable to being appropriated in a variety of different ways. But despite the polysemous nature of their work, Augustine and Kierkegaard's writings are not so indeterminate as to defy any comparison. Both authors provide enough directives and cues to the reader that some things can be asserted with a fair amount of confidence about the purposes of their texts. Because of the specificity of their rhetorical strategies and aims, many parallels and divergences can legitimately be explored. This volume will attempt to pay attention to the rhetorical strategies and pastoral purposes of the writings of these two Christian thinkers in order to give a more nuanced interpretation of Kierkegaard's relationship to Augustine. I will argue that there is some truth in the approach that juxtaposes their works and also some truth in the approach that discovers a basic parallelism. I will conclude that, below the surface, it is the parallelism that is the stronger and more consistent dynamic, even though it is not the parallelism that has usually been discerned by scholars.

The comparison of the two the writers will serve several different pur-

---

4. See Pierre Courcelle, *"Les Confessions" de Saint Augustin dans la Tradition Littéraire* (Paris: Études Augustinienne, 1963).

poses. The most obvious one is to better understand the ways Kierkegaard extended theological trajectories rooted in the thought of Augustine, even when the former was not aware that he was doing so. Because Augustine was so foundational for the theology and spirituality of the Western church, his writings served as a springboard for most subsequent theological developments, including the various ways of doing theology prevalent in early-nineteenth-century northern Europe. Through the impact of the heritage of Augustine on post-Trentine Catholics, Lutheran confessionalists, pietists of all kinds, heterodox mystics, and thinkers as diverse as Hegel, Schelling, and Schleiermacher, Augustinian concepts and modes of thought were simply part of the air that Kierkegaard breathed. Even though Augustine's influence on Kierkegaard was often not direct, Augustine was responsible for much of the framework in which Kierkegaard thought. Situating Kierkegaard in the context of Augustine's legacy will shed light on the rhythms, dynamics, and tensions in Kierkegaard's own work. This will enable us to see that Kierkegaard's work in some ways represented a return to Augustinian themes that had been repressed or deemphasized by official Lutheranism. In certain respects, Kierkegaard was theologically closer to Augustine than he was to Luther. In order to accomplish this central goal of understanding Kierkegaard, we will look back at Augustine from the perspective of Kierkegaard, concentrating on the subjects in Augustine that are particularly relevant for grasping Kierkegaard's theological world. We will examine Augustine's writings insofar as they are the source of theological tendencies that blossomed in Kierkegaard's writings, often bearing unexpected fruit.

Another goal is to gain a better understanding of certain aspects of Augustine's thought. Looking for parallels and analogies between Kierkegaard and Augustine will highlight particular themes in Augustine's work that otherwise might be overlooked or undervalued. The significance of motifs that were implicit or subterranean in Augustine's writings may become clearer when their more explicit elaboration by Kierkegaard is taken into account. In particular, reading Augustine and Kierkegaard side by side will suggest that Augustine's theology was more riddled with dialectical tensions than might otherwise be evident. Moreover, the similarities to Kierkegaard will show that the meanings of Augustine's theological assertions were often dependent on highly specific rhetorical contexts and polemical and pastoral purposes. Reading Augustine through the lens of Kierkegaard is certainly not the only way to engage Augustine, but it is a possible way, and it may shed light on dynamics in Augustine's texts that might not be adequately appreciated, such as the critical importance of divine *kenosis*.

Most importantly, this comparison of Augustine and Kierkegaard will help identify a way of being Christian that avoids some of the mutual negations of most forms of Catholicism and Protestantism. The parallelisms and intersections of Augustine and Kierkegaard, I contend, allowed both of them to transcend many of the binary oppositions that have plagued Christian theology. We will find that both Augustine and Kierkegaard saw no absolute contradiction between affirming that human nature as created by God is oriented toward fulfillment in God and asserting that God's self-giving love comes to humanity as an unanticipated and gratuitous gift. Neither of them regarded human eros and divine agape as mutually exclusive. In fact, the two thinkers concurred that human beings have been created by God in such a way that they can develop an eros for self-giving love and will only be ultimately happy if they do so.

Before we engage in a closer comparison of the two thinkers, it will helpful to consider the two rival genealogical accounts of their relationship in more detail in order to determine exactly what Augustine and Kierkegaard are alleged to have shared — and about what they are alleged to have disagreed. In so doing we will not examine every variety of interpretation of Augustine, or every type of interpretation of Kierkegaard, but only those that either directly compare the two or have an overt bearing on the comparison. We will begin with an examination of the interpretive tendency that dichotomizes the two, for in some ways this construal is the one that most readily suggests itself. Although it has recently fallen into some disfavor, it has enjoyed a venerable history and continues to attract adherents.

Augustine and Kierkegaard Conceived as Opposites

Some commentators locate the putative fundamental divergence between Augustine and Kierkegaard in their markedly different understandings of the respective roles of human and divine agency in the overcoming of the fractures and tensions in the "soul" (Augustine) or the "self" (Kierkegaard). Augustine, according to a very prevalent interpretation, ascribes an almost monergistic efficacy to God's grace in the drama of human salvation. Even when the individual seems to be the voluntary and responsible author of her own faith, it is really God who has irresistibly moved the individual's will. According to this interpretation of Augustine, the individual's ostensible volitional powers are mere instruments that are being wielded by the sovereign divine will. Kierkegaard, however, often described the individual's responsibility to be faithful in such an extravagant way that faith sounded like an act of radical human autonomy. Sometimes these expositors admit that Kierkegaard did suggest that some kind of divine aid is operative in the individual's coming to faith, but then assert that the crucial factor in the process remains the individual's will. Consequently, according to this construal, Kierkegaard's view of human agency had some similarities to the position of Pelagius, Augustine's great nemesis. According to Mark C. Taylor, "[i]t is of central importance for Kierkegaard's argument that man himself be responsible for his faith."[5]

Even more boldly, the older existentialists claimed to detect in Kierkegaard's work a foreshadowing of their own radically volitional view of significant human commitments, and thus a rejection of Augustine's ascription of salvation to divine agency. Taking a more moderate view, Timothy Jackson has argued that Kierkegaard's highlighting of the responsible appropriation of grace resembles the thought of Arminius, the Reformed theologian who proposed that the offer of God's grace can be resisted by the human will.[6] Such an opinion would have had some similarities to the tenets of the so-called semi-Pelagians, whom Augustine stalwartly opposed. But whether Kierkegaard is read as suggesting that the individual initiates the "leap" into faith or as implying that the individual freely cooperates with God's activity, this interpretive trajectory implies that Kierkegaard undercut the emphasis of God's sovereign grace that has been the hallmark of the Augustinian heritage.

Other interpreters have detected different disjunctions separating Kierkegaard from Augustine. For example, George Pattison has argued that Augustine's epistemological speculations differ dramatically from those of Kierkegaard's pseudonymous Johannes Climacus.[7] Augustine formulated a Christian version of the Platonic theme that the truth is recollected, proposing that the light of truth inwardly illumines the mind and makes it receptive to the revelation of divine truth. Augustine's view is very unlike Climacus's ironic exposition of Christianity. Climacus identifies Christian

---

5. Mark C. Taylor, *Kierkegaard's Pseudonymous Authorship: A Study of Time and the Self* (Princeton, NJ: Princeton University Press, 1975), p. 314.

6. Timothy Jackson, "Arminian Edification: Kierkegaard on Grace and Free Will," in Alastair Hannay and Gordon Marino, eds., *The Cambridge Companion to Kierkegaard* (Cambridge: Cambridge University Press, 1998), pp. 235-56.

7. George Pattison, "Johannes Climacus and Aurelius Augustinus on Recollecting the Truth," in Robert L. Perkins, ed., *International Kierkegaard Commentary: Philosophical Fragments and Johannes Climacus* (Macon, GA: Mercer University Press, 1994), pp. 245-60.

faith with an unanticipated encounter with divinely revealed truth communicated by an authoritative teacher. According to Climacus's presentation of Christianity, the receptivity to truth is not a component of human inwardness. (Pattison aptly points out that Climacus's view should not be monolithically identified with that of Kierkegaard, who probably entertained a more nuanced understanding of coming to faith.) Augustine's position would more closely approximate Climacus's description of Socratic religiosity than it would Christian faith. This has generally been the opinion of interpreters who have emphasized the lingering importance of Neo-Platonic epistemology even for the mature Augustine.[8]

Some commentators have portrayed Augustine's work as the ultimate source of Western doctrinal theology — and as the impetus to the consolidation of a rigid orthodoxy.[9] Augustine, it is claimed, strove to unify the church on the basis of corporately held and officially endorsed theological propositions. This, of course, conflicts with Kierkegaard's disparaging remarks about the reduction of Christianity to a doctrine. According to this view, Kierkegaard's insistence that Christianity is an "existence communication" did not mesh with Augustine's concern for defining correct belief against various heresies. Kierkegaard's "subjective turn," it is alleged, stands in opposition to Augustine's efforts to stipulate the objective meaning of concepts such as "original sin," "the Trinity," and the "incarnation."

According to one strand of interpretation, Kierkegaard's natural allies must have been the sectarian and heretical Donatists, who were willing to die for their belief that the Christian community (or at least its leadership) should be rigorously pure, rather than the Augustinians, who promoted a more comprehensive church that was sadly enervated by lax moral expectations.[10] It is often noted that Augustine did come to endorse the imperial government's closing of the churches of the Donatists, thereby implicitly sanctioning state intervention in ecclesiastical matters.[11] It has been recently argued that Augustine's complicity in state coercion was greater than he himself intimates, for he was the leader of a minority party in the churches

8. See Phillip Cary, *Augustine's Invention of the Inner Self: The Legacy of a Christian Platonist* (Oxford: Oxford University Press, 2000).

9. See, e.g., Charles Freeman, *The Closing of the Western Mind: The Rise of Faith and the Fall of Reason* (New York: Vintage Books, 2005), pp. 284-300.

10. Vernard Eller, *Kierkegaard and Radical Discipleship: A New Perspective* (Princeton, NJ: Princeton University Press, 1968), pp. 12-13.

11. For a popular account of this view, see James Carroll, *Constantine's Sword: The Church and the Jews* (Boston and New York: Houghton Mifflin, 2002), pp. 47-48, 208-12.

of northern Africa that triumphed over the majority Donatist party only by establishing an alliance with imperial force.[12] The Kierkegaard who strove to reintroduce Christianity into Christendom must have possessed a fundamentally different understanding of the Christian church from that entertained by the Bishop of Hippo, a high-ranking ecclesiast who had helped invent Christendom. After all, Augustine believed that outside the institutional church there was no salvation, while Kierkegaard doubted whether the Danish church of his own day had any connection at all with New Testament Christianity. Peter Vardy has defined their opposition rather starkly: "Augustine sees Christianity as essentially a communal affair, both in the Church on earth and with the saints in heaven. Kierkegaard emphasizes the individual journey of faith and the priority of the individual in relation to God."[13] Put simply, from this perspective Augustine was a paradigmatic communitarian, while Kierkegaard was a strident anticommunitarian. Kierkegaard could envision the church, at most, only as a gathered community of committed and intentional believers, while Augustine saw the church as a "mixed body" of saints and sinners united by the sacraments.[14] For Augustine, the individual was incorporated into the church through baptism, including the baptism of infants; for his part, Kierkegaard expressed grave reservations by the end of his life about the practice of baptizing babies. In short, Kierkegaard possessed the spirit of a sectarian, whereas Augustine trusted in the church as a sacramental institution.

Still other expositors portray Augustine and Kierkegaard very differently on the issue of the relationship of faith and human speculative capacities. It is often pointed out that Augustine's motto was, "I believe in order that I might understand." The understanding in question, it is alleged, was a speculative grasp of the logical relationships among Christian concepts and their metaphysical implications. The acceptance of revelation provided the basic data, and then the exercise of human reason on those data produced the deeper comprehension. In this view, Augustine used a Neo-Platonic framework to generate a speculative metaphysical theology in a manner that anticipated the way Hegel would use German idealism to cre-

12. For the view that non-Donatist Christianity triumphed in northern Africa because Augustine allied his party with the imperial government, see James J. O'Donnell, "Augustine's Unconfessions," in John D. Caputo and Michael Scanlon, eds., *Augustine and Postmodernism: Confessions and Circumfession* (Bloomington: Indiana University Press, 2005), pp. 218-19, 221.

13. Peter Vardy, *An Introduction to Kierkegaard* (Peabody, MA: Hendrickson, 2008), p. 78.

14. See Eller, *Kierkegaard and Radical Discipleship.*

ate a different kind of speculative system. Kierkegaard, on the other hand, disavowed all speculative metaphysical aspirations and restricted himself to clarifying and evoking the joys and tribulations of human experience in general and Christian experience in particular. From this perspective, Kierkegaard's orientation was existential, while Augustine's was speculative. Augustine's legacy was the disastrous hankering for a Christian philosophy that would render the faith plausible, a prospect that made Kierkegaard shudder. Augustine felt a need to defend Christianity and make it intellectually respectable, while Kierkegaard sought to make Christianity shocking to his contemporaries. Perhaps Augustine had more in common with Hegel than he did with Kierkegaard.

Augustine and Kierkegaard Conceived as Fellow Travelers

In contrast to those interpreters who position Augustine and Kierkegaard as polar opposites, another set of intellectual historians narrate a saga of parallelism and indirect influence. At first blush this may seem odd, for Augustine is often remembered as the consummate theological insider, while Kierkegaard is characterized as the ultimate theological outsider. Nevertheless, existentially oriented thinkers such as Miguel de Unamuno, Nicholas Berdyaev, and Martin Buber have located Kierkegaard in a lineage that began with Augustine, continued through Luther and Pascal, and blossomed in Dostoevsky, Nietzsche, and Kierkegaard. For example, Karl Jaspers described Kierkegaard as Augustine's descendant in that they both "thought with their blood," reflecting on the nature and purpose of human life with self-involving passion.[15] Similarly, William Barrett claims that Kierkegaard walked through the door that Augustine had opened, that door being the "existential" strain in the Christian heritage.[16] Barrett writes: "Where Plato and Aristotle had asked the question, What is man?, St Augustine (in *The Confessions*) asks, Who am I? — and the shift is decisive."[17] Barrett adds that it is this shift that would lead to Kierkegaard. (Augustine himself, according to Barrett, did not entirely enter the existential room because he was held back by his residual Platonism.)

15. Karl Jaspers, *The Great Philosophers*, trans. Edith Ehrlich (New York: Harcourt, Brace and World, 1962-95), 1: 213-14; 4: 190-290.

16. William Barrett, *Irrational Man* (Garden City, NY: Doubleday, 1958), pp. 95-99.

17. Barrett, *Irrational Man*, p. 95.

John Wild proposes that Kierkegaard's "most original conceptions come from classical and Christian, especially Augustinian sources," which inspired Kierkegaard to dismantle the essentialist view of the self.[18] According to this account, the most significant thing about both writers is that they incorporated passionate inwardness and self-reflection into the theological task as necessary conditions. Although Augustine did not use the modern term "the self," he implicitly anticipated the concept by focusing on the individual's introspective self-awareness, self-evaluation, and efforts at self-integration and self-direction (which do, in his estimation, inevitably fail apart from grace). The literary performances of both Augustine and Kierkegaard exemplify the conviction that authentic consciousness of the self requires awareness of God — and vice versa. Moreover, these interpreters point out that both Augustine and Kierkegaard used the spiritual journey of the individual pilgrim as the basic framework for thinking about Christianity. For both theological writers, life should be a *via* toward God, who is simultaneously the source, the support, the path itself, and the destination of the journey. It is noteworthy that, as further evidence for the parallel, both emphasize the fissure that separates the self from God, rendering the journey extraordinarily challenging. In these comparisons of Augustine and Kierkegaard, Augustine is usually identified as the primal font of this "subjective turn" in philosophical and theological writing (though sometimes Paul or Plotinus or even the Stoics are given that credit), and Kierkegaard is then hailed as Augustine's most dramatic modern offspring.

The interpreters who concur that Augustine and Kierkegaard were twin exponents of inwardness, subjectivity, and the fractured nature of the self often disagree about what exactly this self-involving kind of theology entails. Some laud this development, while others critique it. Their particular evaluative perspectives and ideological commitments color the ways each one tells the story. In recent decades Charles Taylor has been one of the most powerful exponents of the view that Augustine was the font of the subjective turn.[19] Taylor established the basic trajectory for any future conversation concerning the relationship of Augustine and Kierkegaard by casting Augustine as the early protagonist of the saga of the evolution of the Western concept of the "self," a concept that would receive one of its

18. John Wild, "Kierkegaard and Contemporary Existential Philosophy," in Howard A. Johnson, ed., *A Kierkegaard Critique* (New York: Harper, 1962), p. 38.

19. See Simon D. Podmore, *Kierkegaard and the Self before God: Anatomy of the Abyss* (Bloomington: Indiana University Press, 2011), pp. 15-19.

most influential modern expressions in Kierkegaard. Subsequent writers tracing the lineage of the "subjective turn," or "interiority," generally debate the merits or demerits of Taylor's account of Augustine and his influence.[20] Because of the influential nature of Taylor's work, I will consider it in some detail as a paradigmatic example of this interpretive tendency.

In *Sources of the Self*, Taylor enthusiastically says: "It is hardly an exaggeration to say that it was Augustine who introduced the inwardness of radical reflexivity and bequeathed it to the Western tradition of thought. This step was a fateful one, because we have certainly made a big thing of the first-person standpoint." By "radical reflexivity" Taylor means the consistent and intentional foregrounding of the self's perspective on itself and its own actions and passions. Augustine, he alleges, turned away from "outer" objects in the public world to "inner" objects available only to the first-person standpoint. According to Taylor, Augustine relocated knowledge of God in this domain of radical reflexivity and in the intimacy of self-presence.[21] Therefore, Augustine's journey to authentic selfhood is simultaneously the journey to God: self-discovery and sanctification are fused. Taylor underscores the enduring significance of Augustine's novel approach. Augustine's turn inward differs from the older Platonic introspection in which the divine ground could be recollected, discovered as always and already present in the depths of the soul. Such recollection has nothing to do with the unique challenges, decisions, and vicissitudes of an individual's life. Platonic recollection does not involve the drama of the self's struggle to relate to itself. In the Platonic scheme the divine ground itself is the true self; the true self is not the activity of relating to that ground. Augustine, however, departed from this picture by making the struggle of self-relating constitutive of the self and of the self's relationship with God.

Moreover, according to Taylor, Augustine further complicates the Platonic picture by insisting that the relationship of God and the self is rendered problematic by sin. God and the self are currently estranged from one another by the self's own activity. Consequently, the reflexive turn does not by itself produce self-certainty and self-mastery or lead to the discovery of the self's autonomous powers. Rather, the effort to relate the self to God initially uncovers the self's incapacity and insufficiency. This floundering

20. See, e.g., Richard Sorabji, *Emotion and Peace of Mind: From Stoic Agitation to Christian Temptation* (Oxford: Oxford University Press, 2000).

21. Charles Taylor, *The Sources of the Self: The Making of Modern Identity* (Cambridge, MA: Harvard University Press, 1989), pp. 131, 134.

of the project of self-knowledge on the reality of sin was part and parcel of Augustine's more general shift of attention from knowing "the good" to personal assenting to "the good." Augustine deprivileged the mind as the exclusive or primary organ for apprehending truth. He came to treat the will as a kind of independent variable determining what we can see and know. Unlike many of his philosophical forebears, for Augustine the will is not just determined by what the mind sees and understands. In conjunction with this highlighting of volition, Augustine locates the source of evil in the soul's tendency to convert self-reflexivity into self-enclosure, in the drive of individuals to make themselves the center of their worlds. Taylor points out that, for Augustine, spiritual healing only comes when the self-aggrandizing soul acknowledges its dependence on God in the very intimacy of its presence to itself. To express it differently, the soul must be enabled to love God; the soul must be swiveled around so that God is the focus of its attention and desire. In other words, Augustine introduced into Western thought the revolutionary theme that love precedes knowledge.[22] Thus, according to Taylor, Augustine was not only responsible for the subjective turn but also for the decisive thematization of the conviction that volition is not determined by cognition, and for the foregrounding of a fatal flaw in volition.

Later in *Sources of the Self,* Taylor argues that all of these themes are echoed, with some modification, of course, by Kierkegaard.[23] According to Taylor, Kierkegaard filters these Augustinian motifs through the modern concept of the creative imagination. Rather than using Augustine's language of divine illumination to explain the transformation in the individual's self-understanding, Kierkegaard uses the post-Romantic view of the capacity of the self to adopt an imaginative stance toward life in general and oneself in particular — and thereby to constitute them. According to Taylor, the transformation of the self in Kierkegaard's pages involves a shift in the way the self imagines its own self, which in turn involves a new construal of the self's relationship to God. The individual chooses to see its life in a novel way, perhaps without actually changing anything about its empirical circumstances. In Taylor's genealogy, the major link with Augustine is Kierkegaard's insistence that this transformation comes from within (even if the motivation is inspired by God) and occurs in the individual's interiority. The new and redeemed life is rooted in a new way of relating to one's own self.

---

22. Taylor, *Sources of the Self,* p. 128.
23. Taylor, *Sources of the Self,* pp. 449-53.

Many other interpreters basically agree with Taylor's tendency to identify Augustine's work as the birth of the modern introspective self that ultimately came to fruition in the writings of Kierkegaard. For many of them, the introspective turn is more or less detachable from its Christian underpinnings and is symptomatic of vast cultural changes that transcend the concerns of Christian communities. In this approach the admittedly different philosophical anthropologies of the two thinkers can be extracted from their Christian presuppositions and treated as independent variables. Martin Heidegger famously differentiated Augustine's helpful analysis of the disclosure of historical being in the forms of angst, care, and self-problematization from Augustine's utterly unhelpful ahistorical ontotheology. It is not accidental that Heidegger did this during the very period in his life when he was absorbing Kierkegaard's work, and his positive description of Augustine is saturated with Kierkegaardian terminology.[24] In a similar way, Wilhelm Anz credited Kierkegaard with being a primary witness to the "ontologically sovereign I."[25] Krister Stendahl famously agreed that Augustine was "the first modern man," and he ascribed to the *Confessions* the honor of being "the first great document in the history of the introspective conscience."[26] Continuing this interpretive trajectory, Mark C. Taylor has proposed that the "epoch of self" was initiated by that staple of the Western canon, Augustine's *Confessions.*[27] Although Augustine's legacy was undermined by Hegel's theory of the culturally constructed self, it was rehabilitated by Kierkegaard. Yet, in spite of their differences, both Hegel and Kierkegaard were indebted to Augustine's seminal account of human life as a journey to selfhood.[28] According to Taylor, Augustine's momentous interiorization of the biblical drama of creation, fall, redemption, and consummation could be cut loose from its scriptural roots. Similarly, Jean-François Lyotard has proposed that Augustine's "I" was the progenitor of the Car-

24. Martin Heidegger, "Augustin und der Neuplatonismus," in *Gesamtausgabe,* vol. 60: *Phänomenologie des Religiösen Lebens* (Frankfurt am Main: Vittorio Klostermann, 1995), pp. 157-299.

25. Wilhelm Anz, *Kierkegaard und der deutsche Idealismus* (Tübingen: J. C. B. Mohr, 1956), p. 70.

26. Krister Stendahl, "Paul and the Interpretive Conscience of the West," *The Harvard Theological Review* 55, no. 4 (1963): 205.

27. Mark C. Taylor, *Erring: A PostModern A/Theology* (Chicago: University of Chicago Press, 1984), p. 35.

28. Mark C. Taylor, *Journeys to Selfhood: Hegel and Kierkegaard* (Berkeley: University of California Press, 1980), p. 5.

tesian *cogito,* and even the ancestor of Edmund Husserl's transcendental ego.[29]

Other interpreters who trace a positive Augustine-Kierkegaard connection are not in complete agreement with Charles Taylor's rendition. Some commentators locate the parallelism not in the analysis of human subjectivity but in the desire of both Augustine and Kierkegaard to illuminate the true meaning of traditional Christian doctrines and virtues. The alleged "subjective turn" is simply part of the effort to elucidate the necessary passional conditions for felicitous Christian communication. These expositors construe the two thinkers as orthodox Christians who were simply clarifying the existential dimensions of standard Christian teachings. For example, in the middle of the twentieth century, Denzil Patrick announced that Kierkegaard "regarded Augustinianism as representing the true Christian position."[30] More recently, David Gouwens has argued that Kierkegaard's "Augustinian narrative understanding of the self" is not rooted in an autonomous psychological interpretation of human inwardness or self-constitution. Rather, Kierkegaard's treatment of selfhood and passion presupposes the pattern of creation/fall/redemption implicit in Christian doctrine in order to clarify the *telos,* failures, and challenges of Christian living.[31] Arnold B. Come agrees with this view and has proposed that Kierkegaard's purpose, like Augustine's, is to present the contents of Christian beliefs in a way that edifies the reader. In order to do this, the author must not only have a conceptual grasp of the doctrines, but also must be personally involved with the subject matter.[32]

Other Christian theologians have narrated a similar saga — but with a more critical intent. They agree with Charles Taylor that Augustine and Kierkegaard did locate all knowledge of God in the self's interiority, but they decry this theological move. For them, the methodological use of subjectivity is a capitulation to the anthropocentrism and even egocentrism of modern culture. The alleged inward turn is a betrayal of the proper focus of Christianity on the objective saving acts of God; it distorts the faith by

29. Jean-François Lyotard, *The Confession of Augustine,* trans. Richard Beardsworth (Palo Alto, CA: Stanford University Press, 2000).

30. Denzil G. M. Patrick, *Pascal and Kierkegaard: A Study in the Strategy of Evangelism,* vols. 1-2 (London: Lutterworth Press, 1947), 2: 322.

31. David Gouwens, *Kierkegaard as Religious Thinker* (Cambridge: Cambridge University Press, 1996), pp. 67-74, 90.

32. Arnold B. Come, *Kierkegaard as Theologian: Recovering Myself* (Montreal and Kingston: McGill-Queens University Press, 1997), pp. 44-46.

interpreting it in the light of the evolution of human subjectivity. For example, Karl Barth lamented that the Augustinian inward turn was transmitted by the pietists to Kierkegaard, who in turn inspired the self-obsession of the existentialists.[33] This subjectivizing strategy had deleterious consequences for Christian thought, because the foregrounding of subjectivity made the *ordo salutis* (the order, or the stages of the process of salvation) the organizing principle of theology. An antecedent analysis of human frustrations and aspirations became the lens through which the significance of all doctrinal affirmations was viewed. As a result, the gospel's concentration on the unanticipated reconciliation accomplished in Christ was displaced by the drama of human spiritual aspiration. Tragically, the Christian message was forced unto a procrustean bed of theories about human nature, and preconceived notions of human flourishing woefully distorted the actual good news of Christianity. The momentum of the current flowing from Augustine to Kierkegaard helped theology metamorphose into anthropology.

More radical interpretations detect not the birth of the self but rather its demise in the inward turn of Augustine and Kierkegaard. Jean-François Lyotard observes that Augustine and Kierkegaard not only write about the self but also construct it through the process of writing.[34] In their respective works the self is a performance, not a preexisting substantive entity. As such it is a fabrication, an imaginative fiction. Moreover, Lyotard proposes that Augustine does not recount an unproblematic story of the journey to true selfhood, but almost inadvertently narrates the repeated loss of self, even at the seemingly advanced stages of spiritual maturation. Following the interpretive trail blazed by Pierre Courcelle, J. J. O'Meara has argued, somewhat more cautiously than does Lyotard, that Augustine generously uses fictional elements in his autobiography in order to give his life a narrative unity that would edify his audience.[35] Joakim Garff has, in a similar way, contended that Kierkegaard's self-presentation in his writings is intentionally fabricated, but nonetheless remains riddled with fissures and

---

33. Karl Barth, "A Thank You and A Bow: Kierkegaard's Reveille," trans. Martin Rumscheidt, *Canadian Journal of Theology* 11 (1965): 3-7. See also Karl Barth, *Church Dogmatics*, trans. and ed. G. W. Bromiley and Thomas Torrance (Edinburgh: T&T Clark, 1957-75), IV/1, p. 741.

34. See Lyotard, *The Confession of Augustine*.

35. J. J. O'Meara, "Augustine's *Confessions*: Elements of Fiction," in Joanne McWilliam, ed., *Augustine: From Rhetor to Theologian* (Waterloo, ON: Wilfrid Laurier Press, 1992), pp. 77-95; see also Pierre Courcelle, *Recherches sur les Confessions de Saint Augustin* (Paris: E. de Boccard, 1950), pp. 188-202.

unresolved tensions.[36] The self performed by Augustine and Kierkegaard is not integrated or coherent; rather, it remains disjointed, fragmented, and motley — in spite of their authorial intentions.

The Elusiveness of the Augustine-Kierkegaard Connection

This overview of interpretive options shows a high degree of variation in the way Kierkegaard's relationship to Augustine has been accessed. On the one hand, sometimes the discontinuities between the two thinkers have been highlighted, with much attention being given to the ostensible divergences concerning the role of free human agency and concerning the function of "objective" doctrinal assertions. On the other hand, sometimes the apparent continuity in the foregrounding of self-relatedness has been emphasized in order to recount a more general story of the turn to the subject in epistemology, ethics, and cultural life. Sometimes a genealogy linking Augustine and Kierkegaard is traced in order to validate a purported parallelism in the use of Christian pathos in the doing of theology. But what is striking and significant about these accounts is the way Kierkegaard figures prominently as either hero or villain in a narrative of cultural history that has its roots in Augustine. Kierkegaard's work is portrayed either as the premier fruit of the Augustinian spirit or as its subversion. Even when the differences between the two are emphasized, those differences are usually presented as Kierkegaard's modification of or reaction against the Augustinian/Lutheran heritage that nurtured him. The one common thread in all of these various accounts is that some kind of important connection is presupposed. In general, this connection has something to do with the respective roles of "inwardness," "subjectivity," and "doctrines" in the two thinkers, and the related issue of the interplay between the self's relationship with God and the self's relationship to itself. For many, the connection, whether it is positive or negative, also has something to do with the critical roles assigned to divine and human agency in the two writers' works.

Oddly, the exact nature of Kierkegaard's relationship to Augustine on these foundational matters has not been extensively studied.[37] Usually

---

36. See Joakim Garff, *Kierkegaard: A Biography,* trans. Bruce Kirmmse (Princeton, NJ: Princeton University Press, 2005).

37. Exceptions to this rule are Robert B. Puchniak, "Kierkegaard and Augustine: A Study in Christian Existence" (PhD diss., Drew University, 2007); see also Puchniak's shorter essays, "Augustine: Kierkegaard's Tempered Admiration of Augustine," in Jon Stewart, ed., *Kierke-*

a few parallels are duly noted, and then either celebrated or decried, depending on the interpreter's ideological sensibilities. But a more nuanced comparison — attending to specific influences, convergences, and divergences — seldom occurs. Often the vaunted similarities and differences are described in very abstract and impressionistic terms, or they are discussed with respect to just one portion of the thinkers' evolving and multifarious writings. Convergences and divergences on specific issues in specific contexts are often not considered; the differences in historical context are often not probed in depth. Another curiosity is the widespread failure to take into account Kierkegaard's explicit statements about Augustine — and the nature of his exposure to Augustine's thought. Even stranger, the internal tensions in the two writers' respective writings are not compared. Given the importance often ascribed to the Augustine-Kierkegaard connection, a closer investigation of the relationship between the two is sorely needed. This is the task that this volume will undertake.

The purpose of this project is not to collate verbal similarities and dissimilarities between Augustine's and Kierkegaard's doctrinal-sounding assertions, as if their words could be detached from their rhetorical contexts and treated like passion-neutral cognitive propositions. The theological articulations of Augustine and Kierkegaard cannot be compared in the way that the doctrinal formulae of a Reformed Scholastic theologian like Francis Turretin or a Lutheran Scholastic theologian like Johann Gerhard can be set side by side. Neither Augustine nor Kierkegaard was a systematic theologian in either the Scholastic or the modern sense. Both were rhetorical thinkers to the core, convinced that literary qualities and conceptual content could not be divorced. Both hoped to achieve certain affective and behavioral purposes through their writing; both sought to edify, console, unsettle, and provoke their readers. Their works were performances, often acts of adoration or confession. Moreover, both writers were highly contextual, responding to specific cultural crises and addressing particular audiences. Sensitive to the particularities of context, audience, and purpose, both Augustine and Kierkegaard produced works in several different genres, ranging from pieces that look like philosophical essays to sermons and prayers.

---

gaard and the Patristic and Medieval Traditions (Aldershot, UK: Ashgate, 2007), pp. 11-22, and "Kierkegaard's 'Self' and Augustine's Influence," in Heiko Schulz, Jon Stewart, and Karl Verstrynge, eds. (in cooperation with Peter Šajda), *Kierkegaard Studies Yearbook 2011* (Berlin: Walter de Gruyter, 2012), pp. 181-94. Another seminal work dealing with Augustine and Kierkegaard is Glenn Graham, "Kierkegaard and the Longing for God" (PhD diss., McMaster University, 2011).

Their selection of literary strategies was very self-conscious, for both writers wanted to move readers to think and feel more deeply rather than merely provide readers with new information, clearer concepts, or more compelling arguments. For both thinkers, the theological import of their words cannot be abstracted from their efforts to nurture the adoration of God and to elicit gratitude for divine grace. Of course, paying attention to the performative force of their texts does not deny that Augustine and Kierkegaard were both advancing substantive theological claims. This reading strategy only presupposes that in the cases of these two intensely literary theologians, both of whom were intent on catalyzing a spiritual transformation of their readers, the theological substance cannot be divorced from the rhetorical purpose.

Conceptual instruction was not an end in itself for either one: both wanted readers to struggle with their texts in order to grow spiritually. Consequently, both Augustine and Kierkegaard often wrote in an odd, elliptical way so that the readers had to examine their own hearts in order to make sense of the text. Augustine remarks in the *Confessions* concerning his own book: "What does it matter to me, if someone does not understand this? Let such a person rejoice even to ask the question, 'What does this mean?' Yes, let him rejoice in that, and choose to find by not finding rather than by finding fail to find you."[38] Augustine even exclaims: "Of this I am certain and I am not afraid to declare it from my heart, that if I had to write something to which the highest authority would be attributed, I would rather write in such a way that my words would reinforce for each reader whatever truth he was able to grasp about these matters, than express a single idea so unambiguously as to exclude others. . . ."[39] Margaret Miles has suggested that Augustine's actual literary practice matched his espoused theory, claiming that he "purposefully wrote in a way that invited multiple interpretations."[40] Augustine's deliberate polysemy and contextual sensitivity make any effort to translate his elliptic prose into univocal doctrinal propositions and systematically arranged formulae a distortion of his writing.

Like Kierkegaard, Augustine was acutely sensitive to the limitations of direct communication between the writer and the reader in all matters of spiritual importance, and he was duly suspicious of the impact of the writ-

---

38. Augustine, *Confessions (Confessiones)*, I, 6 (10), in *WSA* I, 1.

39. Augustine *Confessions*, XII, 31 (42), in *WSA* I, 1.

40. Margaret Miles, *Desire and Delight: A New Reading of Augustine's "Confessions"* (New York: Crossroad, 1992), p. 13.

er's authority. He warns, "Do not think that anyone learns anything from another person."[41] External words are nothing but "useless sounds" unless they prompt the hearer to turn inward and listen for the "Interior Master."[42] For Augustine, indirection and ambiguity are often required for the kind of transformative communication that he treasured. His early Cassiciacum dialogues adopt the dialogic form of Cicero but, as Catherine Conybeare has argued, disrupt that genre with digressions, displacements, and irresolutions.[43] Multivocality pervades these dialogues, peppered as they are with interstices and jolting shifts in perspective. Multiple voices and unresolved disjunctions even appear in *The Soliloquies (Soliloquia)*, his conversations with his own reason. In a different way, ambiguity also pervades Augustine's sermons, for he often disguises their rhetorical structure, forcing the auditor to probe beneath the surface.[44] When it is necessary for his rhetorical purposes, Augustine, the bishop who was vested with ecclesiastical authority, could even announce that he was writing "without authority," a phrase that would later be dear to Kierkegaard. In spite of his frequent condemnations of the aestheticism of the classical rhetorical heritage, Augustine does not hesitate to use his exquisite training in that classical heritage to prod and coax the reader to self-reflection and a heartfelt encounter with the divine.

Augustine's authorial strategies are reflections of his own very deliberate practices of reading Scripture.[45] Though he sometimes insists on fidelity to the more literal and plain sense of a scriptural passage, Augustine frequently celebrates the multivalent possibilities resident within those biblical texts. When commenting on Genesis, which Augustine assumes had been written by Moses, he proposes that Moses may have meant several things in a given passage, and that he may not even have realized all the things that his words could mean.[46] Evidently, for Augustine, meaning was not always tied to the intention of the author. (One must admit that Augustine was very inconsistent in this.) At times he could even claim that the ambi-

41. Augustine, *Homilies on the First Epistle of John (Tractatus in epistulam Ioannis ad Parthos)*, 2, in WSA III, 14.

42. Augustine, *Homilies on the First Epistle of John*, in WSA III, 14.

43. Catherine Conybeare, *The Irrational Augustine* (Oxford: Oxford University Press, 2006), p. 4.

44. Paul R. Kolbet, *Augustine and the Cure of Souls* (Notre Dame, IN: University of Notre Dame Press, 2010), p. 175.

45. See Bertrand de Margerie, *An Introduction to the History of Exegesis*, vol. 3, *Saint Augustine*, trans. Pierre de Fontnouvelle (Petersham, MA: Saint Bede's Publications, 1991), pp. 60-61.

46. See Augustine, *Confessions*, XII, 31 (42), in WSA I, 1.

guity of certain Scripture passages is a spiritual boon because it stimulates different opinions and a dialogic search for truth.[47] Sometimes Augustine recommends a literal reading of a passage, and sometimes an allegorical reading, depending on which reading would help the Christian community grow in love. He was aware that different reading strategies could legitimately be applied to Scripture, and he realized that the meaning of his own texts would also be negotiated by the reader.

Kierkegaard's use of sophisticated destabilizing literary strategies is even more dramatic and obvious than Augustine's. Kierkegaard, of course, is notorious for his use of irony, indirect communication, books-within-books, and pseudonymous voices. His works are saturated with elusive metaphors, interrupted narratives, and strange juxtapositions that frustrate any univocal interpretation. His disorienting style and *heteroglossia* is designed to resist closure and render facile appropriation impossible. Kierkegaard accomplishes the goal of producing a demanding body of work that would force readers to struggle to make sense of it, and by so struggling, be provoked to make sense of their own lives. Kierkegaard succeeded so well in this that some interpreters have denied that his texts have a specific meaning or message at all, thus concluding that his works are simply provocations.[48] While this is surely an exaggeration (because Kierkegaard was trying to encourage certain particular transformations of pathos in his readers, as we shall see), it is nevertheless obvious that edification and literary indirection were correlative for him.[49] Much more than Augustine, he was suspicious that the coercive authority of any writer could subvert the self-reflection that genuine faith requires. Like Augustine, he often deliberately writes in a way that might be amenable to multiple interpretations in order to foster the involvement of the reader in the construction of meaning. Like Augustine, he was convinced that learning to assume responsibility for one's interpretations should be a pedagogy in the more sweeping assumption of responsibility for one's own self (even though that assumption of responsibility is only a preparation for the turn to grace).

Kierkegaard's elusive way of writing had an even deeper motivation. He was convinced that any bit of writing about matters of existential importance acquires meaning only when it is used to nurture the "pathos" and

---

47. See Augustine, *The City of God (De civitate Dei)*, xi, 19.

48. See Roger Poole, *Kierkegaard: The Indirect Communication* (Charlottesville: University Press of Virginia, 1993).

49. See Michael Strawser, *Both/And: Reading Kierkegaard from Edification to Irony* (New York: Fordham University Press, 1993).

"subjectivity" — or "inwardness" — of the reader. Therefore, the shape of the communicative activity must reflect the concerns, feelings, passions, hopes, and fears that are part of its theological message. The pathos must be evident in the form, not just the content, of the communication, because passions cannot be transferred through simple didactic instruction, as if they were neutral data. The attempt to communicate an existential truth must be sensitive to the fact that the desired understanding and the passional process through which it is acquired are essentially linked. Kierkegaard says: "If this [an existential possibility] is communicated in a direct form, then the point is missed; then the reader is led into a misunderstanding — he gets something more to know, that to exist (*at existere*) also has its meaning, but he receives it as knowledge so that he keeps right on sitting in the *status quo*" (JP 1, 633). Authoritative, information-conveying disquisitions inevitably fail to trigger the appropriate pathos. All communication of a capacity to feel and act in new ways must use indirect strategies that destabilize certainties, provoke disquietudes, and stimulate yearnings. Accordingly, as a religious writer, Kierkegaard persuades, cajoles, exhorts, promises, and commands. Concerning the difficulties of being a religious writer, Kierkegaard observes: "The first and foremost task is to create pathos, with the superiority of intelligence, imagination, penetration, to guarantee pathos for the existential, which the 'understanding' has reduced to the ludicrous" (JP 6, 6521). To engage his texts rightly, we must pay attention to his subtle communicative strategies, including his choice of genre, voice, identity of the addressee, and rhetorical force.

In their different ways, both Augustine and Kierkegaard were agreed that the form of a communication had to be appropriate to its content. Of course, there are profound differences between them that cannot be ignored. Augustine, the master classicist, often engages in more overt and sometimes heavy-handed persuasion. When engaged in polemics against alleged heretics, he could even be coercively dogmatic. Kierkegaard, the child of Romantic culture, delights even more than Augustine did in thick irony. Disappointed in the established church, Kierkegaard could not and would not invoke institutional authority. But, in spite of these differences, both write in such a way that their rhetorical strategies are inseparable from the possible meanings of their texts. Consequently, any theological comparison of the two must take into account the passional purposes of any given passage in their works. Similar-sounding doctrinal assertions may not be enough to establish real agreement in the faith, and seemingly divergent propositions may not necessarily be signals of different visions of the Christian life. Therefore, our project is more elusive than any straightforward doctrinal comparison. We can only compare their respective construals of Christian faith and life by paying attention to the metaphors, images, authorial voices, and a host of other literary devices that animate their texts. In any given context, we must take into account the specific pastoral goals that are being pursued by these strategies. Only by heeding the pastoral purposes and rhetorical properties of their writings can we attempt to identify convergences and divergences on specific theological motifs.

In so doing, we may discover that the convergences are more profound and unexpected than a less literary reading would suggest. Some hidden and occluded similarities of a very fundamental nature may become visible. We may also discover that both Augustine and Kierkegaard sought to hold in dialectical tension foundational themes from the Christian heritage that most other theologians have separated and regarded as incompatible, or have inadequately tried to integrate by allowing one to subsume the other. Both writers, we may find, were trying to make room in their depictions of Christianity for both human responsibility and for utter reliance on grace, for both works of love and for faith, for the emulation of Christ and trust in Christ's divine compassion, and for life as a journey to God and for life as God's embrace of humanity. Perhaps Augustine and Kierkegaard were both attempting as best they could to do justice to the complex, multidimensional, and seemingly paradoxical nature of the Christian life. We may even discover that a similar vision of the self-emptying God was at the center of their respective theologies.

The Structure of This Book

In order to identify the points of intersection and divergence between Augustine and Kierkegaard, I will use two different strategies in this book, one historical and the other thematic. First, before we can attempt any thorough interpretation of the relationship of Kierkegaard's thought to Augustine's, we must examine the historical question concerning the character and extent of the sources of Kierkegaard's familiarity with Augustine. Kierkegaard's picture of Augustine may have been partial, and at least somewhat different from our own. What the name "Augustine" suggested to Kierkegaard may well not be the same thing that it suggests to us. Once we have investigated Kierkegaard's exposure to Augustine, we can better appreciate his explicit comments about Augustine and his references to Augustine's works by situating them in his cultural context. We shall discover that Kierkegaard inherited a bifocal view of Augustine: he was seen as both a passionate, self-involving author and as an abstract metaphysician. Kierkegaard embraced the first Augustine and excoriated the second. We shall also discover that Kierkegaard's Augustine was much more systematic and much less rhetorical than the Augustine who has emerged in contemporary scholarship. This is unfortunate, for the Augustine known to many contemporary interpreters bears a more striking similarity to Kierkegaard than did the Augustine constructed by early-nineteenth-century scholars.

Having limned a rough outline of Kierkegaard's portrait of Augustine, I will begin the second, lengthier phase of this project. I will trace particular substantive parallels and divergences between the two thinkers, even when Augustine is not explicitly named as a source or a conversation partner by Kierkegaard.[50] I shall choose the topics to be explored on the basis of their potential fruitfulness for the purpose of comparison — and because of their importance in the work of the two authors. First, and most importantly, I will argue that the theme of desire for God is foundational for both authors: both Augustine and Kierkegaard presuppose that the human heart is restless and that its ultimate *telos* is God as the highest good. Second, I will argue that Augustine and Kierkegaard make "journey" the central metaphor for the Christian life. For both of them, the use of this now hackneyed image was a significant and controversial move, for in the case of Augustine it shifted attention away from the earlier patristic figuring of the Christian life as participation in the story of Christ, and in the case of Kierkegaard it functioned as an alternative to the dominant Lutheran nonteleological understanding of faith. The related motifs of desire/love for God and the Christian life as a journey provide the underlying structure and basic dynamics of each writer's variegated theological production.

In the subsequent chapters I will explore how the themes of "desire" and "journey" inform the ways Augustine and Kierkegaard developed certain key theological concepts. I have selected these particular concepts for special attention because they figure prominently in both Augustine's and Kierkegaard's writings and because they crystallize the differences and similarities between their projects. Because defining "God" solely in terms

---

50. This strategy is used by Robert B. Puchniak in "Kierkegaard and Augustine: A Study in Christian Existence." Puchniak argues that the three forms of despair mentioned in *Sickness unto Death* so closely resemble aspects of Augustine's narrative of the self in the *Confessions* that it is possible that Kierkegaard's text owes an unspoken debt to Augustine's work.

of the ultimate object of desire is purely formal, we will pay particular attention to the ways in which each thinker gives further specificity to the concept "God" by situating it in the unique passions of the Christian life. I will propose that, for both Augustine and Kierkegaard, the desirability of God is identified with God's self-giving love. The attractiveness of God is the beauty of *kenosis*. Philippians 2:5-11 provides the content for their more abstract concepts of God as "the Eternal," "Truth," "Wisdom," and "the highest good." Next I will examine the derailment of the journey toward God by human sin. Here I will argue that both theologians sought to affirm the seemingly oxymoronic themes of assuming responsibility for sin while confessing one's utter incapacity to liberate oneself from its power. Then I will consider Augustine's and Kierkegaard's accounts of the restoration of the possibility of continuing the journey toward God through God's grace. I will argue that both of them paradoxically seek to encourage passionate human striving while simultaneously fostering a sense of absolute reliance on God — as well as a correlative distrust of one's own powers.

Following this, I will investigate the significance and role of Christ, the agent of divine help, in their respective writings. Here I will claim that both writers treat the pattern of Christ's humble descent as the revelation of the nature of God and as the pattern for human life. For both of them, the mystery of the union of the two natures of Christ is clarified by attending to the range of appropriate passional responses to the story of Christ. Next I will examine their portrayals of the Christian life itself, particularly the interplay of trust in God and the performance of loving works. I will propose that, for both Augustine and Kierkegaard, faith and love can only be separated conceptually, for the two virtues are different aspects of attraction to God. Finally, I will consider the two thinkers' very different understanding of the nature and purpose of the church. Here, of course, a sharp divergence between Augustine and Kierkegaard will become evident. I will propose that their parting of the ways is due to their differing assessments of the respective weights of attraction/assurance and risk/uncertainty in the cultivation of the Christian life. For Augustine, unsteady and faltering pilgrims require communal reassurance and positive enticements to keep them on track, while for Kierkegaard, anesthetized and complacent conformists need to be destabilized and jolted into forward movement.

With regard to each topic, I will suggest that both Augustine and Kierkegaard present the Christian life as being animated by pairs of seemingly countervailing dynamics: God as the object of desire and God as an unexpected benefaction; sin as personal culpability and sin as a crippling debility; salvation as a task and salvation as a gift; Christ as God's self-emptying and Christ as a human model of suffering self-sacrifice; the Christian life as receptive trust and the Christian life as active love; and the church as the presence of grace and the church as a catalyst for further striving. In most of these instances both Augustine and Kierkegaard deal with the ostensible conceptual tensions most fruitfully by showing how each of the countervailing themes is embedded in specific forms of pathos, and then by suggesting how these passions can be combined in the living of a life. Treated as metaphysical affirmations, the pairs resist integration. But construed as sets of passions, attitudes, and dispositions, the apparent polar opposites can mutually inform and enrich one another. For example, the efficacy of God's sovereign will and the responsibility of human agency may not be amenable to a conceptual integration, but the passions of relying on God absolutely and striving earnestly to become more godly can be held together.

We must, however, admit that Kierkegaard and Augustine did in some respects differ on this strategy of clarifying seemingly countervailing Christian convictions by contextualizing them in the appropriate forms of Christian pathos. Kierkegaard overtly resisted plotting the dialectically paired theological themes on a metaphysical map; his disdain for "systems," whether they were philosophical or doctrinal, was notorious. Augustine, on the other hand, implicitly showed how metaphysical resolutions of theological conundrums may not be necessary; he did so by simply exemplifying the pastoral uses of contrapuntal doctrinal themes in his writings. The glaring difference between the two theologians is that Augustine continued to think that a metaphysical comprehension of the relationship of seemingly discordant themes may be both desirable and possible. More particularly, he believed that the pursuit of such an "understanding" would be spiritually edifying, for it would focus attention on divine matters, increase delight in divine things, and stabilize the wayward heart. Kierkegaard, needless to say, found such speculation to be spiritually damaging. This difference in attitude was due to Augustine's opinion that pilgrims require reassurance and the prospect of deeper forms of joyful knowledge, which speculation can promise; on the other side was Kierkegaard's conviction that pilgrims need to be kept unsettled and restless, which speculation would subvert.

Through these historical and thematic investigations we may develop a clearer understanding of a theological trajectory that stretches from Augustine to Kierkegaard. My final goal in this book is to offer some tentative assessment of the possible significance of this trajectory. I will suggest that both Augustine and Kierkegaard are representatives of a tendency that refuses to dichotomize delight in God's unmerited presence, and of a passionate yearning to experience God's beauty and grow in Godlikeness. God both immediately blesses the individual with God's self-bestowal in the present moment and lures the individual forward with increased yearning for deeper intimacy and a more profound imaging of God. God is simultaneously the one whose caring and forgiving presence is received in trust, as Luther had proclaimed, and the *telos* of the human pilgrimage, as Aquinas had insisted. Divine agape and human eros are unified here, for it is actually the prospect of God's agapeic love for which humans yearn and which is at the core of God's attractive beauty. This theological vision is different from the synthesis of justification and sanctification in the Reformed heritage, for it has less to do with delight in doing God's will and more to do with loving intimacy with God as a partner. God is not so much the transcendent parent who orders chaos, establishes shalom, and who is lovingly obeyed, as God is the cosmic beloved. (Of course, both Augustine and Kierkegaard generously use parental imagery for God, but this language was mixed with powerful spousal imagery.) Other theologians, in different ways and using different vocabularies, have gestured toward a similar vision, among them Jonathan Edwards and Hans Urs von Balthasar. But Augustine, at the dawn of Christendom, and Kierkegaard, at its twilight, may come closest to articulating a vision of the Christian life that simultaneously rests immediately in God's mercy and is drawn forward toward the beauty of God's love.

PART ONE

Setting the Stage:
Two Pilgrims on the Way Home

CHAPTER 1

Kierkegaard's Tensive Picture of Augustine

Many Kierkegaard scholars have noted, usually with considerable surprise, that Kierkegaard seldom comments on Augustine's work in any sustained way. Neither his journals nor his published writings abound with detailed analyses or critiques of Augustine. In Kierkegaard's pages, Augustine gets much less attention, for example, than does Socrates or even Luther. Moreover, even cursory references to Augustine are not particularly numerous in Kierkegaard's writings. What is most shocking, however, is that Kierkegaard does not explicitly mention the *Confessions*, the book that is usually considered to be most like his own writings — both in style and in substance. Many of the allusions to Augustine that appear in his work seem to be based on lectures about Augustine that Kierkegaard heard or discussions of Augustine in theological and historical textbooks that Kierkegaard read. When Kierkegaard does treat Augustine overtly, he does so unsystematically, often appropriating or attacking themes that are incidental to Augustine's main purpose. This is certainly odd, given the prevalent (but opposed) perceptions that Kierkegaard either revivified the Augustinian heritage or devoted his career to dismantling it.

However, some scholars have suggested that, in spite of the dearth of direct references, a more indirect and unacknowledged presence of Augustine does indeed pervade Kierkegaard's writings, and that the latter may not even have been aware of the true nature and extent of his indebtedness. As early as the 1940s, Ernst Moritz Manasse claimed to detect such a deep parallelism between the two thinkers on the importance of self-consciousness in the life of faith that some kind of mediated influence must be posited.[1] A few years later, Carl Weltzer attempted to demonstrate that both Søren and his brother Peter were inspired by a renaissance of interest in Augustine that had occurred in Denmark in the early nineteenth century.[2] In 1981, Jørgen Pedersen forcefully argued that the structure of Kierkegaard's thought was implicitly based on the presuppositions of the Augustinian tradition.[3] While admitting that Kierkegaard did not engage in any profound study of Augustine, George Pattison, David Gouwens, and many other scholars have suggested that the influence of Augustine was transmitted to Kierkegaard indirectly through the impact that Augustine had exerted on the Lutheran heritage and Western Christendom in general.[4] Robert Puchniak has pointed out that, though Kierkegaard's published works reveal only a few explicit traces of Augustine, his journals do show a more intensive engagement, some of which is appreciative and some of which is critical.[5] Given these considerations, Augustine's influence on Kierkegaard may have been stronger than the relative absence of Augustine in Kierkegaard's published writings would indicate.

To assess the nature of Augustine's impact on Kierkegaard, we must first try to reconstruct as best we can Kierkegaard's acquaintance with Augustine's writings and the picture of Augustine that he inherited from his intellectual environment. In every era, the popular portrayals of Augustine have been highly selective and have reflected the unique concerns of that particular culture, and nineteenth-century northern Europe was no different in this regard. It was not some alleged Augustine-in-himself that influenced Kierkegaard,

---

1. Ernst Moritz Manasse, "Conversation and Liberation: A Comparison of Augustine and Kierkegaard," *Review of Religion* 7 (1943): 361-83.

2. Carl Weltzer, "Augustinus og Brøderne Kierkegaard," in *Festskrift til Jens Nørregaard* (Copenhagen: G. E. C. Gads, 1947), pp. 305-20.

3. Jørgen Pedersen, "Augustine and Augustinianism," in Niels Thulstrup and Marie Mikulvá Thulstrup, eds., *Kierkegaard and Great Traditions* (Copenhagen: C. A. Reitzel, 1981), pp. 54-97.

4. George Pattison, "Johannes Climacus and Aurelius Augustinus on Recollecting the Truth," in Robert L. Perkins, ed., *International Kierkegaard Commentary: Philosophical Fragments and Johannes Climacus* (Macon, GA: Mercer University Press, 1994), pp. 245-60; David Gouwens, *Kierkegaard as Religious Thinker* (Cambridge: Cambridge University Press, 1996), pp. 90-91.

5. Robert Puchniak, "Augustine: Kierkegaard's Tempered Admiration of Augustine," in Jon Stewart, ed., *Kierkegaard and the Patristic and Medieval Traditions* (Aldershot, UK: Ashgate, 2007), pp. 11-22; see also Puchniak, "Kierkegaard's 'Self' and Augustine's Influence," in Heiko Schulz, Jon Stewart, and Karl Verstrynge, eds., in cooperation with Peter Šajda, *Kierkegaard Studies Yearbook 2011* (Berlin: Walter de Gruyter, 2012), pp. 181-94.

but rather Augustine as constructed by a set of nineteenth-century Germans and Danes. This cultural mediation of Augustine is particularly important in Kierkegaard's case, given the fact that he relied heavily on secondary sources. It is also crucial to take this mediation into account because Kierkegaard always appropriated other authors with an eye to their potential use in his own polemical exchanges with his culture.

The reconstruction of Kierkegaard's nineteenth-century picture of Augustine is all the more necessary because Augustine's tentative, rhetorical, and highly contextual writings have uniquely lent themselves to widely divergent appropriations in different eras and different cultural milieus. Although Augustine's work ranged over almost all the topics dear to subsequent theologians, it was not neatly systematic. Nor were his reflections on these theological topics static. In fact, he freely admitted that he had changed his mind about many matters, sometimes drastically, and confessed that much truth remained hidden from him. For example, in recalling his struggle to understand the origin of the soul, Augustine admits: "I did not know then and I still do not know."[6] The influential Augustine scholar J. J. O'Meara has concluded: "In spite of the picture of him [Augustine] as the great definer of doctrines in the West, he was also profoundly questioning, profoundly aporetic."[7] Augustine was so unsystematic that he often exhibited countervailing tendencies. For example, he harbored a deep countercultural streak, including suspicions of the hubris of empire and the incapacity of philosophy to transform the soul. Nevertheless, he was also willing to appropriate the thought forms of the intellectual elite, to court alliances with the imperial authorities, and even to welcome the use of governmental coercion. Exhibiting another tension, Augustine emphasized human responsibility against the Manicheans, but emphasized the power of divine grace against the Pelagians. He critiqued the Donatist hunger for purity in the church, but continued to conceive of human life as a way toward sanctity. Sensitive to these discordant motifs in Augustine's texts, James J. O'Donnell has denied that Augustine's work can be reduced to "a linear, reductionistic narrative of the consecutive transformations of that single personality-entity."[8] According to O'Donnell, Augustine's thought does not

6. See Augustine, *Revisions*, I, 1.3, in *WSA* I, 2.

7. J. J. O'Meara, "Augustine's *Confessions*: Elements of Fiction," in Joanne McWilliam, ed., *Augustine: From Rhetor to Theologian* (Waterloo, ON: Wilfrid Laurier Press, 1992), p. 91.

8. James J. O'Donnell, "Augustine's Unconfessions," in John D. Caputo and Michael Scanlon, eds., *Augustine and Postmodernism: Confessions and Circumfession* (Bloomington: Indiana University Press, 2005), pp. 214-15.

exhibit coherence, control, or integration, for it was a complex composite of seemingly contradictory impulses. Augustine's works cannot be arranged into a neat system of mutually entailing propositions, and the discrepancies among his writings cannot be dismissed as being merely due to the evolution of his thought.

The piecemeal, rhetorical, and context-specific nature of Augustine's work has guaranteed that it would be interpreted in a variety of very different ways through the centuries. The proliferation of discrepant interpretations has been exacerbated by the extraordinary authority that has been ascribed to Augustine's corpus by a host of divergent theological parties. Theologian Mark Ellingsen observes: "Indeed, the entire theology of the post fifth-century Western church might be construed as a commentary on Augustine's thought."[9] Ellingsen adds that Augustine (or different theologically constructed Augustines) have served as the basic springboards for Catholic, Lutheran, Reformed, and even Wesleyan thought. The Roman Catholic heritage has appealed to an Augustine who claimed that God's grace enables growth in love so that the soul can be formed for fellowship with God. The Lutheran tradition has claimed the support of an Augustine who exposed the bondage of the will and realized that even the saints can never satisfy God's law. Reformed Christians have cited the authority of an Augustine who regarded sanctification as an essential component of the Christian life and ascribed all aspects of salvation to the power of God's sovereign grace. John Wesley invoked a pietist Augustine who proclaimed that sincere faith and an intentional life of discipleship are organically intertwined. Theologians as diverse as Thomas Aquinas and Paul Tillich have discerned an Augustine who based his thought on an assumed correlation of reason and revelation. Emil Brunner discovered a very different Augustine, who — at least at his best — explicated the narrative patterns in the biblical texts and used them as a lens to interpret human experience. Paul Ricoeur found an Augustine who delighted in the multiplicity of potentially edifying meanings that are generated when biblical text and contemporary experience interact. Even the heterodox theosophical traditions, from Paracelsus through Jacob Böhme to Franz Baader, found inspiration and support in Augustine. From the fifth century on, different pictures of Augustine have emerged, depending on which of his works have been highlighted and which issues have been taken to be most central. Because of this plurality of construals of Augustine, it will

---

9. Mark Ellingsen, *The Richness of Augustine: His Contextual and Pastoral Theology* (Louisville: Westminster John Knox, 2005), p. 1.

be necessary to determine exactly what pictures of Augustine were common in Kierkegaard's intellectual environment.

The effort to reconstruct the specifics of Kierkegaard's culturally derived picture of Augustine will involve a few different strategies. First, we must attempt to determine which of Augustine's own writings — or at least which passages in them — Kierkegaard did actually read (insofar as that is possible). Next we will investigate what Kierkegaard probably learned about Augustine through his formal studies and through his own, often desultory, reading. Finally, we will examine Kierkegaard's sporadic evaluative remarks about various aspects of Augustine's thought. Having a rough idea of the distinctive characteristics of the German and Danish portraits of Augustine, we can then gauge which of the Augustinian motifs circulating in his culture made an impression on Kierkegaard, and which ones did not. On the basis of these different kinds of evidence we can begin to limn a tentative outline of Kierkegaard's picture of Augustine.

Kierkegaard's Firsthand Familiarity with Augustine's Writings

Although Kierkegaard did not devote the amount of attention to Augustine that he did to such theological giants as Luther, or even the Pietist hymnodist Hans Adolph Brorson, he was by no means ignorant of the Bishop of Hippo and his work. Kierkegaard would have been familiar with at least some of the basic contours of Augustine's life and writings. However, the way Augustine was presented to Kierkegaard led the latter to be more cognizant of certain aspects of Augustine's theology than others — and to interpret them in particular ways. The picture of Augustine that Kierkegaard inherited was shaped by the concerns of early-nineteenth-century northern Europeans and was informed by their particular interpretive propensities, particularly by their tendency to think in terms of a three-way opposition of critical rationality, faith experience, and authoritative doctrines. (Even those theologians who hoped to "mediate" among these poles accepted the notion that they initially seem to be oppositional.) Furthermore, Kierkegaard filtered this material through the prism of his own even more specific interests. Consequently, in order to clarify Kierkegaard's relationship to Augustine, we must first try to determine exactly what he knew about Augustine, including which of Augustine's works he may have actually perused. Next we must explore the portrayal of Augustine that Kierkegaard received from his intellectual environment. Then it will be necessary to investigate

Kierkegaard's explicit evaluative remarks about Augustine. Having done all that, we can, finally, consider the ways that Kierkegaard appropriated or modified the portrait of the Bishop of Hippo that he had inherited.

Kierkegaard did have some limited firsthand acquaintance with Augustine's texts, though the exact extent of that familiarity is impossible to say. He owned a turn-of-the-century Latin edition of the complete works of Augustine in eighteen volumes (which he purchased in May 1843), as well as a different edition of *De doctrina Christiana* that was published in 1838.[10] His published works and journal entries do cite or refer to a few specific passages from Augustine's texts, often quoting them in Latin. Although many of these references are more ornamental than substantive, they may suggest that Kierkegaard did at least occasionally consult particular volumes of Augustine's work.

Kierkegaard's direct quotation of Augustine began in February 1839, when he approvingly mentioned the latter's claim that a marriage that produces children is preferable to a childless marriage because childrearing can be an effective pedagogy in resignation and selflessness (*JP* 3, 2580) — but he did not cite a specific source. It is possible that he discovered this theme in Augustine's *On the Good of Marriage (De bono conjugali)*. However, he may have only encountered a reference to it in Wilhelm de Wette's *Lærbog i den christelige Sædelære*, a textbook mostly consisting of quotations from celebrated theologians that Kierkegaard was using to prepare for his theological examinations.[11] Kierkegaard's dissertation, *The Concept of Irony*, mentions Augustine's concept *beata culpa* ("blessed fault") but does not explicitly attribute it to Augustine. Kierkegaard seems to have found the phrase in *De diligendo Deo*, which was erroneously ascribed to Augustine, though similar phrases occur elsewhere in Augustine's works.[12] Kierkegaard applied the concept not to the fall of Adam and Eve but to the abandonment of the traditional gods by the ancient Greeks. According to Kierkegaard, this defection was blessed because it occasioned the need for Socrates. A journal passage from 1843 mentions Augustine's distinction of proper and improper love, but only cites the entry *amor probus — impro-*

---

10. Augustine, *Augustini Aurelii Opera. Opera et studio Monacorum Ordinis S. Bened. e Congregat*, vols. 1-18, ed. S. Mauri, 3rd edition (Venice: Bassani, 1797-1807); *Sancti Aurelii Augustini, de doctrina Christiana*, ed. Carl Hermann Bruder (Leipzig: Tauchnitz, 1838).

11. Wilhelm Martin Leberecht de Wette, *Lærbog i den christelige Sædelære og sammes Historie*, trans. C. E. Sharling (Copenhagen: C. A. Reitzel, 1835), p. 129.

12. Augustine, *De diligendo Deo* (On the Love of God), *Augustini Aurelii Opera*, XVII, col. 1705.

bus in the index of *Opera Omnia* and does not identify a specific text (*JP* 3, 2400). In his *Prefaces* of 1844, Kierkegaard may be echoing *The City of God* when he remarks that the visible public is like the visible church, being a mixed company of saints and sinners. In *The Concept of Anxiety* (1844), Vigilius, one of Kierkegaard's pseudonymous authors, alludes to Augustine's endorsement of capital punishment for heretics, a practice that Vigilius mentions in order to dramatize the gravity of the demonic rejection of God (*CA,* 121). This is probably a reference to Augustine's epistolary exhortation to a Roman military commander to enforce the imperial decree to shut down Donatist churches (though Augustine did not advocate the execution of Donatists).[13] Also in *The Concept of Anxiety,* Vigilius's question about sexual differentiation before the fall may suggest Kierkegaard's familiarity with the fourteenth chapter of *The City of God* (*CA,* 48).[14] In *Stages on Life's Way* (1845), Kierkegaard refers to *On the Good of Widowhood (De bono viduitatis)* and quotes in Latin Augustine's claim that heaven will be filled more quickly by the practice of celibacy (*SLW,* 147).[15] In *Stages on Life's Way,* Kierkegaard also cites Augustine's comment in *On Christian Doctrine (De doctrina Christiana)* that there would be no difficulty in abstaining from a vice if there were no lust in enjoying it; and in a draft of that text he correctly identifies the exact page in *Opera Omnia* (*SLW,* 338, 601).[16] In 1847, Kierkegaard's observation in *Works of Love* that the virtues of pagans are glittering vices, which he repeats in three different contexts and attributes to "the ancient Church Fathers," could be an allusion to a passage in *The City of God,* though it could also refer to a statement by Lactantius (*WL,* 53, 196, 269).[17] Alternatively, the statement may simply have been a slogan that Kierkegaard heard, unaware of its exact source. However, the fact that Kierkegaard uses it in order to contrast paganism's view of friendship and erotic love with a Christian understanding of love does parallel Augustine's argument in this passage and may indicate familiarity with that passage. In "The Gospel of Sufferings" (also published in 1847), Kierkegaard again refers to the "glittering vice" that the pagans mistook for virtue (*UDVS,* 272). In a draft written in 1846-47 for the projected *Book on Adler,* Kierkegaard cites Augustine's conviction that individuals are forbidden to tell an untruth in order to preserve their chastity (*BA,* supplement, 293). The reference,

13. Augustine, *Letters,* Letter 185, in *WSA* II, 3.
14. Augustine, *The City of God,* XIV, 23, in *WSA* I, 6-7.
15. Augustine, *On the Excellence of Widowhood (De bono viduitatis),* 8 (11), in *WSA* I, 9.
16. Augustine, *Augustini Aurelii Opera,* III, col. 69.
17. See *Sancti Aurelii Augustini,* IX, cols. 750-51.

which he hoped would underscore the need for scrupulous honesty, was to *On Lying (De mendacio).*[18] In 1847, Kierkegaard refers to one of Augustine's sermons, drawing from it the theme that God promises to forgive sins but does not guarantee earthly felicity or longevity (*JP* 2, 1210).[19]

These few references certainly do not indicate that Kierkegaard had much firsthand engagement with Augustine's corpus. In fact, in some cases he may have only seen Augustine quoted in a secondary source. At most, these references may suggest that Kierkegaard was at least somewhat conversant with four or five of Augustine's texts, including *The City of God, On the Good of Widowhood, On Lying, On Christian Teaching,* and an unnamed anti-Donatist work (probably Letter 185). The chronological distribution also implies that Kierkegaard's perusal of Augustine's writings, however superficial and limited it may have been, probably occurred before 1847. Of course, a reference does not necessarily imply that Kierkegaard actually read a particular book, nor does an absence of a reference necessarily demonstrate a total lack of familiarity. But if Kierkegaard did at least glance at these texts, the roster of titles could be significant. Part of the significance concerns the items that are not found on the list. It is notable that Kierkegaard seldom alludes to Augustine's celebrated *Confessions* (a major exception being his paraphrase of the "restless heart" passage [*JP* 1, 65]), the book that is most frequently hailed as the precursor of Kierkegaard's own approach to theological writing and his celebrated subjective turn. Moreover, Kierkegaard seldom quotes from Augustine's doctrinally influential anti-Pelagian writings, even though the issues of original sin, human freedom, and divine grace would loom large in his own writings. (*On the Good of Widowhood* does contain an implicitly anti-Pelagian section in which Augustine urges widows to ascribe their celibacy to the power of God's grace, but Kierkegaard does not refer to that section.) Perhaps less surprisingly, Augustine's rather speculative *The Trinity* is conspicuously absent from the list of Kierkegaard's direct citations and allusions.

The motifs that Kierkegaard encountered in these texts may have shaped his impression of Augustine and influenced the way he appropriated Augustine's work. Many of the volumes emphasized the distinctiveness and rigor of the Christian faith. One of these texts, *On the Good of Widowhood,* emphasizes the superiority of celibate life to married life while admitting that marriage is nevertheless a spiritually valid lifestyle. Another book, *On*

---

18. Augustine, *On Lying (De mendacio),* VII, from *Augustini Aurelii Opera,* VIII.

19. Augustine, *Augustini Aurelii Opera,* Sermon XL.

Lying, develops a defense of a very rigorous view of honesty as a basic virtue. Yet another work, *On Christian Teaching,* argues that the wisdom of Christianity is superior to that of the philosophers, though some helpful insights can be gleaned from those wise pagans. It argues that, although secular learning can be used in a preliminary way in the exegesis of biblical texts, it is faith that makes possible a more profound allegorical interpretation. *The City of God* suggests that the citizens of the general culture are not to be confused with the citizens of the heavenly city, though in this life the constituencies of the two groups are mixed together. These themes about the daunting nature of the Christian life, the uniqueness of Christian wisdom, and the differentiation of true Christianity from the mores of the general culture constitute a definite pattern. All of these motifs would become prominent in Kierkegaard's own writings. Kierkegaard's probably desultory reading in Augustine seems to have acquainted him with Augustine the moral rigorist and the champion of a demanding ideal for the Christian life. Interestingly, Augustine the speculative theologian is not evident in Kierkegaard's list of readings in Augustine that can be documented.

The Secondary Sources of Kierkegaard's Picture of Augustine

Much of Kierkegaard's knowledge of Augustine was gleaned not from these few passages in Augustine's works, but from secondary sources. In his posthumously published journals, Kierkegaard was more likely to cite a textbook account of Augustine's writings than to cite Augustine's writings themselves. These sources of his picture of Augustine were multiple and diverse, for Augustine was woven into the theological fabric of Lutheranism. Kierkegaard encountered references to Augustine when he studied the Lutheran confessions, devotional literature, the history of Christianity, and systematic theology. Secondary sources that mentioned Augustine played an ongoing role in Kierkegaard's theological formation. He was intensively exposed to many of these books very early in his student days, when he was learning to navigate the labyrinthine channels of doctrinal history. But his engagement with textbook accounts of Augustine's thought did not end when he left the university. Even as late in his career as 1851, Kierkegaard was making copious remarks in his journals about a biographical sketch of Augustine that he was currently reading.

Some of Kierkegaard's earliest and most consequential encounters with Augustine were mediated through lectures and tutorials on theology. One of the most potent influences on his development was a series of lectures on dogmatics given by Henrik Nicolai Clausen, a professor of theology at the University of Copenhagen, in the academic year 1833-34. Augustine figured prominently in Kierkegaard's rather detailed notes from this lecture series, which he either recorded himself from lectures that he actually attended or acquired from the compendia of transcribers. Clausen's impact on Kierkegaard's understanding of Augustine may not have ended with these early lectures, for Clausen offered more lectures on dogmatics in 1839-40. During that period Kierkegaard's papers contain additional notes on Clausen, including many references to Augustine. Kierkegaard may have been attending Clausen's new lectures, reading transcripts of those lectures, or at least reviewing his previous notes in preparation for his theology exams. In any case, he was in some way returning to Clausen to reinforce his grasp of the theologians of the early church. In fact, the influence of Clausen may have been even stronger than these notes suggest, for Kierkegaard owned two copies of a popular version of Clausen's lectures published in 1844, as well as a copy of a more detailed version published in 1853.[20]

But Clausen, important though he was, was by no means the only source of Kierkegaard's knowledge of Augustine. Tutorials and lectures by other theologians, philosophers, and church historians supplemented the foundation laid by Clausen. The young Kierkegaard would have been exposed to Augustine in a different way through his theological tutor Hans Lassen Martensen, who would later become the bishop of Copenhagen. Martensen's view of Augustine, presented to Kierkegaard through several different channels, competed with Clausen's in shaping Kierkegaard's concept of the Bishop of Hippo. Only five years older than Kierkegaard, Martensen guided the young scholar in 1834 through Schleiermacher's *Christian Faith*. Kierkegaard's journals from that period express puzzlement about Schleiermacher's apparent affirmation of predestination. This concern about this doctrine would have directed Kierkegaard's attention to Schleiermacher's frequent references to Augustine concerning original sin, grace, and election, for Martensen regarded Schleiermacher as the heir of Augustine on these subjects. Reinforcing the impact of Martensen's construal of Augustine, Kierkegaard attended at least some of Martensen's lectures on speculative dogmatics in 1837-38, and he acquired a copy of subscription notes (notes on the lectures taken by professional transcrib-

---

20. Henrik Nicolai Clausen, *Udvikling af de christelige Hovedlærdomme* (Copenhagen: C. A. Reitzel, 1844); *Christelig Troeslære* (Copenhagen: C. A. Reitzel, 1853).

ers, who then sold them to students) that treated Augustine and Pelagius at length.[21]

While visiting Berlin a few years later (1841), Kierkegaard heard Philipp Marheineke present an exposition of Augustine while lecturing on the history of Christian doctrine (or possibly on dogmatics, for it is not entirely clear which set of Marheineke's two lecture series Kierkegaard actually attended). As we shall see, Marheineke's assessment of the significance of Augustine was very different from Clausen's and Martensen's. Different though they were, all three of these lecture series would have repercussions for Kierkegaard's understanding of Augustine.

In addition to lectures and tutorials, basic textbooks outlining church history and theology were also foundational for Kierkegaard's understanding of Augustine. Throughout his life Kierkegaard frequently consulted the popular textbooks of theology and doctrinal history written by Karl Hase, K. G. Bretschneider, and August Hahn, all of whom devoted much attention to Augustine. Kierkegaard explicitly mentions Hase's *Hutterus Redivivus* as the source of his information about original sin as "sin transmitted from the origin" (*CA, 27*).[22] In addition to these books, Kierkegaard owned a Danish translation of Karl Hase's more general *Kirkehistorie*.[23] He also extensively used as a reference work G. B. Winer's *Comparative Darstellung des Lehrbegriffs der verscheidenen christlichen Kirchenparteien*, a comparison of a wide array of confessional documents, which frequently quotes Augustine as a background authority.[24] In addition, he carefully read Wilhelm Martin de Wette's *Lærbog i den christelige Sædelære*, a history of Christian ethics, during his preparation for his theological examinations, taking many notes on de Wette's exposition of the early church fathers, including Augustine. Also in 1837, Kierkegaard read a discussion of Augustine and Pelagius in Georg F. H. Rheinwald's encyclopedic *Allgemeines Repertorium für die theologische Literatur und kirchliche Statistik*

---

21. See Hans Lassen Martensen, "Lectures on Speculative Dogmatics," in *Papirer* XIII, IIC 28, pp. 74-78; see also Martensen, *Between Hegel and Kierkegaard: Hans L. Martensen's Philosophy of Religion*, trans. Curtis L. Thompson and David J. Kangas (Atlanta: Scholars Press, 1997), p. 63.

22. See Karl Hase, *Hutterus Redivivus oder Dogmatik der evangelisch-lutherischen Kirche* (Leipzig: Breitkopf und Härtel, 1839), p. 205.

23. Karl Hase, *Kirkehistorie. Lærebog nærmest for akademiske Forelæsninger*, trans. C. Winther and T. Schorn (Copenhagen: C. A. Reitzel, 1837).

24. G. B. Winer, *Comparative Darstellung des Lehrbegriffs der verscheidenen christlichen Kirchenparteien* (Leipzig, 1837).

(*KJN* 3, p. 125).[25] His recourse to textbook accounts did not cease in maturity, however, for in 1850 he gleaned more information about Augustine from A. Neander's *Denkwürdigkeiten aus der Geschichte des Christentums und des christlichen Lebens,* which surveyed the history of Christian ethics and social thought (*JP* 2, 1193).[26]

Kierkegaard also encountered material about Augustine in several monographs he owned that dealt with more specific theological topics. In 1837, Kierkegaard read and commented on a critical interpretation of Augustine's doctrine of the fall of Adam and Eve contained in an essay by the Hegelian Johan Eduard Erdmann, who generally tried to integrate Hegelian themes with orthodox Protestant doctrines.[27] In that book he encountered the *felix culpa* theme attributed to Augustine, which Erdmann explained means that sin is a necessary step forward in the evolution of consciousness (*KJN*, vol. 1). In 1838, Kierkegaard took notes on Johann Karl Friedrich Rosenkranz's *Encyklopädie der theologischen Wissenschaften,* in which Augustine and Pelagius were contrasted on the issue of divine and human agency (*KJN* 2, pp. 314-22).[28] Augustine was mentioned in Martensen's *The Autonomy of Human Self-Consciousness in Modern Dogmatic Theology,*[29] and in *Outline to a System of Moral Philosophy,* both of which Kierkegaard read.[30] Augustine also figured prominently in Julius Müller's magisterial tome on original sin, *Die christliche Lehre von der Sünde,* which Kierkegaard used in both the one-volume first edition of 1839 and the two-volume third edition of 1849.[31] In his notes to Marheineke's Berlin lectures of 1841, he mentions Müller's view that the creation of the world was due to freedom,

25. Georg F. H. Rheinwald, *Allgemeines Repertorium für die theologische Litteratur und kirchliche Statistik,* vols. 1-19 (Berlin, 1833-37), vol. 17.

26. August Neander, *Denkwürdigkeiten aus der Geschichte des Christentums u. des christlichen Lebens,* vols. I-II (Berlin, 1823-24).

27. Johann Eduard Erdmann, "Ueber den Begriff des Sündenfalls und des Bösen. Ein Versuch," in *Zeitschrift für spekulative Theologie,* vols. 1-3, ed. Bruno Bauer (Berlin: Dümmler, 1836-1838), vol. 2, no. 2 (1837): 192-214; Erdmann, *Vorlesungen über Glauben und Wissen als Einleitung in die Dogmatik und Religionsphilosophie* (Berlin: Dunker und Humbolt, 1837).

28. Johann Karl Friedrich Rosenkranz, *Encyklopädie der theologischen Wissenschaften* (Halle: C. A. Schwetschke und Sohn, 1831).

29. Hans Lassen Martensen, "The Autonomy of Human Self-Consciousness," in Martensen, *Between Hegel and Kierkegaard,* pp. 76-147.

30. Hans Lassen Martensen, "Outline to a System of Moral Philosophy," in Martensen, *Between Hegel and Kierkegaard,* pp. 246-313.

31. Julius Müller, *Die christliche Lehre von der Sünde* (Breslau: Josef Max, 1839); *Die christliche Lehre von der Sünde,* 3rd ed., 2 vols. (Breslau: Josef Max, 1849).

not necessity, which may suggest some familiarity with Müller at that early date (*KJN* 3, p. 247). He took extensive notes on Müller in 1850, often citing the third edition, which he owned by then, but sometimes referring to the earlier edition, which he had presumably already read, probably before 1844 (*JP* 1, 73; *JP* 2, 1263, 1530, 1531, 1614; *JP* 3, 3093; *JP* 4, 4028, 4030, 4031, 4034, 4555).[32] Kierkegaard's notebooks from 1851 contain many more references to Augustine than usual, for he was carefully reading Friedrich Böhringer's lengthy biography of Augustine in *Die Kirche Christi und ihre Zeugen oder die Kirchengeschichte in Biographie.*[33] More generally, his diffuse reading in Kant, Schleiermacher, Hegel, and the German and Danish Hegelians would have exposed him to further discussions of Augustine.

Augustine According to Kierkegaard's Contemporaries

Many of these authors and lecturers offered similar assessments of Augustine and highlighted the same Augustinian themes. Concerning some aspects of Augustine's thought, an interpretive convergence had emerged in nineteenth-century Protestant Europe. However, in regard to the evaluation of certain more controversial features of his work, two different interpretive tendencies had become evident. One was basically sympathetic, lauding Augustine as the venerable champion of the priority of grace and revelation. A second interpretive tendency was more critical, excoriating Augustine as an obscurantist enemy of responsible human agency. To understand Kierkegaard's picture of Augustine, we will find it helpful to examine the characteristics of the consensus view and of the divergent evaluative trajectories.

H. N. Clausen's lectures deserve careful scrutiny, for he probably provided the basic contours of Kierkegaard's picture of Augustine. Significantly, Clausen's ambivalent portrayal of Augustine illustrates both of the divergent assessments. Clausen had been influenced in different ways both by Kant's critique of speculative metaphysics, as well as by Schleiermacher's analysis of the experience of absolute dependence. Like Kant, Clausen had a tendency to interpret Christianity from the perspective of practical reason,

---

32. See Christine Axt-Piscalar, "Julius Müller: Parallels in the Doctrines of Sin and Freedom," in Jon Stewart, ed., *Kierkegaard and His German Contemporaries,* vol. II: *Theology* (Aldershot, UK: Ashgate, 2007), pp. 153-54.

33. Friedrich Böhringer, *Die Kirche Christi und ihre Zeugen oder die Kirchengeschichte in Biographie,* vols. 1-2 (Zürich: Meyer und Zeller, 1842-55), vol. 1, tome 3, pp. 99-774.

justifying the faith in the light of certain moral principles and dispositions. Like Schleiermacher, he insisted that Christianity presupposes, shapes, and revitalizes an original religious consciousness in human beings. Clausen was generally regarded by his contemporaries as a proponent of an intermediate theological position between rationalism's commitment to critical reflection and supernaturalism's reliance on revelation. He resisted both the fashionable enthusiasm for Hegelian metaphysics, which ascribed too much power to human reason, and also the upsurge of confessional dogmatism, which too severely disparaged human reason. Clausen sought support for his view that biblical revelation must be interpreted and appropriated by critical human reason by appealing to the exegetical practice of Augustine, whose use of a philosophically influenced allegorical interpretation foreshadowed what Clausen considered to be the best practices of moderate nineteenth-century biblical interpreters. In fact, Clausen published a largely appreciative exposition of Augustine's hermeneutics in 1827, praising Augustine for avoiding both historical literalism and reductive rationalism.[34]

In addition to endorsing the spirit of Augustine's hermeneutics, Clausen commended other aspects of Augustine's work in his lectures. He referred approvingly to Augustine's assertion that "God is good without quality, great without quantity, creates without needing to, is present without form, is everywhere without place, is sempiternal without time, makes what is mutable without being moved" (*KJN* 3, p. 74), which was an approximate quotation from *The Trinity*.[35] Clausen was calling attention to Augustine's refusal to confine the infinite God within a limiting, finite conceptuality, while at the same time magnifying God's metaphysical perfections. Similarly, Clausen cited Augustine's proposal — in book 6, chapter 6 of *The City of God* — that time was created along with the world, thereby avoiding both the Alexandrian belief that the world had been created from eternity and the opinion of Methodius of Tyre that the world had been created in time (*KJN* 3, p. 76). In both of these instances, according to Clausen, Augustine was exemplifying an entirely apt sensitivity to God's transcendence of the categories of finitude.

Even more enthusiastically, Clausen lauded Augustine for insisting on an intimate connection between faith and love in the Christian life. By so doing, Clausen was attempting to overcome the tendency of some Luther-

---

34. H. N. Clausen, *Aurelius Augustinus Hipponensis Sacræ Scripturæ Interpres* (Hauniae: Schultz, 1827).

35. Augustine, *The Trinity*, V, prologue, 2.

ans to divorce trust in God's gracious justification of the sinner from the rigors of a life of Christlike love. Clausen found support for his own emphasis of love in Augustine's elaboration of the Epistle of James's teaching that faith and works are inseparable. He approved of Augustine's assertion that the good life is inseparable from faith, and that faith works by means of love (*KJN* 3, p. 55).[36] For both Clausen and Augustine, the inevitable consequence of justification should be diligence in good works and not the juxtaposition of faith and works that Clausen feared was all too typical of popular Lutheranism (*KJN* 3, p. 59). In order to correct the perceived Lutheran tendencies toward antinomianism, Clausen found the support of such a venerable church father as Augustine invaluable.

In spite of this positive presentation of Augustinian themes, Clausen did not hesitate to criticize many of Augustine's other theological proposals. Kierkegaard's notes from the lectures reveal a more Kantian side of Clausen, an antimetaphysical side that led him to portray Augustine in a much more negative light. Much of Clausen's critique of Augustine focused on Augustine's penchant for distracting and irresolvable metaphysical ruminations. For example, Clausen argued that the real *imago Dei* in humanity is the soul's capacity for thought and self-determination, and he objected that this lofty teaching had been obscured by idle and futile speculation concerning the origins of the soul, including Augustine's flirtation with traducianism, the theory that the soul is created with the body and transmitted through reproduction (*KJN* 3, pp. 18-19). Similarly, Kierkegaard records that Clausen maintained that Augustine had helped spawn injurious ruminations about the manner of the resurrection and the nature of the putative intermediate state (*KJN* 3, p. 24). Moreover, Augustine was guilty of constructing a system whose internal logic required him to assert such unknowable and foreboding doctrines as the eternity of punishment for sin (*KJN* 3, pp. 26-27). These criticisms were directed against Augustine's perceived penchant for constructing a system of thought governed by speculative philosophy, a vice that Clausen believed prefigured the misleading vagaries of the contemporary Hegelians.

A great deal of Clausen's discomfort with Augustine involved the seeming incoherence of the doctrine of original sin. According to Clausen, Augustine's theory that Adam and Eve's fall was responsible for the corruption of human nature and for the guilt of their descendants was unintelligible.

---

36. This is a paraphrase of Augustine's *On Faith and Works (De fide et operibus)*, 23 (42), in *WSA*, I, 10.

The notion of a capacity only to choose evil, present at birth, suggested the self-contradiction that sin is on the one hand inherited and innate, but on the other hand is the individual's own fault (*KJN* 3, pp. 29-31). Considered from the perspective of practical reason, an inherited fault cannot render an individual worthy of punishment. Moreover, the doctrine of hereditary sin was not contained in Scripture and did not correlate with the general human experience that sin is due to the difficulty of governing sensuous desire by moral dispositions. Against Augustine's doctrine Clausen objected that humans may be frail, but they remain morally free. Of course, the freedom of individuals to choose the good has not remained unimpaired by deleterious social influences, as Clausen believed that Pelagius, Augustine's nemesis, mistakenly thought.

Augustine was absolutely correct that human beings do need the help of grace, but that need for aid does not imply that humans are totally depraved, Clausen opines. He goes on to say that "the best current in modern theology" has attempted to avoid both "Pelagian frivolity" and "Augustinian abasement" in order to recognize the dialectic of common human frailty and moral freedom (*KJN* 3, p. 31). According to Clausen, this exaggerated view of human sinfulness then forced Augustine to completely divorce grace from nature and reject any notion of human cooperation in salvation. As a consequence, he had to develop a theory concerning the irresistibility of divine grace (*KJN* 3, pp. 64-65). Eventually, the logic of his system required Augustine to articulate the doctrine of predestination, suggesting that God has chosen to rescue some individuals from the general damnation, quite apart from any consideration of their merits, and has elected to infuse those individuals with saving grace. Clausen found this teaching to be particularly abhorrent, for it denied both the universality of grace and the crucial factor of human responsibility. In all these criticisms, Clausen's indebtedness to Kant's conviction that the ascription of moral responsibility requires the presupposition of freedom is evident. Theology must not contradict the certainties provided by practical reason and the religious self-consciousness.

Clausen's ambivalent assessment of Augustine would have a lasting impact on Kierkegaard. On the positive side, according to Clausen, Augustine appreciated God's transcendence of finite categories and the intimate connection of faith and love. Augustine also appropriately recognized human moral frailty and the need for divine assistance. Kierkegaard would take these lessons to heart. However, on the negative side, in Clausen's opinion, Augustine illicitly used speculative philosophy to engage in system building, and he was forced by his own logic to affirm unbiblical and spiritually damaging doctrines. As we shall see, Kierkegaard imbibed Clausen's suspicion of Augustine as a system-builder. Even worse, according to Clausen, Augustine so exaggerated human sinfulness, describing it as an innate corruption, that he utterly negated any sense of human responsibility. Kierkegaard, too, would struggle to preserve the integral role of the self-ascription of responsibility in the Christian life. It must be noted that Clausen's pejorative remarks about Augustine as a speculative systematician paint a very different picture of Augustine from the one drawn by contemporary scholars. The Augustine whom Kierkegaard encountered through Clausen was not the fractured, tentative Augustine of O'Donnell and Conybeare, but the doctrinal propositionalist imagined by seventeenth-century Lutherans, Calvinists, Jansenists, and Jesuits.

The other historians, philosophers, and theologians who influenced Kierkegaard's picture of Augustine would either reinforce or contradict the assertions of Clausen. Some theologians echoed Clausen's view that Augustine was groping for a philosophically informed system, but they regarded this endeavor much more positively than Clausen did. For example, Martensen adopted as his own motto the phrase "faith seeking understanding," which he attributed to Augustine in addition to Anselm.[37] Martensen was convinced that the slogan epitomized the purpose of his own work, which was to philosophically speculate on the contents of authoritative revelation in order to develop a more profound comprehension of theological truth as an organic whole. By presenting himself as a theological heir of Augustine, Martensen gave the impression that Augustine's writings constituted a philosophically informed theological system. In a somewhat more critical way, the mildly rationalistic K. G. Bretschneider reinforced this assessment of Augustine in a textbook that Kierkegaard frequently consulted.[38] According to Bretschneider, Augustine's speculations about the Trinity, like those of many other early theologians, attempted to clarify reason's dim recognition that God must be perfect existence, perfect knowledge, and perfect love. Augustine simply used philosophy to clarify and systematize the intuitions of the religious consciousness, hoping to produce a compendium of Christian wisdom. However, according to Bretschneider, Augustine and his peers had utilized a culturally conditioned conceptuality, now

---

37. Hans Lassen Martensen, "The Autonomy of Human Self-Consciousness," p. 78.

38. Karl Gottlieb Bretschneider, *Handbuch der Dogmatik der evangelisch-lutherischen Kirche*, vols. 1-2, 4th ed. (Leipzig: Johann Ambrosius Barth, 1838), 1: 542-652.

outmoded, that often distorted the kernel of truth contained in his writings. Augustine's doctrines had to be critiqued and modified in order to make them suited to the modern appreciation of the autonomous development of moral character. This Augustine was a formulator of doctrinal propositions whose system could be compared to those of Irenaeus, Origen, and a cavalcade of patristic worthies.

Theologians who rooted theology in an analysis of Christian experience diverged from this portrayal of Augustine as a systematizer who used speculative philosophy to grasp the alleged deeper meaning of faith's contents; they discovered a more interior Augustine. August Neander, for example, praises Augustine for extrapolating the theme of reliance on grace from his own experience.[39] He emphasizes the fact that Augustine's passionate defense of the need for grace was not a mere response to Pelagius's excessive confidence in human capabilities; it was not simply the fruit of the logical requirements of Augustine's alleged system or the polemical politics of his theological situation. Rather, Augustine was a spiritually sensitive thinker who was painfully cognizant of his own incapacity. Augustine simply realized from his own inner life that the internalization of the spirit of Christ was absolutely necessary for regeneration. Augustine's Christian experience gave shape to his theology, even informing his critical appropriation of Platonism (rather than Platonism determining his understanding of Christianity). Karl Hase, a liberal theologian influenced by Kant and Schleiermacher who sought to synthesize modern culture — including critical historical studies — with religious feeling, depicts Augustine as sincerely pious, though somewhat artificial in style.[40]

Friedrich Böhringer's biographical sketch, which Kierkegaard read attentively in the early 1850s, emphasizes Augustine's growing reliance on his religious subjectivity in his quest for truth and his increasing disillusionment with the capabilities of autonomous reason.[41] According to these thinkers, Augustine was a kind of proto-Schleiermacher, or at least an early pietist, basing his theological claims on his own experience informed by revelation. This picture of Augustine begins to resemble the contemporary views that concentrate on his discovery/invention of "inner

---

39. August Neander, *Denkwürdigkeiten aus der Geschichte des Christenthums u. des christlichen Lebens*, vols. 1-3 (Berlin: Ferdinand Dümmler, 1823-24), 2: 241-82.

40. Hase, *Kirkehistorie. Lærebog*, pp. 126-28.

41. Friedrich Böhringer, *Die Kirche Christi und ihre Zeugen oder die Kirchengeschichte in Biographie*, vol. 1, tome 3, pp. 99-774.

space."[42] And this is the Augustine who bequeathed the "subjective turn" to subsequent generations of Christians. Kierkegaard was exposed both to the view of Augustine as the formulator of metaphysically influenced doctrinal propositions and the view of Augustine as the articulator of personal religious interiority. But the late-twentieth-century view of Augustine as a complex, tensive conjunction of many different trajectories was not part of Kierkegaard's cultural heritage.

Rather than arguing about the systematic or expressive nature of Augustine's work, Kierkegaard's teachers and sources often focused on more particular and controversial aspects of Augustine's thought, especially the issue of the relationship of divine grace to human agency. Many writers shared Clausen's more specific ambivalence about Augustine's understanding of sin and grace. For example, Martensen identifies both Augustine and Schleiermacher as advocates of divine determinism, adding that Schleiermacher had reconceived determinism as the unfolding of the individual's own inner necessity. Kierkegaard's former theological tutor juxtaposes Augustine and Schleiermacher's belief in the unilateral efficacy of God's agency to Pelagius's one-sided defense of freedom as arbitrary choice.[43] He also contrasts Pelagius's concept of sinfulness as the free action of individuals with Augustine's view of sinfulness as the corporate nature of the human race operating through the individual. For Martensen, the resulting antinomy must be overcome, for some truth can be found in both positions.[44] He sought to synthesize them by claiming that the individual does organically share the nature of Adam, but that this nature only becomes personal guilt as the individual ego appropriates this tragic legacy as its own and develops it further.[45] Moreover, according to Martensen, Augustine was right to see grace as enabling true freedom, for acting according to our true nature is indeed freedom; but he was wrong to describe grace as a kind of external mechanical force that overrides the human will.[46] This kind of assessment of Augustine was very widespread among European Protestant theologians: Augustine's emphasis of bondage to sin and his consequent affirmation of the efficacy of God's saving grace was indeed one necessary dimension of

---

42. See Phillip Cary, *Augustine's Invention of the Inner Self: The Legacy of a Christian Platonist* (Oxford: Oxford University Press, 2000).

43. See Martensen, "Outline to a System of Moral Philosophy," p. 262.

44. Martensen, "Outline to a System of Moral Philosophy," p. 275.

45. Martensen, *Christian Dogmatics: A Compendium of the Doctrines of Christianity,* trans. William Urwick (Edinburgh: T&T Clark, 1866), pp. 203-5.

46. Martensen, *Dogmatics,* p. 357.

the complex process of salvation, but it was only one dimension. The other dimension, which Augustine sadly neglected but which Pelagius grossly exaggerated, was responsible human agency. The problem of the tension of divine grace and human responsibility that Clausen had impressed upon Kierkegaard was reinforced by his tutorial with Martensen.

There were other thinkers that Kierkegaard read who affirmed this evaluation of Augustine. Georg F. H. Rheinwald's encyclopedic *Allgemeines Repertorium für die theologische Literatur und kirchliche Statistik* contrasts Augustine's ascription of everything to God with Pelagius's concern to preserve free human agency and meritorious action (*KJN* 3, p. 125).[47] Karl Rosenkranz, the influential moderate Hegelian, presents Augustinianism and Pelagianism as polar opposites, with "semi-Pelagianism" emerging as an attempted synthesis of the two (*KJN* 2, p. 320).[48] Semi-Pelagianism was thought to have been a movement that emerged late in Augustine's career and flourished after his death, and maintained that the human will cooperates with grace by accepting it and cultivating it. Kierkegaard's notes on both Rheinwald and Rosenkranz show that he associated semi-Pelagianism with the theologian John Cassian, Augustine's contemporary, and thought that Cassian had emphasized human initiative in the divine-human interaction. Semi-Pelagianism was usually presented by Kierkegaard's sources somewhat sympathetically, for at least it tried to do justice to both God's grace and human responsibility, even though it erred in ascribing too much originating efficacy to the human will.

In this vein, the liberal theological historian Karl Hase also points to the need to mediate the positions of Pelagius and Augustine.[49] Hase regards the development of theology and the entire history of the church as the progressive manifestation of the life of Christ in humanity, and he claims to detect a dialectic of the spirits of the Eastern church and the Western church in that history. Pelagius, who represented the spirit of Eastern Christianity even though he hailed from the British Isles, champions the freedom of the will, while Augustine, who represented Western Christianity, polemicizes for the sovereignty of divine agency. Hase, like the other thinkers, proposes that the themes of dependence on God and free human striving should be combined. Even the conservative August Hahn, an enemy of theolog-

---

47. Georg F. H. Rheinwald et al., *Allgemeines Repertorium für die theologische Literatur und kirchliche Statistik*, 19 vols. (Berlin: Herbig, 1833-60), vol. 17 (1837), pp. 113-19.

48. See Karl Friedrich Rosenkranz, *Encyklopaedie der theologischen Wissenschaften* (Halle: C. A. Schwetschke und Sohn, 1831), pp. 270-77.

49. Hase, *Kirkehistorie*, pp. 122 ff.

ical rationalism and supporter of the neoconfessional movement of E. W. Hengstenberg, proposes that the goal of Protestantism is to avoid the one-sidedness of both Augustinianism and Pelagianism.[50]

August Neander, who tends to parallel Schleiermacher on many issues, extols Augustine's reliance on grace, but laments that the latter had done this one-dimensionally, to the detriment of human agency.[51] Julius Müller's exhaustive treatise on original sin elaborates the same point, praising Augustine for realizing that sin is a characterization of a person as a whole, but criticizing him for failing to explain how this could be regarded as the individual's own personal fault.[52] K. G. Bretschneider, probably the most Kantian of all the writers, also articulates a tensive and mixed evaluation of Augustine on sin, freedom, and grace.[53] Augustine's teachings about inherent depravity were commended in that they point to the enormity of the problem of sinfulness. They validate the prevalent suspicion that human failings are universal and inevitable. Moreover, the language of generational transmission corroborates reason's awareness of the pernicious influence of heredity and culture. According to Bretschneider, Augustine's insistence on sin's inevitability points to the overwhelming power of our sensory nature over the individual's immature rational will in a person's early years. However, Augustine's formulations are archaic and inadequate in that they portray sin as a deterministic power and fail to encourage morally undeveloped children to mature.

It is significant that all of these qualified endorsements of Augustine's emphasis on grace, tempered by the fear that responsible human agency had been subverted, issued from almost the entire spectrum of theologians, from Hegelians to allies of Schleiermacher, and from conservative confessionalists to moderate Kantians. In spite of their theological divergence on many issues, Clausen and Martensen — and even the confessionalists — were basically in agreement in their response to Augustine on sin, freedom, and grace. Kierkegaard could not have avoided inheriting this portrayal that sometimes depicts an unresolved ambivalence in Augustine and sometimes presents him as capitulating to a theory of divine determinism. Some of the nineteenth-century scholars, such as Neander, dimly prefig-

---

50. August Hahn, *Lehrbuch des christlichen Glaubens* (Leipzig: Friedrich Christian Wilhelm Vogel, 1828), pp. 371-410.

51. Neander, *Denkwürdigkeiten aus der Geschichte*, 2: 241-82.

52. Julius Müller, *Die christliche Lehre von der Sünde*, vols. 1-2, 3rd ed. (Breslau: Josef Max und Komp, 1849), 1: 395-406; vol. 2: 45-48.

53. Bretschneider, *Handbuch der Dogmatik*, 1: 542-652.

ured the late-twentieth-century rediscovery of an Augustine whose mature work continued to exhibit unresolved tensions on this issue, while others treated Augustine as a systematician who in his mature period regarded the doctrine of predestination as foundational for his entire theological project.

Diverging from this depiction of an Augustine who failed to do justice to human responsibility, other texts consulted by Kierkegaard do portray Augustine's discussion of sin, grace, and freedom in a more positive light. The Lutheran confessional documents of the late sixteenth century regard Augustine as an admirable articulator of the dialectic of sin and grace, and favorably describe Augustine's view of Adam as the head of the race through whom we have inherited the corruption and guilt of original sin. For almost opposite reasons, Philipp Marheineke, greatly influenced by Hegel, also favorably describes Augustine's treatment of original sin in the Berlin lectures that Kierkegaard attended (*KJN* 3, pp. 250-56). Against supernaturalists like Hahn and Hengstenberg, Marheineke argues that Augustine did not essentially present Adam as being somehow outside the human race because of the peculiarity of his status as the first human being. For Augustine, Marheineke argues, Adam was not just a specific individual whose historical situation, being prelapsarian, was utterly unlike our own. Augustine must have known that if Adam had only a causal and biological relationship to subsequent individuals, rather than a representative relationship, then Adam's sin would seem to necessitate our own. Even more significantly, the story of Adam and Eve's fall could not possibly illuminate the way we all come to be sinners in our own lives, for too many dissimilarities in our respective contexts would abound (*KJN* 3, p. 255). Marheineke vehemently denies that the Augustinian tradition implied the position of the early Lutheran theologian Flacius Illyricus: that the substance of human nature was changed by Adam's fall into something evil. Against this traditional view of Adam as the genetic source of transmitted sin, Marheineke endorses Kant's more symbolic view that the story of Adam should be read as the paradigmatic story of all human beings. Significantly, Marheineke associates Augustine with Kant on this issue, quoting Augustine's statement that "we have all been, we are, that one" (*KJN* 3, pp. 255-56).[54] Marheineke proposes that, for both Paul and Augustine, there is no essential difference between the first and subsequent human beings. The radical contrast between Adam's sin and our own is cancelled as subsequent individuals make Adam's

---

54. Marheineke's quotation seems to be a reference to *The City of God,* bk. 13, chap. 14, where Augustine writes: "[N]os omnes fuimus, sumus ille unus."

sin their own by recapitulating it in their own lives. In effect, Marheineke is construing Augustine's analysis of Adam's sin as the holding up of a mirror in which the individual could see the genesis of the individual's own sinfulness. In a way, Marheineke is pioneering a rhetorical reading of Augustine, for he pays close attention to the religious purpose of Augustine's doctrinal ruminations.

Marheineke was not alone in suggesting that, according to Augustine, Adam and Eve should be seen as prototypes of all sinners. In *The Christian Faith*, Friedrich Schleiermacher also expresses this view that Augustine treated the story of the fall as an "illustration of the universal process of the rise of sin as always and everywhere the same," adding that "it is in this illustrative quality that, for us, the universal significance of the narrative resides."[55] For Schleiermacher, Augustine was right to suggest an original fallibility in human nature that has always cohered with human nature's original potential for religious maturation (though, according to Schleiermacher, Augustine failed to provide a motivational explanation for the susceptibility to temptation, something that Schleiermacher located in the difficulty that the God-consciousness experiences in permeating the sensory self-consciousness).[56] As we shall see, this symbolic way of reading the fall of Adam and Eve, ascribed by Marheineke and Schleiermacher to Augustine, would have profound consequences for Kierkegaard's own treatment of original sin.

The theologians consulted by Kierkegaard who were sympathetic to the theme of holy living often focus on a different aspect of Augustine's life and thought. They portray Augustine as a moral rigorist who sought to recover the early church's exacting view of discipleship during an era of Constantinian laxity. In July 1839, Kierkegaard quoted Augustine's remark that the end of the world would come more quickly if there were no marriage (*JP* 3, 2584; see also *KJN* 2, p. 37). He probably discovered this statement in de Wette's *Lærbog i den christelige Sædelære*, since de Wette quoted this passage from Augustine's *On the Good of Marriage (De bono conjugali)*.[57] During that period Kierkegaard was obviously reading de Wette's history of Christian ethics carefully in preparation for his theological examinations, for he took extensive notes on de Wette's exposition of the early church fathers. In gen-

---

55. Friedrich Schleiermacher, *The Christian Faith*, ed. H. R. Mackintosh and J. S. Stewart, vols. 1-2 (New York: Harper and Row, 1963), 1: 303. Schleiermacher quotes Augustine in Latin, citing *On Genesis, against the Manichees (De Genesi adversus Manicheos)*, ii, 21, in *WSA* I, 13.

56. Schleiermacher, *The Christian Faith*, 1: 293-94.

57. De Wette, *Lærbog i den christelige Sædelære*, p. 129.

eral, De Wette's text tends to emphasize the extraordinarily demanding nature of Augustine's understanding of the Christian life. Friedrich Böhringer, whom Kierkegaard read later in life, also emphasizes the daunting view of Christian discipleship that Augustine advocated, pointing out that for Augustine this discipleship necessarily involved suffering (*JP* 4, 4670).[58] August Neander presented Kierkegaard with a picture of Augustine as not only a strict moralist but also a subtle one, sensitive to the unique features of specific contexts. For example, Neander argued that Christ did not always turn the other cheek, for he reprimanded those who struck him in Gethsemane (*JP* 2, 1193).[59] These works presented Augustine in a different light, not as a systematic Scholastic theologian, nor as a phenomenologist of religious experience, but as an example of the coincidence of a loftily espoused ethic and personal moral seriousness. According to these thinkers, Augustine genuinely walked the path that he wrote about. The correlation of the writer's life and the writer's text made a lasting impression on Kierkegaard.

The similarities in these lectures and texts form the rough outlines of the picture of Augustine to which Kierkegaard was exposed. Most notably, Augustine is identified consistently and primarily as the champion of the doctrines of original sin and of the primacy of grace in human salvation. In fact, some of the textbook accounts of the history of theology devote almost exclusive attention to the Pelagian controversy when discussing Augustine's significance. (The exceptions to this rule were some of the Hegelians and the followers of Schelling, who claim that Augustine's model of the Trinity as God's self-consciousness prefigured their own speculations about Spirit.) This emphasis differs from more recent portrayals of Augustine, which tend to regard his ruminations about hereditary guilt and predestination as more contextual and polemical than foundational. Further, the Augustine who has been constructed by the early twenty-first century is much less likely to be identified essentially and almost exclusively with the doctrines of original sin and predestination, as if they were the basis for everything that Augustine wrote. Many of the nineteenth-century writers and lecturers who influenced Kierkegaard applaud Augustine's position on sin and grace as a necessary corrective to Pelagian optimism, but then protest that Augustine had misleadingly overemphasized divine agency at the expense of human responsibility. Second, many of these interpreters agreed that Augustine was a moral rigorist who helped promote an almost

58. Böhringer, *Die Kirche Christi*, 1: 188 (pt. 3).
59. Neander, *Denkwürdigkeiten aus der Geschichte*, 2: 227-29.

monastic ideal for all Christians. Third, some pointed to the way Augustine intimately connected faith and love, such that love was simply faith in action, or the element of delight implicit in faith. As we shall see, all three of these interpretive trajectories strongly influenced Kierkegaard's appropriation of Augustine.

Disagreements in the secondary literature about Augustine arose over the question of the nature of his approach to theology. For some he was a protosystematician who appropriately utilized speculative philosophy to illuminate the inner coherence of Christian convictions. For others he was indeed a systematician, but lamentably one whose love of speculation produced distortions of the faith. For still others he was not a speculative systematician at all, but a much more existential writer who wove his personal experience and his religious passion into his theological method. This last group of interpreters anticipated contemporary scholars, ranging from existentialists to postmodern theorists, who identify Augustine as the pioneer of the subjective turn. As we shall see, all of these interpreters, both the positive and negative ones, influenced Kierkegaard's appropriation of Augustine and left traces in the former's writings. The tension between Augustine the rationalistic systematician and Augustine the passionately self-reflective thinker would reappear in Kierkegaard's own construal of Augustine,

In general, Kierkegaard's Augustine was a systematic theologian who was saturated with Platonic notions of rationality, who reconceived the Christian faith in such a way that it made sense of his personal struggle to overcome sin and expressed his relief in the help provided by God's grace. On the one hand, this Augustine patterned his theology on the principles of deductive logic; on the other hand, he used that system to express his powerful religious passions. It may be unfortunate that the more dialectical, asystematic, and rhetorical Augustine was not known to Kierkegaard, for he might have recognized in that Augustine an uncanny prefiguring of himself.

Kierkegaard's Explicit Evaluations of Augustine

Before we compare Augustine and Kierkegaard on particular theological issues, we must first consider Kierkegaard's explicitly evaluative comments about the Bishop of Hippo. Kierkegaard's remarks will provide clues about the way he assembled the various bits and pieces of contemporary lore about Augustine and constructed his own portrait of the African father.

Kierkegaard's general understanding of Augustine will provide a context for examining his treatment of the more particular theological themes that he appropriated from Augustine, either through direct reading of Augustine or hearing about Augustine, or indirectly via being immersed in theological traditions that were influenced by Augustine.

Kierkegaard never wrote a comprehensive, in-depth assessment of Augustine's theology. In general, he was not interested in establishing continuity with the thought of any previous theologian, as if that connection would somehow confer credibility on his own writings. For Kierkegaard, appeals to the authority of an individual theologian, even ones as venerable as Augustine and Luther, did not conclusively settle matters about the nature of the Christian faith. At most, such theological giants merely provided some guidance, some inspiration, and much provocation. However, despite his lack of any desire to situate himself definitively in the Augustinian heritage or to distance himself from it, Kierkegaard did make a few rather sweeping evaluative observations about Augustine. The tenor and content of these remarks remained relatively constant throughout Kierkegaard's life, though a few distinctive emphases developed in his later years. From his earliest lecture notes to his latest journal entries, strong ambivalences in Kierkegaard's assessment of Augustine are obvious. Not surprisingly, Kierkegaard focuses on the same theological issues in Augustine's voluminous writings that had been highlighted by his mentors and textbooks, and his response to them reflect the tensions evident in their often contrasting portrayals.

Certain aspects of Augustine's life and work delighted Kierkegaard. Sometimes Kierkegaard echoed the opinion of interpreters like Neander and Hase, who construed Augustine's writings as a felicitous integration of reflection and lived experience. In 1848, Kierkegaard lamented that he knew of no religious thinker who "reduplicated" his thought in his life, except perhaps Augustine (*JP* 3, 3667). This gave Augustine the authority of a genuinely subjective thinker who realized that the truth must be personally appropriated. Moreover, in Kierkegaard's judgment, Augustine understood correctly what this personal appropriation really involved. In 1851, Kierkegaard applauded the fact that Augustine rightly construed the Christian life as a path of affliction and exile (*JP* 4, 4670).[60] Augustine, according to Kierkegaard, aptly acknowledged that Christians must suffer as

---

60. Kierkegaard concluded this from his reading in Böhringer, *Die Kirche Christi und ihre Zeugen*, 1: 188 (pt. 3). Hereafter, volume and page references to this Böhringer work appear in parentheses in the text.

did their prototype, Jesus Christ (*JP* 1, 191). Kierkegaard lauds Augustine for having conceived such an overwhelming love for God that he sacrificed vocational success and familial contentment for the sake of that devotion. Sometimes Kierkegaard admiringly refers to Augustine's candid and unsparing self-criticism, which also testified to his spiritual earnestness. For example, Kierkegaard noted approvingly in 1851 that Augustine recognized that his pleasure in empathizing with victims of tragedy in the theater was superficial, for he was not obligated to relieve their suffering in any way, nor did he have to undergo the actual pain himself (*JP* 4, 4470; Böhringer, 1, pt. 3: 110). Kierkegaard expresses admiration for the early church fathers in general, among whom he always placed Augustine, because their lives expressed the earnestness and pathos that contemporary Christendom so often lacked (*JP* 1, 830). As is evident, Kierkegaard had been attracted to the depictions of Augustine as an earnest disciple of Christ with a passionate piety that had been developed by such scholars as Böhringer, Neander, de Wette, and others.

Kierkegaard was also enthusiastic about the mature Augustine's sense of the authority of revelation and his passion for truth. As early as 1837, Kierkegaard observed that Augustine's "system" required a belief in an inspired revelation (*JP* 1, 29). Kierkegaard claims that Augustine was right that Christianity is the most perfect form of authority, for its authority is rooted in God. If truth is divine, then it is only appropriate that it be communicated through the form of an authoritative disclosure. Echoing Augustine, he warns of the dangers of speculating away all authority (*JP* 1, 181).[61] It was particularly later in his life that Kierkegaard praised Augustine for recognizing that it is part of the perfection of Christianity that it relies on an authoritative revelation rather than on autonomous reason (*JP* 1, 191). In 1851, Kierkegaard cited Augustine's insight that it is good that there is a truth to which the human spirit is subordinate, for only in being subordinate can the spirit become truly free (*JP* 4, 4877; Böhringer, 1, pt. 1: 234-35). He also notes Augustine's argument that it is better to be deceived by an authority than to stubbornly resist all guidance by any authority. By so saying, Augustine was suggesting that the individual's submission to authority can be a virtue and that the acknowledgment of an external authority may be intrinsically valuable (*JP* 2, 1199). While not overtly endorsing Augustine's opinion, Kierkegaard exclaims that Böhringer's exposition of Augustine's defense of authority is worth reading again (Böhringer, 1, pt. 3: 253). In these

---

61. See also Søren Kierkegaard, *Stages on Life's Way* (*SLW*), suppl., p. 601.

journal entries Kierkegaard implicitly downplays the interpretation of Augustine as a speculative theologian who relied excessively on Platonic metaphysics. Rather, Kierkegaard shows a marked preference for the view of Augustine as a faithful expositor of divine revelation that had been promoted by the more conservative commentators, such as Hahn. It is significant that Kierkegaard's enthusiasm for Augustine as the upholder of the authority of revelation became more pronounced in his later years, with many of his most favorable remarks appearing after he had read Böhringer in 1851.

Kierkegaard's view of Augustine was, of course, profoundly shaped by the scholarly discussions of Augustine on the issues of sin, grace, providence, and freedom. Quite early, Kierkegaard expresses a marked preference for Augustine over Pelagius on these matters. In a journal entry of 1837 he observes that, whereas Pelagius addresses himself to humanity as it is, trying to conform itself to the world, Augustine calls for a negation of this empirically given humanity in order to rebuild humanity anew (*JP* 1, 29). Pelagius is an accommodationist who concedes too much to human weakness, while Augustine is a person of hope who trusts in the possibility of a new creation. Kierkegaard points approvingly to Augustine's three-stage view of human history: creation, fall (involving death and spiritual impotence), and new creation (*JP* 1, 29). Because this schematization of human life involves a counterintuitive vision of what humanity could and should become, it can only be based in an inspired revelation, as Augustine well knew. This motif of becoming a new creature, often at odds with ordinary societal norms and expectations, would play a pervasive role in Kierkegaard's own writings. Like almost all of the textbooks that he consulted, Kierkegaard in no way wanted to minimize the sinfulness of the individual.

Kierkegaard also expresses sympathy for Augustine's confidence in God's agency in this process of spiritual re-creation. In 1847 he cited Augustine's conviction that God's providence extends even to the small things of life, not just the large ones (*JP* 1, 179). Also in 1847, Kierkegaard echoed Augustine's reminder that God's benevolent providence is concerned with the individual's salvation, not with worldly felicity or even continued earthly life. Augustine, Kierkegaard admiringly notes, said, "Certainly God has promised you forgiveness — but he has not promised you tomorrow" (*JP* 2, 1210).[62] Augustine had realized that God is the agent at work behind the scenes in the vicissitudes of human lives, prodding and urging humans into Christian maturity. In his own writings Kierkegaard would remain com-

---

62. See Augustine, *Augustini Aurelii Opera*, Sermon XL.

mitted to the notion of divine guidance and even divine governance. Here again he was reflecting the consensus view of Augustine as the theologian who had underscored most forcefully the need for divine help.

Kierkegaard also tended to side more with Augustine than with Pelagius on the subject of free will. In general, he appreciated Augustine's efforts to deflate all grandiose claims about the efficacy of an allegedly self-determining human will. He endorsed Augustine's critique of Pelagius's valorization of an entirely abstract freedom that was independent of context or history. In 1851, Kierkegaard expressed agreement with Augustine that freedom of choice *(liberum arbitrium)*, unconstrained by the past, is a chimera, for the will has a history of prior decisions that has generated a particular momentum and a particular trajectory (*JP* 2, 1268). According to Kierkegaard, Augustine is right that "the particular will is not external to but rather is enclosed within the condition in which the person finds himself" (*JP* 4, 4047; Böhringer, 1, pt. 3: 408). Echoing Augustine's critique of the concept of an "indifferent will" even more clearly, Kierkegaard goes on to endorse Augustine's claim that true freedom, as distinguished from freedom of choice, involves an inner necessity that excludes the thought of another possibility (*JP* 2, 1269; Böhringer, 1, pt. 3: 550). Kierkegaard even approves of Augustine's claim that the individual can sink into sin so deeply as to lose the very capacity to choose. On these issues pertaining to the nature of freedom, Augustine reinforced Kierkegaard's own tendency to see freedom as situated, conditioned, and motivated. Here the influence of Schleiermacher's interpretation of Augustine, probably mediated to Kierkegaard through Martensen, is evident.

Moreover, Kierkegaard applauds Augustine's refusal to allow the acknowledgment of freedom's conditioned nature to mitigate the individual's sense of responsibility and guilt. According to Kierkegaard, Augustine was right that this loss of freedom is itself a punishment for sin and is simultaneously itself a further sin. The intensification of the sinful condition itself is the culpable result of sin; the punishment is not some external sanction contingently imposed on the individual (*JP* 2, 1268). In 1851, Kierkegaard drew further attention to Augustine's theme that abandonment in sin is itself a punishment for sin, noting that according to Augustine, God's question "Adam, where are you?" punitively reminded Adam that he was now "outside of God" (*JP* 3, 3642; Böhringer, 1, pt. 3: 498). Augustine was quite correct that "weakness, ignorance, [and] being overpowered by the sensate" are themselves the condemnable consequences of sin rather than excuses for sin. The debilities that are the necessary results of a voluntary or conscious fault can also properly be regarded as sin. Flaws like the "eclipse of the understanding" should not be regarded as exculpating conditions that motivate sin but as the products of sin (*JP* 4, 4047; Böhringer, 1, pt. 3: 408). In all of these instances Kierkegaard was siding with the more conservative confessionalist assessments of Augustine in order to maximize guilt, distancing himself from Clausen and Martensen, who were prone to seek out nonculpable mitigating circumstances that motivated sin.

Kierkegaard also expressed an appreciation for important aspects of Augustine's exploration of the nature of Christian love. In a journal entry from 1843 he approvingly refers to Augustine's distinction of proper and improper love *(amor probus* and *amor improbus) (JP* 3, 2400).[63] His reference occurs in the context of a reflection on the theme that the biblical mandate to love our neighbors as ourselves assumes that we do indeed love ourselves. Kierkegaard observes that "self-love is egotism unless it is also love for God — thereby love for all," and he goes on to insist that the love in question should be an abiding heartfelt inwardness, and not a concatenation of mere external deeds (*JP* 3, 2399). Only such an enduring, heartfelt love has the power to hide a multitude of sins, a subject that was in the foreground of Kierkegaard's mind at the time and was the subject of one of his edifying discourses. In this passage Kierkegaard links love and faith, claiming that whatever does not proceed from them is sin. Evidently, Kierkegaard found support for at least some of these themes in Augustine's treatment of proper love. The fact that he turned to Augustine to shed light on genuine Christian love may suggest that he had heeded Clausen's suggestion that Augustine had appropriately integrated love and faith.

Augustine's teachings about the strenuous principles of the ideal Christian life also impressed Kierkegaard. As we have seen, in 1839 he recorded in his journal Augustine's remark that without marriage the city of God would be populated more rapidly and the end of the age would be hastened (*JP* 3, 2584). Kierkegaard took Augustine's "ardor for perfection" to be a critique of Christianity's overvaluation of the "physical unity" dimension of marriage and its failure to appreciate Christ's assertion that the saints will be like the angels in heaven. In 1851 he agreed with the Flemish mystic and proto-Reformer Jan Ruysbroek that the secular way of life that prevailed in medieval monastic life was a betrayal of the rule of Augustine, and Kierkegaard interpreted that betrayal as a parallel to the secularization of the faith

---

63. Kierkegaard refers to *Augustini Aurelii Opera,* but only cites the index entry *amor probus — improbus.*

by the Christendom of his time (*JP* 3, 2759).[64] By emphasizing Augustine as a moralist who understood the loftiness of the Christian ideal, Kierkegaard is reflecting the interpretive tradition of de Wette and Neander.

Kierkegaard appreciated the wisdom of Augustine's ethical reflections, even when he did not fully agree with them. Kierkegaard's journals of 1850 and 1851 reveal an intensive wrestling with a cluster of issues related to authority, coercion, force, and nonresistance to evil. In a journal entry from 1850 he approves of Augustine's remark, reported by Neander, that Christ was violating his own commandment to turn the other cheek when he chastised those who struck him (*JP* 2, 1193). Augustine had pointed out that Christ in that episode did not adopt an attitude of meek passivity, at least not verbally. According to Kierkegaard, Augustine realized that a virtue like meekness, when pushed undialectically to the extreme, can be transformed into its opposite — in this case cruelty toward those who attack the innocent. It would actually have been cruel of Jesus to say nothing and allow his tormentors to prolong their abuse of him. This exception to his own rule was motivated by Jesus' compassionate desire to prevent his assailants from acquiring further guilt by striking him again. Kierkegaard also reflects on Augustine's opinion that military service is permissible for Christians (*JP* 2, 1194). Kierkegaard reports that Augustine had "felicitously" stated that it is not the military service that is incompatible with virtuous action, but rather vice. Kierkegaard, an accomplished Latinist, knew that Augustine was punning on *militia* (military) and *malitia* (vice). The Bishop of Hippo, Kierkegaard notes, had justified his defense of military service by appealing to the fact that John the Baptist had not commanded soldiers to discard their weapons, but only to avoid violence, injustice, and greed (Luke 3:14). Kierkegaard ends his reflection with the destabilizing observation that John the Baptist had predated Christianity, implying that John's words might not be an articulation of a Christian ethic. Here Kierkegaard seems to admit the power of Augustine's argument, but he does not hesitate to raise a critical question about it. In 1851, Kierkegaard expressed interest in Augustine's defense of authority and the use of force by the authorities, even though the Dane was himself declaring that the genuinely Christian policy should be to eschew the use of force against injustice and instead disarm injustice by enduring the suffering that it perpetrates (*JP* 2, 1195). In spite of his obvious sympathy for the conviction held (he thought) by some Donatists

---

64. See C. Ullman, *Reformatoren vor der Reformation,* vols. I-II (Hamburg: Friedrich Perthes, 1842), vol. II, pp. 35-61. Ullman discusses and quotes Ruysbroek.

that "Christ has given Christians the prototype not of killing but of dying," Kierkegaard was intrigued by Augustine's argument that "not to use force to compel one to the truth is a 'false and cruel tolerance' " (JP 2, 1195-98). Kierkegaard adds that Augustine was not advocating the use of force to constrain people to come to faith (for faith, he insisted, cannot be constrained), but only to eliminate unnecessary hindrances to faith. Even though this qualified defense of the use of force by ecclesial authorities ran counter to Kierkegaard's vision of the Christian life as the acceptance of weakness in the social realm, he explicitly notes the pages in which Böhringer reports Augustine's argument (JP 2, 1199; Böhringer, 1, pt. 3: 357-68).

In spite of these approving assessments of Augustine, there were other aspects of Augustine's approach to theology that provoked Kierkegaard's scathing censure. Most significantly, Kierkegaard found the speculative dimension of Augustine to be an insidious distortion of genuine faith. In 1853, Kierkegaard bemoaned the contemporary construal of Christianity as a doctrine, "an object for passive, brooding meditation," and associated Augustine with this failure to realize that Christianity is primarily a praxis (JP 4, 3864). The "miserable waste of time" is not alleviated even if the thinker, like Augustine, finally admits that the conceptual matter under investigation is beyond full comprehension (JP 4, 3864). In a journal entry (1854) Kierkegaard's critique is particularly strident, for he accuses Augustine of having "done incalculable harm" because "the whole system of doctrine through the centuries relies essentially upon him — and he has confused the concept of 'faith' " (JP 1, 180). Kierkegaard laments that Augustine had tragically conflated the concept of faith with the concept of knowledge, treating faith as a cognitive system. This "Greek philosophical pagan definition of faith" falsely transposes faith into the alien domain of knowledge. This displacement tends to diminish faith's value, for faith possesses a lesser degree of probability than knowledge proper. Faith, torn from its true context of the "existential," the passionate relationship of a personal subject to a personal God, is thereby transmuted into the intellectualism of Plato and Aristotle. Most tragically, the orienting of faith toward the intellect rather than toward the will obscures the apostolic mandate of obedience. Champions of the "Greek view" of faith, such as Augustine, did not fully grasp the significance of the fact that "God has not made his appearance in the form of an assistant professor who has a few axioms which one must first believe and then understand" (JP 1, 180). According to Kierkegaard, by Augustine's time the church had been corrupted by too much leisure and too much privilege; this privileged situation tempted the church to become scientific and scholarly, and thereby to revert to pagan sensibilities (*JP* 1, 180). Furthermore, Kierkegaard adds in 1854-55, Augustine had confused the concept of faith "by drawing the qualification of his concept 'faith' directly from Plato," and forgetting that faith has an ethical rather than an intellectual character (*JP* 2, 1154). In 1854, Kierkegaard contemptuously cited the "much acclaimed Augustine" as an example of the so-called "Christian philosophers," who were actually a bunch of "muddleheads" (*JP* 4, 4299). Kierkegaard denounces these Christian philosophers, who forgot the critical factor — the single individual. In all of these passages Kierkegaard is echoing the reservations about Augustine the Platonic metaphysician that Clausen had expressed early in Kierkegaard's theological education and that many of his textbooks had repeated.

Kierkegaard sometimes criticizes Augustine for attempting to produce objective arguments to support the probable truth of Christianity. According to one of Kierkegaard's journal entries (1851), Augustine's argument that the truth of Christianity is validated by the unity of Christians in contrast to the disunity found among philosophers is fallacious and misleading (*JP* 3, 3614; Böhringer, 1, pt. 3: 234). Augustine, Kierkegaard believed, overlooked the obvious fact that all religions, not just Christianity, are based on unity and that all philosophy thrives on conflict. In 1854, Kierkegaard berated Augustine for arguing that the mathematical fact that the orthodox Catholic party was the majority in North Africa validated their opinions over against the minority position held by a mere dozen Donatists. Kierkegaard objects to this foolishness: "[Augustine] argues concerning truth on the basis of numbers," as if the prevalence of a belief corroborated its truth (*JP* 4, 4299). This was a colossal mistake that a genuine philosopher like Socrates would never have made. By appealing to impressive numbers, Augustine had failed to realize that Christianity is "related to the category of the single individual" (*JP* 4, 4299). Late in Kierkegaard's life, Augustine began to function for him as the paradigm of the putatively objective Christian philosopher in contrast to the true philosopher, the existentially engaged Socrates. The picture of Augustine the rationalist was beginning to displace the picture of Augustine the passionate pilgrim in Kierkegaard's writings.

Through all of these sometimes vitriolic condemnations of Augustine's lamentable amalgamation of Christianity and Greek philosophy, Kierkegaard is objecting to the "faith seeking understanding" aspect of Augustine's thought. It seemed to Kierkegaard that Augustine had engaged in an ill-advised project similar to that of the speculative philosophers of his own day. More specifically, Kierkegaard is reacting against Martensen's very public appropriation of the Augustinian motto of "believing so that one can understand." Whereas the contemporary generation of theologians had adopted Hegel in order to reconceive the faith, Augustine had used Plato and Aristotle. The mistake in both cases was to think that Christian convictions needed to be recast in a more technical conceptuality that would clarify their meaning and even lead to deeper insight. The problem that Kierkegaard detected in this procedure was threefold. First, the use of alien categories distorted the meaning of the original concepts. Second, the mood of the endeavor was all wrong, for it encouraged objective detachment rather than appropriate passionate involvement. Third, the project's espoused goal of "understanding" the basic teachings more deeply encouraged the false impression that Christian principles were primarily intended to be rationally grasped rather than to be lived out.

Kierkegaard was appreciative but also suspicious of Augustine's teachings about election by grace. In 1854 he confessed that the "idea that a man's eternal salvation is to be decided by a striving in time, in this life, is so superhumanly heavy that it will kill a man more surely than massive sunstroke" (*JP* 3, 2551). He continues: "I now interpret Augustine as having hit upon election by grace simply in order to avoid this difficulty; for in this case eternal salvation is not decided in relation to a striving." Luther, he says, agreed that no human could withstand such anxiety and thus was motivated to affirm salvation by grace. According to Kierkegaard, the problem with this view is not the affirmation of salvation by grace, but rather the impression given by the doctrine that God has lowered the requirement for eternal salvation and no longer expects a sincere striving. Kierkegaard protests that this subverts the despair that individuals should experience and militates against their confession that they "cannot pay the taxes" (the taxes being the honest striving to actualize the Christian ideal). The theme of election by grace that dates back to Augustine gives the misleading impression that the taxes have indeed been lowered and that no one is really expected to pay them anymore. Rather than reveling in such laxity, according to Kierkegaard, we need to honestly admit our inability to live up to God's requirements. Kierkegaard was not denying that we are truly saved by grace, but arguing only that we must not interpret that affirmation in such a way that striving to enact the Christian life (and the consequent despair over the failure to do so) is undermined.

Conclusion

If we put these scattered remarks together, it seems that Kierkegaard entertained two different — almost diametrically opposed — pictures of Augustine. On the one hand, there was the admirable Augustine, the passionately self-involving author who lived out what he believed. That Augustine was the doughty champion of subjectivity who recognized that the proper context for the explication of Christian teachings was the narrative of the motley fears, doubts, offenses, consolations, and joys that characterize the Christian life. That Augustine was committed to striving to actualize the Christian ideal in his life. On the other hand, there was the pernicious Augustine, the speculative philosopher who treated Christian teachings as cognitive objects to be scrutinized, analyzed, and theorized. The villain for Kierkegaard was the Augustine who discerned a commensurability between the teachings of the philosophers and the mysteries of Christian doctrine. Kierkegaard had an allergic reaction to Augustine's suggestion that philosophical speculation and Christian convictions are compatible because they both emanate from the eternal Word. Augustine the speculative philosopher and systematician was the bane of authentic Christianity and, according to Kierkegaard, the precursor of many of its ills during his time.

The two conflicting pictures of Augustine are evident in Kierkegaard's responses to Augustine on the issues of sin, grace, and freedom. On the one hand, there is the devoutly self-abasing Augustine who experienced the despair of moral and spiritual failure and learned to trust only in God's love. That Augustine could aptly sound the alarm about the depths of human corruption and enable the reader to feel the crushing weight of guilt. On the other hand, Augustine the systematician invented the doctrine of predestination in order to conceptualize the interaction of divine and human agencies. That Augustine described sin and grace in such a way that human responsibility seemed to be vitiated.

Both of these pictures of Augustine were supported by Kierkegaard's ongoing formal and informal theological education. In fact, given the ways in which familiarity with Augustine was mediated to him, it was almost inevitable that he would have developed a sharply ambivalent attitude toward the Bishop of Hippo. In the next chapters we shall move beyond Kierkegaard's explicit statements about Augustine and his references to Augustine's writings in order to consider the more thematic correspondences and divergences between the two thinkers. Kierkegaard may have been more or less in accord with more of the basic dynamics of Augustine's work than he realized. Kierkegaard's own assessments of his relationship to Augustine may not have been entirely accurate. As we have seen, any misconstrual on Kierkegaard's part could have been due to the fragmentary nature of his firsthand acquaintance with Augustine's writings, and to the very perspectival interpretations of Augustine that he had imbibed. In any case, in the following chapters we will not be looking for direct genetic connections. Given the limited nature of Kierkegaard's exposure to Augustine, it would be a gross exaggeration to even imply that he derived any of his characteristic theological emphases directly from the African father. Rather, we will explore possible thematic parallels, including the crucial matter of possible parallels of rhetorical and pastoral purpose.

Having abjured any attempt to claim that Augustine exerted a decisive and direct genetic influence on Kierkegaard, we should observe one caveat. Although Augustine's direct influence on Kierkegaard was slight, his indirect influence may have been quite powerful. As we shall see, Augustinian motifs had been woven into the very structure of the theology and spirituality of Western Christianity in general, and of Lutheran theology and spirituality in particular. In multiple profound ways, whether Kierkegaard knew it or not, many of his assumptions about the faith were rooted in Augustine's work. The things that he took for granted about the morphology of Christianity were basically Augustinian. Moreover, Kierkegaard's critique of many of the features of his contemporary Danish Lutheran church implicitly involved a recovery of certain Augustinian themes, even though he might well have been oblivious to that fact. Ironically, Augustine was also the indirect source of many of the aspects of Christianity that Kierkegaard criticized. When the latter was calling for the repristinating of Christendom via a return to New Testament Christianity, it was often aspects of the legacy of Augustine that he wanted to purify and reform. Whether Kierkegaard was retrieving, reforming, or condemning some aspect of Christianity's thought and life, it was the heritage of Augustine that provided the background. For good or ill, the tradition of Augustine was a large component of his ideological world. Perhaps not realizing the full import of his remarks about Augustine, Kierkegaard was right in casting him as both the hero and the villain in his own struggle to grasp the nature of the Christian faith and to live it out. As we shall see, Augustine the hero was more basic to his project than was Augustine the villain. This should not be surprising, for the Christianity in which Kierkegaard had been reared, and which he continued to cherish, was in many ways the fruit of the Augustinian spirit.

CHAPTER 2

Augustine's Restless Heart and Kierkegaard's Desire for an Eternal Happiness

One of the most basic and important characteristics that Kierkegaard shared with Augustine was not something he gleaned from the early-nineteenth-century literature about Augustine: the importance of an implicit desire for God in human nature. Desiring, longing, loving, and yearning for ultimate fulfillment animate the pages of both Augustine and Kierkegaard. To many people, this may sound surprising, for both thinkers are often imagined as brooding introverts, morbidly probing the depths of their own sinfulness, remorselessly exposing hidden reservoirs of guilt, anxiety, and despair. Contrary to this one-dimensional caricature, their respective views of human beings were based on a keen awareness of humanity's yearning for an object that would fill the soul with pure delight. For both Augustine and Kierkegaard, temporal existence is animated by a dimly felt yearning for an unimaginable joy. This positive note was more foundational for both of them than were their exposés of the various ways that this longing can get diverted and thwarted, because their celebrated diagnoses of human malaise were predicated on the assumption of longing for God. The theme of spiritual hunger is the basic thread that runs throughout their portrayals of human life in general and the Christian life in particular. The centrality of the desire for an absolute, transcendent good gives their work an essential but often somewhat covert similarity. In Augustine's writings the pivotal role played by desire is explicit and obvious; in Kierkegaard's writings the crucial importance of desire is sometimes blatant but often it is more occluded. Kierkegaard occasionally uses the Danish word for "desire" *(længsel,* or *ønske),* but more typically he simply describes teleological longing and attraction. Despite differences in terminology, Kierkegaard parallels

Augustine on this theme, sometimes acknowledging the Augustinian lineage but often allowing the debt to remain hidden. To explore the similarities (and differences) between Augustine and Kierkegaard on this crucial theme, we shall first consider the critical function of desire in Augustine's writings.

But before we begin this exploration, I must note that the desire for an absolute, transcendent good need not be regarded as the essential presupposition of the Christian faith. In fact, this understanding of Christianity has often been subjected to severe critique. For example, the foregrounding of such a desire has been pejoratively labeled "eudaemonism" and dismissed as something residually pagan, too tainted by self-concern to be regarded as a fundamental feature of Christianity. Surely, it is sometimes argued, to root the Christian life in a desire for personal beatitude is to succumb to a rarefied form of selfishness. Accordingly, Anders Nygren famously distinguished eros, love motivated by a lack in the soul that seeks to be filled by the possession of a desired object, and agape, Christian love that gives itself to others with no thought of recompense.[1] Eros aims at self-oriented gratification, an *amor sui*, while agape aims only at the well-being of the other. Desire is alleged to be intrinsically acquisitive, possessive, and selfish, rooted in the individual's own subjective needs and wants rather than in sincere concern for the beloved other. Nygren thought that this vice was manifestly evident in the self-absorbed writings of the mystics. According to Nygren, Augustine's concept of *caritas* was a confused and futile attempt to synthesize the two incommensurable forms of love. Christianity, concludes Nygren, should properly strive to incarnate agape and purge itself of the narcissism of eros.

Through the centuries those who have been suspicious of the centrality of desire for God have proposed other candidates for the core of the Christian faith. For some, the heart of the faith has been located in the struggle for the attainment of some purely temporal good, such as societal justice or the satisfaction of basic human needs. For others, Christianity's essence has been the harmonious integration of all aspects of the individual's life and the actualization of all God-given potentials. For yet others it has been obedience to divine imperatives and the satisfaction of knowing that one has been a good and faithful servant. For others the "gospel" has been divine empowerment to navigate and survive the slings and arrows of outrageous

1. Anders Nygren, *Agape and Eros,* trans. Philip S. Watson (New York: Harper and Row, 1969).

fortune and the availability of consolation when tragedy strikes. For yet others, Christianity does indeed provide a transcendent fulfillment, but it is an utterly unexpected and counterintuitive fulfillment that humanity was not yearning for at all. For still others, the kernel of the Christian message is the transcendence of all desire, even the desire for God, epitomized in the old Reformed ordination question, "Are you willing to go to hell for the greater glory of God?"

For most orthodox Lutherans of Kierkegaard's day, the essence of Christianity was God's offer of forgiveness for the individual's moral and spiritual failures — and God's correlative acceptance and embrace of the still sinful self. Lutherans have typically agreed that the theme of justification by grace, not desire for God, is the doctrine on which the church stands or falls. Because of this dizzying variety of construals of the essence of Christianity, we will need to explore what is distinctive about Augustine's and Kierkegaard's understandings of the Christian faith as the desire for an absolute good and an eternal happiness. We must also clarify what they actually meant by those notoriously elusive terms.

Augustine's Restless Heart

The human desire for something that would provide happiness was the driving force in Augustine's work from beginning to end. Augustine's texts are saturated with the language of the heart and the rhetoric of passion. Throughout his writings he generously used metaphors of hunger and thirst to describe the soul's longing for some kind of truth, goodness, and beauty that would bring absolute satisfaction. This entelechy is present in all people, pagan and Christian, whether they are aware of it or not. The craving for happiness is a universal, structural feature of all human beings, uniting the implicit aspirations of the pagans with the explicit hopes of the Christians. In *The City of God*, Augustine insisted that the ultimate purpose of philosophical reflection had always been, even before the advent of Christianity, the attainment of ultimate happiness.[2] In continuity with the aspirations of the philosophers, the Christian's life can be most basically characterized as a "holy desire" or a "fervent spirit."[3] Augustine describes the soul as moaning

---

2. Augustine, *The City of God*, XIX, 1 in *WSA*, I, 6-7.

3. Augustine, *Tractates on the Gospel of John (Johannis evangelium tractatus)*, Homily 2, 4, in *WSA* III, 12.

like a dove and groaning for an ineffable object of desire.[4] The centrality of desire in his work is signaled by the celebrated opening prayer of the *Confessions:* "[Y]ou have made us for yourself, and our heart is restless until it rests in you."[5]

For Augustine, desire is not a passive wishing for some future state of affairs; nor is it an inert sensation of pleasure when contemplating some imagined delightful prospect. Desire is always something dynamic, a motivating action, for it draws an individual like a weight *(pondus)* toward its destination. Augustine writes: "If oil is poured into water it will rise to the surface, but if water is poured onto oil it will sink below the oil; drawn by their weight, things seek their rightful places."[6] Love is like water and oil seeking their proper places where they can find rest. Alternatively, desire is like an arrow in motion seeking its target: it has an internal momentum and directionality. All these metaphors suggest that genuine desire necessarily involves a striving to secure the enjoyment of some object and to actualize some delightful possibility. Consequently, desire must be thought of as being intrinsically and actively goal-directed. To speak of desire is necessarily to speak of motivations, intentions, and purposes. For Augustine, desiring, willing, and acting cannot be hermetically sealed off from one another.

Throughout his writings Augustine often uses "love" and "desire" *(dilectio,* or *desiderium)* and "delight" *(delectatio)* as nearly synonymous terms. In his intellectual culture, "desire" typically suggested a yearning to possess something that the individual does not yet have, but wants. Love often had a stronger nuance of delight in the possession of the object. As we shall see, Augustine saw the two as more closely related than that distinction suggests. He used *amor, caritas,* and *dilectio* interchangeably (as is particularly evident throughout his *Homilies on the First Epistle of John*), all suggesting a present delight in the beloved object but also a movement toward the beloved and a striving to be united with the beloved. The concepts together suggest both the drive to satisfy a lack, to fill a void, but also an attraction elicited by the intrinsic desirability of the beloved. It is not only a deficit in the lover that fuels desire, but also the inherent worth of the beloved, even if the need to experience that worthiness had not been recognized before. This combination of being propelled by an inchoate need and also being drawn by an object whose attractiveness was unanticipated would have im-

4. Augustine, *Tractates on the Gospel of John,* Homily 6, 1-2, in *WSA* III, 12.
5. Augustine, *Confessions,* I, 1 (1), in *WSA* I, 1.
6. Augustine, *Confessions,* XIII, 9 (10), in *WSA* I, 1.

portant consequences for Augustine's vision of the interaction of "nature" and "grace." As we shall see, a parallel relationship of being intrinsically propelled and being contingently drawn would reappear in the writings of Kierkegaard. This two-dimensional understanding of desire would enable both of them to avoid many of the dichotomies that came to afflict Catholicism and Protestantism.

If the desire in human beings is for ultimate happiness rather than for merely relative pleasures, desire has the potential to orient the individual's entire life toward a final fulfillment. Augustine and Kierkegaard both borrowed the term *summum bonum* from the tradition of classical philosophy to indicate the absolute object of desire. The kind of desire that Augustine had in mind is so sweeping and compelling that it has the power to unify an individual's life, prioritizing and integrating all the individual's less than ultimate needs and aspirations. Aristotle had argued in his *Nicomachean Ethics* that every human activity is aimed at some desired good, and that these subordinate goods are desirable by virtue of their contributions to the pursuit of an ultimately desirable good. In his early dialogues, written at Cassiciacum in 386-87, Augustine appropriates this theme, proposing that the human quest for fulfillment must have one true object; and he proceeds to raise questions about the nature of this object to which everything else in life must be subordinated. An individual's most basic desire constitutes that individual's very identity, for desire establishes the underlying directionality of a life. A person is what that person most fundamentally loves.[7]

This effort to understand the object of this desire for happiness would not diminish as Augustine's life progressed. Taking his cues from Cicero's *Hortensius,* Augustine proposes, early in his career as a writer, that all people desire happiness, even if they do not have a clear conception of what happiness truly is. Both Cicero and Augustine (in his Cassiciacum dialogues) tend to define "happiness" negatively, in terms of what it is not. "Happiness" in this context is not a transient affective episode of contentment, satiation, pleasure, or exhilaration. Happiness is a perduring state of living in accord with whatever it is that gives life value and meaning, secure in the knowledge that the deepest aspiration of the human heart has been found. Genuine happiness is not just the acquisition of whatever a person contingently happens to desire at the moment, for most people mistakenly desire things that will ultimately disappoint them. The true object of happi-

---

7. Augustine, *Homilies on the First Epistle of John (Tractatus in epistulam Joannis ad Parthos),* Homily 2, 14; Homily 5, 7, in *WSA* III, 14.

ness must be something that will not deteriorate and cannot be taken away or used up. Because real happiness necessarily includes confidence that the beloved object will continue to provide delight, that object must be immune to the unpredictable fluctuations of fortune and misfortune. Its enjoyment cannot be dependent on external circumstances and the vicissitudes of temporal events. Because the delight in the object must never wane, the elusive object must be something that will be permanently fulfilling, never producing boredom. Consequently, it must be something of absolute and inexhaustible worth. By raising these questions about the nature of happiness, Augustine was not just engaging in a bit of Platonic metaphysics or a phenomenological description of humanity's affective life. Rather, he was prodding readers to feel the inadequacies of all earthly objects of desire, and coaxing readers to begin to long more intensely and consciously for a kind of happiness that this world cannot provide. His literary style was calculated to encourage self-reflection and awaken a sublime discontent with all penultimate earthly goods.

Augustine develops a similar theme in *On Teaching Christianity (De doctrina Christiana),* in which he borrows from the Stoics a distinction between two very different kinds of desire, *uti* and *frui.*[8] *Uti* is the desire to possess something because it is useful for the pursuit of some more important purpose or necessary for the attainment of some ulterior goal. *Frui,* however, is the desire to simply enjoy something, quite apart from questions of utility. To enjoy something is to love that object for its own sake, delighting in its sheer existence, while to use something is to employ it as a means to attain something else that is worth loving for its own sake. Augustine was convinced that there must be a highest value, desirable in itself, that bestows worth on everything else. *Frui* must have an ultimate object that is worthy of absolute love. Kierkegaard, as we shall discover, would repeat many of these motifs in his upbuilding discourses, including his celebrated "Occasional Discourse," often referred to as "Purity of Heart Is To Will One Thing" (*UDVS,* 3-154).

Augustine's strategy prompts the reader to realize that many popular notions of happiness cannot possibly satisfy the reader's heart. Happiness cannot be the possession of any material good, for physical things always fade and die, and even if they do endure for a while, their charms no longer

---

8. See Ola Sigurdson, "The Passion of the Christ: On the Social Production of Desire," in F. LeRon Shults and Jan-Olav Henriksen, eds., *Saving Desire: The Seduction of Christian Theology* (Grand Rapids: Eerdmans, 2011), pp. 35-36.

enchant. Nor can happiness be nothing more than the proper ordering and actualization of a person's potentialities — which was a widespread classical view of the felicity gained via a life of virtue — because the exercise of those powers, no matter how impressive and carefully cultivated, will eventually fail to satisfy. The allures of athletic prowess, rhetorical facility, social intercourse, philosophical discourse, and even abstract reasoning all eventually wane and disappoint. Slowly the reader is guided to recognize that the ultimate *telos* of human desiring can only be something beyond all earthly pleasures and fulfillments: it can only be the contemplation of the highest good, the font of all beauty and truth, which is God. Augustine describes God as "the source of our bliss . . . and the goal of our striving," and he concludes that human lives are brought to fulfillment only through communion with God.[9] For Augustine, the only good that can provide genuine and lasting happiness is the loving contemplation of God and the imaging of God.[10] Augustine asks his readers: "Which do you want, to love temporal things and to pass away with time or not to love the world and live forever with God?"[11] He frequently observes that Jesus' exhortation "You shall love the Lord your God" functions not only as a command but also as a reminder that only through loving God can we attain the goal of happiness.[12] As the ancient philosophers knew, our many earthly loves must be ordered and prioritized according to an ultimate love, and, as Christianity revealed, that primary and most exalted love, the love that fuels all other loves, is our love for God. During his early dialogues, of course, Augustine leaves the concept of God as the object of desire rather vague and abstract. As we shall see, his concept of God only acquires depth and density as he situates it in his thicker descriptions of the passions and aspirations of the Christian life.

For Augustine, the desire for a highest good is not symptomatic of a tragic defect in human nature that should not be there. The longing that is intrinsic to human nature is not merely a negative reaction to human sin; it is more than the wistful yearning to be relieved of the burden of guilt. Moreover, our desire for God is not simply spawned by the tragedies of earthly life, as if a more felicitous created order would be so completely satisfying that an individual would yearn for nothing more. Rather, the restlessness of

---

9. Augustine, *The City of God*, X, 3; see also XIX, 17, in *WSA* 1, 6-7.

10. Augustine, *The City of God*, X, 3, in *WSA* I, 6-7.

11. Augustine, *Homilies on the First Epistle of John*, Homily 2, 10.

12. Augustine, *Explanations of the Psalms (Enarrationes in Psalmos)*, 83:11 (*WSA* III, 14-17).

which Augustine writes is a positive aspect of humanity's ontological structure as it was intended by a benevolent Creator. Emphatically, it is not due to a flaw in our nature or a catastrophe in our development. Far from being an imperfection, the need for God is the source of human fulfillment and joy. (This theme would recur in such discourses by Kierkegaard as "To Need God Is a Human Being's Highest Perfection" [*EUD*, 297-326].) Our insufficiency motivates us to long for what is the basis and support of our very being. It is indeed an ache, but it is a sweet ache. Even if finite life were not ontologically precarious, we would still long for the absolute delight that only God can provide. Augustine often uses images of sensory attraction, describing God as being so fragrant that we are drawn to God's loveliness.[13] God is the exquisitely beautiful vista that we long to behold.

Such reflections on the unsatisfying nature of earthly loves led Augustine to engage in episodic metaphysical speculation. According to Augustine, the disappointment and anxiety that finite loves produce is inevitable, given the basic nature of the universe. Matter is other than the eternal, perfectly actualized God; it is thus mutable, potentially capable of assuming many different forms. That element of potentiality, which can be described as the absence of full actuality, means that matter possesses a dimension of nothingness, though it is not absolute nothingness.[14] In a way, matter is an abyss, for it could become anything or could even become what it should not be. Because it is in principle formless, the material world inherently tends toward chaos (apart from God's ordering activity). It is no wonder that earthly phenomena fail to satisfy. The soul yearns for stability, integration, and eternity. It secretly longs for freedom from anxiety and frustration. These desiderata can never be provided by things that can lose their form and devolve into nothingness.

Augustine's forays into metaphysics, such as these reflections, are designed to help the reader meditate more deeply on the intrinsic inadequacy of earthly loves, and to feel that inadequacy more acutely. Accordingly, he punctuates these cosmological ruminations with personal expressions of disillusion with earthly things and a "panting" for God, writing, "O Truth, illumination of my heart, let not my own darkness speak to me! I slid away to material things, sank into shadow, yet even there, even from there, I loved you."[15] Augustine's technical speculation about unformed matter is

---

13. Augustine, *Tractates on the Gospel of John*, Homily 26, 4 and 5, in *WSA* III, 12.
14. Augustine, *Confessions*, XII, 8 (8), in *WSA* I, 1.
15. Augustine, *Confessions*, XII, 10 (10), in *WSA*, I, 1.

addressed to God as part of an exuberant doxology. Kierkegaard's mentors generally failed to communicate to him a sense of the impropriety of attempting to separate Augustine the metaphysician from Augustine the adorer of God. For Augustine, speculation can be prayerful, and prayer can be speculative. In fact, prayer is the indispensable context for meaningful speculation about divine matters. As we shall see, in the case of Augustine it would be misleading to apply too rigidly the distinction elaborated by Johannes Climacus (Kierkegaard's pseudonymous "humorist" who sympathetically sketched Christian pathos from the outside) between objective and subjective thinking. Augustine's passionate, adoring speculation did not resemble the scientific mood of the Hegelians, though Kierkegaard would not have known this from the lectures he heard by professors such as Henrik Nicolai Clausen.

It is important to note here that Augustine is not negating the value of earthly life; he is not advocating extreme asceticism or dismissing the created order as a source of evil. Augustine had renounced his youthful Manichean dualism; through his spiritual wrong turns he was discovering that the created goods in which he had taken initial delight were not in themselves bad. Rather, it was the tension between their genuine goodness and their limitations that created the problem for him. The goad to Augustine's restlessness was the fact that the limited goodness of finite phenomena made him long for something even better. The pleasure in creaturely beauty stirred up a longing for the source of all beauty. Augustine came to see that the beauty that we love in creatures is really a pointer to the beauty of God, the source of all beauty and the only truly beautiful object. In fact, the more Augustine took delight in the gifts of the Creator, the more his longing for God grew. *Confessions* became the narration of the ways in which his desires were educated, becoming more lofty and even extravagant. His hunger for God intensified, even when he seemed to be retreating from God. Discontent with finite goods was not just the negative fruit of the tragedies and disappointments that frustrate their continuing enjoyment (though the specter of decay and mortality certainly always did haunt Augustine). The impermanence of carnal things is only one dimension of the problem, because even more destabilizing than mortality and decay is the fact that earthly joys simply exacerbate the ache for something even more satisfying, for something of inestimable worth that can produce absolute joy.

Augustine's view of the Christian life, therefore, does not involve the extirpation of desire, but rather its reformation. The spiritual goal is not self-control, volitional autonomy, freedom from all passion, or apathy.[16] Following Lactantius, who invoked Aristotle's contention that the reason for the movement of the will is desire, Augustine rejected what he took to be the Stoic view that the pursuit of virtue requires detachment from the perturbations of the passions. The Stoics alleged that the disorderly passions deflect the mind from concentration on the good, and therefore they should be eliminated or strictly controlled (or so Augustine thought, though he may have been unfair to the Stoics). They heralded the life of *apatheia*, freedom from disturbing episodes of anxiety, infatuation, despair, and anger, as the ideal. Augustine sensed that this tradition did not mesh well with the biblical themes of thirsting for righteousness, loving God with all one's heart, and fearing God's judgment. Moreover, the Stoics could not adequately explain what moved the soul to act. Augustine objected that, without desire, the soul might conceptually entertain a possibility, but would have no motivation to enact it. He excoriated the Stoic virtue of *apatheia* in much the same way that Kierkegaard would later critique purely objective reflection and autonomous will power. If the mind were to be in a state "in which the mind cannot be touched by any emotion whatsoever, who would not judge this insensitivity to be the worst of all moral defects?"[17] According to Augustine's critique of the Stoic view, the task of the individual is to redirect desires toward their proper object. Desire is not to be uprooted, but is rather to be carefully cultivated, channeled, and aimed in the correct direction. For this to happen, humans must be enabled to loosen the bonds of affection that compulsively tie them to lesser goods and feel the attractive power of the highest good. *Cupiditas* must be transmuted into *caritas*. The emotions that originate from love, such as compassion for sufferers, are actually virtues and not disorders of the soul.[18] As we shall see, Kierkegaard was in entire accord with Augustine that passion and desire must be kept front and center in the Christian life.

Because human desires must be transformed and reoriented in order to long for God rightly, desire for God, according to Augustine, does not provide an unambiguous sense of pleasure, at least not while we are still on our earthly pilgrimage. For Augustine, the cultivation of the desire for God and the commitment to a process of reorientation to God do not im-

---

16. See Glenn Graham, "Kierkegaard and the Longing for God" (PhD diss., McMaster University, 2011).

17. Augustine, *The City of God*, XIV, 9, in *WSA* I, 6-7.

18. Augustine, *The City of God*, XIV, 9, in *WSA* I, 6-7.

mediately produce unadulterated joy. God does not promptly ravish the soul with exquisite bliss and comfort. Imaging the beauty and truth of God as a light that attracts the soul, Augustine writes: "What is the light which shines right through me and strikes my heart without hurting? It fills me with terror and burning love: with terror in so far as I am utterly other than it, with burning love in that I am akin to it."[19] The terror is due to the perception of the dissimilarity of the soul and the holy God, coupled with the recognition that God is drawing the soul into a potentially painful process of transformation. The exhilaration of seeking the eternal is qualified by the bittersweet disclosure of God's difference from the unworthy soul.[20] A kind of fear arises as one becomes aware of one's need for God and one's own insufficiency. Although Augustine often describes God as the soul's true source and destination, he also portrays divinity and humanity as being two sides of a chasm. God's immeasurable magnitude can appear so vast that it intimidates the soul. At the same time that it intimidates, the phenomenon of desire for God contains within it the extravagant prospect that the soul, though unlike God, has the possibility to become (in some respects) like God. This transformation into godliness necessarily involves the daunting imperative to reorient one's life away from lesser attachments and to become a new creature, defined by one central love. Consequently, the desire for God both promises absolute fulfillment but also requires the renunciation of cherished aspects of the old worldly self. Because the soul is potentially like God, but currently very unlike God, the prospect of this transformation generates a dialectic of attraction/repulsion in the desire for God. Kierkegaard would later capture this ambivalence in his descriptions of the incarnation as being simultaneously attractive and offensive.

The centrality of desire has profound implications for every aspect of Augustine's theology. It is so woven into the fabric of his thought that it cannot be disentangled from other threads without causing the whole weave to unravel. Of course, Augustine was not interested in constructing a theological system with propositions connected by logical entailments; "desire for God" is not foundational for him in the way that a major premise is foundational for a syllogism. Rather, Augustine was intent on showing how the desire for God pervades every aspect of Christian existence, and he sought to elicit in the reader the various modulations and manifestations of desire

---

19. Augustine, *Confessions*, XI, 9 (11), in *WSA* I, 1.

20. Simon Podmore, *Kierkegaard and the Self Before God: Anatomy of the Abyss* (Bloomington: Indiana University Press, 2011), pp. 64-66.

that jointly constitute the Christian life. While his theology is not a system, it does exhibit a kind of coherence, a coherence given by the omnipresence of the theme of desire. Summarizing his theological vision, Augustine observes: "Now, my weight is my love, and wherever I am carried, it is this weight that carries me."[21]

Perhaps most importantly, the focus on desire colored the way Augustine thought about human motivations, decisions, and actions. For Augustine, humans do not arbitrarily choose their objects of desire by an act of sheer willpower. Augustine was far from being an absolute voluntarist, a fact that would become apparent in his controversy with the Pelagians, who grossly overestimated individuals' control of their volitional and appetitive proclivities and powers. The will does not operate in an affective vacuum. It is not as if individuals are passional tabulae rasae, calmly surveying the spectrum of possible desirable objects and then legislating which objects they will pursue. Rather, we humans always and already find ourselves being attracted to certain objects, and we are defined by those attractions. According to Augustine, love arises through *delectation,* the attractive power of an external reality. Love can be said to seize hold of us, for it draws us out of ourselves and our ordinary, already existing preoccupations. The development of a new desire cannot be accomplished through an exertion of the will, but only through a new experience of the attractiveness of a novel object. Such an experience of a new, deeper, stronger attraction involves both cognitive and affective components.[22] The transformation of desire involves a change of what we perceive to be desirable and a new perception of an object's qualities. Those qualities must evoke a feeling of attraction to that object; only then can the will be moved to choose it. The will merely assents to the attraction and allows its power to be felt by keeping the individual's attention directed to the object. Consequently, if we are to be transformed into lovers of God, it can only be through a more potent perception of God's truth, goodness, and beauty. God's sheer attractiveness must draw the will forward; the will cannot itself initiate the movement toward God, for it would have no motivation to do so. As we shall see, this analysis of the relationship of desiring and willing would have major implications for Augustine's treatment of the relationship of divine grace and human volition. As we shall also see, a parallel treatment of desire and will would much later

21. Augustine, *Confessions*, XIII, 9 (10), in *WSA* I, 1.

22. Margaret Miles, *Desire and Delight: A New Reading of Augustine's "Confessions"* (New York: Crossroad, 1992), pp. 17-38.

appear in the pages of Søren Kierkegaard, becoming particularly evident in *Works of Love.*

Augustine's focus on desire also delegitimizes any valorization of merely objective knowledge as the foundation of the Christian life. For Augustine, the most important things in life can only be learned through loving the subject matter.[23] By saying this, Augustine was not merely voicing a psychological truism about the need for the learner to be sufficiently motivated to remain on task; rather, he was advancing a fundamental epistemological claim. Even with regard to knowledge of the sensory world, without some attraction or interest, our minds would remain fickle and unfocused, unable to concentrate on any object for very long, incapable of distinguishing important features from unimportant ones — and would thus degenerate into chaos and superficiality. With regard to more spiritual matters, love becomes even more crucial for knowledge. In order to know God, our attention must be focused on God, which can only happen through desiring God. Therefore, Augustine speaks of an *intentio cordis,* an intention of the heart that is synonymous with faith's intentionality.[24] With regard to the knowledge of God, Augustine observes: "Give me a lover, and he will know by experience what I am talking about. . . . If on the other hand I am talking to some cold-hearted so-and-so, he has not the slightest idea of what I am talking about."[25]

Augustine caustically contrasts the philosopher who posits God as the explanation for the phenomenon of motion, but feels no impulse to adore God, with the pious believer who longs for God. There is a "difference between presumption and confession, between those who see the goal but not the way to it, and the Way to our beatific homeland, a homeland to be not merely described but lived in."[26] The two types of persons, the philosopher and the faithful believer, are different because of the different qualities of their loves. One desires a comprehensive view of the universe; the other desires to live in ecstatic awareness of God's dazzling beauty and truth. Augustine's language shifts subtly from an intellectual vocabulary to strongly interpersonal imagery. He writes rhapsodically of being healed by God's "fingers," which were gently tending his wounds, and of God's "grow-

---

23. Augustine, *The Trinity,* IX, 2. 2, in *WSA* I, 5.

24. See Lewis Ayres, *Augustine and the Trinity* (Cambridge: Cambridge University Press, 2010), p. 154.

25. Augustine, *Tractates on the Gospel of John,* Homily 26, 4, in *WSA* III, 2.

26. Augustine, *Confessions,* VII, 20 (26), in *WSA* I, 1.

ing sweet" to him.[27] Truly loving God is not simply a matter of drawing inferences from premises or abstracting universal forms from particular instances. Loving God is not to be equated with drawing logically correct formal implications from first principles concerning divine matters. To substantiate his contention, Augustine points out that the demons know at least some true propositions about God but nonetheless fail to love God. Giving cognitive assent to accurate theological propositions is clearly not a sufficient condition for growth in the Christian virtues. Knowledge devoid of passion cannot enable the soul to cleave to God and enjoy eternal blessedness through that bond. Without love, knowledge alone cannot lead to salvation.[28] Climacus's critique of "objective" knowing with respect to religious matters would echo many of Augustine's concerns.

Of course, for Augustine, the desire for God does necessarily possess an epistemic dimension. Throughout his works he insists that an essential dimension of the desire for God is the longing to contemplate divine truth.[29] In his early days of being a Christian, Augustine could even write that we first adhere to God in love and then actually possess God through knowledge, as if knowledge were a higher form of union.[30] The Neo-Platonic tendency to describe the goal of the religious quest in epistemological terms never left him. It was partly this legacy that motivated scholars like Clausen to suspect that Augustine's Neo-Platonism had introduced an alien and abstract conception of truth into his understanding of Christianity. Kierkegaard would inherit that suspicion of Augustine, the Neo-Platonic speculator. But such a characterization of Augustine was misleading, for to Augustine "truth" suggested something far more momentous than the correspondence of propositions to objective states of affairs in the universe. The apprehension of truth is a rapt beholding of the radiant divine mind. In his Cassiciacum writings Augustine proposes that the order sometimes dimly perceived in finite events is a manifestation of the *ordo* in the divine wisdom.[31] Life may often seem like a random pile of colored tiles, but from God's perspective it is a beautifully ordered mosaic. The kind of "knowledge" Augustine speaks of is an "illumination," an apprehension of the single unifying principle that

27. Augustine, *Confessions*, VII, 20 (26), in *WSA* I, 1.

28. Augustine, *Against Two Letters of the Pelagians (Contra duas epistulas Pelagianorum)*, IV, 5 (11), in *WSA* I, 24.

29. See Phillip Cary, *Augustine's Invention of the Inner Self: The Legacy of a Christian Platonist* (Oxford: Oxford University Press, 2000), pp. 71-72.

30. Augustine, *On Free Will (De libero arbitrio)*, II, 16, 41, in *WSA* I, 3.

31. Augustine, *On Order (De ordine)*, I, 1, 2, in *WSA* I, 3.

gives pattern to all things. "Truth" is an insight into what gives meaning to human life and resolves all disquietudes, perplexities, and anxieties. To know the truth is to grasp the significance of things; it is to see how everything is interconnected and has its source in God's "wisdom," and thereby to be filled with contentment and delight.[32] Knowing the truth is a phenomenon that is intensely affectively charged, and the desire for truth is fueled by the prospect of the exquisite joy of illumination. Accordingly, Augustine confesses to God that his desire was "not to be more certain *about* you, but to be more stable *in* you."[33] In several ways, Augustine's passionate, engaged kind of knowing would have similarities to Kierkegaard's descriptions of "earnestness," "pathos," and "subjectivity."

The centrality of desire in Augustine's thought also undermines the concept of the self as being, at least ideally, self-controlled and self-legislating.[34] If our spiritual identities are determined by the objects of our desire, then the self cannot be the self-possessed individual imagined and idealized by the Stoics, much less the Cartesian self that is often claimed as the descendant of Augustine's introspection. Human beings are not essentially self-contained egos, scrutinizing a field of cognizable objects from a transcendent vantage point. Nor are human persons completely autonomous moral agents constituting themselves by their unconstrained decisions. Individuals are not defined by the ability to step back from themselves, detach themselves from the perturbations of desire, and legislate to themselves what their lives shall be. The Kantian struggle to master inclination by adopting the maxims of practical reason is not Augustine's view of human life. Rather, according to Augustine, we are constituted by the relationships of desire that typify our lives. The citizens of the city of God know that the passions rightly ordered and directed are constitutive of the Christian life.[35] Our identities intrinsically involve relationships to things that exist beyond us, affecting us as objects of desire. Most importantly for Augustine, we have been created in such a way that only the love for God can fulfill our

---

32. Here we can discern the influence of the eclectic philosopher Varro, who proposed that God is known through a process of rational thought culminating in reason's reflection on the nature and source of its own powers, rather than the influence of Plotinus, who suggested a more immediate mystical intuition of God. See Eugene TeSelle, *Augustine the Theologian* (New York: Herder and Herder, 1970), pp. 80-83.

33. Augustine, *Confessions*, VIII, 1 (1), in *WSA*, I, 1 (italics in original).

34. For an excellent discussion of this, see Graham, "Kierkegaard and the Longing for God."

35. Augustine, *The City of God*, XIV, 9, in *WSA* I, 6-7.

desiring, relational nature, and that overarching love should integrate, inform, modify, and prioritize all our penultimate loves. The true self is not the self-possessed master of his own internal house, but is a passionately doxological self whose identity is rooted in its joyful adoration of God.[36] Over fourteen centuries later, Kierkegaard's *Works of Love* would articulate this same view of the self's finding its completion in self-abandoning love for God.

The theme of desire also informed the way Augustine came to think of the process of salvation. Because desires cannot be immediately willed into existence, something must happen to the individual to enable the person to develop a new desire, to perceive and experience life differently. We humans are not capable of redirecting and integrating our desires through a self-originating heroic exertion of willpower. The change in perception and attraction must be elicited by something beyond the individual. The object of desire must somehow take the initiative and enable an individual to experience its attractive power. The transformation of desire must come from beyond the self. Consequently, if we are to be transformed into lovers of God, the initiative must come from God. For Augustine, the ability to love God rightly is mediated by the grace of Christ, made available through the sacramental and social practices of the church. Love for God is a response to the manifestation of God's attractiveness; it is not the result of the self-initiated quest for self-integration and self-fulfillment. As the structure of the *Confessions* shows, Augustine came to see God's providence operating behind the scenes in his encounters with Neo-Platonists, his delight in earthly beauty, and even his tragedies, which lured him forward with more provocative and tantalizing glimpses of God's attractiveness. Kierkegaard's view of a new kind of pathos elicited by the incarnate Christ, without whom the new pathos would be impossible, would be the functional equivalent of this dynamic in Augustine's writings.

Thomists have often argued about the relationship in Augustine's thought between natural desire for God and the supernatural gift of *caritas,* the infused ability to love God in a way that transcends ordinary human powers. The concept of *caritas* as a gloriously gracious supplement to creaturely human nature is central to the Thomist tradition. But to sharply differentiate nature and grace in this way is alien to Augustine. The importance of a natural desire for God does not diminish with Augustine's increasing attention to the role of God's grace in redemption. As we have

36. See Michael Hanby, *Augustine and Modernity* (London: Routledge, 2003).

seen, his analysis of desire makes it inevitable that at least some impetus must come from beyond the individual. Accordingly, Augustine does assert that it is God's gracious gift of love that stimulates our hearts and carries them upward.[37] But grace does not give humanity a new *telos,* nor does it add any new supernatural powers to the soul's natural repertoire. As Phillip Cary has convincingly argued, Augustine remained convinced throughout his career that the only destiny suited to human beings is to be bound to God in love.[38] The enjoyment of happiness through beholding God's truth, goodness, and beauty is the only destiny appropriate for an intelligent creature. We were created in such a way that to desire the vision of God is entirely natural to us. According to Augustine, our problem is not the limitations of the human mind, or a deficiency in our ontological structure that requires supplementation, but rather the instability of our will and the waywardness and diffusion of our desires. We repeatedly fail to love God with single-minded and steady devotion. Consequently, we do not need grace to impart a new supernatural capacity; we need grace to heal the nature that we already possess. God's gift of grace refocuses desire, stabilizes it, energizes it, and helps it grow in constancy. As will become evident, much of Kierkegaard's own work can be read as such a therapy of desire.

Finally, the theme of desire had profound implications for Augustine's understanding of growth in the Christian life. For Augustine, desire for God propels the process of sanctification and makes it inevitable that sanctification will be a growth in Godlikeness. Augustine, like many ancient philosophers, was convinced that human beings become like what they desire and love. Knowing God in love is a participatory kind of knowledge that transforms the knower. Consequently, a lover of God will become more like God, reflecting ever more purely God's constancy and single-mindedness. Augustine relates that he "seemed to hear your [God's] voice from on high: 'I am the food of the mature; grow then, and you will eat me. You will not change me into yourself like bodily food: you will be changed into me.'"[39] By spiritually feeding on God, the soul increasingly participates in God's characteristics. Augustine says again and again that the lover of God will be transformed into the image of God; as we draw near to God, we will reflect God's light and holiness more and more profoundly. Because the gaze of the fully mature lovers of God is unshakably riveted on God, they

---

37. Augustine, *Confessions,* XIII, 9 (10), in *WSA* I, 1.
38. See Cary, *Augustine's Invention of the Inner Self,* pp. 67-71.
39. Augustine, *Confessions,* VII, 10 (16), in *WSA* I, 1.

come to reflect the immutability of God. God's lovers become progressively impervious to distractions and fluctuations of mood. In this sense, those who truly love God come to share in God's transcendence of the temporal process and rise above regret about the past and fear of the future. Concerning the "heaven of heaven," which seems to be the created intelligible realm, Augustine writes: "Participating in your eternity, though in no sense coeternal with you, O Trinity, this intellectual creation largely transcends its mutability through the intense bliss it enjoys in contemplation of you, and by holding fast to you with a constancy from which it has never fallen since the first creation, it is independent of the spinning changes of time."[40]

Such freedom from mutability will be the destiny of the souls who contemplate God. Augustine rhapsodizes: "Drinking deeply from you in unswerving fidelity, such a creature shows no trace of mutability at any point, for it is bound fast by the whole strength of its love to you, who are always present to it, and having nothing to expect in the future, nor any memories to relegate to the past, it is neither affected by change nor a prey to distended consciousness."[41] Such changelessness will be the destiny of the saints in heaven. Augustine's language is tentative, for he admits that he is trying to speak of esoteric matters, but the rhetoric crescendoes to the assurance that the reader will understand these mysteries better as she grows closer to God through loving contemplation. Augustine repeats this theme of growing in Godlikeness in *The Trinity (De Trinitate)*, where he confidently declares that the soul is transformed by cleaving to God.[42] He assures readers that insofar as we love God, we will become like God.[43] Later in *The Trinity* he says that love is a "glue" that binds the mind to God.[44] At times Augustine ecstatically exclaims that by adoring Christ, the likeness of God, we become like the likeness. In short, as the soul progresses in love for the eternal God, it will reflect the eternal nature of God.

For Augustine, the growth in Godlikeness and progress in knowing God are correlative. Often he will invert the relationship of the two dynamics and explain that only a soul that has been sanctified and become well advanced in loving God can truly know God and enjoy God's fellowship. In order to be fit for the reception of knowledge of the triune God,

40. Augustine, *Confessions*, XII, 9 (9), in *WSA* I, 1.
41. Augustine, *Confessions*, XII, 11 (12), in *WSA*, I, 1.
42. Augustine, *The Trinity*, VIII, 4, in *WSA* I, 5.
43. Augustine, *The Trinity*, IX, 14–XI, 16, in *WSA* I, 5.
44. Augustine, *The Trinity*, X, 8–11, in *WSA* I, 5.

the soul must be purified and strengthened.[45] Augustine warns that anyone who loves the earth will become earth, while the person who subordinates earthly loves to the love of the eternal God will become capable of understanding divine things.[46] We can behold God only when we have been adequately purged of earthly preoccupations and grown in ardent desire for God. Augustine explains:

> That is why it is necessary for our minds to be purified before that inexpressible reality can be seen by them; and in order to make us fit and capable of grasping it, we are led along more endurable routes, nurtured on faith as long as we have not yet been endowed with that necessary purification.[47]

Rather than knowledge of God and love for God generating Godlikeness in the soul, in these passages it seems that purgation and the concomitant growth in Godlikeness are a necessary condition for knowing God. Life's journey toward the vision of God requires the cultivation of love, and Augustine does not hesitate to admonish the reader to purify his soul so that love for God can intensify. (Even in his anti-Pelagian writings Augustine would not retract this imperative; all he did in those polemics was add the reminder that growth in love is itself a gift from God.) Behind this apparent reversal of the claim that knowing God produces Godlikeness lies Augustine's conviction that "only like can know like," a foundational belief that he inherited from Platonism.[48] In order for the individual to understand God, the individual and God must be like each other. For Augustine, this growth in likeness is a structural potentiality of human nature, for Christ the Logos indwells the human mind. All growth in knowledge is made possible because the mind receives divine light — illumination from the Logos. As the relationship to the Word, the true image of God, is cultivated and restored, we become more like the light and thus are more illumined by it. As we shall see, Kierkegaard's themes of "redoubling" and the "eternal like for like" had antecedents in Augustine's legacy.

The reversibility of the formula that knowing God generates Godlikeness, so that sometimes the soul becomes like God *through* knowing and

---

45. Augustine, *The Trinity*, VIII, 3, 6, in *WSA* I, 5.

46. Augustine, *Homilies on the First Epistle of John*, 2.14, in *WSA* III, 13.

47. Augustine, *The Trinity*, I, 1.3, in *WSA* I, 5.

48. Steven Ozment, *The Age of Reform* (New Haven: Yale University Press, 1980), pp. 44-48.

loving God, and sometimes the soul must become like God *in order to know and love God*, is a pervasive characteristic of Augustine's writings. He expresses the relationship between knowing and loving God differently in different contexts in order to pursue different purposes. When exhorting his readers to strive to become more loving, Augustine reminds them that this growth is necessary for the enjoyment of the desired knowledge of God. Without this growth, they cannot attain their hearts' deepest desire. When enticing his readers to long even more profoundly for the knowledge of God, he proffers the encouraging prospect that this knowledge will transform them and result in the transcendence of mutability and decay. As we shall see, this oscillation between exhorting the reader to become like God in order to know God and promising that likeness to God is the fruit of knowing and loving God, will be inscribed in his controversy with the Pelagians. The Christian life involves both strenuous striving and confident gratitude for God's grace and trust in God's beneficence. As will become obvious, both those notes were also struck loudly by Kierkegaard.

I must note that all this talk of becoming like God through knowing God does not suggest an indiscriminant merging of the self and God, a prospect that was just as alien to Augustine as it would be to Kierkegaard. Although our likeness to God does grow through love, we shall never become what God is ontologically.[49] For Augustine, the goal of our spiritual pilgrimage is the rapt adoration of God, in which the blissful soul remains differentiated from God, the transcendent Other. The eschatological hope is not for a total absorption into the divine being in which all individual identity would be extinguished. Augustine's imagery drawn from the worship practices of the church suggests that the relationship of beatified beings to God remains securely doxological for all eternity. The definitive eschatological activities of praising and worshiping God require the continuation of the Creator/creature distinction. No matter how holy we may become, we will never become Godlike in the sense of possessing the divine power of self-subsistence. Even in the heavenly state, we will continue to need God for our existence and depend on God for our constancy, for Augustine insists that God's grace will still be necessary to stabilize our wills. We will never become self-sufficient (*sibi placere*) in the way that God is; the dependence of the creature on the Creator will never be annulled. Moreover, in Augustine's writings the prevalence of the language of love, including erotic language, to describe the perfect

---

49. Augustine, *On the Catholic and the Manichean Ways of Life (De moribus ecclesiae catholicae et de moribus Manichaeorum)*, 1, 11 (18), in *WSA* I, 19.

relationship of humans to God implies continuing differentiation. Just as two lovers retain distinguishable identities even in their devotion to each other, so also the believer is not absorbed into the beloved God — thus losing all self-identity. Accordingly, Augustine proposes that the saints in heaven will have resurrected bodies that retain gender and other earthly differentiating features. These spiritual bodies will, of course, be purged of all imperfections and will move with indescribable beauty.[50] Needless to say, this embodiment, even if it is a rarified spiritual body, does imply continued differentiation from God. For Augustine, the theme of likeness to God did not suggest becoming divine but rather reinforced for the reader the importance of cleaving to God in love, and it offered the hope of sharing in God's loving fellowship. Like Augustine, Kierkegaard would describe the Christian's relationship to God as an intense intimacy that nevertheless preserves a profound "infinite qualitative difference."

Desire for God, loving God, and knowing God are so foundational for Augustine that they define his teleological view of human life and his vision of the eschatological goal. According to Augustine, desire for God is not a passing feature of the individual's life; it is not a preliminary stage that can be left behind as the individual spiritually matures. Augustine concludes that, in this temporal existence, desire for God can never be fully satisfied. God's beauty can indeed be partially savored in this earthly existence, but God will only be fully known and loved (at least as far as God can be by a finite creature) in the life to come. A person cannot become so filled with the contemplation of God that the hunger for God gives way to satiation. It is not as though, once we have acquired what we have longed for, the desire ceases. In fact, the soul that glimpses a portion of the beauty of God longs to behold more and more of that inexhaustible splendor. The more aspects of God that an individual beholds, the more dimensions the individual realizes are yet to be explored. As we come to know God, we discover that knowing stimulates further desiring, and finding leads to further seeking.[51] This replenishing of desire is a function of the infinity of God's truth, goodness, and beauty. Desire stretches the soul and makes it capable of being even more filled. Consequently, the restlessness of our hearts will continue at least through the duration of this temporal life, and our desire for God will only increase as we seek to satisfy it.

---

50. Augustine, *The City of God,* XXII, 12-21, 30; *The Enchiridion of Faith, Hope, and Love (Enchiridion ad Laurentium de fide spe et caritate),* 23 (87-90).

51. Augustine, *The Trinity,* IX, 1, in *WSA* I, 5.

Augustine is so enthusiastic about desire for God that sometimes he can speak of its continuation even when we eschatologically possess God in love. He often writes as though desire gives way to fulfillment when we behold the splendor of God's light in eternity. Augustine was the heir of a tradition that regarded love as the possession of a desired object, so that desire, fulfilled in love, is superseded by happiness, which is the joy and security of possession. The final state of love should be characterized by delight and peace, not restlessness. However, though Augustine affirms that there is indeed a secure joy in possessing God in love, he proceeds to qualify this tranquil joy. In the case of God, the possession is real and does indeed produce happiness and contentment; but this contentment fuels further desire. Paradoxically, the soul that is at rest in God is simultaneously in restless movement toward deeper intimacy with God. Augustine often elaborates on this theme in order to encourage Christians to continue to seek God and grow in love, for God is still to be sought even after being found.

To conclude, desire for God and love for God, for Augustine, are the essential characteristics of the Christian life. In different ways, almost everything that he wrote was either an attempt to upbuild the reader in love for God or to discredit theological factions that were insufficiently attentive to love. That purpose gives his work a rhetorical unity even if it lacks a systematic unity. The intensive concentration on love for God informs the way that Augustine approached every theological topic and every aspect of the Christian life. For example, with regard to hermeneutics, Augustine's basic principle is that the purpose of the Bible is to build up love in the believer's heart.[52] Consequently, love should be the rule that guides the interpretation of Scripture. Similarly, Augustine maintains that the purpose of participation in the sacramental life of the church is to nurture love, and he warns that the sacraments are not efficacious unless they are appropriated by love.[53] The focus on love also shaped Augustine's approach to ethics, for he insists that no outward behavior, no matter how seemingly righteous, can guarantee that an act is truly Christian; only the presence of love in the heart can be a testimony that the agent is a Christian and that the act is virtuous. From first to last, Augustine was a theologian who was in love with God's love. Love for God provided the framework in which faith, hope, and all other aspects of the Christian life had to be understood. The same could be said of Søren Kierkegaard.

52. Augustine, *On Teaching Christianity (De doctrina Christiana)*, I, 36 (40), in *WSA* I, 11.
53. Augustine, *Homilies on the First Epistle of John*, Homily 5.7; Homily 7.6, in *WSA* III, 14.

Kierkegaard's Desire for an Eternal Happiness

Kierkegaard, with considerably more indirection, parallels Augustine in making desire and love for God the tacit presupposition of his writings. Much of what Kierkegaard wrote would not make sense unless individuals possess a natural hunger for God, however unconscious or repressed it may be.[54] To many readers of Kierkegaard, this claim may seem counterintuitive, for Kierkegaard is often remembered as the advocate of the theme that "there is an infinite, radical, qualitative difference between God and man" (*JP* 2, 1383). Moreover, Kierkegaard does insist that seeking God contains a dimension of "terror," "trembling," and "shuddering," suggesting that God is indeed the awesome, numinous Other (*TDIO*, p. 9). This has often been taken to mean that there is such a yawning ontological gulf separating God and humanity that no longing for God, as an expression of humanity's created nature, could be possible. Surely one cannot yearn for something that is absolutely incommensurable with one's own self. Desiring and yearning, it is claimed, suggest an attraction to some characteristic that the self needs for completion, or that the self admires because it is an intensification of some quality that the self already possesses to a lesser degree, or that the self is already prone to value. In all these instances, there is some common feature uniting the self and the desired object. God's utter transcendence would seem to rule out the continuity of the divine and human that desire appears to require. According to this interpretation, Kierkegaard would have more in common with the "dialectical theology" of the early Barth, insisting on God's absolute otherness, than with Augustine. The qualitatively different God could be worshiped and obeyed, perhaps even trusted, but not really desired. Kierkegaard's words often do seem to encourage this interpretation, as when he remarks, "God and the human being resemble each other only inversely" (*CD*, 292).

However, Kierkegaard's emphasis on God's qualitative difference does not preclude desire for God. Kierkegaard uses the rhetoric of difference in order to promote certain pastoral purposes, mainly to encourage his readers toward humility, thankfulness, and dependence. (We shall examine these pastoral purposes more fully in chapter 4.) As we will see, far from

---

54. See Walter Lindström, *Stadiernas Teologi* (Lund: Haakan Ohlsson, 1943), for an older but still compelling argument that the desire for a relationship to God unifies Kierkegaard's writings. See also Carl Hughes, *Kierkegaard and the Staging of Desire: Rhetoric and Religious Performance in a Theology of Eros* (New York: Fordham University Press, 2013).

being incompatible with desire for God, these virtues that foreground God's qualitative difference are only appropriate because of the more foundational role of desire in the Christian life. For example, we should be humble before God because God possesses to a superlative degree the qualities that we should value and desire, but that we can never adequately instantiate. Kierkegaard warns:

> To love God is the only happy love, but on the other hand it is also something terrible. Face to face with God man is without standards and without comparisons; he cannot compare himself with God, for here he becomes nothing . . . ." (*JP* 2, 1353)

A person would not feel the pain of the disparity between God's holiness and the person's own inadequacies unless God's holiness were loved and desired. God's "qualitative difference" becomes evident only insofar as the individual loves something about God and therefore comes "face to face" with God. By refusing to bifurcate desire for God and an awe-filled appreciation of God's otherness, Kierkegaard was by no means being unique or proposing an idiosyncratic opinion. Nor did Augustine hesitate to link desire for God with the dispositions and passions that underscored God's otherness.

The similarity of Augustine and Kierkegaard with respect to the importance of desire for God is signaled by their common penchant for using romantic and erotic metaphors for the human-divine relationship. Augustine carefully traces continuities and contrasts between his love for God and his love for finite goods, including his mistress, his best friend, his son, and the ordered harmonies of music. The same is true of Kierkegaard. In his writings he illuminates the highly personal relationship with God by comparing and contrasting it to first loves, seductions, and marriage. Daphne Hampson has even remarked: "I find it not too far-fetched to think that Kierkegaard was one of those individuals who in effect had a love affair with God, making celibacy essential."[55] Anti-Climacus, Kierkegaard's pseudonymous Christian to a superlative degree, observes:

> And a believer, after all, is a lover; as a matter of fact, when it comes to enthusiasm, the most rapturous lover of all lovers is but a stripling compared to a believer. (*SUD*, 103)

---

55. Daphne Hampson, *Christian Contradictions: The Structures of Lutheran and Catholic Thought* (Cambridge: Cambridge University Press, 2001), p. 270.

For both Augustine and Kierkegaard, eros is front and center. The exuberant rhetoric of pleasure and delight fills Kierkegaard's pages, as it does Augustine's tomes. Borrowing vocabulary from both classical philosophy and Christianity, Kierkegaard, like Augustine, describes human life as teleologically oriented toward what he variously calls "happiness," "eternal happiness," "the highest good," and "blessedness."[56] Also like Augustine, Kierkegaard insists that this blessedness is of such inestimable worth that it should be thought of as enduring eternally. Most importantly, for Kierkegaard as well as for Augustine, the actualization of our deepest desire, our relationship with the eternal God, brings with it a sharing in God's eternal life. We will explore all these parallels in more detail.

Throughout Kierkegaard's corpus, the concept "God" and the individual's ardent desires and longings require one another in order to be mutually intelligible. God is defined as that which will ultimately fulfill an individual's often inchoate and usually misdirected yearnings. It is no accident that Kierkegaard's metaphors for the relationship with God are drawn from the discourse of romance and marriage, both of which were regarded by various sectors in his culture as avenues to the highest possible happiness. God (or "the good," or "the absolute") is that which satisfies the deepest longings of the human heart. Whatever God is, God is intrinsically and unsurpassably valuable and desirable, pursued not for the sake of an extrinsic reward or to escape earthly unpleasantness. In a journal entry from 1854, Kierkegaard observes:

> As stated elsewhere, an actual relation to God is of such infinite worth that even if it were only for a moment and in the next moment one were kicked, struck, tossed, hurled far away, and forgotten . . . it is still worth infinitely more than everything the world and man have to offer. (*JP* 2, 1442)

Kierkegaard's writings instantiate Augustine's distinction of *uti* and *frui*, with God being identified as that which is desired for its own sake. The otherworldliness, even asceticism, that many have detected in Kierkegaard's works is motivated by his valorization of this hunger for the ultimate Other. Without God, according to Kierkegaard, every earthly joy and delight fails to satisfy. No amount of vocational success, no matter how spectacular,

---

56. The Danish word he typically used was *salighed*. See Abrahim Khan, "Salighed" *as Happiness? Kierkegaard on the Concept* Salighed (Waterloo, ON: Wilfrid Laurier Press, 1985).

could produce absolute contentment. No degree of intimacy, no matter how deep, could inspire a sense of complete fulfillment. No quantity of riches, no matter how vast, could provide a sense of total security. Just as Augustine had contended, our yearnings cannot be stilled by anything finite. In Kierkegaard's terminology, our "eternal happiness" cannot be based on the possession or enjoyment of any temporal good. To understand "God" requires the cultivation of the "restless heart" celebrated by Augustine.

Desire for God in Kierkegaard's corpus most intensively informs *Works of Love,* though it is also inscribed in many of the edifying and Christian discourses. At first blush, this may not be obvious, because the main theme of *Works of Love* seems to be the requirement to love the neighbor, and to see God as the source, support, and imperative force of that love. However, in this text Kierkegaard not only talks about the importance of love for God (which is presumed in all neighbor love), but, more dramatically, he manifests desire for that love in his act of writing. Like Augustine's *Confessions,* Kierkegaard's *Works of Love* (and many of his discourses and other pieces of Christian writing) is a virtuoso performance of longing for God. Most basically, this text attempts to express and elicit a desire for the unique joy that is the fruit of loving God. Kierkegaard does not so much describe or analyze this desire — as one might do in an academic treatise on desire — as try to evoke it. To communicate this eros for God, Kierkegaard often expresses longing for the divine in ecstatic tones, and he invites the reader to identify with the author's yearning. Elsewhere he instructs the reader to read one of his discourses aloud so that the words become the reader's very own (*UDVS,* 5-6); the same can be said with respect to the appropriation of *Works of Love.* Because that book is particularly saturated with implicit yearning and longing, it is an appropriate place to begin the comparison of Kierkegaard with Augustine.

On one level, *Works of Love* seems to deal mainly with the commandment to love the human neighbor rather than explicitly with the phenomenon of longing for God. This could lead one to suspect that Kierkegaard was being typically Lutheran, refusing to speak of an eros for God (and defining the relationship to God in terms of "trust"), and restricting the concept "love" to our relationships with our neighbors.[57] If that were the case, he would indeed be living in a different theological world from the one inhabited by Augustine. However, as we shall see, loving the neighbor is, for Kierkegaard, a manifestation of loving God, for God is love. Kierke-

---

57. For this depiction of Lutheranism, see Hampson, *Christian Contradictions,* pp. 29-30.

gaard makes it clear, as Augustine had, that God is the only proper object of love (*WL,* 19, 108, 121, 130). He explains: "God has truth's and infallibility's infinite conception of love; God is Love" (*WL,* 190). He further clarifies this by saying that "the only true object of a human being's love is *love,* which is God . . . since he is Love itself" (*WL,* 264-65). Although most of *Works of Love* is devoted to helping the reader feel the attractiveness of love for the neighbor, the book presents this love for the neighbor as a manifestation of a more foundational love for God. Kierkegaard explicitly directs his praise to God, whom he describes as the font and "hidden spring of all love" (*WL,* 9). Love for the neighbor is rooted in love for God, and love for God will naturally manifest itself as love for the neighbor. Love for God is the implicit "middle term" in all real love for other creatures (*WL,* 107); without it, love cannot be genuine. Kierkegaard associates the two aspects of the biblical love commandment — to love God and to love the neighbor — very closely, for the God who is loved is the God who loves unstintingly; to love God is to love God's self-giving love, for that love is God's very identity. By adoring that divine love, humans come to participate in it, and consequently express it as love for their neighbors. *Works of Love* is a spiritual pedagogy, leading the reader from ordinary loves to neighbor love and ultimately to the source of all love in God. The book attempts to redirect the reader's longing and desire toward God's love and God's way of loving. Kierkegaard coaxes and entices the reader to see that we were created with an inherent desire for God's kind of love, and that we can only find ultimate happiness through participating in that love. It is thus the life of godly neighbor love that must be presented as the object to be desired, and longing for that life must be elicited. In short, without announcing itself as such, *Works of Love* is an enactment of desire for the kind of love that God essentially is.

To grasp the significance of this theme of desiring the God who is love (and hence of desiring to love the neighbor), we must take *Works of Love's* literary features into account, not just its conceptual content. For Kierkegaard, the rhetorical dynamics of a text such as this are part and parcel of its meaning. The question then becomes: What kind of mood, authorial voice, and genre are appropriate to manifest the desirability of the God of love and God's way of loving? Even an exercise in conceptual clarification — in this case a clarification of "love" — requires the appropriate set of rhetorical conditions in order for genuine communication to occur.

Kierkegaard intentionally chose the literary genre of the "deliberation" for the purpose of fostering a more adequate appreciation of the desirability of Christian love. This choice is significant. According to Kierkegaard, a deliberation is intended to encourage people to consider more deeply a seemingly familiar concept that has not really been fully understood (*WL,* 469). *Works of Love* addresses the problem that the citizens of Christendom, Kierkegaard's intended audience, have succumbed to a spiritual confusion in which they falsely identify Christian love for God and neighbor with the thrill of romance, the comfort of marriage, and the contentment of friendship. Consequently, these befuddled and self-deceived ersatz Christians must be reminded of the distinctive features of genuine Christian love. Kierkegaard's fear was that Christian love was not being passionately desired because the ability to imagine it had atrophied. This clarification of Christian love must include the exhibition of the pathos that is appropriate to the concept, for being able to imagine that pathos is part of what it means to understand any concept. Consequently, in order for readers to truly grasp this poorly understood concept of Christian love, they must be shown the interests, fears, and hopes that are constitutive of its meaning. Readers' passions must be stirred so that they can imagine what it might be like to live a life of love and experience the attractions of that life. Put simply, the reader must become capable of imagining what it would be like to love Love itself. The kind of understanding that Kierkegaard hopes to encourage here is much more monumental than a cognitive adjustment or mental assent to a new idea, for it requires the capacity to imagine a forgotten and repressed kind of desire.

Kierkegaard assumes that the life of love is humanity's highest good — the source of its most profound joy. He writes: "To defraud oneself of [*begrage for*] love [*Kjerlighed*] is the most terrible, is an eternal loss, for which there is no compensation either in time or eternity" (*WL,* 6). According to Kierkegaard, Christianity presupposes that the desire for personal fulfillment, which can be called self-love, is a dynamic animating all people. By his own admission his project is predicated on the premise that this longing for happiness is really an inherent attraction to love itself (*WL,* 154-55). It is central to his exposition of love that all humans have an implicit need to love and be loved (*WL,* 11). Accordingly, throughout the text Kierkegaard addresses the reader as if the reader possesses the intrinsic capacity to be attracted to love. In his terminology, he "presupposes love" in the reader, and he makes this conviction explicit by declaring, "There is a place in a person's innermost being; from this place flows the life of love . . ." (*WL,* 8). According to Kierkegaard, love is no more a "superadded gift" supervenient to created human nature than it was for Augustine. As Augustine had claimed, the desire for love itself (which is God) is intrinsic to our very constitution.

Therefore, for Kierkegaard, the commandment that we should love God and our neighbor is not an arbitrary imposition on human nature. Kierkegaard insists that we must presuppose that the seeds of love have been planted in the individual by the Creator in order for the effort to "love forth love" in the other to be effective (*WL*, 216-17). To think that the motivation for obeying the love commandment is to avoid punishment or to receive some sort of extrinsic reward is to misunderstand it. Rather, the motivational force of the love commandment resides in the sheer attractiveness of the life of love, which is God's very life. This attractiveness is part of the essential meaning of love. If readers cannot even imagine what the joy of loving would be like, they cannot begin to understand the concept. Therefore, a primary strategy for helping another person to understand love is to present love's intrinsic virtues in such a way that the individual can experience their attractions. That is exactly what *Works of Love* sets about doing.

The project of awakening a conscious desire for love determined the literary genre of *Works of Love*. Because the pathos must be encouraged, a philosophical treatise on love would not be apt at all. It could never be enough to supply the reader with a discursive definition of love or a catalogue of allegedly loving acts, if such a catalogue existed. The mood of the coolly dispassionate spectator and analyst of human subjectivity would actually inhibit understanding. Such objective disengagement would give the reader no clue concerning what kinds of passions motivated and inspired the alleged loving actions. Even worse, a pathos-neutral expository essay could give the misleading impression that the passions should be omitted in a consideration of love. In the same way, Augustine had critiqued the dispassionate understanding of the philosophers and pointed out that the demons are cognizant of many propositional truths about God.

Moreover, because God's love, including a life that reflects that love, is the true object of our desire, a simple exhortation to love would be just as inappropriate as a scientific disquisition on the topic of love. Exhortations address the will, calling for resolution and decisive action. The imperative mood assumes that the exhortation has been understood and does not require further elaboration. But that is precisely the problem: the denizens of Christendom do not know what "love" means when they are simply presented with the love commandment. Accordingly, in *Works of Love*, Kierkegaard seldom directly admonishes the reader; the book is not a moralistic harangue. As we shall see, he does often emphasize the imperative force of the divine commandment to love God and neighbor; but he introduces that theme to help steady readers when their resolve begins to waver. Even the authoritative force of the law of love is a gift from God to aid wayward creatures. The fact that "be loving" is a commandment is actually one of love's most attractive features, for it points to God's solicitude. Because the reader must feel the attractiveness of the imperative, Kierkegaard's authorial voice in *Works of Love* is neither judgmental nor accusatory. In fact, the author could not possibly assume a position of moral superiority and still exhibit what love really involves. Because love "hides a multitude of sins," it is not interested in convicting the beloved of reprehensible faults. Kierkegaard cannot exhibit love's attractive passional qualities by scolding or condemning the reader. Rather, God's love, reflected in the love of the author for the reader, must "love forth love." The text itself is a work of love, and its concern for the reader is attractive and is designed to direct the reader to the source of that attractiveness in God (*WL*, 364-65).

Rather than issuing commands himself, Kierkegaard tries to evoke in the reader a sense of the attractiveness of God by praising the life of love (for God is love, as Kierkegaard repeatedly insists). The mood of a deliberation on Christian love must be one of praise, for praise communicates the sense that the object of praise is eminently desirable. Praising something can encourage in others a desire to explore that thing's attractive qualities. Kierkegaard writes:

> To carry it out [the praising of love] has, of course, its intrinsic reward, although in addition, by praising love insofar as one is able, it also has this purpose: to win people to it, to make them properly aware of what in a conciliatory spirit is granted to every human being — that is, the highest. (*WL*, 365)

At crucial junctures in the text Kierkegaard professes that his purpose has been to praise love as best he could in "many times and in many ways" (*WL*, 197, 375). Throughout the book Kierkegaard waxes encomiastic, lauding the life of love as "the highest good" and the "greatest blessedness" (*WL*, 239-41). In so doing he engagingly displays his own exuberant enthusiasm for it, and he hopes that that enthusiasm will be contagious. For all these reasons, the basic tenor of a deliberation about love must be doxological, just as Augustine had assumed. Whereas Augustine had punctuated his works with explicit prayers of adoration directed to God in order to frame his more discursive passages, Kierkegaard more typically expresses to the reader his own personal delight in God's glorious love.

To encourage the reader's ability to imagine the attractiveness of love,

Kierkegaard waxes enthusiastic about the unique passional fruits of a life of love for the neighbor (which is a manifestation of God's love and an expression of love for God). Because this love is not based on the neighbor's intrinsic attractiveness, it is not susceptible to weakening due to changes in the neighbor's attributes. As such it offers the prospect of a life of blessed coherence and continuity. Sounding very much like Augustine, Kierkegaard exults that in this regard Christian love does not suffer from the liabilities that infect romance and friendship, which vainly promise permanence but are powerless to secure it. Love for the neighbor unifies the self, rescuing it from the disintegrative forces of worldly "business" (*WL*, 98). Christian love makes true community possible because it is not based on the reciprocal meeting of needs (*WL*, 159); in Augustine's language, it is not based on the worldly form of *amor sui*. As we have just seen, even the imperative aspect of Christian love is attractive, for the divine command serves as an antidote to the fickle and vacillating nature of the individual's own immediate emotional responses (*WL*, 43). Kierkegaard does not posit any irresolvable tension between pursuing the life of love because God has commanded it and pursuing the life of love because it leads to ultimate happiness. Rather, God commands what will point us fallen humans toward our true fulfillment, and God's commandments can thus be seen as attractive gifts that should be greeted with rejoicing.[58] Most dramatically, Kierkegaard is enthusiastic that genuine love reflects God's eternal nature and is resistant to the vicissitudes of time. He repeatedly proclaims that love is the bond of temporality and eternity (*WL*, 6). Christian love possesses a durability and resilience that resists mutability and decay and thus participates in the perfection of eternity (*WL*, 65). These lyrical outbursts function to galvanize and intensify readers' discontent with their own ephemeral desires and unreliable commitments, and to catalyze a hunger for a love that perdures. The resemblances to Augustine's repeated claims that loving the constancy of God produces constancy in the lover are unmistakable. Kierkegaard was in full agreement with Augustine that we become like the thing we love.

Kierkegaard's rhetorical strategies throughout the book are designed to stimulate the implicit desire for a highest good, and to draw that desire forth into self-consciousness so that the individual can become intentional about it. Throughout the text Kierkegaard seeks to catalyze the readers' concerns about the quality of their own lives. Accordingly, Kierkegaard prods

---

58. C. Stephen Evans, *Kierkegaard's Ethic of Love* (Oxford: Oxford University Press, 2004), pp. 10-22.

readers to examine all their loves, including their immediate attractions, in order to discover within them an inchoate, often unconscious, desire for eternal happiness. He uses reflections on romance and friendship to show how their inadequacies and disappointments point to the deeper satisfactions of neighbor-love and devotion to God. The author enables readers to imagine Christian love by comparing and contrasting it to the delights and sorrows of the more secular loves. Whatever Christian love is, it is on the same continuum as romance and friendship, for all loves are aimed at happiness. The fulfillment that is mistakenly sought in romance and friendship is available only in Christian love, the true *telos* of the human heart. The satisfactions that make the natural loves attractive are more fully realized in Christian love for God and neighbor, for only this love endures, is not contingent on external factors, and is never depleted. Only this love is capacious and comprehensive enough to give significance and direction to all aspects of life. In other words, Christian love satisfies all the criteria for a highest good that Augustine had articulated in his Cassiciacum dialogues. If we comprehended what would truly make us happy (and if we were free of sin), then we would naturally love God and neighbor.[59] Although the radical other-regarding nature of Christian love is offensive to our self-aggrandizing and self-protective sinful proclivities, such love is the only thing that can lead to genuine happiness. In the conclusion of *Works of Love*, Kierkegaard puts these words in the mouth of the Apostle John: "[T]o love people is the only thing worth living for, and without this love you are not really living. Moreover, to love people is the only blessed comfort both here and in the next world . . ." (*WL*, 375).

Paralleling Augustine's assessment of humanity, Kierkegaard's strategy implies that the problem with us humans is that our capacity to love is initially directed toward inadequate objects. He warns: "It is true that love proceeds from the heart, but let us not be hasty about this and forget the eternal truth that love *forms* the heart. No doubt everyone has experienced the fleeting feelings of an indeterminate heart, but in this sense to have a heart by nature is infinitely different from forming the heart in the eternal sense" (*WL*, 12). He adds: "However joyous, however happy, however indescribably confident instinctive and inclinational love, spontaneous love, can be itself, precisely in its most beautiful moment it still feels a need to bind itself, if possible, even more securely" (*WL*, 29). As with Augustine,

---

59. See C. Stephen Evans, *Kierkegaard: An Introduction* (Cambridge: Cambridge University Press, 2009), p. 186.

Kierkegaard roots the inadequacy of earthly loves in their mutability and their multiplicity, and in the inability of a finite good to satisfy an infinite desire. It is impossible to relate with eternal faithfulness and unlimited devotion to something that is not eternal or infinite (*WL,* 313), as Augustine had shown through his reflections on his own friendships. Consequently, the heart, misdirected and malformed as it is, must be rehabilitated, remotivated, and redirected. Like Augustine, who had insisted that faith must be formed by love, Kierkegaard accords a foundational position in his thought to the power of love to form the heart. Kierkegaard, too, was a therapist of desire, and *Works of Love* was part of his therapeutic practice.

Kierkegaard's practice of fostering desire for a life of love, like Augustine's, implicitly rejects the notion that our existential choices are the products either of pure rational deliberation or of disinterested volitional acts. Kierkegaard writes: "Knowledge is the infinite art of equivocation, or infinite equivocation; at most it is simply a placing of opposite possibilities in equilibrium" (*WL,* 231). Reasoning can be indefinitely prolonged, as we take more variables that are possibly relevant into account — and any decision can be indefinitely postponed. Our passions inform and motivate our construals of phenomena, motivating us to pick out what features are significant and what features are irrelevant. Our passions determine when we feel that we have learned enough about a situation and are ready to take action. For example, our assessments of other people are determined by our mistrust of them or our love for them, and in neither case is the mistrust or the love inductively derived from the available information about them (*WL,* 231). Accordingly, Kierkegaard resists any valorization of dispassionate rationality that would dismiss our passions as obstacles to clarity and objectivity. His kind of knowing was just as desire-driven as was Augustine's.

Moreover, we humans can make decisions only because certain options attract us and certain other options repel us. If it were not true that we have specific anxieties, proclivities, hopes, and aspirations, there would be no way to evaluate the merits and demerits of different courses of action. Consequently, the sets of attractions and revulsions that motivate us — our "passions," in other words — are critical for the purpose of giving direction to human lives. Our attractions, concerns, and interests are not simply the products of decisions that we have made, as if we could give ourselves particular desires by a sheer act of will. Rather, they seem to come over us or well up within us. For example, Kierkegaard describes a human's love as arising mysteriously in God's love, "just as the quiet lake originates darkly in the deep spring," rather than as being the product of a dispassionate act of self-legislation (*WL*, 10). Nevertheless, our desires and attractions can be intentionally supported and cultivated, or they can be resisted and allowed to atrophy. An individual is not the sovereign creator of her own passions, though the individual can intentionally decide to welcome, strengthen, or resist them. For both Kierkegaard and Augustine, passion is essential to the task of being an agent who can prefer one course of action over another. Neither of them had any use for the notion of *liberum arbitrium* understood as an abstract, unswayed will equipoised among a constellation of neutral alternatives. Consequently, Kierkegaard wrote *Works of Love* in such a way that the reader is encouraged to cherish and cultivate the passion for the true fulfillment that comes only through loving God and neighbor.

Also like Augustine, Kierkegaard claims that loving God sincerely would foster Godlikeness. Love unites what is dissimilar so that they become similar. In a later journal entry, Kierkegaard says: "What does it mean to love? It is to want to be like the beloved, or it is to move out of one's own [interests] into the beloved's [interests]" (*JP* 3, 2438). Loving God, who is love, necessarily involves enthusiasm for love, and this enthusiasm would be manifested in a reinvigorated life of love. Kierkegaard also says: "[T]he person who loves becomes more and more intimate with the commandment, becomes as one with the commandment, which he loves" (*WL*, 375-76). In Kierkegaard's language, God's love for the individual is "reduplicated" in the individual's genuine human love for the neighbor: "[T]he one who loves is or becomes what he does" (*WL*, 281). When God is loved, the lover begins to love other people in the extravagant way that God does.[60] God's eternal love is redoubled in the temporal lives of individuals. This growth in self-giving love is, of course, growth in Godlikeness, just as Augustine had claimed. This transformation does not happen automatically or suddenly, but is the fruit of a lengthy process of learning to love the God of love more intensively and more consistently. As this transformation progresses, the "veteran" in the life of love understands the love commandment more fully and deeply and actually needs the regulating power of the imperative less (*WL*, 375-76). As Kierkegaard notes, the words of the apostle John in his First Epistle, "Beloved, let us love one another" (1 John 4:7), do not suggest "the rigorousness of duty" but serve as a gentle reminder from one who was "perfected in love" to those who have become "intimate with the com-

---

60. See Andrew Burgess, "Kierkegaard's Concept of Redoubling and Luther's *Simul Justus*," in Robert Perkins, ed., *International Kierkegaard Commentary: Works of Love* (Macon, GA: Mercer University Press, 1999), pp. 39-55.

mandment" and have "become as one with the commandment" (*WL*, 375). Sounding very much like Augustine, Kierkegaard declares that the pure heart that is bound to God begins to take on the limitless character of God (*WL*, 147-48).

Again resembling Augustine, Kierkegaard can portray the correlation of loving God and growth in Godlikeness in two different ways. Sometimes growth in love for God spontaneously germinates in increasing Godlikeness. Sometimes, however, growth in God-likeness (self-giving love) is encouraged so that the individual can know and love God more. Kierkegaard announces that we can become like God, who is love, only through loving, and that without this loving we cannot become like God (*WL*, 62-63). He warns: "God will do unto you exactly as you do unto others" (*WL*, 383), and sometimes he calls this "eternity's like for like" (*WL*, 376). Kierkegaard goes on to explain that we see in God the characteristics that we encourage in ourselves. If we are unforgiving, then we will perceive God as unforgiving. Consequently, the less loving we are, the more God's love will be obscured to our eyes. The imperative force of such remarks suggests that growth in Godlikeness is a human task.

These apparently contradictory themes in Kierkegaard function in the same ways that they do in Augustine's works. When trying to coax an enthusiasm for love in his readers, Kierkegaard emphasizes Godlikeness as the almost unintended and unanticipated fruit that blossoms from loving God. This prospect of Godlikeness adds further luster and allure to the life of love. But when encouraging the reader to strive to be more loving, Kierkegaard depicts knowing and loving God as the result of pursuing the path of Godlikeness. As was the case with Augustine, this vacillation concerning which comes first, love for God or likeness to God, is due to the dual characteristic of any passionate desire. On the one hand, the passion must be elicited by the object, but on the other hand it can be cultivated. Like Augustine, Kierkegaard both elicits love and encourages love's cultivation. Given the highly rhetorical nature of their writings, the relationship between the two themes must be worked out in the lives of the readers, and not in the paragraphs of a theological system.

In *Works of Love*, Kierkegaard was just as insistent as Augustine was that growth in love for God and neighbor is limitless. Kierkegaard declares that "love's element is infinitude, inexhaustibility, immeasurability" (*WL*, 180), and genuine love "never wastes away" (*WL*, 309, 311). Love for God, expressing itself as love for the neighbor, is infinitely expansive, always discovering that it could do more and wanting to do more. For Kierkegaard, as it was for Augustine, finding God does not terminate the longing for God. God perpetually remains a positive lure, never ceasing to draw the heart forward. The desire for God is certainly not just a temporary negative reaction to the deficits of earthly goods.

By no means is *Works of Love* Kierkegaard's only encomium to desire for the God of love and love of the neighbor. Kierkegaard's other writings reflect these themes, particularly his upbuilding and Christian discourses, which often explicitly emphasize the "desire" element that had been implicit in *Works of Love*. Kierkegaard exclaims: "[B]lessed is the person who could truthfully say: God in heaven was my first love; blessed is the person whose life was a beneficent strengthening of this love" (*EUD*, 101). A person should "long for God humbly as one longs for someone without whom one is nothing, fervently as one longs for someone by whom one becomes everything" (*EUD*, 397). His "Discourses at the Communion on Fridays" present the "longing for fellowship with him, the Holy One" at the Eucharist as being central to Christian piety: it is a fellowship that should be longed for with all one's heart (*CD*, 260). He assumes that there are a "stirring within" the communicants and a "heartfelt longing" that bring them to the sanctuary (*CD*, 253). He both describes this "longing" as a gift of the Holy Spirit and exhorts his readers to "grasp hold of the longing" and "hold it fast" (*CD*, 251). This "longing for God and the eternal" is something that is both elicited by grace and something that can be cultivated by intentional human effort (*CD*, 253). Kierkegaard writes glowingly of how the open and welcoming arms of Jesus draw the individual's heart (*CD*, 265-272). "Love's miracle" moves the penitent, fomenting a yearning for deeper companionship with Christ (*CD*, 280).

Many of these discourses identify God as our highest good and the appropriate object of our deepest longings. In a discourse for communion on Fridays, Kierkegaard assures the congregants that their longing "pertains to nothing earthly and temporal, not to your external conditions, not to your future; it is a longing for God" (*CD*, 264). He explains that, for Paul, joy in God is a higher good than all earthly blessings, including friendship (*CD*, 284). In an upbuilding discourse Kierkegaard suggests that a person who "prays aright" cannot really think of anything to request from God "except that I may remain with you, as near as possible in this time of separation in which you and I are living, and entirely with you in all eternity" (*EUD*, 392). The upbuilding discourse "The Thorn in the Flesh" likens the reader to Paul, who was not allowed to remain in the ecstasy of the "highest heaven," but nevertheless remembered that "inexpressible beatitude" and was unsettled by the recollection of what it was like to "have been hidden in the bosom of beatitude, to have been expanded in God" (*EUD,* 336-37). Although other Christians may not have such extraordinary experiences, they, like Paul, do long for this beatitude even in their more mundane moments.

Echoing themes from classical philosophy just as Augustine had done, Kierkegaard does not hesitate to call our desire for God a "need." "To Need God Is a Human Being's Highest Perfection" elaborates on this theme in depth. Kierkegaard urges the reader to realize that the life of prayer should be valued not because it secures benefits but because it intensifies one's focus on God, who is to be desired for his own sake (*EUD,* 297-326). In a Christian discourse he explains that the attractiveness of God is based on our need to be fulfilled through loving something of preeminent and enduring value (*CD,* 188). In another Christian discourse Kierkegaard repeats that we do not love God purely unselfishly — only for God's sake — for we crave what satisfies our longings, and God is our ultimate satisfaction (*CD,* 63-64).

Kierkegaard proceeds to qualify this claim, just as he had done in *Works of Love,* noting that our attraction to God is not just a desire to satisfy an internal lack. Rather, in loving God we encounter something infinitely in excess of any deficiency that had vexed us (*CD,* 16). In "To Need God Is a Human Being's Highest Perfection," Kierkegaard insists that God is not attractive merely because God satisfies a preexistent need. In fact, desire for God is much more than the instinct to alleviate the pain of an experienced deficit from before. Rather, the desire for God is the product of a process in which the object generates a deeper feeling of need (*EUD,* 303). Using the language of attraction from John 12:32, Anti-Climacus expatiates at length about the way in which Christ "draws" individuals to himself, even though the drama of his paradoxical loftiness in abasement can trigger offense (*PC,* 151-262). Desire for God is a grace-induced discontent with anything less than total devotion to God. Just as we have seen in Augustine's writings, Kierkegaard's works describe human beings not only as being structured to yearn for God and to be fulfilled through loving God, but also as being drawn to God by God's unanticipated attraction that stimulates the yearning.

Kierkegaard's discourses more explicitly elaborate the theme touched on in *Works of Love,* that is, that love for God is not a finite hunger that could be sated or a finite void that could be filled. Kierkegaard's discourses are saturated with the Augustinian conviction that desire for God is inexhaustible, for God's loveliness can never be fully comprehended or plumbed. Paradoxically, this kind of love is fueled by its satisfaction, for contact with the beloved only generates an intensified desire to love more constantly and more deeply. Kierkegaard paralleled Augustine's conviction that love for God is not like a stomach that can be filled so that satiation replaces hunger. With earthly goods, satisfaction leads to waning interest in the original beloved object and triggers the quest for a new and different source of enjoyment. But love for God is not like that. It is not exhausted by possession of the beloved; rather, it continues to grow through contact with the beloved (*CD*, 259-260).

Writing about fellowship with Christ at communion, Kierkegaard explains that "it belongs to heartfelt longing that longing is increased through remembrance . . ." (*CD*, 261). The more a person communes with Christ, the more that person longs for him (*CD*, 298). The more intimate one becomes with God, the more one desires increasing intimacy (*CD*, 121). This intensified desire involves a new kind of poignant suffering in wanting even deeper communion. The closer we get, the closer we want to be; the more we know, the more we want to know. Paradoxically, this longing for God increases, not because of God's distance, but because of God's presence. This insatiable yearning is catalyzed by the infinite attractiveness of God, in whose presence the individual's desire never wanes. As Vincent McCarthy has argued, in such contexts Kierkegaard was expressing a longing for the divine beloved in the almost erotic language typical of the Christian mystical traditions of the Middle Ages, much of which were rooted in Augustine's account of the desire for God.[61]

The discourses also echo *Works of Love's* exposure of the ways in which the desire for God gets misdirected. As Augustine warned, finite goods are enticing and can anesthetize the soul. In "To Preserve One's Soul in Patience" and in "Think about Your Creator in the Days of Your Youth," Kierkegaard warns that the individual can fall into servitude to the world and forget the lure of the highest happiness (*EUD*, 183-203, 233-51). Returning again to "To Need God Is a Human Being's Highest Perfection," Kierkegaard alerts the reader to the folly of desiring earthly goods, which can only produce a counterfeit and precarious happiness (*EUD*, 298). Wealth, prestige, attractiveness, and health are all ephemeral and unreliable. Individuals who invest their desire for happiness in such transient goods necessarily become puppets of forces beyond their control, and therefore slaves

---

61. See Vincent McCarthy, "Kierkegaard's Religious Psychology," in Joseph H. Smith, ed., *Kierkegaard's Truth: The Disclosure of the Self* (New Haven: Yale University Press, 1981), p. 238.

to vacillating moods (*EUD*, 308-9). Kierkegaard cautions that it is an act of gross self-deception to imagine that these worldly goods will probably not be taken away. Moreover, he assures the reader that the tribulations of life can teach us, if we are willing to learn, that we do not really need the things that we have vainly imagined that we need. In this context Kierkegaard is not underscoring the pedagogical value of disappointment in order to nurture Stoic self-sufficiency, but rather to direct the reader's attention to the inestimable worth of God's grace (*EUD*, 302). God is not just a consolation to be prized when earthly fulfillment fails, but the true object of desire whose worth becomes more evident as the inadequacies of earthly goods are unmasked. Throughout his literature Kierkegaard strove to debunk the illusory charms of bourgeois complacency in much the same way that Augustine sought to expose the vacuity of vocational success, public acclaim, and material riches.

As in *Works of Love,* so also in his discourses, Kierkegaard assumes that wayward desires are not irredeemable but can be redirected from lesser goods toward the highest good. In spite of the enticements of finite goods, desire for God can be reinvigorated, and the passional life can be reoriented toward its true goal. Like Augustine, Kierkegaard in the discourses assumes that the passions can be cultivated and educated. (This assumption holds even when Kierkegaard insists that the cultivation and education must be construed as gifts from God.) In fact, the cultivation of the appropriate forms of pathos is the purpose of his various series of discourses, and of his entire oeuvre in general. For example, Kierkegaard strives to foster a deeper longing for fellowship with Christ by bringing to the reader's attention the somber realities of the sinful corruption of humanity, the proliferation of atrocities in human history, the uncertainty of all earthly hopes and projects, and the vulnerability of all creatures (*CD*, 260). Similarly, Kierkegaard praises the stunning magnitude of God's mercy in order to nurture joy and comfort in God (*CD*, 295).

Many of Kierkegaard's discourses and journals echo the theme articulated in *Works of Love,* that loving God causes us to become like God (*CD*, 84). The individual is transformed by the object being contemplated and desired. Kierkegaard is keenly aware of the transformative power of the object our "eyes" are "fixed on" (*UDVS*, 184), which is why he advises worried people to look away from the earthly source of anxiety and gaze upward at the birds of the air. As Augustine had proclaimed, the lover becomes the image of the beloved. Kierkegaard writes: "The law of loving is quite simple and familiar: to love is to be transformed into the likeness of the beloved" (*JP* 3, 2450). He explains that to love "is to want to be like [*ligne*] the beloved" (*JP* 3, 2438). Describing a young man who cherished an image of perfection, Kierkegaard says, "And just as it so beautifully happens with lovers that they begin to resemble each other, so the young man is transformed in likeness to this image, which imprints or impresses itself on all his thought and on every utterance by him . . ." (*PC*, 189). As examples of this, Kierkegaard claims that, by blessing the name of the Lord and praising God in the midst of adversity, Job remained "truly the same," just as God remains the same (*EUD*, 121-22). By focusing on the "one eternal object of wonder — that is God" the prophetess Anna's life of expectancy of messianic fulfillment became a model of wonder and joyful surprise (*EUD*, 225-26). Concentrating in prayer on the God who "has no gravity" makes the worshiper "light" (*UDVS*, 182). Loving God with purity of heart produces stability and eternity in the self. Furthermore, love for God also fosters freedom from worldly frustration or anxiety so that the lover begins to share in God's serenity.

The discourses also exhibit the same ambiguity displayed in *Works of Love*, often shifting to the imperative that one must become like what one loves in order to be in communion with it. As we have seen, that identical vacillation ran throughout Augustine's works. Kierkegaard writes: "[O]nly when God has infinitely become the eternal and omnipresent object of worship and the human being always a worshipper, only then do they resemble each other" (*SUD*, 193). He makes it clear that it is the individual's responsibility to cultivate the humility of a true worshiper. Sometimes it is said that we become like God through being in loving communion with God; and sometimes it is said that we must become like God in order to be in loving communion with God. As with Augustine, the choice of theme in Kierkegaard is a function of the particular edifying purpose, whether it be to inspire the reader with the preeminently attractive prospect of Godlikeness or to encourage the reader to strive to be more godly.

Even Kierkegaard's pseudonymous authors express — often indirectly and obliquely — a desire for God. This implicit desire is evident in the celebrated works of the pseudonymous Johannes Climacus, who provides Kierkegaard with an opportunity to explore some dimensions of desire for God not foregrounded in his signed works. For Kierkegaard, the theme of the intrinsic value of longing for God also possesses an epistemological dimension, as it did for Augustine, though it is a paradoxical one. Climacus, who has a penchant for couching issues in epistemological terms, articulates a yearning of reason that to some extent resembles Augustine's passionate rationality. According to Climacus, human reason experiences a profound ambivalence toward God, involving both attraction and repulsion. On the one hand, God is that for which we long, and an aspect of this longing is the hunger for ultimate explanations. In fact, reason yearns for an all-embracing explanation of everything. We yearn to know why things are the way they are, and how they all fit together. On the other hand, an ultimate explanation of everything would have to include an explanation of the nature and purpose of reason, and thus would have to transcend reason. Much to reason's chagrin, no finite explanation that reason could grasp would be ultimately satisfying to it. Paradoxically, our rationality vainly longs for something that is beyond the capabilities of human thought. Climacus, noting that reason frustratingly seeks to go beyond its own frontiers, observes: "This, then, is the ultimate paradox of thought: to want to discover something that thought itself cannot think" (*PF*, 37). This assertion is Climacus's oblique way of provoking the reader to ponder the exceedingly peculiar desirability of a divine revelation.

This yearning for a mode of understanding beyond the cognitive abilities of finite human minds in part accounts for Kierkegaard's celebrated and frequent disparagements of human reason. Earlier generations of interpreters have often regarded his notorious use of the term "paradox" as a rejection of logical principles or as a defense of arbitrary and capricious mental games, and had sometimes even dismissed him as a dangerous "irrationalist."[62] However, for Kierkegaard a "paradox" is not an oxymoronic combination of words like "square circle." Rather, part of the force of the talk of "paradox" is to remind the reader that our dependence on God involves a humble admission of the finitude of our own intellects. Any explanation of our lives that we could understand would be too small and limited to be compelling. God does not conform to our finite expectations and assumptions about what God must be like. (This point becomes particularly important with respect to God's assumption of the form of a servant in the incarnation.) God's transgression of human presuppositions concerning divinity is entirely appropriate, for we would not be genuinely satisfied with a God who did conform to our expectations. Of course, given his theme of illumination, Augustine spoke in a much less disjunctive way of the relationship of human reason to God's rationality; but even Augustine insisted that the divine light transcends the human mind. Augustine's own life showed

---

62. See Walter Kaufmann, *Critique of Religion and Philosophy* (Princeton, NJ: Princeton University Press, 1958).

how the discovery of the limitations of the philosophic quest encourages a hunger for something that reason alone cannot provide, or, in Kierkegaard's language, for something that thought cannot think.

In an ironic and tentative way, this same pseudonymous Johannes Climacus exhibits other aspects of longing for God in *Concluding Unscientific Postscript*. Climacus is a humorist who feels the lure of the infinite strongly enough to realize that the concept of God is not immediately commensurate with finite concerns. Nevertheless, he does not make a decisive decision to relate to God with religious passion (*CUP* 1, 505). In a way, Climacus lives in the ambiguous borderland between ways of life, no longer enthralled with the finite but not yet committed to the infinite. As a humorist, Climacus sees himself as sharing the universal human predicament of living in the tension between the finite and the infinite. Cognizant of the universality of this tension, Climacus refuses to regard himself as spiritually superior to his brothers and sisters. As a humorist, Climacus does not succumb to despair but suspects (or hopes) that some kind of resolution of this tension is possible. Accordingly, he is drawn to the possibility of an "eternal happiness." The ostensible irony of the book is that he appears to speculate about the desire for an "eternal happiness" in a seemingly dispassionate way. He does not engage in the direct praise of God as does Kierkegaard in his own voice in *Works of Love,* nor does he wax enthusiastic about the joys of this "absolute happiness," as Kierkegaard often did in his discourses. This is doubly odd in that Climacus insists that, in order for us to understand "eternal happiness," we must necessarily have the presence of the right kind of pathos, which he also calls "subjectivity."

But Climacus's own posture is not really as neutral or detached as his prose frequently suggests. His fascination with the life of religious passion is blatant, and he can often become quite lyrical in describing it. Climacus even confesses, in the very beginning of the book, his motivations for writing, portraying himself as saying,

> "I, Johannes Climacus, born and bred in this city and now thirty years old, an ordinary human being like most folk, assume that a highest good, called an eternal happiness, awaits me just as it awaits a housemaid and a professor. I have heard that Christianity is one's prerequisite for this good. I now ask how I may enter into relation to this doctrine." (*CUP* 1, 15)

He yearns to know how he can "share in the happiness that Christianity promises" (*CUP* 1, 17). Climacus insists that "to understand oneself in existence" was both the Greek principle and the Christian principle (*CUP* 1, 352); in both cases, the understanding involved the recognition of the need for a highest good. At times he casts himself as a modern Socrates, saying, "This is the way I have tried to understand myself, and even if the understanding is slight and its yield poor, I have in compensation resolved to act with all my passion on the basis of what I have understood" (*CUP* 1, 182). But having confessed this, he immediately undermines it by saying, "This sounds almost like earnestness" (*CUP* 1, 183), and proceeds to give a very sardonic account of how he became a writer in order to alleviate his boredom by making things difficult for humanity. Even with regard to his own authorship, Climacus juxtaposes earnestness and jest, the sublime and the ridiculous. The ambivalence is evident throughout those pages that betray a yearning for this life of committed passion that he continues to hold at arm's length. By adopting this persona (which in some ways is very close to aspects of Kierkegaard's own self), Climacus can identify with the situation of readers who feel uncomfortable with the more shallow conceptions of the religious life current in their culture, but who still cannot allow their religious longings to be unleashed. Climacus accentuates the differences between sincerely passionate religion and its anemic counterfeits in order to exacerbate the discontent latent in his audience and thereby stimulate a deeper longing. Climacus incarnates the reflective but cautiously detached seeker, whose religious passion is only slightly below the surface, ready to burst forth with a bit of coaxing.

Climacus's pathos becomes more overt in his elaboration of the thesis that the "existing subjective thinker is just as negative as positive" (*CUP* 1, 80-93). Using the language of speculative philosophy, Climacus expresses a melancholy yearning for the infinite. While Climacus seems to be describing in rather general terms individuals who long for the infinite, he is also articulating a dynamic gestation in his own heart. Climacus observes that the existing thinker who has recognized the lure of the infinite stirring in his soul exhibits the form of negativity; the desire for the infinite is a disruptive and aching lack. God does not immediately fill the soul with bliss and comfort when the need for the infinite is initially recognized (*CUP* 1, 491). The individual longs for the infinite but is only aware of its incommensurability with the finite. Climacus points out that, according to Plato, "Eros" is the offspring of Poverty and Plenty; desire itself is a synthesis of finite limitation and infinite expansion (*CUP* 1, 92). Desire is simultaneously an anticipated fullness and an experienced poverty. According to Climacus, the ultimate irony is that we finite creatures, existing in time, nevertheless can be content with no worldly achievement, and can find solace in no temporal comfort. Desire for the infinite disturbs all coziness, and destabilizes all sense that one has found fulfillment. This desire manifests itself as ignorance; nothing positive can be said about its goal. Even when the individual undertakes to pursue the infinite, he quickly realizes that no matter how much progress one has made toward the infinite, more progress always lies ahead. The individual faces a life of perpetual sorrow, for it is excruciatingly painful not to be in complete communion with the eternal. The individual wants to express the love for the absolute absolutely, but finitude cannot be made commensurate with it (*CUP* 1, 484). The individual longs to live the life of eternity uninterruptedly, but cannot do so under the conditions of finitude. In such passages Climacus is giving voice, in an indirect way, to Augustine's perpetual ache that accompanied his quest for wisdom. Climacus's personal asides and expressions of frustration interrupt his seemingly cool analysis of the negative moment in desire. These are not mere literary embellishments but are expressions of his personal religious melancholy.[63] Climacus manifests in his writing the way in which eternal happiness, the highest good, is perpetually elusive. He rhetorically enacts the negative moment in desire that Augustine had dramatized in his *Confessions*.

In the course of expressing the melancholy of a desire for God that has not been fully chosen, Climacus echoes many of the sentiments that Kierkegaard articulates in his signed works. These, as we have seen, often bear a marked similarity to themes in Augustine's writings. Most basically, Climacus identifies passion as the key to the quest for an eternal happiness, for "passion is the momentary continuity that simultaneously has a constraining effect and is the impetus of motion" (*CUP* 1, 312). Passion "constrains" by drawing the individual's interest to one object rather than dispersing it among a multiplicity of objects, and it serves as an "impetus of motion" by wanting to possess that object or at least be in communion with it. As with Augustine, so also for Climacus, the passionate thinker aims to "be what he thinks," unlike absent-minded speculative philosophers who forget their own existence (*CUP* 1, 309). In discussing ethical and religious possibilities, Climacus insists that the individual must identify "himself with what is thought in order to exist in it" (*CUP* 1, 339). That identification, which leads to action, is born of passionate interest in what is thought. Climacus assumes that other individuals are, like himself, capable of developing

---

63. For analysis of melancholy as an aspect of desire in Kierkegaard, see Podmore, *Kierkegaard and the Self before God*, pp. 50-89.

a concern for a "highest good" or an "eternal happiness." Christianity, he notes, presupposes that everyone can be "infinitely concerned about himself," and it seeks to activate that concern for one's own ultimate happiness (*CUP* 1, 130). Like Augustine, Climacus distinguishes concern for an absolute good from concern for relative goods, observing, "All relative willing is distinguished by willing something for something else, but the highest τέλος [*telos*] must be willed for its own sake" (*CUP* 1, 394). Paralleling Augustine's distinction of *frui* and *uti,* just as Kierkegaard did in his signed works, Climacus argues that the absolute is not desired for any ulterior purpose but simply for its intrinsic value. Climacus agrees with the discourses that one should give up everything in order to be related to an absolute *telos* and be related only relatively to relative ends (*CUP* 1, 385-87). Articulating the theme that this desire for an eternal happiness is a permanent feature of human nature, Climacus says: "This is just like the Platonic conception of love; it is a want, and not only does that person feel a want who craves something he does not have but also that person who desires the continued possession of what he has" (*CUP* 1, 121). Like Kierkegaard's works signed in his own name, and like Augustine, Climacus equates God with the object of the desire for eternal happiness. Passion for this highest good provides the continuity of action, the "eternity" that the self implicitly desires. Putting all these themes together, Climacus concludes that the proper way to relate to God is with "the infinite passion of need" (*CUP* 1, 201). He promises, as did Kierkegaard in the discourses, that the desire for God awakens ever more desire. Climacus writes longingly of all these themes, portraying their attractions from the perspective of one who has not fully embraced them. It is significant that, shortly after composing *Concluding Unscientific Postscript,* Kierkegaard elaborated the theme of the necessity of "willing one thing" in the discourse popularly known as "Purity of Heart" (*UDVS,* 7-154).

As should now be clear, the theme of desire for God runs throughout Kierkegaard's writings, even in places where its presence is not announced. Sometimes he explicitly recommends desire for God, as in the discourses for communion on Fridays. Sometimes he lovingly parades the most attractive features of this desire for God, such as the expectancy of Anna and the counterintuitive trust of Job. Kierkegaard does this in many edifying discourses, hoping to inspire the reader to personally explore the blessings of a life of yearning for God. But rather than just write about this desire, Kierkegaard more often seeks to instantiate it in his writing. This can take the form of attempting to evoke desire in the reader by praising its object, as he does in *Works of Love.* Here desire assumes the form of doxology. At other times he nurtures desire by displaying the wistfulness of someone who has not yet made a commitment to pursue his heart's longing for an eternal happiness. Here desire assumes the form of the humorist's ambivalence. But, however different these genres are, it is desire that gives them their rhetorical power and thematic cohesion.

Conclusion

In *Works of Love,* his edifying and Christian discourses, and in the pseud-onymous writings, Kierkegaard textually performs many of the themes concerning love for God that had been explicitly articulated by Augustine. Kierkegaard's efforts to evoke and cultivate love for God presuppose that many of Augustine's claims about human nature, desire, and the *summum bonum* are indeed true, even when Kierkegaard does not overtly state or acknowledge them. For both Augustine and Kierkegaard, human beings are primarily creatures defined by the nature of their desires. According to both of them, there is a kind of desire that is not susceptible to unfortunate ep-isodes of affective perturbation. Human beings can nurture in themselves a desire that is not a chaotic welter of moods but a directional momentum that produces coherence and stability. According to both of them, there is a kind of passion that is not reducible to fragmented and wayward emo-tions, but is an enduring disposition and attachment. For both of them, desire motivates the motions of the will and directs the attention of the mind. Most significantly, for both of them, a highest happiness is the true goal of human desire. The two thinkers concur that no ordinary worldly goal can furnish this enduring, absolute happiness. They agree that desire for this highest happiness transforms the desiring self into the likeness of the object of desire. According to both, this desire is perpetually refueled and is never sated. In short, both Augustine and Kierkegaard root their un-derstanding of Christianity in the restlessness of the human heart and its yearning for an eternal happiness. As we shall see in subsequent chapters, Augustine tends to describe the object of desire in Trinitarian language, while Kierkegaard prefers to use the vocabulary of incarnation. But both kinds of discourse point to the sublime attractiveness of God's self-giving love (for those whose hearts have appropriately matured).

It may be tempting to ascribe the parallel between Augustine and Kier-kegaard to their common indebtedness to Plato — or at least to a Christian-ized Plato. Augustine's debt to Platonic and Neo-Platonic notions of eros is notorious, and Kierkegaard's critical appropriation of Plato on this score is also evident, though a bit less overt.[64] Kierkegaard's use of Plato's eros was more cautious than Augustine's, for he did object to the possible Platonic implication that earthly loves might be nothing more than springboards to an utterly abstract (and thus empty) love of God (*CI*, 41-45, 68), and to the seemingly preferential and self-seeking nature of the preliminary forms of eros (*WL*, 264-67). However, the pseudonymous Climacus applauds "the Greek conception of Eros as found in the *Symposium*" for drawing attention to the importance of desiring and striving (*CUP* 1, 121). Indeed, Kierkegaard, often in his own voice, favorably draws on the concept of Platonic eros (e.g., *TC*, 47; *WL*, 175). But in spite of this common fondness for a certain Platonic motif, for both thinkers Plato was primarily significant for providing a vocabulary that could articulate the conviction that human desire can be satisfied with nothing less than the divine. Driving both authors was the theme, rooted in historic Christianity, that God is the source of all love and the ultimate object of all love. A Platonic conceptuality enabled Augustine to express this traditional Christian theme, and a Platonic/Romantic idiom allowed Kierkegaard to declare something very similar. The similarity between the two was due much more to a common commitment to a Christian leitmotif than to a reliance on a Platonic concept.

Augustine's and Kierkegaard's overlapping accounts of love and desire share yet another feature that has profound consequences for their theologies, particularly for the relationship of "nature" and "grace." Both theologians describe desire for God as having an elusive bifocal nature. On the one hand, they both claim — using different vocabularies — that human beings naturally yearn for an eternal happiness. Humans are structured to find ultimate fulfillment only in loving God. That is the way God has created Homo sapiens: it is the *imago Dei* in humanity. This motif makes it sound as though the Christian life is the actualization of a potential inherent in human nature, possibly even a self-initiated task. On the other hand, both authors also describe the desire for God as being elicited by the divine object, and often suggest that the desire could not really be at all functional without that elicitation. As we shall see, both can even describe the desire as being "born" or "created" in the individual through the impact of God's love. That form of discourse makes it sound as though the desire for God is

---

64. See Rick Antony Furtak, "*Symposium:* Kierkegaard and Platonic Eros," in Jon Stewart and Katalin Nun, eds., *Kierkegaard and the Greek World*, vol. I: *Socrates and Plato* (Farnham, UK: Ashgate, 2010), pp. 105-14.

something that happens to an individual — something generated from beyond the individual. In this way of speaking, the desire itself would have to be regarded as a gift. Surprisingly, neither of our two thinkers treated these two themes as antithetical. This seems peculiar indeed, for the issue of the relationship of our created capacities to God's gracious action would divide Western Christendom and set the various Catholic and Protestant parties to warring with one another. In the following chapters I will explore the ways in which Augustine and Kierkegaard negotiate the tension resident in the bifocal nature of their depictions of desire.

CHAPTER 3

Augustine and Kierkegaard on the Road:
Life as a Journey

As we have seen, the writings of both Augustine and Kierkegaard are based on a shared conviction that the Christian life is a teleological movement directed toward a future state of ultimate happiness. They agree that human beings are structured in such a way that they can only find this ultimate happiness in God. This remains true whether an individual pursues this happiness or not, and it even remains true whether the individual is aware of this possibility or not. The centrality of the concept of desire, explicit in the case of Augustine and more implicit in the case of Kierkegaard, implies that this dynamic involves a transition from a state of dissatisfaction to a state of satisfaction. This transition requires intentional effort, for fulfillment is not immediately achieved simply by desiring it. Both thinkers describe a pattern involving an initial potentiality, an impediment to its actualization, and a continued yearning for actualization in spite of the impediment. That movement toward the desired state of affairs, if it happens, is a lengthy, arduous process characterized by progress, detours, backslidings, and, ideally, an arrival at the destination. Human life involves sequential episodes of temptation, sin, repentance, purgation, and sanctification. In other words, life should have a narrative structure with a plot that develops in a specific direction. Hence, for both Augustine and Kierkegaard, the self is intended to become itself through a history that is subject to narration.

The narrative movement from desired happiness through frustration to the attainment of happiness suggested the metaphor of life as a journey to both authors. The fact that talk of "life's journey" has become a common platitude should not blind us to the metaphor's unusual nature. Life has been represented as a struggle, a party, a trial, a confinement, an eternal recurrence, an endurance test, a tale told by an idiot, a box of chocolates, and a host of other things. "Journey" has never been the only way to conceptualize the Christian life. Even the emphasis on desire has not necessarily suggested that life is a journey, because desire could be satisfied in a variety of ways. For example, the object of desire could be immediately encountered, as in the ecstatic traditions. Or the object of desire could be something hidden within, waiting to be uncovered, as in some of the mystical traditions. Or the object of desire could be something promised whose advent the individual merely awaits, as in some of the eschatological traditions. Prior to Augustine, the dominant forms of Christianity, at least in the eastern Mediterranean, tended to think of the Christian life as a deepening participation in the life of Christ, particularly in his glorification.[1] The protagonist of the story is Christ, not we ourselves in our empirical identities. Christ the second Adam perfected human nature in his own person, and that sanctified humanity becomes ours through contemplation and sacramental identification. Our true selves are hidden in Christ, and we are not essentially the disjointed sequences of temporal events that constitute our earthly biographies. In a very different way, Luther also provided an alternative to the journey image, for he suggested that Christianity is not a matter of making spiritual progress but of trusting in God's justification of the sinner. God and the believer meet in the present moment of faith, not at the end of a process of sanctification.[2] (Luther was not always consistent about this, but his reluctance to treat faith as a good work tended to suggest that faith is not a virtue whose development can be narrated.) According to Luther, if there has been a journey, it was principally God's journey to humanity in the incarnation. But both Augustine and Kierkegaard shunned these options, though Augustine retained some elements of the Eastern Christian identification with Christ, and Kierkegaard exhibited some features of the Lutheran nondevelopmental trust. For both Augustine and Kierkegaard, it was the root metaphor of the road that was most suited to the dynamic, future-oriented nature of the Christian life.

1. Rowan Greer, *Broken Lights and Mended Lives: Theology and Common Life in the Early Church* (University Park: Pennsylvania State University Press, 1986), pp. 65-66.

2. Daphne Hampson, *Christian Contradictions: The Structures of Lutheran and Catholic Thought* (Cambridge: Cambridge University Press, 2001), pp. 9-55.

Augustine's Homecoming

The image of a journey to God pervades Augustine's voluminous literature. His writings would help inscribe the theme of life as a *via* (road) and human beings as *viators* (pilgrims) indelibly on Western religion, philosophy, and literature. That metaphor would inspire Dante's movement from the inferno to paradise, Parsifal's quest for the Holy Grail, and the progress of Bunyan's pilgrim. For Augustine, longing for God, striving for God, and finding God can be imagined in geographical terms. He says, for example, "The safest intent, after all, until we get to where we are intent on getting and where we are stretching out to, is that of a seeker."[3] Metaphorically, the inward transformation of pathos becomes an outward odyssey. Augustine constantly mixes the language of spiritual transformation and physical movement, as when he writes: "Let us come not with our feet but with our affections; let us come not by moving from one place to another, but by loving. . . . When someone is transported by the heart he changes his affection by the movement of the heart."[4] Augustine describes the Christian life as a journey toward a homeland, a *patria,* the locus of true felicity and contentment. He often observes that the Neo-Platonists have glimpsed the homeland, but they do not know the route to it.[5] As Augustine explains, we are en route from the earthly city ruled by love of self to the heavenly city ruled by love of God. We begin in a place of exile, a land that is not our true home, in territory quite different from our destination. In the earthly city where we currently find ourselves, we are only strangers and sojourners. Sometimes Augustine describes our life very negatively — as a passage through a desert.[6] The earthly city could not possibly be our permanent abode, for it is riddled with tragedy, decay, and sin. At other times he is a bit less disparaging, picturing earthly life as a wayside inn in which we must use the utensils and comforts provided, but we always remain prepared to leave them behind in order to press on to our destination.[7] For Augustine, our true home is the community of God and the angels, a heavenly city of perfect knowledge and love. We humans were designed and created by God to advance toward this celestial goal, and we will never be happy until we experience homecomng.

3. Augustine, *The Trinity,* IX, prologue, 1, in *WSA* I, 5.
4. Augustine, *The City of God,* IV, 9, in *WSA* I, 6-7.
5. Augustine, *The Trinity,* IV, 15. 20, in *WSA* I, 5.
6. Augustine, *On Teaching Christianity (De doctrina Christiana),* I, in *WSA* I, 11.
7. Augustine, *Tractates on the Gospel of John,* homily 40, 10, in *WSA* III, 12.

The journey is necessarily passion-laden, for it involves an affectively intense process of purgation and transformation: there can be no arrival at the destination without a fundamental passional change in the traveler. For Augustine, the journey along "Charity Street" is a quest for something precious beyond comparison, the finding of which could not possibly be "more advantageous" to the reader.[8] Explicitly linking the foundational themes of desire and journey at the beginning of his classic *The Trinity*, Augustine quotes the exhortation from Psalm 105 that we should "seek [God's] face always,"[9] and he adds at the conclusion of the treatise that we should seek God's face with "ardor."[10] He says: "[G]ive me a man of desires, give me someone who is hungry, give me someone traveling thirsty in this wilderness, and panting for the fountain of eternal life, and he will know what I am talking about."[11] So Augustine constructs his ideal reader as a fellow sojourner. He invites the reader to travel with him:

> Accordingly, dear reader, whenever you are as certain about something as I am, go forward with me; whenever you stick equally fast, seek with me; whenever you notice that you have gone wrong, come back to me; or that I have, call me back to you. In this way let us set out along Charity Street together, making for him of whom it is said, "Seek his face always."[12]

The arrival at the journey's destination is just as passion-charged as was the journey itself, for it is nothing less than the eternal exultant adoration of the triune God.

Augustine wrote the *Confessions* as an attempt to narrate his life with this Christian plot line in mind.[13] The events, issues, and concerns of his life were crafted into a tale of exile, wandering, and homecoming. The fact that the resulting story is a retrospective construction is evident in his repeated confessions that there is no immediate transparency of the self to

---

8. Augustine, *The Trinity*, I, 1. 5, in *WSA* I, 5.

9. Augustine, *The Trinity*, I, 1. 5, in *WSA* I, 5.

10. Augustine, *The Trinity*, XV, Epilogue, 51, in *WSA* I, 5.

11. Augustine, *Tractates on the Gospel of John*, 26, 4, in *WSA* III, 12.

12. Augustine, *The Trinity*, I, 1. 5, in *WSA* I, 5.

13. Augustine scholars constantly debate the degree to which Augustine's reminiscences involve a fictionalizing of his past. See J. J. O'Meara, "Augustine's *Confessions*: Elements of Fiction," in Joanne McWilliam, ed., *Augustine: From Rhetor to Theologian* (Waterloo, ON: Wilfrid Laurier Press, 1992); see also James J. O'Donnell, "Augustine's Unconfessions," in John D. Caputo and Michael Scanlon, eds., *Augustine and Postmodernism: Confessions and Circumfession* (Bloomington: Indiana University Press, 2005), pp. 214-15.

itself. Contemporary scholars debate the degree to which Augustine may have fictionalized his account, or at least heavily stylized it for polemical and pastoral purposes. But in any case, Augustine admits that he did not grasp the significance of the various vicissitudes of his life at the time that he experienced them. According to the retrospective Augustine, the project of making sense of one's own life requires understanding at least the lineaments of the revealed Christian narrative, including the story's beginning, its propelling problematic, and its hoped-for resolution. The Christian narrative provides the interpretive framework for construing the individual's life as having been created by God and having its *telos* in God. When a person does not know that God is the self's source and home, the significance of the events in his or her life will remain opaque and baffling. In recollecting his life according to this schema, Augustine comes to discern the coherence that was due to God, and comes to celebrate even his life's mysteries and tragedies as episodes in a providentially governed journey to God. While the individual continues to travel on this earthly *via*, the autobiographical saga must be constantly renarrated, for the story of a person's life is like an unfinished poem, with new stanzas waiting to be added. New insights into God's gracious activity must be constantly discovered. The unfolding of the story whets the appetite to comprehend the unity of the narrative from beginning to the projected end. For Augustine, this self-narration is a spiritual exercise, because, as he reflects, the writer grows in gratitude, hope, and anticipation. Even more importantly, the writer's example can inspire the reader to engage in the same kind of self-narration, concentrating on the story's origin, ground, and goal in God, and thereby can help the reader grow in the Christian virtues.

The basic plot of the journey is governed by the pattern of creation/fall/restoration/consummation. As we have seen, Kierkegaard was acquainted with this pattern and aware of its association with Augustine; in fact, Kierkegaard used it himself. Augustine had developed the schema by appropriating the history of the human race as a whole from Scripture (particularly the people of Israel) and applying its dramatic framework to individual lives. He says, "The experience of mankind in general, as far as God's people is concerned, is comparable to the experience of the individual man."[14] Individuals progress through the personal equivalents of the various stages of salvation history in order to move from the temporal to the eternal. Although Augustine did occasionally use the language of the ascent of the

---

14. Augustine, *City of God*, X, 14, in *WSA* I, 6-7.

soul, which he had inherited from classical culture, his view of human life was much more horizontal than vertical.[15] Life is more like a quest for a treasure than it is like the Neo-Platonic flight of the soul into the Eternal. For Augustine, the events of this earthly life do play a critical role in the narrative insofar as they serve the pedagogical purposes of educating the soul, shaping the virtues, and stimulating desire for God. As Kierkegaard would note, the way of walking the road is essentially related to arriving at the destination, for the destination involves the perfections of the virtues acquired through the process of journeying.

The starting point of the journey and the characteristics of the pilgrim are relevant to the journey's future trajectory. According to Augustine, human beings are created in the image of God, which he particularly identified with the rational soul. As we have seen, this rationality, which includes affective dimensions, is nothing less than the capacity to know God. To clarify this concept, Augustine used a variety of metaphors, including that of a mirror,[16] an image stamped on a coin,[17] and the imprint of a ring on wax.[18] Continuing the symbolism of responsiveness, Augustine declares that the image of God is so attuned to God that it is receptive only to God's voice.[19] These metaphors suggest an inherent receptivity to something outside the self that can have an identity-defining impact on the self. The metaphors also suggest a dialectic of identity and differentiation. Because we are only the image or imprint of God but not the very being of God, God is both present and absent to the soul, known and yet sought, indwelling yet transcendent. The differentiation of the image of God from God's being is related to Augustine's association of the image of God with the "inner man," which in turn is described in terms of "memory." Memory in this context is the power of self-consciousness, the ability to grasp past, present, and future as a coherent, evolving whole. God is present in the "inner man" as the illumination that enables individuals to see truth, including the truth about themselves and their ideal destiny. It is also this light of God shining in the inner person that inspires the desire to see God, the source of all knowledge, including self-knowledge. To turn to this image is to behold the reflection of God's truth, goodness, and beauty. In short, for Augustine the

15. See Carol Harrison, *Beauty and Revelation in the Thought of Saint Augustine* (Oxford: Clarendon Press, 1992), p. 261.

16. Augustine, *The Trinity*, XV, 2. 8, in *WSA* I, 5.

17. Augustine, *Tractates on the Gospel of John*, Homily 41, 2, in *WSA* III, 13.

18. Augustine, *The Trinity*, XV, 23. 44, in *WSA* I, 5.

19. Augustine, *Tractates on the Gospel of John*, Homily 96, 4, in *WSA* III, 13.

complex trope of the "image of God" suggests an innate potential for knowing and loving God, which is simultaneously a potential for making sense out of one's own life and the cosmos as a whole, without absorbing the individual into God. (We must remember that for Augustine, "knowing" God is an intensely passionate matter. Augustine does not bifurcate "knowing" and "loving" in the way that modernity would with the juxtaposition of "head" and "heart.") Kierkegaard also affirms the inherent orientation of the self to God, and, like Augustine, denies mysticism's volatilization of the self into God. However, as shall become evident, he does not share Augustine's hunger to grasp the overall "truth" about the cosmos as a whole.

As we have seen in Augustine's treatment of desire, he recognized a monumental problem with the current state of this capacity to know God and the self. Augustine saw human life as situated between the rival attractions of higher and lower goods. We are confronted with multiple attractive objects of desire, all vying for our attention.[20] In his early dialogues and treatises Augustine lamented that lesser earthly goods tempt the soul to the vices of carnal desire, pride (the desire for social domination and prestige), and idle curiosity rather than the pursuit of true wisdom. He came to believe that the root vice was pride, the elevation of one's own private, short-term, and apparent good to the status of absolute good. This inflated love of the temporal self displaces the ultimate devotion that is due to God. Egocentrism produces a host of derivative vices, including curiosity about external things that might be useful to the worldly self, as well as concupiscence, the excessive attachment to inferior goods.[21] To make matters worse, our attractions and our commitments are changeable and unsteady. As a result of myopia, fickleness, and narrow self-interest, humans tend to enjoy the things that should only be used. The soul becomes fascinated with the reflections of God in the created order, turns its attention outward rather than inward, and becomes compulsively attached to finite goods. By turning away from the interior image, the soul's attention is dispersed. Earthly beauties and goods should remind the soul of their source in God; instead, they stimulate the desire to possess them. Augustine laments the fact that the attractiveness of earthly things is an adhesive that binds our minds and wills to them so strongly that the bond becomes habitual. Desires for temporal goods become our masters, pulling our will away from the pursuit of our true goal. Earthly desires are a kind of spiritual anesthesia, dulling

---

20. See Augustine, *On Teaching Christianity (De doctrina Christiana)*, in *WSA* I, 11.

21. Augustine, *On Free Will (De libero arbitrio)*, II, 19, 53, in *WSA* I, 3.

our appetite for the only food that will really satisfy us. In spite of this, the memory of a dimly sensed homeland continues to haunt the soul that has been drawn off course by the superficial allures of a multitude of unfulfilling objects. As we shall see, Augustine's analysis of human sinfulness approximates much of Kierkegaard's portrayal of the aesthetic life.

Augustine reiterated his discontent with the temporal dispersion and misdirection of the self in the *Confessions*. In fact, he did much more than describe the loss of direction in our journey toward home; he dramatized it. By no means is the *Confessions* merely a plea for divine forgiveness for particular transgressions; rather, it is an expression of remorse about the soul's repeated derailments on the journey toward God, and it is also a hymn of thankfulness for God's continuing redirection. In the early chapters Augustine recalls the inchoate yearning that unsettled him and initiated his search, causing him to seek relief from his discomfort in a variety of unsatisfying places. He was buffeted from one pleasure to another, his inner world an unstable, inconstant flux. In retrospect he laments: "So I arrived at Carthage, where the din of scandalous love-affairs raged cauldron-like around me."[22] Augustine's imagery parallels the confusing swirl of the outward world with the even more disorienting chaos of his inner world. The sheer instability and emotional disorder resembles the welter of moods expressed by some of Kierkegaard's aesthetic characters. Augustine's restlessness drove him to seek fulfillment in vocational success and the accolades of his peers. It drove him to indulge in the emotional voyeurism of the theater, momentarily delighting in his capacity to feel emotions secondhand. But in spite of these temporary distractions, he unconsciously felt lost and knew that he was meandering in the wilderness rather than making progress toward his home.

According to Augustine, this disorientation is so severe that it can only be remedied by a radical transformation analogous to a geographical redirection. We humans begin life with our desires aimed in the wrong direction. The movement toward God requires a reorientation of desire. In his early dialogues Augustine argues that the virtues must be rightly directed and ordered by the recovery of love for the highest good. Individuals must learn to cherish the proper highest aim above all other goals. We wayward pilgrims must proceed through a period of reorientation to a period of difficult travel and finally to a time of joyful homecoming. We require a pedagogy or therapy of desire, in which our passional lives are refocused on

22. Augustine, *Confessions*, III, 1 (1), in *WSA* I, 1.

God, the genuine *telos* of human longing. We need to engage in the long and arduous process of reeducating our loves so that we will finally learn to love God above all things. As we shall see, this acute awareness of the need to redirect desire inspired Augustine's Platonic-sounding language of an "inward" journey. At times Augustine describes a sequence of stages, beginning with ignorance of the individual's situation, to knowledge of one's sinfulness, to faith and the combat against sin, to a willingness to endure worldly trials and tribulations in order to love God and neighbor, and finally to serenity and beatitude.[23] We begin life having lost the freedom to sin or not sin *(posse peccare, posse non peccare)* so that now it is not possible for us not to sin *(non posse non peccare)*. God then restores the possibility of not sinning *(posse non peccare)*, which is consummated in the inability to sin *(non posse peccare)*. This final state is more glorious than the original possibility of sinning or not sinning that Adam had enjoyed. Kierkegaard would inherit this road map of the individual's journey and give it a few significant tweaks.

Much of Augustine's writing concerns the often painful recovery of the soul from its dispersal in finite goods and its redirection toward the highest good. Most of *Confessions* is the saga of the conflicts between misdirected desire and properly aimed desire. His discovery of Cicero's *Hortensius* challenged the significance of his earthly loves and rechanneled his longing toward wisdom itself, the permanent good that cannot be depleted. He says: "All my hollow hopes suddenly seemed worthless, and with unbelievable intensity my heart burned for the immortality that wisdom seemed to promise. . . . How ardently I longed, O my God, how ardently I longed to fly to you away from earthly things! I did not understand then how you were dealing with me."[24] According to his own account, something mysterious was luring Augustine beyond his inadequate attachments; some force was activating his innate but confused and enervated desire for a more enduring and intense happiness. All the while, Augustine was puzzled about the source of his discontent with temporal pleasures and his new hunger for wisdom. Augustine's reconstruction of his journey suggests that even after he, like all people, had wandered into the wilderness, God used temporal events and experiences to push him back on track. Kierkegaard would later talk gratefully about God's mysterious "governance" of his own life in a similar vein.

---

23. Augustine, *The Enchiridion of Faith, Hope, and Love*, 31 (118-119), in *WSA* I, 8; *On True Religion (De vera religione)*, 26 (48-49), in *WSA* I, 8.

24. Augustine, *Confessions*, III, 4 (7-8), in *WSA* I, 1.

The tension between misdirected desire and appropriately directed desire is not easily resolved, and the journey of reorientation is not a straight line. Much of Augustine's odyssey was a sad tale of looking for an ultimate object to love in all the wrong places. Some of his detours were due to his embrace of faulty ideologies that reinforced his unconscious effort to evade the painful recognition of the true depths of his neediness. His sojourn with the Manicheans eventually triggered the realization that even his own putative quest for wisdom was to some extent a form of self-aggrandizement, for he took pleasure in imagining himself as an enthusiast for truth whose soul participated in the very nature of divinity.[25] But the mythology of the Manicheans failed to satisfy his longing for truth. For a while science, with its universal categories and universal principles, seemed to point to a destination that transcended finite limitations. But the impersonal cosmos described by science failed to provide the home for which his heart yearned.

Augustine's continuing sense of being lost in the cosmos, however, was fueled by much more than misguided ideological commitments. At the same time that he was immersing himself in unsatisfying cosmologies, love for a philosophically inclined friend pulled his heart in another direction. But friends die, as this one did, and the heart remains without a secure home. The very intensity of his grief perplexed and disturbed Augustine. He recalled: "I had become a great enigma to myself, and I questioned my soul, demanding why it was sorrowful, and why it so disquieted me, but it had no answer."[26] By asking this anguished question, Augustine was implicitly urging readers to consider their own losses and griefs, and to ponder the inability of temporal goods to provide a permanent resting place. Augustine models this introspective process by using his devastating sorrow on the death of a friend as a springboard to reflect on the impermanence of all loves directed to the beauties and pleasures of the created order. He opines that finite objects of love that do not endure cannot possibly satisfy the desire for eternal and absolute fulfillment. Even the fellow-feeling of a community of lovers of wisdom is not the soul's final home. The temporal goods that seem close to perfection may delight the heart for a season, but "once perfect, they grow old and perish."[27] Much later, in Book X of the *Confessions*, Augustine generalizes that all creatures on the earth and even the heavenly bodies, no matter how beautiful, prove to be nothing

25. Augustine, *Confessions*, IV, 15 (26), in *WSA* I, 1.
26. Augustine, *Confessions*, IV, 4 (9), in *WSA* I, 1.
27. Augustine, *Confessions*, IV, 10 (15), in *WSA* I, 1.

more than roadside attractions. Kierkegaard would make a similar point in many of his upbuilding discourses; he also hoped to redirect the reader away from excessive concern for worldly fulfillments. By Augustine's self-narration, the reader is led to realize that inordinate attachment to earthly loves inevitably fills the soul with regret and premonition, and diverts the pilgrim from the true course.

Augustine concludes that our dilemma is that we human beings have elevated penultimate goods to the status of absolute goods, and thereby have fallen victim to a self-imposed idolatry, a phenomenon that Kierkegaard would later fear typified both the culture of Christendom and also all individual lives apart from grace. According to Augustine, money, power, popularity, and romance become substitutes for God. Because our ultimate destination is God, and only God can truly satisfy the human heart, all these lesser goods will ultimately disappoint. The objects of misdirected love cannot bear that weight of overattachment and excessive devotion. Nevertheless, our infatuation with our idols has the power to fatally distract us from our true *telos*. When we love created things absolutely instead of God, our progress toward the object of real happiness is reversed, and our lives become disordered.

As we shall explore fully in subsequent chapters, the transitional phase in the pilgrims' journey is the recognition of the magnitude of their lostness and debility. The *viators* must admit that, left to their own devices, they can only wander in circles, race in the wrong direction, or run out of energy. The realization that wayfarers desperately need help is essential for the continuation and successful completion of the journey: the pilgrim requires a guide, fuel, a map, and even a driver. As we shall see, God's grace provides all these things. With grace, the journey takes a new, unexpected, and fruitful turn. According to both Augustine and Kierkegaard, grace enables a new kind of love for God to develop, a longing for radical self-giving.

This account of Augustine's trope of "the journey" may seem to homogenize too neatly the multiple motifs that crisscross his writings. One must admit that the image of the journey forward is intersected by a very different theme. Augustine can speak of an "inward journey" in a way that sounds like Platonic recollection or some contemplative discovery of the truth through introspection. This would suggest that beatitude is not something attained at the end of a process of transformation, but is something that the self already implicitly possesses. Rather than becoming a new creature, the self discovers what it already is. As George Pattison has argued, Augustine's continuing talk about the quest for truth suggests that this truth remains a structural feature of human life even in its fallen state, and it presupposes an innate capacity for God.[28] In a way, the soul already "remembers God" and therefore is able to recognize God when God makes God's self known. Augustine writes: "If I find you somewhere beyond my memory, that means I shall be forgetful of you. And how shall I find you, once I am no longer mindful of you?"[29] Alarmingly for many Christians, it is suspected that the logic of Augustine's thought would obliterate the distinction of the self and God, for divinity is the basis of the soul, or at least is the soul's natural environment. However, though Augustine was steeped in Platonism, he was uncomfortable with the notion that the journey is a simple exercise in recollecting God, of unearthing the immanence of God concealed in the depths of the self. The journey is more than the actualization of a God-oriented potential; it is not like discovering a hidden reservoir of divinity that the soul already possessed. As Pattison notes, the theme of recollection is seriously qualified by Augustine's countervailing theme that God transcends the mind and therefore must furnish the condition that enables God to be known. Augustine writes: "I entered [the innermost places of my being] then, and with the vision of my spirit, such as it was, I saw the incommutable light far above my spiritual ken, transcending my mind. . . ."[30] Therefore, the journey's movement is in an important sense forward, into the future, toward the God who transcends the self as its *telos*.

This mixing of images of journeying inward with images of journeying forward is inspired by Augustine's desire to affirm two different things. First, the self is structured in such a way that it naturally needs God for completion; God is its true home. Second, we wayfaring travelers are not home yet, and we need a great deal of help in getting there. On the one hand, we were created for relationship with God, so that we naturally have an affinity for God; on the other hand, God transcends our relational capacities, must activate them, and offers more than we ever wanted or imagined. To complicate this scenario, the relational capacities that we do possess have been rendered dysfunctional by sin and require divine healing and aid. Kierkegaard's work will display a similar dialectical tension of a trace of God in the soul and the utter transcendence of God.

A similar tension is evident in Augustine's pages concerning the com-

---

28. George Pattison, *Kierkegaard's Upbuilding Discourses* (London: Routledge, 2002), p. 36.

29. Augustine, *Confessions*, X, 17 (26), in *WSA* I, 1.

30. Augustine, *Confessions*, VII, 10 (16), in *WSA* I, 1.

patibility of the theme of the quest for happiness with the doctrine of God's free and unmerited bestowal of grace. Some commentators have complained that Augustine's project remained determined by the eudaemonism typical of classical philosophy. Contrary to the Lutheran emphasis of God's initiation of the very yearning for redemption, the logic of Augustine's position points to a natural human proclivity for God apart from and prior to God's gracious action. According to this critique, in the hands of Augustine, Christianity became another variant of the saga of the human journey to God, rather than the joyous story of God's unanticipated journey to humanity. Even more strongly, such critics object that an independent analysis of human needs and aspirations serves as the alien lens through which Augustine construes Christianity.[31] According to this interpretation, by using this extra-Christian foundational schema, Augustine distorted the main tenets of Christianity. From this perspective, the ultimate root of the perceived problem of anthropocentrism is that Augustine allegedly based his understanding of Christianity on an anthropology in which the goal for humanity is implied by the starting point. The bestowal of unmerited grace by a free act of a transcendent divine agent cannot be easily reconciled with the satisfaction of a desire structured into human nature — or so this critique claims.

However, Augustine is not casting the individual in the role of the self-propelled wayfarer, energized and guided by a structural feature of created human nature. Rhetorically, Augustine tries to accomplish two things by relating the tale of the soul's journey. First, he seeks to reinforce the longing for home so that the individual will not sink down roots in the soil of the earthly city. He does want his writings to push, coax, and lure his readers forward on their own journeys. In doing so he uses the language of the quest for happiness, the fulfillment of innate desires, and even the ascent of the soul. Second, he seeks to foster gratitude as the pilgrim-reader progressively realizes that what seems to be a journey toward God is supported, fueled, and directed toward a surprising goal by the God who has journeyed to the pilgrim. Augustine hopes to encourage both longing and receptivity. He assumes a commensurability between human aspirations and God's self-revelation, a point of contact between God's redemption and humanity as originally created by God. He does not want to erase either God's transcendence of the soul and the priority of God's agency, on the one hand, or the

---

31. See Phillip Cary, *Augustine's Invention of the Inner Self: The Legacy of a Christian Platonist* (Oxford: Oxford University Press, 2000).

importance of human aspiration and striving, on the other. Consequently, for Augustine life's journey is the quest to find something that we cannot specify in advance, but nevertheless can recognize when it encounters us. Retrospectively, we realize that the gift that we are given is exactly what we needed, which we did not know beforehand. The destination cannot be extrapolated from an analysis of the journey's beginning, but the destination does make manifest a potential that was hidden in the beginning. This view accords with Augustine's understanding of how God generally operates in the created order through *rationes seminales,* or immanent capacities for growth in creatures that delimit the field of their possible developmental trajectories without necessitating any single one of those trajectories. God must providentially act on these multiple and open-ended potentialities in order to produce a specific outcome; the subsequent history of the creature is not just the inevitable unfolding of what had been implicit from the beginning.[32] In the case of humans, the created potential makes it possible to view life's journey as a human task, but the providential guidance makes it possible to regard the journey as an unanticipated divine gift. The same juxtaposition of human quest and divine self-giving, and the dialectic of human capacity and unexpected gift, can be found in the works of Søren Kierkegaard.

Kierkegaard's Way(s)

Kierkegaard was well aware of Augustine's use of the journey image from the lectures of Clausen and Marheineke. Familiarity with Augustine's journey metaphor was also mediated to him indirectly from a variety of devotional authors, including the French Catholic theologian Fénelon and the German Reformed theologian Gerhard Tersteegen, both of whom were indebted to Augustine.[33] Kierkegaard came to equal his remote predecessor in his preference for "journey" as the most apt analogy for the individual Christian's existence. Like Augustine, Kierkegaard describes the self as restless, as constantly in motion. He typically uses dynamic metaphors

---

32. Augustine, *On the Literal Interpretation of Genesis (De Genesi ad litteram),* 6, 14 (25)–6, 17 (29).

33. See Peter Šajda, "'The Wise Men Went Another Way': Kierkegaard's Dialogue with Fénelon and Tersteegen," in Roman Králik, Abraham H. Kahn, Peter Šajda, Jamie Turnbull, and Andrew J. Burgess, eds., *Kierkegaard and Christianity: Acta Kierkegaardiana,* vol. 3 (Slovakia: Kierkegaard Society in Slovakia/Toronto: Kierkegaard Circle, 2008), pp. 89-105.

for human individuals, including "wanderer" and "emigrant," and he some-times portrays human beings as "seekers" (*TDIO*, 11-12). Kierkegaard even compares people to projectiles: "Just as the expert archer's arrow leaves the bowstring and has no rest before it reaches the target, so the human being is created by God with God as his aim and cannot find rest before he finds rest in God" (*JP* 1, 65). Echoing the Augustinian heritage, Kierkegaard fre-quently depicts the Christian as a pilgrim struggling to reach a destination (e.g., *EUD*, 343-45; *CD*, 33-34). Kierkegaard sometimes even uses the Latin phrase *theologia viatorum* (theology of wayfarers) to suggest his view of the Christian life (*FT*, 88). To further strengthen the parallel with Augustine, Kierkegaard peppers his works with explicit images of life as a journey.[34] As we have seen, Kierkegaard applauds Augustine for describing earthly life as an "exile" and as an arduous path (*JP* 4, 4670). Moreover, many of the titles of Kierkegaard's discourses incorporate the language of questing and journeying, as in "To Seek after God Constitutes Man's Highest Perfection," which parallels Augustine's theme that our hearts are restless until they rest in God. Perhaps most striking is the title of one of Kierkegaard's most fa-mous pseudonymous books, which portrays life as a "way" with "stages": *Stages on Life's Way*.

Kierkegaard linked the images of spiritual change and directional movement in the same way that Augustine had. Kierkegaard's use of the journey motif is often followed by an explanation that this particular type of journey involves inward transformation. He observes that "there is in au-thorized language a universal, generally accepted metaphor that compares life to a road" (*UDVS*, 289), and he adds that this highway is defined by the way it is walked. According to Kierkegaard, "how one walks life's road," the quality of inner pathos, indicates which road one is traveling (*UDVS*, 290). In another discourse Kierkegaard observes that the road to be trav-eled is within the person, since "the road [is] the continuing transformation of the striving spirit" (*UDVS*, 49). Because of this linkage of progress and inner transformation, Kierkegaard often mixes the journey motif with edu-cational metaphors; for example, in his very last journal entry he describes the Christian life as "the period of schooling, the time of learning," which is "most strenuous" (*JP* 6, 6969). Clear echoes of Augustine and the Chris-tianized version of the classical tradition of *paideia* can be heard.

Kierkegaard's tendency to conflate "journey" with "inwardness" in or-

---

34. See Christopher Ben Simpson, *The Truth Is the Way: Kierkegaard's* Theologia Viato-rum (London: SCM Press, 2010).

der to suggest a progressive transformation of pathos closely parallels Augustine's practice. Kierkegaard's basic affinity for this wayfaring vocabulary manifests an underlying kinship with Augustine that was far deeper than a shared preference for certain literary tropes. By seeing the Christian life as progress along a path, Kierkegaard deviates from the tendency of many strands of his Lutheran heritage to regard salvation as the extrinsic relationship of God to the individual. For the orthodox Lutheranism rooted in the confessional texts of the sixteenth century, the good news of Christianity is the message that God is compassionately disposed toward the individual. God's benevolent attitude toward the sinner is the essence of salvation, and the spiritual evolution of the sinner is thus de-emphasized. God's mercy is a characteristic of God, not of the sinner; it is a reality that remains *extra nos,* and is simply to be responded to with trust. The fundamental component of the individual's religious experience is the moment of faith in which that person grasps God's justification of the sinner. Trust is not the sort of phenomenon that could journey down a highway. According to most Lutherans, trust may come and go, and the individual may experience episodes of relative steadiness or wavering, but trust does not essentially grow. Trust is not teleologically oriented; it is not trying to go anywhere or achieve anything. According to the "Apology of the Augsburg Confession," faith is neither a good work nor an enduring virtue or disposition; it is pure receptivity to God's promises.[35] The "Formula of Concord" insists that faith grasps God's justifying grace quite apart from any "renewal" in the believer.[36] Because the justified individual remains a sinner, the Christian life is more like a permanent dialectical tension between sin and faith than it is like a journey; it is a "continual battle against the flesh."[37] (The "Formula of Concord" would modify this picture slightly by introducing "the third use of the Law" and the prospect of growth in zeal for God's Law; but even then this zeal is described as a fruit of faith rather than as a component of faith.)

Consequently, Kierkegaard's tendency to think in terms of the Christian life as a journey was more daring than it may initially seem. Possibly without knowing it, he was participating in an effort to restore an Augustinian metaphor to a foundational position, and thereby to make directional development much more central to the faith. By emphasizing the journey

---

35. "Apology for the Augsburg Confession," trans. Charles Arand et al., in Robert Kolb and Timothy J. Wingert, eds., *The Book of Concord: The Confessions of the Evangelical Lutheran Church* (Minneapolis: Fortress, 2002), pp. 128-30.

36. "The Formula of Concord," in Kolb and Wingert, *The Book of Concord,* p. 497.

37. "The Formula of Concord," in Kolb and Wingert, *The Book of Concord,* p. 502.

metaphor, Kierkegaard was identifying with the Pietist stream of Lutheranism that had been a powerful influence in his childhood. Kierkegaard valued the catechism of Erik Pontoppidan (issued in 1738 by a Danish Lutheran bishop who had imbibed the piety of the University of Halle). Halle Pietism emphasized the struggle for sincere penitence that precedes conversion, as well as the need to perform good works in order to bolster and discipline the incipient but ever-growing faith that remains vulnerable to fluctuation.[38] Pontoppidan's catechism not only associated faith with a new longing for God but also described Christianity as the "road" to redemption.[39] The orthodox Lutheran tradition, intent on emphasizing the contrast of sin and justification, had affirmed the reality of sanctification but had not intensively probed the way it could be seen as a developmental process involving a new striving. It remained for Pietists such as Pontoppidan to portray both repentance and sanctification as developmental processes and thereby restore the full Augustinian narrative pattern of the Christian life.

Kierkegaard's similarity to Augustine is evident not only in his general fondness for the journey metaphor, but also in the way he sketches the main phases of the journey. Kierkegaard construes human life in terms of Augustine's narrative pattern of first creation, fall into sin, and new creation. (As we shall see, Kierkegaard does modify Augustine's account of the first creation and the fall into sin.) The individual's story begins with prelapsarian unactualized possibilities, it progresses through postlapsarian guilt and debility, and it reaches a climax in a transformation followed by a new striving (*JP* 1, 29). Although Kierkegaard often does not list the final stage of consummation and is more reluctant to speculate about its nature than Augustine was, he does presuppose such a goal and does hold it up as the longed-for destination. In 1837, taking notes on Augustine, Kierkegaard commented about the importance of this plot line (*JP* 1, 29). Kierkegaard habitually uses the more specific categories of the Augustinian narrative, including temptation, guilt, repentance, purgation, justification, and sanctification, for these had become embedded in the theology of the West, including Lutheranism.[40] Clausen's lectures reinforced Kierkegaard's aware-

---

38. Christopher Barnett, *Kierkegaard, Pietism, and Holiness* (Farnham, UK: Ashgate, 2011), pp. 18-21.

39. See Henrik Horstbøll, "Pietism and the Politics of Catechism: The Case of Denmark and Norway in the Eighteenth and Nineteenth Centuries," *Scandinavian Journal of History* 29 (2004): 143-66.

40. See Jeremy Walker, *To Will One Thing: Reflections on Kierkegaard* (Montreal and Kingston: McGill-Queen's University Press, 1972).

ness of the stages of the Augustinian *ordo* or *oeconomia salutis,* even though Clausen was critical of what he feared had become an overstandardization of this plot line in Pietism (*KJN* 3, pp. 60-61). Kierkegaard defined the segments of this narrative in much the same way that Augustine had. Like Augustine, he was convinced that human beings, whether they are aware of it or not, have been structured by God in such a way that their true fulfillment can be found only through relating to God. Also like Augustine, Kierkegaard believed that this relationship is not immediately solidified and must be intentionally actualized. The individual must move from the possibility of a relationship with God to the actuality of that relationship. Hence the self is a development, subject to narration, and susceptible to failure. The self is not a static substance but is a dynamic "becoming" that is enacted before God. It is this teleological dynamic that made the Augustinian metaphor of "journey" so appropriate.

Kierkegaard integrated the narrative of the journey from sinfulness to communion with God with the narrative of the journey of self-understanding. Particularly in this regard, Kierkegaard's writings parallel Augustine's. In Kierkegaard's writings, candid self-knowledge and self-transparency are not immediate givens, a sad reality that Augustine had exposed in the *Confessions.* Consequently, the journey toward God, if it proceeds in the right direction, should also be a progressive clarification of the individual's true identity and goal. As it had for Augustine, so also for Kierkegaard, the project of attaining clarity about oneself requires clarity about the self's ground and *telos.* Like Augustine, Kierkegaard associated the journey toward God with the consolidation and stabilization of the individual's identity. To understand and fulfill oneself, one must understand that one's source and one's home are in God. This fulfillment involves properly relating the various components of the individual's life to one another, such that one's life as a whole is rooted in God and oriented toward God. Continuity and unity are achieved by having a *telos* sufficiently capacious to have implications for every dimension of the individual's life.

Kierkegaard describes the task facing all individuals as the call to develop the eternal aspect of their own selves in the temporal succession of present moments. "Repetition," a category that Kierkegaard frequently invokes, is the continuity of a life lived in the pursuit of such an ideal, renewing its commitment to the goal in every moment. The pseudonym Constantin Constantius, a somewhat jaded aesthete who vainly longs to recapture (or "repeat") the lost thrill of pleasurable experiences, explains that authentic "repetition" involves a qualitative change in an individual brought about through the individual's freedom: in some sense the individual remains the same person, but in another sense the individual has become someone new by striving to actualize an ideal self (*R*, 148-49). Constantius's admitted failure to attain such a "repetition" (due to his implicit refusal to actualize his ideal self), and his evident lack of personal cohesion and directionality, negatively point to the significance of the pursuit of the ideal. An individual's ideal identity must be chosen and enacted, taking into account his concrete history, attributes, and context. Far from being a punctilinear decision, a personal identity is a lifelong task to be performed, for the individual must continuously reaffirm the commitment to actualize the ideal self.[41] By "willing one thing," the person becomes someone definite, with a reliable and enduring character, defined by lasting purposes and aspirations, rather than a fickle, changing reactor to life's multifarious stimuli (*UDVS*, 8-24). Of course, as presented by Kierkegaard's more "aesthetic" pen names, such as Constantius, this task can be described only in purely formal ways. Constantius cannot stipulate what the particular task should be, for he does not share the appropriate pathos.

The specific content of what should be "repeated" throughout a lifetime of love for God and neighbor is supplied by the voices who are explicitly aspiring to be Christian. As we shall see, in different ways they make it clear that love for God and neighbor is the substance of the ideal self that we should seek to actualize. In a way, Kierkegaard is echoing the ancient conviction shared by Augustine that the Christian life is most basically a growth in likeness to God's moral attributes, particularly love. Because human beings are created in God's image *(Billede),* they have God for a prototype *(Forbillede)* and must grow in resemblance to God (*CD*, 41). Identifying the prototype not just as Christ but as God, Kierkegaard says that the "prototype exists before the lowly Christian, and he before his prototype — he can continually grow to resemble it more and more . . ." (*CD*, 42). In his early journals Kierkegaard even speaks of "growing" into the divine through "something which is bound up with the deepest roots of my existence" (*KJN* 1, pp. 20-21). In an upbuilding discourse he overtly speaks of being "transfigured into God," and he explains that life's "victory" is to "reflect the image of God" (*EUD*, 400). When Augustine emphasizes the way the pilgrim would come to be the imprint of God and resemble God, he is sounding the same note.

An analogue to the interpretive controversy concerning Augustine's

---

41. See John J. Davenport and Anthony Rudd, eds., *Kierkegaard after MacIntyre: Essays on Freedom, Narrative, and Virtue* (Chicago: Open Court, 2001).

use of the journey motif has developed concerning Kierkegaard's use of the same trope. According to some interpreters, the "journey" image seems to suggest a knowable starting point and a basic directionality that determines what the destination must be, and even what the intermediate segments of the journey must be. Some of Kierkegaard's remarks (or those of his pseudonyms) have been seized on as evidence to prove that he based some of his writings on an analysis of the teleological dynamics of human life that was conceptually independent of Christian teachings and logically prior to them.[42] According to this view, he formulated a kind of freestanding philosophical anthropology that served as a conceptual foundation for his variegated literature. Kierkegaard's statements (or, rather, those of his pseudonyms) about the nature of the human self — particularly Anti-Climacus's celebrated definition "the self is a relation that relates itself to itself or is the relation's relating itself to itself in the relation" (*SUD*, 13) — have been either praised or condemned (depending on the interpreter's particular theological orientation) as part of Kierkegaard's project to formulate a philosophical anthropology that could then be used to reinterpret basic Christian doctrines. For those who are in sympathy with this effort, Kierkegaard was entirely justified in showing how Christian claims about human nature must be reconceptualized in order to render them intelligible and plausible to modern people. The journey to selfhood, complete with dialectical transitions and contact points between the divine and the human, was an apt framework for reinterpreting the basic message of Christianity.[43] Those who are hostile to such an endeavor criticize Kierkegaard for squeezing Christianity into an alien anthropological framework and thereby grossly distorting it.[44] For still others, the Christian motifs are detachable and unnecessary pious addenda that can be purged in order to uncover a purely areligious view of the self.[45] In all of these assessments, Kierkegaard's con-

42. See Mark C. Taylor, *Kierkegaard's Pseudonymous Authorship: A Study of Time and the Self* (Princeton, NJ: Princeton University Press, 1975); see also John Elrod, *Being and Existence in Kierkegaard's Pseudonymous Works* (Princeton, NJ: Princeton University Press, 1975).

43. See Emil Brunner, *Man in Revolt: A Christian Anthropology*, trans. Olive Wyon (London: Lutterworth Press, 1939); see also Louis Pojman, *The Logic of Subjectivity* (University, AL: University of Alabama Press, 1984).

44. See Karl Barth, "A Thank You and A Bow: Kierkegaard's Reveille," trans. Martin Rumscheidt, *Canadian Journal of Theology* 11 (1965): 3-7; see also Karl Barth, *Church Dogmatics*, trans. and ed. G. W. Bromiley and Thomas Torrance (Edinburgh: T&T Clark, 1957-75), IV/1, p. 741.

45. This is essentially what Martin Heidegger did in *Being and Time*, trans. John Macquarrie and Edward Robinson (New York: Harper and Row, 1962).

cept of "journey" is seen as having at least some extra-Christian roots in Romanticism and/or speculative idealism, just as Augustine's concept did in Neo-Platonism. Needless to say, this contention has sparked the rise of a countervailing interpretive tradition that claims that Kierkegaard's use of the journey metaphor is a legitimate articulation of themes embedded in the depth grammar of Christianity, relatively undistorted by the conceptions he used to express them.[46]

Interpreters who adopt the interpretive view that Kierkegaard developed a foundational anthropology — as well as those who oppose or qualify it — usually argue about the role that the celebrated schema of "the stages of life" *(Stadier)* plays in his writings. This, of course, has been taken to be his archetypal depiction of the journey to selfhood, and thus would be the core to his anthropological theory, if he has one. This proposal has a certain prima facie plausibility. After all, many of the pseudonyms refer to the various stages of life, and many of the pseudonyms seem to instantiate a specific stage in their own writings. For example, Johannes the Seducer appears to be a perfect exemplar of reflective aestheticism, while Judge William seems to be a paragon of the ethical stage. Given all this, a popular interpretive tradition maintains that Kierkegaard's considered view was that life should necessarily progress through a series of stages in a specific sequence toward a goal that was implicit in the beginning of the process.[47] According to many versions of this view, each stage is riddled with inner tensions and disappointments that almost inevitably propel the individuals inhabiting it into the next more fulfilling stage of life. It is claimed that this new stage is also fraught with internal contradictions, motivating a further movement, and so the developmental journey proceeds. An individual's life should exhibit a predictable advance from less satisfying to more satisfying stages of existence, until the structural tensions in the self are happily resolved. In effect, according to this view, Kierkegaard had appropriated the dialectical schema of Hegel and transposed it from world history to the life of the individual. Perhaps Kierkegaard was as indebted to Hegel as Augustine was (allegedly) to Plotinus.

Several questions concerning what Kierkegaard meant by "stages" surface in this discussion. Some theologians take them to be necessary de-

---

46. See David J. Gouwens, *Kierkegaard as Religious Thinker* (Cambridge: Cambridge University Press, 1996); Arnold B. Come, *Kierkegaard as Theologian: Recovering Myself* (Cambridge: Cambridge University Press, 1996).

47. See Taylor, *Kierkegaard's Pseudonymous Authorship;* see also Elrod, *Being and Existence.*

velopment phases through which every individual must progress. Others take them to be loosely defined "spheres" or ways of life, each one governed by its own internal sets of passions, assumptions, and values, which are not necessarily sequential. Because they provide the basic frameworks for thinking and feeling, they are not amenable to any sort of external critique or evaluation. No transcendent standpoint exists beyond them that would make possible an analysis of their interrelationships and respective merits. Some commentators take them to be nothing more than abstractions of characteristics that are combined in motley ways in the actual lives of individuals. Some see them as aspects or dimensions of life that can be integrated in complex patterns. Obviously, the way the "stages" are interpreted has a great deal to do with how Kierkegaard's metaphor of life as a journey is understood. In order to better appreciate Kierkegaard's use of the journey theme, and to grasp the ways his understanding of the journey resembles Augustine's view, we must take a close look at the stages and Kierkegaard's purposes in depicting them.

In general, Kierkegaard is not trying to provide the reader with a conceptually intriguing, empirically plausible, and intellectually satisfying theory of human development. Rather, he is attempting to awaken in the reader the ability to feel the possible delights, satisfactions, anxieties, and despairs that are resident in particular strategies for pursuing happiness that could be expanded into comprehensive ways of life. Kierkegaard does not just describe these ways of life; rather, he displays the pathos that animates them through his various personae. He implicitly invites the reader to imaginatively inhabit these patterned ways of thinking, feeling, and acting, and to explore their attractions and liabilities.

In the first stage that Kierkegaard dramatizes, the aesthetic stage, the individual's life is dominated by the quest to satisfy the momentary desires that just happen to arise in the life of the individual. The texts that present this view of the aesthetic life are primarily found in *Either/Or*, Part I, edited by the pseudonymous Victor Eremita, or "the victorious hermit." Kierkegaard's construction of this editor is significant. Victor, who exhibits a deeply voyeuristic streak, purports to have purchased an antique cabinet on a whim, accidentally discovered a mysterious drawer, and retrieved from it a collection of randomly arranged papers. The papers seem to have belonged to two different men, designated A and B: B's prolix papers are essay-length letters to A. The literary device of the accidental discovery of a hodgepodge of documents sets the stage and proper tone for this exploration of psychic arbitrariness and lack of integration. Moreover, Victor's pleasure in merely observing the passional existence of other individuals enacts a dynamic that manifests itself in the pages of A. These structural features of the text can all be seen as characteristics of the aesthetic life itself. Furthermore, A's papers oscillate erratically between different genres and styles, with no evident literary coherence or thematic development. Some of the individual pieces are themselves a welter of discordant moods. The reader is lured by the evocative language to imaginatively feel pleasure, boredom, ennui, anticipation, titillation, and even despair, all in seemingly random succession. This literary strategy not only illustrates a feature of the aesthetic life, but it encourages the reader to feel it.

In the jumble of essays, memories, and aphorisms, the aesthete's energies are directed toward momentarily attractive objects. Inevitably, however, the desire, the satisfaction, and the object all pass away. The possession (and often consumption) of the desired object produces satiation and boredom. Despite these liabilities, in *Either/Or* the pursuit of these ephemeral pleasures is accorded an absolute value by the aesthete. However, the sensitive reader begins to fear that these delights and titillations cannot ultimately bear such a heavy load of significance. Of course, neither Kierkegaard nor Victor articulates this suspicion directly, but the author drops enough hints so that the reader could, if the reader is invested in the book, notice unsettling tensions in the aesthetic life. (In *Either/Or*, Part II, Judge William will indeed develop these suspicions into many forceful arguments that explicitly critique the aesthetic life, but the reader will be given the responsibility of evaluating the Judge's very perspectival contentions.) For example, much of the satisfaction is due to the self-congratulatory sense of having gotten one's own way and being in control of a situation; but much of the thrill is due to the element of being surprised by an unanticipated pleasure. Consequently, aesthetic satisfaction would seem to require the paradoxical conjunction of being in control and not being in control of one's environment. Moreover, the attention to external circumstances suggests that the immediate aesthetic life is governed to a large extent by necessity or chance, and determined by forces beyond the reach of the individual's influence. In his mood oscillations, the author A demonstrates how he is at the mercy of his own internal fancies and drives, and is also dependent on opportunities for satisfaction that may or may not materialize. It is beyond the individual's power to guarantee that all the factors will always be present that are necessary to ensure gratification. That vulnerability undermines the aesthete's desire to be free of the pain of anxiety.

The prospect of being frustrated if the desire is not satisfied, and of being bored if it is, coupled with the fear of being buffeted by internal and external forces, could move the individual to pursue a more "reflective" form of aestheticism. This way of life is still determined by the satisfaction of desire, manifesting significant continuity with the "immediate" form, but now those desires are intentionally cultivated. The nurturing of sophisticated taste displaces the gratification of purely instinctive urges. Assessing one's current situation, imagining future possibilities, and planning future outcomes become more and more crucial as the reflectively aesthetic life progresses. The movement from the immediate to the reflective aesthetic life is the transition, often by degrees, from spontaneous and immediate episodes of satisfaction to a highly deliberate policy of pursuing enjoyment and planning for it. In this more self-conscious way of life, the individual devises interesting situations, often manipulating others, in order to trigger the desired reactions and passions in the individual's own psyche. The focus shifts from flitting from object to object of the same type to persuading one's own self to be interested in a variety of objects. After a while, the prospect of acquiring yet more objects of the same variety is no longer exhilarating to the veteran collector; the whole project of collecting familiar kinds of objects has become boring. When that state has been reached, it is time to develop a new interest. In extreme cases, an individual might arbitrarily decide to take an interest in seemingly trivial aspects of his environment, like making a hobby of watching the sweat drip off the nose of a boring conversation partner (*EO* 1, 299). In other cases the individual might set out to dominate and direct the emotions of another human being. Such strategies are intended to give the individual more control over the objects of desire. Other people are considered only insofar as they can make the individual's life more pleasurable or more interesting. In an extreme form of reflective aestheticism, the source of delight is the complexity of the individual's own exquisitely refined emotional life. Individuals voyeuristically enjoy observing their own infatuations, anxieties, titillations, and satisfactions. Such a strategy offers the most independence from external circumstances and the vagaries of fortune. This posture, of course, requires transforming oneself into an object of one's own fascinated gaze.

An attentive reader could conclude that reflective aestheticism, like its more immediate precursor, is also contaminated with internal tensions. On the one hand, the nagging consciousness that the thrill is at least partly self-generated militates against the spontaneity that is part and parcel of true pleasure. The effort to force oneself to take an arbitrary interest in whatever happens to be at hand destroys the surprise that pleasure requires. On the other hand, the realization that some external thing or event, even something as inconsequential as sweat patterns, must initially spark the individual's fancy signals that independence from outside factors is far from absolute in this way of life. Moreover, in this reflective stage there are no guarantees that the project of engineering interesting situations or taking interest in trivia will not itself become tiresome and end in the ennui and despair that it sought to avoid.

The similarities of this portrayal of the aesthetic life to Augustine's depiction of the dispersal of the self in the multifarious attractions of the temporal world are obvious. In almost all of his writings Augustine exposes the disappointing and self-defeating features of the life of vulgar materiality. Augustine's remark that "we are powerfully influenced by the feel of things agreeable" suggests the spontaneous attraction typical of the immediate aesthetic life.[48] His conclusion that he stole some pears that he did not really want simply in order to feel the thrill of autonomous power points to an important dimension of the reflective aesthetic life: the desire for control.[49] Furthermore, Augustine's policy of attending theatrical performances in order to be moved to tears was a fairly sophisticated form of reflective aestheticism.[50] The frustrations and disappointments with the diverse types of temporal goods that Augustine had explicitly analyzed are implicitly enacted in Kierkegaard's *Either/Or* and *Stages on Life's Way*. Whereas Augustine had directly said that the life of pleasure leads to psychic disintegration and the loss of purpose and meaning, Kierkegaard shows it.

The second major "stage" in Kierkegaard's pseudonymous literature, the "ethical," is governed by the concept "duty." Devotion to one's duty stabilizes and unifies the fluctuating and dispersed energies of the individual. The pseudonymous author B, or "Judge William," epitomizes not only the life of duty but also the conviction that romantic love can be transmuted into marital commitment and thereby perfected. Here a commitment to do one's duty focuses the self and preserves what was valuable in the life of immediate desire. The free choice to be faithful to the beloved is implicitly an even more momentous decision to live according to the conviction that one's life is one's own responsibility, for which one can be held accountable. The aesthete construes life as an opportunity to pursue a cornucopia of potential enjoyments, but the ethical individual conceives life as a purposeful

48. Augustine, *Confessions,* II, 5 (10), in *WSA* I, 1.
49. Augustine, *Confessions,* II, 6 (14), in *WSA* I, 1.
50. Augustine, *Confessions,* III, 2 (4), in *WSA* I, 1.

task. The individual collects herself from the host of existential possibilities, assumes responsibility for the future direction of her own life, and commits herself to the ongoing actualization of a specific ideal form of life, complete with specific roles, expectations, and obligations.

By such resolution, if it is persistently carried out, the individual achieves concrete definition and permanence. An ideal self-exemplifying fidelity and devotion is posited as the self to be actualized in daily life. An external norm, voluntarily accepted, commands the individual to act dutifully even if passing inclinations suggest otherwise. The requirement to do one's duty not only in one instance but in all instances unifies the disparate episodes of the individual's life, giving it continuity. In this way ethical resolution and decisiveness overcome the flux of passing moods and wayward fancies. Devotion to duty triumphs over the uncontrollable and inconstant external and internal forces that buffet the individual and pull her in divergent directions. Duty can promise an attractive permanence of character, something that the aesthetic life simply cannot secure. Accordingly, Judge William lauds the life of marital duty as the only way to preserve love, by protecting love from the fickleness of immediate desire and the corrosiveness of time (*EO* 2, 22, 138). By so doing, marriage actually fulfills the hopes of romantic love by giving it a developmental history that provides a context for the exploration and discovery of new sources of delight in the relationship with the beloved. According to Judge William, duty is not an external heteronymous imperative, for it only commands what the lovers themselves desire. Moreover, the transmutation of the individual's life into a publicly shared ideal makes it transparent; the community can interpret and sympathetically understand the judge's life, correctly concluding that he is aspiring to be a dutiful husband. The tensions between inclination and duty, freedom and necessity, the private and the public, and the inner and the outer are resolved, according to the judge. The commitment to actualize some goal for the self (like preserving romantic love) requires the cultivation of certain virtues and the assumption of responsibility for becoming the sort of person one should be. This self-chosen task serves to integrate the self and gives it a unifying direction.

Here a loose and partial parallel with Augustine's youthful enthusiasm for Cicero can be detected. Although Augustine certainly did not report any expectation like Judge William's that the life of civic or marital duty would give direction and unity to his life, he did hope that the pursuit of wisdom would give his life coherence. The pursuit of wisdom would enable Augustine to prioritize less than ultimate earthly goods, analogously to the way duty gave form and order to the judge's desires. According to Cicero, the pursuit of wisdom does allow everything of genuine value in the penultimate goods to be preserved, just as the joys of romance were preserved in marriage, according to the judge. As Augustine also learned from Cicero, the self then becomes less conflicted and more serene. The desire for self-integration, and a discontent with the instability and waywardness of the pursuit of pleasure as an ultimate end, were operative for both the youthful Augustine and for Judge William.

Careful readers, having the requisite seriousness about the quality of their own lives, could conclude that the ethical stage also may not be free of inner contradictions. First, it makes a promise that it cannot deliver. It claims to be able to preserve romance, and to nurture romance through its inevitable periods of diminishing excitement. However, duty, by itself, cannot reignite the embers of a passion that are truly dying. Duty is portrayed by Judge William as the regulator and protector of inclination; however, duty is powerless to revitalize waning inclination.[51] Because even a duty-informed inclination remains somewhat at the mercy of forces outside the individual's control, and the ethical life fails to achieve the kind of "equilibrium" that the judge had so desired in regard to his own marriage. Second, the ethical life is sabotaged by the phenomenon of moral dissatisfaction with one's own performance. No provision is made within the life of sheer duty for the inevitable failures to perfectly perform one's duties, and no strategy is available to deal with the consequent experience of guilt. Third, Judge William assumes that individuals are capable of summoning enough willpower to decide to become responsible persons. However, the individuals who have spent their lives in the aesthetic sphere have no history of making such commitments. There is no reason to suppose that they could suddenly begin to exercise their volitional capacities. Of course, the judge does not point out any of these possible liabilities in the ethical life. But sensitive readers of the judge's pages might detect such flaws and begin to suspect that the ethical life will not fully satisfy the longings of the human heart. Similarly, Augustine had famously discovered that his own project of self-integration through philosophy floundered on his own affective waywardness, his guilt, and his volitional incapacity.

Kierkegaard, using the pseudonym Johannes Climacus, outlines a third stage, the religious. As Climacus describes it, this stage is a kind of natural

51. See George Connell, *To Be One Thing: Personal Unity in Kierkegaard's Thought* (Macon, GA: Mercer University Press, 1985).

and generic religiosity that individuals can strive to actualize. This "religiousness A" is an "immanent" form of the religious life, meaning that it is a permanent possibility of the human spirit, rooted in capacities that are inherent in human nature. The ordinary experience of life can evoke and motivate this religiosity; it does not require special doctrinal teachings, a unique revelation, or the initiative of divine agency. "Religiousness A" has important ties to the ethical stage, for it continues to emphasize the individual's life as a task. The difference is that now this task is no longer conceived primarily as the enactment of duties rooted in social roles and interpersonal relationships. Rather, the task is to appropriate an eternal happiness that transcends all such societal factors (*CUP* I, 301-60). Climacus's teleological view of human nature articulated here loosely borrows from Aristotle, but more closely parallels Augustine (*CUP* I, 313). For Climacus, the actualization of the possibility of attaining an eternal happiness is both our *telos* and our duty, for God intends us to become persons characterized by certain passions and virtues. As Climacus declares in his description of the "initial," "essential," and "decisive" expressions of "existential pathos," and in his account of "religiousness A," the commitment to orient one's life absolutely to the absolute good, and only relatively to relative goods, is the determinative feature of this way of life (*CUP* I, 387-561). Because of this relationship to the "absolute," this stage involves the willingness to renounce, if necessary, immediate forms of happiness. The absolute is not just one more desirable good that could be used to supplement other goods, as if they were all logically on a par.

In fact, the willingness to surrender penultimate goods for the sake of the absolute good is one of the major hallmarks of a genuine relationship to the absolute. Even though this orientation toward the absolute does not demand the immediate renunciation of all of life's ordinary joys and satisfactions, the individual must be prepared to give them up if such a sacrifice is required by fidelity to the absolute. This form of religiousness is not a Manichean rejection of finitude and temporality as such. However, a conflict between the absolute good and relative goods is always a possibility, and the individual must be passionally prepared for it. (Similarly, the "infinite resignation" described by de Silentio in *Fear and Trembling* is an inner disposition that everyone should cultivate, even if life does not actually force a particular individual to choose between the highest good and lesser goods.)

Such resignation was no stranger to Augustine. As we have seen, Augustine had warned of the danger of turning toward "the lowest kind of goods" with "immoderate desire," and turning away from "the better and higher."[52] Augustine had learned the lesson of resignation from his reading of Cicero, and it was further reinforced by his study of Plotinus. Even the Manichees, in their exaggerated antimateriality zeal, had agreed that the pursuit of salvation required detachment from concern for earthly goods. But most importantly, Augustine had discerned the call to adopt a posture of resignation in the pages of the Old Testament and had discovered that it is writ large in the story of Jesus. From personal experience, Augustine realized how important — and how arduous — this resignation is. By emphasizing this theme of resignation, Climacus was expressing a conviction deeply engrained in Augustine and the traditions from which he drew.

Climacus says that, because this detachment from immediacy is often painful to achieve, the religious life necessarily involves the twin afflictions of suffering, a "dying to immediacy," and also guilt. The commitment to the absolute will always occur in a context in which the self is already entangled in powerful attachments to lesser goods, and extrication from those entanglements will be difficult. There is an initial and continuing disparity between the way the self is and the way it should be. Part of this suffering is the recognition of the individual's limitations and pathetically wavering will. Furthermore, because it is difficult to subordinate relative goods to the absolute good, guilt will inevitably be felt over not having accomplished this subordination earlier or more thoroughly. Climacus insists that even by attempting to exonerate themselves with regard to specific acts, individuals demonstrate that at some level they experience themselves as having failed to enact the ideal perfectly. As we have observed, the suffering and guilt caused by the difficulty of relating absolutely to the absolute are fundamental motifs running throughout Augustine's *Confessions*. Once again, Climacus and Augustine seem to be running on parallel tracks.

Toward the very end of *Concluding Unscientific Postscript*, Climacus posits one more way of life beyond "religiousness A." "Religiousness B" in Climacus's text is a description of Christianity that emphasizes its marked differences from other forms of religiosity. The decision to enter this Christian stage could be inspired by the disturbing contradictions that the reader can detect within generic spirituality. The most troubling feature of "religiousness A" is the tension between the requirement to surrender everything to the absolute and the resolution to keep striving to do so. The continued striving to surrender makes it seem like the struggle is the individual's own act. Viewed in a certain way, religiousness A could

52. Augustine, *Confessions*, II, 5 (10), in *WSA* I, 1.

be seen as an oxymoronic project of actively trying to embrace passivity. The perceived frustration of attempting to surrender oneself to the absolute through an assertion of will power could foster in a sensitive reader a readiness to consider the alternative of Christianity. As over against generic religiosity, Christianity proclaims the message that eternal blessedness is a gift of grace rather than an accomplishment for which the individual can take credit. This message is a very singular claim about God's surprising attitudes, actions, and purposes that could not be extrapolated from the ordinary experiences of life or discovered in the depths of the soul. In fact, the claim that God is extravagantly gracious is profoundly counterintuitive, even offensive, to ordinary notions of human responsibility and self-worth. Consequently, such a message, which Climacus calls the "dialectical" element in Christianity, would have to be based on transcendent authority — in other words, on a supposed revelation. A reader who has imaginatively internalized the tensions within religiousness A could find this to be good news indeed. Climacus introduces the possibility of forgiveness and unmerited fellowship with God, a prospect that could appeal to a spiritual pilgrim weighed down by guilt and despair. (Alternatively, a reader could well be offended by the disparagement of the efficacy and value of human agency.) In just this way, the travails and failures of a long history of attempts at self-salvation propelled Augustine to the confession that he desperately needed divine forgiveness and help. Kierkegaard's contrast of religiousness A and religiousness B in part paralleled Augustine's differentiation of his own piety from that of Pelagius.

According to Kierkegaard, belief in the Christian claims about salvation necessarily involves the acquisition of a new set of very distinctive passions. Climacus's hypothetical question "What if subjectivity is untruth?" (a question that introduces the discussion of religiousness B) does not suggest that genuine subjectivity or pathos is not a factor in religiousness B. It is not as if Christianity replaces existential earnestness with insouciance about the spiritual health of the self or a dispassionate affirmation of doctrinal propositions. Rather, religiousness B continues to assume an intense concern about the quality and direction of the individual's own life, and in this sense subjectivity continues to be "true." But now that concern is given a new modulation by the specific teachings of a historic religious tradition. One of those central teachings is that the potency of an individual's religious passion is not sufficient by itself to produce eternal happiness. The strength or quality of a person's religious feelings will not save him. At most, all that the individual can attain through his own efforts is the infinitely negative disposition of Socratic irony. Subjectivity is "untruth" in the sense that individuals must not congratulate themselves about the persistence and intensity with which they have pursued their journeys. Such self-referential pride would actually show that they were not engrossed with God at all. To people who acknowledge their own incapacity to make progress on life's journey, the news that God has graciously forgiven and empowered them could, if taken with utmost earnestness, catalyze an entirely new range of passions.

Climacus observes that in religiousness B "the dialectical is decisive only insofar as it is joined together with the pathos-filled and gives rise to a new pathos" (*CUP* I, 555). Oddly, accepting the claim that subjectivity is untruth generates a new, more truthful kind of subjectivity. This new pathos includes trust in God, gratitude to God, resting on God, and hoping in God. Moreover, it also involves a qualification and specification of the eternal happiness at which the individual has been aiming (*CUP* I, 556). The *telos* of the journey is redefined as something more than "inward deepening" and other than the discovery of the eternal within the self (*CUP* I, 570-73). Our desired home is not the Neo-Platonic interior space whose inadequacy Augustine had discovered. Climacus, who is a humorist, can only gesture toward this redefined goal, for it would take a practicing Christian to manifest the pathos necessary for any meaningful talk about the particular characteristics of the journey's end. (We shall consider this specification of the journey's *telos* in the next chapters.) Even with this limitation, Climacus can imagine enough about the Christian life to agree with Augustine's conviction that true faith involves a new and transformed set of passions, dispositions, and virtues. As Augustine had said, refocusing attention on the revelation of God in Christ necessarily involves the development of a new kind of love and a new humility.[53]

It must be pointed out that the possible attractiveness of the Christian life is not simply due to the fact that it promises to satisfy an existential need for self-integration. The motivations to strive for the Christian life are not reducible to the desire to overcome fragmentation and disintegration. If that were the case, Kierkegaard's portrayal of progress on life's way would have been reducible to a Kantian passion for self-integrity, and would not have resembled Augustine's journey of love very much at all. However, for Kierkegaard the Christian life has a positive allure that goes well beyond the prospect of becoming a cohesive, perduring self, and even beyond the promise of the forgiveness of sins. The restless heart is not only motivated

---

53. Augustine, *Confessions*, VII, 20 (26), in *WSA* I, 1.

negatively by a discomfort but is also inspired positively by a desirable good. Traces of Augustine's yearning for something ultimately desirable beyond the self can be detected throughout Kierkegaard's writings, including *Concluding Unscientific Postscript*. What exactly that attractiveness is Climacus cannot really articulate, for he has not embraced Christianity. As we shall see, in other contexts and for other purposes Kierkegaard will display the joy and beauty of the journey's destination.

According to one prevalent understanding of the stages, the inherent passional contradictions within each stage produce such nagging disquietudes that they almost necessitate the individual's adoption of a higher stage. For example, it has often been claimed that Kierkegaard was suggesting that the frustrations of the aesthetic life, once they become conscious, should under ordinary circumstances catalyze the movement into the ethical life, the next stage in the standard progression. Surely, in this reading of Kierkegaard, any individual who understands the liabilities of the aesthetic life would want to adopt the ethical life. Similarly, the recognition of the unresolved discontents experienced in the ethical stage should propel the individual into the religious stage. To continue the dialectical progression, once individuals recognize the tensions that plague the generic religious life, they should be sufficiently motivated to advance toward the final destination, Christianity. Consequently, any person of moderate perspicacity and a healthy desire for happiness must recognize that only Christianity can secure the ultimate felicity that the lower stages had vainly sought but could not actually attain.

If this is true, Kierkegaard was surreptitiously transposing the necessary dialectical movement that Hegel detected in world history into the life of the individual.[54] Of course, interpreters who would argue that usually add the caveat that, for Kierkegaard, the transition from stage to stage is not strictly necessary and does require a free, intentional decision by the individual. Nevertheless, the impression given is that anyone who understands the dynamics of human nature, and recognizes the emotional discomforts to which each stage leads, would certainly not only long to advance to a higher stage but would also resolve to do so. In this view, Kierkegaard was developing an argument to demonstrate that the natural *telos* of human existence is the Christian life, and that a candid examination of human nature can show that this is indeed the case. If this interpretation is correct,

---

54. See Stephen Dunning, *Kierkegaard's Dialectic of Inwardness: A Structural Analysis of the Theory of the Stages* (Princeton, NJ: Princeton University Press, 1985).

Kierkegaard was implicitly suggesting that a compelling objective apologetic for Christianity can be developed on the basis of an analysis of the fundamental dynamics of human nature.[55] The preferability of Christianity over other ways of life could be corroborated by an appeal to a foundational anthropology. Some commentators claim to have found support for this developmental, almost necessity-driven schema of the stages in "A Glance at a Contemporary Effort in Danish Literature," Climacus's survey of Kierkegaard's pseudonymous and veronymous writings (*CUP* I, 251-300).

This fairly common interpretation of Kierkegaard's stages does draw attention to many genuine dynamics in his texts, but it can give a misleading impression. Kierkegaard does write in such a way that readers are encouraged to imaginatively experience the unsatisfying nature of the conflicts and tensions that arise within certain ways of life. Surely he does want readers to feel the attractiveness of Christianity (as well as its offensiveness). Surely he does encourage readers to consider the possibility that Christianity might be able to provide a kind of satisfaction and joy that other ways of life cannot. But the impression of a lockstep dialectical movement from stage to stage in an invariant sequence is supported only by the occasional remarks of a few of Kierkegaard's pseudonymous authors. The notion of an exact sequence of "stages" or "ways of life" that can lead to Christianity is not an integral component of Kierkegaard's edifying and Christian writings — and is utterly absent in many of them. Kierkegaard uses the concept "life view" more frequently than "stage" in his literature as a whole, and he uses it in looser and more mutable ways. The "theory of the stages" in its robust form is articulated by personae like Climacus, who themselves are hardly neutral analysts of human life. The pseudonymous writers interpret the actions and passions of the individual from their own particular vantage points, and they are swayed by their own interests. Even "A Glance at a Contemporary Effort in Danish Literature," which seems to support the view of the stages as a necessary developmental pattern, is only the way that Kierkegaard's assortment of writings looks to Climacus, who is clearly not a purely objective interpreter of these texts. Interestingly, even Climacus himself confesses that his understanding of the corpus is only that of one reader (*CUP* I, 252).

The stages themselves cannot be reduced to univocal, simple definitions; rather, their depictions differ from book to book in Kierkegaard's corpus, according to his particular authorial purposes. For example, the

---

55. See Pojman, *The Logic of Subjectivity.*

aesthetic life sometimes seems to be characterized by immediate impulse gratification, sometimes by social conformity, sometimes by thoughtless habits, sometimes by reflective abstraction, and sometimes by poetic volatilization. Sometimes the ethical stage sounds like conformity to social mores, sometimes like obedience to universalizable moral imperatives, sometimes like the pursuit of the human good embedded in our nature, and sometimes like a combination of all of them. The ethical stage can sound Hegelian, Kantian, or Aristotelian, depending on the context. Even within the very same volume, the presentation of what is usually taken to be a "stage" can vary widely, as is evident in the shifting depictions of the aesthetic life in *Either/Or*. It is unconvincing to attempt to harmonize the variety by claiming that the different pictures of the aesthetic life are simply different stages-within-stages, which themselves allegedly exhibit a dialectical pattern of development from lower to higher forms. Moreover, Kierkegaard's various texts often fail to portray "pure" examples of a stage; rather, features variously associated with the aesthetic, ethical, and religious stages appear to be interwoven in his depictions of specific characters. To further problematize the theory of the stages, it is notoriously difficult to apply the schema to Kierkegaard's upbuilding discourses. In some respects, many of the discourses seem to be examples of Religiousness A; in other respects, however, they seem to be decidedly Christian. In other discourses the ethical and the religious spheres tend to bleed into each other, as they do frequently in Kierkegaard's writings. Obviously, whatever the stages are, they are not ways of life that are hermetically sealed off from one another. This feature of Kierkegaard's work reflects the way Cicero's eclectic Stoicism merges into Plotinus's Platonism and the boundary between a kind of pious Neo-Platonism and Christianity tends to be very porous in Augustine's writings.

Furthermore, Kierkegaard does not reduce the journey to the Christian goal to a single highly standardized pattern. His pages resist the temptation to construe the individuals' pilgrimage as a prescribed dialectical movement through a series of necessary stages. Kierkegaard's corpus as a whole does not consistently depict an invariant, monolithic sequential movement from stage to stage. In *Two Ages*, for example, Kierkegaard describes the lives of two women who live in very different cultural circumstances, both of whom evolve from the romantic love associated with the aesthetic life, through disappointment in their love lives, to a resignation that closely approximates a kind of religiosity (*TA*, 14-20). Neither woman passes through an ethical phase, and neither makes a dramatic decision to live according to the dictates of civic duty. Guilt and moral failure seem to play no role in their development at all. Moreover, neither one embraces a complete resignation in which she abandons all expectation of earthly happiness; nor does either one develop a trust that with God all things are possible. In fact, neither woman deliberately adopts a way of life as an intentional policy in the way that Judge William had; each one's attitude toward existence appears to arise naturally and spontaneously. Instead, an intensification and concentration of romantic passion seem to lead both of them to a kind of qualified, hopeful resignation that shares some important characteristics with the religious life. Kierkegaard describes this disposition toward life as a form of aesthetic existence that is "on the boundary of the religious" (*TA*, 14-20).[56]

Such departures from the expected pattern — and even the depiction of life views that do not exactly match the standard stages — are frequent in Kierkegaard's works. Augustine, too, had recognized the legitimacy of a variety of different paths to genuine faith, for his narratives of the spiritual development of his various friends do not exactly match his own. Moreover, he certainly never insisted that a Ciceronian or Neo-Platonic phase of philosophic detachment must precede the Christian life in all instances.

In Kierkegaard's writings, as in Augustine's, the paths to faith are multiple and idiosyncratic. Their particularity cannot be circumscribed by any single pattern. The twists and turns of all the ways that human lives can spiritually develop cannot be predicted in advance. The human odysseys that emerge in Kierkegaard's pages are too messy and variegated to be categorized so neatly. Similarly, the ways in which people can lose their paths on life's journey are legion and often unprecedented. No Hegel-like structural dynamic of the human spirit propels an advance through a neat, uniform sequence of stages to the goal of the Christian life. The potentially conflicting goals of desire, duty, and religiosity can be combined in a multitude of attempted syntheses, many of which are illustrated by Kierkegaard's diverse characters. He did imagine the ideal life for an individual to be a journey toward a highest happiness, but he did not see this journey as a single path with a predictable progression.

In fact, an even more weighty consideration prevents treating Kierkegaard's presentation of the stages as if it were an argument for an anthropo-

56. See Lee C. Barrett, "Kierkegaard's *Two Ages*: An Immediate Stage on the Way to the Religious Life," in Robert Perkins, ed., *International Kierkegaard Commentary: Two Ages* (Macon, GA: Mercer University Press, 1984), pp. 53-71.

logical theory whose truth could be objectively demonstrated. If the exposure of the tensions within any given stage were so objectively convincing that it compelled any clear-headed reader to adopt the next highest stage, Kierkegaard's strategy of evoking pathos would be subverted. Climacus confesses that he seeks to encourage responsibility and risk, for only then can the pathos appropriate for the religious life blossom. Risk, of course, requires some objective uncertainty, Climacus says, "for without risk, no faith; the more risk, the more faith; the more objective reliability, the less inwardness (since inwardness is subjectivity); the less objective reliability, the deeper is the possible inwardness" (*CUP* I, 209). Climacus's sentiments are echoed throughout Kierkegaard's work in his critique of speculative philosophy's quest for certainty. The voice of Climacus can also be heard in Kierkegaard's disparagement of Grundtvig's attempt to ground the faith in the reliability of the early creeds, and in his critique of the efforts of conservative apologists to base Christianity on the supposedly demonstrable veracity of the apostolic witnesses. Kierkegaard's strategy of maximizing the reader's sense of responsibility undercuts any effort to ground life decisions in a neutral, objective description of human nature. If a reader were to embrace the religious life only because she felt that the accuracy of a particular developmental theory of human life was highly probable, that reader would be acting prudentially, not passionately. It would be nothing more than an exercise in rational self-interest to adopt the religious life if all the alternatives to it could be proven to be recipes for unhappiness. Kierkegaard was not in the business of proffering a theory of human nature whose plausibility could be dispassionately established, for Kierkegaard was not in the business of trying to encourage objective certitude of any kind. It is at this point that we can begin to detect a divergence in the trajectories of Augustine and Kierkegaard. As we shall see, Augustine did not entirely share Kierkegaard's concern to protect and even stimulate the awareness of the lack of objective guarantees that genuine faith requires.

Kierkegaard was careful to develop his writing in such a way that uncertainty and risk would be preserved for the reader. The multivalent literary quality of Kierkegaard's work leaves room for different possible responses. Perhaps readers will identify with one of the voices and conclude that one of these ways of living should be adopted — to the exclusion of others. Or perhaps readers will resonate with different recommendations made by different voices, and decide that their competing demands should be somehow harmonized and integrated. Or readers might determine that the goals implicit in these ways of life should be prioritized according to some hierarchy of value, or that one should be subsumed under another, or that they should be held in a continuous dialectical tension. Perhaps readers should take seriously the suggestion of the title *Either/Or*, that the relationship of the aesthetic life and ethical life is indeed a disjunction. Or perhaps Judge William's advice that an "equilibrium" between them should be sought is worth being heeded. Readers will be attracted to or repelled by the depiction of a particular stage only insofar as they allow their own passional capacities to be cultivated and stretched by the depiction of it. The impact of the portrayal of the stages on readers is not a function of their dialectical plausibility but of the power of that portrayal to engage the reader's imagination and stir the reader's heart. That, of course, has a great deal to do with readers' concerns and interpretive decisions. Kierkegaard throws the responsibility of deciding how to respond to the various stages on the reader. Augustine was less concerned than was Kierkegaard with encouraging anxious self-responsibility and more concerned with offering reassurance and hope that the journey's goal can be attained.

However, even though the alleged theory of the stages is not the conceptual foundation governing all of Kierkegaard's work, the stages cannot be dismissed as peripheral to his writings. For him, the stages function as ideal types that exhibit certain passional dynamics that can be found in varying degrees in most people's lives. This is evident in the fictitious editor Victor Eremita's remark that the papers attributed to the different authors A and B could, for all he knows, have been written by the same person, expressing different aspects of that person's psyche. Nevertheless, for diagnostic purposes, it is helpful to isolate specific sets of passional dynamics and look at them in unadulterated and perhaps exaggerated forms. The descriptions of the stages alert the reader to prevalent strategies for negotiating life's challenges that actual individuals really do use, even if inconsistently. The pseudonymous authors whom Kierkegaard invented do exhibit qualities that, for good or ill, reflect back to us our own characteristics and possibilities. For example, there is a crucial difference between spontaneously pursuing an immediate pleasure and resolving to do one's duty no matter what the consequences. Pleasures, if indulged in with enough frequency, do have a tendency to lose their zest; initial infatuations do tend to fade. Judge William is surely right that duty can provide some continuity and stability to at least certain swathes of a person's life.

Kierkegaard was using the conceptual device of "the stages," a concept that would resonate with the fondness of his educated audience for Hegelian themes, to draw attention to a motley range of emotional dynamics that appear in different ways in different human lives. Most importantly, Kierkegaard used this conceptual strategy to draw distinctions among various passions and concerns that he feared were being conflated in the culture of Christendom. For Kierkegaard, it remained crucial that "categories" not be confused; aesthetic considerations should be distinguished from ethical ones, and both should be differentiated from uniquely Christian categories, even if they all do interact in complex ways. Lives and episodes in a life may not be neatly categorizable as exclusively aesthetic, or ethical, or religious, or Christian; but the differences among these concepts remain in force. In a parallel way, Augustine had sought to dramatize the differences among Neo-Platonic piety, Roman civic virtue, Manichean flight from the world, and true Christian faith. Both thinkers drew distinctions in order to demarcate the uniqueness of the various life options and make room for the sui generis pathos of Christianity.

Besides clarifying the differences among various life choices, the notion of stages of life also captures something important about the Christian construal of life as a journey. The rhetoric of the stages, as well as the definition of the self as a relationship, both point to certain highly general features of any type of profound personal transformation. First, the depiction of the aesthetic life shows that an individual always begins life's journey in a state that combines varying degrees of disorientation, dispiritedness, confusion about the goal, entanglements with impeding factors, obsession with inferior goods, paralysis, and unwillingness to venture forward. Kierkegaard assumes that the developmental odyssey of the self commences in the situation of being governed by immediate urges and desires, with minimal capacity for self-evaluation. For both Kierkegaard and Augustine, this seems to be where we find ourselves as children. In short, the journey begins in some version of the aesthetic life, and the habits, attitudes, and dispositions associated with it continue to plague the wayfarer. Progress on the road necessarily involves purgation and radical transformation. Put in the more theological language favored by Augustine, the journey must include the continuing struggle of repentance, conversion, and sanctification.

Second, because of our premature overattachment to lesser goods, resignation of some kind is needed for any movement beyond the aesthetic life. Kierkegaard and Augustine are agreed that we must be prepared to surrender our overvalued lesser goods if the pursuit of the highest good requires it. Kierkegaard's many and extensive discussions of resignation are motivated by this conviction that earthly goods, no matter how cherished and worthy, must be subordinated to the need to keep traveling toward the human journey's destination. Because of this, God must be described as the highest good, the good for which we are willing to sacrifice every lesser good, a claim that Augustine also made in lauding the lives of the Christian martyrs.[57] In *Fear and Trembling*, Kierkegaard's pseudonymous Johannes de Silentio praises "the knight of infinite resignation," the young lover who relinquishes all expectation of earthly happiness in order to treasure and be faithful to the memory of the beloved princess whose love he can never possess. The lover's willingness to sacrifice everything, including the hope of enjoying an actual relationship with the princess, in order to be faithful to the memory of his beloved serves as an analogy to the religious person who is willing to renounce all earthly goods for the sake of God. Augustine would have understood and appreciated this image, including its foregrounding of love for God, as well as the contrast of the ephemeral nature of earthly loves and the eternal nature of love for God. Elaborating on this theme, de Silentio says:

> His love for the princess would become for him the expression of an eternal love, would assume a religious character, would be transfigured into a love for the eternal being, which true enough denied the fulfillment but nevertheless did reconcile him once more in the eternal consciousness of its validity in the eternal form that no actuality can take away from him. (*FT*, 43)

In the same book, a particular aspect of the shocking tale of Abraham's near sacrifice of Isaac functions as another parable of resignation. De Silentio draws attention to Abraham's willingness to sacrifice Isaac, who not only was his beloved son but was also the heir who would be the font of blessings for all future generations, in order to maintain fidelity to God as the highest priority. God is that for which the individual must be prepared to sacrifice familial ties and personal affections. Of course, this infinite resignation only becomes Christian faith when it is held in dialectical tension with the disposition to rejoice in earthly goods as gifts from God. Abraham was a "knight of faith" rather than a mere "knight of infinite resignation" because he was willing to receive Isaac back again. When it comes to renouncing earthly fulfillment, de Silentio knows what he is talking about. He describes himself as a person who can make this movement of infinite resignation, and his earnest, somber style communicates the gravity of this stance, as well as the

---

57. Augustine, *Sermons*, see sermons 330 and 331 in *WSA* III, 1-11.

"peace and rest" that is found in the pain. Here de Silentio is articulating an aspect of the detachment theme common to many of the strands of classical culture that had shaped Augustine. As we have seen, Climacus, paralleling de Silentio, elaborates the point that the willingness to subordinate all earthly happiness and aspirations to faithfulness to God inevitably involves suffering as the ordinary joys are surrendered (*CUP* I, 431-525). According to Climacus, detachment from earthly sources of satisfaction will inevitably hurt. Climacus adds that the prospect of pain in relating absolutely to the absolute good and relatively to relative goods generates reluctance to undergo the necessary suffering and consequently evokes guilt over that hesitation. These points by Kierkegaard's pseudonymous writers could be read as synopses of major portions of Augustine's *Confessions,* including the latter's admission that he had feared being exceedingly miserable if he were ever deprived of a woman's embrace.[58]

Third, the motif of resignation has yet another aspect, one that gains in intensity as Kierkegaard's writings progress: it destabilizes the idolatrous identification of God with a culture's values, even its most lofty ones. As the journey proceeds into the Christian life or other forms of religiosity, the absolute good, God, relativizes our commonly held social aspirations and norms. In the light of God's surpassing value, all our commitments to such socially beneficial goods as being a dutiful citizen, an industrious worker, an honest business person, or a conscientious parent are of secondary importance, or are only of importance insofar as they are a component of loving God. If God is more valuable than the most noble and lofty ideals of the human community at its best, then the ultimate good could be different from and even conflict with the community's most sacrosanct norms. Because of God's transcending of human *Sittlichkeit,* an exhaustive understanding of God's will could never be gleaned through a compilation of society's moral precepts and codes. God is bigger than the value system of the average bourgeois Christian. The way in which God destabilizes communal ethics is dramatically narrated in de Silentio's multiple retellings of Abraham's near sacrifice of Isaac in *Fear and Trembling.* The meaning of these cryptic reflections has been disputed by scholars perhaps more than any other aspect of Kierkegaard's work, usually in ways that reveal more about the interpreter than about the text.[59] This is probably as it should be,

---

58. Augustine, *Confessions,* VI, 11 (20), in *WSA* I, 1.

59. See John Lippitt's excellent *Routledge Philosophy Guidebook to Kierkegaard and* Fear and Trembling (London: Routledge, 2003) for an exploration of these diverse interpretations.

for the very structure of *Fear and Trembling* raises more questions than it does answers. But whatever else these passages may trigger in readers, at the very least they disrupt the facile identification of God, the destination of our journey, with the cherished norms of any human community.

De Silentio ("from silence") displays in his very demeanor a distancing from the social mores about which he writes. De Silentio exhibits passionate earnestness, wariness about breaking the profundity of silence, a suspicion of popular philosophical systems, and an idiosyncratic fascination with Abraham. All of these factors differentiate de Silentio from ordinary, socially defined human beings. By telling the story of Abraham's near sacrifice of Isaac four different ways — each one accentuating Abraham's struggle against despair — de Silentio encourages readers to identify with Abraham's disorientation and with his own perplexity about Abraham. By dramatizing the shocking character of the tale, de Silentio forces the reader to take seriously the disquieting possibility that fidelity to God could lead to behaviors that flout the most basic and deeply enshrined communal values. De Silentio keeps pointing out that Abraham's devotion to God trumps his parental obligation to preserve the life of his own child, one of society's most fundamental precepts. In the hands of de Silentio, Abraham's unsettling story becomes a vividly painful example of the "teleological suspension of the ethical," the demotion of communally defined or rationally justified ethical duties from the status of highest good (*FT,* 54). Because Abraham believed that Isaac was the child of the promise through whom all future generations were to be blessed, the story forces the reader to reexamine the relationship of devotion to God to concepts of the well-being of the human community as a whole. Of course, this theme of the "teleological suspension of the ethical" by itself could be used to justify any kind of sociopathic behavior. Given the precedent of Abraham, it would seem that a mass murderer could claim that his horrendous deeds were justified by his conviction that he had received a divine command to slaughter people. This was not Kierkegaard's intent. As we shall see, the rest of his writing output provides criteria to make discriminations about the ways in which devotion to God might legitimately put the individual at odds with social mores, as distinguished from mere criminal or deranged behavior.[60] Through this literary strategy, Kierkegaard accentuates the difference between a life oriented toward a religious *telos* and a life aimed at some culturally constructed concept of

---

60. See Gene Outka, "Religion and Moral Duty: Notes on *Fear and Trembling,*" in Outka, *Religion and Morality: A Collection of Essays* (New York: Anchor Books, 1973), pp. 204-54.

collective well-being as the highest good. One of the most painful forms of resignation that the religious life involves is the willingness to distance oneself from the collective consensus.

In a somewhat parallel way, Augustine had also come to distinguish the lesser virtues of loyalty to the polis, the basic unit of classical society, from the ultimate virtues that constitute fidelity to God. Augustine made it clear that the celestial city takes precedence over the terrestrial empire. The absolute value of our true destination, the heavenly community, trumps the securities and contentments of the earthly city. Like Kierkegaard, as Augustine matured he increasingly emphasized the vast difference between the Christianized Roman Empire (the precursor of Kierkegaard's Christendom) and the City of God. Major aspects of the classical culture that Augustine had treasured had to be jettisoned, drastically reconfigured, or relegated to a position of lesser importance. Both thinkers were agreed that our journey is not toward a city built by human hands or sustained by human power. Both were in accord that the life of civic virtue can be in tension with the Christian life, and can impede its progress. Both were also agreed that the task of relativizing the values of the ambient culture could be exceedingly arduous and painful. Whether those cultural goods are the delights of the theater, the attractions of modish philosophies, or even something more foundational, such as the consolations of married life and the comforts of a lucrative career, Augustine and Kierkegaard concurred that they had to be subordinated to the paramount task of progressing toward humanity's chief end. The homeward journey requires a willingness to relegate not only the crasser forms of satisfaction but also the higher and nobler forms to a secondary status.

To conclude this exploration of Kierkegaard's construal of life as a journey, I must emphasize that his use of a variety of literary strategies, ranging from the construction of fictional authors to the formulation of philosophical arguments and schematizations, was designed to stimulate the requisite passional movement. In order to clarify the teleological nature of human life, Kierkegaard drew on the vocabulary and thought patterns of the popular philosophical anthropologies of his day. As a result, at times his description of human life can sound Hegelian, Romantic, or even Schelling-like. These devices were intended to urge readers to reflect deeply on their existence and to consider the possibility that perhaps the human heart can only be satisfied through the life of faith, hope, and love. In his attempt to do this, Kierkegaard did not hesitate to use the concept "stages of existence," often using Hegelian language to describe them. His exposés of possible internal tensions in particular stages function to motivate readers to engage in serious self-examination and to probe their lives in order to determine whether analogous dynamics are at work in their own hearts. Kierkegaard seeks to enable readers to feel more deeply the moods, emotions, and passions that are ingredients of major existential options, and which they may already be experiencing inchoately and dimly. This clarification of the reader's own passional existence may well provide motivations for the reader to proceed to another way of life. Although such a change of a view of life is neither necessary nor inevitable, sensitive, self-reflective readers could come to feel the inadequacies in a particular way of life with such acuteness that it would foster a more intense dissatisfaction. Even though there is no neutral standpoint from which the adequacy or inadequacy of a way of life can be objectively demonstrated, the recognition of internal problems in certain strategies for happiness can intensively stimulate the restlessness of the human heart and catalyze movement.

Kierkegaard used his vast arsenal of literary strategies, including his facility in adapting philosophical schemas to his own purposes, to encourage intentionality about the direction of one's life as a whole. Because the human journey requires intentionality and conscientiousness, Kierkegaard portrays existence as an advance out of unreflective and irresponsible childhood into the spiritual adulthood of self-responsibility and decisiveness. Using a philosophical conceptuality familiar to his audience, he sometimes described this as an advance beyond immediacy into the mediation of dialectical tensions. In order to actualize its potential, the self must synthesize the temporal and the eternal, the infinite and the finite, freedom and necessity. Most famously, his pseudonymous Anti-Climacus, an advanced Christian, appropriates the seemingly arcane language about the self being "a relation that relates itself to itself," a vocabulary common in German and Danish Idealist philosophy suggesting that the life of an individual should aim at synthesizing an ideal self with the concrete characteristics of the individual, including historical location, biological endowments, social context, psychological traits, and so on (*SUD,* 13-42). In a sense, an individual is not born as a "self," but becomes a self by trying to actualize an ideal in the concrete circumstances of a particular life. The individual attains selfhood and becomes "conscious of itself as spirit" by striving to exist "before God" (*SUD,* 46, 77-79). The element of temporality captured by the "journey" motif is evident here, for to be a self requires the effort to synthesize what the individual has been in the past with what the individual aspires to be in the future. The "self" is not something that one immediately is but rather is something that one becomes through the intentional activity of assuming responsibility for the direction of one's life. The individual becomes a genuine self through the earnestness of the journey. Selfhood minimally requires that the individual at least be willing to embark on this journey. Merely ambling aimlessly through life with no direction would be the death knell of the potential self.

Even Anti-Climacus's most abstruse remarks about "the self" can be understood as goads and nudges urging readers to become increasingly earnest about their own pilgrimages. The purpose of moving the reader to deeper self-concern motivates all of Kierkegaard's esoteric theorizing about human nature. His writings can be read as an effort to stimulate the kind of self-reflection that can prepare readers for the pursuit of an eternal happiness. In doing this, his writings also consider the correlative issue of how individuals can get stuck, lost, derailed, or condemned to wander in circles. Instead of presenting the reader with an objective map of human nature and destiny, Kierkegaard prods and cajoles the reader to introspection, to observe humanity, and to make a candid evaluative judgment about the shape and direction of the reader's own life.

Conclusion

Augustine and Kierkegaard were in fundamental agreement that human beings have a restless heart that can only be satisfied by God, and that life is a search for this satisfaction. Life is indeed a journey home — or at least it should be. But the fact that we are on a journey does not stipulate in advance what the homecoming must be like. The true nature and object of the restlessness in human lives can only be diagnosed retrospectively from the vantage point of Christian faith. Knowledge of God, the true object of human restlessness, is not something that can be extrapolated simply from an analysis of the restlessness itself. In fact, it is only from the perspective of the homecoming that the nature of the prior journey can be rightly understood. Consequently, the journey motif used by Augustine and Kierkegaard does not presuppose any foundational theories of human nature detachable from the authors' religious convictions, for even the minimal claim that people are seeking some kind of fulfillment is rooted in their Christian perspective. Logically prior assumptions about the beginning and end points of the journey do not function as a master road map into which the two authors artificially forced Christian concepts and themes. Rather, Christian convictions led both Augustine and Kierkegaard to suppose that some general claims about the teleology of human nature are true.

But this is not to deny that the destination of the journey has a connection to the journey's beginning, and that this connection has some experiential consequences. Both Augustine and Kierkegaard can be read as showing how the Christian concept of salvation meshes with the basic dynamics of human life (as these can be discerned from the perspective of Christianity). The movement away from sin and toward God is simultaneously a movement away from fragmentation and toward self-integration. Admittedly, what the goal of our journey is or how to travel toward it cannot be deduced purely from an analysis of our starting point. We cannot reach the journey's goal by our own locomotion or even know exactly what the destination is like. However, that destination and the way to it are not alien to our created nature and its potentialities. Expressed in more theological terms, creation and redemption fit nicely together, even though redemption is not a mere unfolding of the possibilities latent in creation. Because of this commensurability of creation and redemption, which could also be described as a commensurability of nature and grace, Augustine and Kierkegaard assumed that the Christian message can make contact with certain fundamental aspirations intrinsic to our constitution as human beings. Put simply, the gospel does answer the restlessness of the human heart, even though that restlessness does not in itself imply the truth of the gospel or stipulate what the nature of that gospel must be. Such a conviction of the commensurability of nature and grace suggests that neither Augustine nor Kierkegaard constructed an anthropology that then came to dominate their respective theologies. Kierkegaard's elaboration of the stages and his relational language about the self no more compromised the historic convictions of Christianity than did Augustine's alleged Platonic framework. The tendencies to read Augustine as if he were a Neo-Platonist with a thin veneer of Christianity and to read Kierkegaard as if he were an existential phenomenologist with a Lutheran overlay fail to do justice to the extent to which the Christian *telos* determined the anthropological ruminations of both thinkers.[61] Both were merely searching for a vocabulary about human lives that would enable them to display the attractiveness of the Christian life (as well as its potential offensiveness) and the liabilities of non-Christian options (as well as their ostensible attractiveness). Both Augustine and Kierkegaard were engaging in a kind of passional apologetics, attempting to nurture passions that could lead readers into Christianity. To do this, they

61. See Gouwens, *Kierkegaard as Religious Thinker,* pp. 72-75.

did need to assume that human nature is such that Christianity can awaken and satisfy the deep longings that are potentially available to all persons. Such a minimalist "theory" about human nature does not mean that the understanding of the journey's beginning determines what the end must be.

Both Augustine and Kierkegaard presupposed that human beings are so constituted that transient earthly delights can never fully satisfy them. Both of them assumed that, with some coaching perhaps, individuals could come to feel the discontent with worldly joys and to experience the lure of a mysterious alternative so acutely that they would begin to strive to find that alternative. Both of them assumed that this quest would go through stages and be beset with difficulties. Those shared assumptions led both of them to foreground the venerable image of life as a journey. Most significantly, each was also quite capable of reversing the journey image so that the individual's journey to God became God's journey to the individual, as is evident in Augustine's retrospective discovery of God's governance in the seemingly contingent events in his life and in Climacus's positing of Religiousness B. As we shall see, both Augustine and Kierkegaard treated these two themes of the individual's journey to God and God's journey to the individual as two basic tropes that jointly defined the rhythm of the Christian life.

There was a difference, however, in the ways they presented and developed the journey image. Augustine tended to concentrate on the attractiveness of the destination in order to lure pilgrims forward. Kierkegaard, on the other hand, was much more intent on communicating a sense of the daunting nature of the way and the uncertainty of its viability. This concern accounts for Kierkegaard's adoption of various authorial personae and a presentation of a smorgasbord of life options. Augustine wanted to redirect desire through the power of attraction, while Kierkegaard sought to protect desire from the enervating impact of certitude and security. Augustine sought to reassure, motivate, and guide the faltering and wayward pilgrim, while Kierkegaard wanted to prevent the tranquilized pilgrim from slipping into a spiritual coma. Augustine always returned to the theme that the road leads to the beautiful homeland, while Kierkegaard typically reverted to the message that the path is long, narrow, and uncertain. For Augustine, the main enemy was the self's overattachment to worldly happiness and power, while for Kierkegaard the most pressing foe was complacency and spiritual somnolence. Therefore, Augustine's basic task was to entice and attract, while Kierkegaard's central task was to destabilize and challenge. But in both cases the general purpose was the same: to keep the pilgrim moving.

PART TWO

Signposts on the Journey:
Specific Theological Intersections
of Augustine and Kierkegaard

CHAPTER 4

God: The Attraction and Repulsion
of Boundless Love

The previous chapters have argued that certain parallel purposes and motivations of a very sweeping kind inform the works of Augustine and Kierkegaard. Both see the Christian life as animated by a desire for God and a
longing for a kind of fulfillment that only God can provide. Both regard the
possibility of developing this desire as a structural component of human
nature. Even though the flowering of this desire is a permanent possibility of the human spirit, both also wish to describe it as being elicited and
sustained by its divine object. Neither of them wants to reduce this yearning to an egocentric exercise in spiritual self-gratification. Moreover, both
construe life as a journey toward the fulfillment of this desire in God. Both
detect profound impediments, rooted in the individual's own self, to the
felicitous completion of this journey.

The resonances between Augustine and Kierkegaard are even more extensive and intensive than these highly general similarities might suggest.
Not only do the basic dynamics of their writings parallel one another, but so
do their treatments of more specific theological topics. While certain differences are obvious, on most theological issues the two thinkers often wrestle
with similar dialectical tensions and seek to resolve them in similar ways.
The following chapters will trace these parallels with regard to some of the
major dogmatic loci that have concerned Christian theologians through
the centuries. The order of these chapters, beginning with God and end-
ing with ecclesiology, follows the general sequence in which these loci have
been addressed in traditional expositions of Christian doctrine. This rather
standard order has the advantage of proceeding from themes that are more
basic to ones that are more derivative. In no way do I wish to imply that

either Augustine or Kierkegaard was a systematic theologian in the classical sense, treating Christian convictions as passion-neutral propositions and deducing theological corollaries from doctrinal premises with logical rigor. What I am suggesting is that the issues with which both authors wrestled can conveniently be grouped around the traditional loci common in the history of Christian thought.

So far in our exposition, I have treated Augustine's and Kierkegaard's views of God very abstractly. As I have noted, they both identify God as the "highest good," as the ultimate object of desire and aspiration, and as the source of eternal happiness. However, all such descriptions are purely formal, leaving the concept "God" devoid of particular content. Such formal accounts do not specify exactly what that object of desire or highest good is. All we know at this point is that, whatever God is, God is more desirable than anything else. Augustine himself raises the question of the actual nature of the ultimate object of desire in the *Confessions* after he has related the saga of the development of his love for God, asking, "So what do I love when I love my God?"[1] Nor was Kierkegaard content to leave the concept "God" at the purely functional level, as it had been by the pseudonymous authors of his early writings. As we shall see, Augustine and Kierkegaard both attempted to clarify the concept "God" by exhibiting its more concrete uses in the Christian life.

However, their strategies for accomplishing this sometimes sharply diverged, even though their goals may have remained compatible. According to some interpreters, Augustine approached the topic of God primarily as a Neo-Platonist — that is, intent on cosmological speculation. One interpretive trajectory proposes that Augustine applied this Neo-Platonic framework to the doctrine of the Trinity and gave birth to a tendency to think of God as the dynamic dialectic of unity and differentiation that finds its resolution in identity-in-difference. In this view, the true heirs of Augustine's theology would be the metaphysical ruminations of Jacob Böhme, Friedrich Schelling, and Paul Tillich, all of whom rooted the dynamic tensions of temporal existence in the inner life of God. In contrast to Augustine's alleged cosmological proclivities, Kierkegaard is sometimes construed as a noncognitivist (with respect to God) who avoided saying anything at all about the referent of the concept because to do so would make no sense. In short, Augustine has been cast as an ontologist of the highest order, and Kierkegaard as a radical antirealist. If these characterizations are accurate,

---

1. Augustine, *Confessions*, X, 7-8 (11-12), in *WSA* I, 1.

then surely the two thinkers could have very little in common concerning their respective understandings of "God."

But this dichotomization of Augustine and Kierkegaard is based on a gross exaggeration of dynamics present in their respective theologies. Augustine gives the concept "God" specificity by describing and expressing the yearnings and longings that are part of devotion to God. In these contexts, Augustine shows how the concept is properly used in striving to lead the Christian life and cultivating the pathos appropriate to it. Although Augustine often speaks of "knowing" God in these contexts, this "knowing" is not a detached observational knowledge of God, as if God were a cognizable finite object. Nor is this knowing nothing more than an ineffable mystical intuition of pure being. Rather, this kind of knowing involves specific forms of intimacy, delight in righteousness, mutual love, and interpersonal transparency.[2] When writing in this vein, Augustine's work most closely resembles Kierkegaard's self-involving elaborations of the various Christian passions.

For his part, Kierkegaard was no reductive antirealist who collapsed God-talk into the language of human subjectivity. The concept "God" for Kierkegaard was not a circumlocution for the highest ideals of humanity or a reification of human aspirations. Even when situating language about God in the context of human passions, Kierkegaard writes as if God exists beyond the individual and can act upon the individual. Whatever God is, God can be described as exercising "governance" over individual lives, feeling concern for the spiritual well-being of individuals, and actively loving individuals. Often Kierkegaard does not hesitate to make explicit assertions about the characteristics of this God, including assertions concerning God's Trinitarian nature. Consequently, Augustine's and Kierkegaard's efforts to make sense of the concept "God" cannot be neatly contrasted as a metaphysical/referential approach versus an existential/nonreferential approach. In order to better grasp the similarities and divergences in Augustine and Kierkegaard's approaches to understanding God, we must carefully explore the particularities of the rhetorical and pastoral dimensions of their writings about the transcendent source and goal of human yearning.

2. Augustine, *The Trinity*, IX, prologue and 1.1-8, in *WSA* I, 5.

Augustine's Trinitarian Passions

Augustine's reputation for taking a metaphysical approach to God is not entirely undeserved. Sometimes Augustine does engage in what appear to be attempts to prove the existence of God and thereby stipulate what kind of being God must be. For example, in *On Free Will*, a work written against the Manicheans, Augustine argues that there must be a Truth superior to our minds that grounds the possibility of making true judgments.[3] He even hints at an ontological argument by claiming that existence is a necessary property of perfect Being.[4] However, even these arguments are not dispassionate demonstrations compelling cognitive assent by virtue of their logical rigor; rather, they are an invitation to readers to reflect more deeply on their concerns about truth and being — in order to strengthen the desire for the ultimate good. The so-called proofs function as part of a spiritual therapy, not as part of an academic dispute. Even when Augustine is in his most "objective" mode, his rhetorical purpose is not as different from Kierkegaard's as it initially seems.

Usually when Augustine speaks about God, even when he is using Neo-Platonic terminology and thought patterns, he is using the concept "God" to encourage the growth of the pathos that is constitutive of the Christian life. Most basically for Augustine, knowing and desiring God is linked to a chronic discontent with transience, mutability, decay, and death. Along with the Platonists, he laments the sad fact that by focusing on the passing parade of external objects, the mind has become embroiled in the temporal flux and the inevitable passing away of all things. As we have seen, Augustine yearned for something that transcended this disturbing flux, something nontemporal, immediately accessible, constant, and stable. By turning within, it is possible for us humans to see beyond ourselves and our temporal attachments to the possibility of a transcendent object of love. From the tradition of Plotinus, Augustine inherited this desire to love God directly and immediately, without the love of creatures coming in between to distract and confuse the soul. The degree to which this can be seen as an apt expression of Christian faith depends on what exactly Augustine thinks this love for God involves.

Augustine insists that God must transcend the material realm, for only such a God could be the object of the kind of love that Augustine wanted

---

3. Augustine, *On Free Will (De libero arbitrio)*, II, in *WSA* I, 3.
4. Augustine, *On True Religion*, 31 (57-58), in *WSA* I, 8.

to cultivate. In order to support his assertion of divine transcendence, Augustine often did rely on Neo-Platonic arguments. Moreover, he did use a Neo-Platonic conceptuality to make metaphysical claims about God. This was particularly evident in his early critiques of the view of the Manicheans, who regarded God as a kind of rarefied luminous substance. Such a material God was too beleaguered, too mutable, and too circumscribed to satisfy the longing for ultimate fulfillment. Consequently, Augustine emphasized God's immateriality, invisibility, and immutability. In God, he claims, there is no extension and no divisibility.[5] God is everywhere without being the sum total of all geographic points. God cannot break or deteriorate, for God is simple; in God all the virtues are one, and God's attributes and very being are one. Furthermore, God does not flit from one thought to another in a chronological sequence; rather, God comprehends everything past, present, and future simultaneously.[6] Augustine associates the passage of time with the loss of the past and anxiety about the future. Therefore, it is a blessing that he can be assured that in God there is no temporal movement.[7] These affirmations of God's metaphysical perfections serve to reassure the reader that there is something in the universe that is immune to vacillation, anxiety, and disappointment. We humans may be harried by misfortunes and by our own fickle natures, but God is not. The unchangeableness of God is the antidote to the ephemeral nature of all earthly things. The existence of such a God grounds the possibility that one's own self can come to participate in such a state of blessedness. To hint that God might be vulnerable or mutable would rob life of all hope for serenity and joy. To ascribe the perfections of immutability, self-sufficiency, and unity to God is to cultivate the longing for God's truth, goodness, and beauty. For example, the refrain repeated throughout Augustine's writings that all of God is everywhere functions to reassure the reader of God's universal accessibility.[8] Appropriately, in Augustine's pages these metaphysical assertions about God are usually sandwiched between prayers of adoration. Philosophical speculation is motivated not by curiosity, but by a doxological impulse. God is the beauty and the splendor that will satisfy our mysterious yearnings for a joy that the world can neither give nor take away.

For Augustine, the distinction between necessary being and contingent

---

5. Augustine, *Confessions,* V, 10 (20) in *WSA* I, 1.

6. Augustine, *City of God,* XI, 21, in *WSA* I, 6-7.

7. Augustine, *On True Religion,* 49 (97), in *WSA* I, 8.

8. Augustine, *Confessions,* I, 3 (3); VII, 20 (20), in *WSA* I, 1.

being functions to nurture gratitude for creaturely existence. By encouraging reflection on the precariousness of human life, as well as on the fact that the individual need not have existed at all, Augustine reinforces the appreciative awareness that our continued actuality is entirely due to God's conservation. All creatures, including ourselves, depend on God for their very being. Sober reminders of contingency run throughout Augustine's writings. For Augustine true piety is rooted in an acute sense of one's own nothingness apart from God. To candidly admit this fact and to consciously "become nothing before God" is the beginning of wisdom and is the essence of the virtue of humility. The humble confession of ontological insufficiency is not a cry of despondency or an expression of envy of God's sublime self-sufficiency. Rather, for those who have not yet begun the journey toward God, this recognition is a powerful incentive to commence. For Christians who are on the way, the awareness of frailty should trigger gratitude and joy over the fact that they are sustained by a power beyond themselves. Accordingly, Augustine concludes many of his reflections on God's metaphysical perfections with the joyful exclamation that we are made strong in weakness. That same note would reverberate in Kierkegaard's edifying discourses.

The desire to nurture gratitude and humility led Augustine to use language that conflicted with the way he adoringly described God's changeless and therefore nonsequential perfection. Gratitude to God for particular phenomena inspired Augustine's seemingly speculative ruminations about the nature of God's creative activity and his more general tendency to use agential language (and thus the language of change and temporal sequence) to describe God. Augustine emphasizes that the existence of all things is due to God's active creation out of nothing. That conviction grounds Augustine's insistence that human beings should be grateful for everything that exists, for God's beneficent will is the exclusive source of all things. To secure this point, Augustine argues that God does not create out of necessity. Against the widespread Platonic sensibility, he maintains that the goodness of the created order, including the splendor of the angels, is not an inevitable emanation from the depths of God's being.[9] Augustine's exposition of the doctrine of creation is designed to remind readers of their dependence, that they have been created ex nihilo rather than created out of preexistent matter, or chaos. The notion that the cosmos necessarily emanated from God's being would militate against the feeling of joy and gratitude about

9. Augustine, *The Trinity*, III, 1-18, in *WSA* I, 5.

the fact that anything exists at all. God is indeed the fountain from which all blessings flow, but the fountain flows through intentional, voluntary activity. God is motivated to create and preserve the cosmos solely by self-giving love. Although God was not compelled to do so, God delighted in spreading the bounty of existence. This divine act of extravagant generosity is not something restricted to the initial creation of the universe. Augustine distinguished God's *creatio primitiva* and *creatio continuata*, insisting that God's creative activity continues by upholding all things in being. Although all the materials and possibilities of the universe, including time itself, were created simultaneously, the possibilities are activated over time. Without God's continuing activities of preserving (sustaining the substance, form, and motion of all things) and governing (directing the course of events), all creaturely goods would disappear.[10] Augustine concludes: "The Providence of God, then, guides and governs all things insofar as they are creatures, be they natures or wills."[11] God takes delight in what God has created and invites God's creatures to share that delight. The individual's life and the existence of the entire universe are voluntary gifts from God. Augustine's reflections on the ontology of the Creator and the creature are thus embedded in acts of praise for the gratuitous gift of creation. Such sentiments would recur in Kierkegaard's "What We Learn from the Lilies in the Field and from the Birds of the Air."

To further foster gratitude for sheer existence, Augustine uses strongly agential language to describe God, for God is the active giver of good gifts. Augustine insists that God is always active and "is never inconsistent in . . . action."[12] Interpersonal metaphors of benevolent gift-giving are absolutely essential for the encouragement of the crucial disposition of gratitude. Augustine does not identify the divine with the static eternity of an unmoved mover. God is not the abstract perfection of classical philosophy, eternally passive and self-contained. God is indeed active, for God is constantly sustaining and loving God's creatures. Accordingly, Augustine emphasizes God's will, declaring it to be the source of all change. However, this activity cannot be conceptualized in terms of an earthly temporal sequence, for that would suggest an imperfection in God, as if God had to struggle to accomplish something. Such a view of God as acting within the constraints

---

10. See Stanislaus Grabowski, *The All-Present God: A Study in Saint Augustine* (St. Louis: Herder, 1954).

11. Augustine, *On the Literal Interpretation of Genesis (De Genesi ad litteram)*, 8, 26 (48).

12. Augustine, *Confessions*, XII, 7 (7), in *WSA* I, 1.

of time would jeopardize the attractive sublimity of God. Augustine writes: "[God] does not want this now and that then, nor does he later come to will what formerly he did not will, or reject what previously he wished."[13] Augustine concludes that although God is timeless, this does not mean that in God there is no action, for the giving of love is an action. In order to hold together the themes of gratitude (which suggests divine gracious activity) and adoration (which suggests transcendence of all temporal limitations) Augustine resorts to overtly paradoxical language. Augustine explains that the eternal God does not perform the actions of creation and preservation in a temporal sequence. Rather, God "acts" by being the atemporal creator of temporality and the temporal relationship among events. Sometimes Augustine can even suggest that things happen to God in time, but not in the way that they occur in earthly time, in which change invariably occurs.[14] Elsewhere, Augustine proposes that God is ever in action, yet ever at rest.[15] In all these instances Augustine's rhetoric becomes fractured, riddled with qualifications and retractions. Augustine chose such odd and jarring language in order to affirm two things simultaneously: God is not subject to the wavering and potential disintegration associated with life in time, and yet God is actively and reliably engaged in loving the cosmos, humanity, and the individual. The first affirmation was necessary to encourage longing for God as our true home, and the second to encourage trust and reliance.

In these doxological contexts Augustine affirms the basic goodness of the created order, including its material dimensions. Augustine's spirituality is not a revulsion to life; it is not a yearning to return to nothingness or to dissolve all differentiation into a primal oneness. Far from being an advocate of the total renunciation of earthly goods, Augustine proposes that earthly goods can and should be used to pursue the ultimate goal of the enjoyment of God. In his early work *On the Nature of the Good (De Natura Boni)*, Augustine claims that all created reality shares in some goodness and beauty simply by virtue of being, for existence is a good gift from God. This affirmation is not a mere youthful reaction against the dualism of his Manichean days. Throughout his life Augustine could wax quite lyrical about the beauty of nature and even the legitimate pleasures of earthly life. In his maturity Augustine rhapsodizes: "In each category of your works, when you had said that they should be made and they were made, you saw that

---

13. Augustine, *Confessions*, XII, 15 (18), in *WSA* I, 1.
14. Augustine, *The Trinity*, V, 3.16–4.17, in *WSA* I, 5.
15. Augustine, *On the Literal Interpretation of Genesis*, IV, 16 (27), in *WSA* I, 13.

every particular instance is good."[16] Properly delighting in created goods via being grateful to their Creator is a way of sharing in God's creative joy.[17] As we come to desire God more, we come to see the universe as God does, as an expression of divine love. Rather than being a condemnation of all earthly desires, Augustine's more ascetic admonitions were a critique of the idolatrous misdirection of desire. If we could love God above all else, then we would be freed from the tyranny of idolatrous compulsions and would be liberated to love earthly goods rightly. Even the proper love of self and other people can be achieved through gratefully loving God as the creator of the individual's life and the lives of his neighbors. As we shall see, the theme of proper self-love would resurface in Kierkegaard's *Works of Love*.

To many of his interpreters, Augustine sounds most like a Platonist when he describes God as the source of all truth and intelligibility. Ostensibly, this speculative epistemology would seem to be a point at which Augustine diverges most sharply from Kierkegaard, who was notoriously critical of seemingly cognitive approaches to God. Moreover, this association of God with all human knowing is clearly not peripheral to Augustine's understanding of God. Although this noetic theme was strongest in Augustine's earliest writings, it continued to thread its way through the rest of his work. Because of its centrality in his understanding of God, Augustine's epistemology deserves closer examination.

For Augustine, human beings long to understand the nature and meaning of things. This longing is not doomed to frustration, for the existence of a realm of pure intelligibility makes possible the human quest for truth. Standing in the Platonic tradition, Augustine was convinced that the human mind judges the world of ordinary experience in light of intelligible archetypes. For example, ideal standards of justice precede all particular judgments about justice and make those specific determinations possible. Similarly, the perception of physical beauty presupposes an implicit awareness of appropriate proportions, and thus of ideal harmony, as Augustine argues in his analysis of music. When we claim that our judgments are "true," we are claiming that they are more than expressions of private opinion or personal preference; we are claiming that they correspond to some objective norm. Augustine maintains that it is "illumination" by the divine Word that enables the mind to use these ideals and norms. Interpreters of Augustine have for centuries disputed exactly what he meant by this, with

---

16. Augustine, *Confessions*, XIII, 28 (43), in *WSA* I, 1.
17. Augustine, *Confessions*, XIII, 31 (46), in *WSA* I, 1.

little consensus emerging: some claim that Augustine believes that God imparted knowledge of the archetypes to the human mind; some contend that he believes that God's wisdom is directly beheld by the mind; some maintain that he thinks that God acts through the created powers of the mind; some argue that he proposes that God is the regulative principle governing the mind.[18] However, scholars seem to be in agreement about one thing concerning Augustine's epistemology: in some mysterious way the activity of God in the mind is a transcendental condition for intelligibility. The illuminating activity of the Word is presupposed by the operations of our minds. As Augustine sometimes phrases this theme, it is God's "light" that confers intelligibility on all things.

The sense of God's illuminating activity within the human mind led Augustine, like Plotinus, to turn inward to discern the source of the light. The goal of this inward turn was an immediate intuition of God. Particularly in his early dialogues, which he wrote at Cassiciacum, Augustine seeks a direct apprehension of the divine within, unmediated by external objects and sensory distractions. In the *Confessions,* Augustine claims that if he had followed the "intelligence of the mind" during his Manichean days, he would have realized that God is "more inward than my most inward part."[19] For Augustine, reflection on the nature of knowledge had a pronounced experiential dimension, for it encouraged a hunger for a mystical apprehension of truth in itself, the light that shines in and upon the mind.

These ruminations may make it seem that God is a postulate intended to solve an epistemological problem, or the ineffable content of a mystical experience transcending the polarity of subject and object. However, in these passages Augustine is using philosophical speculation to foster an appreciation for the wonder of knowing. The fact that the human mind can grasp external realities should spark delight and gratitude. It is a marvel that God is the source not only of our being but also of our knowledge. For Augustine, talk of "illumination" functions to draw attention to the ongoing graciousness of God in making possible all human episodes of knowing. In this epistemology God is not just the passive eternity of the ideal realm; rather, God is the active agent in all perception of truth. The capacity to know should be received as a gift of superlative worth. Moreover, the

18. See Charles Boyer, *L'Ideé de vérité dans la philosophie de saint Augustin* (Paris: Beauchesne, 1940); Regis Jolivet, *Dieu soleil des esprits, ou la doctrine augustinienne de l'illumination* (Paris: Desclée, de Brouwer et cie, 1934); Roland J. Teske, *To Know God and the Soul* (Washington, DC: The Catholic University Press of America, 2008).

19. Augustine, *Confessions,* III, 6 (11), in *WSA* I, 1.

knowledge that we do attain in this life should whet our appetite for a kind of knowledge that is purer and more complete.

To make this clear, Augustine identifies the light within us that illuminates the intelligible forms with Christ, the eternal wisdom of God. In all instances in Augustine's writings, talk of Christ signals God's gracious beneficence to humanity.[20] Admittedly, Augustine can occasionally use language that seems to suggest that the intuition of God involves a dissolution of the subject/object polarity, language that makes it sound as if God is simply identified with the deepest dimension of the soul. However, Augustine always qualifies such passages with the reminder that the source of wisdom transcends the soul; the light that enables the mind to perceive is higher than the mind. Augustine concludes these reflections on the indwelling wisdom of God, whose source is beyond us, with exhortations to be grateful for the light of Christ that shines on all intelligible things just as the sun shines on all earthly things.[21]

To conclude, Augustine's frequent forays into metaphysical and epistemological speculation about God function to cultivate devout dispositions and passions in the reader. The ontology serves to stimulate gratitude for the world without, and the epistemology serves to stimulate gratitude for the world within. Praise should be offered to God not only for the world of physical objects, but also for the world of cognitive experience. In both instances, whether reflecting on the dependence of contingent being on necessary being, or on the dependence of acts of knowing on the transcendental conditions of knowledge, Augustine's purpose is primarily doxological, for it is to praise and thank God for God's superlatively good gifts. The reader is tutored by the flow of Augustine's reflections to participate in his offering of gratitude and adoration. As I shall argue later in this chapter, this rhetorical purpose is not so very different from Kierkegaard's aim in *Works of Love* and many of the edifying and Christian discourses.

For Augustine, the passions appropriate to God are not exhausted by gratitude and praise; God is far more than the provident one. Augustine portrays God not only as the ultimately satisfying object of our longing, but also as the source of the imperative to journey toward God. Consequently, life can be imaged not only as a journey but also as a trial. It is not merely true that we can seek our absolute fulfillment in God, as if that were an optional possibility. Rather, we *must* do so, for God has commanded it. In

---

20. Augustine, *On the Teacher (De magistro)*, XI, 38, in *WSA* I, 3.
21. Augustine, *On True Religion*, 31 (57-58), in *WSA* I, 8.

multiple contexts Augustine does not hesitate to talk about God's displeasure, God's judgment, and God's wrath. God demands progress toward the good, and God hates the sickness in people that inhibits that progress.[22] Of course, this wrath should not be construed as an outburst of rage to which God succumbs on certain particularly provocative occasions — but simply as the incommensurability of God's holiness and human sinfulness. Augustine depicts the righteous indignation of God in order to enable the reader to feel the utter importance of the journey to God and the enormity of the failure to pursue that journey. For example, in his *Explanations of the Psalms,* Augustine invokes the image of the Last Judgment and the prospect of eternal damnation to inculcate a sense of the urgency of beginning the journey to God.[23] Augustine warns that what we have become in this life we will be for all eternity. Talk of God as judge is a trope to emphasize how much is at stake in the individual's striving to reach the eternal destination, and how dreadful is the failure to arrive at the terminus of our pilgrimage. As we shall see, Kierkegaard repeated this foregrounding of the theme that the individual's life as a whole is being evaluated by God, and that God's assessment is of ultimate importance.

Even with these qualifications concerning gratitude to God and fear of God's judgment, the concept "God" still remains rather underdetermined. What is the value of the life that we have been given? What is the truth that we are capable of grasping? In light of what norm will God judge our progress? In order to give the concept "God" more robust content, Augustine engages in his lengthy and arduous reflections on the nature of the Trinity. In a way, this is a classic example of faith seeking understanding. But the understanding here is not a better conceptual grasp of a perplexing bit of supernatural information. In seeking to understand the Trinity more deeply, Augustine is not primarily looking for a more adequate definition or map of God's ontological dynamics, as if the doctrine of the Trinity were a cognitive puzzle that had to be solved. Augustine does not want to merely assent to the definition developed at Nicea, but to understand the significance of that affirmation and to use the doctrine in his own life in a meaningful way. Augustine's Trinitarian reflections serve to specify what is so desirable about God, what is so attractive about our destination, and what is so enormously valuable about our earthly journey.

22. Augustine, *On Patience (De patientia),* 19, in WSA I, 10.
23. Augustine, *Explanations of the Psalms (Enarrationes in Psalmos),* CI, 26-27, in WSA III, 14-17.

The doctrine of the Trinity was much on the minds of Augustine's contemporaries because it was still contested by the Arians, who remained a powerful factor in the political and religious life of the empire. The Gothic mercenaries on whom the empire relied for military support were predominantly Arians, and their religion was usually protected by the imperial court. The Arians continued to profess the view that the Logos was the first of God's creatures and thus neither coequal nor coeternal with the Creator. In Milan, Bishop Ambrose, who played such a pivotal role in Augustine's appropriation of Christianity, became the implacable enemy of the Arians and their political patrons. Although these disputes certainly informed and partly motivated Augustine's monumental theological project, *The Trinity* was much more than another exercise in ecclesial polemics. The writing of that book enabled him to explore in depth the meaning of affirmations about God for the Christian life, something that the doctrinal formulae had left unclear. He began working on the book in 400 but did not finish it until about 420. This exceptionally long gestation period is symptomatic of the foundational importance of the subject for Augustine.

These Trinitarian reflections were among Augustine's most sustained efforts to specify the distinctive features of the Christian concept "God." For Augustine, the affirmation that "God is love" was the key to the entire project. (As we shall see, Kierkegaard focused on this same definition of God.) Augustine came to identify God's very nature with love because the biblical phrase "love is from God" suggested to him that our own act of love is the act of the Holy Spirit, and thus an act of the Godhead as such. The fact that God is the ultimate source of all love points to something essential about God's very nature. God should be conceived first and foremost as the font of love, which implies that love is God's very identity. For Augustine, the doctrine of the Trinity was a way of articulating that fact. Therefore, reflection on the meaning of that doctrine would be prayerful meditation on the love of God.

To emphasize the role of love in Augustine's exposition of the Trinity runs counter to many older interpretations of Augustine that have accented his Neo-Platonic roots. It has often been suggested that, because the Neo-Platonists emphasized the divine simplicity as an essential aspect of God's perfection, Augustine thought basically in terms of God's oneness. According to this venerable interpretation, Augustine had difficulty explaining how there could be real distinctions among the three persons. For example, Colin Gunton, expressing the opinion of many others, lambasted Augustine for being the wellspring of the modalism that has haunted the Western churches.[24] According to Gunton, Augustine conceptualized the Trinity on the basis of an analogy to human self-awareness, and thereby reinforced the West's unfortunate tendency to valorize solitary self-consciousness and self-reflection. Augustine's portrayal of God as an eternal act of self-knowledge and self-love sounds suspiciously like the solipsistic interiority that would come to fruition in Romanticism and existentialism. Agreeing with Gunton, the influential Trinitarian theologian Catherine LaCugna argues in more detail that Augustine's assumption that God is a simple substance prevented him from conceptualizing the relational aspect of God.[25]

This interpretive tradition rightly draws attention to the fact that Augustine did use the analogy of human self-reflexivity, but it ignores the purpose to which he put that analogy. At the very beginning of the eighth book of *The Trinity,* Augustine announces that it is love, not intellectual knowledge, that is the key to our understanding of God. We can only understand the Trinity as we consider it in the context of our efforts to grow in love. This focus on love signals that God will not be construed as a self-contained, static monolith.[26]

It is certainly true that Augustine insisted that the persons of the Trinity are identical in regard to their deity; thus did he highlight the divine unity. Each person is fully, equally, and identically God. The singular divine essence is fully present in each of the three persons. Consequently, to understand the Trinity according to the analogy of three separate human individuals who share some common traits would be entirely misleading; the relationship of the persons to the Godhead is not like the relationship of three human individuals to the species Homo sapiens. A subtle and sophisticated variant of this "social" view of the Trinity would become common in the Christian East, suggested by some of the language of the Cappadocian theologians. To further problematize the difference of the Trinitarian persons from one another, Augustine could not fully endorse the more simplistic versions of the "economic" view that differentiated the persons exclusively on the basis of their activities with respect to the created order. Augustine proposes that the actions of the three persons toward the universe are inseparable. For example, in the original work of creation not only the Father but also the Son and the Holy Spirit were active. It is not entirely

24. Colin Gunton, "Augustine, the Trinity, and the Theological Crisis of the West," *Scottish Journal of Theology* 43 (1990): 33-58.

25. Catherine LaCugna, *God for Us: The Trinity and the Christian Life* (San Francisco: HarperSanFrancisco, 1991), p. 102.

26. Augustine, *The Trinity,* VIII, in *WSA* I, 5.

accurate to define the first person as the Creator, for the other two persons were also involved.[27] Having rejected these common ways of distinguishing the Trinitarian persons, Augustine pioneered another strategy. In order to understand the differentiation of the persons, Augustine focuses on the nature of their relationships to one another. He points to the significance of the traditional formulae that the Father begets and the Son is begotten, while the Spirit proceeds from both the Father and the Son. In the theological heritage the three persons are defined by their relationships of begetting, being begotten, and proceeding. This emphatic use of relational language invited reflection on the nature of God's love.

Augustine's talk of identifying persons in terms of their relationships to one another without thinking of them as three individuals remained opaque, and Augustine knew that it was. The notion of relationships that seemed to be logically prior to the separate identities of the terms being related was utterly unlike ordinary discourse about relationships. Without further elaboration, such a conceptual strategy was too esoteric to be helpful to pilgrims on the way to a mysterious destination. Therefore, in the last half of *The Trinity*, Augustine seeks for clarifying vestiges or analogies of the Trinity in human experience. First he uses the analogy of love, for love requires three elements: the lover, the beloved, and the love itself. With respect to the Trinity, this suggests that the Father loves the Son, and the Son loves the Father, and the Holy Spirit is the love that unites them, flowing back and forth between them. According to Augustine, this analogy has its problems and can mislead the reader, for it can suggest the picture of God as a community of separate beings who are united through their love for each other, but otherwise are individuated.

To prevent this misconception, Augustine introduces the analogy of the mind itself, and thereby articulates what became known, for good or ill, as the "psychological model" of the Trinity. This makes perfectly good sense, for Augustine always emphasizes the likeness of the human mind to God, and his theological tradition declares that the mind is the image of God. If God is a Trinity, then the image of God must have a Trinitarian structure. Augustine characterizes this threefold structure of the mind as memory,

---

27. Nevertheless, Augustine adds that the actions of the persons *ad extra* can be distinguished, for, though all of three of them were involved in the event of the incarnation, only the Son was actually incarnate in Jesus of Nazareth; they were all active, but were active in different ways. Different actions seem to highlight the agency of different persons, and thus a particular action can be "appropriated" to that person. For example, the act of creation is usually appropriated to the first person.

understanding, and will, or immediate self-presence, self-concept, and self-love *(memoria sui, intelligentia sui, voluntas sui)*.[28] In doing so, Augustine suggests that the mind is not a static substance but is an activity of self-reflection and self-delight. By analogy, the Father beholds his own image in the Son, and takes delight in that image. To complete the analogy, or image, the Son also takes delight in that of which he is an image, namely, the Father. The Godhead is the mutual delight of the Father and Son, expressing itself as the Holy Spirit. In effect, Augustine was proposing that in God's own self, God is a dynamic activity of joyful love. The Father is the activity of giving life to the Son, and the Son is the activity of offering everything back to the Father. The Father and Son together are this mutuality: they do not exist apart from it.[29] The Holy Spirit is this mutuality that exists only through the love of the Father and the Son. At times Augustine describes the Spirit as the "Gift" of the ineffable communion of the Father and the Son; the Spirit is the enactment of the self-giving generosity of God.[30]

In developing this theme, Augustine was implicitly returning to the language of interpersonal relationships to describe the relationship of the persons. The love that characterizes God is a going forth of the divine self out of itself in attraction to the other, and then discovering that the other, by virtue of having also gone forth from itself, is not really "other." For Augustine, love begins as self-giving and culminates in the mutuality of reciprocal self-giving. This is the joyful movement that lies at the heart of the universe. This love is simultaneously self-oblivious giving to the other but also self-filling desire for the other; it is simultaneously agapeic and erotic. The foundational analogue for God, according to Augustine, is not really the soul — and certainly not the isolated soul — but is the phenomenon of self-giving and self-fulfilling love. As John Milbank has argued against Charles Taylor, Augustine's use of psychological metaphors (which are subordinated to the metaphor of love) does not foster self-enclosed Platonic interiority but rather an ecstatic interrelationality that subverts the dichotomy

---

28. Augustine, *The Trinity*, IX-X, in *WSA* I, 5.

29. John Milbank, "Sacred Triads: Augustine and the Indo-European Soul," in R. Dodaro and G. Lawless, eds., *Augustine and His Critics* (London: Routledge, 2000), pp. 77-102.

30. See Paul Martens, "The Emergence of the Holy Spirit in Kierkegaard's Thought: Critical Theological Developments in *For Self-Examination* and *Judge for Yourself!*" in Robert L. Perkins, ed., *International Kierkegaard Commentary*: For Self-Examination *and* Judge for Yourself! (Macon, GA: Mercer University Press, 2002), pp. 199-222. Martens argues that in Kierkegaard's later work the Holy Spirit is a gift who enables the believer to relate to Christ as prototype and as Redeemer.

of interior/exterior.[31] The analogies that Augustine proposed were merely tentative illustrations, and he frankly admitted their inadequacies.[32] With regard to the Trinity, Augustine's multiple and shifting metaphors, images, and conceptual frameworks were often drawn from different sources and thus did not cohere particularly well. His notorious "psychological model" was just one trope among several, intended as a corrective to some possible misuses of the others.[33] It emphasizes the unity that love embodies, while the interpersonal language suggests the otherness that love requires.

Augustine uses his Trinitarian reflections to invite the reader to participate in God's joy, which is the goal of our journey. That divine joy is specified in these reflections as being God's delight in God's own loving relationality. Therefore, the homeward-bound pilgrim comes to share in God's joy by contemplating God's love and reflecting God's love in the pilgrim's own life. As we have seen, the highest happiness for Augustine is not the reception of earthly benefits from God, but is variously described as the vision of God, the enjoyment of the presence of the God, and even participation in God. *The Trinity* makes it clear that the power that draws the heart is the sheer attractiveness of God's sublime love. The vision of the loving delight of the Father in the Son and the Son in the Father should draw individuals out of themselves and inspire them to begin to love in the way that God loves. Like the persons of the Trinity, we come to unselfishly give ourselves to the objects of our love, and by so doing experience delight and genuine satisfaction. In other words, it is the kind of love enacted by the Trinitarian persons that humans have been yearning for all along.

In order to further clarify what this love manifested in the inter-Trinitarian relationships is like, Augustine turns to its human reflection in human love for the neighbor. Concerning the relationship of love of God to love of neighbor, Augustine writes: "[I]f a man loves his neighbor, it follows that above all he loves love itself. But *God is love and whoever abides in love abides in God* (1 John 4:16). So it follows that above all he loves God."[34] (Kierkegaard would later make almost exactly this same point.) This love for the neighbor, which is a manifestation of love for God, is further defined as brotherly love, which includes the willingness to die for the good of the brethren. This love includes both self-sacrificial concern for the well-being

---

31. Milbank, "Sacred Triads," pp. 90-92.

32. Augustine, *Confessions* XIII, 11, (12), in *WSA* I, 1.

33. See Lewis Ayres, *Augustine and the Trinity* (Cambridge: Cambridge University Press, 2010).

34. Augustine, *The Trinity,* VIII, 5.10, in *WSA* I, 5.

of the other as well as delight in the existence of the other. As with the persons of the Trinity, the ability to receive love and the ability to give love are correlative, although the giving of love is not contingent on the receiving of love. Ideally, love should be mutual; nonetheless, it is given even when it is not reciprocated. It is this vision of God as the source of self-giving love that is the goal of human desire. Those who love God are loving that kind of love; they love the interrelationality that constitutes God's Trinitarian life.[35] To understand the Trinity is not reducible to the ability to use an apt analogy, but is to comprehend the ecstatic nature of love. Understanding the Trinity involves learning to love in the way that God loves, through attaining self-fulfillment through self-giving to the other. The earthly pilgrimage is an intensification of the sojourner's delight in the exquisite beauty of love.

The critique of Augustine, leveled by Anders Nygren and others, that his love for God is nothing more than a selfish drive for personal fulfillment, is seriously misleading. Augustine's account of the attractiveness of the Trinitarian life shows that it is the vision of self-giving and other-regarding benevolence that draws the individual's heart. Love for God is not a means to the end of personal fulfillment; rather, it is the fulfillment itself. Paradoxically, the individual finds fulfillment in delighting in God for the sake of the intrinsic goodness of self-giving love, not for the sake of any self-oriented benefit that the individual might derive from it. Perhaps the strongest tie of Kierkegaard to Augustine is Kierkegaard's repetition of this theme of finding self-fulfillment through self-giving.

The Trinity conceived as the sublimity of love is the capstone of Augustine's theology. To behold and participate in such glorious love is the goal of the earthly pilgrimage. To know God's truth is to grasp the nature of this love by adoring and reflecting it. To be grateful to God for both the outer world of materiality and the inner world of cognition is to rejoice that God has shared this love with God's creatures, making it possible for the "spiritual" creatures to experience the delight of loving in this divine manner. To trust in God is to be confident that God's providence has guided the individual toward the vision of love's splendor. To fear the judgment of God is to dread that one might not reach the precious goal of praising and reflecting the divine love. To affirm God's sovereignty is to trust that it is the invincible power of love that propels and lures the individual forward and animates the entire cosmos. In all these instances the concept "God" is given specificity by clarifying the passions and dispositions that are constitutive of its

35. Augustine, *The Trinity*, VIII, 5.12, in *WSA* I, 5.

meaning. Therefore, for Augustine, God cannot be known through *scientia,* which suggests dispassionate analysis, but only through *sapientia,* which is the engaged, pathos-laden pursuit of wisdom. The passions and dispositions that form the context for meaningful talk about God are various and nuanced, but they are all ordered by the central passion and virtue of love.

Kierkegaard and the Pathos of Knowing God

Kierkegaard's writings do not give any indication that he ever seriously immersed himself in Augustine's ruminations about the nature of God. However, his notebooks show that he was exposed to many of Augustine's teachings about God in general and the Trinity in particular. Through Marheineke's lectures he was aware of Augustine's affirmation of both an original creation from nothing and God's continuing preservation and the consequent need for humans constantly to rely on God (*KJN* 3, 9:1, pp. 256-57). These lecture notes also reveal that he was acquainted with the Augustinian claim that the actions of the three persons of the Trinity outside the Godhead are indivisible (*KJN* 3, 9:1, p. 245). Kierkegaard also learned from Marheineke that, according to Augustine, the persons of the Trinity are *in se invicem,* meaning that they are mutually and reciprocally related (*KJN* 3, 9:1, p. 293). Marheineke proceeded to give this Augustinian theme a Hegelian spin by describing the Trinitarian persons as substance (God-in-itself), subject (God-for-itself), and spirit (God-in-and-for-itself). Despite the Hegelian terminology, Marheineke did successfully express a main theme in Augustine: the claim that the Son is God's self-knowledge and the Spirit is God's self-love. Other authors, including Bretschneider, Hase, and Hahn, reinforced Kierkegaard's familiarity with Augustine's Trinitarian ruminations.

The fact that Kierkegaard apparently was only superficially familiar with Augustine's reflections about God did not prevent Augustinian motifs from appearing in his own writings. In spite of Augustine's penchant for using Platonic vocabulary and for casting issues in metaphysical terms, the edifying purposes of Augustine and Kierkegaard often paralleled each other. With respect to knowing God, both of them sought to encourage similar kinds of religious passions and dispositions in their readers. Moreover, both Augustine and Kierkegaard shared the conviction that the meaning of the concept "God" can only become clear as an individual grows in godliness and learns to use the concept in the individual's passional life. We shall note the multiple ways in which Kierkegaard's efforts to communicate the significance of the concept "God" echo Augustine's attempts — only in a different idiom.

Unlike many other theologians, Kierkegaard refused to explain the meaning of the concept "God" in a mode of objective neutrality. In resisting the disengaged stance of a doctrinal expositor, his work paralleled the self-involving strategy of Augustine. The detached procedure favored by many of Kierkegaard's predecessors and contemporaries, including, he feared, the theologians influenced by Hegel, suggested that God is some type of being who is amenable to scrutiny, analysis, and description. Even if God is said to transcend the categories of space and time, God is still treated as something whose mode of being can be an object for speculation and metaphysical description. According to such a practice, God would have to exhibit recognizable differentiating features and possess attributes that could be compared with the attributes of other beings. But for Kierkegaard, "God" is not the name of any item locatable within the domain of finite beings, or of an entity cognizable by way of contrast to finite beings. Climacus lampoons the notion of cognizing God directly as if God were revealed as a "rare, enormously large green bird, with a red bill" (*CUP* 1, 245-46). Therefore, God cannot be referred to in the way that a geologist might refer to a rock, or an astronomer to a star, or even a child to a mother. Diverging from a certain kind of academic approach to theology, Kierkegaard resisted the tendency to specify the meaning of "God" by compiling an inventory of identifying characteristics, no matter how lofty such characteristics might sound. Kierkegaard does not define God in terms of such daunting metaphysical properties as omnipotence, omniscience, and so forth. Rather, Kierkegaard seeks to give "God" meaning by exhibiting the concept's role in the life of devotion to God. God cannot be described directly, but the pathos of a godly life can be sketched, and this pathos can become the environment in which the concept "God" is used to address a reality beyond the individual. Referring to God can still occur, but it cannot be separated from such activities as worshiping God, obeying God, loving God, and fearing God.[36] All reference to God must be given significance by situating it in the subjective life of the believer. It is not the case that the concept "God" remains the same whether it is treated with objective detachment or with sub-

---

36. See C. Stephen Evans, *Kierkegaard: An Introduction* (Cambridge: Cambridge University Press, 2009), pp. 139-42, for a discussion of the relationship of "dialectical content" and "passions" in Kierkegaard's work.

jective passion. Of course, this recognition is not a denial of the existence of God as a reality beyond the passions of the believer; it is not a denial of God's transcendence or otherness. Kierkegaard was simply assuming that a necessary condition for meaningful discourse about God is the ability to imagine the kinds of hopes, fears, and loves that constitute the natural home for any talk about God.

By so doing, Kierkegaard was sharing Augustine's presupposition that "knowing" God could not be divorced from "loving" God (and also fearing, trusting, and obeying God). Consequently, readers could not learn anything about God unless they could at least begin to imagine what it is like to love God, or, even better, actually begin to love God. Therefore, Kierkegaard and Augustine were also in agreement that any writing that intended to communicate something about God needed to instantiate and illustrate the relevant passions and dispositions that constitute the appropriate context for meaningful talk about God. For both thinkers, the "mood," style, and voice of writing about God had to be suited to the divine subject matter. For both, writing about God should be doxological, penitential, supplicatory, thankful, and grateful. Similarly, writing about alienation from God should be anxious, despairing, fractured, and discordant. In their way of writing, both Kierkegaard and Augustine were careful to display the kinds of pathos appropriate for discourse about God, hoping that this would evoke the reader's own capacity to experience a similar pathos. The thinkers' literary performances show readers the passional qualities associated with knowing God; only by helping readers feel the lure of those passions could the meaning of God be communicated.

Kierkegaard's insistence that God is not the name of an object that could be coolly scrutinized or analyzed has profound consequences for the way God can be known. Kierkegaard was convinced that these consequences must be made evident to cultured individuals who might be flirting with the pervasive enthusiasm for objective knowledge that infects modernity. In *Philosophical Fragments,* the pseudonymous Climacus attempts to expose the insecure foundations of such allegedly objective knowledge of God by adopting the uncommitted stance of his audience and the prevalent style of philosophical reflection. However, underneath his ostensible mood of calm and deliberate investigation, the candor and earnestness about life typical of Socrates shows through. Climacus's very style causes the smug certainties and cool detachment of a "speculative" approach to God to implode.

In his undermining of the speculative approach, Climacus advances philosophical arguments to critique the assumptions of the objectivists, ironically wounding them with their own weapons (*PF*, 103). According to Climacus, the nature and existence of God cannot be objectively demonstrated or even rendered probable by allegedly rational arguments. We cannot know that God exists through inferences drawn from empirical evidence or from reflection on the general nature of the universe. The so-called traditional proofs for the existence of God actually demonstrate nothing, for they violate the distinction of logic and actual existence. More specifically, Climacus argues that the existence of a specific entity is not necessarily implied by any set of empirical phenomena that are its alleged effects. God's existence can no more be inferred from events in the universe than the existence of a person named Napoleon with all of Napoleon's specific characteristics could be inferred from the victories of the French army in the early nineteenth century. Climacus's argument implicitly challenges the celebrated "argument from design," the notion that the harmony and intricacy of the universe imply the existence of a supremely intelligent and benevolent creator. Elsewhere, Kierkegaard (writing under his own name) elaborates that the interconnections of nature do not necessarily reveal divine ingenuity or benevolence or any kind of governance. The intricacies of the ecological system do not require the hypothesis of a cosmic designer. Nature is permeated with violence and apparent chaos; enough apparent randomness abounds to cast doubt on divine intentionality. By no means is providential guidance immediately evident in nature's whirl of chaotic and often destructive events. In the natural world God's activity remains hidden and elusive.

According to Climacus, not only is the existence God not entailed by the available evidence, but it is not required by the supposed laws of thought. Contrary to the "ontological argument" of Anselm, Descartes, and Spinoza, the concept God is neither an innate idea nor a necessary postulate of logic, for logic deals only with formal concepts and their relations. Such matters have no bearing on the question of what actually exists or what the universe is actually like. The argument that the "chain of being," with different classes of entities possessing different degrees of "being," points to the existence of a "highest being" is not convincing. The argument lacks credibility because existence is not a type of attribute that could appear in varying degrees of perfection. In short, unaided reason can determine neither God's existence nor God's attributes. Climacus summarizes: "[T]herefore, whether I am moving in the world of sensate palpability or the world of thought, I never reason in conclusion to existence, but I reason in conclusion from existence" (*PF*, 40). Furthermore,

Climacus's "thought experiment" of imagining a way of life not based on the recollection of truth suggests that, for Christians, God is not the name of an innate dimension of experience or an innate kind of extraordinary feeling. In his various writings Kierkegaard does not even attempt to postulate the existence of God as a necessary condition to account for the possibility of self-integration. Even the yearning that humans experience is not sufficient to posit a God who is the source of it. In short, knowledge of God is not the product of inductive reasoning, abstract speculation, or immediate intuition. Whatever "God" means, it is not something that can be directly and immediately known or experienced.

Kierkegaard's rejection of purely objective knowledge of God bears similarities to Augustine's criticism of loveless attempts to know God motivated by mere curiosity or intellectual hubris. As we have seen, even Augustine's alleged "proofs" are not appeals to the alleged powers of some passionally disengaged deductive capacity. Rather, Augustine's arguments function to reassure and strengthen the faltering pilgrim. The difference between Augustine and Kierkegaard is that Augustine was much more sanguine than was the Dane about the use of metaphysical reflection as a form of contemplative prayer that would focus the mind on God and foster increased love. For Augustine, reflecting about God's nature was a spiritual discipline that should edify the pilgrim. Metaphysical reflection could lead to deeper insight, assurance, and trust. For Kierkegaard, as we shall see, metaphysical reflection tended to reduce the element of risk that true faith requires, and to subvert the mood of passionate engagement. In an edifying discourse Kierkegaard warns:

> There is an upside-downness that wants to reap before it sows; there is a cowardliness that wants to have certainty before it begins; there is a hypersensitivity so copious in words that it continually shrinks from acting; but what would it avail a person if, double-minded and forked tongued, he wanted to dupe God, trap him in probability . . .?" (*EUD*, 381)

For Kierkegaard the longing for metaphysical reassurance was always an evasion of the daunting task of living the life of faith, hope, and love. Augustine engaged in a kind of doxological metaphysics in order to strengthen the love of God in those who lagged and wavered, while Kierkegaard undermined metaphysics in order to unsettle the intellectually smug and the spiritually cowardly. In a way, the two thinkers were addressing different audiences with different spiritual problems.

Rejecting reflection as an avenue to knowing God, Kierkegaard turned to the passions. For Kierkegaard, the characteristics of the passions that are appropriate to God are outlined by Scripture, with its multiple evocative portrayals of God's actions and the apt (and inapt) human responses. Reflecting the multidimensional nature of the biblical narration of God's actions, these passions and dispositions that form the context for understanding the meaning of "God" are manifold, and they interact in intricate ways. As we have already seen, God is that for which we ultimately yearn, whether we are aware of it or not, and that which should be our highest value. However, these identifications of God as the object of longing and as the highest value are both purely formal, as is particularly evident in Kierkegaard's pseudonymous writings. By themselves, they do not specify exactly what it is about God that makes God so valuable or what it is about God that humans long for. Just as Augustine had to provide a thicker description of the longing for God than what was made possible by his Neo-Platonic conceptuality, so also Kierkegaard had to sketch in the particularities of the various Christian passions and dispositions that are aimed at God.

Prominent among the foundational passions and dispositions that inform Kierkegaard's understanding of God is total dependence on God, along with the correlative attitudes of gratitude and trust. An awareness of the individual's ontological fragility and contingency is constitutive of the experience of God. We humans should be viscerally aware of our complete lack of power to secure our own being or worth, and thus be acutely conscious of our neediness and lack of self-sufficiency. Authentic faith involves a profound awareness that we precarious creatures are neither the source of our own existence nor the sustainers of ourselves. In this condition of acute vulnerability, the concept "God" refers to what is to be relied on for all things, to be adored as the source of everything, to be thanked for all blessings, and to be trusted as the foundation of our lives and ultimate well-being. Sounding very Augustinian, Kierkegaard writes:

> You . . . see many forces stirring in nature around you, but the power that supports it all you do not see — and yet it is just as fully certain that he, too, is working, that one single moment without him and then the world is nothing." (PC, 155)

Similarly, many of Kierkegaard's discourses are structured around the contrast between human insufficiency and God's all-sufficiency. In "What We Learn from the Lilies in the Field and the Birds of the Air," Kierkegaard advises the reader "to be contented with being a human being, with being the humble one, the created being who can no more support himself than create himself" (*UDVS*, 177). He proceeds to alert the reader to the dangers of the most insidious spiritual snare, which is the dreadful possibility that a person might "entrench himself, so to speak, in a little or large area where he will not be the object of God's providence and the supporting care of the heavenly Father" (*UDVS*, 178).

Kierkegaard's literary performance in this discourse enacts this dependence, for the author's personal characteristics are not disclosed, as is appropriate for the theme of self-effacement. The reader is not directly admonished or harangued, for an author exhibiting dependence on God should arrogate no such authority to himself. Relinquishing inappropriate power over the reader, the author merely refers to people who might be worried about life's inevitable uncertainties, and might be motivated to trust in their own capacity to establish their own security. In contrast to such illusory self-sufficiency, salutary dependence on God is manifested in the author's reverent dependence on the biblical passage (Matt. 6:24) that he is lovingly elaborating. Also, by not overwhelming the reader with exhortations, Kierkegaard preserves the reader's freedom to disregard the invitation to identify with those who are made anxious by an uncertain future; paradoxically, such a discovery of freedom and thus of personal indeterminacy can foster a longing for something on which the reader can depend.

Woven throughout Kierkegaard's writings is the theme that individuals should strive to become nothing before God, which was particularly prominent in a discourse already discussed in a previous chapter, "To Need God Is a Human Being's Highest Perfection." Kierkegaard says repeatedly that "the highest is this: that a person is fully convinced that he himself is capable of nothing, nothing at all" (*EUD*, 307). This "annihilation" of any trust in human self-sufficiency is the necessary context for understanding the contrasting theme that "God in heaven is capable of all things" (*EUD*, 310). In "One Who Prays Aright Struggles in Prayer and Is Victorious — In That God Is Victorious," Kierkegaard claims that only when an individual "becomes nothing, only then can God illuminate him so that he begins to resemble God" (*EUD*, 399). The relinquishing of self-sufficiency is necessary for transfiguration into the reflection of the image of God (*EUD*, 400). It is an absolutely essential virtue to grow in the recognition of the need for God's grace, and even to recognize that one cannot even generate appropriately pious feelings of insufficiency in one's own self. The appreciation of the priority of God's gracious action, and the incapacity to do anything of

Christian significance by oneself, frames all talk of human striving. Without presuming to assert his own authority or power, the writer shows how talk of God's all-sufficiency requires a context of humble awareness of an individual's powerlessness in the face of life's vicissitudes and spiritual trials.

In Kierkegaard's writings this effort to evoke and express a feeling of radical contingency and lack of self-sufficiency is the functional equivalent of Augustine's praise of God's metaphysical perfections (e.g., omniscience, omnipotence). As we have seen, Augustine was not merely trying to clarify the abstract concept of a "perfect being" by contrasting it with the imperfections of finite existence. Rather, he was attempting to evoke a sense of dependence and fragility in order to foster an appreciation of God's sustaining power. Like Augustine, Kierkegaard describes this dependence on God both in terms of our continuing earthly existence and in terms of our inner journey toward God. Most dramatically, Kierkegaard's protestations that even with respect to our own religious lives we can do nothing at all have striking similarities to Augustine's arguments against the Pelagians.

The theme of dependence on God is intertwined in Kierkegaard's pages with the closely related motif of gratitude, another crucial aspect of the passional context necessary for meaningful talk about God. God is partially defined as that to which gratitude should be expressed for all of life's events, whether they are experienced initially as pleasant or as distressing. To use the concept "God" meaningfully is to greet all earthly vicissitudes with an attitude of thanksgiving. This theme is foregrounded in Kierkegaard's early edifying discourse entitled "Every Good and Every Perfect Gift Is from Above," and in two more discourses of 1843. Again, Kierkegaard does not directly reprimand or exhort. Instead, he describes persons who might be familiar with biblical language about God's providential care for human beings (e.g., James 1:17-22), and yet "go on living as if they had never heard it," in practice attributing their good fortune to their own ingenuity, the support of other people, and luck (*EUD*, 106). At times Kierkegaard addresses a hypothetical "you" and introduces his reflections with "Suppose you. . . ." Without actually accusing the reader of living according to the calculations of worldly sagacity rather than openness to whatever experiences God may provide, the writer gently invites readers to consider the possibility that they may be such ungrateful people. This is rhetorically appropriate, for a discourse about gratitude should not browbeat the reader with guilt. Such a confrontational dynamic would implicitly assert the moral superiority of the author, an attitude inimical to the humble thankfulness essential for this context. Instead of indulging in self-righteousness, the author demonstrates what true thankfulness is like by expressing extravagant thankfulness for the comforting words of the biblical text. Through such literary devices, Kierkegaard contrasts anxious efforts to secure a desired future with receptivity to all aspects of life as gifts from a bounteous, munificent God.

This gratitude should be expressed not only for various forms of earthly well-being, such as physical health, financial prosperity, and a satisfying social life, but also for life's challenges, tribulations, and woes. In both his pseudonymous and veronymous writings, Kierkegaard returns to Job's words: "The Lord gave, and the Lord took away, blessed be the name of the Lord" (e.g., *EUD*, 111-14; *FT*, 197). The misfortunes that befall every individual should be greeted as the discipline of a loving parent who is encouraging the spiritual growth of the child. Sufferings should be experienced as reminders that worldly felicity is not our highest goal. Life's woes can actually be avenues to a more profound intimacy with God, as were Job's afflictions, if they are received with the proper trust. Kierkegaard writes of Job: "[B]ut intimacy with the Lord was still his as before, perhaps more inward than before, for now there was nothing at all in any way capable of drawing his thoughts away from it" (*EUD*, 122). Even the more extraordinary afflictions of social ostracism and persecution that accompany the life of discipleship should be accepted as good gifts, as stimuli to propel growth in Christian earnestness. Finally, throughout his discourses Kierkegaard makes it clear that even the individual's seeming progress in faith, hope, and love should be gratefully regarded as gifts from God rather than as the individual's own Promethean achievements.

One of Kierkegaard's most prevalent themes in his discourses is the spiritual benefit to be gleaned by remaining thankful in the face of suffering. Significantly, Kierkegaard refuses to develop a response to the question of why God allows tragedy and evil. He offers no theory about the role of suffering in God's providential purposes. He does not ruminate about the exact connection between God's will and earthly events. Nor does he speculate about the relationship of primary causes to secondary causes or about the cooperation of divine and earthly causalities. Although Kierkegaard does say that suffering is a God-given impetus for Christians to use in order to detach themselves from worldly culture, he generally refrains from articulating a speculative theodicy to explain why suffering is God's preferred method for weaning the individual away from the fallen world.[37] Although

---

37. See Paul Martens and Tom Millay, "'The Changelessness of God' as Kierkegaard's

Kierkegaard does claim that suffering in general should be accepted with joy as a spiritual pedagogy, he does not attempt to specify what exactly the spiritually beneficial aspects of any particular tragedy might be. Rather, Kierkegaard simply exhorts the reader to be grateful to God in good times and in bad. A metaphysical account of the mechanisms of God's providence or an attempt to second-guess God's purposes would substitute a fatally inappropriate mood of objective detachment for the necessary mood of passionate concern about the quality of the individual's own life. God is not to be regarded as a marionette-master whose manipulations of the strings can be observed, interpreted, and predicted. By reminding his Christian readers that they are living in the time of waiting for the Comforter, Kierke-gaard encourages them to recover from the impatience of wanting to grasp God's providential plan, or experience some immediate and direct comfort (*EUD*, 392). With regard to the question of why our deepest wishes are not fulfilled, Kierkegaard writes, "Or is this the explanation, that God denies him the understanding and requires only faith and consequently wants only the understanding with him that is in the realm of the ununderstandable?" (*EUD*, 395). The effort to produce an "explanation" of suffering is an attempt to subvert the imperative to trust God in all things and to negate the pos-sibility of relating to God in faith. Theodicies replace the struggle to trust with the quest for certainty.

Here Kierkegaard's refusal to produce a theodicy would seem to be sharply at variance with the practice of Augustine. Augustine is notorious for developing not one but several different theories to account for the pres-ence of evil in a universe governed by an all-powerful and infinitely lov-ing God; he did not share Kierkegaard's reluctance to speculate about the purposes of God.[38] Against the Manicheans, who claimed that the material world is controlled by evil forces, Augustine argued that evil is not a thing but is a privation or corruption of something good. Evil does not have an efficient cause but only a "deficient cause."[39] Against the philosophers who doubted God's goodness in creating lower life forms, Augustine had devel-oped the "principle of plenitude," the notion that a fecund Creator would want to fill all the many levels of being. Against the Pelagians, who refused to see God's hand in the more somber events of human history, Augustine

---

Final Theodicy: God and the Gift of Suffering," *International Journal of Systematic Theology* 13, no. 2 (2011): 170-89.

38. See John Hick, *Evil and the God of Love* (New York: Macmillan, 1977), pp. 37-89.
39. Augustine, *The City of God*, XII, 7.

had argued that the appreciation of the good is enhanced by the contrast of good and evil. According to this "aesthetic" theory, the interplay of good and evil constitutes the harmony evident in the composition of the cosmos, just as light and dark tiles contribute the delightful harmony of a floor. All of these proposals would have violated Kierkegaard's stricture against introducing a mood of objective reflection into the individual's engagement with God.

However, by developing these theodicies Augustine was trying to safeguard some of the forms of Christian pathos that Kierkegaard cherished. The argument against Manichean dualism was intended to promote gratitude for the material world and life in general, just as Kierkegaard would have wished. The principle of plenitude was designed to secure thankfulness for the entire panoply of creatures, from inert matter to the glorious angels. The aesthetic theory served to reinforce the sense that even life's ostensible tragedies can be accepted as a part of the goodness of the whole. All of these attitudes would have been applauded by Kierkegaard. The point at which Kierkegaard and Augustine diverged was the basic issue of whether metaphysical reflection had any upbuilding potential at all. Augustine writes as though the individual can be edified by discerning how Christian pathos implies certain claims about the nature of the universe that can then be shown to be plausible. The passions are deepened, strengthened, and focused by metaphysical reflection, if it is done in the appropriately pious mood. Kierkegaard, on the other hand, wrote as if the forms of pathos themselves possess their own attractiveness and plausibility (and also potential offensiveness), and that the power of the Christian passions would only be diluted by resituating them in the alien context of theorizing. Kierkegaard doubted that the mood of earnestness about one's own life could be maintained through abstract speculation. For Kierkegaard, the virtue of trusting in God during times of suffering did not need any metaphysical backing, and in fact would be harmed by efforts to provide such backing. Consequently Kierkegaard abandoned theodicy while Augustine did not, even though their depictions of Christian pathos were surprisingly similar.

Humility before God, another Christian virtue that receives much attention in Kierkegaard's writings, is closely associated with gratitude. Because all of life should be construed as a gift, the individual possesses nothing that could be a basis for self-congratulation. Not even the individual's own apparent accomplishments, including what appear to be noble spiritual exertions, can be a foundation for boasting. Kierkegaard's discourses make it clear that pride should gain no purchase in the individual's life.

The glorification of the individual's own ostensible merits is incompatible with the glorification of God, and it is this glorification that is the core of all genuine edification. In a discourse that celebrates the "joy" of humility, Kierkegaard exuberantly advises that all persons should adopt the motto of John the Baptist, "He [Christ] must increase; I must decrease," and use that motto as the framework for the way they relate to God (*EUD*, 257-89). A sermon attributed to a pastor encapsulates this theme in its very title: "The Upbuilding That Lies in the Thought That in Relation to God We Are Always in the Wrong." The fictional pastor, by virtue of his ecclesiastical endorsement, was empowered to adopt an authoritative voice and directly exhort his audience to adopt a stance of humility before God. Because the pastor's purpose is edification, he neither threatens nor cajoles. Rather than being a goad to stimulate paralyzing guilt, this recognition of inevitable and immeasurable moral inferiority to God is something inspirational, for it underscores the fact that "God's love is always greater than our love" (*EO* 2, 257-89). Admitting the variability and deficiency of one's own love is the other side of resting secure in God's love, the only love that is truly reliable. In order to encourage the requisite humility, Kierkegaard recommends in *For Self-Examination* that his readers always identify with the villains in the biblical stories, for they are the true mirrors of our souls, and they teach us to distrust our own ersatz virtue (*FSE*, 34-44). To show the reader how to do this, Kierkegaard wrote *For Self-Examination* in the voice of a penitent who is candidly confessing that he has failed to enact the Christian ideal. He advises that the prophet Nathan's words to King David, "Thou art the man," spoken after David had seized Bathsheba and arranged the death of her husband, apply to all individuals. Like David, we should recognize ourselves in Nathan's story about the rich man's theft of a poor man's sheep — and in all such paradigmatic tales of vice. Identification with the unsavory characters in the Bible preserves the humility that is necessary for delight in God's excellence. Against the moral self-confidence of the Pelagians, Augustine practiced exactly the same strategy; he used biblical villains as mirrors in which readers can see their own selves. In fact, much of Augustine's dispute with the Pelagians revolved around the need to preserve and nurture humility. On this score Kierkegaard and Augustine were in perfect agreement.

Trust, an unshakable resilience in the face of life's fortunes and misfortunes, is another critical component of the constellation of passions appropriate to the concept "God." Kierkegaard urges the reader who is anxious about many things to rest in God as in a mother's love (*JFY*, 180-81). He lauds the lilies of the field and the birds of the air as exemplars of freedom from the multiple earthly anxieties that burden most creatures (*UDVS*, 155-212). If all things can be construed as gifts from a loving God, then no calamitous event and no threatening force can ultimately harm the individual. No catastrophe could ever separate the individual from the love of God. Sounding very much like Augustine, Kierkegaard insists that ultimate happiness depends on nothing but the enjoyment of God, and that enjoyment cannot be jeopardized by any earthly disaster. Kierkegaard does not attempt to show how ostensible tragedies work for the best in the lives of individuals, nor does he try to demonstrate that life is fundamentally trustworthy. The trust that he calls for is not a response to empirical information about the nature of the universe. Kierkegaard does not present data concerning the average distribution of fortunes and misfortunes. Christian trust is not rooted in a statistical calculation that in all likelihood the individual's basic biological and social needs will be met. Such assessments of probabilities are utterly foreign to the mood exhibited in these discourses and required by any significant talk about God's providence. Rather, by imaginatively portraying the intrinsic contentment of a life of trust, the force of Kierkegaard's rhetoric inspires the reader to want to experience such a life. It is this kind of trust that Augustine had expressed in the *Confessions* as he looked back at his life and saw the hand of God surreptitiously guiding, luring, and prodding him throughout it.

A rather different, more daunting strand is woven into Kierkegaard's various presentations of the meaning of "God." The same strand was evident in Augustine's writings against the Manicheans. Like Augustine, Kierkegaard in many of his voices foregrounds passionate moral striving and deep concern about God's evaluation of that striving as an essential component of meaningful talk about God. Whatever else God may be, God is that norm in light of which our lives are evaluated and judged, and also the agent who performs the evaluation and renders the verdict. Climacus is quite overt in describing God as the source of the ethical task (*CUP* 1, 244). When speaking of God, Kierkegaard's writing abounds with the metaphors of both "law" and "judge." He even insists that the only thing that interests God is "obedience" (*JP* 2, 1436). He declares that "existence is supposed to be an examination," and "God has a very good understanding of what examining means" (*JP* 2, 1439). In the very last journal entry that he ever wrote, less than two months before his death, Kierkegaard says that the person who continues to love God in spite of life-weariness "passes the examination of life," and he likens God to an evaluator who "sits in heaven and listens" to the vocal performances of candidates for the heavenly choir (*JP* 6, 6969).

In many contexts, often located in his discourses, Kierkegaard expresses a sense of earnest and urgent solicitude for the moral and spiritual condition of his readers. To highlight this, he often addresses his readers directly. The author does not himself judge the reader; rather, he exhorts and prompts the reader to treat the discourse as an opportunity to contemplate the momentousness of standing before the divine judge. Comparing the proper reading of a religious discourse to a theatrical performance, Kierkegaard writes:

> [T]he speaker [the author of the discourse] is the prompter; there are no spectators, because every listener should look inwardly into himself. The stage is eternity, and the listener, if he is the true listener (and if he is not, it is his own fault), is standing before God through the discourse. (*UDVS*, 124)

The author's urgent concern for the eternal well-being of the reader is intended to stimulate the reader's own disquietude about the quality of his or her life.

Kierkegaard relentlessly uses the concept of a final judgment to prod the individual to worry with absolute earnestness about the direction of her or his life. We are to live as if we were being judged by "eternity" every moment; phrased differently, each moment is to be lived as if we were standing before the divine judge. According to Kierkegaard, each episode in life is a confrontation with the command to do one's duty. The entire course of the individual's life is a verdict about the individual's eternal destiny. Exemplifying the appropriate anxiety in a discourse about the resurrection of the dead, Kierkegaard warns the reader that "*my* salvation is not yet decided" (*CD*, 212). In the contexts in which these themes appear, Kierkegaard often uses the conceptual contrast of "time" and "eternity," with "eternity" suggesting the ultimate evaluation of the individual's entire temporal life. The quality of our eternal life is determined in this life by our ongoing response to God. It is the obligation to live righteously before God that unites the temporal and the eternal, giving eternal significance to our earthly life in time.

This thought of being observed and evaluated by God inspires and provokes an array of passions and dispositions, many of which Kierkegaard explored in his discourses to prepare penitents to receive Holy Communion. For example, entertaining the picture of a final judgment fosters patience with the ordinary woes of daily living, for their importance pales in comparison with the momentousness of the task of becoming the kind of person of whom God can approve (*UDVS*, 306-20). Conversely, despair about the verdict of eternity haunts the life that cavalierly ignores its divinely appointed goal.

As we have seen, Augustine had also described God as the judge who would pass judgment on our spiritual progress. Human beings will be held accountable for having cultivated love for God or for having failed to do so. Augustine had emphasized the theme of personal responsibility in his critique of the Manicheans, and he continued that motif in his subsequent work, even when arguing for predestination. Like Kierkegaard, Augustine used this image to spur the pilgrim to take life with utter seriousness and to face life-shaping decisions with fear and trembling. For both thinkers, life is not only a journey and a school, but it is also a trial. Usually Augustine used the theme of a final judgment to prod the straying pilgrim back onto the proper path by dramatizing the consequences of departing from it. To motivate the pilgrim to move forward, Augustine was much more likely to use the positive picture of the attractiveness of the goal. However, Kierkegaard — more like John Bunyan — was much more generous in his use of the judgment image. For him it was crucial to emphasize God's ongoing evaluation in order to ensure that the pilgrim did not succumb to the vices of self-satisfaction and assurance that would destroy all passion.

But the motif of trembling at the prospect of God's judgment was tempered by Kierkegaard with other, more ostensibly attractive God-oriented passions. For Kierkegaard, one of the most critical forms of pathos that gives meaning to talk about God is delight in God's love. In his journals Kierkegaard observes: "It is really remarkable that whereas all the other qualifications pronounced about God are adjectives, 'love' is the only substantive . . ." (*JP* 2, 1319). Like Augustine, he frequently interrupts the flow of his books with outbursts of adulation for God's love. Panegyrics to divine love are pervasive in his pages, a fact that his interpreters have all too frequently overlooked. Kierkegaard's dramatic depictions of much more sobering issues, such as human anxiety and despair, have attracted more scholarly and popular attention.[40] Moreover, his insistence on the demanding nature of the Christlike life has given the impression that he was a dour, grim prophet of moral rigorism — perhaps like his own father — rather

---

40. A major exception that does emphasize the centrality of love in Kierkegaard is M. Jamie Ferreira, *Love's Grateful Striving: A Commentary on Kierkegaard's "Works of Love"* (Oxford: Oxford University Press, 2001).

than a poet of God's compassion. However, without the identification of love as God's very nature, much of Kierkegaard's work makes little sense, for the concepts "God" and "absolute good," and so on, are by themselves so abstract as to be vacuous. Contrary to the prevalent description of the gloomy, self-enclosed Danish writer, Kierkegaard can best be understood as a devotee of God's love, for that is the leitmotif that most fundamentally shines through all his works. As it was for Augustine, so also for Kierkegaard, the most important affirmation about God is that God is infinite love. It is this underlying theme that gives specificity and thickness to the concepts of desire for, dependence on, trust in, gratitude to, and fear of God that receive so much attention in his writings.

Kierkegaard's emphasis on the daunting nature of the Christlike life did not prevent him from foregrounding God's gracious love. In fact, he often treated the rigorousness required by Christ as an expression of God's loving solicitude for the individual. Kierkegaard — like Augustine, but to a much lesser degree — treated the doctrine of the Trinity as an elliptical way of highlighting love as God's most essential attribute. In Kierkegaard's theological circles, the doctrine of the Trinity had received renewed attention because of its prominence in the thought of both Hegel and Schelling. Kierkegaard was familiar with Hegel's use of the Trinity to suggest the unity of abstract universality (the Father) and particularity (the Son) in individuality (the Holy Spirit). For Hegel, this synthesis of universality and particularity actualized in the singular, concrete individual is the basic structural dynamic of all reality.[41] In 1838, Frederik Christian Sibbern, a professor of philosophy at the University of Copenhagen, published a critique of what he took to be Hegel's identification of the Trinity with the dialectical movement of universality, individuality, and singularity.[42] According to Sibbern, Hegel at best viewed the Trinity as a pictorial way of suggesting that God attains self-consciousness in the minds of human beings. Sibbern's critique of Hegel sparked heated discussion in Danish scholarly and ecclesiastical communities concerning what the doctrine of the Trinity really means.

Kierkegaard was also very much aware of H. L. Martensen's use of Augustinian themes to modify Hegel's account of the Trinity, pushing it in

---

41. Georg Wilhelm Hegel, *Hegel's Philosophy of Mind*, trans. W. Wallace, ed. A. V. Miller (Oxford: Clarendon Press, 1971), § 566.

42. Frederik Christian Sibbern, "Perseus," *Maanedsskrift for Litteratur* 19, no. 6 (1838): Article III, pp. 46-58. See Jon Stewart, *A History of Hegelianism in Golden Age Denmark*, vol. II: *The Martensen Period: 1837-1842* (Copenhagen: Søren Kierkegaard Research Center and C. A. Reitzel, 2007), pp. 218-25.

a more overtly orthodox direction. Martensen feared that Hegel's view of the Trinity had at best been a hypostasization of an impersonal dialectical movement animating the universe. In his lectures on dogmatics during the summer of 1838 (which Kierkegaard attended), Martensen argued that the Trinity is the eternal ground of the drama of the incarnation enacted in time, and thus the orthodox doctrine was a thematization of God's love. Martensen argued that the revelation of God's self in Jesus Christ shows that God is an infinitely free self-conscious subject, not an impersonal dialectical dynamic.[43] Martensen concluded that the doctrine of the Trinity is the foundation for all Christian belief and practice.[44] God's threefold action *ad extra* in creation, redemption, and consummation are expressions of God's life *in se:* the "economic" Trinity implies the "immanent" Trinity. Later in his *Christian Dogmatics,* Martensen borrows and modifies Augustine's metaphor of self-consciousness to illuminate God's inner life, proposing that God differentiates himself as an "I" (subject) from himself as a "Thou" (object), and then comprehends himself as the reconciliation of both in love.[45] For Martensen, this way of understanding the Trinity underscores the theme that God is most essentially an inner dynamic of love. This love that is internal to the divine life is projected outward to create a universe of finite beings with whom God can be reunited in love. God is, in fact, a threefold fountain of love from which flow three streams of love.

Although Kierkegaard criticized Martensen's fondness for metaphysical systems, he did share Martensen's conviction that God should be conceptualized as love. Of course, Kierkegaard never attempted to develop a speculative account of the Trinity in the grand manner of Hegel or Schelling, or even in the more carefully orthodox ways of Marheineke, Rosenkranz, and Martensen. For Kierkegaard, the marriage of Trinitarian doctrine and metaphysics was a sterile hybrid that served no purpose and undermined the mood of self-involvement that any discussion of God's love requires. Haufniensis overtly criticized Schelling's penchant for positing a dialectic of

---

43. Hans Lassen Martensen, in *KJN* 2, pp. 344, 349.

44. Hans Lassen Martensen, "Rationalisme, Supranaturalisme og *principium exclusi medii,*" *Tidsskrift for Litteratur og Kritik* 1, no. 5 (1839): 465. (English translation: "Rationalism, Supernaturalism and the *principium exclusi medii,*" in Jon Stewart, ed. and trans., *Mynster's "Rationalism, Supernaturalism" and the Debate about Mediation* [Copenhagen: Museum Tusculanum Press, 2009], pp. 127-43).

45. Hans Lassen Martensen, *Den christelige Dogmatik* (Copenhagen: C. A. Reitzel, 1850), p. 111 (English translation: *Christian Dogmatics,* trans. William Urwick [Edinburgh: T&T Clark, 1866], p. 107).

passions in God's inner life (*CA,* 59). In spite of these reservations, Kierke-gaard was convinced, no less than Martensen, that love is the real meaning of the doctrine of the Trinity. The identification of God in terms of personal self-giving pervades Kierkegaard's pages, and it reaches its most mature and thorough articulation in *Works of Love.*

Rather than speculating about God's intra-Trinitarian life or contem-plating the "creative birth pangs of the deity" (*CA,* 59), Kierkegaard at-tempted to engender an understanding of God's love through several less arcane strategies. Sometimes Kierkegaard simply confessed God's love directly, as did Augustine. In his many different voices Kierkegaard often candidly asserts that "God is love" (*FT,* 34; *UDSV,* 101, 267-68, 274, 277; *WL,* 264-65; *CD,* 191, 194, 198), and he overtly identifies love as God's essential attribute. However, more frequently Kierkegaard's understanding of God's love must be extrapolated from his activities of reduplicating God's love in his authorial practice, praising God's love and encouraging the reader to reflect God's love by loving the neighbor. In all of these activities Kierke-gaard does highlight particular features of God's love that may encourage the individual to love God. His efforts to evoke the forms of pathos that are part of loving God imply certain convictions about the nature of God's love. When these are added together, the resulting picture of God's love is surprisingly similar to Augustine's portrayal of the love of God manifested in the relationships of the Trinitarian persons to one another.

We have already seen earlier in this chapter how *Works of Love* func-tions as a stimulus toward a desire and love for God (and thus the neigh-bor). It also demonstrates what God's other-regarding love is like by mir-roring it in the author's textual practice. It is axiomatic for Kierkegaard that genuine Christian love is a reflection of God's love, and thus the two can be used to illuminate each other. To enable an imaginative grasp God's love, the text enacts God's type of love — by being itself a work of love. The reader, unclear about the true nature of divine love, must be shown by the text's own performance what a godly work of love is. The authorial voice of *Works of Love* is significant to its theme, for it expresses the devotion to the well-being of the other that is the essential nature of love. The implied author remains indistinct, refusing to draw attention to himself. His use of a generalized "we" does nothing more than identify him as a member of Christendom's cultured class who has been reared in the basics of the faith (*WL,* 47). For Kierkegaard, this self-erasure is entirely appropriate, for a textual work of love should not draw attention to the lover. Because God's self-giving love is oriented outward toward the beloved, the author should be unobtrusive, directing attention to the neighbor. Accordingly, the most striking rhetorical feature of *Works of Love* is its overt concern for the spiritual health of the reader. The text's solicitude toward the reader is a reflection of God's infinitely more intense concern for human individuals. Because the implied author's love is an image of God's love, the basic thrust of the text suggests that God is first and foremost other-regarding love, intent on nurturing the ultimate felicity of the beloved.

According to Kierkegaard, the most effective way to help another person understand God's love is to lovingly draw attention to love's intrinsic worth so that the other person can begin to experience love's attractiveness. Consequently, the appropriate passional context for speaking of God's love is an attitude of praise, for adoration communicates the sense that the thing being praised is of inestimable value and stimulates a desire to explore the source of the adorer's enthusiasm. Accordingly, in *Works of Love* Kierkegaard addresses God in prayer as the "source of all love in heaven and on earth; you who spared nothing but in love gave everything; you who are love, so that one who loves is what he is only by being in you!" (*WL,* 3). Expressing delight in God's other-regarding love is so important to Kierkegaard that his rhetoric becomes turgid whenever he describes its inexhaustible and unstinting nature. In all these encomia, the feature of God's love that is consistently praised is God's radical self-giving.

The fact that the commandment to love the neighbor is a call to "reduplicate" God's love means that the ideal life of Christian love can be used as a lens for bringing God's love into focus. The ideal form of human love can serve as a template for understanding God because divine love is the ultimate source of all human love.[46] Kierkegaard observes: "Just as the quiet lake originates deep down in hidden springs no eye has seen, so also does a person's love originate even more deeply in God's love" (*WL,* 9). As the individual focuses more and more on God's love, the reader's God-given capacity to become loving will be increasingly enhanced. Like Augustine, Kierkegaard insists that human love is really derivative from God, who is the origin of all love. The water that flows from the fountain of divine love bears the characteristics of the water's source. Therefore, true Christian love can be used as an analogy of God's love.[47]

---

46. See Paul Martens, "'You Shall Love': Kant, Kierkegaard, and the Interpretation of Matthew 22:39," in Robert L. Perkins, ed., *International Kierkegaard Commentary: Works of Love* (Macon, GA: Mercer University Press, 1999), p. 72.

47. See Ferreira, *Love's Grateful Striving.*

This analogy points to the radically other-regarding nature of God's love. Kierkegaard explicitly affirms that God's love rejoices in the sheer otherness of the beloved, even though God's creative love has produced that very otherness (CD, 127; WL, 272). God takes pleasure in the simple fact of the existence of God's creatures quite apart from any benefit that God might derive from them. God's love is not motivated by a desire to gratify some craving for companionship antecedently felt by God, for God does not need anything. Rather, God's love is animated solely by a delight in the other and a concern for the well-being of the other. Christ, the manifestation of God's love, was interested solely in "the other person's benefit," and loved "for the sake of the other person" (WL, 100).

The fact that human love for the neighbor must be active and must bear fruit suggests another crucial feature of God's love. God's love is not just a passive joy about the fact that the beloved exists; it is also an absolutely selfless commitment to promote the well-being of the other (WL, 264). God is not like Aristotle's unmoved mover, who draws individuals through the attractive power of its intrinsic but static excellence, without actively loving them (TM, 272). As Augustine found Plotinus's view of the divine one to be inadequate, so also Kierkegaard rejected the notion common in the classical tradition that the divine moves finite being solely by being the object of desire. God's active love is manifested not only in the gratuity of the gift of life but also in the continuing prevenient nature of God's mercy.

The independence of Christian love for the neighbor from the neighbor's attractiveness or desirable assets shows that God's reconciling love is not a response to the actual or potential spiritual excellence of the beloved object (WL, 44-60). The persistence of God's love is not due to the individual creature's successful cultivation of attractive attributes. God does not love the creature because of the creature's beauty, intelligence, moral virtue, or spiritual accomplishments. God's love is not even contingent on any reciprocity. God will persist in loving the creature even when the creature fails to show appreciation or gratitude, and even when the creature engages in outright rebellion. God does not love the beloved creature because of the beloved's loveliness, but simply because God is loving.

According to Kierkegaard, the nonpreferential nature of Christian love for the neighbor indicates that God's love could not possibly single out favorites. As with the ideal human love that issues from it, God's love is not contingent on the possession of some excellence that certain individuals might exhibit to a higher degree than others. Kierkegaard quips, "If it were love's excellence to love the extraordinary, then God would be, if I dare say so, in an awkward position, since for him the extraordinary does not exist at all" (*WL*, 65). Kierkegaard insists that God's fatherly concern extends even to the least and most inconsequential of God's creatures. He reiterates the conviction that God's nonpreferential love is not lavished more on one particular social or economic class than others. God loves the poor as well as the rich, royalists as well as democrats, and sinners as well as saints. God's love is more radically egalitarian than anything imagined by democratic ideologies. The good news is that no amount of marginalization by human communities could support the suspicion that an individual has been rejected by God.

The love commandment's call for radical self-giving and even self-sacrifice is also a reflection of God's way of loving. In the prayer that introduces *Works of Love,* Kierkegaard addresses God as "you who spared nothing but in love gave everything" (*WL*, 3). Even God's spiritual instruction is an expression of self-giving love, because God the teacher cares for the development of the student's soul, even if that care brings grief to the teacher (*WL*, 377). The divine teacher, who does not covet admiration or any kind of recompense, gives himself sacrificially in his pedagogy. As we shall see, the consistently self-giving and self-sacrificial nature of the life of Christ, which Kierkegaard elaborates repeatedly in his writings, points to these qualities in the Godhead itself. The incarnation, the assumption of lowliness and the acceptance of persecution, is a manifestation of God's eternal self-emptying love. The theme of self-sacrifice, the way of the cross, looms large in Kierkegaard's depictions of the life of discipleship, for that life is a reflection of God's kenotic manner of loving manifested in Christ the prototype.

Other portions of Kierkegaard's writings adumbrate yet more features of God's love. For example, God's self-giving includes radical empathy with creatures who are subject to the manifold joys and tribulations of earthly life. In "To Need God Is a Human Being's Highest Perfection," Kierkegaard explains that God remains with an individual through all of life's vicissitudes as an infinitely caring presence (*EUD*, 322-23). Similarly, in another upbuilding discourse, Kierkegaard declares that God is deeply moved by every struggler's cries of lamentation. Kierkegaard writes:

> [T]he God to whom he [a struggling pilgrim] prays is human, has the heart to feel humanly, the ear to hear a human being's complaint; and even though he does not fulfill every wish, he still lives close to us and is moved by the struggler's cry, by his humble request, by his wretchedness

when he sits abandoned and as if in prison, by his speedy joy over the fulfillment when in hope he anticipates it. (*EUD*, 387)

In a late discourse Kierkegaard described God's love as being "warm," in fact, changelessly warm (*TM*, 280-81). For Kierkegaard, God's intensely interpersonal love is a desire for intimacy with lowly creatures who can offer God nothing.

But this divine love is also a desire for mutuality. For Kierkegaard, the attractiveness of God is not merely the spectacle of sublime divine self-giving. Kierkegaard's view of love is not devoid of the celebration of mutuality, of receiving as well as giving. In all love, including God's, there is an element of joy in receiving love, in knowing that one is beloved. In "To Need God Is a Human Being's Highest Perfection," Kierkegaard expresses a longing to be loved by God, not just to love God. Similarly, in "The Thorn in the Flesh," Kierkegaard elaborates on Paul's wondrous discovery that his true identity is that he is God's beloved. Even Christ wanted not only to love but also to be loved. Because human love is the image of God's love, this delight in mutuality, a desire to receive love in return, is also a dimension of God's love. In journal entries from 1854, Kierkegaard explicitly says: "God loves — and God wants to be loved. These two in equilibrium make true Christianity" (*JP* 2, 1446), and "God is love, and God wants to be loved — this is the Christianity of the New Testament (*JP* 3, 2448).

The motif of God's desire for reciprocity is poignantly illustrated in *Philosophical Fragments* by the parable of the king who wants to love and be loved by a peasant maiden (*PF*, 24-27). Of course, as we have seen, God's self-giving is not contingent on any reciprocation. God will continue to love the individual even if the individual refuses to respond by loving God in return, just as Christ continued to love Peter even while Peter was denying him. Nevertheless, loving mutuality is the ultimate goal of God's love. In fact, God's selfless concern for the well-being of the individual must include the hope and expectation that the individual will reciprocate God's love, for loving God is the individual's highest blessing and intended destiny. God wants the individual to love God, not because God needs some affection but because the individual will experience the highest happiness through loving God.

The meaning of this reciprocity of love that God desires can only be understood if the individual grasps its full gravity.[48] Kierkegaard observes:

48. See Tim Rose, *Kierkegaard's Christocentric Theology* (Aldershot, UK: Ashgate, 2001), pp. 128-29.

"If someone were able to adhere on the greatest scale to the fact that God is love in the sense that God loves him and then came to see the other side, that God wants to be loved — he would become anxious [*angst*] and afraid" (*JP* 2, 1446). Echoing the king/maiden parable of *Philosophical Fragments*, Kierkegaard explains that it would be as if a poor girl realized that a great and powerful man earnestly wanted her to love him. Given the disparity in status, the expectation of reciprocating the love is grievously intimidating. In the case of the individual and God, the prospect that God wants the individual to love God in the way that God loves her or him is potentially frightful. After all, God *in se* is infinite love, but human beings are only finite, fickle, and (as we shall see) sinful. Kierkegaard continues: "[N]othing is more dreadful than to be pulled up to this highest level of existence, where in one sense God's wanting to be loved is so frightfully earnest" (*JP* 2, 1446). Part of understanding the fact that God is love involves realizing what a lofty standard that love is, and feeling how inadequate one's passional abilities are to approximate it. The magnitude of God's love not only attracts but repels. (As we shall see, this is the source of the potential offensiveness of the incarnation.)

God's love, as described by Kierkegaard's many voices, has another unsettling characteristic that often obscures its presence. The very existence of the creature, differentiated from God, is the fruit of God's radically other-regarding bounty. Out of love God establishes the independent life of a genuine "other," an autonomous entity that is not a mere extension of God's own being or will. God limits God's own power and surrenders control over the creature in order to bestow the gift of individuated life. God's love values the otherness of the human creature so much that God refuses to obliterate the distinction of God and the individual. Although a person "wants nothing but to remain with God, as near as possible in this time of separation . . ." (*EUD*, 392), God lovingly maintains some distance so that the person can acquire a coherent self. According to Kierkegaard, one can only give oneself to God if one has a genuine self to give. Because this self-giving is the highest joy possible, God's most loving gift to human beings is the sometimes painful possibility of becoming a self that can give itself in love. This often makes God's love seem odd, disappointing, and even unloving. God provides edification but not immediate beatitude, because only in this way can God lovingly preserve the separate identity of the beloved. Consequently, indirect communication is the appropriate vehicle of divine love, for it makes the beloved's growth possible. This means that God's love is willing to accept the risk and potential pain of being misunderstood by the beloved and provoking the beloved's hostility. This love for human creatures is metaphorically costly for God, for God faces the terrible possibility of rejection by the creature. But God's determination to have a genuine other is so strong that God is even willing to encounter the probable hostility of the beloved.

Because God wants to preserve the independence of individuals, and not coerce or seduce them into loving God by showering them with overt worldly benefits, the beneficence of God must remain partially hidden. We encounter this concealed love of God only indirectly, through the ordinary phenomena of daily life, including the love shown to us by others (including the love for the reader that is exhibited by the author of *Works of Love*). Accordingly, Christians are exhorted to construe events and experiences, no matter how troubling they may seem, as the good gifts of a loving parent, as is evident in Kierkegaard's frequent portrayals of gratitude. Part of what it means to confess that God is love is to be willing to receive both life's blessings and its tribulations with thankfulness, trusting that somehow they are expressions of parental concern.

As it was for Augustine, love is so central for Kierkegaard that he uses it to interpret God's other attributes. For example, he defines God's omnipotence as the power of God's love (*CD,* 127; *SLW,* 144). Similarly, the changelessness of God is the constancy of God's love (*EUD,* 392). Talk of divine immutability simply means that God remains changeless in being committed to the flourishing of God's creatures. God's impassibility is God's constant, steady concern for the other (*TM,* 268; *EUD,* 393); it is not God's inability to experience the griefs of God's creatures. As we have seen, Augustine also maintained that in human beings love is the form of the other virtues. Because the human capacity to love is the image of God, this means that love is also the principle that makes all virtues one in God. Therefore, despite their apparent differences, both Kierkegaard and Augustine concurred that the "metaphysical perfections" of God's power, wisdom, and justice are expressions of God's love.

Although Kierkegaard shied away from the Trinitarian ruminations typical of Augustine, he occasionally did appropriate traditional Trinitarian language in order to discuss God's love. In *Works of Love* and many of the discourses he praises God's external acts of creating, redeeming, and sustaining the individual and the world, and he associates each act with one of the persons of the Trinity, as Augustine allowed with his theory of appropriation. Kierkegaard sees these three activities of God *ad extra* as manifestations of God's internal life of love. First, the individual's sheer existence and all that sustains it are the expression of the love of God the Creator. Although God's creative love is not directly evident in any aspect of nature, the reader can learn to respond to all things and all events as a gift. Second, mercy toward sinners and the provision of a prototype of genuine love are the expression of the love of God the Redeemer. Third, our very ability to grow in faith, hope, and love is the expression of the love of God the Holy Spirit. Implicit in the very structure of the opening prayer of *Works of Love* is this "economic" understanding of the Trinity, minus the metaphysical apparatus. Rather than developing a theory or analogy to clarify how "one nature" can simultaneously be "three persons," Kierkegaard rhetorically enacts three different grateful responses to the three different dimensions of God's love. To believe in the Trinity is to grow in these three modes of gratitude.

Like Augustine, Kierkegaard refuses to allow the three activities of God to be regarded as unrelated to one another. In a journal entry from 1852, he associates the exalted, awesome nature of God with the Father and the attractive accessibility of God with the Son as Mediator (which, of course, can also be offensive). He proceeds to note that the Mediator is also the prototype, whose excellence cannot be adequately approximated, as well as the Atoner, who addresses the problem of failure to follow the prototype. The Holy Spirit helps the individual in striving to be like the prototype (and implicitly the Atoner also, for they are twin aspects of the same Mediator). Kierkegaard says: "It is the Father who directs to the Son, the Son who directs to the Spirit, and not until then is it the Spirit who leads to the Son and the Son who leads to the Father" (*JP* 2, 1432). He adds: "[H]e becomes my Father in the Mediator by means of the Spirit" (*JP* 2, 1432). This complex pattern defies any strict chronological sequence of different experiences of distinguishable aspects of God's activity and suggests that the three Persons act in concert, simultaneously enabling the individual to appreciate God's holiness, God's forgiveness and demand, and God's empowerment.[49] This parallels Augustine's argument that the operations of the persons of the Trinity *ad extra* are indistinguishable, for all of them cooperate in any action upon the universe. The upbuilding point of all this is that the individual should experience the creating, redeeming, and empowering aspects of God in every episode of life.

Unlike Augustine, Kierkegaard does not speculate about the relation-

---

49. See Paul Martens, "The Emergence of the Holy Spirit in Kierkegaard's Thought"; see also Bradley Dewey, "Kierkegaard and the Blue Testament," *Harvard Theological Review* 60 (1967): 407-8.

ships of the persons of the Trinity to one another, or even produce a set of metaphors that could balance one another and thereby trigger deeper insight. Diverging significantly from Augustine here, Kierkegaard does not find that kind of meditation on divine love *in se* to be particularly edifying. Nevertheless, Kierkegaard's encomium to God as the source of all love commits him to the notion that God *in se* is most essentially a dynamic of loving relationality. Rather than contemplating the mystery of how God could be loving in God's own self, Kierkegaard seeks to clarify the nature of divine love by showing how it is reflected in human lives.

This is the heart of the difference between Kierkegaard's and Augustine's strategies for edification. Kierkegaard's strategy chooses to elucidate the meaning of "God" in terms of the ways that the concept "God" functions in the passionate religious life of the individual. Augustine had also insisted on establishing the right worshipful mood for discourse about God, but once this mood was established, he did not hesitate to investigate the plausibility of theological convictions or to generate metaphysical theories on the basis of those convictions. For Kierkegaard, on the contrary, a better understanding of "God" as presented in the Bible is never to be had through trying to conceptualize the attributes of a spectacular but elusive divine being. Definitions of God's perfections and analyses of God's ontological nature will not help the reader understand the Maker of heaven and earth. Rather, the meaning of "God" becomes clearer by imagining a distinctive set of hopes, fears, longings, and joys. The description and indirect textual performance of divine love give heightened specificity to what it is about God that attracts the individual when the individual is attracted to God. It gives content to the theme of desiring God by clarifying what is being desired. Therefore, Kierkegaard avoids the genre of the philosophical treatise and adopts the style of a poetic (and oddly ironic) homily. God can only be spoken of doxologically, penitentially, ecstatically, and fearfully — and never speculatively.

In spite of this profound difference with Augustine, Kierkegaard does echo themes about God's love that had been essential for the Bishop of Hippo. As we have seen, for both thinkers it is the divine love that is the object of human desire — and the destination of the human journey. Both Augustine and Kierkegaard describe love as being delight in the beloved as well as active concern for the beloved's well-being. For both of them, love is ideally the mutual delight of the lover and the beloved, but love nevertheless is not founded on the guarantee or even likely prospect of such mutuality. According to each of these writers, love's extravagant concern for the beloved manifests itself as a self-giving that can take the form of self-sacrifice. Kierkegaard, like Augustine, refuses to bifurcate eros and agape (as those terms have come to be used in the wake of Nygren). For both of them, love for God and the neighbor as self-fulfillment and as other-regarding self-abandonment are not mutually exclusive. Augustine and Kierkegaard are in agreement that the attractiveness of God's love is most evident in God's assumption of the lowly form of a servant in order to enact love for humanity. According to both of them, it is the vision of this radical kenosis that can spark human desire and draw it forward. Individuals can grow in desire for that kind of self-emptying love and yearn to contemplate it and participate in it eternally. Paradoxically, it is self-abandonment that satisfies the restless heart's longing for self-fulfillment. The pages of the works of both Augustine and Kierkegaard characterize the Christian life as an eros for agape.

CHAPTER 5

Sin: Culpable Action and Corrupt State

As we have seen, for both Augustine and Kierkegaard, God is the source, goal, and support of our journey, as well as being the "way" itself. But for both thinkers, that journey to which God calls us is plagued with a lethal problem before it even begins. Both Augustine and Kierkegaard have gained lasting notoriety as the archetypal denigrators of the moral and spiritual capacities of human nature unaided by grace. Augustine stridently opposed the valorization of free will by Pelagius and his allies, and Kierkegaard resisted the chronic optimism of the various forms of culturally accommodated theology that circulated in the early nineteenth century. Neo-orthodox theologians such as Emil Brunner and Reinhold Niebuhr appealed to both Augustine and Kierkegaard as antidotes to the naïve affirmation of innate human goodness that, in their view, had trivialized pre–World War I liberal theologies. Such theologians hail both Augustine and Kierkegaard as the predecessors of psychological theorists, existential playwrights, and naturalistic novelists who sought to probe the disturbing and shadowy depths of the self in the 1940s and 1950s. On the other side, process theologians and devotees of creation spirituality habitually identify Augustine and Kierkegaard as two major fonts of the life-negating sensibility that they fear has infected Western Christianity. Augustine and Kierkegaard, so this critique goes, helped keep Christianity's attention riveted on original sin rather than on original blessing. While caricatures abound, this widespread popular linkage of Augustine and Kierkegaard does contain a fair amount of truth, for both of them were convinced that, without God's gracious intervention, humanity would remain trapped in guilt, spiritual debility, and moral corruption.

The parallel between the two Christian thinkers is even closer than the bare common worry about human sinfulness suggests. Both of them attempted to hold together two equally crucial themes that ostensibly work at cross-purposes. On the one hand, they both sought to portray human beings as universally and inevitably mired in a depravity from which they cannot extricate themselves. Moreover, they both emphasized this plight in order to prepare the individual to rejoice in the offer of forgiveness and new life. On the other hand, they both wanted to preserve a sense of the individual's responsibility and guilt for the fact that the individual is in this predicament. In short, the two theologians sought to affirm that sin is simultaneously both universal corruption and personal guilt; both resorted to paradoxical language and curious rhetorical strategies to combine these two messages; and both have been accused of muddled thinking, self-contradiction, and morbidity. Their language about sin is sufficiently polyvalent to inspire almost contradictory appropriations. On the subject of sin, Augustine has been claimed as a seminal theological predecessor both by Catholics and by their Lutheran and Reformed opponents; Kierkegaard, for his part, has been variously characterized as a faithful Augustinian and as an arch-Pelagian.[1] An examination of both of their writings about sin will reveal many convergences — and some divergences — in the ways they attempted to speak coherently and meaningfully about an elusive matter that seemed to require conflicting vocabularies. A closer examination, however, will show that those ostensibly contradictory discourses might well be complementary.

Augustine and the Totalization of Corruption and Guilt

One of Augustine's most enduring contributions to Christian theology is his critique of the Pelagian trust in the efficacy of human moral and spiritual striving. He has been both extravagantly lauded and bitterly condemned for his diatribes against the Pelagians. As we have seen, Augustine's polemical exchanges with a variety of Pelagian thinkers were the focus of the bulk of

---

1. See Niels Thulstrup, "Adam and Original Sin," in Niels Thulstrup and Marie Milulová Thulstrup, eds., *Theological Concepts in Kierkegaard, Bibliotheca Kierkegaardiana*, vol. 5 (Copenhagen: C. A. Reitzels Boghandel, 1980), pp. 122-56; A. C. Cochrane, *The Existentialists and God* (Philadelphia: Westminster, 1956), p. 39; Gregor Malantschuk, "Kierkegaard's Dialectical Method," in Daniel Conway, ed., *Søren Kierkegaard: Critical Assessments of Leading Philosophers* (London: Routledge, 2002), pp. 140-41.

the secondary literature about Augustine that Kierkegaard read. The Augustine with whom Kierkegaard was familiar was first and foremost the primary originator (often sharing the credit with Tertullian and Cyprian in the textbooks) and advocate of the doctrine of original sin that Lutheranism inherited.

Augustine's thought evolved dramatically on the issue of human sinfulness, perhaps more than it did on any other subject. Augustine's early writings include adamant defenses of individual freedom and responsibility against any hint of determinism. In his early work against the Manicheans, who claimed that a good person will always perform good deeds while an evil person will commit evil deeds, Augustine argues that God did not create evil beings, nor did any other cosmic power produce beings who must sin by necessity.[2] Against the fatalistic view that sin issues inevitably from an evil nature, Augustine sought an alternative explanation for the presence of evil, including the tragic events and the woes that seem to be structured into the natural world. Augustine hoped to counteract the Manichean cosmological dualism that regarded human vice as a manifestation of a destructive power that opposes everything good. Evil, including the human propensity to sin, must not be regarded as a unified force at war with the good. Evil is not a type of virulent entity, for such a view would suggest that God as the Creator is not entirely benevolently disposed toward the created order. No creature's nature was designed by God to be evil, and God did not intend that human individuals would be sinful. At the most general level, evil must be described as some kind of privation, perhaps as a diminishment, a lack, or a corruption of something that is essentially good. Therefore, the source of sin in human beings must be sought elsewhere than in the will of God, the incompetence of the Creator, or the eternal malevolence of a preexisting evil principle.

With regard to human motivations, Augustine concluded that evil is not chosen for its own sake. Evil is always done for the sake of some good, but always at the expense of another — and usually more significant — good. Because humans do love the various goods at hand in disordered and inappropriate ways, they are motivated to choose lesser and inadequate goods. The question then becomes: Who or what is responsible for the derangement of human desires? To explain this, Augustine places the blame on human beings themselves. He insists that human sin is due to the misuse of the human freedom to choose. Augustine locates the problem

---

2. Augustine, *On Free Will*, in *WSA* I, 3.

in the variable will of humanity and the angels, who have freely chosen to disobey God and continue to opt for disobedience. The free will of spiritual creatures is indeed a good gift of God, for it makes possible voluntary obedience to God, which is intrinsic to living rightly. Unfortunately, the freedom to choose to obey God entails the freedom to choose not to obey God. Through this negative power the will itself, not some external factor or necessitating cause, produces its own evil decisions. The voluntary misuse of the will is the source of evil and thus the ground of culpability. Augustine admits that the will's turning to lesser goods is a mysterious phenomenon, for in so doing it is preferring deficiency to fullness. But whatever the motivation, one thing remains clear: God is not the author of sin; disobedient humans and angels are the culprits.

Early in his life Augustine was so intent on asserting the goodness of the created order against Manichean disparagements of it that he tried to discover some good even in the misuse of freedom. Accordingly, he proposed that human vulnerabilities, even the susceptibility to temptation, are actually an incentive to spiritual growth, and that the resulting final state of saved humans who have undergone such a rigorous pedagogy is better than their innocent, created state. By so arguing, the early Augustine was maintaining continuity with a view of the spiritual maturation of humanity that was widespread in the Eastern churches, stretching at least back to the seminal theology of Irenaeus. In this schema, humanity progresses from the immaturity of spiritual childhood, through a period of challenging and chastening experiences, to the goal of full religious adulthood. Sin is either an interruption or retardation of the expected progress or a necessary obstacle to be overcome in order for the proper learning to occur. As we shall see, this developmental pattern would have echoes in the work of the Hegelian theologians, whom Kierkegaard opposed.

However, by the end of his life, Augustine regarded most vulnerabilities as the consequence of the fall into sin, and not as prods initially intended by God for educative purposes. His mature opinion was that human beings cannot, even by means of the enabling power of God's grace, make themselves better than God intended them to be at their creation. In moving toward this conclusion, which uncoupled the fall from the need for spiritual maturation, Augustine modified his early opinions only very slowly. Even by the time of the *Confessions,* he still did not affirm original sin in the robust form that would characterize his later writings. In the *Confessions* he describes a tendency toward sinfulness as being present in the soul from the beginning of the individual's life, but he does not portray it as something to which we are in bondage, totally incapacitating the freedom to not sin.[3] But Augustine does make it clear that there is an inclination toward sin in every individual, due to the mortality of the body, and this inclination becomes personal guilt through the first intentional act of an individual. In the *Confessions* he also begins to claim more robustly that the damaged nature that we inherit from Adam prevents us from being able to eliminate sin from our souls.

But new challenges and controversies were motivating Augustine to emphasize the virulence of human sin more and more strongly.[4] Even before his controversy with Pelagius, during his polemic against the Donatists in 406, Augustine argues that sinfulness persists in the lives of believers.[5] The Donatists had insisted on the purity of the ecclesial hierarchy — and sometimes on the purity of all church members. Against this view, Augustine declares that even mature Christians must continue to depend on the forgiving and empowering grace of Christ. Augustine's purpose is to encourage believers to concentrate on their ongoing incorporation into Christ, and to warn them of the folly of trusting in the power of their own wills. He is urging his readers to cultivate the devotional habit of contemplating Christ and relying on the grace of Christ available through the corporate life of the church and its sacraments. According to Augustine, humility and gratitude remain central virtues even for advanced Christians; self-reliance leads only to spiritual pride, failure, and frustration. In all of this Augustine was attempting to reinforce the recognition that grace is absolutely essential for the individual's recovery from sin. As will become evident, Kierkegaard agreed wholeheartedly with Augustine's proclamation of the need to rely on grace, but he detached that conviction from the sacramental context in which it had been situated in the bishop's thought.

Shortly after this, when arguing against Pelagius and his supporters, Augustine began to strike another, more dramatic note. Pelagius, like Augustine in *On Free Will (De libero arbitrio),* had reacted against the moral determinism suggested by Manichean speculation, in which some people simply have evil natures and therefore perform evil deeds. Augustine's claims about the need for grace seemed to Pelagius to be a Manichean-like denial of freedom and responsibility. Such a denial, he feared, would dissuade Christians from striving for holiness. Pelagius claimed that, by

---

3. Augustine, *Confessions,* II, in *WSA* I, 1.

4. Augustine, *On Baptism (De baptismo),* 1.15.23, in *WSA* I, 21.

5. Augustine, *Tractates on the Gospel of John,* Homilies 4-5, in *WSA* III, 12.

emphasizing human incapacity, Augustine had implicitly reverted to his earlier Manichean position. Somewhat plausibly, Pelagius even quoted the earlier Augustine (in *On Free Will*) against the later Augustine. By arguing in this way, Pelagius sought to avoid exonerating sinful deeds by citing the fragility of human nature. Pelagius reasoned that the freedom of the will to choose not to sin *(posse non peccare)* must still be intact after the sin of Adam, or else the ascription of guilt to subsequent individuals would be impossible. According to Pelagius, though temptations abound and the flesh is weak, the allurements of vice can be resisted. The previous sinful acts of the individual, not to mention the sinful acts of a remote ancestor, cannot blight the individual's basic nature. Sinful deeds do not alter the individual's created nature and therefore do not incapacitate the individual's ability to choose not to sin. The freedom of choice persists in spite of a past history of sin. For a moral rigorist like Pelagius, the possibility of self-reformation is always available for those who want it.

Moreover, according to the Pelagians, God would be unjust to condemn subsequent individuals for a crime committed by Adam. Anyone who incurs guilt by sinning can have only one's own self to blame, for guilt is a nontransferable property. Guilt is an entirely personal matter, for it presupposes that the agent had the power to act otherwise. According to Pelagius, it is not only theoretically possible for an individual to refrain from sin, but also actually possible, for God's grace is available via the goodness of the created order and via the moral teachings and examples of Scripture. These aids to righteous action, however, do not impart any novel or special capacity to obey God, for such a capacity had never been destroyed. To be fair, Pelagius does seem to have admitted that the sinful social environment does adversely affect the individual's resolution. It is to counteract negative environmental influences that God supplies the extra help of positive law, the example of Christ, and the promise of forgiveness. Sin is passed on by imitation, not by propagation. Pelagius wanted to affirm the ability of the individual to respond to God's commandments and the freedom to perform what God commands. Unencumbered by a natural tendency to sin, individuals must assume responsibility for all their deeds.

Caelestius, Pelagius's disciple, added even more controversial claims to the already vitriolic dispute, in some respects pushing Pelagius's thought to its logical conclusion. Caelestius announced that Adam's sin injured only Adam, that infants are born in the same state that Adam enjoyed prior to his fall, that Adam would have been mortal even if he had not sinned (for death is not just a punishment for human sin), and that a person can, if that person so chooses, live entirely without sin. Many of these later propositions had not been expressly articulated by Pelagius himself. They were, however, the logical implications of his position, or so Augustine feared.

Augustine did not carefully discriminate between the authors of these interlocking views. Whether it was Pelagius or Caelestius, Augustine sensed that these claims constituted a theological sensibility incompatible with his own. Against these assertions, Augustine was forced to articulate his own position in *On the Spirit and the Letter (De spiritu et littera), On Nature and Grace (De natura et gratia),* and *On the Grace of Christ and Original Sin (De gratia Christi et de peccato originali).* His tone is often ferociously polemical. The Pelagians, he warns, failed to appreciate the abyss that loomed between the loftiness of the Christian ideal and the weakness of the individual's will. The virulence of Augustine's critique was an indicator of the importance he had attached to the imperative to divest oneself of all illusions of self-sufficiency. For Augustine, nothing less than the preservation of the virtues of gratitude to God and reliance on God's grace was at stake.

In opposing Pelagian optimism, Augustine did not want to imply that the individual will is not active in sinning, as if the individual were nothing more than a passive victim of an alien power. Throughout his writings he continues to insist that we are indeed responsible for our own actions, for sin is never "without will," as he says in a late work.[6] We are not stones or animals devoid of reason and will.[7] Contrary to the accusations of Pelagius, Augustine was not regressing to the determinism of his former Manichean brethren, nor was he embracing Stoic fatalism. However, he did want to point out that our disordered and misdirected loves prevent us from willing the good. Only with the aid of God's grace can the freedom to do the good be drawn forth and stabilized. Augustine's basic conviction was that the sin in us is our own fault, while all the good in us is ascribable to God alone. To substantiate this view, he frequently quotes I Corinthians 4:7: "What do you have that you did not receive?" The Holy Spirit must infuse love into the soul so that the individual can know the good and delight in that good so intensely that the individual's volitional capacity will be drawn to it.

In this context Augustine begins to claim that what he had written about the freedom of the will applied only to Adam before the fall. The advent of "original sin" *(peccatum originale,* a term Augustine had introduced

6. Augustine, *Revisions (Retractationes),* I, 15.2-3, in *WSA* I, 2.

7. Augustine, *On the Grace of Christ and Original Sin (De gratia Christi et de peccato originali),* I, 5 (6), in *WSA* I, 23.

into the theological vocabulary in 398) changes the situation of humanity entirely.[8] According to the mature Augustine, original sin is the lamentable inheritance that Adam bequeathed to all his descendants. Before the fall, Adam had enjoyed the power to not sin *(posse non peccare)* as well as the power to sin *(posse peccare)*.[9] As a result of his fall, Adam lost the possibility of eternal life, the special knowledge of God that he had enjoyed, and the power to not sin. After the fall, Adam was still free, but he was only free to sin. Consequently, through Adam's fault all of his descendants have lost the *posse non peccare*. Like Adam, we subsequent individuals can still choose from among a variety of sinful options. However, the range of our willing is limited, for our will, which is always moved by our desires, is situated in a context in which our desires have been misdirected. Augustine's argument is based on the belief that what we love determines the range of genuine possibilities that will attract us, and thereby establishes the fundamental volitional orientation of the individual. The misdirection of desire can be described as a corruption of our motivational core, infecting all our actions and inclinations. Original sin is essentially the propensity to shift attention from God to earthly delights, from the Creator to the creature. It is an underlying predisposition for *cupiditas* rather than *caritas*.[10] This disordering and malformation of desire toward inferior goods, which Augustine labels "concupiscence," is transmitted to all of Adam's posterity. Because of Adam, the proper relationship of the mind and the will to all the functions of the soul and body has been disrupted from the moment of conception. All people begin their life journeys from a position of sinfulness, and the struggle against sinfulness continues throughout their lives. Even those who do receive God's grace and attain the advanced stages of godliness continue to strive against the lingering propensity to sin. Although the guilt of the concupiscence is removed by baptism, its power remains, continuing to afflict the elect. As a result, humanity can be labeled a "mass of damnation," inheriting mortality, ignorance, concupiscence, and guilt.

Because the individual's horizon of choice has been restricted by a sinful orientation, the individual cannot return to a proper orientation toward the good without help from beyond the self. There is nothing in the self's set of desires powerful enough to effect such a massive reorientation. Some-

---

8. See Augustine, *To Simplicianus (Ad Simplicianum)*, in *WSA* I, 12.

9. Augustine, *On Correction and Grace (De correptione et gratia)*, 12, in *WSA* I, 26.

10. Eugene TeSelle, *Augustine the Theologian* (New York: Herder and Herder, 1970), p. 292.

thing external to the self must awaken the desire for the good and then stabilize that desire. Apart from the intervening of transformative grace, we children of Adam are stuck in our own corruption, utterly incapable of saving ourselves. Almost a millennium and a half later, Søren Kierkegaard would similarly draw attention to the "condition" supplied by God without which we remain bogged down in our own spiritual disability.

Exactly how Adam's corruption is propagated was less important to Augustine than the fact that it is indeed universally disseminated. Augustine was convinced that by the time an individual begins to make conscious decisions, that individual's volitional capacity has already been corrupted. Augustine toyed with various theories to account for the presence of corruption in all individuals without absolutely settling on any one of them. At various times in his life he considered the traducianist theory of Tertullian, the belief that the soul (and not just the body), and hence the soul's corruption, is transmitted from parents to their children in a way that is analogous to how physical characteristics are passed on. In a sense, all subsequent souls are derived from the single soul of Adam. He was uncomfortable with that view, however, for it seemed to suggest that the soul was like some extraordinarily rarified form of matter. Consequently, he usually favored the notion that God directly creates a soul for every individual. He even tended to favorably regard the theory that God has created all individual souls at once, which remain dormant until they are embodied in time. The individual souls acquire bodies either because God wills to incarnate them or because each soul rebels and falls into materiality.[11] This view, however, makes the subsequent individual's solidarity with Adam's sin difficult to explain. As a result, Augustine sometimes proposes that the union of the soul with the body during the act of procreation, when attention is clearly directed away from God, is the factor that disorders the soul. At other times he experiments with the idea that all individuals were seminally present in Adam, contained in his loins, and thus participated in his act and its tragic aftermath.[12] Through all these speculations Augustine remained tentative, for explaining sin's transmission was not as crucial as recognizing that it is somehow passed from generation to generation.

But Augustine did not want to give the impression that this universal

11. For an argument that Augustine long held a Platonic notion of the fall of the soul, see Robert J. O'Connell, *The Origin of the Soul in Augustine's Later Works* (New York: Fordham University Press, 1987).

12. Augustine, *Marriage and Desire (De nuptiis et concupiscentia)*, I, 13 (15), in *WSA* I, 24.

corruption, which we inherit in some mysterious manner, is not also our own personal fault. Although it could appear that forces beyond our control shape our character, we must acknowledge the individual's complicity in the process of deformation. Augustine was convinced that the presence of this corruption in infants, quite apart from their commission of particular sinful acts, should be regarded as their own guilt and is sufficient to ensure their damnation (although their punishment would not be harsh). Adam's progeny choose evil inevitably, but somehow this choice is still their responsibility, and they can legitimately be regarded as culpable. How exactly an individual could be held accountable for an inherited disability was a bit hard to explain.

Obvious incongruities plague Augustine's exposition. He seems to be asserting two incompatible things about original sin. On the one hand, he portrays it as a "state" of corruption; on the other hand, he describes it as culpable action. When emphasizing the "state" aspect of original sin, Augustine often uses metaphors of disease. He elaborates an entire network of related medical images, describing sin as a sickness that is transmitted and God as physician who restores the convalescent to health in the hospital of the church. However, when emphasizing the "act" aspect of original sin, he shifts to moral and legal discourse. The reader is no longer in a convalescent hospital but in a courtroom awaiting sentencing. Clearly the two sets of discourse do not work together without tension. In order to grasp the reasons for this apparent discord, we must take a careful look at Augustine's pastoral purposes in using both the "state of corruption" language and the countervailing "culpable act" language.

The "corruption" vocabulary serves several different upbuilding purposes. Perhaps most importantly, it characterizes the individual's life as a whole. The individual is not to be viewed as merely someone who sins on occasion; rather, the individual is a sinner in general. For Augustine, the corruption language counteracts the tendency of sinners to protest that, though some of their actions have been sinful, their underlying righteous identity has not been affected. Down deep, they are not bad people, they explain; only their actions are bad. To counteract this trivialization of the problem, the ascription of original sin has an identity-defining force. The individual is not just someone who contingently happens to sin; the individual is a sinner. To confess that one's own self is a sinner is to admit that there is something dreadfully amiss with the motivations, inclinations, orientations, dispositions, and goals that govern one's life.

Second, the doctrine of original sin posits the existence of a disordered passional core that accounts for the individual's performance of particular sinful actions. Specific acts are not just atomistic decisions executed by an "indifferent" free will. It is not as if the individual surveys various options for action from a neutral perspective and then makes an uninfluenced choice. Rather, original sin is a motivational propensity prior to all individual decisions. Choices do not occur in an affective vacuum, but are informed by a history of past vice, chronic self-deception and willed ignorance, habitual attractions to inappropriate objects, volitional weakness, congenitally wayward desires, and perverse environmental influences. According to Augustine, all these factors constitute a propensity that endures because of its own momentum, seemingly perpetuating itself. Individual episodes of wicked behavior are mere symptoms of this underlying antecedent condition. Consequently, Augustine can describe original sin as a "fountain" from which sins flow.

Third, according to Augustine's version of the doctrine, sin is universal. No individual can claim to be immune from sin's contamination, and no one can, through his or her own efforts, extirpate sin from the soul. Augustine claims that, after the fall, all humans have lost the freedom to not sin. Without God's healing grace, all of us postlapsarian individuals are free only to sin. This sobering thought serves as an antidote to self-righteousness, for sin's universality prevents people from excluding themselves from the "mass of damnation" and exempting themselves from condemnation. Because all are corrupt and all have fallen short, no humans have the moral authority to claim spiritual superiority over any of their brothers and sisters.

Fourth, sin's presence in an individual is explained through its prior presence in humanity in general. The past history of the human race accounts for sin's persistence in individual lives. In this regard, original sin resembles a birth defect, and Augustine does not hesitate to refer to it as "inherited" sin. He was keenly aware that individuals do not mature in a social vacuum, unaffected by the vices of their ancestors and the disordered passions of their communities. When emphasizing this inherited aspect of original corruption, Augustine can even use language suggesting that sin has a suprapersonal dimension. As we shall see, Kierkegaard affirms all four of these themes associated with original sin as a state of corruption, though he carefully nuances the fourth one.

On the other hand, Augustine also insists that original sin involves personal guilt. At the very least, this means that the persistence of a corrupt motivational core cannot be cited to exculpate the individual from responsibility for the individual sins that are spawned by it. The plea that "original corruption made me do it" is not a valid excuse for any sinful act. But even more dramatically, Augustine argues that the individual is not only culpable for the sinful acts motivated by the corruption, but also for the original corruption itself. The presence of original sin in the soul, even if it does not issue in any sinful acts, renders the individual guilty. The individual should seek forgiveness not only for specific intentional acts of sin, but also for the underlying sinful disposition and its very presence in the soul.

The problem with Augustine's elaboration of original sin is that it appears to mix two incommensurable discourses. Augustine seems to have superimposed a moral conceptuality on a medical conceptuality without adequately integrating them. The Pelagians were quick to point out the nature of the incongruity. Moral discourse, Pelagius claims, presupposes that guilt is a property of intentional actions. In his objections to Augustine, Pelagius implicitly assumes that this principle implies that certain conditions must be satisfied if an act is to be a candidate for religious-ethical approbation or condemnation. For an act to be categorizable as sinful or not sinful, the agent must be the author of that act. The agent must have known what he was doing and have intended to do it. Furthermore, the act must have been performed voluntarily, with an awareness of alternatives, and an absence of necessitating external factors. Of course, the decision to act must be free from coercion and real alternatives must not only be available, but also be known by the agent to be available. It must be impossible to explain the occurrence of the act exclusively in terms of antecedent conditions. Pelagius even declares that the act must not be explicable solely in terms of the agent's prior character or nature.

Given all this, it would seem that guilt can arise only from self-conscious, intentional, and voluntary action, with the possibility of having acted otherwise. Unfortunately, Augustine's talk of an enduring disease that inevitably destroys the possibility of healthy action does not satisfy these conditions. Words such as "corruption," "state," "inheritance," and "disease" make it sound as if original sin is something we are the victims of, not the perpetrators of. If the ascription of guilt requires the fulfillment of the conditions implied by Pelagius, to say that the individual is guilty of original sin would be unintelligible.

Augustine was aware of this problem, and he sought to resolve it through a combination of two conceptual moves that try to explain the guilt of original sin in terms of the history of the human race. First, Augustine locates all the conditions necessary for the attribution of responsible action in Adam. It was Adam who enjoyed the freedom to sin or not to sin. Therefore, his fall was properly culpable. The inception of corruption in humanity was a free, responsible act performed by Adam. Consequently, it could be claimed that Adam was personally guilty for becoming corrupt; in Adam guilt and corruption coincided. Second, Augustine seeks to explain the guilt of all later individuals for having the corruption in their own hearts in terms of their relationship to Adam's act. Somehow Adam's progeny participate in his culpable act and are thus guilty of the ensuing corruption. It is that puzzle that inspired Augustine's various attempts to develop a satisfying metaphysical map of the relationship of subsequent individuals to Adam.

Augustine's attraction to a certain kind of understanding led him not to be content with the sheer givenness of the multiple edifying roles played by the doctrine of original sin in the Christian life. The fact that all the roles and all the types of discourse seemed to be pastorally necessary was not enough for him. He sought a justification for their simultaneous use and an explanation of the possibility of their coexistence. As we shall see, Kierkegaard affirms all the upbuilding roles played by the doctrine of original sin that Augustine had so laboriously identified and elaborated, but the former does not feel the need to explain their compossibility or defend their conjoint use. Kierkegaard's writings about sin are an attempt to see whether Augustine's pastoral goals could be pursued without the metaphysical underpinnings that the latter so desperately sought.

Kierkegaard and the Edifying Possibilities of Original Sin

From the time of his early theological studies, Kierkegaard had certainly become very aware of the Pelagian controversy and Augustine's basic views on original sin (e.g., see *KJN* 3, p. 125).[13] He was taught to regard Augustine positively as the devout penitent who ascribed everything to God, and Pelagius as the Pharisee who ascribed all saving power to human beings. As we have seen, Augustine's anti-Pelagian writings received more attention than any other part of his corpus in the textbooks of Hase, Bretschneider, and Hahn. Moreover, Clausen's lectures covered Augustine's position on original sin with technical precision, situating it in the context of the history of doctrine, as did the lectures by Martensen and Marheineke. At some point in his life, probably by 1844, Kierkegaard became familiar with Julius

---

13. See Georg F. H. Rheinwald, *Allgemeines Repertorium für die theologische Litteratur und kirchliche Statistik*, vols. 1-19 (Berlin, 1833-1837), 17: 113-19.

Müller's influential discussion of Augustine in his voluminous and magisterial *The Christian Doctrine of Sin*. From these and numerous other works, Kierkegaard was well aware that Augustine had described original sin as both the individual's personal guilt and as a perduring state of corruption. He also knew that Augustine had insisted that the debility was universal, inherited, and ineradicable through human efforts. All of his sources emphasized the fact that Augustine taught that all people have sinned in and with Adam, and as a punishment have received a nature capable only of doing evil. None of these themes would have seemed unusual to Kierkegaard, for they were all confirmed and reinforced by the Lutheran confessional documents, catechisms, and liturgies that had shaped him. Augustine's problem of construing original sin as both corruption and as guilt, and therefore as both a state and as an act, would become Kierkegaard's problem.[14]

As we have seen, Clausen set the stage for Kierkegaard's struggle with this issue. Although he basically approved of Augustine's insistence that God's grace is necessary for spiritual healing, Clausen expressed dissatisfaction with Augustine's view that sin is inherited and innate while it nevertheless also involves guilt and merits punishment (*KJN* 3, p. 31). Unfortunately, according to Clausen, the Lutheran confessional document "The Formula of Concord," which was honored in Denmark but not regarded as absolutely authoritative, had mistakenly followed the lead of Augustine and affirmed the doctrine of total depravity. The Augustinian doctrine had motivated the older scholastic Lutheran theologians to develop exotic and implausible theories concerning the imputation of Adam's sin (*KJN* 3, p. 29). Clausen objected that this notion of inherited corruption and guilt contradicts both Scripture and human self-consciousness. Scripture does not teach the total ruination of human nature as a result of Adam's sin, nor does it attribute the responsibility for that ruination to his descendants (*KJN* 3, p. 30). Moreover, the older church fathers agreed that sin is primarily rooted in humanity's sensual nature, not in the mistake of Adam, and that moral freedom remains present in all individuals. Clausen suggested that it was appropriate that Augustine's view provoked a semi-Pelagian reaction, though the semi-Pelagianism of the Council of Trent was conceptually unstable. The best modern theologians avoid the opposite evils of "Pelagian frivolity" and "Augustinian abasement" by proposing that human beings are indeed frail

---

14. See Lee C. Barrett, "Kierkegaard's Anxiety and the Augustinian Doctrine of Original Sin," in Robert Perkins, ed., *International Kierkegaard Commentary: The Concept of Anxiety* (Macon, GA: Mercer University Press, 1985), pp. 35-61.

but nevertheless are morally free, and that in their frailty they do need the help of grace (*KJN* 3, p. 31). According to Clausen, the source of sinfulness is not Adam's fall but a structural feature of human nature, the reality that sensual desire is awakened before the moral disposition can be adequately developed (*KJN* 3, p. 28). The doctrine of sin's proper use is to cultivate a sense of our own weakness and to sensitize us to the need for help.

Much of the theology that Kierkegaard read was adamant in its insistence that the individual's sinfulness must be regarded as the product of freedom.[15] From many sources, including Martensen's lectures, Kierkegaard learned that Kant regarded sin in the individual as the result of the individual's own free leap, though this leap should not be thought of as occurring in the ordinary sequence of temporal events. In notes that he took on a book by Adam Möhler, Kierkegaard records in 1837 that sin must not be construed as a necessary moment in the evolution of the race or the individual (*KJN* 2, p. 325).[16] He echoes Schelling's contention that no system of thought, which by definition must trace necessary connections between phenomena, can ever explain the reality of evil, for evil is that which should not be, and hence can only be ascribed to freedom.[17] Similarly, expositions of Schelling's reflections on the deeper meaning of the story of Adam's fall by Marheineke and Rosenkranz, both of which Kierkegaard owned, agreed that the presence of sin in humanity is a caesura in the scheme of causal explanation.[18]

Most of the textbooks that Kierkegaard consulted reinforced Clausen's view that Augustine was correct to insist on the need for grace but wrong to claim that humans are guilty of the sin committed by Adam.[19] These books filled in Clausen's account by outlining the strategies developed by subsequent theologians, some of which were anticipated by Augustine himself, to mitigate the problem of describing the inherited state of corruption as

15. See Timothy Dalrymple, "Adam and Eve: Human Being and Nothingness," in Lee Barrett and Jon Stewart, eds., *Kierkegaard and the Bible*, vol. I: *The Old Testament* (Farnham, UK: Ashgate, 2010), pp. 3-42.

16. Adam Möhler, *Athanasius der Grosse und die Kirche seiner Zeit, besonders im Kampf mit dem Arianismus*, vols. 1-2 (Mainz: Florian Kupferberg, 1827).

17. See Dalrymple, "Adam and Eve," p. 20.

18. See Dalrymple, "Adam and Eve," p. 20.

19. See Karl Gottlieb Bretschneider, *Handbuch der Dogmatik der evangelisch-lutherischen Kirche*, vols. 1-2, 3rd ed. (Leipzig: Johann Ambrosius Barth, 1828), 2: 1-109; Karl Hase, *Hutterus redivivus oder Dogmatik der evangelisch-lutherischen Kirche*, 4th ed. (Leipzig: Breitkopf und Härtel, 1839), pp. 198-217; August Hahn, *Lehrbuch des christlichen Glaubens* (Leipzig: Friedrich Christian Wilhelm Vogel, 1828), pp. 342-420.

the individual's guilty personal act. It was frequently noted that many later theologians affirmed the transmission of the corruption, but claimed that individuals are only guilty of the acts and dispositions that the corruption foments in them, and are not guilty of the presence of the corruption itself in their souls. Peter Lombard, they typically noted, proposed that the inherited disability is concupiscence, a corruption in the lower powers of the soul, and that this corruption cannot be regarded as personal guilt until these wayward desires are adopted by the will. This led to the theory of "mediate imputation," the notion that Adam's guilt is imputed to individuals only insofar as they declare their solidarity with Adam through their own personal sin. Schleiermacher would later replicate this theory, interpreting original sin as a disposition that is activated by external factors and only then becomes the individual's guilt. Anselm experimented with a different strategy, suggesting that original sin involved the loss of the *donum supernaturale,* the supernatural knowledge of God and rectitude of will that Adam had possessed. Without this, the supernatural acts of faith, hope, and love were utterly impossible, and even the ordinary human moral powers were weakened, making the natural virtues difficult. Consequently, personal sins for which the individual is personally guilty inevitably followed from the loss of the supernatural aid.

The textbooks also pointed out that many subsequent Augustinians remained more faithful to the Bishop of Hippo and attempted to explain how an inherited corruption could legitimately be regarded as personal guilt. According to them, original sin is not just a disordering of the lower appetites or the loss of a supernatural gift of grace. The corruption infects every aspect of a person, and the individual is guilty of harboring all of that multidimensional disease. In their view, it must be shown that the individual somehow participates in the guilt of Adam. The Lutheran and Reformed theologians who followed Augustine generated theories to explain how this could be so. Most of these theories, as we have seen, had been experimented with by Augustine himself. Many Lutheran theologians, including Martin Chemnitz, Johann Gerhard, and Johannes Quensted proposed some kind of biological transmission of both the culpability and the guilt. However, exactly how personal guilt could be biologically transmitted and inherited required further explanation. The traducianist view that predated Augustine, a view holding that the soul of the child is derived from that of the father (or both parents), could explain the presence of the inherited corruption, but not the ascription of guilt to the individual without undermining the notion of God's judgment of fully individuated souls. To address this problem, some theologians proposed that Adam was a "real univer-sal," a kind of Platonic form in whom all individuals participate. As the textbooks explained, other theologians revived Augustine's tentative theory of the "seminal identity" of Adam and his descendants, for all subsequent humans were present in Adam's loins. The "federal theology" proposed that Adam, through a special covenant with God, was the legal representative of all humanity and thus every debt he incurred could legally be charged to the accounts of those he represented. The theory of God's *scientia media* sug-gested that God, who is aware of counterfactual hypothetical possibilities, knew that all individuals would have sinned as Adam did if they had been put in Adam's situation. The textbooks that Kierkegaard used also often spoke disparagingly of these theories, presenting them as examples of the esoteric conceptual convolutions in which those who followed the trajec-tory of Augustine had to engage in order to salvage the hopelessly confused notion that guilt could be inherited.

The lectures by Philipp Marheineke gave Kierkegaard a different per-spective on Augustine's doctrine of original sin, one that treated the story of the fall symbolically (*KJN* 3, pp. 251-56). Marheineke insists that for Au-gustine, Adam's sin is not just something imputed to the individual as a legal debt but is a guilt that is truly the individual's own. This interpretation of Augustine led Marheineke to invoke Kant's insight that Adam was a fig-ure for all human beings (*KJN* 3, p. 255). Marheineke approvingly quotes Augustine's claim that "we all are that one (Adam)," which he regards as a foreshadowing of Kant's use of Adam as a symbol of every individual. According to Marheineke, Paul, Augustine, and Kant were all in agreement that there is no essential difference between Adam and subsequent individ-uals (*KJN* 3, p. 256). The story of the fall of Adam is not a causal, historical explanation of how humanity became sinful once upon a time, but is the archetypal story of what happens in every individual's life. This reading of Augustine would not be lost on Kierkegaard, who would echo some of these themes in *The Concept of Anxiety,* which he published a little more than two years later.

Julius Müller also presents Kierkegaard with a more sympathetic pic-ture of Augustine's reflections on original sin.[20] Müller declares Augustine

---

20. Julius Müller, *Die christliche Lehre von der Sünde* (Breslau: Josef Max, 1839); *Die christliche Lehre von der Sünde,* 3rd edition, 2 vols. (Breslau: Josef Max, 1849). English trans-lation: Julius Müller, *On the Christian Doctrine of Sin,* vols. 1-2, trans. William Urwick (Edin-burgh: T&T Clark, 1885).

to be a "great teacher of the Church" and defends him against the accusation that his doctrine of predestination somehow implies that God had made sin a necessity.[21] Müller opposed the speculative theology of his era because it tended to minimize sin by regarding it as the necessary negative moment in the self-development of the Spirit. According to Müller, this flaw was rooted in the more basic problem of speculative theology's impersonal view of God as the absolute. Such pantheism undercut the experience of the self as a moral agent standing before the righteous divine Other. In opposition to this view, Müller insists that the experiences of sin and guilt are irreducibly individual. He complains that not only Hegel but also Schleiermacher had trivialized sin by making it a phase in the natural development of the individual self-consciousness. For Müller, the individual's freedom, not a structural feature of human development, must be the exclusive origin of sin. Sin does not have a cause, he argues; it presupposes only itself. Just as Pelagius had argued against Augustine, and Augustine had argued against the Manicheans, the ascription of guilt presupposes the presence of freedom and the capacity for responsibility. However, along with Augustine, Müller was convinced that sinfulness also characterizes the individual as such, and not just the individual's particular acts. Also like Augustine, he believed that this identity-establishing disorder of the self must be regarded as the individual's own fault. The individual is the source of the individual's state of corruption, and therefore is guilty of being in that state. Müller praised Augustine for realizing the link between innate corruption and a free responsible act, though Augustine was not able to articulate the insight clearly.[22]

Unlike Augustine, however, Müller did not find it at all plausible to explain this mystery by appealing to the individual's relationship to the free act of Adam. Like Kant, Müller added the qualification that there is no specific point in the individual's temporal life in which the individual can be said to have deliberately chosen to have a corrupt character. At this point Müller himself waxed speculative (but not in a Hegelian way), theorizing about the humans' free self-determination of themselves as sinful in a noumenal realm beyond time. In the transtemporal, noumenal realm the individual has been given a choice to adopt either a sinful or a righteous highest maxim that will govern the individual's empirical life in time, and has foolishly opted for the sinful maxim. Phrased more figuratively, before the

---

21. Müller, *Christian Doctrine of Sin*, 1: 257.
22. Müller, *Christian Doctrine of Sin*, 1: 35.

empirical individual was ever born, the pretemporal soul of that individual has already performed an act that has established the individual's identity as sinful; the individual, through a singular transcendental decision, has chosen to have a sinful character. Kant's distinction of the phenomenal and the noumenal self, and the possibility of locating moral freedom in that noumenal self beyond time, provided Müller with the conceptual resources to articulate this proposal. Müller's strategy had the advantage of dispensing with the notion that it is Adam who establishes the sinfulness of subsequent individuals. According to Müller, each person himself is clearly responsible for his own transition from innocence to guilt.[23] The culpable presence of debilitating corruption in individuals is due exclusively to their free self-determination in the noumenal sphere.

Kierkegaard's response to this literature was complex. He shared the general consensus that Pelagius had foolishly minimized the extent to which human beings need the help of grace to recover from sin. Like the majority of the expositors of Augustine, he was certain that Augustine was correct that individuals are both corrupt and guilty. Like most of them, especially Clausen, Bretschneider, and Müller, he was convinced that talk about being guilty for having inherited a corruption was puzzling and quite possibly not at all useful for the Christian life. The theologians were right that to "inherit" is a category of nature, while "guilt" is an ethical category of spirit. However, Kierkegaard was suspicious of the efforts of Clausen and others to reduce the "corruption" aspect of original sin to the lingering power of sensuousness in the development of the human spirit (*SUD*, 96). That sounded a bit too much like the Catholic theologians of the Middle Ages, who blamed sin on the power of concupiscence. In his own voice Kierkegaard praised Augustine for insisting that concupiscence itself is sinful and is culpable (*JP* 4, 4047). Consequently, Kierkegaard expressed a preference for the orthodox Lutheran dogmaticians, who rejected the notion that sin is due to weakness, ignorance, or sensuousness.

According to Kierkegaard, Kant was right in at least two regards: the ascription of guilt presupposes a freedom that is not subject to any nexus of cause and effect, and, if an individual is to be held responsible for his or her corrupt character, the source of that corrupt character can only be the individual's own free act. Kierkegaard spoke approvingly of Müller's work

---

23. See Christine Axt-Piscalar, "Julius Müller: Parallels in the Doctrines of Sin and Freedom," in Jon Stewart, ed., *Kierkegaard and His German Contemporaries*, vol. II: *Theology* (Farnham, UK: Ashgate, 2007), pp. 153-54.

insofar as Müller did seek to preserve the Kantian conviction that human beings can be held accountable for the basic shape of their moral and religious character. Kierkegaard lauded Müller for being an ethical-religious thinker rather than a mystic-aesthetic thinker. Müller, in fact, was a "very estimable" writer (*JP* 4, 4555) with a "far deeper perception" (*JP* 4, 4556), for he treated original sin as the motivational source of actual sins and realized that there is something dreadfully amiss with our affective core. Müller was entirely right that the "first" sin is not just the numerically first item in a series; rather, the concept "first" suggests an enduring quality in the individual of which actual sins are the effects (*CA*, 30). However, according to Kierkegaard, Müller was no "existential thinker" (*JP* 2, 1531). The effort to explain how the individual could be deemed guilty for having a corrupt heart from birth onward by positing a transtemporal fall was "invented" silliness, showing that Müller had lapsed into useless abstract speculation (*JP* 3, 3093). Moreover, Müller failed to identify a plausible motivation for this fall into sin that allegedly had occurred beyond time, except an inexplicable egocentricity. Ironically, Kierkegaard's response to Müller was very much like Müller's response to Augustine: Müller, in Kierkegaard's estimation, asserted all the appropriate convictions about original sin, but he did so in an inappropriately objective mood. Müller's use of a counterproductive metaphysical conceptuality undermined the edifying truth of his claims. That is exactly what Müller had said about Augustine.

Kierkegaard did enthusiastically approve of Marheineke's effort to read the story of Adam's original sin, and Augustine's interpretation of it, as the paradigmatic representation of the woeful story of all individuals. Kierkegaard was struck by Marheineke's reference to Kant's remark that "we act daily in the same way" as Adam (*KJN* 3, p. 255). Marheineke, as Kierkegaard noted, advised the reader to "change the name [from Adam to your own] and of you the story is told."[24] (Kant actually borrowed the phrase from Horace's *Satires*.) This observation was so important to Kierkegaard that he cited it in both *The Concept of Anxiety* (*CA*, 73) and *Stages on Life's Way* (*SLW*, 478-79). Kierkegaard learned from Marheineke to associate this symbolic view of Adam with Augustine. As we shall see, that insight would play a critical role in Kierkegaard's own grappling with the doctrine of original sin and would provide him with a way to read Augustine sympathetically.

---

24. See Immanuel Kant, *Religion Within the Limits of Reason Alone,* trans. Theodore M. Greene and Hoyt H. Hudson (New York: Harper and Row, 1960), p. 37; see also Dalrymple, "Adam and Eve," p. 17.

Kierkegaard's most thorough treatment of original sin occurs in *The Concept of Anxiety*. This text, much more than *Sickness unto Death*, deals with the origin of a sinful disposition in human beings. In this small but dense book, Kierkegaard's appropriation (and modification) of the Augustinian tradition is obvious. As with all of Kierkegaard's texts, one must pay careful attention to the passional mood and the authorial voice. In this text the pseudonymous author Vigilius Huafniensis, "The Watchman of Copenhagen," explicitly draws attention to this need at the very beginning of the book. Vigilius observes that each domain of discourse possesses its own appropriate mood and requires the presence of that mood in order to communicate intelligibly (*CA*, 9-14). This conviction motivates his careful distinguishing of the domains of psychology and dogmatics. Domains of discourse cannot be homogenized without jeopardizing the types of pathos appropriate to each one. Every concept is embedded in a network of other concepts and cannot be translated into the concepts of another network without volatilizing its meaning. To make communication even more context-dependent, Vigilius contends that the meaning of any concept from any domain of discourse is dependent on the passional qualities of the situations in which it is aptly and typically used. Vigilius argues that it is not the case that an existentially relevant concept or proposition is first grasped cognitively and then translated into pathos. Rather, the pathos is constitutive of its meaning. Therefore, in communicating a concept, one must first evoke the proper mood. If Vigilius's task is to foster some understanding of original sin, he must identify the proper mood and then rhetorically encourage it.

Vigilius's performance implicitly assumes that the proper mood for thinking about original sin is anxiety about one's own self. He remarks that the mood for considering original sin is not that of ethics, for ethics depicts idealities. The mood of ethics is imperative and hortatory, for ethics exhorts people to action, telling them what they should do. The rhetorical force of ethical language is to inspire resolute commitment to action, which is entirely inappropriate for considering the ethical failure and debility associated with original sin. Nor is the proper mood for the clarification of original sin that of psychology, for psychology is embedded in the mood of cool observation. Psychologists are curious about the causal links between phenomena and are intent on discovering demonstrable patterns. Rather than presupposing an atmosphere of resolution or curiosity, meaningful talk about sin requires that the individuals be deeply anxious about the possibility of sin in their own lives.

The question then becomes: How can this necessary anxious self-concern be evoked? Vigilius indirectly and surreptitiously encourages the development of the requisite anxiety in the reader by quite subtly exemplifying it himself. He describes himself as an observant psychologist who scrutinizes human pathos and is interested in the psychological conditions leading up to sin, but not in original sin itself; he reinforces the persona of an observer by his sobriquet "The Watchman." Significantly, he does not identify himself as a pious Christian. Throughout the book his tone is neutral and objective, seemingly detached. He usually sounds didactic, as if he were composing a very tortuous academic treatise; the prevalence of the vocabulary of speculative philosophy heightens the impression of detached scholarship. His intention, he declares, is only to provide a psychological description of the motivation for sin. To do this properly, he must be "disturbed no more than Archimedes" (*CA*, 23).

By his own admission, Vigilius's approach is inappropriate to the nature of his investigation. He had protested that he was not exploring original sin per se, but only the psychological dynamics that precede the fall into sin. A more theological consideration of the doctrine, which is not his intent, would require a mood of repentance and contrition. According to Vigilius, clinical detachment is more appropriate for his kind of psychological investigation. This claim, however, is a bit of a self-contradiction. A few pages earlier he had critiqued the pretensions of passionless speculative objectivity in which the absence of passion prevents the apprehension of existentially relevant content. Presumably, that critique would extend to the project of trying to understand anxiety from a disengaged perspective.[25] Surely, it cannot be the case that only dogmatics requires self-involvement, while psychology does not.

In fact, Vigilius's ostensibly clinical tone is belied by his investment in the subject matter and by his concentration on the story of Adam. He is not really a mere detached observer at all: he is absolutely fascinated with Adam and the phenomenon of anxiety. He admits that anxiety is produced by staring into the abyss of possibility, and he himself certainly does stare into the abyss of the possibilities suggested by Adam's example. What he does in his writing is exactly what he claims that all anxious individuals do.

---

25. Vanessa Rumble, "The Oracle's Ambiguity: Freedom and Original Sin in Kierkegaard's *The Concept of Anxiety*," *Soundings* 75, no. 4 (Winter 1992): 605-25. See also Glenn Kirkconnell, *Kierkegaard on Sin and Salvation: From* Philosophical Fragments *through the* Two Ages (London: Continuum, 2010), p. 41.

By asking the question "Why would anyone want to sin?" he in effect shows that he is anxious about sin as a possibility for his own life. In spite of his protestations of calm objectivity, Vigilius is palpably anxious about anxiety. Even the form of Vigilius's book, with its shift from dogmatics to psychology while constantly circling back to dogmatics, is anxiety-producing. Dissonance is generated in the reader by the text's vacillation between protestations that sin is something incomprehensible and analyses of its understandable motivations. The reader is infected with this agitated, unstable mood, which helps make understanding original sin possible. If anxiety does lead to sin, then anxiety is the proper mood for thinking about sin and its antecedent dynamics.

Kierkegaard has invented an author, Vigilius, who analyzes anxiety rather than the remorse, regret, or contrition associated with guilt because all of those other phenomena presuppose that concern about the quality of one's life is already in place. One cannot foster the self-ascription of guilt if individuals are not already anxious about their ultimate well-being. Anxious concern for the direction and significance of one's life is a precondition for experiencing guilt. Consequently, Vigilius must first shake his readers out of their complacent and self-oblivious spiritlessness before there can be any consideration of guilt. Vigilius suggests that a lack of anxiety is a lack of "spirit," or earnest self-reflection and self-evaluation. Before the story of Adam and his fall can be meaningfully grasped, it must first be a matter of earnest concern to the individual (CA, 186). Through Vigilius, Kierkegaard seeks to unsettle the denizens of Christendom who no longer worry about their guilt or innocence, and who are adept at avoiding any sense of responsibility for themselves.[26] Before the question of guilt can even arise, individuals must recover a sense of human life as an urgent task that can be accomplished or botched. The contentment with bourgeois conformity must be destabilized by a new consciousness of the daunting possibilities that face the individual. The concept of possibility is a thought that "wounds from behind," excising the blockages that prevent an understanding of original sin.

In setting the stage for his exploration, Vigilius expresses marked sympathies for the main themes of the Augustinian heritage. He affirms that original sin is a foundational concept of Christian dogmatics. He treats it as being logically primitive for the Christian faith, irreducible to concepts drawn from other domains. He expresses admiration for the "Smalcald

---

26. See Rumble, "The Oracle's Ambiguity," pp. 605-25.

Articles" and the "Formula of Concord," two Lutheran confessional documents that were strongly Augustinian in their assertions about original sin, because they maximized human culpability (*CA*, 26-27). The accusatory force of these confessional standards is to be commended, for they are "now concerned only with making sinfulness and [the individual's] own participation in it more and more detestable, and in such a manner that no word can be severe enough to describe the individual's participation in it" (*CA*, 26). According to Vigilius, these Lutheran formulations are preferable to the Roman Catholic teachings that define original sin as the loss of original righteousness, the loss of a supernatural gift, the punishment for actual sins, or nonsinful concupiscence (*CA*, 25). Whatever original sin is, it must be ascribed to the individual as grievous personal guilt, a guilt that characterizes the individual's life as a whole.

Vigilius also agrees with Augustine that original sin indicates not only the pervasive guilt of the individual, but also the corruption of the individual's life as a whole. Following the Augustinian tradition, he describes sin as a "state" that the individual is in, or a "quality" that the individual possesses, and not just as an action that the individual performs (*CA*, 28-32). Sin is not a concatenation of episodic wicked actions produced by the individual's arbitrary freedom. Using mysterious language, Viglius says:

> Thus sin comes into the world as the sudden, i.e., by a leap; but this leap also posits the quality, and since the quality is posited, the leap in that very moment is presupposed by the quality and the quality by the leap. (*CA*, 32)

The "quality" here is not just the legal condition of having committed a solitary, isolated sinful action and thereby becoming liable to the verdict of "guilty" for the first time in the person's life. To think that way would trivialize the "first sin" by regarding it as "*one* sin in the numerical sense" (*CA*, 30). If the "first sin" were merely the initial item in a chronological series of sins, then "sin will have no history, either in the individual or in the race" (*CA*, 30). The "first sin" would be something merely "quantitative" and "non-essential" (*CA*, 31). Although becoming sinful is the agent's responsible act, the sinfulness also acquires a kind of enduring power over the agent, perpetuating itself, as Augustine well knew. The "first sin" is not just something that the individual commits, repents of, and then resolves to never do again. If that were the case, the "first sin" would be nothing more than an ethical quality, an individual episode of breaking a rule or exhibiting a vice, rather than a totalizing religious category (*CA*, 17-19).[27] By articulating these convictions early in his treatise, Vigilius affirms both the "sin as a culpable action" and "sin as a paralyzing corrupt condition," themes that were so crucial for Augustine. In Kierkegaard's language, both the "leap" and the "state" aspects of original sin must be confessed. Even more paradoxically, the individual is guilty not only of having committed particular sins, but also guilty of being in the state of bondage to corruption. The state of sinfulness (not just individual acts of sin) is to be construed as the individual's own fault, even though she or he is powerless to overcome it by a resolve to stop sinning.

Although he emphasizes the theme that the individual's sinfulness is not necessitated by the behavior of Adam, Eve, or any other ancestor, Vigilius does not entirely discount the significance of the "inherited" aspect of the Augustinian formulation of the doctrine of original sin. Vigilius, like Augustine, rejects the Pelagian notion that individuals are not influenced by their social contexts or past histories.[28] The self is not hermetically sealed off from the rest of the human race and its legacy of vice. Vigilius writes: "It hardly needs to be said that this view [his own] is not guilty of Pelagianism, which permits every individual to play his little history in his own private theater unconcerned about the race" (*CA*, 34).

In spite of his expressed sympathy for these Augustinian motifs, Vigilius fears that the doctrine's purpose of characterizing the individual's life as a whole had been confused with the attempt to explain how the individual had come to be both corrupt and guilty. The Augustinian tradition had been misguided in its futile struggle to theoretically justify the ascription of guilt for the corrupt state of the individual. Vigilius, like most of the expositors of Augustine whom Kierkegaard had read, critiqued the Scholastic effort to explain the concurrence of guilt and the corruption in terms of the individual's relationship to Adam. According to these implausible theories, we sin because we are somehow connected to Adam, and we are guilty because of a mysterious transfer of Adam's guilt to us. Vigilius adamantly rejects all such causal theories of sin. He explicitly cites for opprobrium the proposal that Adam was the head of the race by nature, by generation, or by covenant. By so doing, Vigilius was rejecting the theories that pictured

27. See David Roberts, *Kierkegaard's Analysis of Radical Evil* (London: Continuum, 2006), pp. 86-87; see also George Connell, *To Be One Thing: Personal Unity in Kierkegaard's Thought* (Macon, GA: Mercer University Press, 1985), p. 183.

28. See Jason Mahn, *Fortunate Fallibility: Kierkegaard and the Power of Sin* (Oxford: Oxford University Press, 2011), p. 69.

Adam as the real universal form of humanity, or posited the seminal identity of humanity with Adam, or proposed that individuals acquire Adam's sinfulness through biological transmission. He singled out the "federal" view — that Adam was the race's legal representative — as being particularly ridiculous, and he condemned it as "historical-fantastic" (*CA*, 25). In addition to being critical of theories of the transmission of Adam's guilt, Vigilius was also critical of theories of the transmission of Adam's corruption. He protests that the corruption present in all of Adam's descendants is not the inevitable consequence of the loss of a supernatural gift, or due to the propagation of concupiscence. Here he even complains that Lutheranism's penchant for the biological motif was misguided. Vigilius fears that all such theories become deterministic, tend to shift the blame to Adam, and vitiate self-accusation and penitence. Alarmed by these tendencies, he concludes:

> Consequently, every attempt to explain Adam's significance for the race as *caput generis humani naturale, seminale, foederale* [head of the race by nature, by generation, by covenant], to recall the expression of dogmatics, confuses everything. (*CA,* 29)

As Vigilius phrases it, the issue is whether we sin because of our relationship to Adam or because of our primitive relationship to sin. For Vigilius, the individual can only become a sinner by sinning, through "a first sin" that establishes a "new quality" in the individual (*CA,* 30). Sin is not an inevitability that afflicts the individual because of something that Adam did; rather, sin enters into every life as a free act. Vigilius maintains that the "new quality appears with the first, with the leap, with the suddenness of the enigmatic" (*CA,* 30). According to Vigilius, the elaboration of these theories of a biological, ontological, or legal connection with Adam has served no edifying purpose whatsoever, because Adam was portrayed as so unlike us that we could not see ourselves reflected in him at all. The theories all imply that only Adam fell from a state of primordial innocence, while we do not. Adam's prelapsarian situation in Eden was so different from our own that his motivation to sin is inscrutable. In the theoretic explanations of the genesis of sin, the story of Adam cannot be used as a mirror to illuminate our own lives, and thus the tale becomes religiously useless.

It is clear that Vigilius seeks to follow Augustine in claiming that we are both pervasively corrupt and are responsible for that corruption; but he did not want to explain how this could be possible through recourse to a speculative theory about the individual's relationship to Adam. He hoped to preserve the "pious feeling (with an ethical tone) that gives vent to its indignation over hereditary sin" (CA, 26), but feared that "as soon as the enthusiasm of faith and contrition disappear, one can no longer be helped by such determinations [the theological theories], which only make it easy for cunning prudence to escape the recognition of sin" (CA, 27). How exactly Vigilius thought that he could retain the piety while jettisoning the genetic explanations of sin has puzzled commentators for over a century. Some, including Torsten Bohlin[29] and Louis Dupré,[30] have concluded that the "sinfulness is a responsible act" and "sinfulness is a corrupt state" themes actually contradict one another. Niels Thulstrup simply regards the combination of propositions as a paradox, particularly when one adds the claim that the corrupt state is inherited.[31]

Other commentators, such as Kresten Nordentoft, treat the "corrupt state" aspect as the dominant factor in the equation and do not pay attention to the issue of the ascription of guilt for that corruption.[32] Kierkegaard, according to Nordentoft, developed a general account of human nature that makes sin the almost inevitable consequence of the structures of finitude. Others, such as Mark C. Taylor, have argued that Kierkegaard really regarded original sin as a nonculpable state that gave rise to free culpable acts.[33] Somewhat similarly, Gregory Beabout claims that the state of anxiety is a necessary but not a sufficient condition for culpable sinfulness; freedom must be added to anxiety about the individual's deleterious social context to generate a voluntary sinful act that then justifies the ascription of guilt.[34] Beabout makes it easy to see how an act may be regarded as sinful and guilty, but difficult to see how an enduring "state" of sinful corruption (the continuation of a corrupt motivational core) could be regarded as culpable. Phillip Quinn had earlier argued, perhaps more tentatively, for a position similar to Beabout's, claiming that the "state" language in Kierkegaard points to psychological and so-

---

29. Torsten Bohlen, Kierkegaards dogmatiska åskådning I dess historiska sammanhang (Stockholm: Diakonistyrelses Förlag, 1925).

30. Louis Dupré, Kierkegaard as Theologian (New York: Sheed and Ward, 1963), p. 61.

31. Niels Thulstrup, "Adam and Original Sin," in Niels Thulstrup, ed., Biblioteca Kierkegaardiana, vol. 5 (Copenhagen: C. Reitzel, 1980), pp. 122-56.

32. Kresten Nordentoft, Kierkegaard's Psychology (Pittsburgh: Duquesne University Press, 1978), pp. 168-74.

33. Mark C. Taylor, Kierkegaard's Pseudonymous Authorship (Princeton, NJ: Princeton University Press, 1975), pp. 268-73.

34. Gregory Beabout, Freedom and Its Misuses: Kierkegaard on Anxiety and Despair (Milwaukee: Marquette University Press, 1996), pp. 49-59.

cial factors that influence and help motivate sin.[35] According to Quinn, anxiety only shows that an act of sin is not an arbitrary choice made from a position of indifference. However, it is also not necessitated and cannot be explained fully by pointing out antecedent conditions, which themselves are nonculpable.

The problem with most of these interpretations is that they attribute to Vigilius (or Kierkegaard) views that he implicitly rejects. Most of them identify the "state" that leads to actual sin as a nonculpable anxiety, and restricts guilt to specific acts and dispositions. This, however, is exactly what Vigilius had found to be inadequate in the Catholic theologians who had identified the corrupt state with nonculpable concupiscence. The modern interpreters of Kierkegaard have simply substituted anxiety for concupiscence. However, as Jason Mahn has suggested, Vigilius was generally trying to do something much more subtle and paradoxical: jolt the reader into self-reflection through the juxtaposition of countervailing discourses.[36] In this context Vigilius advances the discordant claim that individuals should assume responsibility not only for their acts but also for the state of corruption that characterizes their lives as a whole. The ostensible problem with this claim is that "a state of corruption" does not seem to be the sort of thing that is the product of a free and intentional act or even of a series of such acts. We humans do not typically talk about freely choosing our underlying orientations, our most basic passions, and our enduring dispositions, particularly not ones that seem to continue through their own momentum. At most, we may say that we are guilty of the initial actions that put us in a state of addiction, but it makes less sense to say that we are guilty of the continuation of the addicted state, particularly if we are powerless to terminate the addiction. But Vigilius does not restrict our guilt to the initial actions that produced the addiction to sin, and in fact praises the Augustinian tradition for extending our guilt to the continuation of our corrupt state.

In order to show how this paradoxical affirmation can be meaningful, Vigilius rejects all the explanatory theories suggested by the doctrinal traditions as idle speculation. The problem is not the conceptual inadequacies of any particular one of these theories; rather, it is the folly of attempting to address this seeming conundrum through the production of theories at all. In his journals Kierkegaard sarcastically observes:

35. Phillip Quinn, "Does Anxiety Explain Original Sin?" *Nous* 24 (1990): 227-44.
36. See Mahn, *Fortunate Fallibility,* pp. 53-85.

To say that the church teaches original sin, that the Catholic church teaches it thus and the Protestant church thus, to erect a speculative concept which explains original sin and sin at all — that is indeed the task of the learned and wise in our time. The more concrete understanding of it in the individual, that is to say, the way I have to understand it, is a simpler, less complicated task, which I have chosen. (JP 2, 1248)

These theories give the impression that a deeper understanding of original sin can be gleaned through the discovery of more illuminating metaphors or more lucid conceptual schemes. However, like the attempt to comprehend sin through speculative metaphysics, such a theoretical posture encourages detachment and destroys the essential mood of self-concern, making any real understanding of original sin impossible.

What Vigilius was trying to do was encourage the development of the various passions and concerns that provide a different kind of understanding of original sin, one not available from theories. The presentation of these passions serves as an alternative clarifying lens to the explanations produced by the speculative accounts of humanity's unity with Adam. For Vigilius, the individual will know what the language about original sin as a "leap" and original sin as a "state" really means when individuals can use that language in their own passional lives. One set of passions is associated with sin as a free "leap," and another set is associated with sin as a "state." Consequently, the problem of correlating the two types of discourse about sin becomes the problem of integrating the two types of passions in a single life.

To accomplish this, Vigilius made two conceptual moves that distinguish his work from Augustine's. First, Vigilius uncoupled the "What is my identity?" question from the "Why and how did I become a sinner?" question. It is one thing to be earnestly concerned about one's religious identity in the eyes of God; it is quite another thing to seek a genetic explanation of the factors that produced one's religious identity. The problem with Augustine was that he failed to adequately distinguish the religious identity question from the genetic question, and he seemed to think that the identity issue would benefit from an answer to the genetic question. In effect, Augustine remained somewhat uneasy about construing the individual's identity as corrupt and culpable unless a theory could explain and justify those attributions. Kierkegaard, on the other hand, had no such compunctions: he was quite content to talk about sin as defining an individual's total identity without basing this on any metaphysical foundations.

Second, Kierkegaard approached the "How did (and do) I become a sinner?" question from a different angle. Rather than speculate about Adam's prehistory, or the individual's earliest childhood, or the relationship of the history of the human race to the individual, Kierkegaard sought to evoke the psychological states that can give rise to sin and encourage the reader to fear them. In order to address the "How did I become a sinner?" question, Kierkegaard turned away from metaphysics and toward an ironically edifying psychological deliberation. Whereas Augustine had sought the answer in some metaphysical connection of the individual with Adam, Vigilius addresses the issue by helping people to better understand the motivational factors operative in their own lives. We shall consider Kierkegaard's approach to the "How did I become a sinner?" question first.

Much of Vigilius's work is devoted to the psychological, motivational question of the origin of sin's culpability and corruption. Like Augustine, Vigilius wants to condemn sin as something culpable but also see it as arising out of a predisposing condition. The problem, of course, is that motivational explanations can be used to exonerate an action by making it seem necessary. Vigilius struggles to avoid justifying sin by explaining its passional roots, for that will discourage individuals from confessing their own personal guilt. To avoid suggesting any hint of determinism, Vigilius carefully separates the tasks of psychology and dogmatics: dogmatics deals with the ascription of identity; psychology deals with motivations. Vigilius distinguishes the identity-ascribing force of the doctrine of original sin from its function as an analysis of the motivational roots of sin.

His text enables readers to imaginatively experience how sin arises as a possibility in the life of every individual rather than explaining its origin via a historical or metaphysical narrative. In order to help people appreciate how sin is motivated, Vigilius cultivates in the reader a negative capacity for anxiety. In spite of his recognition that subsequent individuals have a history and a context that encourage sin, Augustine had implicitly made the mistake of treating Adam as abstract *liberum arbitrium*, the power to either sin or not sin, independent of antecedent factors. Because he lived in a state of innocence, Adam — in the Augustinian tradition — seemed to sin for no intelligible motive. Even Augustine's claim that pride, the selfish desire to be powerful in the way that God is powerful, had motivated Adam was not satisfying, for it remained unclear how or why Adam would have been vulnerable to the temptation to covet God's self-sufficiency. Why would Adam have felt the lure of pride if Adam had enjoyed knowledge of God and basked in loving fellowship with God? Attributing sin to selfishness does not explain how selfishness arose (*CA*, 76-79). To claim that *concupiscentia* (inordinate desire), or desire for forbidden objects, or sheer delight in breaking the rules is the motivation for sin similarly begs the question, for it is not clear how such factors could gain a purchase in the heart of an innocent person (*CA*, 38-41).

Instead, Vigilius retells the saga of Adam's fall as a paradigmatic tale, just as Marheineke had suggested. For Vigilius, it is the archetypal story of the way anxiety motivates sin in all humans; for him, the individual is potentially "spirit," or the power of actualizing different possibilities. He also describes this potential spirit as "the power of being able" (*CA*, 44-45). Vigilius is not being completely novel here, for Augustine himself had claimed that the desire to exercise power, "a shady parody of omnipotence," was one of the primary motivations for sin.[37] Anxiety is an ambivalent or dialectical state that arises in response to the individual's growing sense of having possibilities. The anxiety is catalyzed by the recognition of the indeterminacy of one's own freedom and the open-endedness of possible futures. Anxiety is the state of being torn between the comfort of security and the lure of the unknown. The prospect of possibility both titillates and terrifies the self. The anxiety is augmented exponentially if the perceived possibilities on the horizon involve an ethical prohibition, even if the difference between good and evil has not been grasped. The prohibition signals the possibility of dire consequences and alerts the individual to the fact that immediate unity with God's will could be ruptured. In anxiety the self experiences the potential differentiation of the individual agent from God. Prior to this recognition of possibility, God had been the assumed environment in which the self had lived; but now the self must acknowledge that God is distinguishable from the self. The resulting anxious vertigo can motivate the individual to sin simply in order to end the ambivalence. Vigilius describes this psychological dynamic so powerfully that he tends to make the fall into sin seem highly probable. In fact, he associates the transition to sin with "dizziness" and "fainting," phenomena that do not seem to be qualities of fully intentional, responsible acts. Sin appears to be something that comes over an individual, for the individual is said to swoon in "feminine weakness" and "succumb" to sin (*CA*, 61). The unsettling depiction of the strength of the motivation to sin and the seeming powerlessness of the swooning individual serves to further potentiate the anxiety welling up in the reader.

Throughout *The Concept of Anxiety*, Vigilius tries to elicit anxiety by

37. Augustine, *Confessions*, II, 6 (14), in *WSA* I, 1.

describing it. The reader is encouraged to experience the transition from innocence to sin not as ancient history but as an ever-present reality in the reader's own life. The primeval history of Adam is not an abstract characterization of the race as a whole or an empirical identification of the source of an epidemic. Rather, Adam can be discovered within one's own life. Adam's succumbing to anxiety presents a possibility that we could enact — and thereby stimulates our anxiety. Vigilius implicitly goads the reader to look inward and begin the process of self-examination. He confesses the nature of his authorial purpose by claiming: "How sin came into the world, each man understands solely by himself. If he would learn it from another, he would *eo ipso* misunderstand it" (*CA*, 51). Even more vehemently, he warns the reader:

> So when the single individual is stupid enough to inquire about sin as if it were something foreign to him, he only asks as a fool, for either he does not know at all what the question is about, and thus cannot come to know it, or he knows it and understands it, and also knows that no science can explain it to him. (*CA*, 50)

In the concluding chapter of his book, Vigilius admits that he regards anxiety as being the educator of humanity. By implication, Kierkegaard, if not Vigilius himself, has been trying to educate humanity. According to Vigilius, "Whoever has learned to be anxious in the right way has learned the ultimate" (*CA*, 155). Such a person has recovered the primary condition for understanding sin: the sense of the possibility of failing and falling. By triggering anxiety, Vigilius has supplied one of the forms of pathos necessary for understanding original sin: individuals must be worried about the quality of their lives as a whole and realize that their lives could be botched.

The persistence of anxiety is Vigilius's functional equivalent of the perduring state from which sin arises about which Augustine had speculated. Sin does not arise from the individual's relationship to Adam, but from the individual's own anxiety. Some of the roles played by the "state of corruption" language in Augustine are performed by Vigilius's analysis of anxiety as an ongoing condition that motivates sin. A significant difference between Vigilius and Augustine is that Vigilius insists that this particular condition, the phenomenon of anxiety, is nonculpable. Vigilius warns: "Further than this, psychology cannot go . . ." for psychology does not possess the appropriate mood to understand the sin and guilt that arise from anxiety (*CA*, 45).

Even when exploring anxiety as a predisposition to sin, Vigilius does not lose sight of the second theme emphasized by Augustine, that is, sin as culpable act. Augustine's early focus on personal responsibility and guilt is not lost in Vigilius's analysis of anxiety as a motivating precondition. The transition from anxiety to sin is not necessary: Adam could have remained in a state of unresolved anxiety or opted for trust in God. Vigilius consistently rejects all suggestions that anxiety somehow necessitates sin. This informs his pervasive critique of Hegelianism, in which sin is not personal guilt so much as it is the negative moment in the evolution of spirit and thus necessary for the dialectical process of maturation (CA, 11-14, 30, 35). Vigilius protests that the immanent movement of logic should not be confused with the temporal becoming of the individual. The immediate harmonic state of Adam in the Garden of Eden did not have to be superseded by oppositional individuation in order to give birth to self-conscious Spirit. Even with the disruption of immediacy by anxiety, innocence could have endured if the individual had opted for trust rather than sin (CA, 36-37). The evolution of Spirit does not require the sinful opposition of subject and object, self and world, in order to provide the conditions for a higher reconciliation. Differentiation need not involve destructive hostility. Similarly, Vigilius rejects Romanticism's celebration of sin as a healthy and inevitable assertion of the individual's autonomous identity. In these contexts Vigilius emphasizes the "leap" nature of sin and its incomprehensibility. Like Adam, every individual begins with the possibility of not sinning. In Vigilius's exposition, the insistence that anxiety does not inevitably lead to sin functions to forestall excuses and to encourage the self-ascription of responsibility.

Some interpreters of Kierkegaard have claimed that Vigilius may have inadvertently introduced a different kind of necessity into his account of sin, a necessity that is theological rather than metaphysical. Vigilius emphasizes the value of repentance so strongly that it begins to seem as though the fall into sin — or at least the failure to live without moral guilt — is a positive good, for it sets the stage for that blessed repentance.[38] Vigilius often says curiously positive things about anxiety, describing the possibility of sin as a kind of fortunate fallibility, for it does make faith possible.[39] The felix culpa (or perhaps felix fragilitas) theme sometimes appears to suggest that the fall into sin prepared the way for redemption, and hence was a

38. See Arnold Come, Kierkegaard as Theologian: Recovering Myself (Cambridge: Cambridge University Press, 1996), pp. 138-40.

39. See Mahn, Fortunate Fallibility, pp. 53-85.

necessary condition for a greater good than the innocence of Eden. The paradise that is regained is more wonderful than the paradise that was lost. In his own voice in "Every Good and Perfect Gift Is from Above," which he published in tandem with *The Concept of Anxiety*, Kierkegaard reiterates that the sufferings initiated by Adam make possible redemption, for one learns through doubt, suffering, and guilt to need God (*EUD*, 31-48).[40]

The confession of sin serves the purpose of drawing individuals closer to God, or at least those individuals who are willing to be educated by humility. Kierkegaard even announces that one must pass through anxiety in order to rest in faith in God's providence and the atonement (*CA*, 161-62). These encomia to the pedagogical value of anxiety and even sin have suggested the view that Kierkegaard introduced a new kind of necessity or strong predisposition to sin based on the crucial role of sin in God's plan to bring about the glory of redemption, which could imply that God had planned the fall into sin.[41] However, the fact that the self-awareness of sin is closer to redemption than is spiritlessness does not mean that sin is justifiable or necessary in the *ordo salutis*. Such speculation would be utterly alien to Vigilius (and Kierkegaard). In fact, he wishes that "no reader would be so profound as to ask: What if Adam had not sinned?" for such a question points readers away from the task of becoming earnest about the quality of their own lives (*CA*, 50). To say that the individual can come to see sin as being productive of the possibility of redemption is not to deny that sin is utterly horrible or that its advent must always be lamented.

Let us now turn from the "How did I become a sinner?" question to the "What is my identity?" question. As we have seen, for both Augustine and Vigilius the doctrine of original sin has an identity-ascribing force: the individual not only sins but is a sinner. Vigilius does not regard this transition from anxiety to sinfulness as exclusively a quality of isolated acts that the individual has performed, or as a single act occurring only at the beginning of the individual's moral life. Vigilius encourages readers to see their lives as a unity, and therefore as a continuing transition from anxiety to sin. In claiming that the individual's life as a whole is sinful, and is both corrupt and guilty as a whole, Vigilius was entirely in agreement with Augustine. But unlike Augustine, Vigilius dispenses with all theories that would explain the metaphysical grounds of sinful personal identity. The unity of the

---

40. See Kirkconnell, *Kierkegaard on Sin and Salvation*, pp. 40-57.

41. See John S. Tanner, *Anxiety in Eden: A Kierkegaardian Reading of* Paradise Lost (Oxford: Oxford University Pres, 2002), pp. 72-74.

sinner's life is not based on an enduring corruption lodged in the individual's substantival soul. Sin should not be thought of as a self-perpetuating substance or as an automatic mechanism that operates without the individual's volition. The ongoing identity of the sinner is certainly not due to a singular deed of adopting an evil highest maxim in the noumenal realm (Kant), or to a pretemporal decision to give oneself a sinful character that would then manifest itself in time (Müller).

Rather than formulating a theory about the grounds of personal unity, Vigilius strives to enable the individual to imagine this unity by becoming anxious about the future repetition of sin. Vigilius points out that because the individual has sinned in the past, the possibility of sinning in the future can never be discounted. By sinning, the individual has demonstrated what the individual is capable of doing. A more specific kind of subjective anxiety is posited as a consequence of sin (CA, 56), for "the nothing that is the object of anxiety becomes, as it were, more and more a something" (CA, 61). Vigilius observes: "If I am anxious about a past misfortune, then this is not because it is in the past but because it may be repeated, i.e., become future" (CA, 91). Vigilius encourages readers to see the individual's continuing identity as rooted in the possibility of repeating certain acts. The sinful act reveals an underlying proclivity: it manifests a possibility that is always present, infecting the dynamics of life as a whole. The individual knows that what he has done in the past he could always do again. Anxiety about sin's repetition provides continuity to his life. The individual comes to fear that he sins because of the kind of person he is, and not merely because he once made a bad decision. This is the first step toward the assumption of responsibility for the basic shape of one's life. In effect, Vigilius is exhorting the reader to extend the sense of culpability usually associated with specific actions to his life as a whole. The sense of personal identity as a sinner is not something based on the acceptance of a theory, but rather is a passional achievement.

In a similar way, Vigilius affirms the universality of sin as a state, just as Augustine had done. Unlike the Pelagians, Vigilius does not regard humanity as a collection of radically isolated individuals; rather, he sees sin as uniting individuals in the race. However, diverging from Augustine, he refuses to even try to explain that universality through a theory of the corporate nature of humanity. According to Vigilius, belief in the universality of sin is not based on tabulated surveys of the widespread incidence of sinfulness or on metaphysical speculation about Adam as the head of the human race. Rather than outlining a metaphysics of species unity, Vigilius seeks to enable the reader to be anxious about the individual's relationship to other people's sinfulness. The reader is warned that it is anxiety that unites the human race, an unsettling prospect that makes the reader even more anxious. What is a possibility for someone else is a possibility for anyone. Vigilius urges the reader to admit "rightly and profoundly to oneself that what has happened to one human being can happen to all" (*CA*, 54). Anxiety that the sins of others reveal one's own potential sins is at the root of the corporate sense of sinfulness. Vigilius's corporate language encourages us to see the acts of others as revealing what we each are capable of doing. Consequently, not only the example of Adam, but also the example of any sinner (including Vigilius himself) can reveal as in a mirror what is in the individual's own heart. The corporate language about sin also prevents self-congratulatory comparisons of the self to seemingly more heinous reprobates, for even their egregious misdeeds are manifestations of one's own perverse capabilities. Vigilius admonishes his readers not to worry about the status of the others with respect to salvation, but only about one's own. In this way, even talk about the universality of sin is used to reinforce anxiety about sin in one's own self and thus helps make genuine earnestness possible.

Many of these themes are not unique to Vigilius, but are echoed elsewhere in Kierkegaard's writings. Their frequent recurrence suggests that these traces of the Augustinian heritage concerning original sin were not a minor or isolated aspect of Kierkegaard's oeuvre. In many of his edifying and Christian discourses, Kierkegaard emphasizes the surprising passional benefits of personally appropriating the seemingly somber doctrine of original sin. To celebrate the hidden joys of believing in original sin was something that Vigilius, the detached (but inwardly anxious) psychologist, was not in a position to do. Unlike *The Concept of Anxiety,* the works that Kierkegaard signed with his own name concentrate on the attractiveness of a life lived in the light of the Augustinian doctrine. To be able to imagine these passional blessings is part of what it means to understand original sin.

In "Every Good and Perfect Gift Is from Above," the discourse of 1843 referred to above, Kierkegaard proposes that possibility disrupts the immediate unity of God and the self. In the prelapsarian state of innocence, no reflective knowledge of God was possible, because God and the self had not been differentiated. Consequently, both doubt and faith were impossible. But the recognition of possibility posits a difference between the self as it currently is and the self as it could be. We differ from Adam only in that we exist in a derived environment in which the split between God and the self has already occurred. Unlike Adam, we are presented not just with an inchoate, abstract sense of possibility, but with concrete examples of possible sinful ways of life in our social environment. Of course, this dawning of a sense of possibility does not necessitate sin, for even the quantitative accumulation of sin in the surrounding society does not compel a leap into sin. The parallel to *The Concept of Anxiety* is blatant: here the reader is encouraged to accept the possibility of doubt and temptation, for they are the inevitable concomitants of the possibility of faith.

In "The Upbuilding That Lies in the Thought That in Relation to God We Are Always in the Wrong," a sermon that Kierkegaard puts in the mouth of a Jutland pastor, the preacher proclaims that the individual can never be certain that he or she has done enough to approximate God's ideal (*EO* 2, 344-45). Located in *Either/Or*, after Judge William's exhortation to fulfill marital duties, the sermon serves to undermine all confidence in anyone's ability to satisfy God's law, including the ability of the judge and the reader. The reader is led to realize that episodes of ethical failure are symptoms of a deeper malaise. The resulting contrition and humility are the first steps toward the happiness of relying exclusively on God, a virtue that Judge William did not notably exhibit.

The Jutland preacher then extols the hidden virtues of the willingness to accept one's state of being in the wrong before God. The admission that we sinners suffer as guilty removes the possibility that God might be unfair in allowing us to be plagued with misfortune. It is better for one's self to be in the wrong than for the beloved — in this case, God — to be cast in that role. The willingness to assume guilt is motivated by love for God, while the desire to exonerate oneself betrays an unloving, self-centered orientation. Under his own name, Kierkegaard repeats this theme in the discourse "The Joy of It That in Relation to God a Person Always Suffers as Guilty," in which the renunciation of the project of self-justification is portrayed attractively as an aspect of loving God (*UDVS*, 264-88). Acknowledging that one is a sinner removes doubts about God's goodness, for no one suffers innocently. The desire to establish one's own rectitude in some particular matter is symptomatic of spiritual self-aggrandizement. Kierkegaard applauds the totalizing force of the Augustinian view of guilt:

The guilt of the person in relation to God is not guilt of this or that — the relation cannot be summed up that way. He is eternally guilty and therefore always guilty; whenever he so wills, God can assert the fundamental guilt . . . . (*CA,* 286)

This same motif is woven throughout "States of Mind in the Strife of Suffering" in *Christian Discourses* (*CD*, 93-159). In the sermon and the discourses, Kierkegaard rejects all attempts to justify the ways of God through a theodicy, as if the existence of human suffering were a conceptual problem that could be resolved through a better theory; instead, he encourages the reader to embrace a kind of joy that can only be experienced through confession. Ironically, the acceptance of the Augustinian doctrine of pervasive guilt and depravity can bring with it a type of comfort, in this case an unshakable confidence in God's goodness.

In all these instances Kierkegaard was using the doctrine of original sin to foster a habit of self-emptying. The self-ascription of guilt for one's life as a whole was part of the broader task of renouncing the project of self-justification. To genuinely believe in original sin is to turn from trust in the self to trust in God. The doctrine is part of the struggle to "become nothing" so that the individual can be refocused on God and be filled with love for God. To do this, Kierkegaard had to use two different sets of discourse, one to encourage earnest self-concern and the self-ascription of responsibility, which required the language of "act" and "leap," and the other to extend that concern to the shape and direction of one's life as a whole, and to see that life as blighted with a spiritual disability, which required the language of "state" and "condition."

Conclusion

Kierkegaard's relationship to Augustine's views concerning original sin was complex and nuanced, but largely approving. Most importantly, the two thinkers were agreed that the individual's autonomous struggle for self-integration and quest for self-fulfillment always and everywhere fails. According to both Augustine and Kierkegaard, this failure is neither the product of a necessary mechanism that operates apart from the individual's will nor the result of a series of atomistic, unmotivated leaps. Both agreed that the individual must assume responsibility for this failure at the same time that the individual recognizes that she is in bondage to it. The two writers agreed that sin has the qualities both of an enduring state and the qualities of culpable action. Both were in accord that the penitential attitude should be extended to cover the individual's life as a whole. Both encouraged the cultivation of critical self-examination, moral humility, repentance, discontent with the shape of one's life, and a longing for forgiveness and help. Augustine and Kierkegaard were in harmony concerning the forms of pathos that constitute the true significance of the doctrine of original sin.

But Kierkegaard often objects to the mood of speculation that Augustine had introduced into the discussion of original sin. And he denounces the proliferation of fanciful theories that had been spawned by Augustine and his theological heirs. Kierkegaard dismisses the efforts to explain the unity of the sinful life, the transmission of sin, the solidarity of the race, and the grounds for the ascription of guilt to individuals. In short, Kierkegaard objects to Augustine's attempt to resolve the tensions between the "state" language about sin and the "leap" language about sin by having recourse to metaphysics. Instead of theorizing, Kierkegaard seeks to preserve the edifying potential of Augustine's theology without lapsing into an inappropriate speculative mood. Unlike Augustine, he does not try to explain how or why the individual can be held responsible for a total state of corruption. He refuses to answer such questions as "What would have happened if Adam had not sinned?" or "How is it that we are guilty for our lives as a whole?" Rather than trying to gain insight through speculation, Kierkegaard hopes to evoke in the reader the passions that would show what the doctrine of original sin means in the living of the Christian life. Most significantly, he seeks to encourage various forms of anxiety about the quality of the individual's life. It would seem that the fundamental difference between Augustine and Kierkegaard is that Augustine seeks to understand original sin by means of locating it on a conceptual map, while Kierkegaard strives to understand it by eliciting the proper kind of self-concern. From Kierkegaard's perspective, this would be a substantive difference between them, for transferring a Christian concept into the realm of speculative theory undermines its meaning.

But perhaps juxtaposing the two thinkers in this way would be a gross oversimplification. Perhaps the two theologians were not as far apart as Kierkegaard sometimes thought. As we have seen, Augustine was no stranger to the notion that Christian teachings make sense only in the context of the appropriate pathos. Augustine, the superb rhetorician, knew full well that the passional force of a communication is part of its meaning. Augustine's more abstract musings about humanity's connection to Adam always appeared as part of a more basic purpose to move the reader, to transform the reader's passions. In fact, we can discern the effort to stimulate anxiety as a component of grasping the doctrine of sin in Augustine's writings. His reflections on the roots of his own sinfulness in the *Confessions* leap from one kind of vice to another, and from one possible motivation to another, unsettling the reader with their lack of closure and generating a kind of vertigo. The explicit linkage of anxiety and sin is also found in Augustine, for example, in his discussion of the fall of the angels. According to Augustine, the angels were uncertain about their destiny and fell victim to an unhealthy self-concern.[42] They became anxious about their possible future when they surveyed their environment. The formless matter that they beheld expressed the nothingness of indeterminate possibilities, for unformed matter could become anything at all, or even nothing. An abyss of indeterminate possibility lies at the heart of all finitude, threatening individual beings with dispersion, fluidity, and chaos.[43] If even the angels can be destabilized by anxiety, then surely anxiety plays a role in the fall of human beings. Augustine describes this in such an unsettled, agitated way that the reader begins to feel the anxiety being described. Augustine's literary practice and his concern to evoke the appropriate pathos are not unlike Kierkegaard's. Both of them were edifying authors, and both of them found much edification in the self-abnegation encouraged by the doctrine of original sin. The specific difference between them is that Augustine believed that speculation could be put to passionate purposes, while Kierkegaard feared that such a strategy would only subvert the necessary mood of earnestness.

---

42. Augustine, *City of God*, XII, in *WSA* I, 6-7.
43. Augustine, *Confessions*, XII, in *WSA* I, 1.

CHAPTER 6

God's Gracious Response to Sin: The Enigma of Divine Sovereignty and Human Responsibility

According to Augustine and Kierkegaard, Christianity is essentially a religion of salvation from sin. Moved by love, God graciously makes it possible for sinful individuals to recover from their woeful derailment into depravity and to resume their journeys toward eternal blessedness. This divine offer of salvation inevitably raises the question of the respective contributions of God and human beings to the final attainment of beatitude. In the process of redemption, what exactly does God's agency achieve and what does human effort accomplish? This question of the relationship of divine and human agencies arises with regard to every aspect of the journey toward the individual's ultimate home, including the inception of the recovery from sin, the subsequent growth in faith, hope, and love, and the attainment of the final destination. Whether the issue is the origins of faith in God's forgiveness, the strengthening of love for God and neighbor, or hope in the prospect of eternal salvation, neither Augustine nor Kierkegaard could evade this question: Is salvation an unconditional gift from God or the product of human striving?

Augustine and Kierkegaard have both gained lasting notoriety for their understandings of the roles of human agency and divine agency in the individual's pursuit of eternal blessedness. On this subject, however, their positions have most often been contrasted. Augustine has been hailed as the champion of irresistible divine grace that generates saving faith, while Kierkegaard has been characterized as a defender of an autonomous human "leap" into faith. Augustine has been portrayed as the architect of a deterministic system, while Kierkegaard's leap has been identified as the precursor of Sartre's radical self-positing. Kierkegaard has even been labeled the "arch-Pelagian of all time," for he allegedly valorizes the self-cultivation of fear and trembling as a human work that wins salvation.[1] However, a closer examination reveals that such a simplistic juxtaposition is misleading. Augustine retained an enduring concern for responsible human agency, while Kierkegaard sought to affirm complete reliance on God's gracious action. The dual affirmation of the assumption of the responsibility to grow in the Christian life and the humble, grateful, and total dependence on God's agency characterized both thinkers. Moreover, both were fully aware of the tension between these themes.

Augustine on Divine Predestination and Human Spiritual Striving

To complicate the issue, Augustine's thought on this matter evolved dramatically, just as it did with regard to sin. In ascribing an opinion to Augustine based on one of his particular works, one must always pay attention to when it was written — and in what polemical context. Moreover, Augustine's vocabulary was sufficiently fluid and elusive that he can legitimately be interpreted in a variety of different ways. Reformed Protestants and many Dominicans have preferred to read him as a consistent advocate of the priority and irresistible efficacy of God's grace, while most post-Trentine Catholics have interpreted him as leaving some room for human cooperation with grace. Meanwhile, Lutherans have debated whether he was a monergist or a synergist, and Wesleyans have wondered if he could legitimately be classified as a qualified Arminian and claimed as one of their own.

In his earlier writings Augustine forcefully defends the importance of free, responsible human decisions and actions in the individual's attainment of blessedness. In the period from 387 to 391, Augustine vehemently opposed the fatalistic views of the Manicheans in *On the Greatness of the Soul (De animae quantitate), On Free Will (De libero arbitrio), On the Teacher (De magistro), On True Religion (De vera religione),* and in a commentary on Genesis *(De Genesi adversus Manicheos).* Against their apparent determinism, Augustine argued for the reality of free will, undetermined by internal nature or external circumstances. His rhetoric suggests that the redirection of our desire away from the world and toward God is at least promoted through our own self-transformative efforts. The implication is that the desire for God can be cultivated through intentional activity.

---

1. Hans Frei, in conversation with the author, July 1984, Yale University.

During this period Augustine argued that the journey to God required an initial recognition of the superiority of the soul to the material world, and a turning within the soul in order to rest in oneself rather than in transitory phenomena. Although this was not an absolute rejection of worldly interests, it was an intentional subordination of earthly concerns to the higher value of knowing God. According to Augustine, the individual must choose to perform these foundational activities of polishing the image of God in the soul.[2] Because the attachment to earthly goods with which we begin life becomes habitual, rigorous effort is required to break their power.[3] The virtues of temperance, fortitude, justice, and prudence, all of which are necessary to properly order and direct love, can combat the allure of carnal things. At this point Augustine seems to claim that these virtues can be willed into existence, even though their flourishing will take time and resolve. The virtues are the fruits of our own efforts and are the fulfillment of our being.[4] Augustine's language in these writings is overtly voluntaristic, and his tone is exhortatory. Although the goal of discerning and loving the good cannot be achieved by a single act of will, the necessary attention and openness to the good are under one's own control.

Even here Augustine by no means ascribes the attainment of blessedness entirely to the efficacy of human exertions. The power of God's attractiveness, drawing the soul like a magnet, is an even more basic factor. Augustine was merely claiming that the soul had to overcome the obstacle of distracting worldly attachments so that the beauty of God could then be more clearly discerned. God is indeed acting in the individual, for God is always disclosing God's self in the human soul. This immediate consciousness of God is both the *telos* of human life and the catalyst for the further transformation of desire. Although the episodes of profound awareness of God that occur through contemplation are momentary, and thus are not genuine beatitude, the memory of them draws the heart to God more strongly. In this way Augustine, even in his early writings, did claim that God's active self-disclosure is the ultimate font of the *caritas* that attracts humans to God.[5]

As Augustine matured, his focus on God's role in the drama of human salvation intensified. He ascribed more and more of the initiative in sal-

---

2. Augustine, *On the Greatness of the Soul (De animae quantitate)*, 28 (55), 35 (79), in *WSA* I, 4.

3. Augustine, *On Free Will*, II, 13, 37, in *WSA* I, 3.

4. Augustine, *On Free Will*, I, 12, 26, in *WSA* I, 3.

5. Augustine, *On True Religion*, 12 (25); 55 (112-113), in *WSA* I, 8.

vation to God, and expanded God's role beyond God's luring of the soul. In *Confessions,* Augustine retrospectively discerned God working within and behind the circumstances that had motivated Augustine to take certain actions and that had shaped his emotions and dispositions. God, he concluded, had been operating through the seemingly mundane factors in his life that had propelled him on his journey, including personal illnesses, vocational opportunities, disappointments with philosophic and religious movements, separations from intimate companions, and ostensibly fortuitous encounters with potential mentors. Through what he initially experienced as his own self-generated actions and decisions, divine providence was surreptitiously leading him home.[6] Appropriately, the mood of *Confessions* shifts repeatedly from the penitential confession of Augustine's wayward actions to the joyous expression of gratitude for God's providential direction. The basic rhetorical dynamic in the *Confessions,* the movement from the recollection of seemingly self-initiated deeds to praise for God's potent initiative, signals a growing appreciation of the power of God's grace. *Confessions* is Augustine's hymn to the clandestine operation of God's prevenient grace in his own life. At about the same time, in *To Simplicianus (Ad Simplicianum),* Augustine overtly declares that the operation of God's grace precedes free human action so efficaciously that all our godly thoughts, inclinations, and deeds must be credited to the power of grace.[7] Only God's agency can save humanity, for humanity is a mass of corruption that has lost the capacity for healthy spiritual action and even the right to salvation.

During the period when he was writing *Confessions,* Augustine seemed to believe that God's prevenient grace operated by providing individuals with vivid impressions that arouse certain inclinations, to which those individuals can then assent. God must take this kind of initiative to free the will from the power of the strong worldly inclinations that frustrate its redirection toward God. God accomplishes the reorientation of the individual's heart by providing opportunities for new, more God-oriented inclinations to arise and be embraced. In *Confessions,* Augustine writes as if the individual can freely resist or consent to the awakening of these new inclinations. Therefore, it appears that before the year 418, Augustine understood God's saving activity to be nothing more than God's efforts to move the individual's will by providentially ensuring that the individual be exposed to positive suggestions and attractions. When God provides the appropriate

---

6. Augustine, *Confessions,* V, in *WSA* I, 1.

7. Augustine, *To Simplicianus,* I, 2.16, in *WSA* I, 12.

inducements, an act of turning to the good can be elicited if the individual voluntarily consents. However, as he further matured, Augustine began to suggest that God knows exactly what factors will effectively elicit the desired free act, so that the individual's positive response will be assured. His progressive emphasis of the divine initiative was intended to discourage the twin vices of spiritual smugness and trust in one's own moral prowess. The increasing focus on the power of grace promoted Augustine's general project of shifting the soul's attention away from its own seeming excellences to God's attractive love. Accordingly, he describes God's attractive grace gratefully, passionately, and adoringly.

Augustine's quarrel with Pelagius would provide the former an opportunity to further clarify his understanding of the relationship of the divine and human agencies in the matter of salvation. Just as Pelagius had emphasized the individual's agency and responsibility with respect to sin, so also he emphasized the freedom and efficacy of the individual's will with respect to salvation. To be fair, Pelagius did not claim that individuals pull themselves up by their own bootstraps while God merely observes their exertions. Pelagius admitted that God is somewhat active in the process of salvation, for God does attempt to persuade the sinner to convert to the good by furnishing inspiring examples of righteous lives. Nevertheless, for Pelagius, the crucial factor in the situation is the human will's decision to either heed the examples or ignore them, and whether to emulate them or discount them. The focus for Pelagius always fell on the free, responsible actions of the individual, who thus bears the burden of his own salvation. The major credit for salvation goes to the stalwart resolve of the individual, just as the blame for sin must go to the individual's volitional failure. In the face of Pelagius's valorization of human agency, Augustine began to emphasize the role of the Holy Spirit in infusing the individual's soul with a delight in the good. He began to claim that God's grace does not merely elicit new inclinations through providing external attractive goods; it also arouses new inclinations by working within the individual's soul, infusing a "victorious delight" in the good.[8] Augustine explains: "If we are to call this grace 'teaching,' we should certainly mean by it the teaching which we believe God pours out with an ineffable sweetness in the depths and interior of the soul, not merely through those who externally plant and water, but also through himself who gives the increase secretly. In that way he not merely reveals

---

8. Augustine, *Against Julian, An Unfinished Work (Contra Julianum, opus imperfectum)* I, 107; II, 217; II, 226, in *WSA* I, 25.

the truth, but also imparts love."[9] God gives us new affections so that we can then enact them freely.

This shift to an affirmation of the direct interior working of grace through the Holy Spirit led Augustine to maintain that grace operates infallibly, and at least at one point he did assert that it works irresistibly. Augustine says: "One should, therefore, have no doubt that human wills cannot resist the will of God who in heaven and earth has done everything he willed and who has brought about even those things which are in the future."[10] The birth of new, righteous inclinations in the Christian's soul is not in any way the fruit of the individual's own heroic activity. There is nothing for which the individual can take credit, and there is no reason for the individual to be proud of any spiritual accomplishments. By articulating the theme of the potency of grace, Augustine was encouraging the reader to avoid the vice of spiritual self-congratulation, which would only mire the individual more deeply in self-regard. Because the essence of the individual's problem is the turn away from God to self-gratification and self-aggrandizement, the antidote to the problem can hardly be further esteem for the self. The self-reliance advocated by Pelagius would be a self-defeating strategy if the goal is to love God more ardently.

But even as he emphasized the priority of God's grace with increasing vigor, Augustine could still use the language of human freedom, willing, and responsibility. For example, in his anti-Pelagian *On the Spirit and the Letter,* Augustine insists that, though the incentive and the ability to have faith are God's gift, faith nevertheless is an act of freedom.[11] God does not act apart from our volitional capacities, but rather acts through them. In this context of exhorting believers to live the Christian life, Augustine adds that human beings have the capacity to respond to God's gift. This remark has been construed by many Catholic theologians to suggest that God offers the grace that enables individuals to will in a new, more godly manner, but that this new ability to will rightly can be either resisted or accepted. Consequently, Augustine could be implying that the human will must in some way cooperate with grace and does contribute something to salvation. On the other hand, Augustine may only have been claiming that God's grace works through our volitional capacities, effectively motivating them to make the desired deci-

---

9. Augustine, *On the Grace of Christ and Original Sin (De gratia Christi et de peccato originali),* I, 13 (14), in *WSA* I, 23.

10. Augustine, *Rebuke and Grace (De correptione et gratia),* 14 (45), in *WSA* I, 26.

11. Augustine, *On the Spirit and the Letter (De spiritu et littera),* 34 (60), in *WSA* I, 23.

sions. But no matter how these passages are construed, Augustine continues to insist in most contexts that the recognition that God is the source of our new ability to grow in faith, hope, and love does not imply that the human will is merely passive in this transformative process.[12]

As the controversy evolved, Augustine came to emphasize divine agency even more strongly and in more ways. Against the so-called semi-Pelagians, Augustine composed *On the Predestination of the Saints (De praedestinatione sanctorum)* and *On the Gift of Perseverance (De dono perseverantiae).* Some theologians in southern Gaul, such as John Cassian, a monk who had settled in Marseilles, were alleged to be articulating the opinion that God gives grace to those who have shown some initiative in inaugurating the development of holy dispositions in their souls, and that it is the responsibility of individuals to preserve and cultivate the gift of grace once it is bestowed. Through the exercise of our freedom we can either enhance the virtues that grace imparts, allow them to atrophy, or entirely lose them. Because we are the agents in our response to grace, we deserve some credit or blame for the flourishing or languishing of grace in our souls. Augustine objected that this view robs God of the gratitude due God for our continuing growth in sanctification. Our perseverance in holiness should be received as a gift from God, not as an occasion for boasting. With regard to our continuation on the journey to God, the emphasis should be on God's persistent faithfulness. God's elect can never lose their promised salvation, for perseverance is accomplished by God, not by our own feeble efforts to cooperate.[13] Augustine sought to encourage trust in God's power and gratitude for God's support in every dimension of the process of salvation, from its beginning to its end. The beginning of faith in conversion, the perseverance in faith, the growth of faith, and the culmination of faith in the beatific vision were all attributed to the power of God. Every stage of the individual's spiritual maturation is a divine gift.

This desire to maximize trust and gratitude led Augustine to articulate what became famously known as his doctrine of predestination. The question inevitably arose: If salvation is due entirely to God's grace, why are some people saved rather than others? Augustine and his readers clearly recognized that not all people become new creatures who exhibit faith, hope and love. The answer of the Pelagians to the question of God's election of some people and rejection of others was simple: predestination is

---

12. Augustine, *Letters (Epistulae),* letter 157, 2 (10), in *WSA* II, 3.
13. Augustine, *Rebuke and Grace,* 13 (40), in *WSA* I, 26.

nothing more than God's foreknowledge of human decisions. God "elects" those whom God foresees will indeed use their freedom wisely. Augustine, of course, could not credit human agency with such a determinative role in salvation. Our seemingly noble striving does not merit either the gift of grace or final salvation. If an individual does attain salvation, all the credit must go to God. Augustine explicitly and emphatically denies that the election of individuals to salvation is based on God's foreknowledge of their future virtue.[14] Therefore, if some people attain salvation and some do not, the only explanation can be that God had chosen to work efficaciously in some and not in others. As early as *To Simplicianus (Ad Simplicianum)*, Augustine had argued that God's choice of Jacob over Esau was not a function of God's foreknowledge of the subsequent courses of their lives but was simply God's sovereign but inscrutable determination to prefer one over the other. God's choice of Jacob happened beyond time and was not a response to foreseen events in time. By the period of his polemical exchange with Julian of Eclanum, Augustine was insisting that we are predestined not only to receive grace but also to receive the glory that awaits us at the pilgrimage's end.[15] He maintains:

> Faith, then, both in its beginning as in its completeness, is a gift of God, and let absolutely no one who does not want to be opposed to the perfectly clear sacred writings deny that this gift is given to some and not given to others.[16]

At times Augustine even declares that God actively hardens the hearts of the nonelect,[17] though in some contexts he explains that God merely does not extend his grace to or withdraw it from those whom God has not chosen.[18] In any case, according to the inscrutable divine will, God has mercy on whom God will have mercy and passes over whom God will pass over.

As Augustine aged, the language of synergism — that somehow the human will cooperates with God's action and thereby contributes some-

---

14. Augustine, *The Enchiridion on Faith, Hope, and Love (Enchiridion)*, 25 (98), in *WSA* I, 8.

15. Augustine, *On the Gift of Perseverance (De dono perseverantiae)*, in *WSA* I, 26; *Against Julian, An Unfinished Work*, in *WSA* I, 25.

16. Augustine, *On the Predestination of the Saints (De praedestinatione sanctorum)*, 8 (16), in *WSA* I, 26.

17. Augustine, *On the Predestination of the Saints*, 19 (38)–20 (40), in *WSA* I, 26.

18. Augustine, *Tractates on the Gospel of John*, XLVIII, 3-4, in *WSA* III, 12.

thing essential to the outcome — receded into the background. But the language of human responsibility never entirely vanished. Even in his late anti-Pelagian writings, he continues to exhort his readers to actively make use of the gift of perseverance that had been granted them, and to warn them that God would be displeased if they failed to appreciate, cultivate, and exercise that divine gift. Augustine is aware of the tension in his position, for he does confess that both the efficacy of grace and the importance of the human will must be taught. Both must be proclaimed, for both motifs are woven throughout the Bible.[19]

Augustine's doctrine of predestination does not function in his writings as the foundation of a theological system whose most basic and most important principle is divine determinism. The doctrine was not deduced from the premise of God's omni-causality, as it would be for some later hyper-Calvinists. Augustine did not reason that God is the ultimate cause of all events and hence must be the cause of the salvation and damnation of human individuals. Further, he does not assert the supralapsarian view that God ordained the fall of Adam and Eve into sin; the tragic reality of sin is the fruit of human freedom, not of divine ordering. He insists that the decree of election occurred after (logically "after," though not chronologically "after") the fall of Adam and Eve, for it was not God's original intent that any humans be lost. It was not God's original desire that there should be sin so that grace may abound, and thus Augustine avoids portraying sin as a necessary feature of a closed universe determined in all its details by God.

As I have pointed out, Augustine's use of the doctrine of predestination is highly dependent on specific pastoral contexts and purposes. He warns that preachers should address the topic of predestination with caution and sensitivity. The proper locus for the introduction of the subject of election is the issue of gratitude for the individual's salvation. Augustine's mature doctrine of election was not an invitation to speculate on who was saved and who was not, nor was it intended to be a depiction of inevitable future torment that would be useful for terrifying the nonelect during their earthly sojourn. According to Augustine, the doctrine should not be invoked to afflict reprobates with the horrible thought that they have been chosen to be hated by God. Reprobation should never be proclaimed in the second person, but only mentioned in the third person — and then only hypothetically. In fact Augustine advised that the doctrine of predestination should not be taught to those who were not mature in their faith and might be alarmed by

19. Augustine, *On the Spirit and the Letter (De spiritu et littera)*, 30 (52), in *WSA* I, 23.

it.[20] Rather, the basic purpose of the doctrine was to reassure believers that their salvation was entirely in God's hands. The faithful should not worry whether they were among the elect or not, but simply trust that their salvation is due to God's reliable and invincible love.[21] Furthermore, the doctrine served to glorify God for being powerfully beneficent in every phase of the process of salvation. Augustine's view of predestination did not arise from reflection on God's omnipotence, but from the celebration of salvation as the unmerited gift of divine love.

However, Augustine did not restrict himself to extolling the trustworthy and all-sufficient power of God's grace in the appropriately edifying contexts. Given his desire to seek a "deeper" understanding of his Christian convictions, he could not help but spell out what seemed to be the necessary theological and metaphysical presuppositions of the pathos that he was trying to nurture. For Augustine, the logical implication of giving God all the credit for the salvation of an individual was that God must have chosen that individual for salvation. This tenet then had to be reconciled with the empirical observation, supported by biblical passages, that not all are saved. These two premises entailed the conclusion that it must be true that the unsaved are not saved because they were not among the chosen. If someone is not saved, it can only be because God did not choose to be gracious to that person. To Augustine, the passional purpose of encouraging utter reliance on God seemed to imply divine predetermination of every significant factor pertaining to an individual's salvation.

Kierkegaard's Stereoscopic View of Salvation as a Human Task and a Divine Gift

Kierkegaard was aware of the contours of Augustine's teachings about grace and predestination from Henrik Clausen's lectures, which devoted a significant amount of attention to them (*KJN* 3, p. 64). According to Clausen, Augustine opposed nature and grace in order to emphasize human incapacity in all things related to salvation. Augustine's view was presented as an innovation, for Clausen pointed out that the affirmation of free cooperation with God's grace had been the accepted position of the church until Augustine. But Augustine's acute sense of human spiritual disability led him

---

20. Augustine, *On the Gift of Perseverance*, 22 (61); 23 (58), in *WSA* I, 26.
21. Augustine, *On the Predestination of the Saints*, 11 (21), in *WSA* I, 26.

to formulate the doctrine of irresistible grace, limit salvation to Christians, and champion predestination. Pelagius's conviction that individuals were capable of self-correction in spite of humanity's fall into sin contradicted Augustine's own experience. The Augustinian "system," Clausen continued, was enormously influential in Protestant circles. It was privately adopted by all the Reformers and became a dominant theme in Calvin. Clausen wrote at length about medieval and modern Roman Catholic developments, claiming that Augustine's system in all its aspects had never gained absolute acceptance in the church, but had always hovered like a cloud over the vestiges of care-free Pelagianism (*KJN* 3, p. 81). This interpretation betrayed Clausen's own theological sensibilities, for he regarded Augustine as a useful corrective to excessive confidence in unaided human abilities — but also as a corrective that went too far.

Between the two poles of Augustinianism and Pelagianism, Clausen outlined a spectrum of more subtle intermediate options. He proposed that most Catholics had become semi-Pelagians, believing that morally good acts in the natural order could be performed, which God would then reward with grace. Although the human will's ability to choose the good has been severely impaired by original sin, it has not been totally destroyed. Semi-Pelagianism contended that, in the *ordo salutis,* human agency takes the initiative, sincerely strives to live righteously in spite of its disability, and yearns for divine assistance. God then rewards the individual's genuine but faltering efforts to grow in virtue with an infusion of grace that supplies a new spiritual energy with which the person can pursue sanctification more robustly. This, he noted, became the basis for the nominalist doctrine of "congruous" merit, the theory that God accepts as meritorious those acts that, though sincerely aiming at virtue, fail to satisfy God's rigorous standards of holiness (*KJN* 3, p. 66). In other words, God lowers expectations and regards as meritorious works that are only partially righteous. The Council of Trent in the late sixteenth century, Clausen opined, was an attempt by Catholics to find a mediating position between Augustinianism and semi-Pelagianism, because it rejected Augustine's claim that free will was totally lost by the fall into sin, and it declared instead that it had only been weakened. Consequently, not all human works prior to the individual's justification deserve God's displeasure; humans do contribute something to their own salvation (*KJN* 3, p. 65). Clausen pointed out that the "Formula of Concord," which was respected in Denmark even though it was not an official doctrinal standard, affirmed Augustine's view of depravity, but it did not endorse his view of irresistible grace.

In this exposition of doctrinal history, Clausen clearly approved of Augustine's insistence that humans need divine help and that salvation is not merited, but feared that Augustine had obliterated all human responsibility and agency. He shared semi-Pelagianism's desire to reintroduce some human cooperation with grace, but was still Lutheran enough to have an allergic reaction to the suggestion that such cooperation was in some sense meritorious. It is not surprising that Clausen spoke favorably of the "synergism" of the "Formula of Concord" and even the Council of Trent, for this view suggested that in some mysterious way God's grace makes possible a genuinely free human response without necessitating it (*KJN* 3, pp. 65-66). The synergist view, intimated by Philipp Melanchthon, agreed with Augustine that God initiates the process of salvation by offering grace, soliciting a positive response, and inviting the cooperation of the human agent. The Arminians, a Dutch Reformed theological party mentioned by Clausen, articulated a similar view by proposing that God restores the individual's freedom to respond to Christ's offer of grace, a freedom that had been lost through sin, and then permits the individual to freely accept grace (which an individual may choose not to do).

Other theologians whom Kierkegaard read spoke more favorably of Augustine's doctrines of election and grace. For example, Philipp Marheineke agreed with Augustine that God does indeed elect persons for salvation, and that it is crucial to affirm this fact (*KJN* 3, pp. 294-97). This election cannot be based on God's foreknowledge of merit or conditioned by any human response. Such a theory would divorce God's knowledge from God's will and destroy the unity of God's perfections. However, Marheineke added, God has elected humanity as such rather than specific individuals. It is the responsibility of individuals to recognize their election and live out their divinely intended destiny (which some may fail to do). While departing significantly from Augustine's particularism, Marheineke did, at least, suggest that Augustine's view had the virtue of emphasizing God's gracious initiative and the unconditional nature of God's love.

Kierkegaard's explicit statements about election and predestination reflect the countervailing assessments of Augustine expressed in his readings and in the lectures that he heard. Quite early in his journals Kierkegaard began to devote serious attention to the relationship of divine and human agency. Many of his remarks were scathingly critical. In 1834 he complained:

The concept "predestination" must be regarded as a thoroughgoing abortion. Doubtlessly having originated in order to relate freedom and God's omnipotence, it solves the riddle by denying one of the concepts and consequently explains nothing. (*JP* 2, 1230)

Later that same year he repeated that predestination had failed to reconcile "the conception of human freedom" with the "conception of God's governance of the world" (*JP* 2, 1231). The doctrine of predestination inevitably "brings a man into self-contradictions" (*JP* 3, 3545), and gets a person "entangled in the worst contradictions" (*JP* 3, 3543). Kierkegaard credited the doctrine of "desperate election by grace" with generating "the most dreadful split in humanity" (*BA*, 290). Kierkegaard's hostility to the doctrine was motivated by his fear that it would foster passivity. In 1836 he observed that any system of necessity suggests that the "crooked way" of the world is the cosmic system's fault, thereby relieving the individual of responsibility (*JP* 2, 1232). Three years later he objected to the doctrine of predestination's easy confidence that salvation is already assured for the elect (*JP* 3, 3548). Much later in his life he denounced the doctrine of predestination as "a dogma of sedentary piety" and as "an unmistakable sign of how the existential momentum has been diminished" (*JP* 3, 3550) because the doctrine contributed to the "softness" of contemporary Christianity by transmuting earnest Christianity into an innocuous doctrine. He also complained that "fatalistic election by grace" jeopardized subjectivity by making everything, including faith and the desire for faith, a gift from God (*JP* 4, 4551). In 1850, moreover, Kierkegaard condemned doctrines of election as valorizations of the sphere of being and as legitimizations of what is (*JP* 4, 3852); that is, the doctrine encourages a metaphysical-aesthetic sensibility that discourages ethical striving and the self-ascription of responsibility demanded by the sphere of becoming.

However, many of Kierkegaard's other journal entries speak favorably of the sovereignty of grace and even of election. In 1834 he warned, "If predestination is explained solely as grounded in foreknowledge, one comes to assume that man deserves grace" (*JP* 3, 3546). Of course, for a Lutheran like Kierkegaard, the notion of humans deserving or meriting grace had to be scrupulously avoided. Throughout his journals Kierkegaard castigates Pelagianism for indulging in prideful self-glorification because the vain effort to claim some credit for the self's agency contradicts the basic Christian imperative to become as nothing before God. In another journal entry of 1834, Kierkegaard observed that the divide between Catholic theologians and Protestants revolved around the issue of whether one can receive grace without first being inwardly prepared by the Holy Spirit to do so (*JP* 2, 1463).

The illusory celebration of the alleged contributions of human agency to salvation fails to grasp the significance of the atonement. Kierkegaard declares: "Christ's Atonement is everything, unconditionally, because it makes no difference, after all, what a man does" (*JP* 2, 1469). Positions that valorize human agency flout the basic Christian imperative to rely absolutely on God's grace. And, sounding almost predestinarian, Kierkegaard even advises that an individual "must rest in the blessed assurance that everything is already decided," a conviction that is paradoxically necessary in order to have the courage to strive (*JP* 2, 1473). Perhaps Kierkegaard and Augustine did not differ as much on the issue of grace and human responsibility as Kierkegaard may have thought.

Some passages make explicit the tension between the need to rely on God and the requirement to diligently strive, thereby expressing a certain ambivalence on Kierkegaard's part. Toward the end of his life Kierkegaard remarked: "The idea that a man's eternal salvation is to be decided by a striving in time, in this life, is so superhumanly heavy that it will kill a man even more surely than massive sunstroke. The weight of it is so great that it is impossible even to begin . . ." (*JP* 3, 2551). Augustine, he adds, "hit upon election by grace simply to avoid this difficulty" (*JP* 3, 2551), which, of course, was detrimental to the development of genuine earnestness. But in this journal entry, the conjunction of these statements betrays a strong and enduring ambivalence about the doctrine. On the one hand, the doctrine of predestination seems to deny human responsibility and striving; on the other hand, the denial of predestination appears to open the door to works-righteousness and an unbearable anxiety about salvation. The conceptual vertigo is evident in Kierkegaard's youthful confession: "It seems to me that the doctrine of predestination, like an ant lion, pulls me down into a funnel; the first downfall conditions all the subsequent ones with a horrible consistency" (*JP* 3, 3542).

Like Augustine, Kierkegaard assumes throughout his writings that the movement toward blessedness requires the individual's heartfelt, intentional transformation, and that this transformation is itself the product of God's redemptive activity. As in Augustine's works, the conjunction of these two themes opens a Pandora's box of perplexing issues. On the one hand, faith necessarily involves a new way of thinking, feeling, and acting, all of which require the individual's earnest cultivation. On the other hand, these new capacities must be regarded as gifts from God. The ostensible tensions between these themes paralleled the ones with which Augustine wrestled in his deliberations about grace, freedom, and election. To deal with these strains in the Augustinian heritage, Kierkegaard engaged in a sustained consideration of the passional dimensions of faith. For Kierkegaard, the appropriate way to integrate self-responsibility and gratitude for God's action was not to invent a conceptual map of the relationship of divine and human agencies, but to elicit certain passions and dispositions and invite the reader to synthesize them.

The issue of the relationship of God's action and human action usually arose for Kierkegaard in regard to how an individual comes to have faith and how the individual should continue to nurture it. His understanding of faith was partly animated by his deep and abiding antipathy to objectivizing types of discourse. Therefore, whatever faith is, it must be a mode of passionate subjectivity. This theme was most clearly articulated by the pseudonymous Johannes Climacus, though it recurs throughout Kierkegaard's writings. As we have seen in Climacus's discussion of subjective truth, faith cannot be identified with cognitive assent to doctrinal propositions; nor can it be reduced to objective certainty about the reality of a special kind of supernatural entity; nor can it be equated with justified true belief in the occurrence of particular historical events. Faith in God is not the entertainment of a more or less probable hypothesis about the existence of a being with certain marvelous attributes. For Kierkegaard, faith has less to do with calculations concerning the possible existence of an object, and much more to do with the quality of the individual's relationship to the object. The individual should not ask whether God exists or whether a particular object is God, but rather concentrate on how the individual is engaged with that allegedly divine object (*CUP* 1, 199). Faith is a quality of the relationship, a quality of the passion that constitutes the relationship. Consequently, faith involves a kind of intense concern about the individual's relationship to whatever it is that the individual takes to be absolutely important. In short, Christian faith is a mode of the passionate subjectivity described earlier, a distinctive form of pathos that is part and parcel of a distinctive way of living. Faith is not a matter of speculating about truth, but rather is a matter of living in the truth. Faith is the embrace of a way of living even when the validity of that way of living is objectively uncertain. This conviction is encapsulated in Climacus's slogan, "subjectivity is truth" (*CUP* 1, 189-207).

Even though Kierkegaard consistently regards faith as a distinctive kind of subjectivity that is ingredient to a unique way of life, his writings seem to exhibit a certain ambiguity about the source of this subjectivity. Sometimes he uses the rhetoric of an extreme voluntarist, describing faith as the individual's own self-generated heroic act. Faith in these contexts appears to be a "leap" executed through the exercise of sheer willpower. Here the individual seems to be the principle, and perhaps the exclusive, agent in the production of faith. It was this dimension of Kierkegaard that captured the imaginations of the existentialists and also earned him the negative reputation of being an advocate of criterionless — and thus irrational — commitments.[22] At other times Kierkegaard uses a vocabulary that sounds almost predestinarian, declaring faith to be a "gift" given by God to a recipient who is not even expecting the gift. His assertion that faith is born through total reliance on God's grace could suggest that God is the sole and irresistibly efficacious agent in faith's production, and possibly imply a full-blown doctrine of predestination. The reader can legitimately express confusion when Climacus insists that "faith *(Tro)* is not an act of will" (*PF,* 2), but then goes on to declare in the same volume that belief *(Tro)* is "an act of freedom" (*PF,* 83). Because both the language of faith as a gift from God and the language of faith as a human task are found in both his pseudonymous and veronymous texts, Kierkegaard could be criticized for entertaining two opposing views of the relationship of human and divine agency.

Given this oscillation of themes in his writings, some expositors have concluded that Kierkegaard entertained a Pelagian view of the faithful life, seeing it as the product of human exertion.[23] At the very least, it is argued, Kierkegaard's opposition to predestination was often voiced so stridently that he must have been a champion of a position like Kant's that foregrounded moral freedom.[24] Other interpreters have construed him as a thoroughgoing Augustinian who saw faith as a new capacity graciously and unconditionally implanted in the individual by God.[25] Still other commentators have adopted a middle-of-the-road position, identifying Kierkegaard as some sort of "Arminian" or "synergist." These interpreters propose that God offers faith to the individual, and perhaps even restores the freedom of the individual; but then they add that the individual must then use that

---

22. Alasdair MacIntyre, *A Short History of Ethics* (New York: Macmillan, 1966), pp. 217-18.

23. See Mark C. Taylor, *Kierkegaard's Pseudonymous Authorship: A Study of Time and the Self* (Princeton, NJ: Princeton University Press, 1975), p. 314.

24. See Ronald M. Green, *Kierkegaard and Kant: The Hidden Debt* (Albany: State University of New York Press, 1992), pp. 180-81.

25. See M. Holmes Hartshorne, *Kierkegaard, Godly Deceiver* (New York: Columbia University Press, 1990), pp. 28-44; Gregor Malantschuk, *Kierkegaard's Thought,* trans. Howard and Edna Hong (Princeton, NJ: Princeton University Press, 1979), pp. 143-44, 246-58.

freedom to accept the gift of faith.[26] According to this rather large group of expositors, Kierkegaard accepted the Kantian position that moral responsibility implies freedom from external, necessitating causes — including divine ones. In this view, therefore, Kierkegaard must have assumed that individuals can freely cooperate with grace, or at least freely refrain from resisting grace. At the very minimum, Kierkegaard must have presupposed that individuals have the capacity to freely use grace once it has been bestowed.

As we have seen, Kierkegaard was aware of the historic theological disputes about the relationship of human and divine agency in the genesis of faith. In his context these arguments were not merely episodes in the church's ancient history — that is, of antiquarian interest only. Controversies about the relationship of grace and human agency were prevalent among contemporary theological factions of all stripes, including rationalists, pietists, idealists, and confessionalists. The possibility of controversy was rooted in the ambiguity of the Lutheran confessional document "The Formula of Concord," which states that the human will is "neither totally, halfway, somewhat, nor in the slightest and smallest bit" responsible for conversion; nevertheless, it does not affirm the Calvinist tenet that God's gracious agency is irresistible.[27] Many conservative Lutheran confessionalists, including Andreas Gottlob Rudelbach, the "Old Orthodox" Danish theologian who exchanged copies of his books with Kierkegaard, continued to echo Luther's insistence that the human will is in bondage to sin, concluding that only an act of God could engender the faith that would liberate the individual from sin's paralyzing clutches.[28] Some interpreted the doctrine of election to mean that, with respect to salvation, the divine will somehow determines the human will; as the Calvinists had explicitly affirmed, the operation of God's grace in the soul is irresistible. Schleiermacher himself was widely perceived as teaching that grace works on the

26. Here I disagree with Timothy Jackson's "Arminian Edification: Kierkegaard on Grace and Free Will," in Alastair Hannay and Gordon Marino, eds., *The Cambridge Companion to Kierkegaard* (Cambridge: Cambridge University Press, 1998), pp. 235-56.

27. "The Formula of Concord," Robert Kolb and Timothy J. Wingert, eds., *The Book of Concord: The Confessions of the Evangelical Lutheran Church*, trans. Charles Arand et al. (Minneapolis: Fortress, 2002), pp. 519, 549. Although "The Formula of Concord" was not officially adopted by the Danish Church, it figured prominently in Kierkegaard's theological education.

28. See Søren Jensen, "Andreas Gottlob Rudelbach: Kierkegaard's Idea of an 'Orthodox Theologian,'" in Jon Stewart, ed., *Kierkegaard and His Danish Contemporaries*, vol. II: *Theology* (Farnham, UK: Ashgate, 2009), pp. 303-33.

individual through some kind of necessity without the free cooperation of the self-determining ego. For example, H. L. Martensen complained that "Schleiermacher, as well as Augustine and Calvin, has taken a one-sided view of the truth that man is 'a vessel' for grace."[29] Martensen gave Kierkegaard the impression that most Reformed theologians, including Schleiermacher, believed that all phenomena were necessitated by God's will. In opposition to this opinion, many rationalists championed Kant's contention that free agency, unconstrained by antecedent factors, is a necessary condition for the moral responsibility that faith presupposes.

Adopting a more mediating position, the Pietists of Halle University developed the view that the free self-cultivation of sin consciousness is the prerequisite for the reception of grace.[30] They usually described this struggle to achieve heartfelt penance *(Busskampf)* as the individual's own act. In a way, this view was a return to the *facere quod in se est* doctrine of the medieval nominalists, who claimed that God grants the grace that creates faith to those who use their natural moral and spiritual abilities as best they can, particularly in the cultivation of despair over sinfulness.[31] Such an attitude became widespread in Denmark during the mid-eighteenth century due to the influence of the Pietist catechism written by Erik Pontoppidan. Dissenting from both of these views, other Pietists and moderate Lutherans embraced the synergist compromise that God assists the sincere but inevitably deficient efforts of the sinner to become faithful. In that view, repentance is partly the fruit of the individual's own resolve, which God aids and supplements with an infusion of a new power to trust and obey. This had been the opinion of Melanchthon and Strigelius, and it seemed to be the position of Clausen. Bishop Mynster suggested something like this by proposing that the individual must strive for religious maturity so that God's grace can become efficacious.[32]

This synergistic view also appeared in Balle's catechism, which Kierkegaard studied as a child: in this textbook the catechumen was instructed that God will assist the struggling individual with grace when the individ-

---

29. H. L. Martensen, *Christian Dogmatics: A Compendium of the Doctrines of Christianity,* trans. William Urwick (Edinburgh: T&T Clark, 1866), p. 365.

30. See Christopher B. Barnett, *Kierkegaard, Pietism, and Holiness* (Farnham, UK: Ashgate, 2011), pp. 18-19.

31. See Karl Gottlieb Bretschneider, *Handbuch der Dogmatik der evangelisch-lutherischen Kirche,* vols. 1-2, 3rd ed. (Leipzig: Johann Ambrosius Barth, 1828), 2: 475-76.

32. See Bruce H. Kirmsee, *Kierkegaard in Golden Age Denmark* (Bloomington: Indiana University Press, 1990), pp. 100-135.

ual sincerely tries to repent.[33] To further complicate matters, the Pietists of Herrnhut emphasized the attractive power of Christ's love and the internal working of the Holy Spirit; but they were also capable of describing conversion as the individual's own act. Expanding the theoretical options, H. L. Martensen, Kierkegaard's tutor and later the primate of Denmark, proposed the even more nuanced theory that sinners are free only to resist God's grace, but not free to surrender to grace or assist grace; all spiritually positive freedom is the gift of God.[34] Martensen was thus echoing the view of the seventeenth-century Reformed theologian Jacob Arminius, who differed from the Lutheran synergists by making it clear that the will is not free to positively cooperate with grace, for the ability of the will to turn toward God has been destroyed by sin. When God offers grace, the offer itself elicits a new freedom to respond, which, if it is not resisted, will produce faith. However, it is true that the will is free to resist this offer of grace. Like Roman Catholic understandings of the efficacy of the sacraments, Arminius was arguing that God's grace is efficacious unless the human will places an impediment in its path. If the individual comes to have faith, God should receive all the glory, but if the individual refuses faith, the individual is entirely to blame. Each of these theological factions developed a different vocabulary to describe the interaction of the divine and human agencies, seeing God's act as necessitating, inviting, initiating, or urging human action.

No matter how much these factions differed from one another, they nevertheless shared the common yearning for a speculative solution to the problem of the relationship of divine and human agencies. Each position theorized about God's agency and human agency as if they were two comparable forces, like the exertions of a horse and a mule yoked to the same plow. Because the two agencies were thought to be comparable, their respective roles in the genesis of faith could be identified and analyzed. In order to do this, the theologians usually borrowed some kind of metaphysical conceptuality to explain how the two very different kinds of agencies, one finite and the other infinite, could interact. Theologians experimented with Aristotle's distinction of primary and secondary causality, and with Kant's distinction of noumenal and phenomenal agency. All of these theologies assumed that talk about faith as a gift from God and talk about

---

33. Nikolae Edinger Balle, *Lærebog i den Evangelisk-christelige Religion* (Copenhagen, 1791).

34. Martensen, *Christian Dogmatics*, p. 359.

faith as one's own responsibility should be taken as potentially conflicting assertions that required harmonization through the offices of a technical conceptual framework.

However, Kierkegaard did not quite fit the popular description of an orthodox Augustinian, or a standard Pelagian, or a Lutheran synergist, or even an Arminian. He neither argued for divine determinism, nor for free, untrammeled human agency, nor for a cooperation of the two. His understanding of the way Christian concepts come to have meaning rules out such a systematic resolution. As we shall see, Kierkegaard dismissed the effort to factor out and to analyze the respective contributions of divine and human agencies in the birth and growth of faith. For Kierkegaard, the ostensible paradox of grace and free will is not the kind of issue that is amenable to a theoretical resolution. Instead, the resolution of what is really an existential challenge rather than a cognitive conundrum is achieved in the living of the Christian life. By approaching the issue of grace and freedom in this way, Kierkegaard was able to do justice to the twin trajectories in Augustine's thought that Augustine had such difficulty articulating simultaneously.

The issue of the relationship between divine and human agencies arises in Kierkegaard's writings when he distinguishes what could be called generic religiosity from more specifically Christian faith. He often portrays the development of generic religiosity as the product of human effort, while he describes Christian faith as the result of God's action. However, the situation usually becomes more complicated as Kierkegaard's exposition develops. Usually he proceeds to show how some of the aspects of generic religiosity are preserved in Christian faith. In other words, some of the themes related to human agency are preserved even in his elaborations of the distinctively Christian focus on divine agency. In this way, both Kierkegaard's pseudonymous and veronymous works invite the reader to use "act" and "gift" language in intricately interacting ways in the daily life of faith. Because this dual focus becomes obvious in Climacus's discussion of faith as a "condition" given by God, in de Silentio's reflections on the "knight of faith," in the edifying discourses' exploration of "becoming nothing before God," and in Kierkegaard's veronymous account of the composition of his writings, we need to examine all four portions of Kierkegaard's work in some detail.

The way the "human task" and "divine gift" aspects of faith are differentiated and then simultaneously affirmed is most evident in Climacus's *Philosophical Fragments*. Of course, Climacus does not address the issue of divine grace and human agency as a traditional systematic theologian. Climacus's pervasive antipathy toward "systems," evident in the book's very title, applies to theological systems just as much as it does to philosophical systems. By using the guise of a "thought experiment," Climacus, the self-described "loafer," indirectly suggests how the "gift" and "task" aspects of faith can be integrated in the living of the Christian life (*PF*, 7). Presenting itself as a response to the epistemological question of how truth can be learned, the small volume can also be read as an investigation of the active and receptive aspects of faith. By approaching this question from an epistemological angle, Climacus is tapping into the general cultural fascination with questions of doubt and certainty, thereby capturing the cultivated reader's attention. But as the text develops, it becomes increasingly clear that epistemology is merely the springboard for an engagement with even deeper issues.

Climacus surreptitiously introduces the question of the origin of faith via the device of exploring the differences between construing "the truth" as something individuals discover within themselves, and thus can be "recollected," and construing "the truth" as something brought by a teacher (*PF*, 9-13). In the case of "recollection," the moment of encounter with a teacher would be no more than an accidental occasion for discovering the truth within — without decisive significance. Climacus poses this exploration as a thought experiment, asking the hypothetical question: What would need to be the case if the moment of encounter with the teacher is to be decisive in the discovery of truth, rather than the encounter with the teacher being a mere occasion for accessing an inner wisdom? In other words, Climacus structures this inquiry as a fanciful search for the conditions of the possibility of a decisive moment of encounter with the teacher. As this project develops, it becomes clear that part of this issue is the difference between truth as something resident in the individual and truth as something extrinsic to the individual that would require revelation. Much of the argument is aimed at highlighting the difference between innate wisdom, or at least an innate capacity for wisdom that only requires activation, and the historic revelation of God in Christ.

But *Philosophical Fragments* does much more than distinguish truth as revealed from truth as innate. The revealed/innate contrast raises the further question of how a revealed truth could be recognized and appropriated. Presumably, the ability to understand and appreciate the content of the revelation would require a receptive capacity involving a certain type of subjectivity. So even if the truth is based on an external revelation (in this case, the life of Jesus), a subjective "condition" for understanding that truth would need to be operative in order for an individual to comprehend its significance (*PF*, 62, 100). "Condition" in this context suggests a set of passions, concerns, and attitudes that pervade a person's life so thoroughly that they predispose the person to notice certain things, believe certain things, trust certain things, and make certain commitments. Put simply, the question becomes: What is the source of this passional condition, this faith? Is the "condition for understanding" (faith) an intrinsic capacity of the individual or is it a new ability given to the individual?

In *Philosophical Fragments,* Socrates' pedagogical practice and his own passionate inwardness, including his protestations of ignorance, epitomize the position that the individual already possesses a latent capacity for truth that awaits actualization through a free decision. Socrates' inwardness is presented as a disposition toward life that he freely adopted and maintained, and which the reader could also adopt and maintain. The truth of Socrates' life is his own act. As *Philosophical Fragments* progresses, this self-generated and self-sustained pathos of Socrates provides the foil for Climacus's construction of a dramatic alternative. If knowledge of the eternal is regarded as a capacity in the self, confidence in the power of one's own agency would be entirely appropriate. The Platonic theme that the truth is latent within the individual valorizes the individual's own ability to discover it for herself. If learners can delve within themselves and recollect the truth, then they already possess the potential for truth, and the teacher merely stimulates them to activate that potential. With the help of a little pedagogical catalyst, a human being is capable of resolving her own passional malaise. Such a conclusion would suggest that humanity itself holds the key to spiritual health. Enthusiasm for the spirituality of Socrates implies extravagant confidence in human abilities. Even if the consideration is added that what Socrates discovers is his own ignorance, the adoption of a life of Socratic ignorance would still be an example of trust in the individual's subjective potentialities, for even the embrace of self-skepticism is an intentional act. Choosing honesty and humility by negating one's claims to know anything would still be one's own heroic deed. Because of this, even the pure emulation of Socrates reduces spirituality (and thus Christian faith, if faith is construed as a variation on the theme of Socratic subjectivity) to a kind of work.

Climacus contrasts the Socratic view that knowing truth is a capacity in the learner, merely waiting to be activated through the provocation of a teacher, to the proposal that understanding the truth involves a new birth, becoming a new person. If the moment of transformation is to be regarded as decisive, the Socratic sensibility is insufficient. The hypothetical religion that Climacus constructs in contrast to the Socratic position is transparently a cipher for Christianity. Generic religiosity, even of the refined Socratic sort, would militate against the dual Christian themes that salvation is an unmerited gift from beyond the self and that it involves a "new birth." Christianity assumes that the relationship with the divine is not grounded in the intrinsic power of human subjectivity.

According to Climacus's hypothetical construction of a non-Socratic religion, faith, the appropriation of the truth, is not the awakening of a latent power. In fact, Christianity assumes that humanity is in a state of error. Humanity would not even suspect that it was in this woeful condition if it were not informed of it by an external authority. In Climacus's language, the individual needs "the god" in order to realize "that the god is absolutely different from him" (*PF*, 6). If Christianity is to be differentiated from Socratic subjectivity, even the consciousness of sin must be regarded as a gift that comes to individuals from outside themselves. The difference between God and humanity cannot be discovered by us; we cannot know through the power of our own insight how different from God we are. Far from knowing the truth, human beings do not even ask the right questions, for asking appropriate questions presupposes some awareness of the range of possible answers. Climacus concludes:

> Now if the moment is to acquire decisive significance, then the seeker up until that moment must not have possessed the truth, not even in the form of ignorance, for in that case the moment becomes merely the moment of occasion; indeed, he must not even be a seeker. (*PF*, 13)

The view articulated by Climacus suggests that in the inception and growth of faith the individual does nothing for which the individual could take credit. Humanity cannot be regarded as moving toward truth, but rather as resting content with illusions. For Climacus, the logic of absolute gratitude for the teacher requires the denigration of any ability or inherent capacity to yearn or question rightly. The possibility of faith is not even suspected, anticipated, or sought. In the language of dogmatics, sinners are not preparing themselves for the grace that will awaken faith in their hearts. The individual can take no credit for self-generated remorse, the penitential state that the Scholastic tradition had called "attrition," as if the cultivation of a sense of guilt predisposed the individual to receive God's grace. Of course, elsewhere in his corpus Kierkegaard does encourage the reader to engage in the preparation for grace by separating from the crowd, looking in the mirror of Scripture, and so forth. But here the rhetorical emphasis falls on taking no credit for the initiation of those efforts. By rejecting self-initiated preparation for grace, Climacus is parting company with the Pietists and other Lutherans, such as Clausen and Mynster, who inclined toward the synergist position. To this extent, the religion that Climacus outlines resembles Augustine's rejection of the semi-Pelagian argument that the individual must prepare to receive grace.

According to Climacus's constructed religion (which is really Christianity), humanity needs to be reborn. Self-actualization is not sufficient to correct the severity of the human problem. The Socratic progression from ignorance to self-discovery is not the kind of radical new birth that Christianity envisions. Faith, the condition for grasping the truth, is not an act of the individual but an act of God, for it is discontinuous with the individual's old capacities and dispositions. In Climacus's language, the teacher must supply "the condition" for understanding. The "condition" in this context is not the external revelation, for Climacus has already discussed that; rather, it is the inner capacity to understand and appropriate that revelation. In explaining this, Climacus argues:

> Now, if the learner is to obtain the truth, the teacher must bring it to him, but not only that. Along with it, he must provide him with the condition for understanding it, for if the learner were himself the condition for understanding the truth, then he merely needs to recollect, because the condition for understanding the truth is like being able to ask about it — the condition and the question contain the conditioned and the answer. (*PF*, 14)

The giving of the condition is a "transformation," not a "re-formation," of the learner, and can be described as a "rebirth," making the learner a "new creature." This rebirth, ascribed to the teacher's (God-in-Christ's) agency, is a requisite for understanding the content of the revelation. This "condition" is much more than a capacity to process previously obscure data. Rather, it is a new matrix of concerns, aspirations, and hopes; in other words, it is the pathos of faith (*PF*, 15).[35] Climacus is implying that faith cannot be regarded

---

35. See Tim Rose, *Kierkegaard's Christocentric Theology* (Aldershot, UK: Ashgate, 2001), p. 47.

as the individual's own self-generated achievement. Faith is not a matter of herculean acts of resolution; rather, faith is a gift from which a new way of living flows. Climacus claims: "It is easy to see, then . . . that faith is not an act of will, for it is always the case that all human willing is only efficacious within the condition" (*PF*, 62). To ascribe the awakening of faith to God, to regard faith itself, the "condition," as a gift, is to trust in something beyond the self. To have faith is to eschew reliance on the strength of the individual's own volitional powers. To construe faith as a gift is to maximize gratitude and to take no credit for anything. The perspective of faith, Climacus implies, ascribes even the individual's own progress in developing a new pathos to grace alone. Though the pedagogy is surreptitious, *Philosophical Fragments* is designed to coax the self-satisfied Socratic reader to imagine the attractiveness of a life of gratitude for God's grace. In this context it is significant that Climacus does not write about the need to mobilize reserves of willpower in order to accept "the condition" (the grace that creates faith) when it is offered. Such a concern would trigger the speculation that there must already be a latent condition in the individual that enables him to accept the offered condition. An infinite regression of conditions for other conditions would loom menacingly on the horizon. Nor does Climacus say that God restores the freedom of individuals, which they must then exercise. Hints of Lutheran synergism and Arminianism are strikingly absent. Instead, Climacus simply encourages gratitude for the gift of grace. The mood is one of sheer receptivity. In a way, *Philosophical Fragments* is a sustained but covert celebration of the priority and gratuity of God's grace, teasing the reader to consider the possibility of a life of gratitude.

However, *Philosophical Fragments* also functions as a goad for readers to assume responsibility for their responses to the teacher (Christ), whether that response is faith or offense. Besides indirectly encouraging gratitude, Climacus also attempts to foster a self-concern that will result in some kind of active engagement with the divine teacher. His rhetorical strategies are designed to maximize the sense of the momentous significance of the individual's response to the teacher. As he hints, the need to rely on God for truth can also offend the human desire for self-mastery. Accordingly, Climacus warns readers about the fearful possibility of being offended by the teacher, and he implies that readers must assume responsibility for succumbing to offense. He overtly claims that "offense is always an act, not an event" (*PF*, 50). He also alerts readers to the need for vigilance in the maintenance of faith. In this context Climacus describes faith as a "leap," a choice of vocabulary that would long be taken to encapsulate the essence of Kierkegaard's thought. Faith, it would seem, is an act that the individual performs (*PF,* 43). Here Climacus does characterize any kind of belief as "an act of freedom, an expression of will" (*PF,* 83). Both doubt and faith are intentional dispositions that an individual can adopt. Climacus alerts the reader to the need to decide whether to be offended by the paradox of the incarnation or to embrace it with faith — "the happy passion." The premonitory warnings about the possibility of offense suggest that something of monumental consequence hinges on the individual's decision. In this way, Climacus unsettles readers by using strongly "agent" language at the same time that he describes faith as a gift that the individual gratefully receives. So, even if faith is a gift from God, in some sense it can also be seen as the individual's responsible act. But in spite of the evident paradox, Climacus does not attempt to dissect faith in order to determine who exactly is doing what in faith's genesis. Climacus simply juxtaposes the two different kinds of discourse that Augustine had used.

Philosophical Fragments is not the only text by Climacus that exhibits this juxtaposition. As he had done in *Philosophical Fragments,* Climacus repeats this odd pattern of describing generic religiosity as a type of human work in *Concluding Unscientific Postscript,* then contrasts it to Christian faith, which he describes as a gift, and then suggests that in some ways the "work" language is still applicable within Christianity. Once again, the neat contrast of faith as the product of human activity and faith as a gift from God is sharply drawn and then rendered more complicated and problematic. In the case of *Concluding Unscientific Postscript,* the "task" and "gift" aspects of faith are initially distinguished through the device of Climacus's contrast of the claims that "subjectivity is truth" and that "subjectivity is untruth." Unlike *Philosophical Fragments,* here the focus is not so much on the issue of whether knowledge is innate or is revealed from beyond the individual; rather, this book concentrates attention on the issue of the role of self-involving passion in the pursuit of truth.

To decipher what Climacus means by affirming the seemingly contradictory propositions that "subjectivity is truth" and "subjectivity is untruth," let us first examine his assertion of the truth of subjectivity. As it did for Augustine, "truth" here suggests much more than the epistemic validity of propositions about states of affairs. Truth is what gives meaning and value to human life, enables the individual to make sense out of existence, and resolves anxieties and disquietudes about life's worth and purpose. By claiming that subjectivity is truth, Climacus, like Augustine, is denying that an individual must first attain cognitive certainty through purely objective procedures, and then must adjust his or her emotions accordingly. Climacus is rejecting the academic prejudice that regards passion as a disruptive force that clouds clear vision and disturbs calm deliberation. Like Augustine, Climacus (and certainly here he speaks for Kierkegaard) is convinced that passion is necessary for any engagement with matters of existential consequence. Without passion — or desire, as Augustine usually phrased it — the mind would not even know what to focus on, and the concentration that knowledge requires would be impossible.

In elaborating the content of this passionate "truth," Climacus outlines a generic type of religiosity, "Religiousness A," which involves the resignation, suffering, and guilt that are components of any genuine "existential pathos." The description of Religiousness A parallels to a large extent Climacus's earlier account of the "Socratic" position, which is based on the premise that "subjectivity is truth." Such a religious life is true, possessing a true pathos born of a true set of priorities. In order to relate to God within the individual, "everything that is in the way is cleared out, every finitude" (*CUP* 1, 561). This life of resignation, suffering, and guilt is presented as a mode of existence that the individual actively embraces in choosing to relate absolutely to the absolute and only relatively to the relative. Consequently, the life of Religiousness A as an ideal is described as the individual's own act, the product of the individual's own decision and resolution. Even "self-annihilation" (the annihilation of the finite self with its finite concerns) is regarded as the individual's responsibility (*CUP* 1, 572). In general, Climacus describes "becoming subjective" as a task that should be performed; in fact, it is "the highest task assigned to a human being" (*CUP* 1, 129). This task of transforming the individual's life by willing the absolute *telos* requires the assumption that the individual is free to perform it (*CUP* 1, 137-39, 183, 244). In this regard, the life lived in the light of the theme that "subjectivity is truth" has "passed through the ethical" and retained its self-ascription of responsibility (*CUP*, 1, 388). In many ways, Religiousness A could serve as a description of a lofty type of Pelagianism.

To this truthful pathos Climacus juxtaposes Christianity. According to Climacus, "Religiousness B," an incognito for Christianity, assumes that subjectivity is not the truth, for the truth must come from God as a gift. Because of human sin, there is no "immanental underlying kinship between the temporal and the eternal" (*CUP* 1, 573), which means that there is no eternity within the self that could be recollected or activated. Humans lack the "condition" for understanding the truth, and must become "a new creation" (*CUP* 1, 573). Here the structural and thematic parallels to *Philosoph-*

ical Fragments are not only particularly evident, but they are pointed out by Climacus himself. Not only must the truth be revealed to human beings, but they also must be given the capacity to appropriate it.

Climacus, at least in part, offers the hypothesis of subjectivity's untruth in order to engender in the reader a suspicion of the life of self-generated pathos. Climacus, like any good Lutheran, implicitly challenges the conviction that the attainment of the appropriate kind of spirituality is the deciding factor that determines an individual's eternal well-being. When Climacus says that "subjectivity is untruth," "subjectivity" refers to the cultivation of inwardness as the individual's own project and achievement. Climacus is not suggesting that Christian faith does not require the passionate inwardness of authentic subjectivity. He is certainly not advocating a reversion to detached objectivity and cognitive assent to doctrinal propositions. By proposing the untruth of subjectivity, Climacus seeks to prevent the reader from succumbing to any Pelagian self-congratulation for spiritual athleticism and profundity. "Subjectivity is untruth" suggests that it is not the case that an individual can please God or experience spiritual fulfillment by mustering the requisite degree of passion. Being right with God is not the result of successful efforts to cultivate the necessary amounts of renunciation, suffering, and guilt. Implicitly, Climacus is drawing attention to the possibility that humans may be so subtly perverse that even the self-negation required by the cultivation of resignation, suffering, and guilt could become grounds for self-assertion. Resignation and guilt could be prized as odd types of good works, for humans are all too prone to take pride in anything, even in the depth and sincerity of their own guilt feelings. Climacus's claim that "subjectivity is untruth" presents individuals with the potentially offensive prospect that God may freely give an eternal happiness that they could not win for themselves. Whatever Christian subjectivity may be, it is not merely an intensification or extension of a generic religious quest; rather, it is a new form of pathos that the individual cannot self-generate. Accordingly, Climacus can even declare that "existing before God" and "seeking God" are the kinds of things that come over the person, that "seize" a person.

Of course, the prospect that the individual can do nothing to bring about a "true" relationship with God is potentially offensive to human self-esteem. The sheer gratuitousness of salvation scandalizes the ordinary human propensity to take credit for one's own spiritual exertions and struggles. Consequently, appreciating the untruth of subjectivity involves the self-ascription of a new kind of guilt (*CUP* 1, 581-85). The individual comes to see the predisposition to take offense at God's grace as one's own fault. According to Climacus, this profound dissatisfaction with one's own self is the full-blown concept of "sin" in the Christian sense. Climacus insists that the meaning of "sin" cannot be reduced to guilt over particular acts or ignorance of the good, but can only be explicated in terms of the concept of the incarnation and the consequent possibility of offense at the gratuitous gift of God's love. In the Christian sense, "sin" is not just moral depravity or the failure to renounce earthly joys as one's highest good; rather, sin is the failure to gratefully receive God's grace.

Ironically, the theme that "subjectivity is untruth" itself encourages a more Christianly truthful subjectivity, which Climacus describes as a "sharpened pathos" (*CUP* 1, 581-85). By fostering the suspicion that the individual's seemingly admirable striving for the highest good is actually a subtle form of self-assertion, the appreciation of subjectivity's untruth can stimulate an even more profound form of self-abnegation. Accordingly, Climacus uses the "subjectivity is untruth" motif in contexts where self-satisfaction about the quality of one's own inwardness is a temptation. A new discontent with one's own spiritual exertions and a new yearning to rely totally on God must emerge before "subjectivity is untruth" makes sense. The untruth of subjectivity does not negate the earlier contention that faith is a mode of subjectivity. It merely means that faith should not be construed as the individual's own meritorious act: one should not have faith in the power of one's faith.

Climacus writes in a way that indirectly encourages the reader to cultivate this refined religious subjectivity that is the passional matrix of Christian convictions. Not only does the language of pathos return in the discussion of the untruth of subjectivity, but so does the language of responsible agency. Paradoxically, Climacus disabuses the reader of all notions of doing anything that could produce salvation at the same time that he coaxes the reader to actively cultivate total reliance on God. Ironically, he encourages the individual to responsibly strive to take no credit for striving. In the conclusion of *Concluding Unscientific Postscript*, Climacus repeats the perplexing juxtaposition of two different discourses that had characterized *Philosophical Fragments*: the language of human responsibility and the language of absolute reliance on God.

Climacus is not the only one of Kierkegaard's pseudonymous writers who boldly contrasts generic religiosity (and human agency) and Christianity (and divine agency), and then proceeds to complicate the distinction. A similar strategy is operative in Johannes de Silentio's *Fear and Trembling*, in which "infinite resignation" is compared to "faith" (*FT,* 38-51).[36] The exemplar of infinite resignation is a young swain who has fallen in love with an unattainable princess. The ardent lad has recognized that the prospects for an actual union with the princess are nonexistent, but he has vowed to himself to cherish and remain faithful to the memory of the princess. This knight of infinite resignation's intentional devotion to an unattainable beloved involves the cultivation of an inwardness that resembles many of the aspects of Climacus's Religiousness A. Through his own exertions, the lover shall maintain his love in spite of the recalcitrance of the external world. A felicitous relationship to "immediacy," the prospect of earthly happiness, has been denied him; in response, he has made the "infinite movement." The actual events of his life, all the slings and arrows of outrageous fortune, will no longer determine his emotional states. The lover has achieved independence from life's vicissitudes by deciding to remain faithful to his beloved whether he is united to her or not. In fact, an actual life with the beloved has become a matter of indifference to him. The breach with immediate happiness spawned by his disappointed love affair is universalized into a distancing from all actuality. Indifferent to the success or failure of any earthly projects, unmoved by any dreams for earthly fulfillment, he rests tranquilly in the enduring quality of his own resolution to love faithfully. The permanence and invulnerability of his loving disposition are the presence of the eternal in him. His love has become his religion. In his own way, the knight of infinite resignation has discovered the truth of subjectivity so lauded by Climacus and has attained an "eternal consciousness." De Silentio observes:

> He does not need the erotic titillation of seeing the beloved etc., nor does he in the finite sense continually need to be bidding her farewell, because in the eternal sense he recollects her. . . . He has grasped the deep secret that even in loving another person one ought to be sufficient unto oneself. He is no longer finitely concerned about what the princess does, and precisely this proves that he has made the movement infinitely. (*FT,* 44)

For our purposes, it is most significant that in the cases of both Socrates and the knight of infinite resignation, the resulting passionate inwardness

---

36. See Sharon Krishek, *Kierkegaard on Faith and Love* (Cambridge: Cambridge University Press, 2009), pp. 75-108, for a somewhat similar account of the dialectic of renunciation and affirmation/trust in faith.

is depicted as the individual's own act. As de Silentio remarks, infinite resignation is a movement "I venture to make when it is demanded of me and can discipline myself to make . . ." (*FT,* 48). In both cases, strenuous internal effort must be exerted in order to sustain this disposition.

The "knight of faith," however, is different. Rather than instantiating the passionate subjectivity of generic religiosity, his form of pathos resembles that of Christianity. After performing the movement of infinite resignation, he then proceeds to execute a second movement of embracing the possibility of receiving back God's earthly gifts, a movement that does not seem to be under the control of the knight's will. Unlike the knight of infinite resignation, gratitude in response to God's gifts becomes this knight's salient characteristic. Consequently, the pathos of this exemplar of faith is exquisitely dialectical. At the same time that he is prepared to surrender all earthly happiness to God, he also hopes that God will bless his earthly life. To illustrate this tensive "double movement" (*FT,* 27-53), de Silentio turns to the example of Abraham. The incomprehensible thing about Abraham is that he was willing to sacrifice his son Isaac, his hope for earthly fulfillment, at the same time that he hoped that God would somehow restore Isaac and all the happiness he was willing to surrender. Abraham's greatness, according to de Silentio, was his "mad" faith that God would somehow be faithful to God's promise to make him blessed through the very Isaac whom God was commanding him to sacrifice. Abraham makes a "double movement," one in which he renounces everything and one in which he trusts that he shall receive everything. In the story of Abraham, world-renunciation and world-affirmation go hand in hand. The "absurd" content of Abraham's faith is the wager that "with God all things are possible," including this paradoxical confluence of renunciation and affirmation. Mirroring Abraham, all knights of faith accept actuality as a gift from God, genuinely delighting in ordinary life's simple pleasures; and at the same time, they inwardly resign them. After describing the knight of faith's renunciation of all prospects for earthly happiness, de Silentio continues:

> But then the marvel happens; he makes one more movement even more wonderful than all the others, for he says: Nevertheless I have faith that I shall get her — that is, by virtue of the absurd, by virtue of the fact that with God all things are possible. (*FT,* 46)

The crucial thing to note here is that this confidence in God's bounty is not the product of the individual's intentional action. De Silentio is clearly fascinated by Abraham's pathos, and even seems to be drawn to it. But because he himself is not a faithful individual, he finds Abraham to be totally mystifying. De Silentio can only limn the contours of faith from the outside — as an external but intrigued observer. No matter how much de Silentio may be attracted to (and repulsed by) the prospect of faith, he cannot generate faith in himself by an act of will. He admits with evident regret, "[B]ut this movement I cannot make. As soon as I want to begin, everything reverses itself, and I take refuge in the pain of resignation" (*FT,* 50). De Silentio confesses that the advent of faith can only be described as something beyond his own capacities. Although infinite resignation is a "movement I make all by myself," the movement of faith can be made only "by virtue of the absurd," which one cannot do by oneself (*FT,* 48-49). Simultaneously renouncing the world while yet affirming it requires a potency not naturally available to people like de Silentio; it requires the gift of empowerment from God.

Just as Climacus had problematized the original disjunction of Religiousness A and Religiousness B, so also de Silentio complicates the contrast between the pathos of the knight of infinite resignation and the knight of faith. The knight of faith has renounced the prospects of worldly happiness, just as much as the knight of infinite resignation had done. Presumably this movement of resignation in the dialectic of faith must be described as the knight of faith's own act. Renouncing the world continues to be construed as a task, though the ability to receive the world back is a mysterious gift. To complicate matters even further in regard to that gift of faith, Abraham is still admired for his courage, trust, and hope in receiving Isaac back. Evidently the gift of faith is something that should not be regarded as a power in the individual that works automatically. It seems to be the kind of thing that one should be encouraged to intentionally exercise and cultivate. De Silentio simultaneously marvels that Abraham has been given this gift to perform a dialectical movement beyond ordinary human powers, and he admires Abraham's active exercise of that gift. Faith seems to be both something that one receives and something that one does. It is significant that de Silentio does not clarify matters by adding that God offers the capacity and then Abraham must responsibly accept and use it. He simply uses the two different types of language conjointly, without being synthesized. The structural and thematic similarity to both *Philosophical Fragments* and *Concluding Unscientific Postscript* is obvious. Moreover, one can clearly hear echoes of Augustine's two ways of describing the Christian life as a gift and as a task.

This dialectical juxtaposition of responsible human agency and God's gracious activity is not just an idiosyncrasy of the pseudonymous writings, for it recurs in writings that Kierkegaard signed his name to. Even the early edifying discourses, which Climacus labels as expressions of the categories of "immanence" (*CUP* 1, 256), complicate the exhortation to assume responsibility for one's life with very Christian reminders that only God, and not the self, can accomplish anything of existential importance.[37] The tension is evident in his first edifying discourse of 1843, entitled "The Expectancy of Faith." On the one hand, Kierkegaard declares that faith can be acquired "only by personally willing it," in order to distinguish faith from romantic toying with possibilities (*EUD*, 13). The essay makes the reader feel the enormous responsibility of tending to one's own faith. To drive this point home, Kierkegaard reiterates that no one can receive faith from another human being. On the other hand, he just as forcefully reminds the reader that faith can be learned only through an absolute reliance on God (*EUD*, 28). Rhetorically, the attention shifts from trusting in the individual's spiritual exertions to trusting in God, the provider of faith. The ultimate ground of "faith's expectancy" in the face of life's uncertainties is God, not the feeble self. In his next edifying discourse, "Every Good and Every Perfect Gift Is from Above," Kierkegaard similarly first encourages his readers to receive every gift from God with thankfulness, implying that the reader has the power to nurture this receptivity; then he claims that even the willingness to receive spiritual gifts from God is itself a gift (*EUD*, 44). He continues:

> In repentance, you receive everything from God, even the thanksgiving that you bring to him, so that even this is what the child's gift is to the eyes of the parents, a jest, a receiving of something that one has oneself given. . . . God is the one who does everything in you and who then grants you the childlike joy of regarding your thanksgiving as a gift from you. (*EUD*, 46)

Our offering of thanksgiving to God is not our own act. In "Strengthening in the Inner Being," Kierkegaard again first encourages the reader to develop concern about the meaning of the reader's own life, even inviting the reader to be God's "co-worker" in this project of "strengthening the in-

---

37. Thomas C. Anderson, "Is the Religion of *Eighteen Upbuilding Discourses* Religiousness A?" in Robert L. Perkins, ed., *International Kierkegaard Commentary: Eighteen Upbuilding Discourses* (Macon, GA: Mercer University Press, 2003), pp. 51-75.

ner being" (*EUD,* 86). But then he concludes by citing Paul's reminder that "nobody can provide this strengthening for himself" because "the witness itself is a gift from God" (*EUD,* 98). Repeating this pattern in yet another discourse of 1843, Kierkegaard first encourages the reader to be receptive to God's gifts, then reminds the reader that "God is the only one who gives in such a way that he gives the condition along with the gift" (*EUD,* 134). In all of these instances, Kierkegaard initially presents receptivity to God as an attitude that the individual can freely adopt, even claiming that resolution can bind a person to the eternal, and then he confesses that this receptivity is something that only God can instill in the individual's heart. As always, Kierkegaard refuses to integrate these motifs in a semi-Pelagian, synergistic, predestinarian, or Arminian way.

In other discourses Kierkegaard emphasizes the frustration and failure that any striving for self-integration and self-mastery will inevitably encounter. In "To Need God Is a Human Being's Highest Perfection" (1844), Kierkegaard warns that the purpose of relying on God is not merely to give individuals access to an additional source of power to enable them to attain their spiritual goals (*EUD,* 309). Grace is not to be thought of as an assisting infusion of spiritual energy. Rather, through the struggle to reorient themselves, individuals should learn that they are capable of doing nothing at all. God is not merely a helpful higher power that assists in the making of momentous decisions (*EUD,* 322). Kierkegaard concludes that the struggle for self-mastery is an exercise in egotism that only produces a deeper self-enclosure. In "The Thorn in the Flesh," Kierkegaard advises even more forcefully that every vestige of self-confidence must be eradicated (*EUD,* 345). In the pursuit of the religious life, the allegedly autonomous self must be humbled by anxiety, despair, and disintegration; in short, the self must become nothing before God. Similarly, in "One Who Prays Aright Struggles in Prayer and Is Victorious — In That God Is Victorious," Kierkegaard explains that this particular spiritual victory is the recognition that the individual has already lost the battle of self-salvation. The struggle to live in relationship with God generates the prideful impatience of wanting to quickly reach an "understanding" with God, a situation of mutual transparency. Kierkegaard observes:

> Whom should the struggler desire to resemble other than God? But if he himself is something or wants to be something, this something is sufficient to hinder the imbalance. Only when he himself becomes nothing, only then can God illuminate him so that he resembles God. However

great he is, he cannot manifest God's likeness; God can imprint himself in him only when he himself has become nothing (*EUD*, 399).

According to Kierkegaard, the self-centeredness and self-enclosure that afflict humanity cannot be remedied through self-assertion. The enclosed heart of the spiritual Prometheus must be broken open by the divine Other. Ironically, in all these discourses, Kierkegaard still exhorts the individual to strenuously labor to become as nothing, even though the attempt to transform one's own self is delusional and arrogant. Kierkegaard's effort to foster self-abnegating reliance on God continues to use the language of personal agency and exertion.

The tension between the Christian life conceived as a task and the Christian life construed as a gift recurs in the discourses for communion on Fridays (*CD*, 251-300). Kierkegaard typically begins each discourse with an exhortation to the reader to engage in a rigorous program of "inward" action. It is a matter of utmost urgency that readers should assume responsibility for cultivating the pathos necessary for receiving the Eucharist. Although the longing for fellowship with Christ is planted in the individual's heart by the Holy Spirit, "the person himself shall do everything to use rightly what God gives" (*CD*, 254). Kierkegaard does not specify if this is a longing implanted in the individual's heart at birth, or if it is aroused at some later time in the individual's life, but in either case it is something that the individual must diligently tend. The gift of grace must be actively nurtured so that it "might become the strong but also well-tested, heart-felt longing that is required of those who worthily want to partake of the holy meal of Communion" (*CD*, 251). The ways in which the communicant must strive to be worthy are multiple. For example, the reader who aspires to be rightly prepared for communion should meditate on the vanity and unreliability of all temporal phenomena. Furthermore, potential communicants should struggle to develop sincere attitudes of repentance for their lives as a whole. To make the task even more daunting, conscientious individuals should also resolve to cherish and make use of the offer of grace, as well as nurture a permanent consciousness of being in the presence of Christ. Readers approaching the communion table must foster in themselves an appropriate self-suspicion, without allowing their own anxiety and guilt to engulf them. Moreover, communicants should strive to appreciate the magnitude of God's mercy and implore God's blessing on all their labors. In all of these specific exhortations to develop the virtues appropriate for participation in the Eucharist, Kierkegaard is implicitly insisting that the invitation to the communion table presents the potential communicant with a task. At the beginning of the first discourse, Kierkegaard even makes this explicit, observing that although God does give persons a longing for reconciliation, that longing must be grasped and cultivated by the individual (*CD*, 251). He repeatedly mentions that a response to God's gracious presence in Holy Communion is a "requirement," and he uses a barrage of imperatives to underscore the need for action. Taken by itself, this motif of the self-cultivated preparation for an encounter with God's grace suggests that Kierkegaard's natural allies would be the synergists who posited the need for cooperation with God's gracious activity in the individual's heart. Some of his sentiments might even reflect the Pietist view that the sinner's act of contrition must precede God's act of bestowing grace. Perhaps Kierkegaard had more in common with John Cassian than with Augustine.

However, these very same discourses also declare in no uncertain terms that the individual can do nothing with respect to the eucharistic encounter with Christ. At the same time that the discourses call for action, they shift the focus to the gracious power of God that precedes, supports, supplements, overwhelms, and generally displaces human striving. Paradoxically, at the same time that Kierkegaard encourages the reader to get busy with the task of preparation for communion, he also develops the countervailing theme of increasing reliance on God's grace and distrust of one's own efforts. In fact, the theme of reliance on God's agency crescendoes as the discourses develop. Kierkegaard introduces this motif by insisting that the presence of longing for God in our soul is not due to our own exertions; we do not give ourselves a hunger for God. Then Kierkegaard shifts readers' attention from the dubious quality of their spiritual preparation to the reliability of the work of Jesus. The reminder of Jesus' fidelity to the fickle individual should comfort readers whenever doubts about their own spiritual integrity grow and become paralyzing. The reader's appropriate self-doubt should be countered with the certainty that Christ is faithful to us in spite of our unfaithfulness. Next, Kierkegaard adds that we cannot hope to maintain our own penitence by our own power, cautioning that "not even in this dare we trust in our own strength" (*CD*, 275). We are not justified by the strength and authenticity of our own remorse, for that remorse is not our own self-generated act. When we imagine that we are spiritually surviving a divine test, and are inclined to take credit for it, we must remember that it is really God who is sustaining us through it. Kierkegaard confesses: "[W]e know very well that in the moment of the ordeal you yourself must hold on to us, we know very well that *fundamentally* we are faithless and that at every moment *fundamentally* it is you who are holding on to us" (*CD*, 286).

In a variety of ways Kierkegaard reiterates the point that faith is not a good work that we perform. Analogously, even in our most arduous spiritual trials, it is God who is holding on to us, preventing us from falling, and pushing us forward (*CD*, 298). Even when we seem to be taking our own steps forward in the development of a faithful life, we must not be so presumptuous as to congratulate ourselves. Kierkegaard concludes that the more a person becomes involved with God, the more it will become clear to that person how little she is capable of doing. Kierkegaard admonishes:"You cannot be Christ's coworker in connection with the reconciliation, not in the remotest way" (*CD*, 299). That is certainly not the language of synergism. Kierkegaard adds: "Alas, no, you are capable of nothing, not even of holding your soul by yourself at the peak of consciousness that you stand totally in need of grace and blessing" (*CD*, 300). His rhetoric here seems to rule out any semi-Pelagian or pietistic preparation for grace through attrition. In fact, Kierkegaard even refuses to allow for self-congratulation in regard to Arminian-style nonresistance to God's gracious action. To summarize, Kierkegaard insists that those who come to Holy Communion should realize how utterly incapable they are of contributing anything at all to their own spiritual health. In general, we should simply confess our extreme incapacity, rejoice in God's strength, and be silent. When viewed retrospectively, the life of faith should be construed as a sheer gift rather than as an achievement. This dynamic in Kierkegaard's discourses surely sounds like the celebration of God's sovereign power found in Augustine's predestinarian treatises.

By the end of this series of discourses, the reader has been admonished to assiduously cultivate several different virtues and then exhorted to entirely distrust their efficacy. The reader encounters a puzzling combination of words of warning and words of comfort. On the one hand, Kierkegaard uses a multitude of rhetorical strategies to provoke the reader to dread the frightful prospect of going to the communion table unworthily, and to admonish the reader to do everything possible to avoid such a spiritual catastrophe. On the other hand, he uses an equally extensive set of literary ploys to erode the reader's confidence in the possibility of doing anything of religious significance — and thereby fosters a confidence in God alone. Even in the same discourse Kierkegaard sometimes exhorts the reader to earnestly struggle and sometimes nurtures self-oblivious confidence in God. Prompted by the author's paradoxical directives, readers should strive earnestly at the same time that they put no confidence in their own fledgling efforts. Readers must simultaneously work out their own salvation in fear and trembling, and must also trust only in God, taking no credit for anything, including the cultivation of penitential attitudes. The ostensible problem with this dialectical tension is that the provocation of concern about one's own worthiness presupposes a sense of responsible human agency, while the encouragement of trust in God requires a concentration on the exclusive reliability of divine agency. In juxtaposing these themes, Kierkegaard does not even attempt to explain how God's agency relates to human agency; he does not describe God's action as assisting, overriding, guiding, urging, compelling, or eliciting a human response.

This now-familiar pattern of juxtaposing the language of human responsibility with the language of divine sovereign action is encapsulated in the structure of "Christ as the Prototype" in *Judge for Yourself!* After exhorting his readers to follow the demanding path of Christ the prototype (a path that is the narrow way of ostracism, persecution, and crucifixion), and quoting Jesus' intimidating ultimatum that no one can serve two masters, Kierkegaard abruptly turns to a consideration of the care-free trust in God exemplified by the insouciant lilies and the birds. The discourse of strenuous human action is suddenly placed against the discourse of passive reliance on God's providential activity. The obvious tension between the two types of language raises the question of the relationship of divine grace and human responsibility in a particularly acute way. To address this issue, Kierkegaard offers the analogy of little Ludvig, a child who seems to be pushing a stroller through his own exertions, though it is really the mother who is supporting and propelling him. Kierkegaard says:

> Yet the mother has hit upon something new that will definitely delight little Ludvig even more: would he like to push the stroller by himself? And he can! What! He can? Yes, look, Auntie, little Ludvig can push the stroller himself! Now, let us be down to earth but not upset the child, since we know very well that little Ludvig cannot do it, that it is his mother who is actually pushing the stroller, and that it is really only to delight him that she plays the game that little Ludvig can do it himself. And he, he huffs and puffs. And he is sweating, isn't he? O my word, he is! The sweat stands on his brow, in the sweat of his brow he is pushing the stroller — but his face is shining with happiness . . . . (*JFY*, 185)

After drawing attention to the seemingly sole efficacy of divine action suggested by the poignant parable (for Ludvig's agency seems to be purely an illusion), Kierkegaard returns to the theme of the need to imitate Christ and to suffer for the faith as he did. He emphasizes that the follower of Christ must actively "will" to suffer, and he reverts to strongly volitional language (*JFY*, 201). Once again the essay oscillates between stern imperatives and reminders that we cannot really do anything, just as it oscillates between the suffering prototype on the one hand and the lilies, the birds, and little Ludvig on the other. We have seen a similar oscillation in Augustine's anti-Pelagian writings.

Finally, even Kierkegaard's posthumously published *The Point of View for My Work as an Author* exhibits this same juxtaposition of the Christian life as a task and the Christian life as a gift. On the one hand, this notoriously polysemous work reads like a confession of Kierkegaard's authorial intentions. Viewed in one way, his writing output was his own very deliberate action, and he had a plan that was operative from beginning to end. Kierkegaard describes his work as "a task" of self-denial that required much "fear and trembling" (*PV*, 25). His literary productivity was his own self-oblation that he offered to God. The language in the early sections of the essay implies that his creative action was designed, initiated, and sustained by human agency, with divine agency merely providing auxiliary aid (*PV*, 24, 43). His self-disclosure is addressed to "earnest seekers" who will appreciate the arduousness of his authorial labors to promote genuine Christianity. The foregrounding of human agency in these contexts, with a suggestion of divine assistance, is fully compatible with semi-Pelagianism.

However, in the third chapter Kierkegaard begins to assign a more prominent role to God's "Governance" of his project. God gave him "the ability and the energy" to work on a staggeringly grand scale (*PV*, 72). Moreover, "Governance" bore down on him when he began to go astray and provided boundaries and direction (*PV*, 72-74). God was even active in the ostensibly fortuitous things that happened to him, ensuring that he would be in the proper mood for a particular segment of his literary endeavors. Kierkegaard reflects: "From the very beginning I have been as if under arrest and at every moment sensed that it was not I who played the master but that it was someone else who was the master . . ." (*PV*, 74). He does not describe his obedience to Governance as something that he chose to do, or even as something that he could have resisted. The rhetoric is not suggestive of Arminianism. Kierkegaard muses that "in one sense all the writing has had an unbroken evenness, as if I had done nothing other than to copy each day from a printed book" (*PV*, 76). As the essay progresses, the verbs suggesting divine action become stronger as he portrays himself as having been "constrained" and "used" by Governance. Looking back at his writing career, Kierkegaard simply confesses, "I could not do otherwise" (*PV*, 86). There is no talk of having been able to consent to God's overtures or of having been able to resist God's promptings.

This strand in *Point of View* parallels Augustine's tendency to ascribe all efficacy to God and to take credit for nothing. But, as with Augustine, Kierkegaard never completely abandons the language of human intentionality in his authorial self-disclosure, for it resurfaces even when he is waxing most encomiastic about the power of Governance. Two agencies seem to be operative in the production of his writing: some passages highlight human agency, while other passages focus on divine agency. That ambivalent duality, of course, is exactly what Augustine had inscribed into the *Confessions*.

To summarize this comparison of different portions of Kierkegaard's authorship, a recurrent pattern of juxtaposition is evident in all of these examples from the pseudonymous writings, as well as from the texts signed in his own name. Put simply, he portrays faith as both a gift and a task. To have genuine faith, the individual must depend entirely on grace, and at the same time actively cultivate faithful dispositions and passions. We should recognize that before God we can do nothing, which sounds receptive and passive, while we also attend to the quality of our subjectivity and way of life, which sounds active. This conjunction seems oxymoronic, or at least disturbingly tensive. Furthermore, this tension recurs throughout Kierkegaard's writings in the internal structure of many of his exhortations. He repeatedly encourages readers to regard themselves as nothing before God, but adopting this stance appears to be plagued by an inner contradiction. Surely the effort expended in striving to see oneself as nothing would make a person something. If our ultimate task is to become as nothing, to put aside our willfulness, that task nevertheless requires an exertion of will on our part. The reader is left fearing that Kierkegaard may be recommending mutually exclusive attitudes, and may begin to long for a clarifying explanation of how our actions and God's action interact. Does the human will cooperate with grace, or are our actions governed by divine determinism? Can our will resist God's offer of grace, or is God's activity irresistible? Is Kierkegaard at heart a synergist, believing that the human and divine wills work together, or a monergist, claiming that God's will alone is efficacious? Does he presuppose a theory of dual agency or single agency?

The frustrated reader will be disappointed, for Kierkegaard provides no such theory. He resists the temptation to transpose the urgency of the life of faith into the realm of speculation. As we have seen, Kierkegaard will not attempt to clarify the respective roles of God's action and human action through recourse to a metaphysical or theological theory. Kierkegaard refuses to regard the divine and human agencies as comparable factors in a theological algebra. He does not flat-footedly claim that God makes the first move in faith's birth by infusing a new capacity into the individual's soul, and that the individual then freely makes the second move of accepting it. Nor does he say that God gives the condition irresistibly. Any such calculus would be too "scientific" and too "objective" to be meaningful. Kierkegaard was not a deterministic Calvinist, a semi-Pelagian, a Lutheran synergist, or an Arminian. Given his convictions concerning the conditions for meaningful communication, he could not have been any of those. Outside specific contexts of fostering a specific kind of pathos, the concepts of "grace," "freedom," and "faith" lose their meaning. Rather than trying to develop an abstract conceptual schema, Kierkegaard seeks to nurture the practical wisdom of recognizing when it is appropriate to emphasize which theme. Perhaps the activities of being grateful for God's action and of assuming responsibility for one's passions are not incompatible, if the contexts of their use and their purposes are taken into account. As we have seen, by emphasizing both the "gift" and "task" aspects of faith in the same texts, sometimes almost on the same page, he dramatizes the need to combine both themes in the individual's life — without collapsing one into the other.

Kierkegaard uses both the "task" view of faith and the "gift" view of faith as complementary models that serve different purposes with respect to the same phenomenon. He treats the two models as being neither mutually exclusive nor synthesizable. In Kierkegaard's writings the "human task" and "divine gift" models of faith are irreducibly different; nevertheless, both are necessary. Admittedly, Kierkegaard does not explicitly defend or even articulate this strategy of complementarity, but he certainly does consistently practice it. He even did at least gesture toward this practice of maintaining a dialectical tension when he quoted a sermon by Luther in which the venerable Reformer compared the world to a drunken peasant who, when he is helped up one side of a horse, falls off the other side (*FSE*, 24). Rather than conceptually integrating the themes, the individual needs to develop skill in discerning when to use which one. On the one hand, when tempted toward pride by self-aggrandizing comparisons to one's worldly neighbors, the incipiently self-righteous Pharisee should have recourse to the gift model. Similarly, when the anxious individual succumbs to brooding fears about the inadequacy of his spiritual progress, desperately looking for reassuring signs of sanctification, the gift model should be used as an antidote. On the other hand, when the individual is tempted to become spiritually smug, prematurely content with minimal growth in love, the task model can function as a corrective prod.

In short, the individual must discern when it is edifying to talk about human agency and when it is edifying to talk about efficacious grace. The cultivation of these skills of discernment is subject to the same stereoscopic perspective, for the cultivation itself can be seen as both a gift and a task. The combined use of the two models could counteract tendencies toward spiritual self-aggrandizement while it still encourages the effort to live a genuinely faithful life. Individuals learn to express gratitude even for their own efforts to grow in faith, hope, and love for God and neighbor — and for progress in the Christian life. Used in tandem, the two models could subvert the project of self-salvation without discouraging the responsible effort to live faithfully. By simultaneously entertaining the "gift" and "task" views of faith, Christians can nurture responsible gratitude and grateful responsibility.[38] It is this complex, bifocal pedagogy that Kierkegaard's writings attempt to provide.

Conclusion

When we read Kierkegaard's remarks about "predestination," "grace," "freedom," "divine sovereignty," and related concepts in the light of various pastoral purposes, we may perceive that Augustine and Kierkegaard were not as different on the issue of divine grace and human freedom as Kierkegaard or his subsequent interpreters sometimes thought. Both theologians wanted to encourage individuals to strive to grow in the Christian virtues, and both wanted individuals to do that with passion and earnestness. When exhorting or coaxing their readers to get busy with the task, both Augustine and Kierkegaard use the language of free, responsible human agency. As we have seen, Augustine even continued to do this during his most vehemently anti-Pelagian period. Moreover, both thinkers also wanted individuals to put no trust in their own spiritual exertions but to rely on God's grace, take no credit for anything, and receive God's love with unadulterated gratitude. When doing this, both Augustine and Kierkegaard use a vocabulary that highlights God's agency alone. Their pastoral goals of fostering both responsible striving and self-abandoning reliance on God are parallel. In

---

38. See M. Jamie Ferreira, *Love's Grateful Striving: A Commentary on Kierkegaard's Works of Love* (New York: Oxford University Press, 2001), for a somewhat similar point.

pursuing these twin but tensive goals, the two thinkers use two counter-vailing discourses simultaneously that could not be synthesized in a grand metaphysics of divine and human agency.

Perhaps many of the apparent differences between Augustine and Kierkegaard were due to their differing contexts — and their differing assessments of the problematic nature of those contexts. After combating Manichean fatalism, Augustine came to fear the threat posed by the self-righteousness of the Pelagians and Donatists as an even greater danger. The most effective strategy to use against them was to emphasize the need to rely on divine agency. For Kierkegaard, on the other hand, the most pressing problem was the smugness and spiritual lethargy of Christendom. Against that complacency it was more appropriate to emphasize the need for genuine human striving. Consequently, each thinker tends to give rhetorical priority to a different element of the dialectic. Of course, neither writer neglected the recessive pole, for Augustine continued to encourage responsible action, and Kierkegaard consistently urged reliance on God's grace. In fact, it could be argued that Kierkegaard's writings indirectly emphasize reliance on God's agency just as much as do Augustine's.

But perhaps there was an even deeper disparity between them than a possible difference in emphasis, a disparity that was evident in our earlier chapters. Augustine was much more prone to attempt to develop a metaphysics of divine and human agencies — as an instance of faith seeking understanding. He found meditation on the mysteries of the God/human relationship to be not only meaningful but also edifying. That proclivity led Augustine to formulate his various proposals about predestination and the various operations of grace. This penchant also motivated Augustine to sometimes use strongly necessitarian language when describing God's saving actions. All of this aroused Kierkegaard's suspicion and disapprobation. Yet, in spite of this significant difference, the rhetorical and pastoral instincts of Augustine remain congenial to Kierkegaard's own. The rhetorical Augustine is sensitive to the varying contexts and purposes of theological statements, and thus he continues to mix discourses and vocabularies. Like Kierkegaard, that rhetorical Augustine knew that the real integration of responsibility and gratitude occurs in the Christian's life, not in a theological system.

CHAPTER 7

Christology: The Allure of Lowliness

The preceding discussion of Augustine's and Kierkegaard's reflections on divine agency and human responsibility with regard to the genesis of faith did not address the crucial issue of the content of that faith. In their pages the faith that is simultaneously a gift and a task is not a generic spiritual experience or an amorphous religious disposition. For both thinkers the Christian life is shaped and defined by the unique object of the individual believer's trust, hope, and love. Both Augustine and Kierkegaard regarded Jesus Christ as the crucial factor in the *viator's* journey from sin toward blessedness. Both insisted that without Jesus Christ the journey of faith could not proceed, nor could it even begin. To make the connection of Christ and the journey theme explicit, Augustine often uses the phrases "Christ the way" and "Christ the homeland."[1] Quoting John 14:6, Kierkegaard also frequently refers to Christ as "the way" (*JP* 1, 361). Similarly linking Christ to the journey motif, Kierkegaard observes:

> When a ship is to put to sea, the end of a cable is cast out and fastened to a tugboat — and in this way the ship is drawn. When a human life is to be commenced and continued without too much dependence upon the temporal, a cable must be cast out. . . . But Christ above all is the drawing power from eternity to eternity. (*JP* 1, 311)

However, the exact nature of the role that Jesus plays in the writings of each theologian, respectively, has been a matter of some debate. For decades

---

1. See Goulven Madec, *Le patrie et la voie: Le Christ dans la vie et la pensée de saint Augustin* (Paris: Desclée, 1989).

some theologians have accused both Augustine and Kierkegaard of being inadequately attentive to the significance of Christ in general, or of failing to appreciate the union of the two natures of Christ, or at least of ascribing inordinate importance to just one of the natures.

The critics of Augustine often admit that the Bishop of Hippo did espouse a belief in the humanity and divinity of Christ, but they then add that one of the two natures did not play a foundational role for him. Exactly which nature is deemed to have been neglected depends on the theological proclivities of the particular interpreter. The influential historian Adolf von Harnack famously argued that Augustine, in spite of disclaimers, focused mostly on Christ's humanity, particularly the receptivity of his human soul to God's action, as the source of humanity's new power to overcome sin.[2] Harnack was thus able to claim that Augustine's early humanistic "Photinianism" (Photinius was a fourth-century theologian who was believed to have taught that Jesus was a human being who had been adopted into sonship by God), which he never entirely outgrew, had anticipated Harnack's own liberal Christology. Taking a very different view, Otto Scheel, in his classic study of Augustine's Christology, argues that Augustine's piety was really focused on the Logos and the eternal ideas contained in it; the humanity of Jesus was merely a pointer to the divine Word.[3] Scheel's argument was an elaboration of the earlier suggestion by Isaak Dorner that Augustine's denial that Jesus experienced concupiscence was symptomatic of a type of Docetism.[4] Other Augustine scholars have similarly claimed that the fact that created human nature is naturally oriented toward God, coupled with the fact that the Logos illumines the mind in any act of knowledge, tends to reduce the importance of the incarnation for Augustine.[5] Augustine, they conclude, remained much more theocentric than Christocentric. For a very different reason, Rowan Greer has proposed that the incarnation as a whole was undervalued by Augustine, for he "shifts the emphasis in this

---

2. Adolf von Harnack, *History of Dogma*, trans. J. Millar (London: Williams and Norgate, 1898), 5: 128-29.

3. Otto Scheel, *Die Anschauung Augustins über Christi Person und Werk unter besonderer Berücksichtigung ihrer verschiedenen Entwicklungstufen und ihrer dogmengeschichtlichen Stellung* (Tübingen: J. C. B. Mohr, 1901).

4. See Isaak August Dorner, *The History of the Development of the Doctrine of the Person of Christ*, Division 2 (Edinburgh: T&T Clark, 1880), 1: 77-79.

5. Rudolf Lorenz, "Gnade und Erkenntnis bei Augustin," in Carl Andersen, ed., *Zum Augustin-Gespräch der Gegenwart* (Darmstadt: Wissenschaftliche Buchgesellschaft, 1981), 2: 43-125.

general perspective from Christ's story to the Christian's" and thus "a set of anthropological issues begins to dominate."[6] According to Greer, Augustine highlights the drama of salvation and considers the significance of Jesus primarily with respect to soteriology. By doing so, Augustine reversed the healthy tendency of the early church to focus on the person of Christ and to interpret salvation in the light of the incarnation.

Turning our attention to Kierkegaard, we find that similar critiques have been launched against his views on Christology. K. E. Løgstrup argues that the Dane was mostly interested in the paradox of the incarnation, and not as much in the actual historical human being Jesus of Nazareth or in the work of Jesus.[7] According to Løgstrup, the sheer fact of the incarnation and the mystery of the person of the God-man eclipsed the particularities of the earthly human life of Jesus. Other scholars have found the picture of Christ the "prototype" to be the key to Kierkegaard's Christology, and thus they ascribe to him an almost exclusive interest in Jesus' imitable human nature. More precisely, Kierkegaard's earlier focus on the paradox of the incarnation is said to give way in his later works to an emphasis on the way of life of the human being Jesus of Nazareth.[8] More radically, Christoph Schrempf, the German translator and editor of Kierkegaard's works, proposes that the principle that "subjectivity is truth" should have led Kierkegaard to be suspicious of the conviction that Jesus was the incarnation of God.[9] Early in the twentieth century, Karl Barth leveled a complaint against Kierkegaard that resembled Greer's analysis of Augustine, proposing that Kierkegaard had reduced Christ to his role in the soteriological drama of the individual.[10] Wanda Berry has agreed with Barth that Kierkegaard's reflections about Christ were governed by the need to "redouble" Christ's life in the lives of believers, a strategy with which she, unlike Barth, sympathizes.[11]

6. Rowan Greer, *Broken Lights and Mended Lives: Theology and Common Life in the Early Church* (University Park: Pennsylvania State University Press, 1986), p. 68.

7. Knud Ejler Løgstrup, *Opgør med Kierkegaard* (Copenhagen: Gyldendal, 1968).

8. See Johannes Sløk, *Da Kierkegaard tav. Fra forfatterskab til kirkestorm* (Copenhagen: Reitzel, 1980).

9. See Christoph Schrempf, *Sören Kierkegaard: Ein unfreier Pionier der Freiheit,* intro. Harald Høffding (Frankfurt am Main: Neuer Frankfurter Verlag, 1907).

10. Karl Barth, "A Thank You and A Bow: Kierkegaard's Reveille," trans. Martin Rumscheidt, *Canadian Journal of Theology* 11 (1965): 3-7.

11. Wanda Warren Berry, "Practicing Liberation: Feminist and Womanist Dialogues with Kierkegaard's *Practice in Christianity,* in Robert L. Perkins, ed., *International Kierkegaard Commentary: Practice in Christianity* (Macon, GA: Mercer University Press, 2004), pp. 303-41.

Again, soteriological concerns are said to determine what can be affirmed about Christ. In short, Kierkegaard, like Augustine, has been variously accused of privileging the metaphysics of the incarnation at the expense of the humanity of Jesus, privileging the human life of Jesus at the expense of the incarnation, and of emphasizing the saving work of Christ at the expense of the significance of the person of Christ.

But these criticisms are misleading. Both Augustine and Kierkegaard return again and again to the themes of Jesus Christ as the presence of God in human form, as well as Jesus Christ as the perfection of human nature. Both thinkers frequently narrate the story of Jesus' earthly life, and both frequently elaborate on the theme of the descent of God the Son. Moreover, both writers foreground these themes at crucial junctures in their works. For Augustine and Kierkegaard, the twin affirmations of Christ's divinity and humanity play a foundational role in the Christian life. In neither case is the interpretation of the significance of Christ merely extrapolated from a prior understanding of the human journey; in fact, for both theologians, Christ introduces an unanticipated and unsettling variable. Both seek, in different ways, to clarify what the doctrine of the incarnation means by portraying the various uses of the two ways of talking about Jesus Christ in the cultivation of Christian pathos. As we shall see, it was a shared understanding of the incarnation that gave content to both of their formal definitions of God as the ultimate object of love and desire. For Augustine and Kierkegaard, the God who is loved is the God revealed in Jesus Christ. Christ manifests what it is about God that draws the heart to God and propels the pilgrim's journey. As we shall see — first with regard to Augustine and then with regard to Kierkegaard — it is God's self-giving and self-emptying love that constitutes God's attractive sublimity. Both identify the beauty of God with the kenotic pattern articulated by Paul in Philippians 2:6-11, the hymn-like passage that was foundational for both of them.

Augustine and the Beauty of Kenosis

Augustine's emphasis on the need to rely on the grace of God was rooted in his convictions about Jesus Christ. In spite of a widespread view of Augustine as an inveterate Neo-Platonist who remained focused on the transcendent One beyond time and space,[12] Augustine's mature understanding

---

12. See Scheel, *Die Anschauung Augustins.*

of God was a function of his construal of the narrative pattern of the life of Christ.[13] Jesus Christ was much more for Augustine than the human being in whom receptivity to God's benevolence was paradigmatically enacted. The incarnate Jesus Christ was also much more than a signifier directing attention to the eternal forms resident in the Logos. For the mature Augustine, the soul's apprehension of God is not an immediate intuition detachable from the life, death, and resurrection of Jesus Christ. Although he produced no single, exhaustive treatise on Christology, his reflections on the Trinity, grace, sanctification, the church, and eschatology were all based on a christological foundation.[14] According to Augustine, Jesus Christ reveals what exactly it is about God that is so sublimely attractive that it enables God to draw us to God as our highest good. Jesus Christ provides the specific content for the picture of humanity's ultimate *telos,* which had been so very abstractly defined. As we shall see, that content is very similar to Kierkegaard's depictions of Jesus as the enactment of God's self-emptying love.

During Augustine's lifetime, the identity and significance of Jesus Christ were still hotly contested matters. Arianism regarded the Son as a creature of God and tended to highlight the humanity of Jesus. Arianism still enjoyed some imperial protection and was favored by most of the Germanic tribes, many of whom served as mercenaries in the Roman army. Meanwhile the Manicheans kept alive the countervailing tendency to deny the humanity of Jesus. The Council of Chalcedon that authorized the classic formula that Christ is the union of the divine nature and human nature in one person would not occur until 451, over two decades after Augustine's death. (And, in fact, the language of the Chalcedonian formula would be greatly indebted to Augustine and his continuing influence.) The Council of Ephesus, which affirmed the unity of Christ's person, would not take place until 431. The general uncertainty about Jesus was thus reflected in Augustine's own spiritual development. During his Manichean period Augustine had imagined Christ to be a purely spiritual being uncontaminated by lowly human nature, a view common among Christian Docetists. Augustine admitted that in his subsequent early Neo-Platonic days he had believed that Jesus had been a supremely wise human being, and therefore could serve as an imitable model of ascetic dis-

---

13. See Basel Studer, *The Grace of Christ and the Grace of God in Augustine of Hippo: Christocentrism or Theocentrism?,* trans. Matthew J. O'Connell (Collegeville, MN: Liturgical Press, 1997).

14. See Brian E. Daley, S.J., "A Humble Mediator: The Distinctive Elements of Saint Augustine's Christology," *Word and Spirit* 9 (1987): 100-117.

cipline.[15] As Augustine well knew from personal experience, according to some Christians in the fourth century, Jesus was nothing more than the most profound human sage who had ever lived, while according to others, Jesus was the God who had come to earth and assumed a human body. In the first instance Jesus' human life should be emulated, while in the second instance Jesus should be adored. As Augustine matured, he came to believe that Jesus should be both emulated and adored.

According to the theologically seasoned Augustine, Jesus was both the perfectly faithful human being and the presence of God with sinful, wayward humanity; Jesus was both our role model and the enactment of God's love. Significantly, Kierkegaard would later describe Christ in a similar fashion as the prototype and the Redeemer. For Augustine, Jesus' dual role implied that Jesus had to be regarded as both fully human and fully divine. But, according to Augustine, it was also crucial to affirm that Jesus was one person, and not two separate beings, because, without that affirmation of personal unity, Jesus could serve neither as our role model nor as the assurance of God's love. Therefore, Augustine had two reasons for affirming the oneness of Christ in the incarnation. First, only by being joined to divinity could the human nature of Jesus be transformed and become the source of our own transformations. Much of Augustine's piety presupposes the fact that the Word's assumption of a human soul had transfigured Jesus' human affections, making them godly. For example, at the Last Supper, Jesus was grievously disturbed and anxious in a very human way, but the divinity within him transformed that perturbation into resolution.[16] By being united to Christ by grace, we can have that transformation occur in our own souls. Second, Augustine's spirituality was also predicated on the conviction that God the Son had come to earth in order to establish loving fellowship with finite human beings. In order for that fellowship to be genuine, God the Son had to live as a human creature, that is, the divine person had to be in intimate contact with human nature.

Both of the christological dynamics that Augustine cherished required a real coming together of the divine and the human. Furthermore, in order for divinity to come into contact with full humanity, it was important to Augustine that Jesus possessed both a human soul and a human body — not just a human body, as the Apollinarians proposed.[17] The threat of

---

15. Augustine, *Confessions*, VII, 19 (25), in *WSA*, I, 1.

16. Augustine, *Tractates on the Gospel of John*, Homily 60, 2, in *WSA* III, 13.

17. Augustine, *On Eighty-Three Varied Questions (De diversis quaestionibus octoginta tribus)*, LXXX in *WSA* I, 12.

Apollinarianism was evidenced by the fact that in their younger days both Augustine and his friend Alypius had erroneously assumed that most Catholics denied that Jesus had a human soul, a denial that had greatly troubled the spiritually questing youths. In order for humanity to be transformed by divine power, it was important to Augustine that the eternal God, maker of heaven and earth, had touched finite human nature and sanctified it. Both the healing and the solidarity required a union. Consequently, in his theological maturity, Augustine came to describe Jesus as two natures in one person, the formula that would be made normative at the Council of Chalcedon.[18]

In order to explain what this union was and how it could be possible, Augustine uses a variety of images and concepts, many of them informal and fluid. He frequently turns to the motif of love that is so central to his theology and that we have already seen operative in his discussion of the Trinity. By at least 411, Augustine was teaching that the human soul or mind of Jesus was wedded to the eternal Word by such an intensity of love and the concomitant immediate intuition of the Word that it became like the Word in all respects.[19] The difference between Jesus' union and that of ordinary humans who love God is that Jesus' union was so complete that Jesus possessed God's wisdom, while other humans merely participate in it.[20] The human nature of Jesus, prepared and supported by God, was uniquely receptive to the Word, though Augustine clearly assumed that the union did not prevent Jesus from having a distinct human life, with human thoughts and even a susceptibility to temptation (even though the sustaining power of God always enabled him to resist temptation).[21] The one person experienced all the tribulations and limitations of being human.[22] Furthermore, Augustine's writings reveal a continuing emphasis on the fact that Jesus had a fully functional human soul, for it was through Jesus' human soul that the eternal Word made contact with the bodily, finite, historical individual from Nazareth. For Augustine, the locus of the union of divinity and humanity was the human soul of Jesus, because the Eternal Word should not be imagined to have been circumscribed by Jesus' material body.[23] At times

---

18. Augustine, *Letters,* Letter 137, 9, in *WSA* II, 2.

19. Augustine, *Letters,* Letter 137, in *WSA* II, 2.

20. Augustine, *On Faith and the Creed (De fide et symbolo),* 4 (8-10), in *WSA* I, 8.

21. Augustine, *Explanations of the Psalms,* Exposition 2 of Psalm 32, verse 1 and 2, in *WSA* III, 15.

22. Augustine, *Letters,* Letter 137, 8-9, in *WSA* II, 2.

23. Augustine, *On Faith and the Creed,* 4 (10), in *WSA* I, 8.

Augustine could even speak as if Jesus had two sources of volition, which were, however, in perfect harmony.

This tended to portray the incarnation as a phenomenon in Jesus' consciousness rather than as an ontological union. God was present to Jesus' soul, which directed his body. This kind of "soulish" union was by no means insignificant, for as we have seen, Augustine regarded the soul as the center of self-consciousness, agency, and desire. This model of a union of the natures through love served in Augustine's writings to highlight the way human nature becomes godly via loving God, as well as the initiative of God in establishing the loving bond of absolute solidarity. God's love clearly has priority in the affectional interaction, for it elicits the love of the human nature of Jesus. Interestingly, this model of incarnation did point in an indirect way toward the Christology of Friedrich Schleiermacher, who located the incarnation in Jesus' uninterrupted God-consciousness (though Schleiermacher, given his Reformed background, focused on Jesus' feeling of absolute dependence rather than Jesus' love). From his tutorial with Martensen, Kierkegaard would have been well aware of this view, but perhaps not of its roots in Augustine.

Later in his life Augustine began to treat the union of the natures in Jesus' soul as at least partially parallel to the operation of God's grace in a human individual.[24] However, he was quick to point out that Jesus should not be thought of as an already existing human individual who was suffused with grace at some point in time and thereby became divine. Unlike ordinary human individuals, Jesus' very existence was due to the presence of God in him. The Holy Spirit united the human Jesus to the Word from the very inception of his life. The fact that the union was effected before the human Jesus had merited any such glorious honor by a demonstration of righteousness manifests the gratuity of grace. The incarnation dramatizes the way God's self-giving makes possible the perfection of human nature. In Jesus Christ, God shares God's life with humanity so that human beings can attain the goal of God-likeness. But in spite of the colossal *lack* of analogy between Jesus and his human brothers and sisters, Jesus could be cited as a model of openness to God's grace. For Augustine, the pastoral force of this model was to exhort individuals to be receptive to grace in the way Jesus was, and to inspire them to do so with a dramatic picture of God's benevolence in giving grace. To a certain extent, Harnack in the early twentieth century did indeed detect this important christological trajectory in Augustine's writings. This theme

24. Augustine, *On the Predestination of the Saints*, 15 (31), in *WSA* I, 26.

is crucial to our purposes, for the motif of Jesus as the prototype of human openness to God would be paralleled in the works of Kierkegaard.

Augustine also used the analogy of the soul and the body to clarify the nature of the union of divinity and humanity in Christ.[25] This was, of course, only an analogy, and was by no means intended to suggest that Jesus did not have a human soul. Rather, the analogy was designed to make one crucial point about the relationship of the Word to Jesus' human soul: the Word directed and governed Jesus' human soul just as the soul of any human being directs and governs that person's body. The force of the analogy was to suggest that the incarnation was not a union of equal partners; the executive power in the life of Jesus was the Word. Augustine often described the Word as acting through the human nature of Jesus. Therefore, the earthly life of Jesus makes the transcendent God knowable to finite human minds. This tended to identify the divine Word as the primary subject and agent in the incarnation, expressing itself through Jesus' humanity. This priority of the Word was reinforced by Augustine's use of the analogy of the "word in a person's heart" to the spoken word to clarify the relationship of Jesus' divinity and humanity. Augustine explains that Jesus' human obedience and humility were motivated by the humility shown by the Word in its willingness to obey the Father's will and assume lowly human nature:

> The fact that he came down from heaven was the cause of such great obedience of the human being whom he bore, obedience totally free of any sin.[26]

Because of this condescension of the Word into a human being, the humanity of Jesus draws the soul toward the divine nature. Augustine proclaims: "Through Christ as human you make your way toward Christ as God. . . ."[27] Here the spiritually edifying purpose of this model is to encourage the reader to see the narrative pattern of Jesus' life as the enactment and manifestation of God's relationship to human beings in general, which is a relationship of self-giving. Augustine urges his readers to look to Jesus to see what God is like. Over fourteen centuries later, Kierkegaard would persuade his readers to do the very same thing.

---

25. Augustine, *Letters*, Letter 137, 3 (9), *WSA* II, 2.

26. Augustine, *Against an Arian Sermon (Contra sermonem Arianorum)*, 7.6, in *WSA* I, 18.

27. Augustine, *Sermons (Sermones)*, Sermon 261.7, in *WSA* III, 7.

Troubled by the Apollinarian heresy that Christ, the divine Word clothed in human flesh, did not possess a human mind and therefore lacked an essential dimension of human being, Augustine increasingly favored (after 411) the use of the term "persona" to suggest the unity of Christ as a single acting subject, who nevertheless possessed both divine and human natures.[28] "Persona," a concept originally drawn from the world of drama and law, had a nuance of playing a public role. In Augustine's writings "persona" suggests not only the role but also the center of agency behind the actions. By using this term, Augustine is drawing attention to Jesus' pattern of self-conscious, intentional agency. That pattern of intentional action was revealing of Jesus' identity; Jesus' identity was something that was essentially a matter of enactment. This understanding of "persona" would give Augustine a warrant for elucidating both Jesus' humanity and Jesus' divinity in terms of the shape of the New Testament narrative of his actions and passions. As with the analogy of soul and body, the purpose of this terminology is to draw attention to the revealing power of the narrative, both in disclosing Jesus as the perfection of human being and Jesus as the presence of God.

For centuries scholars interested in doctrinal precision have been puzzled about what exactly Augustine's multiple analogies and images suggest about the union of the two natures of Christ. Even in his own day it was not entirely clear where Augustine should be located on the spectrum of the current prevalent Christological theories. In Augustine's era, two different christological tendencies had become evident, one associated with the city of Alexandria and one with the city of Antioch. In general, the Alexandrians emphasized the union and communion of the two natures, while the Antiochenes emphasized the distinction between the two natures. According to the Alexandrians, the properties of one nature can be ascribed to the other nature (the *communicatio idiomatum*), so that the divine properties like omniscience are shared by Jesus' human nature, and human suffering is somehow shared by the divine nature (without actually entailing that God suffered). But according to the Antiochenes, Jesus' human nature continued in at least some important respects to operate within the bounds that define the lives of finite creatures. Much to the chagrin of doctrinal purists, Augustine was capable of using both sets of theological discourse. When emphasizing the way Jesus' life was the enactment of God's self-giving love,

---

28. Augustine, *Commentary on the Letter to the Galatians (Expositio Epistulae ad Galatas)*, 27, in *WSA* I, 17.

Augustine can sound very much like an Alexandrian. In these contexts he declares that, before assuming the form of a servant in the incarnation, the person of Christ, the second person of the Trinity, existed for all eternity in the form of God. He claims that the Son of God was crucified on the cross and that Jesus in his earthly life was the "human God."[29] However, when exhorting Christians to imitate Christ, Augustine can sound like an Antiochene, insisting that Jesus' human nature is like ours, having been vulnerable to temptation, anxiety, and despair, and thus is imitable in its spiritual struggles.[30] Augustine's penchant for shifting from one conceptuality to another, depending on his rhetorical purpose, is so strong that sometimes he claims that Mary is the "Mother of God" (not just the mother of Jesus' human nature), and sometimes he denies that very proposition.

Augustine does not indulge in this paradoxical way of talking about Jesus, riddled with elliptical images that do not neatly cohere, merely because he is curious about the metaphysics of the incarnation. Quite the contrary, he insists that reflecting on the incarnation requires trembling in fear over the possibility of one's own salvation, a sentiment that Kierkegaard would echo.[31] The two natures of Christ — and their relationship — are central to Augustine's piety because of the role they play in the drama of redemption and in the pursuit of the Christian life. For Augustine, Jesus' saving work is complex, having several different aspects. Humanity's sinful condition produces several different dire predicaments from which human beings need to be rescued. Therefore, the saving work of Christ has several aspects, and many of these aspects require a different kind of discourse in order to be articulated and comprehended. Moreover, appropriating each of these aspects of Christ's salvation involves the cultivation of a different kind of pathos, and the discourse about it has to express the singularity of that pathos.

Most importantly, for Augustine, the incarnation as a whole and the crucifixion in particular reveal the nature and extent of God's love for humanity. Augustine was attracted to the venerable theme of *kenosis,* the self-emptying of God suggested by Paul in Philippians 2. In his polemics against the Arians, Augustine makes this passage central to his efforts to show that biblical passages that seemed to talk about the Son's subordination to the Father were referring only to this state of having assumed the form of a servant. This hermeneutical move was so crucial to Augustine that one

---

29. Augustine, *The Trinity,* I, 4.28-31, in *WSA* I, 5.

30. Augustine, *On Faith and the Creed,* 4 (8-9), in *WSA* I, 8.

31. Augustine, *Confessions,* VII, 21 (27), in *WSA* I, 1.

interpreter, Lewis Ayers, has christened it Augustine's "panzer."[32] According to Augustine, God's mercy is so profound that God deigned to leave power and glory behind in eternity in order to redeem sinful humanity. The humility of God is most fundamentally manifested in the Word's assumption of human nature in the womb of Mary.[33] This divine condescension manifests the radically self-giving nature of God's love, a kind of love that Augustine discerns in the relationships of the persons of the Trinity to one another. Jesus' willingness to be persecuted and crucified by humanity repeats this incarnational pattern, for it shows that the divine love would rather suffer when confronted with opposition, rejection, and violence than retaliate. Christ's voluntary humiliation is the opposite of our sinful pride and undermines all our self-serving attitudes and values. When Augustine describes the conversion to Christianity of the celebrated Neo-Platonic rhetorician Victorinus, he emphasizes the difficulty the proud Victorinus had in accepting the lowly sacraments and lowly scriptures of the church instead of the proud sacrifices and proud gods of paganism.[34] Throughout the narration of the story of his own conversion Augustine highlights the theme of the lowliness of the Christian life as being a reflection of the lowliness of Christianity, which in turn reflects the lowliness of Christ.

The importance of *kenosis* in Augustine's theology cannot possibly be exaggerated, for it is absolutely foundational for his understanding of the Christian journey and destination. It is the spectacle of this extravagantly self-giving love that attracts our heart. The enactment of the splendor of other-regarding love evokes a new kind of love and desire in fallen humanity. According to Augustine, the best way to elicit a loving response in an individual is to show him how much he is loved by someone of higher status, who loves him like an equal in spite of the inequality.[35] To do this in a way that necessarily entails the voluntary acceptance of suffering manifests love in the most powerful manner imaginable. For this reason Augustine often described the self-emptying eternal Word as the basic subject, the "I" in the incarnation, and not Jesus' human soul.[36] The story of Jesus Christ is most essentially the story of the God who came to earth. That Word came

32. Lewis Ayers, *Augustine and the Trinity* (Cambridge: Cambridge University Press, 2010), pp. 144-47.

33. Augustine, *On Faith and the Creed*, 4 (6-8), in *WSA* I, 8.

34. Augustine, *Confessions*, VIII, 2 (4), in *WSA* I, 1.

35. Augustine, *On the Instruction of Beginners (De catechizandis rudibus)*, 7, in *WSA* I, 10.

36. William Mallard, "Jesus Christ," in Allan D. Fitzgerald, ed., *Augustine Through the Ages* (Grand Rapids: Eerdmans, 1999), p. 469.

into the world not in majesty but in poverty, so that weak human beings would not be overwhelmed by the divine glory.[37] As we shall see, this same kenotic motif would recur throughout Kierkegaard's writings and receive its most poignant expression in the parable of the king and the maiden in *Philosophical Fragments*. In fact, we shall also see that it was the need to identify the basic agent in the Incarnation as the self-emptying God the Son that led both Augustine and Kierkegaard to often adopt Alexandrian-sounding discourse.

Furthermore, this kenotic theme emphasizes the reality of the Word's identification with humanity; in the incarnation God did not merely pretend to share the human condition. In some sense, the Word that constituted Jesus' identity must be said to have hungered, been thirsty, suffered agony, and despaired. Frequently Augustine could apply language to the one person of Christ that strongly suggested human liabilities and human struggles. That way of speaking about Jesus seemed to point to an Antiochene Christology in which the human nature of Jesus retained its vulnerabilities precisely because it was not suffused with the divine perfections. It was this rhetorical trajectory that had led Harnack to claim that Augustine tended to emphasize the human soul of Jesus. To safeguard the humanity of Jesus without compromising the perfection of his divinity, Augustine could not sharply differentiate the natures and jeopardize the unity of Jesus' person, as the Antiochenes attempted to do, for that strategy would subvert the entire concentration on the reality of God's solidarity with humanity. Augustine continued to speak of the person of Jesus as being the second person of the Trinity. However, attributing genuine suffering to Jesus, as Augustine insists on doing, seems to contradict the conviction that the second person of the Trinity enjoys the invulnerable perfection of the Godhead. Therefore, Augustine proposed that throughout the incarnation the Word voluntarily willed to be vulnerable to human frailties.[38] Afflictions did not befall the Word contrary to the Word's own will, in the involuntary way that they afflict us. This proclamation of the Word's voluntary vulnerability was a discourse designed to further highlight God's extravagantly self-giving love and even more strongly draw the self-oriented sinner's heart. As we shall see, such a discourse would become prominent in the christological reflections of Kierkegaard — for the same reasons.

Finally, the theme of the humble self-giving of the eternal Word in-

---

37. Augustine, *Confessions*, VII, 18 (24), in *WSA* I, 1.
38. Augustine, *Explanations of the Psalms*, 87.3, in *WSA* III, 14-17.

forms much of Augustine's treatment of the saving work of Christ. The divine *kenosis* of becoming incarnate is recapitulated in the kenotic pattern evident in Jesus' earthly career. Jesus' crucifixion, in fact his entire life as a human, can be seen as a reflection of the divine self-giving. Just as God offered God's life to humanity in the incarnation, so also as a human being Jesus offered his life back to God. To emphasize this, Augustine often uses sacrificial and priestly language to describe the atonement accomplished by Christ. Jesus is the perfect sacrifice, an offering of total devotion to God and absolute affection for God. By participating in Christ through grace, we who are Christ's brothers and sisters can share in that perfect self-offering. Even Augustine's talk of Jesus being a ransom paid to Satan serves to reinforce the theme of self-giving love. For Augustine, Satan was the epitome of virulently aggressive pride. It is this pride that enthralls human souls. By delegitimizing the power of self-assertion through the "ransom" of suffering love, Jesus exposes pride's vacuity and impotence.[39] By refusing to use Satan's own strategy of overwhelming force, God reveals that the power of self-sacrifice breaks the demonic power of self-aggrandizement.

For Augustine, this profligate display of self-sacrificial love is the essential expression of God's truth, goodness, and beauty. The drama of love narrated in the Gospels gives specific content to Augustine's more formal descriptions of God's attractiveness. The true nature of the beauty for which Augustine had yearned only becomes clear in the form of the humble incarnate God. Augustine combined the phrase "the most beautiful among the sons of man" (Ps. 44:3[45:2]) with the statement that "he had no form or comeliness" (Isa. 53:2) and applied them to Christ, concluding that the tortured Christ had no physical beauty, for his body had been ruined, but that he did radiate the "inner beauty" of self-sacrificial love.[40] The absolute beauty of Christ in "the form of God," the bridegroom, assumed the lowly form of his beloved in order to reestablish the loving relationship. Augustine waxed enthusiastic: "The Bridegroom made Himself ugly for the sake of the ugly Bride, in order to make her beautiful."[41] He even says that Christ assumed deformity in order to restore humanity's proper form, and that by doing so he revealed that the true form of beauty is the willingness to accept deformity for the sake of the beloved. Paradoxically, the beauty of God is

---

39. Augustine, *Confessions*, IX, in *WSA* I, 1.

40. Augustine, *Homilies on the First Epistle of John*, 9.9, in *WSA* III, 14; *Explanations of the Psalms*, 43, 16, in *WSA* III, 14-17.

41. Augustine, *Sermons*, 95.4, in *WSA* III, 4.

both hidden and revealed in the ostensible ugliness of the crucified body of Christ. Christ does not cease to be God in assuming the form of a servant; rather, the form of God is simply hidden from carnal, sinful eyes that cannot perceive the inner beauty of self-emptying love. Because only the genesis of faith can enable the individual to appreciate this beauty, Christ's state of humiliation is thus both a revelation and a concealment. God in Christ descends to the lowly condition of the beloved sinner in order to awaken her love and elevate her heart. It is in the vision of self-emptying love that the restless heart finally comes to rest; therefore, the divine agape is the *telos* of humanity's eros.[42] As will become evident, this tensive dialectic of revelation and concealment would recur in a potent way in the writings of Kierkegaard.

But gratitude and delight over the divine self-giving are not the only forms of pathos that are associated with the incarnation. The principle of *kenosis* governs not only the theme of Jesus as the revelation of God but also Jesus as the perfection of human being.[43] The self-emptying pattern of Jesus' life also functions as a model to be emulated by the disciple. Augustine never jettisoned his early focus on Jesus as teacher and example. The story of Jesus is not only the story of divine condescension, but is in addition the story of the human response to grace. In Jesus, the image of God — marred by sin — is restored so that humanity can move forward toward the original goal of participatory knowledge of God and loving fellowship with God. The spectacle of Jesus as the perfection of human virtues, in his own life transforming anxiety into courage, pride into humility, folly into wisdom, and the chaos of desires into order, is more than an external example. Rather, Jesus' human life inspires admiration, affection, and delight, all of which have an impact on the soul and move the will. Christ is the attractive, magnetic paradigm of humble openness to God. As we have seen, Augustine sometimes describes one aspect of the incarnation as the unwavering acceptance of God's grace by a fully human person, Jesus of Nazareth, from the moment of conception on throughout his life. As such, the humanity of Jesus could serve as a model for all believers (who, unlike Jesus, however, are not protected by God's grace from ever experiencing alienation from God). The humility and self-giving evident in the contours of Jesus' human

---

42. See John Burnaby, *Amor Dei: A Study in the Religion of Saint Augustine* (London: Hodder and Stoughton, 1938), p. 158.

43. See Augustine, *On Faith and the Creed (De fide et symbolo)*, 4 (6), in *WSA* I, 8; *Commentary on the Letter to the Galatians (Expositio Epistulae ad Galatas)*, 24 (10).

life define the road to truth and beatitude. The "way" is revealed to be the path of self-abnegation in order to love the other. The truth to which the Neo-Platonists desired to ascend is paradoxically revealed to be the pattern of descent. Augustine muses:

> If you walk along the humble Christ, you will arrive at the exalted Christ; if in your sickly health and debility you do not spurn the humble one, you will abide in perfect health and strength with the exalted one.[44]

This reveals the same "inverse dialectic" that Kierkegaard would later use with such dramatic results.[45] The soul ascends by descending; loftiness is attained through lowliness. Augustine writes:

> He who for us is life itself has descended here. . . . Life has come down to you, and are you reluctant to ascend and live? Surely after the descent of life, you cannot fail to wish to ascend and live? But where will you ascend when you are "set on high and have put your mouth in heaven"? (Ps. 73:9). Come down, so that you can ascend, and make your ascent to God. For it is by climbing up against God that you have fallen.[46]

As the disciple follows the path of the master who took the form of a servant, the imitation of the prototype causes the desire for the self-emptying God to grow even stronger. For Augustine, as Kierkegaard would later agree, the entire Christian life most essentially should be an imitation of Christ's prototypical humiliation.

The imitation of Christ's humility toward God and reliance on God's grace are then linked by Augustine to love for the neighbor. Receptivity to the self-giving love of Christ reproduces itself in self-giving to fellow human beings. For Augustine, Jesus is the perfect exemplar of neighbor-love; Jesus as a human being fulfilled all righteousness by obeying the love commandment.[47] Augustine, like Kierkegaard, focuses on the commandment to love God and neighbor as the epitome and essence of God's law, and he shows little interest in a moral casuistry based on rigid adherence to specific precepts. Jesus as a human most dramatically adhered to this love

---

44. Augustine, *Sermons*, 142.2.2.

45. See Sylvia Walsh, *Living Christianly: Kierkegaard's Dialectic of Christian Existence* (University Park: Pennsylvania State University Press, 2005).

46. Augustine, *Confessions* IV, 12 (19), in *WSA* I, 1.

47. Augustine, *Against Julian, An Unfinished Book*, Book IV, in *WSA* I, 25.

commandment when he suffered persecution and nonetheless continued to love his tormentors. Augustine closely associates following Jesus' example of neighbor-love with the willingness to suffer, and particularly suffer from sinful society's hostility. To emphasize this, Augustine quotes Peter: "Christ suffered for us, leaving us an example to follow in his steps" (1 Pet. 2:21).[48]

To summarize, Augustine makes *kenosis* central to every aspect of his Christology. The self-giving of God is the aspect of the divine that draws the human heart to its homeland in Christ. In order to make this divine self-emptying clear, we must emphasize that the subject in the life of Jesus of Nazareth is the second person of the Trinity. With respect to the work of Christ, it is the power of self-giving that defeats Satanic pride and disarms human pretensions. Moreover, the spectacle of Jesus' suffering love for his enemies has the capacity to evoke a response of love. For this reason, the reality of Jesus' sufferings — and thus his true humanity — has to be affirmed. Finally, it is the life of humble receptivity to God's self-giving, and the consequent impulse to give oneself to the neighbor, that is the content of the theme of following Jesus' example. In order to follow Jesus, we must insist that Jesus was fully human and thus imitable. Therefore, to understand all this arcane language about natures and persons is to develop the appropriate set of kenotic passions. The pilgrim learns what the christological affirmations mean as the pilgrim grows in the appreciation of the beauty of God's self-giving, cultivates a yearning for that sublime self-emptying, develops a self-abandoning reliance on this loving God, and more and more reflects Jesus' pattern of self-giving in the pilgrim's own life.

Kierkegaard and the Attractions of Lowliness

Like Augustine, Kierkegaard's intense interest in Jesus Christ was motivated by the recognition that human beings are utterly powerless to extricate themselves from their sinful predicament. That is, we cannot pull ourselves up by our bootstraps, and we cannot heal ourselves. If remediation is going to occur, it must come to us from a source outside our ordinary experience and capacities. Consequently, Kierkegaard highlights God's redemptive work through Jesus Christ, whose life, death, and resurrection constituted an act of radical love that rivaled the divine beneficence manifested in God's original act of creation. Because this love is so undeserved and so unex-

---

48. Augustine, *Sermons*, 101.5.6.

pected, Kierkegaard frequently says in almost all his voices that knowledge of this love can only be communicated through a revelation. For example, concerning the revelation of God's self-emptying love in the incarnation, Climacus writes: "[F]or if the god gave no indication, how could it occur to a man that the blessed god could need him?" (*PF,* 36) Such a wonderful but utterly improbable thought could not naturally arise in any human being's heart.

As with all other theological topics, for Kierkegaard the mood must be right in order to consider the themes of incarnation and atonement, the two principal doctrines that historically have served to articulate the self-giving love of God in Jesus Christ. According to Kierkegaard, the revelation of God in Christ is not a set of propositions about a mysterious being that must be grasped and affirmed by a dispassionate intellect. Rather, the revelation of God in Christ makes available a new way of life replete with new emotions and passions. Most importantly, in order to understand the incarnation, individuals must be plagued by a sense of their own failure and bemoan their inability to change themselves. Only in such a mood of repentance will the individual be able to grasp the import of teachings concerning God's redemptive act and experience the appropriate wonder over the unfathomable nature of God's love. In short, repentance, hunger for Christlikeness, and gratitude for divine love are necessary conditions for any meaningful talk about Christ. Kierkegaard's authorial task was to situate the standard christological doctrines in these highly specific passional contexts so that the doctrines could acquire meaning for the reader. Part of the force of saying that knowledge of the Christian God must be revealed is to suggest that the pathos appropriate to belief in the Christian God is so distinctive that it is not naturally elicited by life's ordinary vicissitudes. The hopes and fears that are part and parcel of believing in the God who became incarnate in Christ are exceedingly unusual, so unusual that many of them are counterintuitive. A writer who hopes to illuminate the meaning of the incarnation must use extraordinary literary devices to foster these utterly distinctive passions.

In many ways, Kierkegaard's christological reflections parallel Augustine's understanding of the incarnation as God's gracious and costly enactment of self-emptying love for a hostile humanity. In fact, the similarities are striking, beginning with the centrality of the kenotic hymn in Philippians 2, for both of their understandings of Christ. This parallelism is unusual given the fact that the secondary sources that Kierkegaard used said very little about Augustine's Christology. Clausen's lectures on the development of christological doctrine do not mention Augustine (*KJN* 3, pp. 37-39). The early nineteenth century did not remember Augustine as a profound contributor to the church's understanding of the person and work of Christ. In all likelihood, Kierkegaard's family resemblance to Augustine was due to the incorporation of Augustinian themes into Lutheran Christology, the tradition of christological piety that Kierkegaard had thoroughly imbibed. Kierkegaard was aware of the analogies of the relationship of soul and body and the indwelling of the Holy Spirit to explain the union of the two natures of Christ, but he did not know that one of their sources was Augustine (*KJN* 3, p. 37). He was also aware of the claim that the person of Christ suffered, though that suffering must not be attributed to the divine nature; but again, he was not aware of the connection of this formula with Augustine (*KJN* 3, p. 39).

However, this Augustinian christological orientation that Kierkegaard inherited through Lutheran mediation was alleged to be haunted by a perplexing and possibly fatal conceptual problem. As essentially Augustinian themes were appropriated and increasingly refined by the medieval church and later by Lutheran theology, the doctrine of the union of the two natures of Christ came to be articulated in a way that produced an apparent conundrum. In accordance with the orthodox teaching promulgated by the Council of Chalcedon, whose language Augustine had profoundly influenced, Christ was declared to be the union of a divine nature and a human nature in one person. By the time of Lutheran Scholasticism, the concept "nature" had come to suggest the essential attributes common to a species, and "person" had come to suggest the underlying principle of concretion and self-subsistence, though these connotations had by no means solidified during Augustine's own lifetime. Of course, the essential attributes of humanity and the essential attributes of divinity seem to be mutually exclusive, for human power, virtue, and wisdom are finite, while those of God are infinite. If Jesus was indeed the union of these two natures, Jesus would have simultaneously known everything according to his divine nature and yet not known everything according to his human nature. Moreover, he would have been able to do everything and yet not able to do everything. The list of mutually exclusive predicates could go on and on. To make matters more perplexing, the doctrinal tradition taught that the union of the two natures was not to be imagined as their hybridization into an intermediate being, a *tertium quid,* that perhaps was more powerful than humans, but not as powerful as God. According to orthodox teaching, the glory and power of the divine nature were not compromised, nor was the vulnerability of the humanity reduced to an illusion. Lutherans, even more than other traditions, exacerbated the conceptual difficulties by emphasizing the unity of the person of Christ rather than the differentiation of the natures. In order to highlight Jesus as the love of God come to earth, Lutheran theologians identified his "person," the principle of his self-subsistence, as the second person of the Trinity. By so doing, they were extending one christological trajectory suggested by Augustine himself. Not only all the actions appropriate to divinity, but all Jesus' human actions and passions, must be ascribed to the divine person in the way that predicates are attributed to a subject. Because the Lutherans had also inherited Augustine's conviction that Jesus' sufferings were genuine human emotions, Lutheran theologians would speak of the divine person as suffering through its human nature (even though the divine nature in itself cannot suffer). Moreover, because they emphasized the intimacy of the union of the natures in the person of the Word, the Lutherans had to accept the notion of the *communicatio idiomatum* and its implication that the divine perfections were communicated to the human nature. The divinity was totally "in the flesh," suffusing Jesus' humanity with divine omniscience and omnipotence. This claim inevitably evoked the question of how Jesus, whose human nature was saturated with divine perfections, could then undergo anything resembling ordinary human experiences, particularly the negative ones such as anxiety, sorrow, or loneliness.

To resolve this problem and explain how Jesus could suffer, Lutheran theologians developed the theme of Jesus' "state of humiliation," which itself had roots in Augustine's kenotic reflections. According to this theory, the eternal Logos, the person of Jesus, voluntarily renounced the use of divine power, and chose to share human suffering. Jesus freely exposed himself to opposition, ridicule, degradation, and even the experience of God's wrath against sin. This obedient renunciation of self-will, this self-emptying, blossomed into Jesus' exaltation as God's faithful child in whom human nature was glorified. This pattern of humiliation/exaltation, in which the potential for power and glory was surrendered in order to enact the true glory of an obedient, humble, and self-giving life, became the defining characteristic of the incarnation. In Lutheranism this kenotic pattern served as the theological foundation for the crucial doctrine of justification by grace, for God's acceptance of sinners is a fruit of this divine self-giving. The recessive theme was also voiced that this self-giving love could then serve as the pattern for the lives of all Christians. Once again, the legacy of Augustine is obvious.

In this complex conceptuality, the concepts of "nature" and "person" get strained to the breaking point. Whereas "nature" had referred to what kind of thing an individual entity (or "person") might be, and "person" had simply indicated the existence of an entity, now the two concepts were treated as if each one referred to a kind of thing. The person of Jesus was said to be divine, rather than being the bare referent of the noun to which the predicates "divine" and "human" were ascribed. In other words, not only was Jesus' divinity divine, but so was his person. Subjects were getting mixed up with predicates, and predicates with subjects. In his lectures, Clausen had alerted Kierkegaard to this conceptual muddle and its unedifying consequences, warning that the mystery of the union of the two natures in Christ was "just as far from dogmatizing theories on the essence and constitution of this union as it is from dissolving the historical truth into rhetorical symbols or fantastic speculation" (*KJN* 3, p. 37). He added that speculation about the nature of the unity of Christ's person had led to "various kinds of ideas that occasioned intense conflicts and, in time, a series of dogmatic definitions that could not promote real insight into the nature of the mystery and so the character of the mystery was often distorted and new difficulties thereby generated" (*KJN* 3, p. 37). As much as Kierkegaard would diverge from Clausen, he retained Clausen's suspicion of the speculative nature of dogmatizing Christological "theories."

Like Clausen, Kierkegaard found this conceptual labyrinth to be decidedly unedifying. Instead of trying to formulate a more sophisticated theory of "natures" and "persons," as the theological tradition had typically done, Kierkegaard sought to clarify the mystifying talk about Jesus' humanity and Jesus' divinity by situating it in the appropriate forms of pathos. He continued to cherish the passions and dispositions that the Lutheran doctrines were intended to safeguard, but he jettisoned the distracting conceptualities that attempted to explain how two natures could be united in one person. Kierkegaard's reliance on edification rather than metaphysical explanation is evident in the advice he offers in his journals: "Believe that Christ is God — then call upon him, pray to him, and the rest comes by itself" (*JP* 1, 318). To help the reader make sense of the paradoxical language about Christ, Kierkegaard seeks to show when it is appropriate to speak of Jesus as God, and for what purpose, and when it is appropriate to speak of Jesus as human, and for what purpose. Having done that, he then seeks to show when it is appropriate to speak of Jesus as the unity of both, and for what purpose. These various purposes involved the exploration of the passional situations in which Jesus is aptly confessed both as the savior of humanity and as the pattern for human life.[49] By doing so, Kierkegaard is implicitly returning to Augustine's strategy of using different christological vocabularies in different contexts for different purposes.

Like Augustine, Kierkegaard's christological reflections foregrounded the schema of Jesus' two states of humiliation and exaltation suggested by Philippians 2. For the motif of divine humiliation to be evident, Kierkegaard had to make it clear that the humble, earthly Jesus was God. Therefore, like Augustine, Kierkegaard does not hesitate to identify Jesus as one person, the divine second person of the Trinity, describing him as "he who was equal with God," "he who could command legions of angels, indeed, could command the world's creation and its destruction," and "he who was lord of creation" (*UDVS*, 224). Kierkegaard even suggests that it is God who through the God-man says, "My God, my God, why hast thou forsaken me?" (*JP* 1, 333) In his discourses and explicitly Christian books, Kierkegaard draws attention to the divine person of Christ when he adopts the voice of a penitent addressing other potential penitents in order to reassure them of the possibility of forgiveness, or the voice of an enthusiast for Christianity in order to praise the sublimity of God's self-emptying love (and warn of the concomitant possibility of offense). Through these authorial voices, Kierkegaard extols the divinity of Christ in order to underscore the magnitude of the self-abnegation enacted in the life of Jesus. Motivated by love, the almighty God voluntarily renounces the use of power, making God's own self vulnerable to disappointment and rejection, and this ultimate example of self-emptying manifests the true nature of God's love.

In celebrating the divinity of Christ, Kierkegaard puts the venerable Lutheran theme of *anhypostasia* to an upbuilding use. *Anhypostasia* was the doctrine that Jesus did not have a human "person" that functioned as the subject of his human predicates. Rather, the divine second person of the Trinity served that role. Over the centuries, through many mediations, this theory had been extrapolated from some of Augustine's remarks about Jesus' "person" being divine. Instead of elaborating a speculative explanation as the theological tradition had done, Kierkegaard simply shows how the purpose of this kind of talk is to foster gratitude for God's radical conde-

---

49. See Lee C. Barrett, "The Joy in the Cross: Kierkegaard's Appropriation of Lutheran Christology in 'The Gospel of Sufferings,'" in Robert Perkins, ed., *International Kierkegaard Commentary: Upbuilding Discourses in Various Spirits* (Macon, GA: Mercer University Press, 2005), pp. 275-85.

scension. Kierkegaard preferred his Augustinian Christology without the incrustation of metaphysics that he found to be so deadening.

To illustrate this in the form of a parable, Climacus, in *Philosophical Fragments*, narrates the tale of the king who yearns for a genuine relationship of mutuality with a peasant maiden and thus must share the life of a peasant. Climacus, given the literary premise that his book is an exploration of the contrasting ways that truth can be learned and also of the contrasting kinds of teachers, gives the story an epistemological twist, couching the dramatic tension in terms of the king's desire to be understood by the maiden — without deception. Climacus writes:

> Likewise, the king could have appeared before the lowly maiden in all his splendor, could have let the sun of his glory rise over her hut, shine on the spot where he appeared to her, and let her forget herself in adoring admiration. This perhaps would have satisfied the girl, but it could not satisfy the king, for he did not want his own glorification but the girl's, and his sorrow would have been grievous because she would not understand him . . . . (*PF*, 29)

The maiden would simply be dazed and overwhelmed if she were suddenly exalted to the status of her radiant monarch in his realm of glory. Climacus then declares: "If, then, the unity cannot be brought about by an ascent, then it must be brought about by a descent" (*PF*, 31). To perform this descent, the king must actually leave behind his royal prerogatives and not merely pretend to be a peasant. The king must genuinely lower himself to the status of a humble peasant, sharing the life of a peasant, and to some extent resembling the way Socrates had to identify with the ignorant in order to help them discover the truth within them. Of course, a king cannot really enact that kind of extreme identification without abdicating the throne; but God can do this without ceasing to be God. Climacus observes:

> For this is the boundlessness of love, that in earnestness and truth and not in jest it wills to be the equal of the beloved, and it is the omnipotence of resolving love to be capable of that of which neither the king nor Socrates was capable, which is why their assumed characters were still a kind of deceit. (*PF*, 32)

Kierkegaard repeats this theme in a journal entry of 1847, where he says that "[Christ's] self-abasement was in earnest. It was not like a pope's washing the feet of the poor, when everyone knows that it is the pope . . ." (*JP* 1, 309). God can and must dwell with humanity as a servant in order to bring about a relationship of real mutuality. It is the fact that God's love seeks equality and understanding with the beloved that demands the kenotic pattern described in Philippians 2. Consequently, humanity must relate to God as the lowly, humble one, and not primarily as the exalted, majestic one. Just as the parable requires the identification of the protagonist's genuine identity as the king (and not just a peasant or a deposed monarch), so also the Gospel story requires the identification of Jesus' core identity as the heavenly Word. Understanding this involves wonder, amazement, gratitude, and joy. Echoes of Augustine's similar encomium to God's self-humbling desire for mutuality are unmistakable, even if Kierkegaard was unaware of them.

True to his antispeculative convictions, Kierkegaard refuses to treat God's abasement as a conceptual riddle. During the mid-nineteenth century, Lutheran theologians such as Gottfried Thomasius reopened the historical question of whether the eternal Son had refused to use certain of his metaphysical perfections during the incarnation, or used them in secret, or whether the Son's infinitude did not exclude concentrating itself in finitude.[50] Thomasius was convinced that somehow the Son had divested himself of the divine mode of being in glory while retaining everything essential for divinity.[51] In the seventeenth century these issues had bitterly divided the schools of Tübingen and Giessen, and debates about Christ's *status exinanitionis* had continued to flare up (*KJN* 3, p. 53). Kierkegaard insisted on only two points: the voluntarily abased Jesus really is the presence of God with human beings, and in Christ God did somehow participate in human suffering. To ask how that was possible was to evade the real task of responding to the God who came to earth.

Climacus's literary strategies dispensed with the old metaphysical puzzlement about the incarnation only to spawn a new, more serious kind of disquietude. The new challenge to comprehension is that God's love, willing to go to such extreme lengths, is even more unimaginable than the confluence of God's metaphysical perfections with a finite human life. Contrary

---

50. See David Gouwens, *Kierkegaard as Religious Thinker* (Cambridge: Cambridge University Press, 1996), pp. 169-170; Tim Rose, *Kierkegaard's Christocentric Theology* (Aldershot, UK: Ashgate, 2001), pp. 111-17.

51. See Thomas R. Thompson, "Nineteenth-Century Kenotic Christology: The Waxing, Waning, and Weighing of a Quest for a Coherent Orthodoxy," in C. Stephen Evans, ed., *Exploring Kenotic Christology: The Self-Emptying of God* (Oxford: Oxford University Press, 2006), pp. 74-111.

to expectations, God does not want to be adored as the all-powerful cosmic potentate who performs spectacular miracles and controls all events. To make God's love even more unthinkable, the divine compassion is utterly gratuitous. God does not need to love or bless humanity. God is not like Socrates, whose love for his students was motivated by an internal need to be a teacher. Being gracious to humanity does not satisfy an antecedent need in God to be fulfilled through a relationship with finite creatures, as if God suffered from a social lack. (Augustine, we must recall, had similarly argued that God is not moved to love by a lack thereof.) God's kind of love is utterly shocking. The real paradox is not the cognitive difficulty of conceptualizing how the finite could be united with the infinite or how eternity could be united with temporality. Rather, the real paradox is the incredible nature of the claim that the unchanging God entered time as a vulnerable human bring in order to love humanity.

This portrayal of God as the lowly one flouts ordinary human expectations concerning how divinity should behave. The incarnation is an offense to humanity's natural conceptions of transcendent power. The claim that God seeks fellowship with the lowly by becoming lowly is not plausible; it violates our commonplace understandings of divinity. According to Kierkegaard, particularly in his later discourses and Christian writings, those ordinary conceptions of what God should be like are not innocent, for they are rooted in human longings for power. In these contexts, Kierkegaard, adopting the voice of a penitent, concentrates on the motivations for humanity's negative reaction to Christ in order to provoke the reader to look inward and discover the same hostile reaction in his own heart — and perhaps begin to repent. Humans, Kierkegaard suggests, vainly imagine that God must be the perfect instantiation of the qualities they secretly covet for themselves (*JFY*, 174-82). Because humans crave the power to satisfy all their desires but lack the power to do so, they imagine an omnipotent God free of those liabilities, a God who is the epitome of everything that they would like to be. The prospect of a God who humbles God's own self is the deepest kind of offense to the relentless human drive for self-exaltation. In *Confessions*, Augustine had narrated his own offense at the lowliness of Christianity with its inelegant Scripture and plebeian membership. The kenotic God who encountered him in Jesus Christ was not the kind of God that Augustine, the youthful, upwardly mobile seeker had expected.

For Kierkegaard, like the mature Augustine, the theme of God's self-emptying had profound implications for the way that God can be known through Christ. These implications dovetailed nicely with his conviction that traveling the Christian road necessarily involves uncertainty and risk — and thus maximal passion. If God has appeared among us in the form of a servant, contrary to all expectations, the divinity would not have been immediately recognizable (*PF*, 63-71). The incarnation is a kind of divine incognito: given the counterintuitive and shocking nature of God's love, the revelation of God in Christ must appear to worldly eyes to be a form of concealment. Even to those attracted to it, the revelation is ambiguous. Even if Jesus had appeared in a more spectacular guise, the presence of divinity in him could not have been immediately perceived or deduced from empirical evidence. Not the performance of astounding miracles and not even the resurrection from the dead and the ascension into the heavens would function as conclusive proof of divinity. No act performed by Jesus could indubitably demonstrate divine identity, for a sensational and marvelous event is not necessarily the effect of a divine cause. Miracles, resurrection, and ascension, if these could be somehow corroborated, would only demonstrate that Jesus was very extraordinary. To accentuate the uncertain character of the incarnation, Climacus argues that neither the testimony of contemporary witnesses nor the longevity and remarkable spread of Christianity across the globe proves that Jesus is divine. Other religions have been around for a long time and have won vast hordes of adherents. Other religions possess ancient documents that testify to their alleged truth. Even if they had been probative, all of these alleged evidences of the truth of Christianity would have been nothing more than demonstrations of divine power, testifying to the might of a cosmic potentate.

But that is not the kind of God who is revealed in the self-abasement of Jesus Christ. The humble form of the incarnation dramatically exacerbates the problem of unrecognizability, for the presence of God in a lowly, suffering human being is doubly immune to direct observation and verification. Kierkegaard writes:

> But just as the essentially Christian always places opposites together, so the glory is not directly known as glory but, just the reverse, is known by inferiority, debasement — the cross that belongs together with everything that is essentially Christian is here also. (*JFY*, 161)

Consequently, the incarnation of God in the lowliness of Jesus could be ignored, doubted, denied, and rejected, even by the eyewitnesses of his life. In this way, the inverse dialectic that we had seen in Augustine recurs in Kierkegaard's pages in the form of revelation through concealment, which itself is a function of exaltation through abasement.

Ironically, the very ambiguity of the revelation, the fact that it is just as much concealment as it is revelation, is a further indication of the depth of God's love. In the incarnation God accepts the risk, and even the likelihood, of being misunderstood. "Ah, the soul-anguish of misunderstanding!" Kierkegaard exclaims in regard to Christ (*JFY*, 173). God suffers the pain of knowing that God's efforts to be in fellowship with humanity might backfire by causing offense (*WA*, 63-64). Nevertheless, God loves humanity enough to become vulnerable in a relationship that would certainly not blossom in mutuality in all instances, and could even turn lethal.

In many works, including *Christian Discourses* — "Does a Human Being Have a Right To Let Himself Be Put to Death for the Truth?" and *Judge for Yourself!* — Kierkegaard expands the concept of God's condescension to include the overarching narrative pattern of Jesus' interactions with his followers and his enemies. The kenotic dynamic of the Word becoming flesh was replicated in the episodes of Jesus' earthly life. In many passages Kierkegaard criticizes the prevalent sentimentalized view of Jesus as the beloved shepherd who serenely accepted the adoration of his flock. In opposition to this picture of a benign, avuncular Christ, Kierkegaard offers the more brutal image of Jesus as the rejected, crucified one. The self-abasement that consistently characterized Jesus' earthly ministry was greeted with hostility and persecution, and thus the crucifixion was simply the logical conclusion of this trajectory. Christ refused to seek anything for himself, including his refusal to accept political power and become king, as the crowd demanded. It was Jesus' flagrant renunciation of power that enraged the homicidal mob members who cherished the augmentation of power as the highest good. The story of Jesus reveals the tragic and damning reality that sinful human beings simply cannot tolerate the spectacle of self-emptying love. Kierkegaard makes this clear in "Does a Human Being Have a Right To Let Himself Be Put to Death for the Truth?" in which an unnamed person who is zealously attempting to emulate Christ writes: "He was crucified precisely because he was love, or to develop it further, because he refused to be self-loving" (*WA*, 79). Similarly, in *Practice in Christianity*, Kierkegaard describes the antagonism that Christ provoked and lamented: "And he, this abused one, he was love; he wanted only one thing — to save humankind. He wanted it on any terms, would leave heavenly glory because of it; he wanted it on any terms — would sacrifice his life for it" (*PC*, 170-71). Jesus' implicit message that self-abnegation is a characteristic of divinity itself provoked the crowd to a fever pitch, for the world hates self-abnegating love with unrestrained ferocity. The incarnation of absolute self-denial offends because it exposes humanity's own precious drive for self-aggrandizement. The human world is scandalized by the incarnation because the selfless ways of God are incompatible with the selfish ways of world. By emphasizing this point, Kierkegaard repeats Augustine's essential contrast of Jesus' self-giving humility with humanity's self-serving pride.

Besides using the language of Jesus' divinity to nurture gratitude for God's self-giving love, Kierkegaard uses the traditional christological vocabulary to accomplish other purposes, particularly to encourage the confidence and hope that this daunting path is indeed the true road to blessedness. He uses the concept of Jesus' divinity to underscore the authority of Jesus' example and thus the reliability of the path of costly discipleship. To declare Jesus to be divine is to say that his path of suffering love is the definitive road to ultimate fulfillment. Appeals to the divine authority of Christ serve to encourage the reader's resolution to persevere on the path, confident that it is not a delusion. Talk of Jesus' divinity bolsters the flagging spirits of those who have been worn down by the world's incomprehension and hostility. As we have seen, this purpose of fostering hope and reassurance had precedents in Augustine's writings, though Kierkegaard may not have been aware of them.

The theme of Jesus' life and death as a manifestation of God's kenotic love informs Kierkegaard's treatment of the redemptive activity of Jesus and the host of issues that had usually been addressed under the rubric of "atonement." The claim that God's love was enacted in human history in the life, death, and resurrection of Jesus Christ did not capture the entire scope of redemption for Kierkegaard. The work of Jesus was much more than the objective establishment of God's solidarity with humanity; the love of God manifested in Jesus was intended to have a transformative impact on the life of the individual. God did not become incarnate simply to enjoy fellowship with humanity in a way that would be undemanding and require no response. Many of Kierkegaard's calls to become contemporaneous with Christ were designed to combat such theological detachment. Accordingly, Kierkegaard did not expatiate about the conceptual intricacies and puzzles of the popular "objective" views of Christ's atoning work that suggested that the purpose of Christ's redemptive career was to change the legal situation of humanity vis-à-vis God's justice or to change the cosmic environment by defeating evil principalities and powers.[52] Admittedly, when Kierkegaard discusses Jesus as the Redeemer from sin, he often does use Anselm's lan-

52. Augustine sometimes describes the atonement as the defeat of Satan, but by this he

guage of Jesus' satisfaction of God's justice as well as the even more ancient description of Jesus as a sacrifice for sin, neither of which sound on the surface like a foregrounding of divine love (except that God's love is the background motivation for these cosmic transactions).[53]

But no matter how much Kierkegaard does speak of Christ's passion as the atonement for human sin and guilt, he does not propose a theory concerning the mechanics of this atonement. Instead, he typically describes the cross as manifesting God's forgiveness rather than as bringing about that forgiveness by a legal or economic transaction. The enactment of God's merciful and suffering love on the cross can stir the human heart, motivate repentance and transformation, and thereby bring about salvation. Though Kierkegaard can describe Jesus as a "satisfaction" of divine justice, he prefers to explore the ways in which Jesus' work can change individual lives. In so doing, his edifying practice resembles that of Augustine, who had also presented the self-giving of the human nature of Jesus to God not only as a model for the individual Christian's own self-offering, but also as a tableau that can stir the individual's heart.

In an ironic reversal, Jesus' rejection and crucifixion contribute to the ability of his story to transform the individual. In Kierkegaard's reading of the passion story, God's forgiveness is manifested through the confluence of two narrative patterns. First, Jesus' death reveals the extent of human perversity and guilt, for the intentional execution of the most loving person who ever lived exposed the fact that the sinful world cannot tolerate love (*WA,* 79). Augustine, too, had regarded the crucifixion of Jesus as the decisive revelation of human sinfulness, without which we human beings would not grasp the extent of our depravity. For both theologians, this stark exposé of humanity's opposition to love, an opposition in which the reader is implicated, should engender profound self-examination and remorse. In these contexts Kierkegaard urges his readers to imagine themselves as members of the murderous mob that crucified Jesus. He insists that if we had been present at Golgotha, we, too, would have demanded Jesus' death.

Second, while the behavior of the crowd exposes sin, Jesus' forgiveness of his enemies is a revelation of the startling depths of God's mercy. Jesus' love is so extreme that not even his crucifixion by those to whom he had

---

usually means the triumph of the apparent weakness of self-abnegation over the self-assertive desire for domination.

53. See Lee C. Barrett, "Anselm of Canterbury: The Ambivalent Legacy of Faith Seeking Understanding," in Jon Stewart, ed., *Kierkegaard and the Patristic and Medieval Traditions* (Farnham, UK: Ashgate, 2008), pp. 167-81.

tried to manifest his love could provoke him to retaliation. Only those who have developed a deep sense of dissatisfaction with the direction of their own lives are in a position to understand and appreciate this forgiveness. For example, in "Thorn in the Flesh" (*EUD*, 338), Kierkegaard describes how paralyzing self-accusation can be healed by the awareness of being loved by God. Individuals, he observes, can create a gap between themselves and God through relentless self-condemnation, which can become an egocentric enclosing reserve. To believe in the "atonement" is, among many other things, to abandon the project of cherishing one's guilt. For Kierkegaard, as for Augustine, the yearning for forgiveness is one of the passions that draws the heart to the crucified one.

Like Augustine, Kierkegaard also discovered transformative power in the portrayal of Jesus as a human being. Even when viewed as the life of a human being, Jesus' story exhibits a kenotic pattern, just as Augustine had said. For Kierkegaard, Christ was not only the incarnation of God's forgiving love, the Redeemer, but also the "prototype" who inspires and commands "following after" and imitation. Phrased in the language of pietism, Christ is not only the savior of the individual but also the lord of the individual's life. The significance of the prototype is dramatized in Kierkegaard's recounting of the tale of a young boy who, when shown a picture of the crucified Jesus, responds with consternation and anger after it is explained to him that the crucified man was the most loving person who has ever lived (*WA*, 55). However, as the boy matures, his righteous indignation morphs into a desire to become like the man in the picture and suffer for the sake of loving humanity just as that man, Christ, had suffered. This desire to mirror Christ's compassion was partly motivated by gratitude for forgiveness, but it was fueled even more strongly by the sheer attractive power of the depiction of extravagant love. Christ as the one who loved radically and suffered persecution as a consequence functions as the paradigm of the Christian life, simultaneously attracting through the beauty of love and repelling through the offense to self-aggrandizement. Ideally, the reader, like the man in story, should be moved by love's beauty and also become willing to suffer persecution for the faith. By suggesting this, Kierkegaard is drawing on one venerable strand of Lutheran theology that had described the Christian life as the way of the cross, as an imitation of Christ's passion. This tradition, of course, had deep roots in Augustine's emphasis on the believer's participation in Christ's adoption of the form of a servant. For Augustine, as for Kierkegaard, that life of servanthood would inevitably alienate the world and provoke its persecution. For both Kierkegaard and

Augustine, the Christian life is patterned after Jesus' earthly career of on-going self-sacrifice, which was itself a manifestation in time of the eternal divine self-emptying. According to Augustine and Kierkegaard, the story of Jesus clarifies the ideal human life and inspires commitment to that ideal.

In many instances, the motif of Christ as the prototype of scorned and persecuted love is introduced in order to comfort Christians who are suffering because of their emulation of Christ. The world's fierce opposition can cause many who have dared to love their neighbors to doubt God's love for them (*UDVS*, 264-88). The hostility that they encounter — and their consequent disappointment and pain — raises the suspicion that God is indifferent to their sincere efforts to follow Christ's path. Kierkegaard observes that such individuals who face persecution or ostracism often feel like they are walking the path of love by themselves, ignored by God (*UDVS*, 226-27). Reflection on Christ's rejection by the world is intended to inspire such readers to reconceptualize their sufferings as a source of joy. Readers must be reeducated to experience their sufferings in a new way. Kierkegaard seeks to fortify these doubters with the reminder that suffering is absolutely necessary if one is going to follow Christ. Those Christians wrestling with despair can be comforted with the assurance that the world's opposition testifies that they are indeed following after Christ, and can be encouraged to find joy in the knowledge that Christ walks with them. Strengthened with such knowledge, Christians can even accept the pain of being misunderstood by their own friends and alienated from their families. The joyful thought hidden in the anguish of ostracism and persecution is that this christomorphic suffering is certified to be the path to eternal happiness. Here Kierkegaard's reflections on the comforts of Christlike suffering parallel Augustine's encomia to the joys of the martyrs.

As it was in Christ's own life, the humiliation of Christ's followers is the obverse side of their exaltation. Kierkegaard does not dwell on the exaltation of Christ, and thus does not foreground the corresponding exaltation of Christ's followers, because he fears that he might distract the reader from the urgent task of following Christ in the present moment by diverting attention to future glory. Such a shift in focus to the exalted state may even encourage a spiritually pernicious desire to walk the path of self-emptying love simply in order to attain the heavenly reward. Such a self-serving motivation would be inimical to the genuine love for the neighbor that Christ enacted. By keeping the focus on the suffering that is intrinsic to the Christian path, Kierkegaard seeks to alert the reader to the mysterious connection between humiliation and exaltation, between suffering for

Christ and joy in the Lord. The worldly sagacity that can discern no connection between suffering and intimacy with God must be countered with the reassurance that Christians are educated by suffering to rely on God and to surrender self-will. Paradoxically, this surrender is not only painful but also joyful, for Christians experience the bliss and serenity of loving purely. The faithful individual is not just recompensed with joy in some future state, for the peace and satisfaction associated with eternity can be experienced now through the daily growth in love. Meditation on Christ's painful rejection by humanity is, however, not encouraged for masochistic purposes but is recommended as part of a strategy to purge the reader of despair over life's unfairness and to kindle a desire for the self-forgetful joys of neighbor-love. Kierkegaard, echoing a long tradition that prominently included Augustine, depicts the road to blessedness as the path of suffering, persecuted love, and hails Jesus as the perfected human exemplar of this difficult way.

In many contexts Kierkegaard adds another edifying note and emphasizes Jesus' humanity in order to reassure readers that they, too, can walk the path that Jesus traveled, in spite of frailties and hesitations. The life of love, no matter how daunting, should not be dismissed as a fanciful utopian ideal unrelated to the actual capacities of human beings as they were created by God. If Jesus' humanity were to be ignored — and Jesus were to be described only as a divine being who possessed superhuman powers — we finite and fragile humans could not hope to emulate him at all. A purely divine being could not serve as a realistic pattern for any human being's maturation. But, according to Kierkegaard, when Jesus' life is construed as a genuinely human saga of self-denial, it can indeed function as a model that an individual can hope to emulate. Kierkegaard's frequent recountings of the human struggles of Christ and his exhortations to become contemporaneous with Christ serve to encourage readers to take up their cross and follow. Kierkegaard reminds readers that, in Gethsemane, Jesus as a human being learned obedience through facing the fearful prospect of crucifixion and spiritual tribulation. Jesus had to struggle to overcome anxiety, and that human struggle in the garden should be reflected in the lives of his followers. For the very same reasons, Augustine had affirmed the authentically human emotions of Jesus, and presented his triumph over anxiety and despair as a model of Christian striving.

Of course, in many ways Jesus cannot be imitated, particularly not in his role as Redeemer. For this reason the discourses about Christ as divine and Christ as human must be carefully differentiated. Kierkegaard warns that we should not impudently try to emulate Jesus' bearing of the sins of others or his saving of humanity, for those are uniquely divine actions (*CD*, 278). Such an arrogant ambition would utterly destroy the mood of gratitude for God's love that the Christian life of service requires as its foundation. In order to discourage the hubris of trying to save the world, Kierkegaard reiterates the theme that Jesus' burden was heavy so that ours might be light. We guilty sinners do not bear Jesus' heavy burden of knowing that his suffering was unjust, nor do we feel the full sting of God's seeming indifference. Unlike Christ, we mere followers, who know ourselves to be guilty, cannot claim that we do not deserve the misfortunes that befall us. No one besides Jesus has been in a position of legitimately doubting God's goodness, for no other person has suffered innocently. No other person possesses the moral authority to fear with any justification that God may not be just or benevolent. Consequently, we cannot and should not try to emulate the Redeemer's confrontation with the specter of divine condemnation. Moreover, as the essay "Does a Person Have the Right to Let Himself Be Put to Death for the Truth?" illustrates, the continuing infection of sin disqualifies even the most spiritually ambitious imitator of Christ from ever pursuing a messianic career (*WA*, 55-89). With this serious qualification to the way in which Christ can function as the prototype, Kierkegaard subverts any lingering Pelagian aspirations to become a perfected saint through one's own efforts. Like Augustine arguing against the Donatist vision of a pure church, Kierkegaard always returns to the sobering thought that perfection in this life is not attainable.

To summarize, Kierkegaard jettisoned the effort to clarify the significance of Jesus through metaphysical speculation about "natures," a practice in which even Augustine, he feared, had unfortunately dabbled and which subsequent Catholic and Lutheran Scholastics had practiced with unseemly vigor. Kierkegaard's writings are innocent of the mystifying technical terminology of Scholastic theology, and he eschews the attempt to produce a logical calculus to show how concepts like "person" and "nature," and "finite" and "infinite" can interact. For Kierkegaard, the relationship of the infinite and the finite in Christ, or in the individual's own self, is not amenable to a detached conceptual resolution. In his pages there is no speculation about the conceptually puzzling relationship of the glorified humanity of Christ to Christ's susceptibility to suffering. Instead, Kierkegaard simply shows how the apparently contradictory teachings about Jesus' divinity and Jesus' humanity can be connected to one another in the way that receiving a gift of mercy can be connected to following an example. Gratitude for forgiveness and the resolve to emulate a "prototype" are certainly different, but they are not contradictory. Kierkegaard shifts attention away from the construction of conceptual systems to the task of integrating a rich and complex family of interactive passions. Rather than reconciling the ostensible tension between the divine and human aspects of Christ through a more sophisticated set of definitions and distinctions, Kierkegaard coaxes the reader to forge the spectrum of Christ-directed hopes, resolutions, and joys into a coherent life. The old doctrines remain in force as second-order descriptions of the edifying purposes of Christian language about Jesus Christ and as imperatives to pursue those purposes. But in order to understand those doctrines, Kierkegaard proposes that skill in integrating passions must replace skill in manipulating ciphers in an abstract conceptual grid. The picture of Christ that emerges is both repellent because it challenges self-protective and self-aggrandizing instincts, but also mysteriously attractive in its sublime self-giving.[54]

Conclusion

As we have seen, though Kierkegaard's scattered christological reflections do not constitute a new theory of the logistics of the hypostatic union, the main christological themes that informed the piety of Augustine, as well as the entire Lutheran heritage that was so indebted to the African father, were given new expression in Kierkegaard's writings. For both Augustine and Kierkegaard, the content of the highest good is the self-giving love most evident in Christ's embrace of lowly human beings and even his enemies. According to both theologians, this love should be adored as the revelation of God's nature and emulated as the ideal human life. For both, this following of the way of Christ will stand in sharp antithesis to the world's preferred way of pride and self-aggrandizement — and will probably provoke hostility and suffering. In short, the christological reflections of both theologians were elaborations of the theme of divine *kenosis,* and the reduplication of that *kenosis* in the life of the believer. To communicate the dual themes of delight in the divine self-giving and the imperative to follow Christ, both Augustine and Kierkegaard use literary strategies that are rhetorical, pastoral, and highly imagistic.

The most significant thing about their two elaborations of the signifi-

---

54. For a discussion of this ambivalence, see Bradley R. Dewey, *The New Obedience: Kierkegaard on Imitating Christ* (Washington, DC: Corpus Books, 1968), pp. 73-101.

cance of Christ is the centrality of *kenosis*. Both Augustine and Kierkegaard were enthralled with the "form of a servant" theme in Philippians 2, and it is this motif that gives specificity to their discussions of God and their talk about the *telos* of the human journey. The God who is desired is the self-emptying God. Without this, their language about the highest good remains purely formal and abstract. As we have seen, self-giving was the basis for Augustine's account of the Trinity as love, and self-giving was the basis for Kierkegaard's analysis of the attractiveness and offensiveness of the incarnation. Therefore, it would be accurate to claim that, for both thinkers, the pattern of Christ's agape is the object of our eros.

The revelation that the ultimate object of desire is the divine self-giving love comes as a surprise in the works of both Augustine and Kierkegaard. Augustine did not anticipate this during his youthful meanderings through various philosophical and religious options; nor do the characters depicted by Kierkegaard suspect this. According to both Augustine and Kierkegaard, an analysis of the human quest for God does not reveal that the prospect of divine self-giving is the destination. Both, therefore, emphasize the disjunction between the revelation of God's love and ordinary human aspirations and expectations. In fact, Kierkegaard — more than Augustine — goes out of his way to emphasize how deeply offensive and counterintuitive it actually is. Nevertheless, if the appropriate forms of pathos are in place, the picture of God's radical self-giving love can have a mysteriously attractive power. If we do not resist its allure, the picture of divine self-giving proves to be not alien to the human longing for fulfillment. Shockingly, it turns out that this is what the human heart has always yearned for, even though there was no way of predicting this.

CHAPTER 8

Salvation: Faithful Love and Loving Faith

According to the depth grammar of Christianity articulated in the structure of doctrinal textbooks, the work of Christ must be appropriated by the believer through the development of such virtues as faith, hope, and love. This subjective appropriation of the work of Christ in an individual's life has often been treated under the rubric of "salvation," the state of being in ultimate communion with God. The writings of Augustine and Kierkegaard on the Christian life and salvation have been just as controversial and contested as every other aspect of their writings. On the one hand, many Protestants, particularly Lutherans, have viewed both Augustine's and Kierkegaard's portrayals of salvation with great suspicion. On the other hand, many Catholics have been delighted to detect a similarity between Augustine and Kierkegaard on this very issue, and they have sometimes embraced Kierkegaard as a fellow traveler. The contentious issue concerns the relationship of the believer's justification (or acceptance by God) to that believer's sanctification (or growth in the Christian life).

The Lutheran worry that Augustine and Kierkegaard may have undermined the foundational status of faith in God's justifying grace has largely set the agenda for the discussion of justification and sanctification in the two thinkers. Augustine has been identified by Lutherans as a primary source of the Catholic inversion of the proper relationship of justification and sanctification, and Kierkegaard has been criticized as a renegade who attempted to re-Catholicize Protestantism. Lutherans have feared that both authors, no matter how much they insist on grace as the propelling force in the individual's progress in sanctification, depict acceptance by God as something contingent on the achievement of a certain degree of Christlikeness. If salvation is defined as communion with God, then in this sense salvation happens at the completion of the process of sanctification. This, it is claimed, is evident in Augustine's preference for the basic image of the pilgrim to characterize the Christian life, and in Kierkegaard's foregrounding of the image of the disciple or follower. By privileging these root metaphors, Augustine and Kierkegaard were valuing the individual's growth in love as the most essential and foundational aspect of the Christian life. After all, the pilgrim must arrive somewhere in order to be in a fully satisfying relationship with God. According to this critique, this focus on growth in love militates against the centrality of the conviction that God accepts the sinner apart from any works, including works of love: love for God and neighbor displaces trust in God's merciful acceptance as constituting the essence of the gospel. This objection holds even when we recognize that for Augustine and for Kierkegaard, growth in love was made possible only by God's grace. Even if God is only crowning with salvation the gifts that God has graciously given the individual, it is still the case that the crown is given to the gifts, and is not given until the journey has been successfully completed. It is not the sinner who is justified, but the saint, even though the saint could not have become a saint without God's grace. The healing of the sinner seems to precede the sinner's final acceptance by God; justification appears to be contingent on sanctification, even if both are the fruit of grace. In the terminology of Melanchthon, justification by grace alone was not being respected as the doctrine by which the church stands or falls. Giving voice to this suspicion, John Elrod proposes that Kierkegaard had "nothing but contempt and derision for [Lutheran Christendom's] emphasis on the acceptance of unmerited grace as a sufficient condition for salvation."[1]

To make matters even more complicated, various types of Catholics and Protestants have differed among themselves, tending to relate the virtues of "faith" and "love" in very different ways. Because of this diffusion, they have developed divergent understandings of the relationship of justification and sanctification. Given the suggestive and often tentative nature of his work, Augustine has been claimed by many of these divergent parties as the font of their own theological vision. Part of the problem is that the technical definitions of "justification" and "sanctification" had not yet stabilized during Augustine's era. Augustine sometimes used "justification" in ways that would later be associated with "sanctification," thereby opening

---

1. John Elrod, *Kierkegaard and Christendom* (Princeton, NJ: Princeton University Press, 2001), p. 230.

the door to erroneous interpretations. In order to resolve this ambiguity, we need to closely examine his writings to determine exactly what he was trying to accomplish in his diverse discussions of salvation. Only then will we be able to compare the thrust of his work with that of Kierkegaard.

Augustine and the Symbiosis of Faith and Love

As with many of the theological themes that we have already discussed, Augustine said strikingly different things in different contexts about the relationship of being regarded as righteous by God *(iustitia)* to being made righteous by God *(sanctificatio)*. He also said different things about the correlative issue of the relationship of faith in God's acceptance of the sinner to the sinner's actual growth in love for God and neighbor. In some contexts, often when arguing against the Pelagians, Augustine could sound positively Lutheran, exhorting his readers to trust that God deems sinners to be righteous.[2] Here it seems as though this divine declaration of righteousness is independent of and precedes any spiritual improvement in the individual. In other contexts, Augustine similarly states that God's graciousness is not contingent on the spiritual rectitude of the individual, though it is not entirely clear whether "grace" here refers to God's full acceptance of the sinner or to God's granting the sinner the power to become righteous. For example, when comforting those in despair, Augustine assures readers that God's grace is not granted because of any putative merits that the individual could claim to possess.[3] God loves us not because we are righteous, but so that we will become righteous. In the same vein, Augustine came to vehemently argue — against the Pelagians — for this prevenience of God's grace. God's love, which could be construed as God's acceptance of the sinner, precedes any re-formation of the sinner's life, for Augustine insists that God seeks sinners before they ever seek God. The beginning of faith in our souls is a gift from God.[4] He further clarifies that God's favor is not bestowed on us because God foresaw our future virtues or realized that we would use that grace productively. In fact, because sinfulness continues even in God's elect, no one during this earthly journey can ever claim to deserve God's love. When encouraging humility, Augustine even described the individual to

2. Augustine, *On the Spirit and the Letter*, 26 (45), in *WSA* I, 23.
3. Augustine, *The Enchiridion on Faith, Hope, and Love*, 30, in *WSA* I, 8.
4. Augustine, *Grace and Free Choice*, 14 (28), in *WSA* I, 26.

whom God has given grace as still being totally sinful.[5] Sin does continue to contaminate the individual after baptism, even though its guilt is not imputed. To some degree, in this life God always loves the individual in spite of the individual's sin. All of these motifs tend to foreground justification, seemingly apart from sanctification, making it possible for Lutherans to legitimately claim Augustine as an ancestor.

In another vein, Augustine also described salvation as growth into the likeness of Christ, the epitome of love. The love of God that is graciously given to us is a love that makes us lovers of God.[6] Augustine even describes justification as a marriage of the soul and Christ, a bond so intimate that Christ's properties are transferred to the soul.[7] The soul is transformed by this union so that it begins to love in the unstinting way that Christ loves. A blessed exchange occurs between Christ and the believer, with Christ taking on the believer's sinfulness and giving the believer his own righteousness. The implication is that justification is not something imputed to the sinful individual, but is something imparted. Sinners are not merely *declared* to be righteous; they are actually *made* righteous. Rather than being a legal transaction, justification is a spiritual re-creation of the believer and a reorientation of the believer's heart. Occasionally Augustine even implies that justification is a state of the believer's soul that increases as the believer progresses in the Christian life.[8] This could mean that Christians become more acceptable to God as their love for God grows.

To further complicate matters, Augustine treats sanctification in a variety of different ways. When encouraging a deeper appropriation of the Christian virtues, Augustine shifts attention from justification to what would be more consistently labeled sanctification and the performance of works of love. In these contexts Augustine observes that there can be no faith without love, for faith is attachment to Christ, who is the epitome of love. Faith without works is not only dead, but it also does not save, for it is not really faith.[9] Consequently, the works that flow from grace can be said to be necessary for salvation. Augustine even suggests that the works of love, even though they are motivated by grace, are meritorious and are appropriately rewarded by God. In a similar way, he maintains that knowledge of God must be informed by charity in order to have any saving value.

5. Augustine, *On the Predestination of the Saints,* 4 (8), in *WSA* I, 26.

6. Augustine, *On the Spirit and the Letter,* 32 (56), in *WSA* I, 23.

7. Augustine, *Letters,* Letter 188, in *WSA* II, 1-3.

8. Augustine, *Sermons,* Sermon 158.5, in *WSA* III, 5.

9. Augustine, *Homilies on the First Epistle of John,* Homily 2.8, in *WSA* III, 14.

Augustine argues that there is no tension between Paul's panegyrics to faith and James's valorization of works of love, for James was speaking of the loving works that issue from faith, while Paul was talking about works done apart from faith.[10] As we shall see, Augustine's refusal to pit Paul against James presaged Kierkegaard's own desire to reintroduce James into his predominantly Pauline context.

Augustine did not simply juxtapose Paul on faith and James on love; rather, he sought to clarify how faith in Christ generates works of love directed toward the neighbor. According to Augustine, faith is a kind of certitude based on trust in God's declarations and promises rather than on immediate vision.[11] Faith in this context is not restricted to trust in God's justification of the sinner; it extends to all aspects of God's self-revelation through Scripture and the life of the church. To have faith is to focus attention on Christ and to regard Christ as the reliable embodiment of God's love. This acceptance of the picture of Christ as revealing God awakens love for God in the Christian's heart. To love God, who is love itself, is to love God's commandment to love the neighbor. Consequently, it is not possible to have faith in God without loving God, and it is not possible to love God without loving God's children.[12] As Augustine sometimes phrases it, to love the head of the body of Christ requires loving the members of that body. Our love for the neighbor reflects the Trinitarian nature of God, for any human act of love presupposes a lover (the individual), the object of love (the neighbor), and love itself (God). In loving the neighbor we are really loving love itself; conversely, we cannot love love itself without loving the neighbor. Our love should reflect God's love so deeply that it stretches itself beyond love for our neighbors to include love for our enemies. According to Augustine, we should embrace those who are our foes not because they already possess lovable characteristics, but so that they might become lovable.[13] We must do so because that is the extravagant manner in which God loves us. In fact, love for neighbors and enemies is the radical kind of love that we are adoring when we adore God. For Augustine, loving God and the human other is the affective and volitional dimension of knowing God in faith, and thus faith and love can only be conceptually distinguished. As we shall see, Kierkegaard links faith and love in much the same way Augustine

10. Augustine, *On Eighty-Three Varied Questions*, LXXVI, 2, in *WSA* I, 12.

11. Eugene TeSelle, "Faith," in Allan D. Fitzgerald, ed., *Augustine through the Ages* (Grand Rapids: Eerdmans, 1999), pp. 347-50.

12. Augustine, *Homilies on the First Epistle of John*, homily 4.3, in *WSA* III, 14.

13. Augustine, *Homilies on the First Epistle of John*, homily 10.7, in *WSA* III, 14.

did. Moreover, Kierkegaard would similarly repeat Augustine's contention that in loving God we are loving love itself, and that therefore love for the neighbor will flow from our enchantment with love.

Augustine's more detailed discussions of the way in which sanctification (growth in love) occurs exhibit a certain ambiguity, just as his general treatment of the relationship of being declared righteous by God and being made righteous had manifested an ambiguity. The ambiguity concerns the relationship of God's law, contrition, forgiveness, and growth in love. At times Augustine can sound a note that is congenial to many Lutheran ears concerning the spontaneous character of love for God and neighbor. He often claims that the motivation to love God and neighbor should not be the coercive power of God's law or the fear of punishment for violating it. Christians, he reminds his readers, have been liberated from the law's condemnation. Instead of obligation motivating obedience, love should spontaneously produce good works, moving the will with delight in the sheer goodness of God. Gratitude for justification, God's unmerited acceptance of the sinner, should naturally bear the fruit of loving works. This conviction was the source of Augustine's celebrated advice that Christians who love God may do what they will.[14] Sometimes this upsurge of love is described as a grateful response to the prospect of being loved by God; the soul simply becomes inebriated by the plenitude of divine love and overflows with loving deeds.[15] Of course, Augustine recognizes that this joyful eruption of love must assume the form of a life of sacrifice, but this willingness to sacrifice is made possible by the soul's growing delight in the beauty of self-giving love.[16] In these contexts the detailed precepts of God's law neither motivate works of love nor even guide the Christian in discerning how to go about loving the neighbor.

Sometimes, particularly when writing against the Pelagians, Augustine can sound even more like an anticipation of certain moods of Luther. He occasionally writes as if the primary or only function of the law is to expose sin and bring it to self-consciousness.[17] The law's purpose is accusatory and condemnatory. It helps foment the guilt and sense of helplessness that is the necessary passional prerequisite of gratitude for God's grace. On occasion, Augustine would even observe that the law actually exacerbates sinfulness,

---

14. Augustine, *Commentary on the Letter to the Galatians*, 57 (4), in *WSA* I, 17.

15. Augustine, *On the Christian Struggle (De agone Christiano)*, 10 (11), in *WSA* I, 10.

16. Augustine, *City of God*, X, 6, in *WSA* I, 6-7.

17. Augustine, *To Simplicianus*, I. 2-3, in *WSA* I, 12.

for it incites a rebellious delight in breaking God's rules. The individual's recognition that she not only violates the law but perversely enjoys doing so should be the basis for a deeper sense of spiritual incapacity. The law in these contexts only condemns; it does not heal or even assist in healing. The law brings knowledge of sin, but not the power to resist sin.

However, in other contexts Augustine can describe sanctification quite differently, making it seem less spontaneous and more intentional. For example, when encouraging the faithful to live the Christian life more profoundly, Augustine does ascribe a positive use to God's law. Growth in the Christian life does require discipline, which in turn requires principles and practices. Augustine does not hesitate to exhort his readers to avoid such vices as lechery and drunkenness, and he implies that the law is a helpful disciplinarian.[18] More specifically, the imitation of Christ does require more than loving Christ; it also involves heeding Christ's precepts and holding up Christ's life as an example.[19] Although we cannot hope to fulfill the law without grace, with the presence of God's grace in the soul the believer is empowered to strive to fulfill the law. God's grace enables us to be lovers of God's law, which for Augustine is revealed primarily in the life and teachings of Jesus.[20] The law of love proclaimed by Jesus provides guidance for wayfaring and sometimes wayward pilgrims, keeping them oriented in the right direction. The law is also a companion and an aid to the freedom to love.[21] By presenting the law in such an attractive light, Augustine implicitly suggests that sanctification is not always the fruit of justification. It is not the case that gratitude for forgiveness is the only motivation for growth in love; sometimes the prospect of obedience exerts its own attractions. Sometimes discipline and regulations can edify, strengthen, and encourage. As we shall see, Kierkegaard would similarly regard the law of love as a gift from God to inspire and stabilize the flagging and inconstant will.

This theme of the law as a disciplinarian points to other ways in which growth in love is an intentional and arduous process. According to Augustine, the temptations and tribulations with which Christians are afflicted should be accepted as another example of God's discipline, weaning them away from reliance on earthly goods. The sufferings of Christians serve the

18. Augustine, *Homilies on the First Epistle of John,* Homily 3, in *WSA* III, 14.

19. Augustine, *Confessions,* XIII, 21 (30); *Sermons* 235 (408), 1; *The Enchiridion for Faith, Hope, and Love,* 53, in *WSA* I, 8.

20. Augustine, *Grace and Free Choice (De gratia et libero arbitrio)* 18 (38), in *WSA* I, 26.

21. Augustine, *On the Grace of Christ and Original Sin (De gratia Christi et de peccato originali),* I, 13 (14), in *WSA* I, 23.

salutary purpose of reminding them of how dependent on God they are, and making it clear that this earth is not their ultimate home. The lives of the martyrs are particularly instructive in this regard, and should be held up for emulation. Because their willingness to accept persecution as an opportunity to grow in love manifests a profound truth about the need to receive all things, even ostensible calamities, as gifts of a gracious God. Kierkegaard would be in complete sympathy with this sentiment.

Augustine does, however, temper his emphasis of the need to grow in love with a major caveat. According to Augustine, it is not possible from the observation of outward works to determine if they have been performed in a spirit of love or not.[22] The same act can be done for several different motivations and with several different intentions, some of which may be loving, but many of which may not be. Consequently, love is hidden in the recesses of the individual's heart, known only to God with certainty. Augustine introduces this consideration in order to prevent any unseemly speculation about who is saved and who is not, and to discourage self-congratulatory comparisons of one's own putative virtues to other people's vices. Therefore, one's own perceived progress in sanctification should not be the basis for one's hope for salvation.

When describing sanctification, Augustine does make it sound as if fellowship with God is the goal attained at the end of the process of spiritual growth. If it is true that "only like can know like," then the pilgrim must be transformed into the image of God's self-giving love in order to know God. According to this principle, mutuality requires commonality, which in this instance would be a common ability to love and a common delight in love. To perfect this capacity to love, we need to perform works of love over the course of a lifetime in order to form and strengthen the soul. At this point Augustine would, of course, interject that the works themselves are the fruits of God's grace, and not of the pilgrim's heroic exertions. Nevertheless, the works are still necessary to reach the goal, no matter how they are produced. Given their importance in forming the soul, works of love should be intentionally encouraged and disciplined (though it must be remembered that the discipline is a gift from God), and not regarded as the spontaneous products of gratitude. Consequently, works of love would be a necessary means to the end of loving reciprocity with God. In these moods, Augustine implies that salvation comes at the end of the road, after the successful completion of the journey of sanctification.

---

22. Augustine, *Homilies on the First Epistle of John,* homily 8.10, in *WSA* III, 14.

To summarize, Augustine uses the language of "justification" and "sanctification," as well as the vocabulary of "faith" and "works of love," in different ways in different contexts in order to pursue a variety of purposes. These discourses diverge from each other and are not easily integrated. He emphasizes justification when he wants to encourage hope and confidence in the power of God's love. The struggling — often staggering — pilgrims must be reassured that they are already being sustained by God's love, and that Christ is already walking with them and will not desert them. Such vexed and self-doubting *viators* must be reminded that the presence of Christ with them is not contingent on their merits or their progress. In these contexts Augustine also emphasizes faith as a settled conviction about a truth that cannot be immediately apprehended in our current circumstances, but whose future possession has been assured. Faith here is closely associated with gratitude for God's support in spite of our woeful incapacity, and with hope that the promised beatitude will be achieved. Therefore, if salvation is defined as the state of being sustained by God as God's beloved, then in this sense salvation is a present reality while we are yet on the road. In other words, justification precedes sanctification.

Augustine shifts to the language of sanctification when he seeks to remind pilgrims that they are not yet at the journey's end and thus need to keep moving forward. In these contexts he also redoubles his efforts to present the attractiveness of the full beatitude that we do not yet enjoy so that the glimpse of the homeland will lure us toward it. Because this beatitude is fellowship with the God who is self-giving love, it requires the cultivation of love in the soul. To share in a relationship of reciprocal love with God, we must learn to love in the way that God loves us. Augustine uses these themes to urge readers to increase their diligence and resolutely move forward toward the goal (while reminding them that this very perseverance is also a gift). To encourage this maturation of love, in these contexts Augustine valorizes discipline, the law as a guide, and even the educative potential of suffering — all as gifts of grace. Accordingly, if salvation is defined as the state of being in ultimate communion with God, then in this sense salvation happens at the completion of the process of sanctification. Justification, understood as God's complete embrace, is the product of sanctification.

Kierkegaard and the Dialectic of Faith and Love

Kierkegaard was exposed to Augustine's reflections on the relationship of faith and love — and the correlative theme of the relationship of justification and sanctification — initially through the lectures of Clausen. Clausen, who was sympathetic to Augustine on this matter, introduces the issue by drawing attention to James's view of the inseparability of faith and works (*KJN* 3, pp. 54-55). According to Clausen, Augustine, like James, maintains that the good life, which is the life of love, is inseparable from faith. Faith, he adds, quoting Augustine, works by means of love (*KJN* 3, p. 59). He proceeds to explain that Augustine is claiming that the inevitable consequence of faith is diligence in good works. By emphasizing this, Clausen is trying to correct what he perceives to be a classic Lutheran suspicion that valorizing the virtue of love might encourage some form of Pelagian works-righteousness. The Lutheran motto *sola fide* was commonly thought to divorce faith from love — to the detriment of love.

Kierkegaard shared Clausen's desire to reconceptualize faith in such a way that love would be seen as integral to the Christian life. In *For Self-Examination,* Kierkegaard expresses concern about the appropriateness of Luther's extravagant celebration of God's justifying grace in Christendom's current situation. As the church and the general culture succumbed to spiritual and moral indolence, Luther's emphasis on justification merely encouraged further complacency. Kierkegaard proposes that in such a smug environment the imperative to actually obey God's law needs to be reintroduced into Christendom. He remarks that, if justification by grace through faith is the major premise of Lutheranism, then in this current environment of lassitude, "it certainly becomes most proper to pay a little more attention to the minor premise (works, existence, to witness to and suffer for the truth, works of love, etc.), the minor premise in Lutheran doctrine" (*FSE,* 24). Like Clausen, Kierkegaard objects to Luther's denigration of the Epistle of James and its salutary focus on works of love, and proposes that if Luther were alive today he would proclaim that "the Apostle James must be drawn forward a little" (*FSE,* 24).

In fact, Kierkegaard concentrates so much on James's injunction to be "not only hearers of the Word but doers of it" (James 1:22) and the imperative to love the neighbor that he has been accused of reintroducing a covert form of works-righteousness into a Christian tradition that had been defined by its confidence that sinners are justified by God's grace alone, apart from works. In so doing, some would say, Kierkegaard compromised Lutheran "solafideism" and destabilized the traditional Lutheran antinomies of faith and works, and law and gospel (or grace).[23] He has even been accused of being the arch-Pelagian of all time, and quite possibly the most dangerous, for his version of justification by works is subtle and attractive.[24] According to this critique, Kierkegaard not only treats love as a meritorious work, but he also emphasizes the individual's heightened sense of anxiety and despair so much that he elevated the cultivation of this depressing self-knowledge into a curious kind of self-justification. In this view, Kierkegaard inadvertently implies that we are justified by the power of our own honesty about ourselves rather than by God's grace. Moreover, according to a slightly different interpretation, it is Kierkegaard's equation of the Christian life with the imitation of Christ that jeopardizes the Lutheran conviction that we are saved by grace alone through faith alone. Kierkegaard, it is suggested, was advocating a new ethical standard with new stringent requirements that the individual would have to satisfy in order to be right with God.[25] Because of the controversy surrounding Kierkegaard's vigorous emphasis of works of love, we must explore his treatment of the themes of God's law, grace, justification, and sanctification more carefully. Given the fact that Clausen had portrayed Augustine as trying to hold faith and love together, a comparison of Kierkegaard's work with Augustine's may illuminate each of their approaches to these thorny issues.

Actually, Kierkegaard frequently affirms Luther's theme of "grace alone." He confesses that "Lutheran doctrine is excellent, is the truth," and he advises that Lutherans' prioritization of faith and grace should not be "abolished or disparaged" (*FSE*, 24). As we have seen, such an emphasis of grace is writ large in Kierkegaard's own depiction of faith as a gracious gift. But Kierkegaard certainly also wants to introduce a new rigor into Christianity as a corrective to the smugness and laxity of bourgeois Christendom. Against the current complacency, Kierkegaard protests that Luther's doctrine of justification by grace should not be taken to mean that God is a lenient parent who simply tolerates the infractions of God's naughty children. By elaborating the theme of grace apart from the continuing obligation to fulfill God's law, Lutheran theologians had failed to take seriously the lofty ideal of the life of love to which Christians are called (*FSE*, 15-25). As a re-

23. See Hermann Diem, "Kierkegaard's Bequest to Theology," in Howard A. Johnson and Niels Thulstrup, eds., *A Kierkegaard Critique* (New York: Harper, 1962), pp. 262-63.

24. This view was suggested by Hans Frei, in a conversation with the author, March 1984.

25. See Anthony Rudd, *Kierkegaard and the Limits of the Ethical* (Oxford: Clarendon Press, 1993), pp. 168-69.

sult, subsequent Lutherans were unable to recognize the extent to which the old worldly life and the new loving life are not commensurate. Kierkegaard feared that this made them blind to the fact that the Christian life does not grow out of natural virtue, and does not evolve out of natural human capacities. Moreover, without an appreciation of the rigorous demands of Christian love, contemporary churchgoers did not really experience the terrified conscience that had so afflicted Luther and that had served as the necessary presupposition for the longing for forgiveness. For Kierkegaard, a profound disquietude with one's own guilt is an absolute prerequisite for valuing God's justifying grace — and even understanding what it means (*CD*, 251ff.). But "grace," in Kierkegaard's view, had been debased into a code word for the lowering of moral and spiritual expectations that typified the established church. Like Dietrich Bonhoeffer a century later, Kierkegaard recoils at this prospect of "cheap" grace divorced from God's expectations.[26] To rectify this imbalance, Kierkegaard reemphasizes the crucial significance of responsible, intentional works of love for the Christian life. In order to avoid a reversion to works-righteousness, he seeks to accomplish this goal without undermining the conviction that salvation is a free, unmerited gift from God. As he had done throughout his writings, Kierkegaard strives to do this by illustrating and evoking the passions that constitute the context for talk of grace, faith, and works without attempting to integrate the relevant doctrines into a logically organized systematic theology. In so doing, he ends up sounding a great deal like Augustine.

In order to show how both "grace" and "works" are essential for the Christian life, Kierkegaard has to distinguish the respective roles of the assurance that God already accepts the sinful individual and the imperative to grow in love for God and neighbor. In other words, the different functions of the doctrines of justification and sanctification would have to be clarified. These two different motifs in the Christian life require two different ways of talking about "works" and God's requirements, or "law." To avoid conflating these two discourses, Kierkegaard implicitly borrows the distinction of the "second" and "third" uses of God's law from Lutheran confessional theology. This distinction is more often associated with the Reformed tradition, but it is clearly articulated in the Lutheran "Formula of Concord" and in

---

26. Murray Rae, "Kierkegaard, Barth, and Bonhoeffer: Conceptions of the Relation between Grace and Works," in Robert L. Perkins, ed., *International Kierkegaard Commentary: For Self-Examination and Judge for Yourself!* (Macon, GA: Mercer University Press, 2002), pp. 143-67.

the systematic tomes of the seventeenth-century Lutheran Scholastic theologians. The two uses are rooted in the practice of Augustine, even though he does not use the terminology. As Kierkegaard knew from the textbooks of Bretschneider, Hase, and Hahn, the "first" use of God's law is simply to restrain sin. By this the theologians meant the law's capacity to frighten sinners into obedience through the threat of dire sanctions. Kierkegaard says little about this use, for it pertains only to the regulation of overt behavior, and has nothing to do with the transformation of the heart.

The second use of God's law, also known as its "theological" use, is to expose sinners' failure and incapacity to fulfill the law, exacerbate guilt, and thereby motivate repentance. As we have seen, Augustine did sometimes write about God's law in this way, often in his polemics against the Donatists and Pelagians. In this second use, the law should accuse inadequately contrite individuals and terrify their consciences, preparing them to be receptive to the good tidings of justification by grace. The third use of God's law, however, was much more positive. According to the third use, God's law is intended to provide necessary principles of godly living to the saints, those believers who delight in doing God's will in the world. The rules of a righteous life should be welcomed by the faithful in the way that an avid musician welcomes the guidance of a musical score. The musician does not experience the structure of the score as an external imposition that impedes his freedom, but rather as the necessary condition for a joyful performance. The law should be an aid to the process of sanctification. Augustine, too, had described the example of Christ's life and Christ's precepts in this way and had highlighted their role in nurturing the development of Christian love. As is evident, the second and third uses of the law were exceedingly different in purpose, for one inspired receptivity to justification, and the other encouraged sanctification. The possibility of conflating the two threatened to reintroduce the Pelagianism that orthodox Lutherans desperately sought to avoid, and the preservation of the distinction required unrelenting vigilance. As a result, the third use of the law often received scant attention in contemporary Lutheran circles, except by the Halle Pietists.

Kierkegaard was the heir of the conviction that justification and sanctification are different but equally important, and that the second and third uses of the law are different but equally important. His writings frequently pursue pastoral goals associated with both of these two uses; but, like a good Lutheran, he carefully keeps these goals distinct. His use of the law of love in the third way is responsible for the perception that he was jeopardizing the principle of *sola gratia*. In effect, all he was doing was reviving in a particularly vivid way a recessive element in his own theological heritage. By doing so he was also implicitly recovering a crucial component of the Augustinian heritage and restoring the theme of sanctification, or growth in Christlikeness, to a position of prominence in the Christian life.

Many of Kierkegaard's writings indirectly focus on justification by enacting the second use of God's law, the encouragement of guilt and re-pentance. He departs from the Lutheran tradition by using the example of Christ to convict the individual of sin, rather than by using the Ten Com-mandments or natural law, as had been the case in the older theological heritage. For Augustine, too, the life of Christ was the epitome of God's commandment to love God and neighbor, and the most profound guilt was provoked by the perceived failure to approximate that ideal. Kierkegaard feared that those less rigorous ethical norms discoverable by reason and en-shrined in the Old Testament had been co-opted by Christendom to lower moral standards to a level that most moderately decent citizens could attain, thereby fostering the self-flattering illusion of holiness. In much the same way, Augustine had struggled to make it clear that the virtue of Christian love was not reducible to the virtues of Roman citizenship or the pursuit of philosophy. For both Augustine and Kierkegaard, the true essence of God's law is epitomized in the command to serve one master, and that master is the pattern of self-giving love evident in the life of Christ. Kierkegaard often depicts the strenuousness of the life of the "prototype" Christ in such an intimidating way that the reader must despair of ever living up to it.

But in these contexts Kierkegaard does not emphasize the loftiness of this standard because he expects that his readers will be ashamed of them-selves, successfully correct their lives, and become absolutely Christlike (*FSE*, 24). Rather, Kierkegaard emphasizes the extreme unselfishness of Christian love in order to evoke continuing repentance. Kierkegaard writes: " 'The prototype' must be presented as the requirement, and then it crushes you" (*JP* 1, 349). For Kierkegaard, receptivity to the central Lutheran mes-sage that fallen human beings are forgiven even though they are sinners presupposes the anguish of a contrite conscience (*PC*, 67). Tragically, in the present age the citizens of Christendom do not feel particularly guilty, and thus they lack the passional presupposition for rejoicing in the unmer-ited forgiveness promised by God. In such an environment of moral laxity, the proclamation of justification by grace merely encourages further indo-lence and spiritual smugness. It is to counteract this spiritual numbness that Kierkegaard turns to the Epistle of James to accentuate the full rigor and seriousness of God's imperative, the daunting proclamation of the law that could catalyze an appreciation of the need for grace (*FSE*, 24). In this context, works of love must be emphasized in order to stimulate the pained awareness of how far individuals fall short of God's ideals. In this way, Kierkegaard's encomia to Christlike love help readers experience their own incapacity, and then long for forgiveness and spiritual help.

In his various texts Kierkegaard uses the law of love to stimulate remorse over many different things in different stages and aspects of the Christian life. In all of these instances we can find parallels in Augustine's writings. When attacking the complacency of Christendom, Kierkegaard insists that the individual must first admit to herself that she is not even trying to approximate the divine standard. Law-induced guilt is necessary for the initial recognition of the need for forgiveness and for any progress in Christian faith. Kierkegaard writes: "Christianly the emphasis does not fall so much upon to what extent or how far a person succeeds in meeting or fulfilling the requirement, if he actually is striving, as it is upon his getting an impression of the requirement in all its infinitude so that he rightly learns to be humbled and to rely upon grace" (*JP* 1, 993). However, he adds this warning: "But if someone does not have a true conception of the magnitude of the requirement, he cannot have a true conception of the magnitude of grace — he really takes grace in vain" (*JP* 2, 1497). Then, as the individual does begin to strive to more closely approximate the ideal, the continuing recognition of failure inspires further humility and preserves the proper gratitude for forgiveness and the awareness of the ongoing need to rely on God. As individuals pursue the life of love, they gain a deeper understanding of what love requires, and the ideal of Christian love becomes more elevated and distant. Kierkegaard agrees with Luther that "the more one does his best to do good works with the idea of being saved, the more anxious he becomes" (*JP* 2, 1485). When the aspiring saint takes his good works before God, he "sees them transformed into something miserable and base" (*JFY*, 154). As one makes progress in the Christian life, the law then serves to forestall the inception of spiritual pride. The law convicts both the lethargic, self-satisfied bourgeois citizen and also the religious zealot intent on taking heaven by storm. Augustine had used the law in a similar way to erode the self-satisfaction of the allegedly virtuous pagans and the spiritual athleticism of the Pelagians. In a similar way, for Kierkegaard, the law continues to teach us to discount even our most sincere and ostensibly impressive strivings and to be suspicious of our tendency to exaggerate the worth of our own performance. This deflation of spiritual pride was a crucial task in Kierkegaard's religious context. According to some of his contemporaries, including many Pietists and Grundtvigians, the individual needs forgiveness less and less as the individual advances in the Christian life. Moving toward perfection, the individual could trust more in the potency of the inner experience of regeneration and the sanctified works flowing from it, and would need to trust less in the mercy of God. The need to counteract this disparagement of God's grace fueled Kierkegaard's repeated reminders of the loftiness of the Christian ideal and the impossibility of attaining it, just as it had inspired Augustine's reminders that perfection is not attainable in this life. Kierkegaard had his own Pelagians and Donatists to combat.

In defending the need to rely on God's grace, Kierkegaard cites two different reasons for the impossibility of fulfilling God's law. The first, and more obvious, is the weakness of sinful human nature. Given the hidden self-serving motivations that contaminate all our actions, even our seemingly most noble and altruistic deeds are imperfect. But a second reason is implied in Kierkegaard's pages: God's demand is infinite; consequently, no matter how loving an individual has been, the individual could always have been more loving (*WL*, 134). An infinite distance yawns between God's perfect love and our paltry imitation. For Kierkegaard, this is not a depressing thought. The infinite distance reminds us that we are nothing compared to God, and that distance thereby encourages the appropriate dispositions of gratitude, humility, and trust in God alone. He would even go so far as to suggest that we should rejoice that the law cannot be fulfilled, for this failure makes the need for humility more evident. The appreciation of God's forgiveness of our faulty performance is more edifying than any delight in our own good works, for it fosters ecstatic gratitude and adoration of God's beneficence. The evident impossibility of fulfilling the law dispels the illusion that obedience to the law could ever produce blessedness and inspires rejoicing over the sheer gratuity of salvation. Here Kierkegaard is echoing the *felix culpa* theme (or at least a "fortunate fallibility" theme), attributed to Augustine, that in a paradoxical way the fall into sin is a blessing in disguise, for it makes the joy of redemption possible.[27] However, neither Augustine nor Kierkegaard believed that this made the fall into sin soteriologically necessary; neither was a supralapsarian, one who argued that God had ordained Adam's fall. All that they meant was that, given the reality of the fall, the sinner must first experience the darkness of the abyss of alienation from God before the individual can delight in the radiance of divine forgiveness.

---

27. See Jason Mahn, *Fortunate Fallibility: Kierkegaard and the Power of Sin* (Oxford: Oxford University Press, 2011).

This joy of rejoicing in God's sublime gratuitous love was at the core of Augustine's own piety.

In addition to emphasizing the use of the law to expose sin and stimulate repentance, Kierkegaard's works even more frequently emphasize sanctification and thus use the law in its "third" function, a strategy that corresponds to Augustine's ubiquitous exhortations to grow in love. Like Augustine, Kierkegaard portrays Christ as the "prototype" for the Christian life. Christlike works of love should characterize the Christian's life, for the life of love is humanity's true *telos* and most profound joy. The imitation of Christ's life of suffering love is intrinsically valuable, not just instrumentally valuable in producing guilt and repentance. Particularly in *Works of Love,* Kierkegaard adopts the voice of an ardent encomiast of love in order to enable the reader to imagine the positive attractions and unique blessedness of a life of obedient, self-giving discipleship (*WL,* 197, 375). In much of Kierkegaard's writing, the law of love serves as a stimulus and a guide to the loving works that should be the fruit of faith. By doing so, Kierkegaard is only emphasizing the continuing significance of the law and works in nurturing the joyful love of the neighbor, and not introducing an alien Pelagian element into Lutheranism. In a way, he is calling Lutheranism back to a recessive aspect of its more authentically Augustinian heritage.

Of course, Kierkegaard warns that loving works are not meritorious and should never be incentives to self-congratulation. The imitator of Christ is no religious athlete winning heavenly laurels; the faithful disciple does not take heaven by storm. When discussing the life of love, Kierkegaard insists that the aspiring lover of God and neighbor should never be motivated by the prospect of reward, no matter how transcendent that reward might be. The imitation of Christ is fueled not by the expectation of personal benefit but by thankfulness for the love shown by God and by attraction to that extravagant love. Like a good Lutheran, Kierkegaard frequently repeats that works of love contribute nothing to salvation, and he identifies "salvation" with the acceptance of the unworthy by God. After praising works of love and calling for their performance, he cautions, "Ah, the first thing you learn when you relate yourself to God in everything is that you have no merit whatever" (*WL,* 385). He confesses: "I am deeply and humbly aware that if I am ever saved I will be saved by grace, just as the robber on the cross" (*JFY,* 15). In a journal entry he says: "Christianity requires everything, and when you have done this, it requires that you understand that you are nevertheless saved simply and solely by grace" (*JP* 2, 1480). For Kierkegaard, grace provides the context in which the law, even in its third use, must be understood. Similarly, Augustine had insisted that the individual cannot take credit for growth in love, for our loving works are the fruit of grace. However, Augustine does imply that God is pleased by our grace-motivated works of love and does accept them.

Two very different dynamics are operative in Kierkegaard's works: we must have faith in God's unmerited mercy, and we must strive to love with all our might. The duality raises the question of how faith and love — or justification and sanctification — are related. At times in Kierkegaard's pages, works of love and faith simply appear to be parallel phenomena. This pattern would suggest a passional bifurcation, with faith and love being discrete dispositions with separate motivations. At other times loving works are described as being the fruit of faith in the atoning work of Christ. Christ's enactment of costly love for humanity spontaneously motivates imitation. Kierkegaard writes: "Imitation or discipleship does not come first, but 'grace'; then imitation follows as a fruit of gratitude, as well as one is able. . . . [I]t begins with joy over being loved — and then comes a striving to please, which is continually encouraged by the fact that even if he does not, he is still loved" (*JP* 2, 1886). In these contexts Kierkegaard is repeating a theme from his own Lutheran heritage that had deep roots in Augustine's writings: that gratitude for God's unmerited forgiveness elicits love for Christ. Kierkegaard and Augustine were in agreement that love for God is a response to God's self-giving. In *Works of Love,* Kierkegaard makes it clear that we humans are enabled to love only because God has first loved us. Or, as some Lutheran theologians had phrased it, justification typically inspires sanctification.

However, in Lutheran dogmatics it had never been entirely clear how or why gratitude should express itself as obedience to God's law. Even the specification that the law in question here is the law of love did not clarify matters. At most, the implication given by the confessional documents was that the forgiven sinner would surely want to please the divine benefactor by performing any tasks that the benefactor required. That view, however, made the connection between gratitude and the performance of works of love entirely contingent. God could have required anything, and whatever it was, the pardoned and relieved sinner would have gratefully done it. The motivation for performing works of love would have been a self-interested relief over escaping punishment. Obedience to God would have been a submission to a heteronomous will in order to preserve the potentate's benevolent disposition. The problem with this scenario is that the motivation to engage in works of love is prudential, and hence not really loving. Though

Kierkegaard certainly does regard obedience to the law of love as a duty, the motivation for doing one's duty is not to secure one's own felicity.

Given his interest in forming the religious subjectivity of individuals, Kierkegaard cannot allow either the ambiguity about motivation or the suggestion of a prudential motivation to continue, and he attempts to exhibit a natural connection between faith and love in his writing. Consequently, he describes faith with active, vital metaphors. As we have seen, faith is not dispassionate assent to cognitive propositions; rather, it is a passion for God that necessarily involves dispositions to act in certain ways. In an imaginary conversation, Luther says to the author of *Works of Love*:

> I have indeed been observing your life, and you know that faith is a restless thing. To what end has faith, which you say you have, made you restless, where have you witnessed for truth, where against untruth, what sacrifices have you made, what persecution have you suffered for your Christianity, and at home in your domestic life where have your self-denial and renunciation been noticeable? (*FSE*, 18)

Given Kierkegaard's conviction that passions involve an impetus toward action, faith will manifest itself in public, observable ways. Kierkegaard insists that love delights in opportunities to express itself so that it can be known by its fruits (*WL*, 10-16). Therefore, love must make itself visible; it must be seen by the world.

The motivational connection between grateful faith and obedience to the law of love becomes clearer in Kierkegaard's discussion of Christ's love and the individual's imitation of that love. Kierkegaard frequently observes that Christ's love "reduplicates" itself in the individual (*WL*, 280-82). This is not surprising, for it is the very nature of love to seek to become like the beloved. In this case the beloved is Christ, the epitome of the life of extravagantly self-giving love. Because Christ loved all of his neighbors, including every sinful individual, the grateful and trusting appreciation of that love will inspire its redoubling in the believers' love for their neighbors. The enticement to grow in love is not just joy about being accepted by God, but is even more powerfully delight in the beauty of the love manifested in the forgiveness of the sinner. The lover's attraction to the beloved, in this case Christ, who is the epitome of the life of love, generates a desire to become like the beloved. Accentuating this note of sheer delight, Kierkegaard writes lovingly and poetically in praise of love. Without this immediate appeal of a life of love, the exhortation to emulate Christ the prototype would be the heteronomous imposition of an imperative alien to human nature. Love as a purely external command would necessarily backfire, for an external command focuses one's attention on one's own efforts to fulfill it, and fails to direct attention to the neighbor, who is supposed to be the object of love. Accordingly, in Kierkegaard's writings, the vocabulary of gift and gratitude frames the rhetoric of obligation; works of love flow naturally from trust and delight in God's love for sinners. Kierkegaard's view that faith in God's love revealed in Christ spawns a desire to imitate it was functionally equivalent to Augustine's conviction that love for God, which is a necessary concomitant of faith's focus on God's love, naturally exhibits the characteristics of the divine beloved. On this crucial matter Augustine's and Kierkegaard's statements are often interchangeable.

However, Kierkegaard is not content to describe the life of love as a matter of pure spontaneity, and in this he once again resembles Augustine. For Kierkegaard, the "Royal Law" to love God with all one's heart, mind, and strength and to love one's neighbor as oneself is not just an internal impulse welling up in the individual's heart due to enthusiasm for Christ. In many contexts he describes this Royal Law as a commandment, based on external authority, which the individual has a duty to obey. In fact, about one-third of his *Works of Love* is devoted to the obligatory dimension of love for the neighbor. The desire to become like the beloved, potent as it may be, is not sufficient by itself to ensure the steadiness, resolution, and single-mindedness that love requires. Even those who are in love with Christ's life of love still need the stabilizing influence of the law. Given the individual's volitional unreliability, God's law is a blessing that supports the will when spontaneous benevolence is insufficiently powerful (*WL*, 24-43). The law provides welcomed aid by commanding steadfastness, for even the ardor of those who are enamored of Christ can wane. The followers of Christ should not just wait passively for feelings of compassion to arise inside them or remain quiescent until the urge to act stirs them. The law's imperative force continues to function as the necessary counteraction to the individual's stubborn inclinations toward self-protection and self-gratification. The law's demand "you shall love" safeguards love through the inevitable periods of enervation and waywardness. In this life no one is so spiritually mature that he or she is continuously and consistently motivated by spontaneous loving feelings.

When addressing the need to stabilize the will and solidify resolution, Kierkegaard sounds very much like a divine command theorist. But, as we have seen, when emphasizing the need to cultivate the appropriate motivations to love, Kierkegaard sounds like some kind of virtue theorist. Noting this, Robert C. Roberts has concluded: "Neither the divine command nor the virtue that it enjoins has the kind of hierarchical privilege in Kierkegaard's thought (or in Christian ethics more generally) that it would need to function as the base of a moral theory."[28] Roberts adds that, in Kierkegaard's works, moral concepts like love are an array of themes that exhibit "mutually supporting complexity" and invite "multidirectional, dialectical exploration."[29] That "mutually supporting complexity" is evident in the fact that sometimes Kierkegaard presents love for God and neighbor as a duty, and sometimes he presents them as the *telos* of human yearning. In both respects, he sounds like Augustine, who also exhibited a multidirectional dialectic of duty and attraction. For both Augustine and Kierkegaard, God lures us with the attractiveness of love, and steadies us with the commandment to love. Moreover, the two theologians agreed that the Royal Law can both command and attract because what God commands is also what will satisfy our restless hearts and fulfill our souls.[30] Through obedience to the law of love, the self becomes the self that God had created it to be.

Some interpreters have claimed to detect a shift in Kierkegaard's writing concerning this public enactment of faith through loving works.[31] This shift, if it is as severe as is sometimes claimed, would tend to throw more weight on the "commandment" aspect of Christian love and diminish the yearning dimension. This would seriously erode the perception of a deep parallelism between Augustine and Kierkegaard with regard to sanctification. The argument that Kierkegaard essentially changed his view begins with the observation that in his earlier literature Kierkegaard had talked about Christianity as a religion of "hidden inwardness" in which the critical factor is the intensity and quality of the individual's religious passions. This inwardness could not be definitively linked with specific external actions. In general, a third party can never know with certainty what is transpiring in another person's heart. Kierkegaard frequently cautions that no ostensible fruit of the spirit is by itself sufficient evidence of God's grace. Even regarding the ethical life, Judge William had observed that "the ethical lies so

28. Robert C. Roberts, "Kierkegaard and Ethical Theory," in Edward F. Mooney, ed., *Ethics, Love, and Faith in Kierkegaard* (Bloomington: Indiana University Press, 2008), p. 90.

29. Roberts, "Kierkegaard and Ethical Theory," p. 90.

30. See C. Stephen Evans, *Kierkegaard's Ethic of Love* (Oxford: Oxford University Press, 2004), p. 135.

31. See John W. Elrod, *Kierkegaard and Christendom* (Princeton, NJ: Princeton University Press, 1981), pp. 249-53.

deep in the soul, it is not always visible, and the person who lives ethically may do exactly the same as one who lives aesthetically, and thus it may deceive for a long time . . ." (*EO* 2, 257). This general difficulty is exacerbated in Christianity, because no particular set of actions uniformly flows from the paradoxical passion of faith. No combination of behaviors could count as conclusive evidence that a person was simultaneously renouncing earthly happiness in order to be faithful to God, and also poised to receive happiness as a gift from God. In *Fear and Trembling,* de Silentio retells the story of Abraham's near sacrifice of Isaac in three different ways, in which Abraham's external behavior remains pretty much the same, but his emotions are entirely different. Abraham's faith is clearly not identifiable with a set of actions, not even the dramatic one of preparing to slaughter Isaac. According to the interpreters who emphasize the incommensurability of inwardness and action in the early Kierkegaard, his later insistence that faith must manifest itself as overt imitation of Christ signals a rejection of his youthful theme of "hidden inwardness."

Another possible interpretation, however, would argue that the change in rhetoric may be symptomatic of nothing more than a shift in purpose. As it turns out, Kierkegaard continues to insist that faith requires inwardness, and to warn that no single set of actions can ever be a sufficient condition for asserting that a person has faith. Moreover, he continues his critique of Pietism's identification of the Christian life with the performance of specific righteous duties and the avoidance of certain sinful behaviors. Rather, the real change in Kierkegaard's works is his suggestion that actions that exhibit a certain pattern are a necessary but not sufficient condition for faith. Action is never an adequate demonstration of the presence of faith, but faith can never be without action. As Kierkegaard matured, he became increasingly convinced that the actions inspired by faith had certain common, publicly identifiable features. This development drew him even closer to Augustine's concern with distinctive spiritual practices as expressions and supports of the Christian life.

As Kierkegaard's career as a writer progressed, he identified the life of love more closely with suffering. He had always set the standard for the life of love quite high in order to differentiate Christian love from its cultural counterfeits. The loftiness of the ideal generated the spiritual challenge that he labeled the "double danger." This double danger was the likelihood that the individual's inner anguish concerning the renunciation of self-interest would be compounded by the further suffering triggered by society's inevitable incomprehension, hostility, and rejection. A growing tension becomes evident in Kierkegaard's writings between his depiction of the Christian life as the holy acceptance of life as God's good gift (with, of course, the willingness to surrender this gift if love requires it) and a one-dimensional portrayal of Christianity as a total renunciation of the world and an unqualified embrace of suffering. Some passages exuberantly celebrate blessedness and joy, while others warn of inevitable earthly anguish. Sometimes the Christian life is identified with the serenity and felicity that accompanies works of love — and sometimes with the renunciation and suffering that love requires. In some of Kierkegaard's earlier works, rejection by the world seemed to be a tragic byproduct of the life of love, but in later writings such rejection seems to be a part of love's very essence. Earlier, Kierkegaard had seemed to distinguish Christian heroes who are called to literally renounce everything from the average believers, who only need to confess their failure to do so; but in his final writings he insists that everyone must renounce the world and "die to every earthly hope" (*FSE*, 77). Many interpreters have supposed that, in these later texts, Kierkegaard was jettisoning his earlier depiction of the Christian life as a dialectic of celebration and self-sacrifice, and positing a stark conflict between fulfillment in this world and fulfillment in the realm of the eternal.[32] Undoubtedly, toward the end of his life the accent had clearly fallen on world-renunciation rather than world-affirmation. Rather than exhorting the reader to imitate Christ's love (which would involve both joy and suffering), the later Kierkegaard tended to exhort the reader to imitate Christ's suffering. Like certain forms of pietism, the spotlight was riveted on the necessity to share Christ's rejection and follow the dolorous way of the cross. According to some commentators, this shift in focus raises the ugly possibility that Kierkegaard had drifted toward a view of God as a cosmic torturer, with world-negation becoming his somber, dominant note.

As I see it, it was Kierkegaard's increasing sense of human society's inveterate antipathy toward love that inspired his tendency to identify suffering (rather than a willingness to suffer if necessary) as a necessary constituent of Christian love (*WA*, 67-72). In his later writings, love entails witnessing to the world about the value of love, a testimony that inevitably triggers persecution and suffering. Simply living the life of love functions as a witness to the surrounding society; the witnessing will happen inevitably due to the public character of loving acts. What the world beholds in

---

32. See Valter Lindström, *Stadiernas Teologi: En Kierkegaard-studie* (Lund: Gleerup, 1943).

a life of love will antagonize it in several different ways. Loving behavior will be a visible testimony to the dismantling of the individual's old needy and assertive self that had lived out of its own resources. As the individual grows in love, the public will behold the blossoming of a new hospitable and generous self, negligent of its own self-interest. This new self trusts in God alone, confident that God paradoxically blesses the faithful by helping them acknowledge their lack of power. The reliance on God rather than one's own strength will be evident to the public and will challenge the public's delusion of self-sufficiency.

Works of love will thus provoke society's implacable hostility (*FSE,* 59-64). Moreover, the life of love requires the rejection of calculations of probable outcomes and cost-benefit analyses, or else the individual would only love the neighbor insofar as it is prudent and not terribly inconvenient. Further, the life of love can prosper only if individuals renounce all self-serving sagaciousness, a renunciation that will be obvious to all. The world will be scandalized by this kind of active self-abnegation and the abandonment of strategies for earthly success (*FSE,* 60-64, 84). In short, the Christian goal of self-emptying, of becoming nothing before God, runs counter to the basic instincts of human society and will therefore incur its wrath. Being the target of society's ire robs an individual of ordinary earthly joys, a price that the Christian witness must be willing to pay. For these reasons, obedience to the law of love intrinsically involves the imitation of Christ's passion: suffering becomes a necessary component of sanctification and an expression of the law's third use. Much of Kierkegaard's later fascination with the theme of martyrdom was motivated by his conviction that the cultured reader had probably been desensitized to the likelihood of society's opposition, and had been socialized into an anemic, domesticated version of Christianity with all the unpleasantness conveniently removed. A preacher may declaim eloquently about martyrdom (a jibe at Bishop Mynster), but if any one of his parishioners actually heeded his words, the preacher would trivialize the message by advising the congregant to "travel, find some diversion, take a laxative" (*WA,* 67). In this context Kierkegaard's intensifying focus on suffering caused by social opposition was an amplified version of Augustine's own call to renounce many of the delights of pagan culture even if that would provoke social ostracism and derail a promising career.

Although allegations of a drastic shift in Kierkegaard's writings may be somewhat exaggerated, his tendency to emphasize the third use of the law while still advocating its second use did indeed produce tensions in his writings. Most obviously, his continuing desire to revitalize repentance (and thus to identify the individual as a sinner) tended to compromise his promotion of the life of active love, including witnessing and suffering. As we have seen, the imitation of Christ's passion is essential to authentic witnessing. Witnessing necessarily involves the reduplication of the crucifixion in the lives of the witnesses. The problem is that sinners do not possess the requisite innocence to reduplicate Christ's suffering love. Sinners cannot witness to "the truth" because they are not "in the truth," which is to say that they do not truly love. Because the seed of sin remains even in regenerated persons of faith, the would-be witnesses can never be certain of the rectitude of their own motivation. The Lutheran theme of *simul justus et peccator*, with its roots in Augustine's anti-Pelagian writings, seems to render the intentional imitation of Christ's passion an impossibility. One of Kierkegaard's fictional authors, a person earnestly longing to grow in Christlikeness, expresses this conundrum in its most provocative form: Does anyone have the moral authority to allow himself to be put to death in order to emulate Christ? (*WA*, 55-89). By extension, one could also ask: Does anyone have the moral authority to allow himself to be persecuted by society in order to emulate Christ?

The willingness to accept persecution and even martyrdom could be motivated by a self-interested desire for personal spiritual integrity and purity, in which case the resolution to suffer would not be a true witness to love because it was not an authentic act of concern for the neighbor. Therefore, the aspiring martyr for love can never be certain that she really is more loving than the loveless population to whom she hopes to witness. Kierkegaard's perplexed pseudonymous author asks: "Do I dare say that I am good or holy?" (*WA*, 76) The ultimate paradox here is that if love is self-emptying, then witnessing to love can never take the form of an assertion of moral or spiritual superiority. Augustine had made much the same point in his arguments against the self-righteous Donatists, who, he claimed, were notably deficient in love.

Kierkegaard does not resolve this issue through any revision of the *simul justus et peccator* doctrine or through the development of a theological anthropology designed to clarify the boundaries of the saintly and the sinful dimensions of the self. Instead, he demonstrates how to deal with the issue through his own act of writing. The essay by a perplexed follower of Christ is itself an act of witnessing that shows how genuine witnessing can be done by abject sinners. Ironically, by confessing that one is not worthy to be a witness, one has already witnessed. The confessor has renounced all claims to self-justification and has thereby surrendered the self-sufficiency that inhibits love for the other. Even something as seemingly innocuous as the confession of the failure to live lovingly is a renunciation of a kind of power, namely, the power of self-salvation. It is a rejection of the religious variant of the ideology of personal initiative and achievement. This humiliating recognition of incapacity in regard to the most important aspect of life has the potential to infuriate any human society that is enamored of self-sufficiency. The confessor did not intend to invite persecution or to emulate Jesus' martyrdom, but the hostility of the world may well be the byproduct of the confession of incapacity. In this paradoxical way, even sinners are capable of an indirect and inadvertent witnessing.

Through the dynamic tensions that exist among his diverse texts, Kierkegaard dramatizes for the reader two countervailing passions that typify the Augustinian heritage: rejoicing in God's free forgiveness apart from all human works, and joyful striving to enact love for God and neighbor. Together these interactive dynamics of gratitude for grace and growth in love constitute salvation. Sometimes individuals need to be sensitized to their need for forgiveness, and sometimes they need to be energized to bear fruit; sometimes they need to be totally receptive, and sometimes they need to exert themselves. As we have seen, these same two dynamics had permeated Augustine's writings. It is the possible conflict between these two poles that threatens to paralyze the Christian life and has inspired a host of attempts to integrate justification and sanctification in a doctrinal formula. Consistent in his antipathy to theological theorizing, Kierkegaard did not seek to demonstrate how justification and sanctification could be integrated through a more conceptually sophisticated doctrinal statement. Yet his writing is an education concerning when and how to be grateful, and when and how to get active. It also teases and provokes the reader to be sensitive to contexts in which humble gratitude is the appropriate sentiment, and to contexts in which vigorous exertion to love the neighbor is most apt. If a happy integration is possible, it will be actualized in the coordination of the passions and the dispositions of the faithful individual — not on paper.

Conclusion

Augustine and Kierkegaard both sought to do justice to the twin foci of the Christian life: the trust that one is already loved by God and the desire to grow in love for God. Like Augustine in his anti-Pelagian polemics, Kierkegaard uses the daunting ideal of God's law to evoke the repentance that spawns receptivity to God's offer of grace. Both of them identify this divine imperative with the Royal Law, the exhortation to love God and one's neighbor. Moreover, both of them regard the impossibility of satisfying it as an incentive to abandon spiritual self-reliance and depend on God. For both Augustine and Kierkegaard, God's love is available now, while we are pilgrims on the road, still sullied and wounded by sin. Like Augustine writing to struggling *viators,* Kierkegaard also uses God's law to encourage positive growth in loving works (sanctification). Both agreed that the law of love serves both as an enticement (because God's love and the life that reflects it are beautiful) and as a disciplinary corrective (because it has imperative force).

Despite these striking parallels, an apparent difference remains. Augustine sometimes (though not consistently) speaks of God's absolute acceptance of the pilgrim (justification) as occurring at the end of the journey, when the pilgrim has sufficiently grown in love (sanctification). This makes sense, given Augustine's conviction that mutuality requires likeness. Kierkegaard, however, insists that God's full acceptance occurs now, while the journey is in progress and the pilgrim remains imperfect and sinful. He insists: "In order to gain the courage to strive, he (the struggling individual) must rest in the blessed assurance that everything is already decided, that he has conquered — in faith and by faith" (*JP* 2, 1473). If God's acceptance of the sinner is what justification means, then justification is not contingent on sanctification. This sensibility informs Kierkegaard's repeated protestations that not even the final attainment of saintliness is in any way meritorious. Augustine, of course, was often quite content to speak of the meritorious nature of a grace-inspired life.

However, the discrepancy between Augustine and Kierkegaard on the relationship of justification and sanctification may not be as profound as it initially seems. Everything hinges on what "justification" is taken to mean. Catholics have tended to identify it with suitability for a relationship with the God of perfect reciprocity; Lutherans, on the other hand, have tended to identify it with the divine acceptance of the sinner. Significantly, both Augustine and Kierkegaard affirm the crucial nature of both. Augustine makes it clear that God is already in a loving relationship with the struggling pilgrim. In this sense, the pilgrim has been "accepted" by God and enjoys God's reconciling love. Conversely, Kierkegaard makes it clear that the goal of Christianity is the attainment of loving mutuality with God. Both of them concur that, in one way, God is with us during the journey, and, in another way, with us at the journey's end. Augustine and Kierkegaard attempt to hold together themes that Catholics and Protestants have tended to separate. Significantly, both of them tended to give the most weight to the way that God is with us at the end of the journey, for that is our goal. If Kierkegaard has a "catholic" moment, this is surely it.

CHAPTER 9

The Church: A Parting of the Ways?

All of the similarities between Augustine and Kierkegaard concerning their respective paths to blessedness that we have seen to this point cannot be fully appreciated without taking the role of the church into account. We must approach this task carefully and cautiously, for it is with the volatile issue of ecclesiology that most commentators are likely to detect not just a divergence between the two thinkers, but an unbridgeable chasm. Indeed, this is where their roads do seem to veer off in opposite directions. Augustine died in his ecclesiastical post, refusing to desert it even though his city was being besieged by Vandals. Kierkegaard died a year or so after having vowed to attend no more worship services (*JP* 6, 6943). Surely the bishop who sanctioned the use of imperial coercion to "compel" Donatists to return to the true church could have little in common with the dying layperson who refused to receive communion from a minion of the state church. By the end of his life, Kierkegaard's contempt for the kind of ecclesiology popularly associated with Augustine was undisguised and bitter. The vehemence of the former's critique of the Danish church establishment inevitably raises the question of whether he and the powerful Bishop of Hippo ever had much in common at all. If the layman and the ecclesiast ended up having such antithetical attitudes toward the church as an institution, then surely the seeds of that divergence must lie in the fundaments of their respective theologies. Differences in historical context certainly could not entirely account for such flagrantly opposed ecclesiastical sensibilities. Or could they? Or might it be that the numerous intersections of their paths that I have suggested thus far are illusory or at least exaggerated?

We should not minimize the differences between Augustine and Kierkegaard on the nature and purpose of the church. Augustine has been rightly remembered as a fervent proponent of the corporate nature of Christianity. Many of his images and conceptual motifs informed the ecclesial visions of such diverse Christians as Martin Luther, John Calvin, and Cardinal Bellarmini, all of whom were the heirs of his magisterial view of the church. Augustine has become celebrated (and vilified) for advocating Cyprian's claim that there is no salvation outside the church. In fact, Richard Price, an Augustine biographer, has noted that his understanding of Christianity was so thoroughly communal that he proposed that the goal for individual Christians should be to have no feeling that was not generally shared by the community of the saints.[1] In Augustine's rhapsodic descriptions of the perfected saints enjoying the vision of God, it is difficult to see how the celestial worshipers are at all individuated. And, though Augustine is often credited with inventing the Western interior self, his descriptions of the church are saturated with collectivist metaphors. Clearly, the individual pilgrim cannot become or remain a Christian without total immersion in the preaching, sacraments, discipline, and fellowship of Christian communities, both local and global.

Kierkegaard, on the other hand, has been accused of being not only an archindividualist, but also an anti-ecclesiastical zealot. More damningly, he has been stigmatized as being thoroughly anticommunal. In 1936, Martin Buber lambasted Kierkegaard for emphasizing the individual's relationship to God so one-sidedly that he succumbed to *acosmism* and *ananthropia*.[2] According to Buber, Kierkegaard was so enthralled with the self's relationship to itself that his much-vaunted love for the neighbor could not be a constitutive structure of selfhood, but was a mere appendage to the interior drama. Similarly, Mark C. Taylor has written that, for Kierkegaard, "the birth of individuality requires severing the umbilical cord of sociality through the difficult labor of differentiating self and other. The one who undertakes this spiritual pilgrimage ever remains a lonely wayfarer."[3] In Taylor's view of Kierkegaard, we must all walk that lonesome highway, and we must walk it by ourselves. More recently, John D. Caputo has lamented that Kierkegaard's final years were infected with a pervasive world-weariness and a suspicion of human communities that was "grim, even masochistic."[4]

1. See Richard Price, *Augustine* (New York: HarperCollins, 1996), p. 82.
2. Martin Buber, *Between Man and Man* (New York: Macmillan, 1965), pp. 211, 213.
3. Mark C. Taylor, *Journeys to Selfhood: Hegel and Kierkegaard* (Berkeley: University of California Press, 1980), pp. 179-80.
4. John D. Caputo, *How To Read Kierkegaard* (New York: W. W. Norton, 2007), p. 112.

Because Kierkegaard could not appreciate the positive role of human communities in the journey to selfhood, he certainly had no comprehension of the constructive possibilities of ecclesial life.

Even those interpreters whose assessments are more moderate discern a sharp divergence between Augustine and Kierkegaard with regard to ecclesiology. Peter Vardy concludes that Augustine saw Christianity as "essentially a communal affair, both in the Church on earth and with the saints in heaven," while "Kierkegaard emphasizes the individual journey of faith and the priority of the individual in relation to God."[5] Augustine champions the notion that the practices of the church community enable its members to become genuine individuals, while Kierkegaard argues that in order to have a genuine community its members must first have become individuals. In many assessments of Kierkegaard, ecclesial community is at most the product of an already healthy individual relationship to God, a view that Augustine could not have fathomed.

To engage in some fanciful anachronistic speculation on the basis of these views, it could be proposed that Kierkegaard would have aligned himself with the enemies of Augustine in most of the church-related controversies of the fourth and fifth centuries. The influential Augustine scholar Eugene TeSelle has noted:

> But from the *social* point of view both Donatism and Pelagianism, in their different ways, represent an attempt to hold on to the Church of the earlier centuries, a Church which did not countenance compromise with the spirit of the age and which anticipated with equanimity remaining in the position of a minority . . . [but] by resisting too close a scrutiny of the actions of the Church and the Empire and the implications of their mutual involvement, Augustine helped open a way to the absorption of semi-pagans, among both the aristocracy and the populace, into the church and an easy alliance of throne and altar.[6]

Like the Donatists and Pelagians, Kierkegaard wanted to "hold on to the Church of the earlier centuries," refused to "countenance compromise with the spirit of the age," and resisted the "easy alliance of throne and altar." He certainly opposed any lessening of the rigor of the Christian life in order to accommodate contemporary "semi-pagans." It could be plausibly argued

---

5. Peter Vardy, *An Introduction to Kierkegaard* (Peabody, MA: Hendrickson, 2008), p. 78.
6. Eugene TeSelle, *Augustine the Theologian* (New York: Herder and Herder, 1970), p. 273.

that in Kierkegaard's dispute with Hans Lassen Martensen and the legacy of Bishop Mynster, Augustine would have identified with Mynster and Martensen. After all, it was Mynster who wanted to open the doors of the sanctuary and invite in the unworthy so that they might experience the church's solace and embrace. It was Mynster and Martensen who were advocates for a comprehensive church and opposed the restriction of the church to a cadre of sincere, ardent imitators of Christ. Mynster and Martensen kept alive Augustine's dream of the church as a hospital for sinners, intentionally including in its fellowship the hypocritical, the lax, and the indifferent. On the other hand, Kierkegaard's enthusiasm for a more stringent "New Testament Christianity" would have situated him with the Donatists, or perhaps in an even more extremely rigoristic category of ecclesiology.

To further corroborate this oppositional view of the two theologians, the underlying differences between Augustine and Kierkegaard on the church resurface with regard to a number of more specific points. For example, Augustine cites the worldwide expansion of the church and Theodosius's decree against idols as validations of the truth of the church, for they were the fulfillment of God's promise to Abraham. Kierkegaard, of course, had no use for any such argument based on ecclesial success. Not only was the logic of the argument invalid, but it implicitly promoted a theology of ecclesial triumphalism, which Kierkegaard found repellent. Furthermore, Kierkegaard was drastically at odds with Augustine's willingness to rely on imperial support for the church. After initially opposing the use of force to close Donatist churches and compel the Donatists to worship in Catholic sanctuaries, Augustine had concluded that God sometimes uses coercive discipline as well as persuasion to draw people to God. Kierkegaard, of course, would have denounced coercion as being utterly inimical to the growth of the sincere passion that the Christian life requires. Finally, Kierkegaard refused to receive communion from priests who were unworthy due to their authorization by the establishment, while Augustine had contended for the objective validity of the sacraments regardless of the spiritual qualities of the officiant or those who authorized him.

In light of these considerations, the perception of a profound difference between Augustine and Kierkegaard in the area of ecclesiology cannot be cavalierly dismissed. However, the exact nature of that difference remains elusive, as do the theological reasons for it. We need to make a careful comparison of the two thinkers in order to determine how such a divergence could have developed from their often surprisingly similar understandings of God, Christ, and the Christian life. Moreover, only such a comparison can reveal the significance of this seeming parting of the ways and its importance for assessing the relationship of Augustine and Kierkegaard.

Augustine: The Church as Mother

Augustine's myriad and scattered reflections on the church are governed by two very different themes. The first is that the church is an extension of the self-giving activity of God enacted in the life, death, and resurrection of Jesus Christ and in the work of the Holy Spirit in the imparting of grace. The second theme is that the church is the corporate dimension of the journey toward God, and thus can be construed according to the model of the individual Christian's striving. The first theme portrays the church as God's gift, while the second theme depicts the church as a human task. For Augustine, the church must be viewed stereoscopically, for it is both a divine benefaction to be received and an ideal to be approximated. Needless to say, this introduces yet another dialectical tension into Augustine's work.

The theme that the church itself is a gift of grace has a certain priority over the theme of the church as a pilgrim society. This concept is so important to Augustine that he can even sometimes describe the church as an extension of the incarnation. The very existence of communities of Christians who gather to praise God, hear the gospel, and celebrate the sacraments is a sheer gift of God to humanity. It is the product of the same extravagantly generous divine intention that assumed human nature in the incarnation. In fact, this motif is yet another expression of the "divine self-giving" dynamic that we have seen permeating Augustine's writings as a whole. As we might expect, many of the subthemes that Augustine had introduced in the discussion of Christ and grace reappear in his doctrine of the church. Accordingly, parallel paradoxes also appear.

Perhaps most importantly, Augustine insists that the Trinity is the primary agent at work in the church, just as the Logos was the primary agent in the incarnate life of Jesus. The existence of the church is not primarily a human achievement, just as God's presence in Jesus was not the fruit of his human virtue. Augustine declares, repeatedly and passionately, that the church is established and preserved by God's activity, not by feeble human efforts. It is God who has instituted the church and continues to draw people into it through the attracting power of Christ's love.

In a similar way, Augustine's analysis of the gratuity of divine love resurfaces in his discussion of God's love for the church. He claims that

God's life-giving solicitude and concern for the church are not based on any internal deficiency or lack in God, as if God needed the companionship of a group of human beings. God does not need a human community to worship and adore God, just as God did not need to create the universe or become incarnate. According to Augustine, God's love in creating and sustaining the church is just as totally gratuitous as was the incarnation. In this sense, the church can be said to be an expression of the life of the Trinity and the free self-giving of the persons of the Trinity to one another in love. Consequently, Augustine describes the church as the "temple" of the Trinity, for it is indwelt by all three persons and thus by the intra-Trinitarian love.[7] The most significant thing about Augustine's use of this kind of discourse is its identification of the church with God's self-giving love and the encouragement of gratitude for that love and reliance on it.

Related to this "temple" image and the focus on the priority of divine action is Augustine's penchant for describing the church as the body of Christ. Augustine repeatedly reminds his readers that Christ is the head, and the church is his body. Once again, Augustine's elaboration of this image involves the use of themes from his doctrine of the incarnation. Just as in the incarnation the two natures of Christ could exchange properties, so also here the properties of Christ can be attributed to the church as his body.[8] Just as the incarnate Lord possesses two natures that cannot be divorced, so also the "whole Christ" is the head together with its members.[9] The wholeness of the body is constituted by all the members together with the head, a point that Augustine makes in order to discourage schism.[10] To further emphasize the intimate nature of this communication, Augustine also describes the church as the bride of Christ.

Because of this communication of properties, the love of God the Son is reflected in the love of the members for God and for one another. Therefore, the church is first and foremost a society of brotherly and sisterly love. For Augustine, love is the church's most essential and definitive attribute. In describing the heavenly city that is the eschatological fulfillment of the church, Augustine insists that the heavenly city is characterized by perfect love of God, and not by the love of self that typifies the earthly city. Love for God manifests itself as genuine love for the neighbor, so that concern for

---

7. Augustine, *Enchiridion*, 15 (56), in *WSA* I, 8.

8. Augustine, *Sermons*, Sermon 341, in *WSA* III, 10.

9. Augustine, *Sermons*, Sermon 62, in *WSA* III, 2.

10. Augustine, *Homilies on the First Epistle of John*, Homily III.4, in *WSA* III, 14.

the well-being of fellow members of the body of Christ is a principal mark of the church, and unselfish love for God and neighbor is thus the vital characteristic that differentiates the church from all other human communities. According to Augustine, this love should be visible and obvious, for it is this love that attracts restless hearts to Christianity and points to the source of love in God.[11]

Not only the existence of the church, but also the oneness of the church, is God's work, just as the oneness of the person of Christ is established by the Logos. Only God's gracious activity can unite Christians of all times and places into one community. Consequently, the unity of Christ's person is reflected in the gift of the unity of his members. Over against the Donatists, Augustine argues that the gift of love undergirds a unity that cannot be broken without forfeiting that love. For Augustine, love — the presence of God in the church — and communal unity are all correlative: where there is no love there can be no unity, and where there is no unity there can be no love. By emphasizing this, Augustine is combating the aspiration of the schismatics to preserve the alleged purity of the church by severing ties with those whom they perceived to be morally and spiritually deficient. He is proposing that the exclusivity and censoriousness of the Donatists were evidence of a fatal lack of love in their hearts. The Donatist preference for images of exclusion to symbolize the church, such as an "enclosed garden" or an "arc," betokened their communal self-centeredness.[12] According to Augustine, unity and love are more important than uniformity of behavior, for love is decisive for salvation and reflects the very being of God.[13] Because he wanted to avoid the exclusivity of the Donatists, Augustine declared their sacraments to be valid, and he concluded that Donatists did not require rebaptism in order to join the Catholic fold. However, he also concluded that their sacraments were not effective, for the Holy Spirit cannot dwell in a church if there is no love in it. It was for this reason that Augustine endorsed Cyprian's claim that there is no salvation outside the church, for he envisioned the church as a fellowship of love.

The incarnation also grounds Augustine's claims about the universality of the church. Because the love of Christ is universal and nonpreferential,

---

11. Augustine, *On Faith and the Creed,* 9-10 (21), in *WSA* I, 8; *Homilies on the First Epistle of John,* Homily X.3, in *WSA* III, 14.

12. See Maureen Tilley, *The Bible in Christian North Africa: The Donatist World* (Minneapolis: Fortress, 1997), pp. 104-13.

13. J. Patout Burns, "Appropriating Augustine Appropriating Cyprian," *Augustinian Studies* 36 (2005): 1-16.

the fellowship of Christian congregations is also global and nontribal. This tenet served as the basis for Augustine's critique of the Donatists' reluctance to show concern for the churches beyond North Africa. For Augustine, the universality of Christ's love could tolerate no such parochialism. The cohesion and vitality of the church are not based on ideological like-mindedness (such as the Donatists' traditional Punic suspicion of the Romanized elite), shared class interests, or ethnic loyalties, for the church's identity is not rooted in ordinary commonalities of blood and culture or any narrow regionalism. With respect to this point, Kierkegaard was in wholehearted agreement, as his critique of both the Danish church establishment and Grundtvig's attempt to synthesize Christianity and Scandinavian folk culture shows.

The priority of the grace of Jesus Christ also grounds Augustine's understanding of the "objectivity" of the sacraments, a term that was still fluid in Augustine's milieu. As we have seen, for Augustine the sacraments are valid apart from the character of the officiant. It is the power of Christ that is at work, not the piety of the human celebrant. It is Christ himself who baptizes, just as it was the gracious power of God that effected the incarnation and awakens faith, hope, and love in individual hearts. Similarly, Augustine declares that in the Eucharist it is Christ who is the true priest.[14] Moreover, it is the voice of God that speaks through the pastor's sermons. Augustine consistently reinforces the point that God's grace is made available to individual pilgrims through the objectivities of ecclesial ritual and practice. The objectivity of God's action through preaching and the administration of the sacraments parallels the objectivity of God's presence in Christ and the objectivity of God's impartation of grace to sinners. The actuality of grace in these ecclesial mediations thus depends solely on God's ordination, not on the merit of the human actors. Any attempt to make the availability of grace contingent on the worthiness of the church's members or leaders would jeopardize the reliability of God's gift and undermine trust, confidence, and reliance on God. Of course, Augustine believed that the purpose of these means of grace was to nurture Christian passions and virtues in the faithful, but he was convinced that the transformation of pathos occurs through participation in the church's worship practices. As he elaborates in his homilies on the First Epistle of John, the visible church has objective marks that identify it, including the preaching of the forgiveness of sins, the offering of grace through sacramental rituals, the reading of Scripture, and acts of

---

14. Augustine, *Sermons*, Sermon 229.2, in *WSA* III, 6.

charity. As we shall see, Kierkegaard also wanted to encourage trust in the reliability of God's grace, but he did not tightly associate that reliability with trust in the church's rituals.

Furthermore, the theme of the objective mediation of grace can be found in Augustine's discussion of the other functions of the church. For example, he maintains that it is Christ, not the bishop, who teaches in Christ's school, the church.[15] The bishop is really a fellow student who is being used by the divine pedagogue to instruct the other pupils. In the same way, Christ proclaims himself through the words of the preacher. Even with respect to discipline and witnessing, it is Christ who is the ultimate agent, for Christ suffers in the travail of the martyrs. Just as Jesus was persecuted during his earthly life, so he is still being persecuted in his ecclesial body; persecution will be the church's lot.[16] Kierkegaard would at least agree about persecution and martyrdom as being reduplications of Christ passion, though he would describe it with the vocabulary of imitation rather than participation. About the operation of divine agency through the church's teaching and preaching, he would be more qualified. As we shall see, the affirmation that God is active depends on the context, and who exactly is preaching and teaching, and what exactly they are saying.

In all these ways Augustine sees Christ's activity of attracting the heart and fueling the pilgrim's journey home as operating through the practices of the church. The church is God's nurturing grace at work. Augustine writes: "[U]nless, therefore, our faith has its roots within a community and a human society, it will not attain full fruition."[17] Because of the primacy of this nurturing function, Augustine likens the church to a mother's milk, whose nourishment we need.[18] For Augustine, this maternal metaphor is crucial for appreciating the role of the church. The church is the mother of our faith: it is in the womb of the church that our love for God gestates. Elaborating on this image, Augustine proposes that because of the unity of Christ and his members, all the faithful who constitute the body of Christ can be said to be the mother of faith collectively. This language is designed to sensitize the reader to the fact that it is the nurturing power of love that makes the church indispensable for spiritual growth.[19]

These many claims about the christological grounding of the church

---

15. Augustine, *Sermons,* Sermon 33A.3, in *WSA* III, 2.

16. Augustine, *Explanations of the Psalms,* Ps. 61.4, in *WSA* III, 14-17.

17. Augustine, *On Faith and the Creed,* 9-10 (21), in *WSA* I, 8.

18. Augustine, *Tractates on the Gospel of John,* 101.5, in *WSA* III, 13.

19. Augustine, *Explanations of the Psalms,* Ps. 47.13, in *WSA* III, 14-17.

and the priority of God's agency in the church have specific rhetorical and edifying purposes: they function as encouragements to trust in and to be grateful for the incarnation of God's grace in the form of a human community. Augustine is persuading the reader to view the church as a social context in which God's gracious presence can be received, celebrated, appropriated, and enacted. In this sense, the church is an extension of the availability of God that commenced with the incarnation, and should be regarded with analogous delight and thankfulness. Christ is present through the corporate acts of supplication, praise, proclamation, and service. If a pilgrim wants to progress in love for God, and feel the lure of love more strongly, that pilgrim must discern God's availability in all the messy details of the church's practices, rituals and structures.

Augustine adds one more crucial christological parallel to this maternal theme: the church reflects the abasement of Christ. It is through the life of the church that the pilgrim learns the humility and self-giving that typifies God's love. Because Augustine was so acutely aware of the temptations of spiritual pride, he countered the impetus toward self-salvation by foregrounding the need to humbly admit debility. The self-propelled flights of the philosophers cannot carry the aspiring pilgrim to the homeland. Augustine criticizes the Platonists, who in their pride did not recognize the incarnation of God in Christ because they refused to admit their need for help.[20] The humility of Christ is an antidote to sinful pride, and that humility is reflected in the life of the church. Augustine writes: "The high priest, you see, who dwells in this house, our Lord Jesus Christ, was pleased to offer himself as an example of humility, to ensure the return of humankind which had gone out from paradise through pride."[21] In a parallel way he exclaims: "Forbid it, Lord, that rich personages should ever be more welcome in your tabernacle than the poor, or the nobility than lowly folk, when your own preferential choice fell upon the weak things of this world in order to shame the strong, upon lowly things, contemptible things and nonentities, as though they really were, to set at naught the things that are."[22] In narrating the story of Victorinus's conversion, Augustine makes the point that it is not walls that make a church, but rather the holy mysteries "instituted by [God's] humble Word."[23] To inspire pilgrims to renounce

---

20. Augustine, *City of God*, X, 29, in *WSA* I, 6-7.
21. Augustine, *Sermons*, Sermon 50.8, in *WSA*, III, 2.
22. Augustine, *Confessions*, VIII, 4 (9), in *WSA* I, 1.
23. Augustine, *Confessions*, VIII, 2 (4), in *WSA* I, 1.

the ways of pride, the church must make its humility visible. Consequently, Augustine opposes the Donatist contention that the church is holy because of the spirituality and virtue of its members. Such a flattering corporate self-understanding would be the quintessence of pride. Rather, according to Augustine, the church is holy because it admits its incapacity and humbly has fellowship with those backsliders and hypocrites whom the Donatists proudly disdained. Charity is made visible by the fact that it covers a multitude of sins. For Augustine, the doctrine of *kenosis,* Christ's self-abasement, points to the need for an inclusive church that does not scruple to embrace the impure.

The second root metaphor that Augustine uses to explicate the nature of the church is that of the Christian life itself. In a way, his use of the incarnation as a lens through which to view the church already suggests this second motif. Just as the Logos assumed ordinary human nature, complete with a human body, so Christ continues to be active and available through a body of ordinary human beings. But the analogy of the church and the incarnation is not perfect. In the incarnation the assumed human nature was free of sin, while that is hardly true in the case of the church. As Augustine insists against the Donatists, the human nature found in the church remains infected with corruption and continues to struggle against its own pride, folly, and worldliness. Therefore, Augustine switches to the metaphor of the pilgrim on the road to the city of God. The church itself, not just the individual wayfarer, is a pilgrim. Just as the metaphor did with regard to individual lives, this motif suggests a movement toward an eschatological *telos:* the church grows into being the perfect body. It has not yet arrived at its destination, but it is en route. Its holiness and blessedness reside in its head — and is only slowly permeating the members.

This metaphorical shift was crucial for Augustine, for it enabled him to argue against the Donatists that righteousness is not the church's mark.[24] Just as the life of the pilgrim on earth manifests a mixture of sin and saintliness, so does the life of the church as a corporate body. Therefore, like individual pilgrims, the church is perpetually engaged in a struggle against the sin that it discovers in itself. The two cities, rooted in two different loves, will continue to strive against each other in the visible church. As it will in the earthly histories of individuals, this corporate struggle within the church will continue until the end of the age. For Augustine, the perdur-

24. Augustine, *Letters,* Letter 93, in *WSA* II, 1-3.

ing presence of sin rules out perfectionism with respect to both individual and corporate lives. It was this metaphor of the pilgrim church, perpetually struggling to overcome the residual sinfulness in itself, that grounded Augustine's claim that the holiness of the human leadership or the general membership is not essential for a true church, for Christian faith and hope are fixed not on sinful human beings as they now are, but on the eschatological power and promise of God to perfect them.[25]

The metaphor of the pilgrim church reinforced Augustine's claim that the church is a mixture of inveterate sinners and genuine lovers of God progressing toward sainthood. The sin/saintliness polarity does not just typify the church's ethos as a whole. The problem of sin in the church is not merely the lamentable fact that many of the saints remain manifestly deficient in sanctity and still have much ground to travel. In addition to this, the sinner-saint distinction divides the membership of the visible church into two categories. The church is a mixed body, inclusive of obdurate sinners bound for damnation and saints headed for the beatific vision. In the visible church on its earthly journey, the tares grow among good grain.[26] Not everyone who is a member of the visible church on earth is among the elect. Only the invisible church, including the saints and angels, is the community of the elect purged of the tares.

The analogy of the church and the individual pilgrim's life also provided a device for Augustine to maintain that the church itself remains in a state of constant dependence on God for justification and sanctification. Against the Donatists, whose rigor allowed for little forgiveness, Augustine portrayed the church as the recipient of God's mercy. Augustine's distinction of the church as it is now, encumbered by sin, and as it later will be, perfected in love, paralleled the theme of sanctification in the individual's life. Sanctification has a corporate dimension as well as an individual one, and in both instances the process will only be completed beyond earthly history. For Augustine, sanctification possesses this irreducibly corporate aspect partly because "whenever joy is shared among many, even the gladness of individuals is increased, for all are affected by the common enthusiasm and they catch the flame from each other."[27] The passions of the Christian life are contagious, as is evident in Augustine's reliance on the inspirational impact of stories of exemplary Christian lives. Even more powerfully, corporate

---

25. Augustine, *Letters,* Letter 53, in *WSA* II, 1-3.
26. Augustine, *Sermons,* Sermon 88.19, in *WSA* III, 3.
27. Augustine, *Confessions,* VIII, 4 (9), in *WSA* I, 1.

actions — preeminently worship — stimulate, channel, and reinforce the longings of the individual's heart.

This second motif of the church as a pilgrim people thus suggests that the church is our task as well as our gift from God. Of course, it is God's grace that is the ultimate agent in the pursuit of that task, but it is a task nonetheless. The church is a challenge as well as a comfort. As the body of Christ, the church should not only receive grace from Christ its head, but as a pilgrim people it should also enact that grace. The church should strive to instantiate faith, hope, and love more thoroughly in its corporate life. The imperative implicit in this metaphor is that the church should be characterized by the intention to grow in obedience, trust, heartfelt compassion, and desire for God.

Augustine's two different root metaphors for the church point in different directions. One foregrounds the objectivity of God's gracious presence with the church, and the other highlights the need for demonstrable growth in Christian virtues. One theme encourages reassurance, confidence, and trust, and the other motivates intentional effort. As Augustine made clear with regard to the individual's life, the first theme is not contingent on the second. The church remains the body of Christ even when its spiritual growth is anemic, faltering, and unsteady. Augustine was no more able to develop a theoretical account of the relationship of these two images of the church than he was able to explain the mystery of the relationship of God's grace and human responsibility in the lives of individuals. Throughout his works those two images of the church are not collapsed but remain held in dialectical tension.

In spite of the irreducible difference, the first image of the church as the body of Christ enjoys a certain priority in Augustine's writings, just as the Logos does in the incarnation and grace does in the Christian life. The church's primary mission is to nurture, which includes providing consolation, reassurance, reconciliation, guidance, and direction. Augustine emphasizes the church as a provider of comfort and support rather than the church as an agent of provocation and challenge. He does not feel a need to emphasize provocation because he presupposes that individuals already possess a restless heart. Therefore, it is not the church's task to stimulate desire and longing, for those dynamics reside in human subjectivity. The church's task is basically to reorient desire in the appropriate direction, largely by displaying the attractiveness of its object that can draw the heart and by offering spiritual power (grace) to augment internal motivation. In imagining his ideal audience, Augustine envisions people like himself who longed for a highest good but did not know the path to it and could not attain it by themselves.[28] His multiple recountings of other people's "conversions" assume that they were already yearning for the light. In Augustine's eyes, human beings are too weak to reach the homeland; to make matters worse, if they are left to their own devices, they do not even realize that they need help. Consequently, they need institutional instrumentalities, the ordinary ecclesial means of grace, to nurture and discipline them. These considerations led Augustine to affirm that God works through a community to provide the necessary support and guidance. The church does not need to go out of its way to generate uncertainty or risk, for those things can be presupposed. It was at this point that Kierkegaard would most sharply diverge from the Bishop of Hippo.

Kierkegaard and the Church as an Eschatological Hope

Even the most cursory reading of Kierkegaard's later writings will reveal that his discourse about the church is very different from Augustine's extravagant language of nurture. After the death of Bishop Mynster in 1854, and Martensen's subsequent lionization of the latter as "a truth-witness," Kierkegaard launched his infamous no-holds-barred critique of the Danish ecclesiastical establishment. Far from nurturing faith as a mother, he said, the state church is such an egregious distortion of authentic Christianity that it actually militates against the development of true Christian pathos. Kierkegaard denounced "the established order" as "a crime" and declared it to be "Christianly indefensible" (*TM*, 69-70). With considerable venom he attacked its baptisms, confirmations, marriages, preaching, and clergy, and he declined to participate in the church's institutional life. Much of his scathing critique was founded on his claim that genuine Christianity involves a life of persecution and socially induced suffering, while the aberrant established church identifies the Christian life with social conformity and bourgeois felicity. In the heat of his assault, Kierkegaard located much of the problem in the church's "leniency," "mildness," "coddling," and its indiscriminate and unqualified offer of worldly comfort. This kind of discourse would appear to be a far cry from Augustine's maternal imagery.

Given the intensity of its rhetoric, the later "attack" writings have attracted the most attention of those trying to decipher Kierkegaard's un-

28. Augustine, *Confessions*, X, 3 (3)-4 (6), in *WSA* I, 1.

derstanding of the church. Much of the spirited — and sometimes vitriolic — interpretive debate has revolved around the issue of the extent to which "the attack" either is or is not a development of Kierkegaard's earlier attitudes toward the church. Some scholars have found these late writings to be a significant departure from Kierkegaard's previous works. For example, N. H. Søe proposes that the perceived shift was attributable to an emotional disturbance that Kierkegaard could no longer master in his last years.[29] This ascription of the late writings to a psychological problem had even been suggested by Kierkegaard's elder brother Peter at Søren's funeral. Anthony Rudd finds the late writings to be so at odds with Kierkegaard's earlier work that they are a heretical rejection of not only sociality but finitude.[30] Taking a more moderate approach, Valter Lindström discerns a shift toward regarding persecution as an essential feature of the Christian life, and a movement away from seeing self-denial for the sake of neighbor as the form of suffering that Christian love requires.[31] Further, Otto Bertelsen locates the change in Kierkegaard's work even more basically in his growing attention to the visibility of the Christian life, which was a departure from his earlier insistence on the hidden inwardness of faith.[32] In these views, Kierkegaard's final understanding of Christianity was so ascetic and individualistic that it really had no room for an empirical Christian community.

Disagreeing with the trajectory of the above interpretations, other scholars have concluded that Kierkegaard's attack on Christendom was the culmination of the rigorous view of Christianity that he had always held.[33] Niels Thulstrup argues that Kierkegaard's thought was always dichotomous and always emphasized the incompatibility of the lofty Christian ideal with ordinary forms of social life.[34] David Law has pointed out that throughout his writings Kierkegaard uses irony as a tool to critique the idolization of

29. N. H. Søe, "Søren Kierkegaard og kirkekampen," in Gregor Malantschuk and N. H. Søe, eds., *Søren Kierkegaard's Kamp mod Kirke* (Copenhagen: Munksgaards Forlag, 1956), pp. 45-75.

30. Anthony Rudd, *Kierkegaard and the Limits of the Ethical* (Oxford: Clarendon Press, 1993), pp. 168-69.

31. Valter Lindström, *Efterföljelsens Teologi hos Sören Kierkegaard* (Stockholm: Svenska Kyrkans Diakonistyrelses Bokförlag, 1956), pp. 136-62.

32. See Otto Bertelsen, *Den kirkelige Kierkegaard og den "Antikirkelige"* (Copenhagen: C. A. Reitzel, 1999).

33. Gregor Malantschuk, "Søren Kierkegaard's Angreb paa Kirken," in Malantschuk and Søe, *Søren Kierkegaard's Kamp mod Kirke*, pp. 7-47.

34. Niels Thulstrup, *Kierkegaard and the Church in Denmark* (Copenhagen: C. A. Reitzel Forlag, 1984), pp. 257-59.

social entities, using it as a negative moment to clear the ground for healthier growth.[35] Timothy Dalrymple also contends that the late writings are not as radically different from the earlier ones as they first appear to be, for they are designed to expose the disparity of the actual church and ideal Christianity, a project that had always been central to Kierkegaard's work.[36]

The disparity and variation in assessments of the relationship of Kierkegaard's earlier works to his final writings suggests that his reflections about the church were complex and probably evolving. To move beyond a flat-footed contrast of Augustine and Kierkegaard, we must consider the reasons for Kierkegaard's critique of the Danish church establishment and explore the possible roots of those reasons in broader themes in his theological vision. As we shall see, the sources of his discontent were multiple, though often interconnected. Only by untangling the various strands can we attempt a more nuanced comparison with Augustine.

Oddly, given the extreme vitriol of some of his broadsides, one of Kierkegaard's primary motivations in critiquing the established church was to preserve the radical nature of Christian love. Augustine and Kierkegaard were in agreement that the love commandment should guide any effort to understand the nature and purpose of the church. As his writing progresses, Kierkegaard maintains more and more forcefully that Christian love must be active (even though its roots remain hidden) and thus visible in the public arena. Augustine was in entire agreement. As we have seen, Kierkegaard also increasingly emphasizes the sad reality that the "world" is implacably hostile to Christian love. The selfish values of ordinary human society and the self-giving values of Christianity are antithetical and incompatible. So far, Kierkegaard is in continuity with Augustine's schema of the two divergent cities with their two divergent loves. According to Kierkegaard's final critique of the Danish church, Christianity is "precisely what the natural man is most opposed to, is to him an offense" (*TM,* 169).

A few years earlier Kierkegaard had asserted much the same thing, lamenting that Christianity and the world "have the very opposite views, that what the one calls good the other calls evil" (*JFY,* 96), and warning that the aspiring Christian must learn that "love is not loved, that it is hated,

35. David Law, "Irony in the Moment and the Moment in Irony: The Coherence and Unity of Kierkegaard's Authorship with Reference to *The Concept of Irony* and the Attack Literature of 1854-1855," in Robert L. Perkins, ed., *International Kierkegaard Commentary: "The Moment" and Late Writings* (Macon, GA: Mercer University Press, 2009), pp. 71-100.

36. Timothy Dalrymple, "On the Bronze Bull of Phalaris and the Art and Imitation of Christ," in Perkins, *"The Moment" and Late Writings,* pp. 165-98.

that it is mocked, that it is spat upon, that it is crucified in this world" (*FSE*, 84). This theme was not even new in the early 1850s, for Kierkegaard had expressed the same sentiment in *Works of Love* (*WL*, 192), "The Gospel of Sufferings" (*UDSV*, 329-330), and "Does a Human Being Have a Right to Let Himself Be Put to Death for the Truth?"[37] As we have seen in the discussion of sanctification, his sensitivity to the antithesis of Christianity's love and the world's lovelessness increased over the years. This perception of a fundamental valuational dichotomy was responsible for Kierkegaard's growing valorization of the martyr as the Christian ideal. For Kierkegaard, therefore, the imitation of Christ's humility and abasement, which are necessary dimensions of Christ's self-giving love, inevitably leads to the requirement to be prepared to imitate his passion. The "requirement" of leading such a life, in which society's animosity could turn lethal, is implied by the love commandment. In order to witness to Christ through works of love, the Christian must be prepared to suffer at the hands of society. Kierkegaard's problem with the Danish established church was that the venerable institution seemed to be intent on obscuring this requirement — in fact, was busy trying to nullify it.

This conviction about the suffering, persecuted nature of the Christian life inspired many of Kierkegaard's more specific critiques of his contemporary church. Most shockingly, in his view, pastors failed to even proclaim this requirement or alert their flocks to the connection between suffering and the effort to live a life of love (*TM*, 4-6). Their sermons about suffering for the faith wrongly identified suffering with the ordinary woes that afflict all human life, and dissociated suffering from the controversial practice of witnessing through works of love. At most, the aesthetic admiration of the sufferings of Christ displaces the proclamation that the Christian life is the way of the cross.

To compound the problem, pastors did not lead a life of self-sacrifice themselves; therefore, when they did mention the sufferings of Christ or Christian discipleship, their words were evacuated of meaning. As we have seen, Kierkegaard insists that the way an ethically or religiously significant message is communicated helps constitute its meaning, for the appropriate form of pathos (including behavioral dispositions) must be exhibited. Because pastors do not live self-sacrificially, and thus do not attract the hostil-

---

37. See Sylvia Walsh, "Dying to the World and Self-Denial in Kierkegaard's Religious Thought," in Robert L. Perkins, ed., *International Kierkegaard Commentary: For Self-Examination and Judge for Yourself!* (Macon, GA: Mercer University Press, 2002), pp. 169-97.

ity of the surrounding loveless society, their sermons about the sufferings of Christ are vacuous. The clergy, conforming to the ethos of economic individualism, have devised a scheme to make a comfortable living off the fact that someone else was flogged (*TM*, 84). Kierkegaard snarls contemptuously that the clergy "lives on Jesus Christ's having been crucified" (*TM*, 31) rather than imitating the crucifixion. Such a disjunction of life and speech renders it virtually impossible to acquire a clear understanding of Christian concepts.

Returning to a theme discussed above: part of Kierkegaard's discontent with the church's proclamation was due to its undialectical emphasis on grace. Kierkegaard laments: "The official 'proclamation' [taking the word in its double meaning] here in this country, if placed alongside the New Testament, is, in my opinion, a perhaps well-meant attempt to make a fool of God . . ." (*JP* 6, 6943). The conviction that God is gracious to sinners was translated as meaning that "God has no expectations." Basking in God's acceptance undercut the notion that the individual should strive in fear and trembling to actualize an extraordinarily elevated ideal. According to Kierkegaard, in the context of "Golden Age" Copenhagen, this comforting association of the church with the notion that God's grace makes no real demands merely reinforced bourgeois complacency and encouraged romantic self-indulgence. Surely Augustine would have been just as alarmed as Kierkegaard was at the implicit message that the Christian life does not involve strenuous intentional striving.

Kierkegaard also condemns the close alliance of church and state as another factor contributing to the erosion of the ideal of the Christlike life of suffering, persecuted love. That unholy marriage of throne and altar and the consequent conferral of a privileged status in the civil society to the clergy broadcast the implicit message that the Christian life is fully compatible with prosperity, power, and prestige. Kierkegaard warns:

> Then the Way . . . has become something else, not the one in the New Testament: in abasement, hated, abandoned, persecuted and cursed to suffer in the world — No, the Way is: admired, applauded, honored, and knighted to make a brilliant career! (*TM*, 22)

To be a Christian is to be rewarded with worldly honors and perhaps a handsome salary. The radical demands of love for the neighbor are commuted to the much less onerous expectations of domestic felicity.

It was not just the fact of official establishment that disarmed the church, but also the church's accommodation to popular sensibilities. As David Law has noted, Kierkegaard's polemic against the established church was partly a function of his critique of bourgeois liberalism and the way that economic individualism had infiltrated the church.[38] This diabolical amalgamation of the bourgeois ideology of self-gratification with the message of the church blinds potential pilgrims to the educational potential of suffering. According to Kierkegaard, suffering at the hands of society can teach individuals to rely on God, not the world. It can also be a clarification that the goal of the Christian life is the attainment of a loving character, not acclamation and success. By associating "God's blessings" with prosperity, the church's proclamation and example incapacitated individuals from discerning the loving pedagogy of God in their sufferings.

Furthermore, the identification of being Christian with being born and baptized in Denmark further obscured the rigorous nature of the Christian requirement. The illusion that one is a Christian by birth discouraged inwardness and the striving to actualize an ideal. Christianity degenerated into a tribalism that celebrated the immediate possession of God's favor and forgot that Christianity posits an arduous pursuit of a lofty *telos*. Rather than realizing that they were on the road, Danish Lutherans thought that they were already at the destination.[39] In his attempt to destabilize this complacent cultural Christianity, Kierkegaard was returning to his theme in *Practice in Christianity:* that the church on earth is always militant — and never triumphant (*PC*, 215-17). Surely Augustine would have agreed.[40]

Kierkegaard also complains that the church's focus on the objectivity of grace in the sacraments and proclamation of the gospel encouraged complacency and a failure to appreciate the demands of suffering love. In 1851 he criticized the Augsburg Confession for identifying the church with the right teaching of the Word and the celebration of the sacraments, because the definition omitted the "existential" factor (*JP* 1, 600). This undialectical trust in objectivity turned Christianity into paganism. Long before the final attack, Climacus had cautioned that without subjective appropriation,

---

38. Law, "Irony in the Moment," pp. 66-68.

39. See Sylvia Walsh, *Kierkegaard: Thinking Christianly in an Existential Mode; Kierkegaard's Dialectic of Christian Existence* (University Park: Pennsylvania State University Press, 2005), pp. 187-91.

40. See Jack Mulder, Jr., "The Catholic Moment? On the Apostle in Kierkegaard's 'The Difference between a Genius and an Apostle,'" in Robert L. Perkins, ed., *International Kierkegaard Commentary: Without Authority* (Macon, GA: Mercer University Press, 2006), pp. 203-34.

the practice of infant baptism misleadingly gives the impression that one becomes a Christian through the efficacy of an external ceremony (*CUP* 1, 363-68). It is significant that this critique of the church is not focused on the issue of this establishment or the amalgamation of the church and the surrounding culture. This criticism seems to cut to the heart of Augustinian/Lutheran understandings of the church. At this point Augustine's response to Kierkegaard would be more nuanced, with many qualifications introduced. While Augustine would agree that some faith must be present in the recipient in order for the sacramental acts of the church to be efficacious, he would protest that the objectivity of God's offer of grace must also be emphasized. Individuals need to be encouraged to trust the church as a means of grace in order to grow in Christlikeness.

All of these critiques are aimed at aspects of the life of the church that discourage the recognition of the full depth and rigor of the love commandment and the persecution that inevitably follows from trying to live it out. According to Kierkegaard, this obfuscation of the requirement makes repentance and the appreciation of grace impossible. Kierkegaard is not denying the doctrine of justification by grace, nor is he minimizing the need for grace to grow in love for God and neighbor (*CD,* 187; *PC,* 227). He never claims that loving works, persecution, or even martyrdom could be in any way meritorious. Rather, Kierkegaard is arguing that the forgiveness aspect of God's gracious disposition toward humanity does not abrogate God's requirement (*TM,* 47). At times Kierkegaard claims that all he wanted was a little "honesty," for the church to admit that the lives of its members fall woefully short of the ideal. By not proclaiming and trying to live out the implications of the love commandment, the church had sabotaged the Lutheran terrified conscience and the more general Augustinian sense of the need to rely on God's grace in all things.

Augustine probably would have had some sympathy with many of Kierkegaard's criticisms of the ecclesial establishment. Most of them focused on the failure of the church to proclaim the gospel and to live out the gospel; most of them involved the accusation that the church had diluted the gospel through its alliance with the state and the surrounding culture. The church, Kierkegaard feared, had sold out to the world, and the world's allergic reaction to self-sacrificial love had infected the church. In different ways, the church has accommodated itself both to the conservative culture of the crown and to the more modern culture of the crowd. In Augustinian terms, the terrestrial city, with its love of self, had come to dominate the visible church and had thereby obscured the vision of the celestial city. But these criticisms were mostly targeted at abuses of the church. Presumably these issues, though very serious, could be corrected through a program of thorough-going reform and spiritual renewal of the church. In principle, Augustine could well have agreed with all of this without retracting his claim that the church is the body of Christ and our spiritual mother. There is nothing about the nature of the church that makes such a colossal distortion of the gospel inevitable, unless it is assumed that individuals are so thoroughly depraved that they will always corrupt the church in this outrageous manner. That would imply that the church is so severely vulnerable to sinful distortions that nothing can be done to protect or correct it. Kierkegaard evidently did not believe that, for he continued to write as if his words might have some salutary impact on the church. Even in his attack literature he continued to hold up the examples of New Testament Christianity and the church of the martyrs as correctives. His practice implied that some sort of alternative form of community was possible. Augustine, too, was no stranger to ecclesial reform, and he came to be critical of the Eusebian marriage of Christianity and the ideology of empire. Perhaps the divergence of Augustine and Kierkegaard on the issue of the church has been grossly overestimated.

Such a conclusion would be premature. There were deeper issues that divided Augustine and Kierkegaard. These deeper issues were not restricted to matters of reform or the disengagement of the church from the culture. Rather, they revolved around the basic nature of the relationship of individuals to communities in general, including church communities. These differences are much more difficult to negotiate.

Perhaps Kierkegaard's most troubling critique of the church is that an individual's overidentification with a communal ethos inevitably squelches passion. According to Kierkegaard, collectivities like the animal herd, or the modern crowd, are passionless. For example, by assuming that the popular opinion of the moment is the unquestioned truth, the "public" has eliminated uncertainty. People no longer seriously wonder how they can find an eternal happiness, assuming instead that happiness is the state of being just like all the others. If one is in doubt about the meaning of life or the nature of the highest good, all one must do is consult a newspaper with a wide circulation and adopt the opinion of the editor. The truth is plain, and the public knows what it is, thanks to the new magisterium of the popular press. Without uncertainty, risk evaporates — and without risk, passion dissipates. Kierkegaard's exposure of the passionlessness of the "crowd," which is a modern invention, applies to any collectivity that guarantees indubitable truth. The church as a homogeneous, ideologically uniform society could manifest the same group-think tendencies typical of the crowd. Kierkegaard feared that this was indeed the case, for uncertainty and risk were discouraged by the church. He complains that the problem with Mynster was that he had "never been out in 70,000 fathoms of water and learned out there" (*JP* 5, 5961). Kierkegaard found the variety of ecclesial "rest and peace" that Mynster promised to be spiritually stultifying. Similarly, he feared that Martensen's conviction that the exalted and glorified Christ provides certainty to the members of his body would induce spiritual slumber.

In opposition to this ethos of assurance, Kierkegaard claims that the "individual" is a "higher determinant" than "fellowship" (*PC,* 223). He declares this not because of any commitment to bourgeois individualism (with which he had no sympathy) but because the human lifespan is supposed to be a time of individual testing. He explains:

> Christianly, struggling is always done by single individuals, because spirit is precisely this, that everyone is an individual before God, that "fellowship" is a lower category than "the single individual," which everyone can and should be. . . . But this life is indeed a time of testing, of unrest, and therefore "the congregation" does not belong in time but belongs first in eternity, where it is, at rest, the gathering of all the single individuals who endured in the struggle and passed the test. (*PC,* 223)

The eschatological congregation will be a collection of individuals who all faced risk and uncertainty, and consequently developed passion. At most then, the earthly, visible congregation could be nothing more than a gathering of spiritually struggling individuals. This anticollectivist streak in Kierkegaard was a function of his suspicion that communities encourage consensus, and consensus undermines uncertainty and risk, and consensus thus subverts the passion that the Christian virtues require.

A closely related factor contributed to Kierkegaard's suspicion of communally shaped identities. In Kierkegaard's view, the individual's identification with a collectivity militates against the self-ascription of responsibility. By submerging one's identity in a group, the individual loses the urgency and singularity of standing alone before God. Kierkegaard relies on the image of God's Judgment Day to insist that life is an examination, and that the individual episodes in our lives — and the shape of our lives as a whole — are being evaluated by God. God's judgment is exquisitely individualized: it is not families, congregations, or nations that will stand before the ultimate throne of judgment; rather, judgment intrinsically differentiates individual from individual, separating sheep from goats.

In Kierkegaard's view, which here diverges sharply from Augustine's, the nurturing image of the church community works at cross-purposes with the need to develop self-responsibility. The image of the church as nurturer inflates the type and degree of spiritual help that one person can expect to receive from another. It is axiomatic for Kierkegaard that there are limits to the kind of aid that individuals can offer each other in religious matters. Because faith is a matter of passionate subjectivity, involving personal risk and the self-ascription of responsibility, no person can be the decisive factor in another person's coming to have faith. By suggesting that membership in an institution confers or promotes salvation, even if the codicil is added that the membership must be a sincere matter of the heart, an inflated view of the role of that institution is encouraged. Rather than assuming responsibility for the individual's own God-relationship, the individual will begin to trust in the ideological consensus and contagious emotions of the group.

Finally, and most damningly according to Kierkegaard, any immersion of the individual in a corporate entity would make authentic love impossible. For Kierkegaard, love involves self-giving, and self-giving requires that there is a self in place to give. The love of the members of any group for one another is really a sophisticated form of self-love, for the putative love is based on the perception of commonality or on the reciprocal meeting of needs. Christian love always has the individual's relationship to God as a "middle term," and that relationship is always individuating. Moreover, Christian love is other-regarding, for it is intent on helping the neighbor, quite independently of the interests of the lover. Kierkegaard frequently suggests that such an other-regarding orientation is an impossible stance to maintain in a collectivity, for any collectivity is based on corporate self-interest. That self-interest could be quite rarefied, such as the desire to appear to be philanthropic, but it is self-interest nonetheless.

These criticisms of the church cut deeper than Kierkegaard's more limited and focused objections to the church's capitulation to hegemonic cultural values. And the criticisms seem to apply not only to the established church but to any church. Vernard Eller may have been a bit too optimistic when he hailed Kierkegaard as an advocate of classic Protestant sectarianism and of the notion of a gathered church of committed believers.[41] As

41. See Vernard Eller, *Kierkegaard and Radical Discipleship: A New Perspective* (Princeton: Princeton University Press, 1968).

Christopher Barnett has shown, Kierkegaard's reservations about ecclesiastical communities would pertain to sectarian churches, such as the Hutterites, or the free congregations, such as the Grundtvigians, just as much as to an established church.[42] Kierkegaard carefully and consistently distances himself from the self-righteousness of the sectarian groups and from the ecclesial romanticism of the Grundtvigians. He had no more sympathy for separatism than he did for the establishment, for he was suspicious of the power of any collectivity to minimize individual responsibility and passion. At times Kierkegaard tends to link the need for congregational life with the more basic human need for sociality, which he identified as a mere animal instinct. Consequently, the church can be described as a divine concession to our animal nature (*JP* 4, 4341). Such remarks have led Bruce Kirmmse to conclude that Kierkegaard's view of Christianity is too unsocial to have much use for the concept "congregation" at all.[43] This apprehension was a world apart from Augustine's enthusiasm for the church's nurturing potential.

But Kierkegaard's suspicion of collectivities and his lack of interest in sketching an alternative ecclesiology does not mean that he had no use for any kind of church community or any of the functions traditionally performed by the church. He frequently describes himself as a "gadfly" whose mission was to reform the church and perhaps trigger an awakening. As we have seen, Kierkegaard uses the prayer books, hymnals, catechisms, and confessions of the church, is well aware of their value, and often commends them for devotional purposes. Also, he insists that Christian pathos requires the communication of authoritative concepts and schooling in the use of those concepts. As we have seen, Climacus describes a new kind of subjectivity that was only made possible by an authoritative "dialectical" element. In practice, "Christian concepts" point to the basic doctrinal heritage of the church, which he took to be a roughly accurate exposition of biblical themes.[44] He remarks that "a Christian dogmatics is a development out of Christ's activity" (*JP* 1, 412). Of course, he was certainly Protestant enough to insist on the primary authority of the Bible, but in practice he

---

42. See Christopher Barnett, *Kierkegaard, Pietism, and Holiness* (Farnham, UK: Ashgate, 2011), pp. 111-212.

43. Bruce Kirmmse, "'But I am almost never understood . . .' Or, Who Killed Søren Kierkegaard?" in George Pattison and Steven Shakespeare, eds., *Kierkegaard: The Self in Society* (Basingstoke, UK: Macmillan, 1998), p. 188.

44. See Arnold Come, *Kierkegaard as Theologian: Recovering My Self* (Montreal: McGill-Queen's University Press, 1996), pp. 27-36.

read the Bible through the lens of the church's historic teachings. In all of this it is clear that Kierkegaard valued the church as a transmitter of the Christian tradition. Some agency needs to present the attractive and offensive picture of the self-offering God to humanity.

Ironically, the same understanding of Christian love that led Kierkegaard to critique the church also provided some clues for a possible Christian community that would be acceptable to him. The basis of any genuine Christian community would, for Kierkegaard — like any true Augustinian — have to be love.[45] It is significant that in the midst of his bitter attack on Christendom, Kierkegaard published a sermon that he had delivered a few years earlier, "The Unchangeableness of God," which highlights God's love as the fundament. He reiterates his perennial theme that God, out of love, wants to transform us, and he suggests that our transformation may be fostered by some social channels. These themes have roots in his much earlier *Works of Love*. In that volume he describes the band of disciples as "a society of love" (*WL*, 122), and he observes that their purpose was "not mutual flattery but mutual assistance to humility before God" (*WL*, 122). This remark suggests that communities can help build up a person in humility — and presumably also in love. This possibility coheres with Kierkegaard's central contention, in *Works of Love,* that to love someone is to help build him up in love. Kierkegaard proposes this: "To love another person means to help him to love God and to be loved means to be helped." Notice the implication of reciprocity, which could serve as the basis for a new kind of Christian community. The goal would be a church based on neighbor-love, with each member seeking to build up the others in love.

Of course, there would need to be limits set on the kind of help that can be offered. The most loving thing that one person can do for another is to help that person stand alone before God. That goal would require a church that functioned in the way that Kierkegaard's work did, for the aim of his writings was always to help individuals stand alone before God. This reconceived role of the church would require the indirect stimulation of self-concern and self-responsibility, the preservation of risk and uncertainty, and the presentation of both the attractiveness and the offensiveness of the Christian life. Part of this ecclesial activity would involve "presupposing love" in the other so that love could be "loved forth." This kind of ecclesial mission would also require a community that made clear the nature of the

45. David Gouwens, *Kierkegaard as Religious Thinker* (Cambridge: Cambridge University Press, 1996), p. 226.

Christian ideal, which would in turn require exemplary leaders who were active imitators of Christ, all risking persecution and suffering.[46] The combination of qualities identified here might be very difficult to encourage and harmonize, but it is not utterly impossible. In theory at least, structures and strategies could be developed that could foster conditions in which individuals could encourage one another to freely give themselves to God and their neighbor in love.

Conclusion

But even with the envisioning of an appropriately Kierkegaardian kind of ecclesial community, it must still be admitted that Kierkegaard does sharply diverge from Augustine on the relationship of the individual to the congregation. Even if it is possible to imagine both of them agreeing that the purpose of the church is to promote growth in love, they would see the church doing this in very different ways. Augustine views the individual Christian life as the fruit of God's grace operating through the practices of the community. His own "conversion" involved his willingness to submit to that corporate discipline and nurture. According to Augustine, the prideful individual, intent on self-salvation, is healed by encountering the lowly Christ through the lowly church. The church is an active agent in exposing the individual to the picture of the self-giving God — through its proclamation, its sacraments, and the love enacted within it. What individuals need is to be humbled and then loved. God offers this attractive love through a community and its practices; that is the primary tool that God uses to draw the heart. The restless heart needs to be redirected, focused, and attracted.

For Kierkegaard, however, the single individual's relationship to God cannot be seen as primarily the product of God's working through a congregation. The individual's relationship to God determines the individual's relationship to the congregation (*JP* 1, 595), not vice versa. This is not to say that the individual cannot be challenged and provoked by the church, or informed by the church, or presented with the picture of the attractive/offensive Christ by the church. But all the church can really do is help the individual to stand alone before God, and then get out of the way.

Behind this difference in ecclesial sensibilities between Augustine and Kierkegaard lies a difference in their assessments of what is wrong with peo-

---

46. See Barnett, *Kierkegaard, Pietism, and Holiness.*

ple. Augustine presupposed the viability and strength of the restless heart, and he wanted to redirect, attract, and shape it. Kierkegaard, however, is worried about the restless heart's impairment. For Kierkegaard, the most urgent problem is that contemporary people have difficulty developing the requisite concern about one's own self and the sense of responsibility for the direction of one's own life. The culture and the church have developed a spiritual anesthesia that tranquilizes the restless heart. For Kierkegaard, that passionless somnolence is the root problem generated by Christendom. But Kierkegaard extends his critique to conclude that excessive reliance on any community would discourage passion. To prevent that from happening, Kierkegaard emphasizes the uncertainty and offensiveness of Christianity over against Augustine's concentration on the church's enactment of Christ's nurturing love.

Both Augustine and Kierkegaard regarded the Christian life as a gift and as a task, and both wanted the dialectic of those two themes to be recapitulated in the church. But given their different contexts, they emphasized different poles of the dialectic. Augustine's main concern was to combat pride and concupiscence, while Kierkegaard's main concern was to combat passionlessness. However, the suspicion remains that the difference between them in emphasis was not just due to a difference in historical context and thus a difference in perceived threats. Augustine consistently gives a certain priority to the gift aspect of God's grace, and Kierkegaard consistently responds that the gift will not be appreciated unless a risky task is being pursued. As a result, Augustine imagines a church that is like a nurturing mother, and Kierkegaard imagines (at least his writings contain the resources for him to imagine) a church that is like a spiritual provocateur.

CHAPTER 10

Conclusion: Two Edifying Theologies of Self-Giving

The trajectories of Augustine's writings and Kierkegaard's writings are partly parallel and partly divergent, but perhaps not as divergent as they initially appeared to be. The two thinkers, in fact, were not as different as Kierkegaard himself sometimes thought they were. Admittedly, Kierkegaard's explicit comments about Augustine do seem to alternate between a profound appreciation of his work and a deep suspicion of it, applauding some aspects of his thought and decrying other aspects. In so doing, Kierkegaard was often reflecting the ambivalence in the largely Lutheran-mediated picture of Augustine that he had inherited. However, when we compare Kierkegaard's writings to Augustine's on the wide variety of theological topics that we have examined, a definite pattern becomes evident in the vacillation of approbation and condemnation in Kierkegaard's overt assessments of the Bishop of Hippo. The comparison of Kierkegaard's and Augustine's works reveals a consistent pattern of substantive agreement about the edifying purposes of their various theological assertions, whether the issue at hand is the doctrine of God, original sin, Christology, soteriology, or whatever.

This parallelism is evident in the theological topics that they chose to highlight and the issues that they chose to address. As we have seen, both writers implicitly organized their theological reflections around the theme of the individual's journey home to God, a journey that is really a function of the more basic journey of God to the individual through the self-giving of Christ. Because of the centrality of this journey motif, the narrative of salvation informing the individual's life, extending from creation by God through the fall into sin and on to reconciliation with God and growth in faithful love, furnishes the depth structure of their writings. In this basic

379

pattern based on the individual's life, they treat God as the source, support, and goal of the journey, and they consider Christ to be the crucial enabler and inspirer of the movement forward toward the goal. Because of this, I have chosen to organize this volume around the theological topics prominent in any discussion of the drama of creation, fall, and salvation. I believe that this strategy has been appropriate because it was this very structure that became the standard way of organizing most theological textbooks, including the ones that Kierkegaard used. The conventional sequence of topics, governed by the dynamics of the individual's religious life, was, of course, inspired by Augustine's reflections.

Moreover, a further parallelism is evident in the way the two thinkers approach the theological task in bringing pastoral and therefore rhetorical concerns to the forefront. Kierkegaard may well have not intended this substantive and sometimes rhetorical parallelism, and probably was not even conscious of its extent. But these parallels far outweigh the divergences. Even when Kierkegaard disagrees with his venerable predecessor, he is consistent in the way he parts company with him. Almost always — except with regard to the church — it is only Augustine's penchant for using these theological themes as a springboard for speculation that provokes Kierkegaard's ire.

These parallelisms invite some summary reflections concerning the general relationship of the two bodies of work. Having taken a close look at Augustine and Kierkegaard on the specific theological topics that implicitly structure their works, I shall now explore more synoptically the global similarities and differences between them. In doing so, I shall highlight the aspects of their works that most dramatically seem to diverge or converge, and the aspects that have triggered the most interpretive controversy. First, I shall consider the issue of the relationship of doctrinal convictions and existential passions in their writings. This, of course, was an issue that gripped Kierkegaard himself and has subsequently inspired much heated scholarly debate. Next I shall examine the relationships of edification and speculation in Augustine's and Kierkegaard's respective writings, for it is here that they most sharply seem to part company. Then I shall shift attention to the content of the pathos that they sought to encourage, again looking for overlaps and contrasts. Finally, I shall consider a unique and somewhat unsettling feature of the pathos that permeates the literary output of both — the dialectical nature of their efforts to edify the reader.

Doctrines versus Passions?

As we have seen, Kierkegaard was well aware of the plurality of interpretations of Augustine in his own Lutheran culture and somewhat aware of the diversity of perspectives within Augustine's own pages. Kierkegaard imbibed the ambivalence about Augustine present in his intellectual environment. From a variety of sources, including Neander, de Wette, and Böhringer, Kierkegaard was introduced to an Augustine who was a passionate penitent and an ardent lover of God. That was the Augustine who prayed, cried, rejoiced, hoped, and praised, and by so doing showed his readers the existential import of Christian doctrines. Kierkegaard was almost always in agreement with that passionate Augustine, as his explicitly laudatory remarks reveal. More importantly, his expositions of the passions and dispositions that are associated with particular doctrinal themes usually parallel Augustine's own presentations. The edifying purposes of Augustine and Kierkegaard usually mirrored each other. (The issues of the church and the sacraments were the notable exceptions.)

But Kierkegaard had also been made aware of a different Augustine, an Augustine who sought to philosophically comprehend divine mysteries. Kierkegaard acquired his own reservations about Augustine from an interpretive tradition indebted to the antimetaphysical aspects of Kant, and to some extent Schleiermacher. From Clausen and others he learned to be suspicious of Augustine as an abstract speculator who distorted the faith with an infusion of Platonism. Kierkegaard's criticisms of Augustine on specific topics almost always amount to the accusation that the kind of "understanding" of the faith that Augustine sought was too detached from the cultivation of the hopes and fears that constitute the Christian life. Unable to entirely shed his Platonism, Augustine lured individuals into an inappropriate mood of detached reflection. This posture of objectivity was not just a mistake in authorial strategy on Augustine's part. Rather, Augustine's project of striving to "understand" what he had merely "believed" failed to do justice to the passional factors that are necessary for successful Christian communication. In Kierkegaard's view, whenever Augustine got the mood wrong, he emptied Christian concepts of their meaning. This critique of Augustine is implicit even when Kierkegaard does not name the African father but attacks the musings of Lutheran theologians who had extended Augustine's speculative tradition. For Kierkegaard, the ghost of the Bishop of Hippo hovered over the shoulder of a more modern bishop, Hans Lassen Martensen.

The tension between Kierkegaard's simultaneous appreciation and critique are evident in a journal entry from 1839 (*JP* 3, 3548), in which Kierkegaard concludes that the doctrine of predestination "is simply an attempt to make fear and trembling, which has its truth in the life of the individual, into a scholarly-dogmatic qualification." This entry warrants consideration because it exemplifies what Kierkegaard liked about Augustine — and what he did not. Kierkegaard contrasts the errors of the adherents of predestination and Montanism, which was an exceedingly rigorist movement in the early church. According to their spokesperson, Montanus, backsliders who had abandoned the faith no longer possessed the possibility of conversion: their damnation has been sealed irrevocably. Kierkegaard contrasts the ominous claim of Montanus with the assertion of the predestinarians that salvation is assured for those whom God has elected. (It must be remembered that Kierkegaard almost always associated predestination with Augustine.) In the case of a potential Montanist backslider, the individual would be forewarned that he could not regain salvation if he fell. In the case of an individual already convinced of his elect status, but facing temptation, he would know that he could not possibly lose his salvation. According to Kierkegaard, there is something right about each position and something dreadfully wrong. The value in each theological stance is its emphasis on a theme that is truly vital for the Christian life. The Montanists appropriately highlight the fear and trembling over the prospect of possible damnation that should be a dimension of any Christian's journey. The predestinarians (including Augustine), conversely, emphasize the confidence in the reconciling power of God that should be resistant to anxieties about future felicity. The problem with both positions is that they take aspects of legitimate forms of Christian pathos and transpose them into a dogmatic concept. With the Montanists a healthy spiritual self-concern is translated into a "scientific" certainty that, under certain circumstances, an individual can be known to be damned. With the predestinarians, the virtue of trust in God's fidelity is translated into a conviction that the individual's election is an objectively knowable fact. In both cases, passions that are essential to the Christian life are inappropriately metamorphosed into "scientific" and "dogmatic" certitudes.

By extension, Kierkegaard suggests that the pathos embedded in the doctrinal formulae articulated by theologians like Augustine can often be affirmed. However, the translation of that pathos into a passion-neutral, seemingly objective proposition analogous to ordinary statements about matters of fact is detrimental to the faith. What Kierkegaard attempts to do throughout his writings is apply this principle to Augustine. Augustine the passionate pilgrim striving to instantiate the dynamics of the Christian life must be distinguished from Augustine the contemplator of propositions that are alleged to convey certainties.

In the light of these considerations, it would be tempting to oversimplify the differences between Kierkegaard and Augustine by characterizing Kierkegaard as a literary writer and Augustine as a doctrinal writer. It would be tempting to regard Augustine as a propositionalist who thought that Christianity is based on the one-to-one correspondence of theological propositions with objective states of affairs, while Kierkegaard was a nonpropositionalist who identified the meaning of doctrines with their existential use. Augustine and Kierkegaard could then be contrasted using the polarities objective/subjective, realist/nonrealist, cognitivist/expressivist, and so on. It would be tempting to assume that Kierkegaard could only appropriate Augustine by squeezing the doctrines out of him and leaving only the piety. All this would be tempting, but it would be wrong.

The first problem with this possible picture of the Augustine-Kierkegaard relationship is its construal of Kierkegaard as being undialectically opposed to doctrines as an essential component of Christianity. This perception of Kierkegaard is by no means hypothetical, for recently many interpreters of Kierkegaard have argued that the essential thrust of his work is incompatible with any acceptance of the authority and referential force of the doctrinal teachings of the Christian heritage. These exposés of the alleged incommensurability of doctrinal convictions and Kierkegaard's project ascribe the inherent opposition to an array of factors. One of the most often cited is the "poetic" or "literary" quality of his texts. That is, irony, humor, multiple voices, digressions, gaps, aporias, and all the strategies of indirection sabotage the discursive force that doctrines are thought to require, and they prevent appropriating Kierkegaard's body of work as though it were a compendium of propositional teachings.[1] His broken images, fractured structures, and promiscuous mixing of genres open up a plethora of interpretive possibilities, and thereby they subvert the apprehension of an authoritative and univocal meaning that a doctrinal system presumably should communicate.

Another much-touted consideration is the yawning gap between lan-

---

1. For examples, see Louis Mackey, *Kierkegaard: A Kind of Poet* (Philadelphia: University of Pennsylvania Press, 1971); Roger Poole, *Kierkegaard: The Indirect Communication* (Charlottesville: University Press of Virginia, 1993).

guage and the immediacy of experience that prevents doctrines from adequately expressing the rich indefiniteness of faith.[2] From this point of view, Kierkegaard's corpus dissolves all stable doctrinal meanings into a vortex of undecidable intertextual associations.[3] A different critique of the supposition that Kierkegaard was sympathetic to ecclesial doctrines concerns the incompatibility of ethical and religious pathos with doctrinal certainty and closure. According to this view, religious pathos requires an absence of tidy closure and a radical openness to the enigmas, tensions, and possibilities of existence.[4] In a somewhat related way, other interpreters of Kierkegaard claim that the authoritative force of doctrinal assertions discourages the agency of the individual and undermines the imperative to work out the meaning of one's own life for oneself.[5] According to this perspective, adherence to obligatory doctrines transmutes subjectivity into objectivity, stifles passion, and spawns the spiritless conformity to Christendom that Kierkegaard so abhorred. Other expositors of Kierkegaard argue that he was deeply suspicious of the tendency of doctrines to naturalize and domesticate otherness, and that he was fully aware that the real purpose of religious language is to witness to an alterity that cannot be represented by propositions.[6]

The portrayal of Kierkegaard as an enemy of doctrinal teachings is thus inspired by a variety of considerations, ranging from the "literary" nature of his writings, to his sensitivity to the "problem of language," to his concern to foster the initiative and self-involvement of the individual agent, to his appreciation of the open-endedness required by religious pathos, and finally to his desire to preserve the otherness of the object of religious language. All of these arguments assume that accepting doctrinal teachings necessarily involves the imposition of principles that dampen pathos by subverting uncertainty, resolving all ambiguities, and trammeling the creative initiatives of the individual. In most of these critiques, doctrines

---

2. See Steven Shakespeare, *Kierkegaard, Language and the Reality of God* (Aldershot, UK: Ashgate, 2001), pp. 56-63; Michael Strawser, *Both/And: A Reading of Kierkegaard from Irony to Edification* (New York: Fordham University Press, 1997), p. 85.

3. Mark C. Taylor, *Erring: A Postmodern A/theology* (Chicago: University of Chicago Press, 1984).

4. See Pat Bigelow, *Kierkegaard and the Problem of Writing* (Tallahassee: Florida University Press, 1987).

5. Benjamin Daise, *Kierkegaard's Socratic Art* (Macon, GA: Mercer University Press, 1999).

6. Mark C. Taylor, *Alterity* (Chicago: University of Chicago Press, 1987), pp. 342-43.

are assumed to be passion-neutral propositions that refer to supernatural states of affairs, propose a one-to-one correspondence between assertions and transcendent facts, demand cognitive assent, are endorsed by a magisterium, and are supported by the coercive authority of an ecclesiastical tradition. If doctrinal convictions do indeed preclude striving, risk, uncertainty, self-investment, and otherness, then the conclusion that Kierkegaard was not a doctrinally oriented theologian would be legitimate. Throughout his writings Kierkegaard clearly insists that the pursuit of the religious life intrinsically involves risk, struggle, and uncertainty. The dynamic and always unresolved "how" of Christian pathos cannot be allowed to devolve into the comfortable complacency of "objective" convictions.

The interpretation of Kierkegaard as having a basically critical attitude toward ecclesial doctrines (and thus as someone who could have little in common with Augustine) is given credence by many of Kierkegaard's own statements about the significance of Christian doctrine *(Lære)*. For example, he exclaims: "But good Lord, Christianity is no 'doctrine'" *(JP* 3, 2870), and he complains that "dogmatics as a whole is a misunderstanding, especially as it now has been developed" *(JP* 1, 627). Kierkegaard bemoans the "superficial sanctity of the modern age" that is manifested "when a preacher prides himself on teaching what is orthodox or when he is busy looking for still more precise definitions against those who believe in another way" *(JP* 1, 660). The root problem with Christendom is that "people have completely transferred Christianity from being an existence-communication to being a doctrine" *(JP* 1, 676). The notes Kierkegaard wrote in 1847 for a proposed series of lectures on communication carefully distinguish an authentic understanding of Christianity from familiarity with doctrinal formulae *(JP* 1, 650). A recurrent theme in his reflections on communication is that Christianity cannot be taught didactically, for Christianity is an "existence communication" and not a system of doctrinal definitions. For Kierkegaard, therefore, the content of an existential communication is not an object but a passionate capability, in this case a capacity to dramatically reconfigure one's whole life *(JP* 1, 649). Kierkegaard writes: "In the communication of knowledge there is only the dialectical transition (therein the truth of immanent necessity); in capability, especially in ethical capability and the religious, the transition is pathos-filled" *(JP* 1, 284). Recapitulating this theme, he observes: "This means that truth in the sense in which Christ is the truth is not a sum of statements, not a definition etc., but a life" *(PC,* 205). These considerations would seem to rule out doctrines as essential ingredients of Christianity, for learning doctrines is surely only a "dialectical transition."

However, the picture of a consistently nondoctrinal Kierkegaard fails to take into account another motif that runs throughout his writings. Kierkegaard writes just as approvingly of the concept "doctrine" as he does critically. For example, he confesses that "on the whole the doctrine as it is presented is entirely sound" (*JP* 6, 6702), and he declares that "the doctrine in the established church and its organization [is] very good," nor does it need to be reformed (*JP* 6, 6727). Similarly, Kierkegaard congratulates the Lutheran heritage, declaring that "Lutheran doctrine is excellent, is the truth" (*FSE*, 24). This approbation of doctrine is not restricted to his signed writings, for the pseudonymous Vigilius Haufniensis praises the Lutheran confessional documents and disavows any interest in doctrinal revision (*CA*, 14, 23, 26-27). As we have seen, much of Kierkegaard's work assumes the validity of such foundational doctrines as the Trinity, original sin, the incarnation, and the atonement.

The duality in Kierkegaard's observations about doctrine is a function of the fact that he used the concept "doctrine" in two different ways. His negative assessments of doctrine occur in contexts in which doctrines are thought of as passion-neutral formulae that are part of an abstract conceptual calculus. Throughout all his writings Kierkegaard is adamant that Christian teachings are not bits of information that should be appropriated in the way that someone could digest data about historical events. His negative sense of "doctrine" suggests a body of data that could be coolly examined, analyzed, and situated in a historical or metaphysical schema. Treating doctrine in this way casts the individual in the role of the detached scientist who interrogates and evaluates data from a position of mastery. Kierkegaard always objects that becoming a Christian is not becoming more facile with articulating precise dogmatic definitions or more adept at tracing logical arguments within a theological system. The clinical detachment of the academic approach to doctrine holds Christian convictions at arm's length as though they were objects to be cognized. When Kierkegaard uses "doctrine" in this negative way, he is engaging in a critique of doctrinal systems that is analogous to his critique of metaphysical systems. All of Kierkegaard's suspicions of a metaphysical system apply equally strongly to a doctrinal system. In both cases, attention is diverted away from the self. Kierkegaard's unsettling literary tropes and disconcerting rhetorical strategies are designed to counteract the pernicious disengaged understanding of doctrine.

But Kierkegaard saw a more positive — indeed, an essential — role for doctrines in the Christian life. The purpose of doctrine in the positive sense is to sketch the contours of a new possibility for existence, an unforeseen possibility, and to invite individuals to personally and passionately appropriate it. Kierkegaard describes doctrines as being "dialectical" in the sense that they propose something to be believed that does not naturally arise out of the individual's own experience, such as "God loves sinners" or "suffering, self-giving love is the highest joy." They make reality claims about the way the universe really is, such as "God was in Christ," and they propose a new way of thinking.[7] However, doctrinal formulations make these reality claims in order to encourage the pursuit of a new and highly unusual way of life characterized by a distinctive pathos. To grasp the meaning of a set of doctrines involves the capacity to imagine the distinctive passional qualities that are essential to that way of life, and the ability to consider the new patterns of thought, action, and feeling that constitute it. The individual must be able to experience these passions and dispositions as possibilities for one's own self, and imaginatively feel their attractions and repulsions. Because doctrines can be used either negatively as speculative distractions or positively as life-shaping stimuli, they are significant only when the appropriate passion is present. The meaning of a Christian conviction is not an inherent property of a doctrinal sentence; the significance of a doctrine cannot be read off its linguistic form divorced from a context of passional use.

We must note that understanding the doctrinal concept and being able to imagine the correlative passion are not related sequentially. One does not first cognize the doctrinal concept and then imagine the correlative pathos. The imaginative grasp that doctrinal understanding requires can only be achieved if individuals are concerned about the shape and quality of their own lives, including their deepest hopes, fears, and values. Understanding a doctrine in the positive sense requires the cultivation of earnestness about oneself just as much as it requires attention to the ostensible subject matter.

Kierkegaard's use of indirect literary strategies, his concern with nurturing certain kinds of pathos, and his doctrinal purposes, rather than being inimical to one another, actually reinforce each other. Even his destabilizing literary maneuvers are necessary for successful doctrinal communication. As Kierkegaard observes, meaning is not just a matter of "what" is said, but also of "how" it is said (*JP* 1, 657). Therefore, the literary, passional, and often oblique character of Kierkegaard's work cannot be cited

---

7. See C. Stephen Evans, "Realism and Antirealiam in Kierkegaard's *Concluding Unscientific Postscript*," in Alastair Hannay and Gordon Marino, eds., *The Cambridge Companion to Kierkegaard* (Cambridge: Cambridge University Press, 1998), pp. 154-76.

as evidence that he was somehow allergic to Christian doctrines. Pitting an antidoctrinal Kierkegaard against a doctrinal Augustine is an injustice to Kierkegaard.

It is also an injustice to Augustine. By emphasizing the importance of pathos for understanding doctrines, Kierkegaard was actually doing something similar to Augustine's typical practice. Admittedly, Augustine did sometimes suggest that the purpose of a theologian was to render the figurative language of the Bible into more explicit and unambiguous forms.[8] But that was not the main thrust of his own practice. It must be remembered that Augustine was steeped in the rhetorical tradition of Rome, with deep roots in Cicero. Moreover, Augustine regarded preaching as one of the central duties of the episcopal office, and he saw the bishop as a kind of Christian public orator.[9] Rhetoric was the science of persuasion, and rhetoricians were thus highly attentive to the relationship between assertions and the affectivity of auditors.[10] In Rome, one of the perceived purposes of rhetoric was to promote civic virtue and wisdom, and this required forms of communication that addressed the emotions. That the auditor only understands a communication when the appropriate emotions are aroused and when the auditor grasps how to enact its implications was a commonplace of the rhetorical tradition. Augustine's work pays attention to subjectivity just as much as Kierkegaard's does. Augustine puts the classical rhetorical tradition to a Christian use by claiming that any exposition of Scripture must either fortify *caritas* or discourage *cupiditas*.[11] Similarly, he declares that belief in the contents of faith necessarily involves a delight in them that draws the soul to give its assent. Faith, in the sense of accepting the tenets of Christianity, must be formed by love and made active by love. For Augustine, believing the doctrines (the *ea quae creduntur*) must involve faithful thought, action, and experience, and thus cannot be divorced from the practice of piety. Both Augustine and Kierkegaard present doctrinal motifs in a way that encourage the development of genuine religious pathos. For this reason, Kierkegaard may not have been as far removed from Augustine as some interpreters have alleged.

Even the rhetorical strategies of these two exceptionally rhetorical authors were often similar. Both adopted sophisticated literary styles that were

8. Augustine, *On Teaching Christianity*, Book III, in *WSA* I, 11.

9. Augustine, *On Teaching Christianity*, Book IV, in *WSA* I, 11.

10. See Stephen Andrew Cooper, *Metaphysics and Morals in Marius Victorinus' Commentary on the Letter to the Ephesians* (New York: Peter Lang, 1995), pp. 10-15.

11. Augustine, *On Teaching Christianity*, Book III, 10 (15), in *WSA* I, 11.

designed to engage the passions of the reader. Both mixed genres in order to frustrate the genre expectations of the reader, to throw the reader off balance, and thereby to open the reader to a new vision. They both shift the addressees of their writings, sometimes talking to the hypothetical reader, sometimes to God, and sometimes to themselves. They both use philosophical argument in ad hoc ways for limited edifying purposes. They both exhibit in their style of communication the passions that they sought to nurture in their readers. Their writings are even peppered with many of the same images, such as "the road," "exile," "struggle," "the fountain" (of love), and an entire range of romantic metaphors. They both use all these strategies to provoke readers to reflect more intently on the unresolved tensions and dissatisfactions in their own experience and to evoke an enthusiasm for a new way of life. In short, both Augustine and Kierkegaard regarded the nurturing of a distinctive type of pathos as the purpose of doctrines and were convinced that the ability to imagine (and, better yet, live out) the appropriate kinds of pathos is a necessary condition for understanding specific doctrines.

Edifying Speculation?

Having emphasized the parallelism of Augustine and Kierkegaard, we must admit that they were not always in accord. One of the decisive points where Kierkegaard and Augustine diverged was the basic issue of whether metaphysical reflection had any upbuilding potential or not. Augustine writes as though the individual can be edified by discerning how Christian pathos implies certain claims about the nature of the universe. If those implications can then be shown to be plausible, Christian faith is bolstered and understanding is enhanced. For Augustine, the passions can be deepened, strengthened, and focused by metaphysical reflection, if it is conducted in the appropriately pious mood.

Kierkegaard, on the other hand, writes as though the forms of pathos themselves have their own attractiveness and plausibility (and also potential offensiveness), and that the power of the Christian passions would only be diluted by resituating them in the alien context of theorizing. Kierkegaard doubts that the mood of earnestness about one's own life can be maintained through abstract speculation. For Kierkegaard, the virtue of trusting in God during times of suffering, for example, did not need any metaphysical backing at all, and in fact would be harmed by efforts to provide such backing. Kierkegaard abandoned theodicy while Augustine did not, even though their depictions of the Christian virtue of trust are surprisingly similar. According to Kierkegaard, speculation not only encourages the wrong mood, but it also aims at a kind of closure that would make the risk of faith impossible.

However, even the metaphysical Augustine may have been more similar to Kierkegaard than the latter realized. Kierkegaard's negative assessment of Augustine as a systematician may have been based on exaggerations in the secondary literature that he had read, including Clausen's lectures. Kierkegaard heard about the pernicious abstractions of Augustine's Platonism, but he never really engaged Augustine's texts to see how that Platonism really functioned for him. It is certainly true that Augustine does engage in metaphysical speculation, and it is true that he tries to defend Christianity with philosophical arguments. But Augustine philosophizes prayerfully and pastorally, always putting the argument to some edifying use. For example, he expresses anticipation of the so-called ontological argument for the existence of God in order to encourage an adoring appreciation of God's plenitude. Even when Augustine speculates about the nature of time, a quintessentially metaphysical issue, he situates time in a passional context, noting its connection to anticipation, recollection, regrets, remorse, nostalgia, hopes, and fears. In general, Augustine's myriad philosophical arguments and digressions function as catalysts for repentance, spiritual growth, and devout contemplation of God's sublimity. We must remember that Kierkegaard, at least in the guise of Climacus, is also not above resorting to philosophical arguments in order to move his readers. The difference between Augustine and Kierkegaard may have been the degree to which each found this ad hoc strategy to be useful, and the extent to which each feared its possible misuses. As was the case with regard to their respective understandings of the church, the root difference between them may have been Augustine's almost instinctive desire to direct, nurture, and reinforce frail and wayward pilgrims, and Kierkegaard's passion to destabilize and agitate prematurely complacent pilgrims in order to keep them moving.

Two Theologians of Love

Augustine and Kierkegaard are not only similar in their common concern for the passional requisites necessary for understanding Christian teachings; they are also strikingly similar with respect to the types of pathos that they emphasize as constituting the Christian life. Most important, both make desire for God central to their vision of the Christian life. By so doing, they are both the heirs of the classical heritage and the concept of eros for the divine. Moreover, both associate growth in love for God with the increasing clarity about the nature of one's own true self. For both, self-transparency requires loving knowledge of God, and loving knowledge of God requires a passionate hunger to understand oneself. In this sense, Charles Taylor was correct that both Augustine and Kierkegaard encourage attention to subjectivity. However, Taylor may have failed to appreciate the extent to which their motive for doing so was to illuminate the meaning of Christian convictions, which only makes sense in the context of certain passions.

Augustine and Kierkegaard see the self as created to desire, know, and love God. Both discern the possibility of "becoming nothing" and being ecstatically open to God in adoration and praise as part of humanity's created nature. But they also regard God's gracious work in bringing about a state of mutual love through God's self-giving as a free and unexpected gift. Creation is teleologically oriented toward redemption, but redemption is not the mere actualization of a potential resident in creation. The fact that the self-giving God fulfills our created nature can only be known retrospectively. Concerning the presence of a "theology of creation" in Kierkegaard, George Pattison has observed:

> And yet a theology of creation is still a theology. If it implies that all human beings, by virtue of the relationship of creature to Creator, are potentially open to the fulfilled God-relationship of faith, it also suggests that to understand this is only possible once one has stepped into the theological circle.[12]

Surprisingly, Augustine and Kierkegaard relate creation and redemption, and nature and grace, in similar ways: nature does not prescribe what grace must be, but grace does satisfy the longing of nature in a way that nature did not anticipate. By so doing, both theologians avoided the tendency of some forms of Catholicism to reduce grace to the completion of nature, and the tendency of some forms of Lutheranism to dichotomize the two.

Both Augustine and Kierkegaard use "journey" as a root metaphor for

---

12. George Pattison, "Philosophy and Dogma: The Testimony of an Upbuilding Discourse," in Edward F. Mooney, ed., *Ethics, Love, and Faith in Kierkegaard* (Bloomington: Indiana University Press, 2008), p. 161.

the Christian life. "Journey" reinforces the developmental and directional nature of the Christian life as progress toward the goal of reciprocal love for God. For Kierkegaard, this involves shifting the emphasis in his own Lutheran tradition away from justification to sanctification. It is, of course, important to him that God's forgiveness and acceptance are promised in this life and are made available to the sinner, but the perfection of love for God and neighbor should be the primary focal point of Christianity. For Kierkegaard, justification is not contingent on sanctification, but sanctification is the Christian's ultimate concern, for it is the actualization of the loving mutuality that will be our ultimate fulfillment. The centrality of love construed as mutual understanding and delight accounts for both Augustine's and Kierkegaard's penchant for romantic images to portray the individual's relationship with God, rather than the exclusive use of images of trust in a parental figure. In this way Kierkegaard was steering his Lutheran heritage back toward Augustine.

"Journey" is not the only metaphor for life that the two authors evoke. They both temper "journey" with metaphors of "trial," "school," "hospital," and "test." All of these images suggest that the journey is a difficult struggle against an obstacle that has come between the starting point and the destination. The purpose of these themes is to suggest the need for diligence, rigorous self-evaluation, the assumption of responsibility, and repentance. They also point to the need for help, which the metaphor of journey by itself does not do. Sin is a disruption of the journey, and a devastating complication of it, but the need to move from sin to forgiveness is not the most basic motivation for the journey, nor is forgiveness the journey's main point or goal.

Perhaps the most striking and startling parallelism of Augustine and Kierkegaard is their common conviction that the ultimate object of desire is the self-giving love of God. This accounts for their joint fondness for the kenotic hymn in Philippians 2. For both of them the aspect of God that most forcefully draws the heart is the divine self-emptying. Both of them structure much of their writing around the contrast of highness and lowness, or exaltation and abasement. The theme of self-giving informs both of their understandings of the nature of God, including Augustine's most abstract reflections about the Trinity. The concept of self-giving undergirds their understandings of the significance of the person and work of Jesus Christ. For both of them, abasement is evident in the very fact of the incarnation of the Word, and is repeated in the human life of Christ. This same motif reappears in their parallel contrasts of pride and humility in human life and the struggles of the pilgrim. Both of them see faith and love as being directed toward the divine self-giving, and thus as two sides of the same coin: both insist that the divine movement is reflected in the life of the Christian.

This is the most significant result of the comparison of Augustine and Kierkegaard. Their solution to the putative tension between eros and agape is shockingly simple: the proper object of eros is the divine agape. The longing for self-fulfillment that seems to be part of our created nature is satisfied by the adoration and reflection of God's self-giving. Eros goes astray when it pursues with ultimate passion any penultimate object that is less than the sublimity of self-giving. The restless heart comes to rest in the form of a servant. In this way Augustine's work is innocent of many of the dichotomies that would later divide Catholics and Protestants, and Kierkegaard can be credited with deconstructing them after they had been solidified. A bishop living at the dawn of Christendom and a layperson living at its dusk strangely shared a common vision of the co-implication of nature and grace, creation and redemption, faith and love, and justification and sanctification.

Dialectical Edification

Augustine and Kierkegaard parallel each other in yet another surprising way. Both of them foreground the "dialectical" nature of most forms of Christian pathos. In this context, "dialectical" suggests a tension between two motifs, both of which must be affirmed, but which resist synthesis. Both of their sets of writings are stranger than an integrated theological system. The two thinkers consistently portray the dispositions and passions that constitute the Christian life as typically coming in tensive pairs. Kierkegaard articulates this insight explicitly while Augustine inscribes it implicitly in his writings. The same pattern of affirming apparently contradictory doctrinal themes, without theoretically synthesizing them, occurs throughout their respective writings.

For example, both Augustine and Kierkegaard claim that sin is a state of corruption in which the individual is stuck, but it is also the individual's fault and a responsible act. For both of them, the Christian life is a task to be strenuously performed, but it is also a gift to be celebrated. During his theological maturity, Augustine insists that every aspect of the Christian life is the product of God's gracious agency, for which the individual can take no credit; at the same time, he continues to call for responsible action. In a parallel way, Kierkegaard sometimes sounds like an extreme voluntarist, describing faith as a kind of heroic "leap" that a person can perform through sheer will power. At other times Kierkegaard almost sounds like a predestinarian, such as when he describes faith as a "gift" unilaterally bestowed by God that the individual passively receives. Moreover, both Augustine and Kierkegaard agree that God's law, the imperative to live a Christlike life of love, cannot be fulfilled and should drive the individual to repentance and openness to divine aid. On the other hand, they both also insist that the law's valorization of love does stir the heart and inspire the continuing striving for the fulfillment of love's requirements. In a similar way, both portray Christ as both the daunting prototype and the lenient Savior. A similar dialectical tension is evident in the twin claims that creaturely life should be accepted with gratitude as a blessing from God — and should be constantly given up.

Because both the language of absolute reliance on God and the language of strenuous striving are found in both their texts, Augustine and Kierkegaard seem to be operating with two opposed sets of theological discourses. In all these instances, Augustine and Kierkegaard have urged their readers to pursue seemingly contradictory policies, for example, to diligently cultivate several different pious attitudes and then to distrust them, trusting exclusively in God's agency. Following their cues, readers must simultaneously work out their own salvation in fear and trembling, and also trust only in God, taking credit for nothing at all, not even cooperation.

To complicate matters, neither author produces a theological metatheory that could show how the two sets of countervailing dynamics could be harmonized. Augustine sometimes attempts to do this (as in his musings about Adam and Eve), but he never quite succeeds, and Kierkegaard, on principle, never even tries. Whether either writer realized it or not, their common conviction that understanding a theological concept or doctrine requires the cultivation of the appropriate form of pathos points to the utter impossibility of a speculative integration of all doctrines and the resolution of their dialectical tensions. The problem is that each doctrinal concept requires its own very specific passional context in order to be meaningful. Without the presence of the particular hopes, fears, and yearnings associated with a doctrine, the meaning of that doctrine evaporates. The specificity of the passions that help constitute the meaning of a doctrine undermines the possibility of a detached systematic overview of the whole network of doctrines. For example, "original sin" and "grace" cannot be grasped together because the passional context appropriate to "sin" is repentance, while the passional context appropriate to "grace" is joy. The theologian does not have access to a passion-neutral metaperspective from which all the interconnections of predestination, original sin, free will, justification, sanctification, prevenient grace, or any other doctrine can be surveyed. Kierkegaard realized that the longing for an omniscient God's-eye perspective from which the logical tensions among the various doctrines could be surveyed and resolved is futile. Augustine may have sought such a perspective, but he never attained it, and he always fell back on the eliciting of particular passions for particular pastoral purposes. In practice, both Augustine and Kierkegaard write as if the integration of the diversity of passions corresponding to the plurality of doctrines should primarily be achieved in a person's life, rather than on paper. Augustine, the preacher-cum-rhetor, and Kierkegaard, the theologian-cum-ironist, both looked for the felicitous combination of these tensive themes in the individual's struggle to forge a coherent religious life.

Robert C. Roberts has noted a similar unsynthesized plurality of discourses in Kierkegaard's writings about ethics. Roberts concludes: "Instead [of a systematic integration of divine command theory and virtue ethics], the picture of moral concepts suggested by Kierkegaard's writings — pseudonymous and signed — is that of an array that has a jewel-like hardness of mutually supporting complexity, inviting, as the only right philosophical response, a multidirectional, dialectical exploration of the kind that is exemplified in Kierkegaard's many books. . . ."[13] Roberts's point about Kierkegaard's ethical discourse could be extended to include the doctrinal discourses of both Augustine and Kierkegaard. For both thinkers, the values, ideals, affirmations, and imperatives that give shape to the Christian life are a web of motifs that are "multidirectional" and exhibit a "mutually supporting complexity" without organizing themselves in a neat hierarchy of logical priority or a deductive system of entailments. The dialectically paired doctrines cannot possibly provide any systematic closure, for they point in different directions. As a result, exactly how such convictions should be combined in a single individual's life cannot be stipulated with the help of a metaprinciple.

Although the various discourses resist synthesis, and remain in tension with each other, they are not necessarily mutually exclusive. They might

---

13. Robert C. Roberts, "Kierkegaard and Ethical Theory," in Mooney, *Ethics, Love, and Faith in Kierkegaard*, p. 90.

well be complementary, as Roberts suggests about ethical discourses. This use of complementary ways of speaking to do justice to the complexity of a single phenomenon is not unique to Augustine or Kierkegaard. The use of complementary models for the purpose of explanation has antecedents in the history of philosophy and science. Immanuel Kant uses complementary models to account for human action when he proposes that, according to theoretical reason, human actions must be regarded as determined by prior causes, while, according to practical reason, those same actions must be regarded as free and undetermined. In physics both "wave" and "particle" models must be used to understand different aspects of the behavior of electrons.[14] In certain contexts — and for certain purposes — it is heuristically useful to conceptualize the behavior of electrons as if they were tiny interacting particles; in certain other contexts — for certain other purposes — it is heuristically useful to regard their behavior as if they were waves. For our purposes, the significant consideration is that no metamodel can be developed to integrate the wavelike features and the particlelike features. Moreover, the insights of neither model can be expressed in the terms of the other one. The "wave" and "particle" models remain irreducibly different but equally necessary for different explanatory purposes. Scientific wisdom involves an ability to make judgments concerning when to use which model — and for what purpose. Understanding the relationship of the models is a kind of practical skill concerning their appropriate uses.

Something similar can be said of Augustine's and Kierkegaard's uses of theological themes. The virtues, dispositions, and passions that Augustine and Kierkegaard encourage come in paradoxical pairs. The ostensible incompatibility at the level of theoretical understanding may not be as problematic at the level of practice. The seemingly irreducible dialectical tensions between such polar theological themes as sin as corruption and sin as an act, or faith as a gift and faith as a task, may be resolved in the living of a life when they cannot be in a text. The integration of the themes could occur as the individual Christian develops skill in knowing exactly when and how to be absolutely grateful, and when and how to push oneself as rigorously as possible to be more loving, hopeful, and faithful. The individual can learn how to integrate in a single life sheer receptivity to God and the assumption of responsibility for one's own moral and religious character. The pilgrim can develop insight into how to live in such a way that con-

14. See Ian Barbour, *Myths, Models, and Paradigms* (New York: Harper and Row, 1974), pp. 71-92.

tinuing repentance is synthesized with the continuing pursuit of Christlikeness. The tensions among these themes do make it impossible to definitively map out their interconnections in an abstract system, be it philosophical or theological. The picture of the Christian life, informed by doctrinal teachings, is open-ended, perpetually unfinished, fraught with uncertainty, and continuously renegotiated. Struggling to make sense of the doctrines by living them out in a way that approximates the ideal of self-giving love involves all the risk and passion that Kierkegaard could ever want, and has all the allure that Augustine needed.

Bibliography

Bibliography of Works about Augustine

Ayers, Lewis. *Augustine and the Trinity*. Cambridge: Cambridge University Press, 2010.

Böhringer, Friedrich. *Die Kirche Christi und ihre Zeugen oder die Kirchengeschichte in Biographie*. 2 vols. Zürich: Meyer & Zeller, 1842-55.

Boyer, Charles. *L'Ideé de vérité dans la philosophie de saint Augustin*. Paris: Beauchesne, 1940.

Brown, Peter. *Augustine of Hippo: A Biography*. Berkeley: University of California Press, 1969.

———. *Power and Persuasion in Late Antiquity: Toward a Christian Empire*. Madison: University of Wisconsin Press, 1992.

Burnaby, John. *Amor Dei: A Study in the Religion of Saint Augustine*. London: Hodder and Stoughton, 1938.

Burns, J. Patout. "Appropriating Augustine Appropriating Cyprian." *Augustinian Studies* 36 (2005): 1-16.

Cary, Phillip. *Augustine's Invention of the Inner Self: The Legacy of a Christian Platonist*. Oxford: Oxford University Press, 2000.

Chadwick, Henry. "On Re-Reading the Confessions." In *Saint Augustine the Bishop: A Book of Essays*, edited by Fannie LeMoine and Christopher Kleinhenz, 139-60. New York: Garland Publishing, 1994.

Conybeare, Catherine. *The Irrational Augustine*. Oxford: Oxford University Press, 2006.

Cooper, Stephen. *Augustine for Armchair Theologians*. Louisville: Westminster John Knox, 2002.

Courcelle, Pierre. *"Les Confessions" de Saint Augustin dans la Tradition Littéraire.* Paris: Études Augustinienne, 1963.

―――. *Reserches sur les Confessions de Saint Augustin.* Paris: E. de Boccard, 1950.

Daley, Brian E., S.J. "A Humble Mediator: The Distinctive Elements of Saint Augustine's Christology." *Word and Spirit* 9 (1987): 100-117.

De Margerie, Bertrand. *An Introduction to the History of Exegesis.* Vol. 3: *Saint Augustine.* Translated by Pierre de Fontnouvelle. Petersham, MA: Saint Bede's Publications, 1991.

Ellingsen, Mark. *The Richness of Augustine: His Contextual and Pastoral Theology.* Louisville: Westminster/John Knox Press, 2005.

Ferrari, Leo C. *The Conversions of Saint Augustine.* Villanova, PA: Villanova University Press, 1984.

Frend, W. H. C. *The Donatist Church: A Movement of Protest in Roman North Africa.* Oxford: Clarendon, 1952.

Gilson, Étienne. *The Christian Philosophy of Saint Augustine.* Translated by L. E. M. Lynch. London: Victor Gollancz, 1960.

Grabowski, Stanislaus. *The All-Present God: A Study in St. Augustine.* St. Louis: Herder, 1954.

Greer, Rowan. *Broken Lights and Mended Lives: Theology and Common Life in the Early Church.* University Park: Pennsylvania State University Press, 1986.

Gunton, Colin. "Augustine, the Trinity, and the Theological Crisis of the West." *Scottish Journal of Theology* 43 (1990): 33-58.

Hanby, Michael. *Augustine and Modernity.* New York: Routledge, 2003.

Harrison, Carol. *Beauty and Revelation in the Thought of Saint Augustine.* Oxford: Clarendon Press, 1992.

Heidegger, Martin. "Augustin und der Neuplatonismus." In *Gesamtausgabe,* vol. 60: *Phänomenologie des Religiösen Lebens,* 157-299. Frankfurt am Main: Vittorio Klostermann, 1995.

Hick, John. *Evil and the God of Love.* New York: Macmillan, 1977.

Jolivet, Regis. *Dieu soleil des esprits, ou la doctrine augustinienne de l'illumination.* Paris: Desclée, de Brouwer et cie, 1934.

Kolbet, Paul R. *Augustine and the Cure of Souls.* Notre Dame, IN: University of Notre Dame Press, 2010.

Lorenz, Rudolf. "Gnade und Erkenntnis bei Augustin." In *Zum Augustin-Gespräch der Gegenwart,* vol. 2, edited by Carl Andersen, 43-125. Darmstadt: Wissenschaftliche Buchgesellschaft, 1981.

Lyotard, Jean-François. *The Confession of Augustine.* Translated by Richard Beardsworth. Stanford: Stanford University Press, 2000.

Madec, Goulven. *Le patrie et la voie: Le Christ dans la vie et la pensée de saint Augustin.* Paris: Desclée, 1989.

Mallard, William. "Jesus Christ." In *Augustine through the Ages,* edited by Allan D. Fitzgerald, 463-70. Grand Rapids: Eerdmans, 1999.

Manasse, Ernst Moritz. "Conversation and Liberation: A Comparison of Augustine and Kierkegaard." *Review of Religion* 7 (1943): 361-83.

Markus, Robert A. *Conversion and Disenchantment in Augustine's Spiritual Career.* Villanova, PA: Villanova University Press, 1989.

———. "The Legacy of Pelagius: Orthodoxy, Heresy, and Conciliation." In *The Making of Orthodoxy: Essays in Honour of Henry Chadwick,* edited by R. D. Williams, 214-34. Cambridge: Cambridge University Press, 1989.

Milbank, John. "Augustine and the Indo-European Soul." In *Augustine and His Critics,* edited by R. Dodaro and G. Lawless, 77-102. London: Routledge, 2000.

Miles, Margaret. *Desire and Delight: A New Reading of Augustine's "Confessions."* New York: Crossroad, 1992.

O'Connell, Robert J. *Imagination and Metaphysics in St. Augustine.* Milwaukee: Marquette University Press, 1986.

———. *The Origin of the Soul in Augustine's Later Works.* New York: Fordham University Press, 1987.

O'Donnell, James J. *Augustine: Confessions.* 3 vols. Oxford: Oxford University Press, 1992.

———. *Augustine, Sinner and Saint: A New Biography.* London: Profile Books, 2005.

———. "Augustine's Unconfessions." In *Augustine and Postmodernism: Confessions and Circumfession,* edited by John D. Caputo and Michael Scanlon, 212-21. Bloomington: Indiana University Press, 2005.

O'Meara, J. J. "Augustine's *Confessions:* Elements of Fiction." In *Augustine: From Rhetor to Theologian,* edited by Joanne McWilliam, 77-95. Waterloo, ON: Wilfrid Laurier Press, 1992.

Pedersen, Jørgen. "Augustine and Augustinianism." In *Kierkegaard and Great Traditions,* edited by Niels Thulstrup and Marie Mikulvá Thulstrup, 54-97. *Bibliotheca Kierkegaardiana,* vol. 6. Copenhagen: C. A. Reitzel, 1981.

Price, Richard. *Augustine.* New York: HarperCollins, 1996.

Scheel, Otto. *Die Anschauung Augustins über Christi Person und Werk unter besonderer Berücksichtigung ihrer verschiedenen Entwicklungstufen und ihrer dogmengeschichtlichen Stellung.* Tübingen: J. C. B. Mohr, 1901.

Sigurdson, Ola. "The Passion of the Christ: On the Social Production of Desire." In *Saving Desire: The Seduction of Christian Theology,* edited by F. LeRon Shults and Jan-Olav Henriksen, 31-54. Grand Rapids: Eerdmans, 2011.

Stendahl, Krister. "Paul and the Interpretive Conscience of the West." *The Harvard Theological Review* 55, no. 4 (1963): 199-205.

Stock, Brian. *After Augustine: The Meditative Reader and the Text.* Philadelphia: University of Pennsylvania Press, 2001.

Studer, Basel. *The Grace of Christ and the Grace of God in Augustine of Hippo: Christocentrism or Theocentrism?* Translated by Matthew J. O'Connell. Collegeville, MN: Liturgical Press, 1997.

TeSelle, Eugene. *Augustine.* Nashville: Abingdon, 2006.

————. *Augustine the Theologian.* New York: Herder and Herder, 1970.

————. "Faith." In *Augustine through the Ages,* edited by Allan D. Fitzgerald, 347-50. Grand Rapids: Eerdmans, 1999.

Teske, Roland J. *To Know God and the Soul.* Washington, DC: The Catholic University Press of America, 2008.

Tilley, Maureen. *The Bible in Christian North Africa: The Donatist Worl.* Minneapolis: Fortress, 1997.

Wills, Garry. *Font of Life: Ambrose, Augustine, and the Mystery of Baptism.* Oxford: Oxford University Press, 2012.

Bibliography of Works about Kierkegaard

Agacinski, Sylvaine. *Aparté: Conceptions and Deaths of Søren Kierkegaard.* Translated by Kevin Newmark. Tallahasse: Florida State University Press, 1989.

Anderson, Thomas C. "Is the Religion of *Eighteen Upbuilding Discourses* Religiousness A?" In *International Kierkegaard Commentary: Eighteen Upbuilding Discourses,* edited by Robert L. Perkins. Macon, GA: Mercer University Press, 2003.

Anz, Wilhelm. *Kierkegaard und der deutsche Idelaismus.* Tübingen: J. C. B. Mohr, 1956.

Axt-Piscalar, Christine. "Julius Müller: Parallels in the Doctrines of Sin and Freedom." In *Kierkegaard and His German Contemporaries,* vol. II: *Theology,* edited by Jon Stewart, 143-60. Farnham, UK: Ashgate, 2007.

Barnett, Christopher. *Kierkegaard, Pietism, and Holiness.* Farnham, UK: Ashgate, 2011.

Barrett, Lee C. "Anselm of Canterbury: The Ambivalent Legacy of Faith Seeking Understanding." In *Kierkegaard and the Patristic and Medieval Traditions,* edited by Jon Stewart, 167-81. Farnham, UK: Ashgate, 2008.

————. "The Joy in the Cross: Kierkegaard's Appropriation of Lutheran Christology in 'The Gospel of Sufferings.'" In *International Kierkegaard Commentary: Upbuilding Discourses in Various Spirits,* edited by Robert Perkins, 275-85. Macon, GA: Mercer University Press, 2005.

————. "Kierkegaard's Anxiety and the Augustinian Doctrine of Original Sin." In *International Kierkegaard Commentary: The Concept of Anxiety,* edited by Robert Perkins, 35-61. Macon, GA: Mercer University Press, 1985.

————. "Kierkegaard's *Two Ages:* An Immediate Stage on the Way to the Religious Life." In *International Kierkegaard Commentary: Two Ages,* edited by Robert Perkins, 53-71. Macon, GA: Mercer University Press, 1984.

Barth, Karl. "A Thank You and A Bow: Kierkegaard's Reveille." Translated by Martin Rumscheidt. *Canadian Journal of Theology* 11 (1965): 3-7.

Beabout, Gregory. *Freedom and Its Misuses: Kierkegaard on Anxiety and Despair.* Milwaukee: Marquette University Press, 1996.

Berry, Wanda Warren. "Practicing Liberation: Feminist and Womanist Dialogues with Kierkegaard's *Practice in Christianity.*" In *International Kierkegaard Commentary: Practice in Christianity,* edited by Robert L. Perkins, 303-41. Macon, GA: Mercer University Press, 2004.

Bertelsen, Otto. *Den kirkelige Kierkegaard og den "Antikirkelige."* Copenhagen: C. A. Reitzel, 1999.

Bigelow, Pat. *Kierkegaard and the Problem of Writing.* Tallahassee: Florida University Press, 1987.

Bohlen, Torsten. *Kierkegaard's dogmatiska åskådning I dess historiska sammanhang.* Stockholm: Diakonistyrelses Förlag, 1925.

Burgess, Andrew. "Kierkegaard's Concept of Redoubling and Luther's *Simul Justus.*" In *International Kierkegaard Commentary: Works of Love,* edited by Robert Perkins, 39-55. Macon, GA: Mercer University Press, 1999.

Cain, David. "A Star in the Cross: Getting the Dialectic Right." In *International Kierkegaard Commentary: For Self-Examination and Judge for Yourself!* edited by Robert L. Perkins, 315-34. Macon, GA: Mercer University Press, 2010.

Come, Arnold. *Kierkegaard as Humanist: Discovering Myself.* Montreal: McGill-Queens University Press, 1995.

———. *Kierkegaard as Theologian: Recovering Myself.* Montreal: McGill-Queen's University Press, 1996.

Connell, George. *To Be One Thing: Personal Unity in Kierkegaard's Thought.* Macon, GA: Mercer University Press, 1985.

Crites, Stephen. *In the Twilight of Christendom: Hegel vs. Kierkegaard on Faith and History.* Camersbury, PA: American Academy of Religion, 1972.

Daise, Benjamin. *Kierkegaard's Socratic Art.* Macon, GA: Mercer University Press, 1999.

Dalrymple, Timothy. "Adam and Eve: Human Being and Nothingness." In *Kierkegaard and the Bible,* vol. I: *The Old Testament,* edited by Lee Barrett and Jon Stewart, 3-42. Farnham, UK: Ashgate, 2010.

———. "On the Bronze Bull of Phalaris and the Art and Imitation of Christ." In *International Kierkegaard Commentary: "The Moment" and Late Writings,* edited by Robert L. Perkins, 165-98. Macon, GA: Mercer University Press, 2009.

Davenport, John, and Anthony Rudd, eds. *Kierkegaard after MacIntyre.* Chicago: Open Court, 2001.

Dewey, Bradley. "Kierkegaard and the Blue Testament." Harvard Theological Review 60 (1967).

———. *The New Obedience: Kierkegaard on Imitating Christ.* Washington, DC: Corpus Books, 1968.

Diem, Hermann. "Kierkegaard's Bequest to Theology." In *A Kierkegaard Critique,* edited by Howard A. Johnson and Niels Thulstrup, 244-65. New York: Harper, 1962.

Doody, John. "Kierkegaard." In *Augustine through the Ages: An Encyclopedia,* edited by Allan D. Fitzgerald, 484-86. Grand Rapids: Eerdmans, 1999.

Dunning, Stephen. *Kierkegaard's Dialectic of Inwardness: A Structural Analysis of the Theory of the Stages.* Princeton, NJ: Princeton University Press, 1985.

Dupré, Louis. *Kierkegaard as Theologian.* New York: Sheed and Ward, 1963.

Eller, Vernard. *Kierkegaard and Radical Discipleship: A New Perspective.* Princeton, NJ: Princeton University Press, 1968.

Elrod, John. *Being and Existence in Kierkegaard's Pseudonymous Works.* Princeton, NJ: Princeton University Press, 1975.

———. *Kierkegaard and Christendom.* Princeton, NJ: Princeton University Press, 2001.

Emmanuel, Steven. *Kierkegaard and the Concept of Revelation.* Albany: State University of New York Press, 1996.

Evans, C. Stephen. *Kierkegaard: An Introduction.* Cambridge: Cambridge University Press, 2009.

———. *Kierkegaard's Ethic of Love: Divine Command and Moral Obligations.* Oxford: Oxford University Press, 2006.

———. *Kierkegaard's "Fragments" and "Postscript": The Religious Philosophy of Johannes Climacus.* Atlantic Highlands, NJ: Humanities Press, 1983.

———. *Passionate Reason: Making Sense of Kierkegaard's "Philosophical Fragments."* Bloomington: Indiana University Press, 1992.

———. "Realism and Antirealism in Kierkegaard's *Concluding Unscientific Postscript.*" In *The Cambridge Companion to Kierkegaard,* edited by Alastair Hannay and Gordon Marino, 154-76. Cambridge: Cambridge University Press, 1998.

Fenger, Henning. *Kierkegaard: The Myths and Their Origins.* Translated by George Schoolfield. New Haven: Yale University Press, 1980.

Ferreira, M. Jamie. *Kierkegaard.* Oxford: Wiley-Blackwell, 2009.

———. *Love's Grateful Striving: A Commentary on Kierkegaard's Works of Love.* Oxford: Oxford University Press, 2001.

———. *Transforming Vision: Imagination and Will in Kierkegaardian Faith.* Oxford: Clarendon Press, 1991.

Garff, Joakim. *Søren Kierkegaard: A Biography.* Translated by Bruce Kirmmse. Princeton, NJ: Princeton University Press, 2005.

Gouwens, David. *Kierkegaard as Religious Thinker.* Cambridge: Cambridge University Press, 1996.

———. *Kierkegaard's Dialectic of the Imagination.* New York: Peter Lang, 1989.

Graham, Glenn. "Kierkegaard and the Longing for God." PhD dissertation, McMaster University, 2011.

Green, Ronald. *Kierkegaard and Kant: The Hidden Debt.* Albany: State University of New York Press, 1992.

Hall, Amy Laura. *Kierkegaard and the Treachery of Love.* Cambridge: Cambridge University Press, 2002.

Hannay, Alastair. *Kierkegaard: A Biography.* Cambridge: Cambridge University Press, 2001.

Hannay, Alastair, and Gordon Marino, eds. *The Cambridge Companion to Kierkegaard.* Cambridge: Cambridge University Press, 1997.

Hartshorne, M. Holmes. *Kierkegaard, Godly Deceiver.* New York: Columbia University Press, 1990.

Hughes, Carl. *Kierkegaard and the Staging of Desire: Rhetoric and Religious Performance in a Theology of Eros.* New York: Fordham University Press, 2013.

Jackson, Timothy. "Arminian Edification: Kierkegaard on Grace and Free Will." In *The Cambridge Companion to Kierkegaard,* edited by Alastair Hannay and Gordon Marino, 235-56. Cambridge: Cambridge University Press, 1998.

Jegstrup, Elsebet, ed. *The New Kierkegaard.* Bloomington: Indiana University Press, 2004.

Jensen, Søren. "Andreas Gottlob Rudelbach: Kierkegaard's Idea of an 'Orthodox Theologian.'" In *Kierkegaard and His Danish Contemporaries,* vol. II: *Theology,* edited by Jon Stewart, 303-33. Farnham, UK: Ashgate, 2009.

Khan, Abrahim. *Salighed as Happiness? Kierkegaard on the Concept Salighed.* Waterloo, ON: Wilfrid Laurier University Press, 1985.

Kirkconnell, Glenn. *Kierkegaard on Sin and Salvation: From* Philosophical Fragments *through the* Two Ages. London: Continuum, 2010.

Kirmmse, Bruce. "'But I am almost never understood . . .' Or, Who Killed Søren Kierkegaard?" In *Kierkegaard: The Self in Society,* edited by George Pattison and Steven Shakespeare. Basingstoke, UK: Macmillan, 1998.

———. *Kierkegaard in Golden Age Denmark.* Bloomington: Indiana University Press, 1990.

Krishek, Sharon. *Kierkegaard on Faith and Love.* Cambridge: Cambridge University Press, 2009.

Law, David. "Irony in the Moment and the Moment in Irony: The Coherence and Unity of Kierkegaard's Authorship with Reference to *The Concept of Irony* and the Attack Literature of 1854-1855." In *International Kierkegaard Commentary: "The Moment" and Late Writings,* edited by Robert L. Perkins, 71-100. Macon, GA: Mercer University Press, 2009.

———. *Kierkegaard as Negative Theologian.* Oxford: Clarendon Press, 1993.

Leon, Celine, and Sylvia Walsh, eds. *Feminist Interpretations of Søren Kierkegaard.* University Park: Pennsylvania State University Press, 1997.

Lindström, Walter. *Efterföljelsens Teologi hos Sören Kierkegaard.* Stockholm: Svenska Kyrkans Diakonistyrelses Bokförlag, 1956.

———. *Stadiernas Teologi.* Lund: Haakan Ohlsson, 1943.

Lippitt, John. *Kierkegaard and Fear and Trembling.* London: Routledge, 2003.

Løgstrup, Knud Ejler. *Opgør med Kierkegaard.* Copenhagen: Gyldendal, 1968.

Mackey, Louis. *Kierkegaard: A Kind of Poet.* Philadelphia: University of Pennsylvania Press, 1971.

———. *Points of View: Readings of Kierkegaard.* Tallahassee: Florida State University Press, 1986.

Mahn, Jason. *Fortunate Fallibility: Kierkegaard and the Power of Sin.* Oxford: Oxford University Press, 2011.

Malantschuk, Gregor. *Kierkegaard's Thought.* Translated by Howard and Edna Hong. Princeton, NJ: Princeton University Press, 1979.

———. *"Søren Kierkegaard's Angreb paa Kirken."* In *Søren Kierkegaard's Kamp mod Kirke,* edited by Gregor Malantschuk and N. H. Søe, 7-47. Copenhagen: Munksgaards Forlag, 1956.

Marino, Gordon. *Kierkegaard in the Present Age.* Milwaukee: Marquette University Press, 2001.

Martens, Paul. "The Emergence of the Holy Spirit in Kierkegaard's Thought: Critical Theological Developments." In *International Kierkegaard Commentary: For Self-Examination and Judge for Yourself!* edited by Robert L. Perkins, 199-222. Macon, GA: Mercer University Press, 2002.

———. "'You Shall Love': Kant, Kierkegaard, and the Interpretation of Matthew 22:39." In *International Kierkegaard Commentary: Works of Love,* edited by Robert L. Perkins, 57-78. Macon, GA: Mercer University Press, 1999.

McCarthy, Vincent. "Kierkegaard's Religious Psychology." In *Kierkegaard's Truth: The Disclosure of the Self,* edited by Joseph H. Smith. New Haven: Yale University Press, 1981.

———. *The Phenomenology of Moods in Kierkegaard.* The Hague: Martinus Nijhoff, 1978.

Mercer, David. *Kierkegaard's Living Room.* Montreal: McGill-Queens University Press, 2001.

Mooney, Edward. *Knights of Faith and Resignation: Reading Kierkegaard's "Fear and Trembling."* Albany: State University of New York Press, 1991.

———. *On Søren Kierkegaard: Dialogue, Polemic, Lost Intimacy, and Time.* London: Ashgate, 2007.

———. *Selves in Discord and Resolve: Kierkegaard's Moral-Religious Psychology.* London: Routledge, 1996.

Mulder, Jack, Jr. "The Catholic Moment? On the Apostle in Kierkegaard's 'The Difference between a Genius and an Apostle.' " In *International Kierkegaard Commentary: Without Authority,* edited by Robert L. Perkins, 203-34. Macon, GA: Mercer University Press, 2006.

Nielsen, H. A. *Where the Passion Is: A Reading of Kierkegaard's "Philosophical Fragments."* Tallahassee: Florida State University Press, 1983.

Nordentoft, Kresten. *Kierkegaard's Psychology.* Pittsburgh: Duquesne University Press, 1978.

Outka, Gene. "Religion and Moral Duty: Notes on *Fear and Trembling.*" In *Religion and Morality: A Collection of Essays,* 204-54. New York: Anchor Books, 1973.

Patrick, Denzil G. M. *Pascal and Kierkegaard: A Study in the Strategy of Evangelism.* 2 vols. London: Lutterworth Press, 1947.

Pattison, George. "Johannes Climacus and Aurelius Augustinus on Recollecting the Truth." In *International Kierkegaard Commentary: Philosophical Fragments and Johannes Climacus,* edited by Robert L. Perkins, 245-60. Macon, GA: Mercer University Press, 1994.

———. *Kierkegaard: The Aesthetic and the Religious.* London: Macmillan, 1992.

———. *Kierkegaard's Upbuilding Discourses: Philosophy, Literature, and Theology.* London: Routledge, 2002.

———. "Philosophy and Dogma: The Testimony of an Upbuilding Discourse." In *Ethics, Love, and Faith in Kierkegaard,* edited by Edward F. Mooney, 155-62. Bloomington: Indiana University Press, 2008.

Perkins, Robert L., ed. *International Kierkegaard Commentary.* 21 vols. Macon, GA: Mercer University Press, 1984-2009.

———, ed. *Kierkegaard's "Fear and Trembling": Critical Appraisals.* University: University of Alabama Press, 1981.

Podmore, Simon. *Kierkegaard and the Self before God: Anatomy of the Abyss.* Bloomington: Indiana University Press, 2011.

Pojman, Louis. *The Logic of Subjectivity: Kierkegaard's Philosophy of Religion.* University: University of Alabama Press, 1984.

Polk, Timothy. *The Biblical Kierkegaard: Reading by the Rule of Faith.* Macon, GA: Mercer University Press, 1997.

Poole, Roger. *Kierkegaard: The Indirect Communication.* Charlottesville: University of Virginia Press, 1983.

Puchniak, Robert. "Augustine: Kierkegaard's Tempered Admiration of Augustine." In *Kierkegaard and the Patristic and Medieval Traditions,* edited by Jon Stewart, 11-22. Aldershot, UK: Ashgate, 2007.

———. "Kierkegaard and Augustine: A Study in Christian Existence." PhD dissertation, Drew University, 2007.

———. "Kierkegaard's 'Self' and Augustine's Influence." In *Kierkegaard Studies Yearbook 2011,* edited by Heiko Schulz, Jon Stewart, and Karl Verstrynge, in cooperation with Peter Šajda, 181-94. Berlin: Walter de Gruyter, 2012.

Quinn, Phillip. "Does Anxiety Explain Original Sin?" *Nous* 24 (1990): 227-44.

Rae, Murray. "Kierkegaard, Barth, and Bonhoeffer: Conceptions of the Relation between Grace and Works." In *International Kierkegaard Commentary: For Self-Examination and Judge for Yourself!* edited Robert L. Perkins, 143-67. Macon, GA: Mercer University Press, 2002.

Roberts, David. *Kierkegaard's Analysis of Radical Evil.* London: Continuum, 2006.

Roberts, Robert C. *Faith, Reason, and History: Rethinking Kierkegaard's "Philosophical Fragments."* Macon, GA: Mercer University Press, 1986.

———. "Kierkegaard and Ethical Theory." In *Ethics, Love, and Faith in Kierkegaard,* edited by Edward F. Mooney, 72-92. Bloomington: Indiana University Press, 2008.

Rosas, L. Joseph. *Scripture in the Thought of Søren Kierkegaard.* Nashville: Broadman and Holman, 1994.

Rose, Tim. *Kierkegaard's Christocentric Theology.* Aldershot, UK: Ashgate, 2001.

Rudd, Anthony. *Kierkegaard and the Limits of the Ethical.* Oxford: Clarendon Press, 1993.

Rumble, Vanessa. "The Oracle's Ambiguity: Freedom and Original Sin in Kierkegaard's *The Concept of Anxiety.*" *Soundings* 75, no. 4 (Winter 1992): 605-25.

Šajda, Peter. "'The Wise Men Went Another Way': Kierkegaard's Dialogue with Fénelon and Tersteegen." In *Kierkegaard and Christianity* (*Acta Kierkegaardiana*, vol. 3), edited by Roman Králik, Abrahim H. Kahn, Peter Šajda, Jamie Turnbull, and Andrew J. Burgess, 89-105. Slovakia: Kierkegaard Society in Slovakia/Toronto: Kierkegaard Circle, 2008.

Schrempf, Christoph. *Sören Kierkegaard. Ein unfreier Pionier der Freiheit.* Introduction by Harald Høffding. Frankfurt am Main: Neuer Frankfurter Verlag, 1907.

Shakespeare, Steven. *Kierkegaard, Language and the Reality of God.* Aldershot: Ashgate, 2001.

Simpson, Christopher Ben. *The Truth Is the Way: Kierkegaard's* Theologia Viatorum. London: SCM Press, 2010.

Sløk, Johannes. *Da Kierkegaard tav. Fra forfatterskab til kirkestorm.* Copenhagen: Reitzel, 1980.

Søe, N. H. "Søren Kierkegaard og kirkekampen." In *Søren Kierkegaard's Kamp mod Kirke,* edited by Gregor Malantschuk and N. H. Søe, 45-75. Copenhagen: Munksgaards Forlag, 1956.

Stewart, Jon. *Kierkegaard's Relations to Hegel Reconsidered.* Cambridge: Cambridge University Press, 2003.

Strawser, Michael. *Both/And: Reading Kierkegaard from Irony to Edification.* New York: Fordham University Press, 1997.

Tanner, John S. *Anxiety in Eden: A Kierkegaardian Reading of* Paradise Lost. Oxford: Oxford University Press, 2002.

Taylor, Mark C. *Erring: A PostModern A/Theology.* Chicago: University of Chicago Press, 1984.

―――. *Journeys to Selfhood: Hegel and Kierkegaard.* Berkeley: University of California Press, 1980.

―――. *Kierkegaard's Pseudonymous Authorship: A Study of Time and the Self.* Princeton, NJ: Princeton University Press, 1975.

Thulstrup, Niels. "Adam and Original Sin." In *Theological Concepts in Kierkegaard, Bibliotheca Kierkegaardiana,* vol. 5, edited by Niels Thulstrup and Marie Mikulová Thustrup, 122-56. Copenhagen: C. A. Reitzels Boghandel, 1980.

―――. *Kierkegaard and the Church in Denmark.* Copenhagen: C. A. Reitzel Forlag, 1984.

Vardy, Peter. *An Introduction to Kierkegaard.* Peabody, MA: Hendrickson, 2008.

Walker, Jeremy. *To Will One Thing: Reflections on Kierkegaard.* Montreal and London: McGill-Queen's University Press, 1972.

Walsh, Sylvia. "Dying to the World and Self-Denial in Kierkegaard's Religious

Thought." In *International Kierkegaard Commentary: For Self-Examination and Judge for Yourself!* edited by Robert L. Perkins, 169-97. Macon, GA: Mercer University Press, 2002.

————. *Living Christianly: Kierkegaard's Dialectic of Christian Existence.* University Park: The Pennsylvania State University Press, 2005.

————. *Living Poetically: Kierkegaard's Existential Aesthetics.* University Park: The Pennsylvania State University Press, 1994.

Watkin, Julia. *Kierkegaard.* London: Continuum, 1997.

Weltzer, Carl. "Augustinus og Brøderne Kierkegaard." In *Festskrift til Jens Nørregaard.* Copenhagen: G. E. C. Gads, 1947.

Weston, Michael. *Kierkegaard and Modern Continental Philosophy.* London: Routledge, 1994.

Westphal, Merold. *Becoming a Self: A Reading of Kierkegaard's "Concluding Unscientific Postscript."* West Lafayette: Purdue University Press, 1996.

————. *Kierkegaard's Critique of Reason and Society.* University Park: The Pennsylvania State University Press, 1991.

Wild, John. "Kierkegaard and Contemporary Existential Philosophy." In *A Kierkegaard Critique,* edited by Howard A. Johnson, 22-39. New York: Harper, 1962.

Index